PRACTICING TEXAS POLITICS

2015–2016 Edition

1974

Lyle C. Brown   Baylor University

Joyce A. Langenegger   Blinn College

Sonia R. García   St. Mary's University

Ted A. Lewis   Pellissippi State Community College

Robert E. Biles   Sam Houston State University

Ryan Rynbrandt   Collin College

Veronica Reyna   Austin Community College

CENGAGE
Learning·

...zil • Mexico • Singapore • United Kingdom • United States

CENGAGE
Learning·

Practicing Texas Politics, 2015–2016 Edition

Lyle C. Brown, Joyce A. Langenegger, Sonia R. García, Ted A. Lewis, Robert E. Biles, Ryan Rynbrandt, Veronica Reyna

Product Manager: Carolyn Merrill

Content Developer: Jennifer Jacobson

Managing Developer: Joanne Dauksewicz

Associate Content Developer: Jessica Wang

Product Assistant: Abigail Hess

Media Developer: Laura Hildebrand

Marketing Manager: Valerie Hartman

Content Project Manager: Cathy Brooks

Art Director: Linda May

Manufacturing Planner: Fola Orekoya

IP Analyst: Alexandra Ricciardi

IP Project Manager: Brittani Morgan

Production Service and Compositor: Cenveo

Text and Cover Designer: Rokusek Design

Cover Image: Glass Building: © Natalia Bratslavsky/Shutterstock.com;

Barn Building: © Kevin Webb/Shutterstock.com

Chapter Opening Image: © Ken Hurst/Shutterstock.com

Chapter Background, Cowboy Image: © Alan Poulson Photography/Shutterstock.com

For product information and technology assistance, contact us at
Cengage Learning Customer & Sales Support, 1-800-354-9706
For permission to use material from this text or product, submit all requests online at **www.cengage.com/permissions**.
Further permissions questions can be emailed to
permissionrequest@cengage.com.

Library of Congress Control Number: 2014943027

Package: 978-1-285-85310-9

Text-only edition: 978-1-285-86105-0

Loose-leaf edition: 978-1-305-63387-2

Cengage Learning
20 Channel Center Street
Boston, MA 02210
USA

Cengage Learning is a leading provider of customized learning solutions with office locations around the globe, including Singapore, the United Kingdom, Australia, Mexico, Brazil, and Japan. Locate your local office at **www.cengage.com/global**.

Cengage Learning products are represented in Canada by Nelson Education, Ltd.

To learn more about Cengage Learning Solutions, visit **www.cengage.com**.
Purchase any of our products at your local college store or at our preferred online store **www.cengagebrain.com**.

Printed in Canada
Print Number: 01 Print Year: 2014

Australia • Bra

Brief Contents

Contents

List of Selected Readings

Letter to Instructor

Dear Texas Government Instructor:

Texas is a state in transition. The economy and tax system hold fast to the Lone Star State's land-based roots, while the Austin area is often called the new Silicon Valley and biotechnology and nanotechnology flourish in the state's metropolitan areas. Although Texas's population is now majority minority, Anglos continue to hold almost all statewide offices, seats in the state legislature, judicial benches, local offices, and appointive positions on boards and commissions. At the same time the state has eight emerging universities vying for Tier 1-university status, it continues to have the highest number of high school dropouts in the nation. Texas's current economic success attracts thousands of new residents each week, but limited water resources and a decaying infrastructure threaten the state's economic success and growth. Government will play an active role in negotiating and resolving these issues. The students in our classrooms will be the ones who select the policymakers and policies to deal with the multiplicity of concerns that face the Lone Star State in the 21st century. Understanding their government is critical to our students' future role as active, informed citizens.

- *Practicing Texas Politics* analyzes **the practices and policies** of the Lone Star State by giving students a realistic introduction to how public policymaking is conducted in Texas. The state's individualistic and traditionalistic political culture is referenced throughout to aid students in placing policy decisions in a historical and cultural context. Students are introduced to current policymakers, their decisions, and the impact of the resulting policies. The roles of political parties, special interest groups, voters, and the media in influencing public policy are also explored. Policymaking and process are integrated within each chapter throughout the book with a special emphasis on public education, higher education, social services, and infrastructure needs both as policy issues in Chapter 10, "Public Policy and Administration," and from a budgetary perspective in Chapter 13, "Finance and Fiscal Policy."

Through learning outcomes, learning checks, and other pedagogical features, students are given an organizational structure that helps them learn, understand, and remember the material.

New to This Edition

- Numbered learning objectives drive each chapter's organization with a learning objective tied to each major section and each paragraph of the chapter summary. Critical thinking questions are now presented with nearly every photo and figure, offering plentiful opportunities for instructors and students to meet this important Texas GOVT 2306 required core objective.

- A **new Chapter 6, "The Media and Politics,"** integrates scholarship with application on the roles and influence of the media, incorporates history as it relates to current roles and issues, and juxtaposes how Texas reflects national patterns with how it differs from them.

- A **new Chapter 11, "The Judicial Branch,"** is dedicated solely to a discussion of the Texas judicial system and the court structure.

- A **new Chapter 12, "The Criminal Justice System,"** focuses on the criminal and juvenile justice systems in the state.

- Updates of new laws passed by the 83rd regular and special sessions are included.

- A timely **selected reading—11 are new**—appears at the end of every chapter prior to the chapter-ending pedagogy. Readings include two Learning Check questions.

- Endnotes have been moved from the end of each chapter to the end of the book.
- Marginal **social media icons** signal new coverage of the use and transformative role of electronic technology, and particularly social media, in Texas politics.

MindTap

As an instructor, MindTap is here to simplify your workload, organize and immediately grade your students' assignments, and allow you to customize your course as you see fit. Through deep-seated integration with your Learning Management System, grades are easily exported and analytics are pulled with just the click of a button. MindTap provides you with a platform to easily add in current events videos and RSS feeds from national or local news sources. Looking to include more currency in the course? Add in our KnowNow American Government Blog link for weekly updated news coverage and pedagogy.

Our goal, first and foremost, is to help you develop your students into active, informed participants in their democracy. We have attempted to present a realistic and up-to-date picture of how Texas politics is practiced in all branches and at both local and state levels of government. We welcome your feedback on any material or feature in this book.

Sincerely,

The Practicing Texas Politics Author Team

Letter to Student

Dear Student:

Welcome to Texas government. Whether you're a native-born Texan or a newly arrived Texan, you can feel the energy of change all around you. You live in a state that no longer has a majority population from any race or ethnic group and in a few short years will have a majority Latino population. Despite the economic downturn that affected the rest of the world, you're in a state that created more new jobs than any other state for five consecutive years (2009–2013). Job growth has occurred in two economic sectors: energy and technology. The number of people who live here increases by almost 1,100 every week. The fastest growing metropolitan area by number of new residents (Houston-The Woodlands-Sugar Land) and the fastest growing city by rate of growth (Austin-Round Rock) are here in the Lone Star State. This same state, however, has the most uninsured children in the nation, the highest dropout rate in the country, and one of the greatest gaps in earnings between the wealthy and the poor in the United States. A decaying transportation infrastructure and depleted water resources will require multi-billion-dollar solutions. And who will solve these problems? You, the future voters and taxpayers of Texas will have that responsibility. That's why you need to understand your role and how the system works so you can keep Texas the vibrant state we all want it to be. Helping you become an effective participant in that system is why we wrote *Practicing Texas Politics*.

In this book you'll be introduced to today's important policymakers and learn what we all have a right to expect of them. You'll meet students, just like you, who have chosen to get involved and make a difference at their colleges, in their communities, and in this state. You'll learn about ways you can become involved through internships and other programs, as well as by voting and through political campaigns. You'll see how Texas compares to other states, and you'll be exposed to the diversity of the Lone Star State–home of the first all-female Supreme Court (all the way back to 1924), a host of musicians from Los Lonely Boys to Beyoncé to Willie Nelson, and four former U.S. presidents (Dwight Eisenhower, Lyndon Johnson, George H. W. Bush, and George W. Bush). You'll come to understand what this state could be in the future and how you can shape the outcome.

- Updated **"Students in Action"** features in each chapter help you make a personal connection to the content, highlighting how Texas students like you have participated in the community or providing information on internships and other opportunities for interested students.

- **"Point/Counterpoint"** examines a key controversial issue in Texas politics from both sides of the controversy and asks you to consider your position on each issue.

- **"Learning Checks"** provide a few factual questions at the end of major sections and at the end of each chapter's reading for you to use in checking your knowledge. Answers are provided at the end of the chapter.

- **"How Do We Compare?"** boxes compare Texas with other states.

- A **Marginal Glossary** allows you to access terms as they are needed for easier understanding of the text.

- Following the Selected Reading, **end-of-chapter materials** include a conclusion that wraps up the chapter and offers final thoughts for you to consider, a chapter summary organized by learning outcome, Key Terms, and Learning Check answers.

- Critical thinking questions ask you to think about your political opinion and beliefs on a variety of important issues in this state.

- Charts, graphs, and maps are used to give you a visual image for understanding concepts.

- Social media icons mark explanations of the ways social media is influencing government, affecting political campaigns, and transforming the media.

The Benefits of Using Mindtap as a Student

As a student, the benefits of using MindTap with this book are endless. With automatically graded practice quizzes and activities, automatic detailed revision plans on your essay assignments offered through Write Experience, an easily navigated learning path, and an interactive eBook, you will be able to test yourself in and outside of the classroom with ease. The accessibility of current events coupled with interactive media makes the content fun and engaging. On your computer, phone, or tablet, MindTap is there when you need it, giving you easy access to flashcards, quizzes, readings, and assignments.

You are the people who will guide Texas through the 21st century. It is our hope that when you understand how to get involved in Texas politics, you will choose to do so. And that once you are involved, you will use your vote and influence to create the kind of Texas in which you want to live. It is to you, the students of Texas, that we dedicate this book.

Sincerely,

The Practicing Texas Politics Author Team

Resources for Students and Instructors

Students...

Access your *Practicing Texas Politics* resources by visiting **www.cengagebrain.com/shop/isbn/9781285853109**

If you purchased MindTap or CourseReader access with your book, enter your access code and click "**Register**." You can also purchase the book's resources here separately through the "**Study Tools**" tab or access the free companion website through the "**Free Materials**" tab.

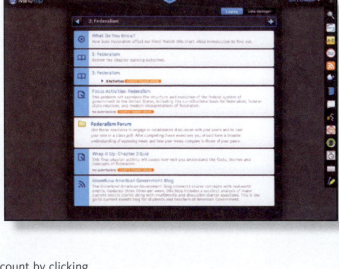

Instructors...

Access your *Practicing Texas Politics* resources via **www.cengage.com/login**.

Log in using your Cengage Learning single sign-on user name and password, or create a new instructor account by clicking on "**New Faculty User**" and following the instructions.

Practicing Texas Politics – Text Only Edition

ISBN: 9781285861050
This copy of the book does not come bundled with MindTap.

Personal Learning Experience

MindTap for *Practicing Texas Politics*

ISBN for Instant Access Code: 9781285872780
ISBN for Printed Access Code: 9781285860640
MindTap for *Practicing Texas Politics* is a highly personalized, fully online learning experience built upon Cengage Learning content and correlating to a core set of learning outcomes. MindTap guides students through the course curriculum via an innovative Learning Path Navigator where they will complete reading assignments, challenge themselves with

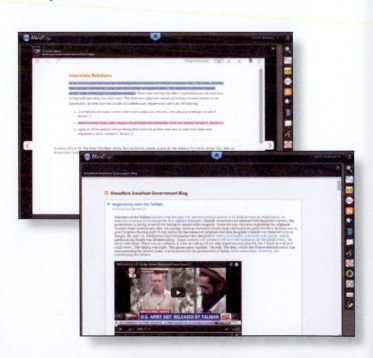

focus activities, and engage with interactive quizzes. Through a variety of gradable activities, MindTap provides students with opportunities to check themselves for where they need extra help, as well as allowing faculty to measure and assess student progress. Integration with programs like YouTube, Evernote, and Google Drive allows instructors to add and remove content of their choosing with ease, keeping their course current while tracking local and global events through RSS feeds. The product can be used fully online with its interactive eBook for *Practicing Texas Politics*, 2015-2016 Edition, or in conjunction with the printed text.

Instructor Companion Website for *Practicing Texas Politics*—for instructors only

ISBN: 9781285872766

This Instructor Companion Website is an all-in-one multimedia online resource for class preparation, presentation, and testing. Accessible through Cengage.com/login with your faculty account, you will find available for download: book-specific Microsoft® PowerPoint® presentations; a Test Bank compatible with multiple learning management systems; an Instructor Manual; Microsoft® PowerPoint® Image Slides; and a JPEG Image Library.

The Test Bank, offered in Blackboard, Moodle, Desire2Learn, Canvas, and Angel formats, contains Learning Objective-specific multiple-choice, critical thinking short answer questions, and essay questions for each chapter. Import the test bank into your LMS to edit and manage questions, and to create tests.

The Instructor's Manual contains chapter-specific learning objectives, an outline, key terms with definitions, and a chapter summary. Additionally, the Instructor's Manual features a critical thinking question, lecture launching suggestion, and an in-class activity for each learning objective.

The Microsoft® PowerPoint® presentations are ready-to-use, visual outlines of each chapter. These presentations are easily customized for your lectures and offered along with chapter-specific Microsoft® PowerPoint® Image Slides and JPEG Image Libraries. Access the Instructor Companion Website at www.cengage.com/login.

IAC Cognero for *Practicing Texas Politics*, 2015–2016 Edition – for instructors only

ISBN: 9781305081321

Cengage Learning Testing Powered by Cognero is a flexible, online system that allows you to author, edit, and manage test bank content from multiple Cengage Learning solutions; create multiple test versions in an instant; and deliver tests from your LMS, your classroom, or wherever you want. The test bank for *Practicing Texas Politics*, 2015-2016 Edition contains Learning Objective-specific multiple-choice, critical-thinking short answer, and essay questions for each chapter.

CENGAGE**brain**.com

Free Companion Website

ISBN: 9781285872773

This free companion website for *Practicing Texas Politics*, 2015-2016 Edition is accessible through cengagebrain.com and allows students access to chapter-specific interactive learning tools including flashcards, glossaries, and more.

CourseReader for
Texas Politics

ISBN for CourseReader 0-30 Instant Access Code: 9781133350279
ISBN for CourseReader 0-30 Printed Access Code: 9781133350286

CourseReader: Texas Politics allows instructors to create their reader, their way, in just minutes. This affordable, fully customizable online reader provides access to thousands of permissions-cleared readings, articles, primary sources, and audio and video selections from the regularly-updated Gale research library database. This easy-to-use solution allows instructors to search for and select just the material they want for their courses. Each selection opens with a descriptive introduction to provide context and concludes with critical-thinking and multiple-choice questions to reinforce key points.

CourseReader is loaded with convenient tools like highlighting, printing, note-taking, and downloadable PDFs and MP3 audio files for each reading. CourseReader is the perfect complement to any Political Science course. It can be bundled with your current textbook, sold alone, or integrated into your learning management system. CourseReader 0-30 allows access to up to 30 selections in the reader. Instructors should contact their Cengage sales representative for details. Students should check with their instructor to see if CourseReader 0-30 is required for their specific course.

Acknowledgments

We are indebted to many personal friends, government officials and their staffs, political activists, lawyers, and journalists who have stimulated our thinking. Likewise, we owe much to librarians and archivists who located hard-to-obtain facts, photos, and new readings. We also appreciate the professional assistance rendered by the editorial, production, and marketing staff of Cengage Learning. Without the benefit of their publishing experience, this textbook and its ancillaries would be of much less value to students and instructors.

Of course, expressions of appreciation are due to spouses, family members, and many others who helped to produce this new edition of our book and have learned to cope with the irregular working hours of authors struggling to meet deadlines. We are especially grateful to the many students who assisted us in writing *Practicing Texas Politics*, especially those who willingly gave of their time and expertise in the production of the *Students in Action* feature, as well as those who assisted us by providing input to some of our early drafts. We give special thanks for the assistance and support of Janice Hitchcock, Alexandra Fleming, and Jonathan Armstrong, all of Collin College; Jessica Thibodeau from the University of Texas at Austin; and Kirsten Anderson of Austin Community College.

We would also like to thank Patrizio Amezcua from San Jacinto College–North, for authoring this edition's Instructor's Manual, and author Ryan Rynbrandt from Collin College, for authoring this edition's Test Bank. Our hope is that through the efforts of all, this book will help Texas students better understand the practice of Texas politics and their role as participants.

Reviewers

We would also like to thank the instructors who have contributed their valuable feedback through reviews of this text:

Previous Edition Reviewers:
Mario Marcel Salas, *Northwest Vista College*
Brian R. Farmer, *Amarillo College*
Billy Hathorn, *Laredo Community College*
Amy S. Glenn, *Northeast Lakeview College*
Jim Startin, *University of Texas at San Antonio*

New Reviewers:
Sandra Creech, *Temple College*
Patrizio Amezcua, *San Jacinto College—North*
Debra St. John, *Collin College—Preston Ridge Campus*
Evelyn Ballard, *Houston Community College—*
    Southeast College
Aaron Knight, *Houston Community*
    College—Northeast College

About the Authors

Lyle C. Brown, Professor Emeritus of Political Science at Baylor University, served as departmental director of graduate studies and director of Baylor's Foreign Service Program. His international academic experience includes teaching at Mexico City College (now University of the Americas) and postgraduate study at the Instituto Tecnológico de Monterrey in Mexico. He received his M.A. from the University of Oklahoma and Ph.D. from the University of Texas at Austin. Dr. Brown served as president of the Southwest Council of Latin American Studies. His writing experience includes co-editing *Religion in Latin American Life and Literature* and authoring numerous articles.

Joyce A. Langenegger teaches government at Blinn College and is the college's Director of Professional Development. She received M.A. and J.D. degrees from Baylor University and an M.A. and Ph.D. from Fielding Graduate University. Dr. Langenegger has been named to "Who's Who Among America's Teachers" and received a NISOD Award for Teaching Excellence, Teacher of the Year for Blinn College-Bryan, and "Most Valuable Player" award from San Jacinto College for her work as a professor and administrator at that institution. She is a frequent workshop presenter on innovative teaching strategies. Before beginning her teaching career, she practiced law in Houston.

Sonia R. García is a Professor and Coordinator of Women's Studies at St. Mary's University in San Antonio. She has also served as Chair and Graduate Director of the Political Science Department. Dr. García received her Master's from the University of Arizona and her Ph.D. from the University of California, Santa Barbara. She has published articles on Latina politics and is a co-author of *Mexican Americans and the Law: El Pueblo Unido Jamás Será Vencido* and lead author of *Políticas: Latina Public Officials in Texas.*

Ted A. Lewis taught government at Texas colleges for more than 25 years before becoming Vice President for Academic Affairs at Pellissippi State Community College in Knoxville, Tennessee. He holds an M.S. from the University of North Texas, and a doctorate from the University of Texas at Austin. Dr. Lewis has conducted workshops on Texas election procedure for the Texas Secretary of State. He has served as a county party chair, on state executive committees, and on campaign advisory committees. A frequent workshop presenter, he has also published articles on political science and student-oriented course design and learning strategies. Dr. Lewis is listed in both "Who's Who in American Politics" and "Who's Who Among America's Teachers."

Robert E. Biles, Professor Emeritus and former chair of Political Science at Sam Houston State University, has taught college students about Texas politics in Texas, Colombia, and Ecuador. He received his M.A. and Ph.D. from The Johns Hopkins University-School of Advanced International Studies. Dr. Biles is the author of numerous books and articles. His involvement in politics includes serving as a school board member, county party chair, county election supervisor, and staff member of the U.S. Senate Foreign Relations Committee. He has advised state agencies and held leadership positions in statewide lobbying groups and professional organizations. Dr. Biles has received four Fulbright grants as well as awards for his research, teaching, and administrative service.

Ryan Rynbrandt is a Professor of Political Science and former Director of the Honors Institute at Collin College in Plano, Texas, where he teaches courses in American and Texas Government. Professor Rynbrandt works to increase student civic engagement. He is especially committed to initiatives that bring the resources of higher education to bear in addressing problems in the broader community. He received his master's degree from the University of Michigan in Ann Arbor, where he received multiple teaching awards and served as President of the Graduate Association of Political Scientists. He has been active in politics at the local, state, and national levels.

Veronica Reyna is Associate Professor of Government and Assistant Dean of Social and Behavioral Sciences for Austin Community College. She has been faculty advisor to a civil rights organization at ACC. Professor Reyna earned her M.A. in Political Science from St. Mary's University in San Antonio, where she taught as adjunct faculty. Her political involvement has included interning for Congressman Ciro Rodriguez, working as a union organizer, and volunteering in various Texas campaigns. She has also taught Texas politics at colleges and universities in San Antonio.

QUICK START GUIDE

1. To get started, navigate to: www.cengagebrain.com **and select "Register a Product".**

A new screen will appear prompting you to add a Course Key. A Course Key is a code given to you by your instructor - this is the first of two codes you will need to access MindTap. Every student in your course section should have the same Course Key.

2. Enter the Course Key and click "Register".

If you are accessing MindTap through your school's Learning Management System such as BlackBoard or Desire2Learn, you may be redirected to use your Course Key/Access Code there. Follow the prompts you are given and feel free to contact support if you need assistance.

3. Confirm your course information above, and proceed to the log in portion below.

If you have a CengageBrain username and password, enter it under "Returning Students" and click "Login". If this is your first time, register under "New Students" and click "Create a New Account".

4. Now that you are logged in, you can access the course for free by selecting "Start Free Trial" for 20 days, or enter in your Access Code.

Your Access Code is unique to you and acts as payment for MindTap. You may have received it with your book or purchased separately in the bookstore or at CengageBrain.com. Enter it and click "Register".

NEED HELP?

The Environment of Texas Politics

Learning Objectives

1.1 Describe how political culture has shaped Texas's politics, government, and public policy.

1.2 Explain the differences among the geographic regions of Texas.

1.3 Analyze the relationship between the social history of Texas and the political characteristics of the state's diverse population.

1.4 Describe both the four land-based industries that formed the historic basis for the Texas economy and the diversification of the modern Texas economy.

1.5 Identify five major policy challenges Texas faces in the 21st century.

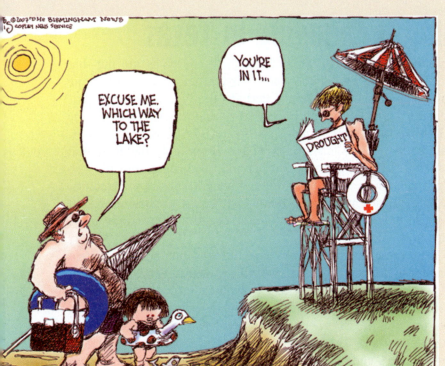

The drought that began in 2011 has had major implications for Texas politics and governance.

Scott Stantis/Town hall

CRITICAL THINKING

What impact has the drought that began in 2011 had on the Texas economy and government?

I have said that Texas is a state of mind, but I think it is more than that. It is a mystique closely approximating a religion. And this is true to the extent that people either passionately love Texas or passionately hate it and, as in other religions, few people dare to inspect it for fear of losing their bearings in mystery or paradox. But I think there will be little quarrel with my feeling that Texas is one thing. For all its enormous range of space, climate, and physical appearance, and for all the internal squabbles, contentions, and strivings, Texas has a tight cohesiveness perhaps stronger than any other section of America. Rich, poor, Panhandle, Gulf, city, country, Texas is the obsession, the proper study and the passionate possession of all Texans.

–John Steinbeck, 1962

Everything Is Changing in Texas

They say everything is bigger in Texas. Even the stereotypes are big—big trucks, big belt buckles, big hair—but if that's all you know about the Lone Star State, you don't know today's Texas. Perhaps the biggest things about Texas are the changes it has seen and the diversity that has resulted. It's the land of Willie Nelson, for certain; but it's also the land of Los Lonely Boys, Pantera, Erykah Badu, Kelly Clarkson, the Geto Boys, and the Reverend Horton Heat. It's still the land of cattle barons and oil tycoons; but it's also the land of high-tech pioneers, international traders, defense contractors, manufacturers, and service providers. Texas's stunning growth in recent decades has brought massive transformation and breathtaking variety in its people, economy, and politics.

If you live here, these transformations and the way our political system handles them have a significant impact on your life. Better understanding your home state and its political system will help you navigate these changes and contribute to the development of a better government. If you don't live here, pay attention anyway; the Texas experience is a preview of the changes facing the United States as a whole. The Lone Star State's successes and failures in negotiating these changes and balancing diverse interests will provide lessons for the rest of the nation. And you'll probably end up moving here anyway—everyone else seems to be. Nearly 8 million people since 1990 have told their place of origin what David Crockett allegedly told the people of his district: "You may all go to hell, and I'll go to Texas." This growth increases both opportunities and challenges, like the persistent water shortages referenced in the cartoon above. Because of the sheer size of Texas, what happens here also has an impact on the direction of the United States as a whole.[1] The 2010 census ranked Texas second largest among the 50 states, with a population that has now exceeded 25 million. That places the Lone Star State between California with its 37 million residents and New York with 20 million.

Substantial changes and diverse interests put democratic institutions of government to the test. The increased population of the Lone Star State includes more than 18 million men and women of voting age (18 years or older). Our analysis of the politics of Texas's state and local governments will help you understand political action and prepare you to be an active and informed participant in the political life of the state and its counties, cities, and special districts. As Texas Congresswoman Barbara Jordan once said, "The stakes are too high for government to be a spectator sport." It's time to suit up and play. To help you play effectively, we will introduce you to the playing field (government, political culture, land, and economy of the state), the players (citizens, activists, politicians, public employees, and opinion leaders), and the rules of the game (constitution, laws, and political processes).

Political Behavior Patterns

★ **LO1.1** Describe how political culture has shaped Texas's politics, government, and public policy.

There has never been full agreement in democratic societies about the proper size and role of government. Views on that question vary widely and are held deeply. Yet aside from a handful of anarchists, there *is* agreement that society needs rules, or "public policies," by which to live. Making, implementing, and enforcing these policies is the job of **government**. The government of the State of Texas is modeled on that of the United States, with the power to make policy divided among legislative, executive, and judicial branches. Each branch has its own powers, and each has some check on the power of the others. The state government also delegates some policymaking power to local governments, including counties, cities, and special districts. As a result, **public policies** take different forms.

Government, Politics, and Public Policy in Texas

Many policies are laws passed by the legislature, approved by the governor, implemented by an executive department, and interpreted by the courts. Others are constitutional amendments proposed by the legislature and ratified by the voters of Texas. Some policies derive from rules promulgated by state agencies and ordinances passed by local governments. What all of these efforts share in common is that they are attempts to meet a public need or reach a public goal. Government tries to meet public needs by allocating resources. In practice, resources are allocated when a state or local government formulates, adopts, and implements a public policy, such as raising taxes to pay for more police protection or better streets and highways. Government tries to meet public goals by using policy to encourage or discourage specific behaviors. The state can encourage some behaviors using incentives—for example, establishing scholarships or student loans to encourage getting an education. It can discourage other conduct with punishments, such as imposing penitentiary time for selling drugs. In addition, the government can encourage or discourage behaviors through public relations and information campaigns such as the famous "Don't Mess with Texas" campaign against littering.

government
A public institution with authority to formulate, adopt, implement, and enforce public policies for a society.

public policy
Government action designed to meet a public need or goal as determined by a legislative body or other authorized officials.

In the political realm, you may think of public policy as the product, and government as the factory in which it is made. If that's the case, then **politics** is the process that produces public policy. In fact, the government has at times been compared to a sausage factory—even if you like the product it produces, the process isn't always very pleasant to watch. The politics of policymaking often involves conflict among government officials, political parties, interest groups, media figures, citizens, noncitizen residents, and other groups that seek to influence how policies in Texas are enacted and implemented. Such conflict over power and resources can encourage the worst behavior in people, and opportunities for corruption and greed abound. Yet politics also requires cooperation and can inspire noble and courageous action. In sum, politics is the moving force by which government produces public policy, which in turn determines whether and how we use the power of the state to address our challenges and take advantage of our opportunities.

Political Culture

Politics is influenced by a **political culture** that consists of the values, attitudes, traditions, habits, and general behavioral patterns that develop over time and shape the politics and public policy of a particular region. Political culture is the result of both remote and recent political experiences. According to political scientist Daniel Elazar (1934–1999), "Culture patterns give each state its particular character and help determine the tone of its fundamental relationship, as a state, to the nation."[2] Elazar identified three distinct cultures that exist in the United States: moralistic, individualistic, and traditionalistic.

In the **moralistic culture** that originated in Puritan New England, people view government as a public service. The role of government is to improve conditions for the people and to create a just society. The people expect government to provide goods and services that advance the public good. Citizens see it as their duty to become active in governmental decision making through participation in politics and government, and they hold the government accountable to their high expectations.

The **individualistic culture** grew out of westward expansion throughout the 19th century. Frontier areas to which settlers moved had no government to provide goods and services for them. They became more self-reliant, and the notion of the "rugged individualist" emerged. The business community also advanced the individualistic culture, often viewing government as an adversary that taxed and regulated them; therefore, they wanted to limit its size and scope. Individualistic culture does not consider government a vehicle for creating a just society and believes government intervention in private life should be limited. Today, the individualistic culture is dominant in a majority of the midwestern and western states.

The **traditionalistic culture** grew out of the Old South and is rooted in feudal-like notions of society and government that developed in the context of the agrarian plantation economy. In the slave states, property and income were unequally dispersed. Governmental policymaking fell to a few powerful

politics
The process of policymaking that involves conflict and cooperation between political parties and other groups that seek to elect government officials or to influence those officials when they make public policy, such as enacting and interpreting laws.

political culture
Attitudes, habits, and general behavior patterns that develop over time and affect the political life of a state or region.

moralistic culture
This culture influences people to view political participation as their duty and to expect that government will be used to advance the public good.

individualistic culture
This culture looks to government to maintain a stable society but with minimum intervention in the lives of the people.

traditionalistic culture
A product of the Old South, this culture uses government as a means of preserving the status quo and its leadership.

families or influential social groups who designed policies to preserve the social order, and a one-party system developed. The poor and minorities were often disenfranchised. In the traditionalistic culture, government is a vehicle for maintaining the status quo and its hierarchy. Today the traditionalistic culture remains dominant throughout the South.

Texas Political Culture

Texas exudes pride in its own uniqueness. The state's distinctive historical, geographical, and cultural identity has created a political culture that influences the Lone Star State's style of government, politics, and policy. As with all states, this culture is a mix of moralistic, individualistic, and traditionalistic subcultures. Although elements of each subculture exist in Texas, individualists and traditionalists have historically dominated the state and controlled the direction of the political system.

Texas Moralism The moralistic subculture in Texas has historically been the domain of those who lack power, yet moralists have helped shape Texas as well. Throughout its history, Texas has seen movements to use government for the betterment of society. The Radical Republicans of the post–Civil War era sought to use government to end a white supremacist political system and achieve racial equality. Radical Republican Governor E. J. Davis's aggressive use of state government power in an effort to protect African American political participation made him many enemies in the white power structure that regained control of the government when Reconstruction ended. Reaction to his administration resulted in the decentralized, weak government established by the 1876 Texas Constitution, which is still in operation today.

In the late 19th and early 20th centuries, **progressive** groups like the Farmers' Alliance, the Populist Party, and even the Socialist Party surged in popularity in Texas as they challenged government to control the damaging effects of rising corporate capitalism.[3] Throughout the 1800s and into the early 1900s, a powerful Temperance movement in Texas sought to use government to end the sale and consumption of alcohol. From the earliest days of the civil rights struggle, **African Americans** and **Latinos** in Texas engaged in organized political activism to change the traditionalistic political structure of the state.

For most of its history Texas has been a one-party-dominant state. Whether the dominant party was Democratic or Republican, conservative majorities faced opposition from liberals who support the use of government to improve the lives of middle- and low-income Americans, one of the key identifiers of a moralistic political subculture.

Texas Individualism Daniel Elazar asserted that the political culture of Texas is strongly individualistic, in that those in positions of power have tended to believe that government should maintain a stable society but intervene as little as possible in the lives of the people.

progressive
Favoring and working for progress in conditions facing the majority of society or in government.

African American
A racial classification applied to Americans of African ancestry. The term is commonly applied on the basis of skin color, omitting white Americans whose ancestors immigrated from Africa and including black Americans whose ancestors immigrated from the Caribbean, Latin America, and Europe.

Latino
An ethnic classification of Mexican Americans and others of Latin American origin. When applied to females, the term is Latina. We will use this term throughout the book in addition to the term "Hispanic," which refers to people who trace their ancestry to Spanish-speaking countries.

An important source of Texas's individualism is the Anglo settlers' frontier experience. In the early 19th century, a growing number of colonists from the United States entered Texas individually or because they were recruited by *empresarios*, such as Stephen F. Austin. These settlers, without significant government backing, established farms and communities and persevered through extreme hardships.[4] With this objective, settlers displaced Native Americans from a large region. Resistance by Native Americans led to thousands of Native Americans as well as settlers—men, women, and children—slain on the Texas frontier from the 1820s to the mid-1870s. This period of frontier warfare lasted longer in Texas than in most other states.

After the Texas frontier was secured, the task of establishing law and order remained. In some areas, range wars, cattle rustling, and other forms of violence continued into the 20th century. Without an extensive government structure for imposing order, many Texans grew accustomed to struggling for survival and using force to settle disputes. In 1995, when the legislature legalized the licensed carrying of concealed handguns, some interpreted the action as another influence of frontier days, when many Texans carried concealed weapons or wore pistols openly in holsters. Two assumptions, often advanced by gun rights groups, underlie the concealed weapons law: first, that Texans do not need to rely on law enforcement for protection; second, that citizens of the Lone Star State have an individual right to possess and carry weapons.

The power of Texas individualists is reflected in the government structure they helped create and continue to dominate. Compared with other heavily populated states, Texas has a limited government with restricted powers: a legislature that meets biennially, with low salaries that can be increased only after approval by Texas voters; a governor who has limited budgetary, appointment, and removal powers; and an elected judiciary. Government spending for social services and public education on a per capita basis is consistently among the lowest in the nation. Including independent school districts, Texas has more than 3,000 special districts that perform services not provided by city or county governments.

The public perception of government and elected officials remains negative, although this viewpoint appears more directed to the federal government. Recent Texas governors have been elected to multiple terms in office. In 1998, George W. Bush became the first Texas governor elected to a second four-year consecutive term (although he resigned two years into his second term, following his election as U.S. president in 2000). In 2010, Rick Perry was elected to an unprecedented third four-year term, making him the longest serving governor in Texas history.

Texas Traditionalism The dominance of traditionalistic culture in Texas also can be traced to the early 19th century. The plantation system thrived in East Texas, and cotton was king. Before Texas's entry into the Confederacy, much of its wealth was concentrated in a few families. Although slave owners represented only a quarter of the state's population and one-third of its farmers, these slave owners held 60 to 70 percent of the wealth and controlled state politics.[5] After the Civil War (1861–1865), **"Jim Crow"** laws limited African Americans' access to public services. In the late 19th and early 20th centuries, poll taxes and all-white primaries further restricted voting rights.

Today, many Texans are the descendants of migrants from traditionalistic states of the Old South, where conservatism, elitism (upper-class rule), and one-party politics were entrenched. Although urbanization and industrialization, together with an influx of people from other states and countries, are changing Texas, Elazar insisted that the traditionalistic influence of the Old South lingers. Participation in politics and voter turnout remain low. Turnout is less than 50 percent for presidential elections and is consistently less than 30 percent for gubernatorial elections. Elazar noted that many Texans have inherited southern racist attitudes, which for a century after the Civil War were reflected in state laws that discriminated against African Americans and other minority groups. It was not until 2000 that two Confederate-themed Civil War plaques were removed from the Texas Supreme Court building, as demanded by the National Association for the Advancement of Colored People (NAACP). Similar symbols of Texas's role in the Confederacy remain in public places throughout the state and continue to cause controversy.

The traditionalistic influence of Mexico is also discernible among Texans of Mexican ancestry, who were affected by a political culture featuring the elitist **patrón** (protective political boss) **system** that dominates certain areas of South Texas. For more than four decades, however, the old political order of that region has been challenged—and, in many instances, defeated—by new generations of Mexican Americans.[6] Compared with other areas of the state, however, voter turnout remains much lower in counties along the Mexican border.

The traditionalistic culture can also be seen in the state's economic conservatism and deference to the power of wealthy individuals and corporations. Texas has a climate favorable to business owners. It remains one of the few states without a personal or corporate income tax and has adopted **"right to work"** laws, which make it difficult to form and operate labor unions. City councils have drawn criticism for publicly financing corporate ventures or providing certain businesses with property tax abatements. The City of Arlington drew attention for its use of local tax dollars and **eminent domain** to remove people from their homes to make way for Jerry Jones's new Dallas Cowboys stadium.[7] Other powerful individuals and families continue to play an important role in local and state politics and influence public policies.

A Changing Culture?

Since the mid-1970s, Texas has experienced massive population influx from other areas of the nation and from other countries. Many of these new Texans come from places with more heavily moralistic political cultures. This in-migration raises an important question: How long will the historical

Jim Crow laws
Ethnically discriminatory laws that segregated African Americans and denied them access to public services for many decades after the Civil War.

patrón system
A type of boss rule that has dominated areas of South Texas and Mexico.

right to work laws
Laws that limit the power of workers to bargain collectively and form and operate labor unions, increasing the power of employers relative to their employees.

eminent domain
The power of the government to take private property for public uses, so long as just compensation is paid.

Texas State Capitol Building

Courtesy of the Texas House of Representatives

CRITICAL THINKING

In what ways is Texas's political culture (moralism, individualism, and traditionalism) reflected in politics, policies, and the people's attitudes about, and expectations of, government today?

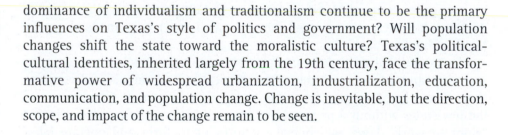

1.1 Learning Check

1. True or False: The goal of public policy is to influence people's behavior.
2. Which two types of political culture have traditionally been dominant in Texas?

Answers on p. 39.

dominance of individualism and traditionalism continue to be the primary influences on Texas's style of politics and government? Will population changes shift the state toward the moralistic culture? Texas's political-cultural identities, inherited largely from the 19th century, face the transformative power of widespread urbanization, industrialization, education, communication, and population change. Change is inevitable, but the direction, scope, and impact of the change remain to be seen.

The Land

LO1.2 Explain the differences among the geographic regions of Texas.

Texas's politics and public policy have always been shaped by the state's size. Its large area and diverse physical geography create strong regional interests and distinct subcultures. The state is bounded by New Mexico to the west; Oklahoma to the north; Arkansas, Louisiana, and the Gulf of Mexico to the east, and borders Mexico to its south. This international boundary follows the Rio Grande (known as Rio Bravo del Norte in Mexico) in its southeastern course from El Paso to Brownsville and the Gulf of Mexico.

Size

With more than 267,000 square miles of territory, Texas is second only to Alaska (570,640 square miles) in area and is as large as the combined areas of Florida, Georgia, Alabama, Mississippi, and Tennessee. Connecting the more than 1,200 incorporated cities in Texas requires approximately 222,000 miles of roadways, including more than 80,000 miles of major highways constructed and maintained under the supervision of the Texas Department of Transportation. The state's massive size has an impact on political campaigns as well. Running for statewide, and in some instances district-level, office requires a significant investment of financial resources. Despite the rise of **social media** as an inexpensive and effective campaigning and organizing tool, traveling the state for rallies and fundraisers while targeting 20 media markets with advertisements is an expensive undertaking that requires extensive fundraising.

Regions

Because of the state's vast size and geographic diversity, Texas developed a concept of five areas—North, South, East, West, and Central Texas—as five potentially separate states. In fact, the United States congressional resolution by which Texas was admitted to the Union in 1845 specifies that up to four states "in addition to said state of Texas" may be formed out of its territory and that each "shall be entitled to admission to the Union." Over the years, various plans for carving Texas into five states have been proposed to the Texas legislature. Few Texans have taken those plans seriously. Physical geographers have identified four distinct regions: the Texas Great Plains (a part of the Great Plains originating at the Canadian border), the Gulf Coastal Plains (extending along the Gulf of Mexico to Florida), the Interior Lowlands, and the Basin and Range Province (extending to California). The Texas Comptroller's office identifies 13 separate economic regions in Texas. For simplicity, we condense these 13 regions down to six (Figure 1.1).

The West Texas Plains Agriculture is the economic bedrock of the West Texas Plains, from the sheep, goat, and cattle production in its southern portions to the cotton, grain sorghum, and feedlot cattle in the north. The area depends heavily on the continually depleting and environmentally sensitive Ogallala Aquifer. The careful management of this underground water-bearing rock formation will be crucial to the region's future. Below the Cap Rock Escarpment, oil production forms the economic base of cities like Odessa and Midland.

From the Panhandle down to Odessa, West Texas is known for its social, economic, and political conservatism. Dominated by white **Protestant fundamentalism**, agriculture, and oil, West Texas is fertile soil for the Republican Party. Democrats have little electoral success here even in the larger cities of Lubbock and Amarillo.

The Border South and Southwest Texas border Mexico. The region produces citrus fruits and vegetables, but increasingly it is international trade that is

social media
Websites and computer applications that allow users to engage in social networking and create online communities. Social media provide platforms for sharing information and ideas through discussion forums, videos, photos, documents, audio clips, and the like.

Protestant fundamentalism
A socially and politically conservative form of Protestant Christianity that arose in the late 1800s as a reaction against modernism. Protestant fundamentalists insist that the Christian Bible is literally true in both religious and historical terms.

1. **West Texas Plains**
2. **The Border**
3. **Central Texas**
4. **North Texas**
5. **East Texas**
6. **The Gulf Coast**

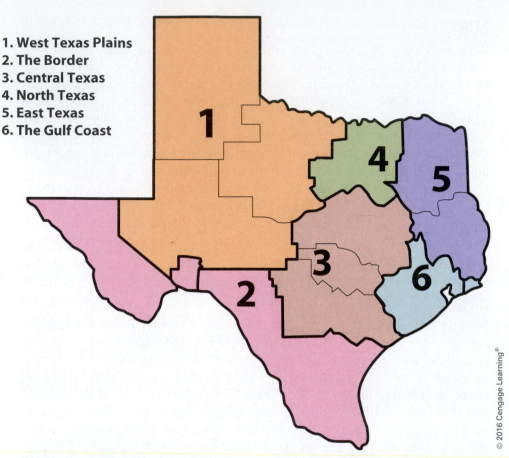

© 2016 Cengage Learning®

Figure 1.1   The 6 Regions of Texas

CRITICAL THINKING

How does Texas's large geographic size affect its politics and governance? How do the state's regions differ in culture, politics, and economy?

vital to its economy, which can thus be sensitive to swings in the Mexican economy. In 1994, the **North American Free Trade Agreement (NAFTA)** lowered trade barriers among Mexico, the United States, and Canada. The resulting rise of *maquiladoras*, or American factories on the Mexican side of the border, meant that U.S. companies could take advantage of Mexico's inexpensive labor pool and lax regulation there. Much cross-border investment resulted.

From El Paso to Brownsville, many Texans near the border have deep ties with Mexico and are strongly linked to it through family, friends, media, and trade. Spanish is the primary language in many cities, and the Catholic Church is a major part of everyday life. With a large Latino population, the Democratic Party has substantial electoral success here.

Central Texas Waco, Austin, and San Antonio are all in Central Texas. The region is dominated by universities and colleges, the high-tech sector,

North American Free Trade Agreement (NAFTA)

An agreement among Mexico, the United States, and Canada designed to expand trade by eliminating tariffs among the three nations.

the state government, tourism, and major military bases. It is also home to the German Hill Country, an agricultural region that holds onto its Central European cultural identity and its social and political conservatism.

Despite being the capital of a conservative state, Austin is politically and socially liberal and self-avowedly "weird." With a boom in the high-tech industry, a major university, and a thriving art and music scene, Austin has experienced rapid growth and in-migration from all over the country and the world, but particularly from highly educated former residents of the Northeast and West Coast. Austin also has the highest concentration of millennials in the nation.[8] As a result, the Democratic Party does well in Austin, and also in San Antonio, though surrounding areas tend toward Republican conservatism.

North Texas This region is home to the Dallas–Fort Worth metroplex dividing East and West Texas. This metropolitan area has seen decades of explosive growth and economic development as national and international corporations continue to move their headquarters here. Although Fort Worth still embraces its cowboy past, Dallas seems to prefer diving headlong into the future. Both cities have become modern centers for high-tech industries, financial services, defense contractors, and food production.

Fort Worth is home to Wendy Davis, who was the Democratic Party's candidate for governor in 2014. Democrats sometimes find electoral success in the urban centers of the metroplex, but the suburban and rural parts of the region are conservative Republican strongholds.

East Texas Cotton production, a constant in East Texas for nearly all of its history, continues in the region but has declined along with oil as the backbone of a struggling economy. Timber production in the Piney Woods, cattle and poultry farming, and some manufacturing have helped fill the gap while other economic diversification continues.

The westernmost extension of the Deep South, East Texas can seem a world apart, as references to life "behind the Pine Curtain" suggest. The area remains racially segregated and dominated by Protestant fundamentalism and powerful families with deep historical roots in the area. It is firmly a part of the Republican "Solid South."

The Gulf Coast The coast of the Gulf of Mexico stretches from the Louisiana border to the Rio Grande. Shipping and fishing are naturally important to the economy, but so are manufacturing and the presence of major corporate headquarters. The Spindletop oil well at Beaumont launched the oil age in Texas, and petrochemicals remain fundamental to the region's economy. It has thus been sensitive to oil booms and busts, including the 2001 collapse of Enron, which had been deeply integrated into the life of the region before the deep corruption of its executives led to its downfall.

Anchored by Houston, the state's largest and most diverse city, the area also has the highest concentrations of unions in Texas. As a result, Democrats have some electoral wins in the urban areas. Rural parts of the Gulf Coast remain reliably Republican, however.

1.2 Learning Check

1. What is the impact of the Lone Star State's size on Texas's politics?
2. True or False: All the regions of Texas depend economically on the same industries, and thus are nearly identical in culture and politics.

Answers on p. 39.

The People

......................................★ **LO1.3**   Analyze the relationship between the social history of Texas and the political characteristics of the state's diverse population.

> *I am forced to conclude that God made Texas on his day off, for pure entertainment, just to prove that all that diversity could be crammed into one section of earth by a really top hand.*
>
> —*Mary Lasswell*

In every decade since 1850, Texas's population has grown more rapidly than the overall population of the United States. According to the federal census estimate of 2013, Texas's population totaled 26,448,193—a stunning increase of 27 percent from 2000. (At the national level, the total population estimate in 2013 was 316,128,839—an increase of approximately 11 percent from 2000.) Texas also had five of the fastest-growing metropolitan areas in the nation between 2000 and 2010. By 2014, seven of the 15 fastest growing cities with populations of at least 50,000 were in Texas.

Population Distribution

Just as Texas's physical geography makes the state a land of great contrasts, so does the distribution of its inhabitants. At one extreme is Harris County in the southeastern part of the state, with approximately 4 million inhabitants. At the other extreme is Loving County, on the New Mexico border, where the 2010 census counted only 82 people. Today, Texas's four most populous counties (Harris, Dallas, Bexar, and Tarrant) have a combined population of more than 10 million people. These four urban counties (along

How Do We Compare...in Population?

2013 Population Estimates as Reported by the U.S. Bureau of the Census

Most Populous U.S. States	Population	U.S. States Bordering Texas	Population
California	38,332,521	Arkansas	2,959,373
New York	19,651,127	Louisiana	4,629,470
Florida	19,552,860	New Mexico	2,085,287
Texas	**26,448,193**	Oklahoma	3,850,568

CRITICAL THINKING

How does a large and rapidly growing population create both opportunities and challenges for Texas?

with Travis County) are located within the Texas Triangle, roughly outlined by segments of interstate highways 35, 45, and 10.

Texas has seen large demographic movements from rural to urban areas and from large cities to the suburbs and back. Although the shift from rural to urban areas and the growth of exurbs (extra-urban areas beyond suburbs) has continued into the 21st century, a repopulation of inner cities has revitalized downtowns and attracted new residents. Some rural areas in the Lone Star State have recently experienced rapid population growth as a result of a resurgence in oil and natural gas production.[9]

Urbanization Migration from rural regions to cities results in urbanization. Texas was 80 percent rural at the beginning of the 20th century, but today more than 85 percent of the state's population is urban. Urban areas are composed of one or more large cities and their surrounding suburban communities. A suburb is a relatively small town or city, usually outside the boundary limits of a central city. The early history of suburbanization was marked by racial segregation, with Anglos in more affluent suburbs and historical minority groups in the inner city and less affluent suburbs. Federal government policies of "**redlining**," interstate highway designs, and "**urban renewal**," along with state and local policies like **exclusionary zoning** and **racial covenants**, were used purposefully to ensure residential segregation. Even when laws and court decisions moved official policies away from racially discriminatory practices, economic inequality, the phenomenon of "white flight," and the practice of some realtors and lenders "steering" their clients into segregated neighborhoods kept integration from fully happening. Today, de facto racial segregation (segregation by fact) remains, especially with regard to suburban areas, though to a lesser extent than in the past.[10] Between 1980 and 2010, Texas suburbs experienced explosive growth and spread into rural areas.

Metropolitanization Suburbanization on a large scale creates a metropolitan area, or a core city surrounded by a sprawl of smaller cities and towns. Metropolitanization concentrates large numbers of people in urban centers that become linked with suburbs in a single geographic entity. Although socially and economically integrated, a metropolitan area is composed of separate units of local government, which include counties, cities, and special districts. Since 1910, federal agencies have defined metropolitan areas for census purposes. The U.S. Office of Management and Budget establishes statistical areas, currently dividing them into Micropolitan Statistical Areas (mSA), with a population of 10,000–50,000 and Metropolitan Statistical Areas (MSA), with a population of 50,000 plus.

By 2010, Texas had 42 mSAs and 44 MSAs. Cities are eager to obtain the highest possible statistical designation because many congressional appropriations are made accordingly. For example, to qualify for mass transit funds, an area must be a Metropolitan Statistical Area (MSA).

Texas's rate of population growth is consistently greater in the MSAs than throughout the state as a whole. Most of these population concentrations are

redlining
A discriminatory rating system used by federal agencies to evaluate the risks associated with loans made to borrowers in specific urban neighborhoods.

urban renewal
The relocation of businesses and people, the demolition of structures, and the use of eminent domain to take private property for government development projects.

exclusionary zoning
The use of local government zoning ordinances to exclude certain groups of people from a given community.

racial covenants
Agreements by a group of property owners, subdivision developers, or real estate operators in a given neighborhood, binding them not to sell, lease, or rent property to specified groups because of race, creed, or color for a definite period unless all agree to the transaction.

metropolitanization
The development of a residential pattern centered in a core area containing a large population nucleus together with adjacent communities economically and socially integrated with that core.

within the Texas Triangle. The Lone Star State's MSAs contain more than 80 percent of the state's population but fewer than 20 percent of the state's 254 counties. It is politically significant that these 48 counties potentially account for about four of every five votes cast in statewide elections. Thus, governmental decision makers are answerable primarily to people living in one-fifth of the state's counties. Urban voters, however, are rarely of one mind at the polls; they do not tend to overwhelm rural voters by taking opposing positions on all policy issues.

Demographics Is Destiny

Like the population of the nation, Texas's population is aging as the baby-boom generation (born between 1946 and 1964) enters retirement age. The Census Bureau estimates that the population of Texans older than 64 will exceed 5 million by 2030. The elderly are the most powerful and most conservative voting bloc, voting and participating in other ways at higher rates than any other age group and represented by the nation's largest interest group—the American Association of Retired Persons (AARP).

Texas is also diverse in racial, ethnic, and cultural terms. More than one-half of all Texans are either African American or Latino. The remainder are predominantly **Anglos** (non-Hispanic whites), with a small but rapidly growing **Asian American** population and approximately 170,000 **Native Americans**. More than one-third of all Texans speak a language other than English at home.[11] In 2012, the Houston metropolitan area replaced New York City as the most ethnically diverse city in the country.[12]

Texans Throughout History: From Conflict Toward Cooperation

The politics of democracy is about forging a path for diverse groups with sometimes opposing interests to live together peaceably. One of the remarkable facets of Texas is that, though racial and ethnic tensions still exist, its diverse population lives together peacefully. Historically, peaceful coexistence was difficult. Texans have a reputation for toughness, and that reputation was formed over hundreds of years of surviving an often unforgiving terrain, made harsher by a social atmosphere that historian and political scientist Cal Jillson has called "breathtakingly violent."[13]

The First Texans Few specifics are known about the people who inhabited what would become the Lone Star State for more than 10,000 years before Spanish explorers planted the first of Texas's six flags here in the 1500s. When the Spaniards arrived, the land was inhabited by more than 50 Native American tribes and nations. Population estimates vary widely, ranging from 50,000 to perhaps a million people. In East Texas, the Caddo lived in organized villages with a complex political system. The state's name comes from the word *tejas*, meaning "friendly," which was the tribal name for a group of Indians within the Caddo Confederacy. The Comanches were arguably the most important tribe in shaping Texas history. Excellent horsemen

Anglo
As commonly used in Texas, the term is not restricted to persons of Anglo-Saxon lineage but includes those of European ancestry more generally. Traditionally, the term applies to all whites except Latinos.

Asian American
An ethnic classification for persons whose ancestry originates in the Far East, Southeast Asia, or the Indian subcontinent.

Native American
A term commonly used for those whose ancestors were living in the Americas before the arrival of Europeans and Africans. Another commonly used term in the United States is "American Indian" or in Canada "First Nations."

and valiant warriors, they maintained a successful resistance to the northward expansion of Spaniards and Mexicans and the westward expansion of Anglos. Native American tribes were not unified. For example, the Tonkawa of Central Texas often allied with Anglos in fights against the Comanches and the Wichitas, another important South Plains tribe.

European Colonization Accurate estimates of the Native American population may not be available, but whatever the true size, their numbers declined rapidly after European contact in the 16th century. With Spanish explorers and their African slaves came diseases like cholera that spread through native communities. Though Spain and France claimed Texas, neither country actively ruled the territory. Their activities were mostly exploring, surveying, and fighting. The area remained sparsely populated through the Mexican Revolution against Spain in 1810. In 1824, three years after Mexico overthrew Spanish rule, the area that is now Texas became part of a federal republic for the first time.

Mexican Texas Around the time of Mexican independence, Anglo American settlers began coming to the Mexican province of Tejas in greater numbers. Although the first non-Spanish-speaking immigrants to Texas were largely of English ancestry, some were Scottish, Irish, or Welsh descendants. Others were French, Scandinavian, and Eastern European, with a few Italians, Greeks, and other European nationalities. The arrival of Anglo settlers sped the decline of the Native American population, which had already been reduced to 20,000-30,000 people. Violence between the native population and immigrant whites was constant and pervasive. Despite the Mexican government's authorization of Stephen F. Austin to offer free land to settlers willing to work it, government officials were concerned about the immigrants. Many Anglo newcomers resisted the constitution and laws of Mexico that established Catholicism as the state religion and abolished slavery. (See chapter 2, "Federalism and the Texas Constitution" for more discussion of the historical context).

When General Antonio López de Santa Anna was elected president of Mexico in 1834, most Texans did not expect that he would repudiate the principles of the federal democratic republic he was elected to serve. When he did, a result was the Texas Revolution, with its famous battles at Goliad, the Alamo, and San Jacinto. A great deal of blood was shed to establish the independent Republic of Texas in 1836 that received diplomatic recognition by the governments of the United States, England, France, Holland, and Belgium.

The Republic of Texas The elected presidents of the Republic, Sam Houston (twice) and Mirabeau B. Lamar, and the Texas Congress struggled to establish Texas as an independent nation, even as many in the government sought to join the United States. The demands of establishing and maintaining an army and navy, operating a postal system, printing paper money, administering justice, and providing other governmental services were made difficult by conflicts within and without the Republic's borders.

Anglo-Indian warfare continued because of increased immigration from the United States, and because some Texan Anglo leaders pursued policies of removal and extermination. The fighting was so fierce that two decades after independence, one observer in 1856 estimated the state's Native American population at about 12,000, with most having been killed or driven from the state.[14] And while many Tejanos had fought for Texas's independence, Cal Jillson notes that "some Texas leaders sought to equate Indians and Mexicans and urge the expulsion or extermination of both."[15] From the time of Texas independence until 1900, immigration from Mexico all but ceased. Latinos remained concentrated in settlements such as San Antonio that were founded during the 18th century, and within Central and South Texas. Conflicts, in some cases violence, among Anglo Texans, Native Americans, and Tejanos continued into Texas's statehood, which came about in 1845, less than a decade after its independence.

The Lone Star State In South Texas, Latinos comprised a majority of the population despite the increased number of Anglo arrivals after the Mexican War of 1846–1848 (which followed admission of Texas into the Union). Anglo immigration, by contrast, dominated much of the rest of the state. Before the Civil War, more than one-half of the state's Anglo residents had migrated from Alabama, Arkansas, Georgia, Kentucky, Louisiana, Mississippi, Missouri, and Tennessee.[16] It was no surprise, then, that the Republic of Texas legalized slavery and entered the union as a slave state. By 1847, African Americans accounted for one-fourth of the state's population, and most were slaves.

Yet slavery was not universally accepted in Texas. Some estimates suggest that as many as 24,000 German immigrants and descendants settled in the Hill Country of Central Texas by 1860. Most opposed slavery on principle, whereas others simply had no need for slaves. As a result, 14 counties in the Texas Hill Country voted 40 percent or greater against secession in 1861. Despite Sam Houston's opposition, the secessionists won and Texas joined the Confederate States of America in February of that year. In the ordinance of secession and in an official explanation of the causes of secession issued the following day, Texas leaders repeatedly cited northern attacks on the institution of slavery, along with the failure of the federal government to protect Anglo Texans against Mexican and Indian banditry and other grievances.[17]

The Civil War and Reconstruction

Though Texas saw less fighting than other southern states in the Civil War, it nonetheless felt the ravages of combat. In addition to battle with Union troops, Central Texas was scarred by what has been called "a civil war within a Civil War,"[18] as hundreds of opposing Union and Confederate sympathizers died in armed confrontations. The Confederacy lost the war and Texas was brought back into the Union, but not fully until the end of Reconstruction, a period in which the United States government sought to remake the political and economic structures of southern states.

Governor Edmund J. Davis's heavy-handed tactics used to enfranchise freed slaves during Radical Reconstruction temporarily made political participation safe for freed slaves and disenfranchised many leading Anglo citizens who supported the Confederacy. This even led to a small wave of freedmen migration into Texas.

The Great State of Texas

Texas was fully readmitted to the United States in 1870, but civil strife continued. Although Anglo migration into the state declined during the Civil War and Reconstruction, it resumed by the 1870s. Westward settlement further displaced Native Americans and converted the prairies into cattle and sheep ranches. A combination of Anglo in-migration and African American out-migration reduced the percentage of African Americans in the population from 31 percent in 1870 to 13 percent by 1950.

Those African Americans who remained in Texas faced great difficulty. Slavery was replaced for many by a different form of servitude in the form of sharecropping, in which they farmed land as tenants for a portion of the crops grown. De jure segregation, or segregation by law, resulted in denial of adequate education and economic opportunities. Texas saw almost 340 lynchings of African Americans between the end of Reconstruction and World War II.[19]

Early in the 20th century, waves of immigrants escaping the Mexican Revolution and its aftermath fed the American need for seasonal laborers. Many Latinos worked as farm and ranch laborers. The Great Depression and the resulting competition for work greatly increased anti-immigrant sentiment and policy in Texas, and violence sometimes erupted as a result.[20]

After World War II, many Latinos left agriculture and sought manufacturing work in cities. Most of them experienced improvements in wages and working conditions in unskilled or semiskilled positions. A growing number of Latinos entered managerial, sales, and clerical professions.[21] In the 1960s, the federal government began to enforce the desegregation decisions of the U.S. Supreme Court, and Texan President Lyndon Johnson signed a series of new antidiscrimination civil rights laws. Public schools, workplaces, and some neighborhoods, especially in urban areas, were integrated.

Integration has reduced, but not eliminated, intergroup tension in Texas. Dramatic incidents such as the dragging death of James Byrd[22] and statistics demonstrating continued discrimination in housing, employment, and criminal justice illustrate that conflict and inequality still exist in the Lone Star State. Yet historical minority groups have made major strides in education, employment, and political representation in recent decades. In increasing numbers, Texans of varied backgrounds work, live, socialize, date, and marry across racial, ethnic, and religious differences. Evidence suggests that young people use more social media than other groups and that people who use social media websites like Facebook or Twitter have more racially and ethnically diverse social networks.[23] Polling data indicate that today's young people are more likely than their elders to reject racism and celebrate diversity.[24] This viewpoint is developing as Texas moves from a majority-minority state, with no racial or ethnic majority, to a majority Latino state.

The U.S. Census Bureau projected racial categories in Texas for 2013 at the following percentages:

White/Anglo	44.0
Hispanic/Latino	38.4
Black/African American	12.4
Asian	4.3
American Indian or Alaskan Native	1.0
Native Hawaiian or other Pacific Islander	0.1
Two or more races	1.8

Texans Today

Texas ranks among the most racially and ethnically diverse states in the nation. There really is no such thing as a "typical Texan." Five groups comprise the major racial or ethnic groups in the state: Native American, Asian American, African American, Latino, and Anglo.

Native Americans Although some counties (Cherokee, Comanche, Nacogdoches), cities and towns (Caddo Mills, Lipan, Waxahachie), and other places have Native American names, by 2010, Texas Native Americans numbered only around 170,000. Most live and work in towns and cities, with only a few on reservations. Approximately 1,100 members of the Alabama-Coushatta tribe reside on a 4,351-acre East Texas reservation. On the U.S.-Mexican border near Eagle Pass, a few hundred members of the Kickapoo tribe are allowed by the governments of Mexico and the United States to move freely between Texas and the Mexican state of Coahuila. At the far western boundary of the state, the 1,700-member Tigua tribe inhabits a reservation near El Paso.

Asian Americans The Lone Star State is home to one of the largest Asian American populations (nearly 1 million) in the nation. Most of Texas's Asian American families immigrated from Southeast Asia (Cambodia, Laos, and Vietnam in particular), but a growing percentage are U.S. born. Vietnamese-born Hubert Vo (D-Houston) became the first Vietnamese American elected to the Texas House of Representatives in 2004 and has been reelected five times.

Most Asian Americans live in the state's largest urban centers—Houston and the Dallas–Fort Worth metroplex. Fort Bend County near Houston has the greatest percentage of Asian Americans in the state at 17 percent. Approximately one-half of Texas's first-generation Asian Americans entered this country with college degrees or completed their degrees after arrival. The intensity with which the state's young Asian Americans focus on education is revealed by enrollment data for the University of Texas at Austin. Although Asian Americans account for less than 4 percent of the total population of the state, they comprised 15.4 percent of the undergraduate enrollment at the University of Texas at Austin and 19 percent of the enrollment at the University of Texas at Dallas in the fall 2013 semester.

African Americans By 2014, Texas had approximately 3 million African Americans, more than 11 percent of the state's population.[25] The African American population has continued to grow, but more slowly than other ethnic groups. Today, Texas has the third-largest number of African Americans in the nation, after New York and California. Most reside in southeast, north central, and northeast Texas, concentrated in large cities. In recent years, a significant number of Africans seeking employment and a higher standard of living have immigrated to the United States and settled in Texas. More than one-half of the state's African Americans reside in and around major urban areas. Although African Americans do not constitute a majority in any Texas county, according to the 2010 census, Jefferson County (Beaumont) had the greatest percentage of African Americans at 33.5 percent.

In recent decades, the political influence of African American Texans has increased in local, state, and national government. From the years following Reconstruction until 1958 (when Hattie White was elected to the Houston School Board), no African American held elective office in the state. In 1972, Barbara Jordan became the first African American since Reconstruction to represent Texas in Congress; and in 1992, Morris Overstreet became the first African American to win a statewide office when he was elected to the Texas Court of Criminal Appeals. In 2009, Ron Kirk was appointed by President Obama to be the U.S. Trade Representative.

Latinos In the 1980s, Texas saw an increase in immigrants from Central America, South America, and the Caribbean. Still, more than 84 percent of Texas Latinos are of Mexican origin. By 2014, Texas Latinos numbered almost 10 million, approximately 39 percent of the state's population.[26] Latino births now account for more than one-half of all newborns in the state. Based on current population trends, some demographers suggest that by 2040 Latinos will comprise 58 percent of the state's population.[27] Texas ranks second in the nation behind California in the number of Latino residents. The majority of the population in 50 Texas counties is Latino. In seven counties in the Rio Grande Valley and along the border, more than 90 percent of the population is Latino. Though poverty rates are significantly higher for Latinos than Anglos, Texas's Spanish-surnamed citizens are gaining economic strength.

As Latinos continue to be the fastest-growing ethnic group in Texas (in terms of numbers), their political influence is also increasing. Between 1846 and 1961, only 19 Latino politicians were elected to seats in the Texas legislature. Since 1961, however, Latinos have won election to many local, state, and national positions. In 1984, with the election of Raul Gonzalez to the Texas Supreme Court, the first Latino won a statewide office. By 2010, Texas had more than 2,300 Latino elected officials, the largest number of any state. This figure represents more than 40 percent of all Latino elected officials in the country. Organizations such as the League of United Latin American Citizens and the Southwest Voter Registration Education Project have worked to increase voter registration and turnout among Latinos in recent years.

An estimated crowd of 25,000 march through downtown Dallas to City Hall in support of immigration reform, summer 2010.

Rodger Mallison/MCT/Landov

CRITICAL THINKING

What challenges and opportunities does racial and ethnic diversity present the Texas government? How can government best respond to the challenges and seize the opportunities?

Anglos According to the 2000 census, more than 52 percent of Texas's population was composed of "non–Hispanic whites." However, that percentage dropped to less than 50 percent in 2004, when Texas joined Hawaii, New Mexico, and California as majority-minority states. By 2014, the Anglo population of Texas reached almost 11.5 million, or about 44 percent of the state's population.[28] Projections indicate that the percentage of Anglos in the state will continue to decrease and the percentage of other racial/ethnic groups will continue to increase.

Despite a decreasing numerical majority, poverty rates among Texas Anglos remain dramatically lower than other groups, and incomes remain significantly higher. The poverty rate for Texas Anglos was 12 percent in 2013, compared to 29 percent for African Americans and 19 percent for Latinos.[29] In 2013, African American and Latino households had median annual incomes in the $35,000 range, whereas Anglo and Asian households averaged $59,000 to $64,000.[30] Anglos own almost two-thirds of all businesses in Texas. Anglos also continue to hold most local, state, and national political offices in the Lone Star State.

Implications of Increasing Diversity The changing demographics of Texas led many to speculate that the partisan makeup of Texas will soon be changing. "Demographics is Destiny," as the saying goes. With Hispanics as the largest minority in Texas, many point to Democratic President Barack Obama's winning 70 percent of the Latino vote to Republican Mitt Romney's 29 percent in 2012 as evidence that Texas will soon become a Democratic state. Some commentators have observed that if Latino voter turnout suddenly rose to the same level as that of non-Hispanic whites, Texas would instantly become a battleground state, in which Democrats would be competitive. Because of the size of its population, a Democratic Texas could assure presidential victories and increased Senate majorities for the Democrats. The Democratic Party is so encouraged by the prospect that they have launched "Battleground Texas", an organizing effort to register and turn out Democratic supporters. In 2014, Battleground Texas had more than 12,300 followers on Twitter and 43,600 likes on Facebook.[31]

Yet the ascendance of Democrats over Republicans in Texas is not a foregone conclusion. Latino voting rates remain consistently low. In addition, Republican candidates have averaged nearly 40 percent of the Latino vote in statewide races since 2000 and are making efforts to improve those numbers. Even if those efforts fail, a Democratic Texas may still be a decade in the future. Analyzing demographic trends and voting results, political observers argue that voter turnout rates suggest Texas Democrats will not reach parity with Republicans until 2024.[32]

Steve Murdock, a former state demographer and former director of the U.S. Census Bureau, has identified several negative economic implications of the current population trends. Latinos and African Americans account for the largest population growth in numbers and have the highest poverty and school dropout rates. The challenge for Texas will be to improve opportunities for these groups or face widespread poverty, lower education levels, and a declining economy.[33]

✔ **1.3 Learning Check**

1. True or False: The rate of population growth in Texas's Metropolitan Statistical Areas is greater than throughout the state as a whole.
2. How has the size and political power of Texas's Latino population changed in recent decades?

Answers on p. 40.

The Economy

★ **LO1.4**   Describe both the four land-based industries that formed the historic basis for the Texas economy and the diversification of the modern Texas economy.

The Lone Star State's economic success has relied heavily on land-based industries. These days, the Texas economy is vastly more diverse and includes 21st century industries like high technology and international trade.

The Texas Economy Through History

Much of Texas's early history was dominated by cattle, cotton, timber, and minerals (oil and gas). These four industries remain important sectors of the Texas economy and culture.

Cattle Cattle ranching began with the Spanish conquest, with later settlers continuing to bring livestock into Texas. Plentiful land and minimal government interference encouraged huge cattle empires, established by entrepreneurs such as Richard King and Mifflin Kenedy. Today, King Ranch covers more than 825,000 acres in South Texas.[34]

In 1865, an estimated 5 million cattle ranged over Texas's nearly 168 million acres of land. During the 25 years after the Civil War, approximately 35,000 men drove nearly 10 million cattle and 1 million horses north along the Chisholm and Goodnight-Loving Trails to Kansas railheads. By the late 1880s, when the railroads were built closer to Texas ranches, the cattle drives ended. In time, the economic impact of the beef business leveled off in the wake of newly emerging industries. Although the severe drought in 2011 and its aftereffects forced a reduction in the number of cattle in the state, Texas still leads the nation in cattle production. The inventory of approximately 11 million cattle is more than twice as many as the next largest producer. Cattle production accounts for more than 70 percent of livestock cash receipts and approximately one-half the total for all agricultural products in the state. Texas also leads the nation in the production of sheep, goats, wool, and mohair.[35]

Cotton Although popular culture romanticizes the 19th-century cowboys and cattle drives, cotton formed the backbone of the state's economy in that era. Before Spaniards brought cattle into Texas, cotton already grew wild in the region. Rich, fertile soil led to the crop's easy cultivation, begun by Spanish missionaries. In the 1820s, Colonel Jared Groce and other settlers began growing cotton, including a new hybrid variety, in East and Central Texas. Here soil and weather conditions most closely resembled those in the Old South. Before the Civil War, when slaves performed much of the field labor, cotton production spread. During that war, revenue from the sale of Texas cotton to European buyers aided the Confederacy. As more frontier land was settled, cotton production moved westward and increased in volume.

The Lone Star State leads the country in exported cotton, much of which is shipped to South Korea and Taiwan. Darren Hudson, director of the Cotton Economics Research Institute at Texas Tech University, estimates that Texas produces about 50 percent of U.S. cotton and approximately 10 percent of the world's cotton. In fact, Texas produces so much cotton that if you lined up all the cotton bales produced in the past 10 years end-to-end, they would circle the earth two-and-a-half times! Although cotton is grown throughout the state, the High Plains region of West Texas accounts for approximately 60 percent (more than 3 million bales) of the state's annual cotton yield. During the 2011 drought, estimates projected that cotton production in West Texas fell from a 10-year average of about 4.5 million bales per year to fewer than 1.5 million bales. This reduction represents a financial loss of more than one-third of the U.S. cotton crop ($2.2 billion).[36] Continuing drought, along with hail and blowing sand, destroyed millions of acres of cotton in 2013. By 2014, the Texas cotton yield had dropped by 50 percent, and the Great Plains was forecast to experience a 12 percent drop in production from 2012.[37]

Timber East Texas includes the Piney Woods and the Big Thicket, a densely wooded area that was largely uninhabited until the 1800s.[38] Following Texas's independence in 1836, immigrants built new communities, creating a construction industry that needed timber. By the mid-1800s, more than 200 sawmills were in operation from East to Central Texas.[39] As the population grew, creation of new towns and railroad lines increased demand for timber. This "bonanza era" for the timber industry continued well into the 20th century. By the early 1900s, the timber industry was the state's largest employer, manufacturer, and revenue generator. Estimates indicate that from the 1880s until the 1930s about 18 million acres of pine timber were logged in Texas, producing more than 59 billion board feet of lumber.[40]

The impact of timber on the state and national economies declined by the 1920s, as clear-cutting by some logging companies depleted the availability of timber in many parts of East Texas. Thousands of acres of woodlands were also cleared for exploration following the discovery of oil in this region. In 1933, the Texas legislature authorized the federal government to purchase more than 600,000 acres for four national forests (Angelina, Davy Crockett, Sabine, and Sam Houston). In addition, the timber industry began to implement reseeding and sustainable logging practices. At the end of the

20th century, Texas was the nation's tenth largest timber producer, generating more than $12.9 billion annually.[41]

The effects of the 2011 drought resulted in the loss of between 100 and 500 million trees throughout the state. Texas Forest Service officials estimated that more than 166,000 acres of trees in East Texas need to be replanted, at a cost of $57 million.[42] An additional 1.5 million trees on more than 16,200 acres were destroyed in a catastrophic wildfire in Bastrop County in late 2011, leading one Texas Parks and Wildlife Department official to predict that it would take more than half a century to fully recover from the loss.[43]

Oil and Gas Long before Europeans arrived, Native Americans used oil seeping from the Texas soil for medicinal purposes. Early Spanish explorers used it to caulk their boats. In the late 19th century, thousands of barrels were produced from crudely dug wells across the state. But it was not until 1901, when the Spindletop Field was developed, that petroleum ushered in the industry that dominated the state's economy for nearly a century. During the next 50 years, more wells were drilled, bringing industrial employment on a grand scale to rural Texas and offering tens of thousands of Texans an immediate and attractive alternative to life "down on the farm." Many of the major oil companies, such as Humble (now ExxonMobil Corporation), Magnolia Petroleum Company, Sun Oil Company, Gulf Oil Corporation, and the Texas Company, were created. (Gulf Oil Corporation and the Texas Company [Texaco] now are a part of Chevron.) In 1919, the Texas legislature gave the Railroad Commission of Texas limited regulatory jurisdiction over the state's oil and natural gas industry.[44]

At its peak in the early 1980s, the Texas oil and gas industry employed half a million workers, who earned more than $11 billion annually. Oil and natural gas production and related industries accounted for almost one-third of the state's economy. Over the next two decades, fluctuating prices reduced revenue. The discovery of major natural gas deposits in South, Central, and North Texas in the early 21st century, along with the advent of new recovery methods such as hydraulic fracturing, has launched an oil boom that helped insulate the state's economy from the global recession that began in 2008. Texas now accounts for more than 30 percent of total U.S. oil production, and if it were its own country would be the 11th largest producer in the world.[45] Revenues from taxes on oil and gas are helping Texas fill its Rainy Day Fund, complete highway construction and maintenance, invest in education through the Permanent University Fund, and fund the State Water Plan.[46] About 250,000 Texans worked in this industry in 2012, and even more Texans depended on energy-related industries for their employment. Most oil and gas jobs (including those in refineries and other petrochemical plants) pay relatively high wages and salaries.

Still, with increased economic diversification and oil prices under $100 per barrel in 2014, the oil and gas industry accounts for less than 6 percent of the state's economy and is not expected to regain its former level of influence. Meanwhile, awareness is growing that fossil fuels (including oil, gas, and coal) burned for industrial purposes and in automobiles, trucks, buses, and airplanes are the world's principal source of air pollution, contributing to significant human health problems.[47]

New Economic Directions

The devastation of plunging oil prices in the 1980s made the dangers of reliance on a single industry clear to Texas's business and government leaders, who subsequently pursued a restructuring and diversification of the state's economy. Texans have launched new industries that have quickly spread across the state, bolstering the Texas economy and playing an important role in the national economy. In 2006, for the first time, more *Fortune* 500 companies were headquartered in Texas than in any other state. In 2014 California ranked first with 54 and Texas was second with 52.[48] Texans today are employed in a variety of enterprises. A continuing struggle to provide jobs and market goods and services, however, requires effective public policies, an educated and productive labor force, an adequate supply of capital, and sound management practices.

Energy Four of the five largest corporations headquartered in Texas in 2014 were energy and energy related.[49] Using recent advancements in hydraulic fracturing (or "fracking"), energy producers have ushered in a second energy boom. Environmental and health concerns have accompanied this recovery method. (See Point/CounterPoint on p. 33: Should Oil and Gas Drillers Use Hydraulic "Fracking?").

Environmental concerns and fuel costs cause many people to resort to alternative fuels. In recent years, growth of renewable energy sources has outpaced the growth of coal, natural gas, and other energy sources. Renewables made up only 1 percent of Texas's energy supply in 2001, but that rose to more than 10 percent in 2013, with the overwhelming share being wind power.[50] Most of Texas's wind farms are located in West Texas. Although the Texas legislature twice refused to create financial incentives to encourage the solar industry in Texas, this action has not deterred the industry's development. One of the nation's largest solar photovoltaic generation farms began operations in December 2011 near Webberville to generate power for Austin Energy, the nation's ninth largest community-owned electric utility.[51] In 2014, two out-of-state companies announced plans to build large solar energy farms in Texas.[52]

Anticipating the need for workers in alternative energy technologies, several institutions of higher education in the state (including Texas Tech, Texas A&M, West Texas A&M, the University of Texas at Austin, the University of Houston, and Texas State Technical College in Sweetwater) offer renewable energy programs and classes in wind and solar power. In 2013, the U.S. Department of Energy and Vestas Wind Systems joined with Sandia National Laboratories to break ground on a new state-of-the-art wind turbine test facility at Texas Tech.[53]

High Technology The term *high technology* applies to research, development, manufacturing, and marketing of a seemingly endless line of electronic products like computers, smartphones, drones, and medical equipment. Although high-technology businesses employ less than 6 percent of Texas's labor force, these enterprises contribute about 10 percent of all wages paid to private sector employees. Most "high-tech " jobs are in manufacturing firms like Motorola, Dell, Hewlett-Packard, Texas Instruments, and Applied Materials. Approximately 85 percent of all high-tech employment in Texas is centered in the state's major cities.

More than one-third of all high-tech jobs are in professional, technical, and managerial positions, and wages and salaries are nearly twice as much as the average for other private sector positions. The Texas Emerging Technology Fund, administered by the state, provides funding for research and development activities and the relocation of companies from other states (especially California) in emerging technology industries. During the first decade of the 21st century, however, in cities such as Houston, Dallas, and Austin, jobs in semiconductor, computer, and circuit board manufacturing actually declined. Several high-tech companies relocated to other states and countries in pursuit of lower labor costs; predictable regulations; and access to markets, incentives, and a skilled workforce.[54] Despite this trend, by 2014, approximately 485,000 Texans held high-tech jobs, and Texas continues to rank second only to California in the size of its high-tech workforce.[55]

Additionally, **biotechnology** is a multibillion-dollar industry producing new medicines and vaccines, chemicals, and other products designed to benefit medical science, human health, and agricultural production. In the past two decades, biotech-related jobs have increased four times faster than the overall increase in employment in Texas. Home to more than 4,500 biotechnology firms, manufacturing companies, industry consortia, and research university facilities, Texas employs more than 100,000 workers in the biotech sector at an average annual salary of more than $74,800.

Supported by big biotech companies, scientists at Texas A&M University have aided in research leading to the production of genetically modified organism (GMO) crops, such as corn, soybeans, and cotton. Environmental and consumer protection groups, however, have opposed GMOs and called for labeling all foods containing them.[56] Security is a concern for this industry. The Texas A&M Center for Innovation in Advanced Development and Manufacturing, established in 2012 to lead the nation's biosecurity research efforts, is a public-private partnership likely worth $1.5 to $2 billion. The initial federal

Richard Ellis/The Image Bank/Getty Images

CRITICAL THINKING

What industries are essential to sustain and continue to develop the Texas economy in the 21st century?

biotechnology
Also known as "biotech," this is the use and/or manipulation of biological processes and microorganisms to perform industrial or manufacturing processes or create consumer goods.

grant of more than $175 million is the largest sum of federal money awarded to Texas since NASA.

Services Employing one-fourth of all Texas workers, service industries continue to provide new jobs more rapidly than all other sectors. Service businesses include health care providers (hospitals and nursing homes); personal services (hotels, restaurants, and recreational enterprises such as water parks and video arcades); and commercial services (printers, advertising agencies, data processing companies, equipment rental companies, and consultants). Other service providers include education, investment brokers, insurance and real estate agencies, banks and credit unions, and merchandising enterprises. Many high school and college students work in the service sector as restaurant and bar wait staff, retail store sales associates, and the like.

Influenced by an aging population and the availability of new medical procedures, health services employment has steadily increased. According to the Texas Workforce Commission, as of 2012 private and public health care services employed about 1.1 million workers (including 624,000 in ambulatory health care services, 297,000 in hospitals, and about 174,000 in nursing and residential care).[57] The Texas Workforce Commission projects that these positions will be among the fastest growing occupations over the next several years.[58]

Most service jobs come with few or no benefits and pay lower wages and salaries than manufacturing firms that produce goods. Thus, the late journalist Molly Ivins warned that "the dream that we can transform ourselves into a service economy and let all the widget-makers go to hell or Taiwan is bullstuff. The service sector creates jobs all right, but they're the lowest paying jobs in the system. You can't afford a house frying burgers at McDonald's, even if you're a two-fryer family."[59]

Agriculture Texas ranks second in the nation in agricultural production (behind California). It leads the country in total acreage of agricultural land and numbers of farms and ranches, as well as in production of beef, grain sorghum, cotton, wool, and mohair. Other important cash crops include corn, hay, rice, cottonseed, peanuts, soybeans, pecans, and fresh market vegetables and citrus.

Gross income from the products of Texas agriculture amounts to about $22 billion annually, making agriculture the second largest industry in Texas. Mexico is the largest purchaser of Texas's farm and ranch products, and Japan is a major consumer of Texas-grown wheat and corn. Beef is the state's most important meat export. Despite these impressive statistics, however, farming and ranching provide less than 2 percent of the state's jobs and total income. Furthermore, most agricultural commodities are shipped abroad or to other parts of the United States without being processed in Texas. Consequently, Texas needs industrial development for the processing of food and fiber to derive maximum economic benefit from its agricultural products.

Over the past eight decades, the number of farms and ranches in Texas has decreased from more than 500,000 to fewer than 250,000, and the average acreage has increased from 300 acres to approximately 527 acres.[60]

These developments largely reflect the availability of labor-saving farm machinery and chemicals. Small family farms are also being rapidly replaced by large agribusinesses or sold for development. When farm commodity prices are low (because of overproduction and weak market demand) or when crops are poor (as a result of drought), many farmers end the year deeply in debt. Some must sell their land—usually to larger farm operators and sometimes to corporations. But some wealthy individuals purchase agricultural property (especially ranchland) as a status symbol—even though their land generates little or no income. Some use their agricultural property ownership to qualify for various exemptions and reductions in local, state, and federal taxes. In addition, much farm and ranchland near expanding cities is lost to urban sprawl. According to the U.S. Department of Agriculture, every minute, a half-acre of Texas farmland is converted into part of a road, shopping mall, or subdivision.

The Texas drought in late 2011 was the worst single-year Texas drought since recordkeeping began. It may also prove to be one of most devastating economic events in the history of the Lone Star State. Texas AgriLife Extension Service reported a record $7.62 billion in agricultural losses in 2011 as a result of the drought. In November 2013, the drought officially became the second longest drought in Texas history.[61]

Trade By reducing and ultimately eliminating tariffs during the 15-year period from 1993-2008, the North American Free Trade Agreement stimulated U.S. trade with both Canada and Mexico. Because more than 60 percent of U.S. exports to Mexico are produced in or transported through Texas from other states, expanding foreign trade produces jobs for Texans, profits for the state's businesses, and revenue for state and local governments. It also means that Texas benefits from peace and prosperity across its southern border, and suffers when those conditions are absent.

Maquiladoras (partner plants) on the Mexican side of the border typically use cheap labor to assemble imported parts for a wide range of consumer goods and then export these goods back to the United States. Under NAFTA, these exports are not taxed. Consequently, Texas border cities (especially Brownsville, McAllen, Laredo, and El Paso) attract many manufacturers who set up supply and distribution facilities in Texas that serve the maquiladoras in Mexico.[62] A United Nations report revealed that labor policies at maquiladora assembly plants endanger women in Ciudad Juárez, a Mexican city across the border from El Paso, where hundreds of women and girls have disappeared or have been raped and murdered in recent years.[63]

NAFTA has both benefited and harmed the state's and the nation's economy. The nation exports more services than it imports from Canada and Mexico. Conversely, the nation imports more goods than it exports to its partner nations.[64] Texas's garment industry has been adversely affected by NAFTA, especially in border counties. Likewise, some Texas fruit and vegetable producers have been hurt by Mexican competition. In addition, increased trucking on highways between Mexico and Canada contributes to air pollution and causes traffic problems that make road travel slower and more dangerous.

maquiladora
"Partner plant" on the Mexican side of the border that uses cheap labor to assemble goods and then exports these goods back to the United States.

Since 1995, a succession of political and economic crises in Mexico has raised serious questions concerning NAFTA's future. Mexico has seen assassinations of public figures, kidnappings of wealthy businesspeople, drug-related corruption of government officials, attacks on tourists, widespread unemployment and hunger in both urban and rural areas, and acts of armed rebellion.[65] A more prosperous and stable Mexico usually means fewer jobless workers migrating to the United States and more trade between the two countries.[66] In 2006, Mexico's voters selected Felipe Calderón as president. He began a military assault on criminal drug cartels soon after taking office, and violence over the next few years reached record levels.[67] In January 2012, the Mexican government reported that 47,515 people had been killed in drug-related violence since President Calderón's election, with others estimating as many as 80,000 dead.[68] In July 2012, Enrique Peña Nieto was elected to serve as president until November 30, 2018. President Peña Nieto has made some changes in violence prevention programs and security reorganization, but his approach to organized crime strongly resembles that of Calderón. The Peña Nieto administration's claims of reduced violence are hard to corroborate, as reporting on crime has been limited both by his government and by drug cartels seeking to silence reporters. Most statistics suggest a decrease in homicide and an increase in extortion and kidnapping.[69]

Important as it is, Mexico is far from Texas's only trading partner, as Texas does business with countries all over the globe, even some that are controversial. Several Texas politicians, including former Agriculture Commissioner Todd Staples and U.S. Senator John Cornyn, have advocated for increasing trade with Cuba. Although Cuba has been designated as a sponsor of terrorism, Texas agriculture exports to the island continue to grow.[70]

1.4 Learning Check

1. What are the four land-based industries that were important to the Texas economy in the past?
2. Which economic sector is currently creating the most jobs for Texans?

Answers on p. 40.

Meeting New Challenges

LO1.5   Identify five major policy challenges Texas faces in the 21st century.

Clearly, Texas has experienced rapid and dramatic change in recent decades, and though change provides opportunities, it also brings challenges. Texans are greatly affected by public policy decisions concerning immigration and Texas's workforce, protection of the ecological system, job-creating economic development, technological changes in communications and industry, and restructuring and financing of the state's public schools and institutions of higher education.[71]

Immigration: Federal and State Problems

Since Texas became part of the United States, immigration has been the source of many controversies that affect state, national, and international politics: how to control the flow of immigrants, the length of time a nonresident may remain within U.S. territory, the type of labor nonresidents may perform, and other issues. Some immigrants are undocumented and come across the border in violation of federal immigration law or overstay legal visas. Although Texas employers attract immigrants as a source of cheap labor, this system can depress wages for all workers and provide often unwanted competition for jobs. Because Texas relies largely on consumption and property taxes to fund state and local government services, even **undocumented immigrants** pay state taxes when they buy goods and services or rent or buy property. Yet many Texas citizens wonder if they pay enough to cover the social services they sometimes use. (For a discussion about immigration's impact on Texas's economy, see this chapter's Selected Reading, "Immigrants' Economic Strength Increases." on p. 36.) As with each wave of immigration in American history, prejudices along with economics produce heated controversy in politics.

In 1986, President Ronald Reagan signed into law the Immigration Reform and Control Act that granted amnesty to any immigrant who entered the country illegally before 1982. The law also included measures to restrain the flow of new illegal immigrants into the United States. Penalties were provided for employers who knowingly hired undocumented immigrants; and it authorized more enforcement personnel for the Immigration and Naturalization Service, the agency then in charge of controlling immigration. Despite this act, thousands of undocumented immigrants continued to enter Texas each year, and those who employed illegal immigrants rarely faced serious consequences. Today, many undocumented people are arrested, detained, and expelled from the country; and families are often separated in the process. Others have voluntarily returned home after earning money to support their families. Thousands remain in Texas and often arrange for family members to join them. Some of these workers are exploited by employers, merchants, and landlords. Others receive fair wages and humane treatment. All live and work in fear of arrest and deportation.

Despite increasing anti-immigrant sentiments nationally in the 1990s, in June 2001 a substantial bipartisan majority in the Texas legislature passed and Governor Perry signed the Texas DREAM Act, which allows undocumented immigrants who were brought to Texas as children by their parents to pay in-state tuition at public colleges and universities if they graduated from high school or received a GED in the state. Available to those who have at least three years of residency and are seeking legal residency, this provision has benefited thousands of Texas students.

Following the terrorist attacks of September 11, 2001, Congress passed the Enhanced Border Security and Visa Entry Reform Act of 2002, which President George W. Bush signed into law. In addition to provisions regarding terrorist organizations, this act also concerns the tracking of international students at U.S. educational institutions, the issuance of visas, and other details regarding foreign nationals. In 2006, President Bush signed the Secure Fence Act authorizing, among other barriers, more than 700 miles of fencing along the almost 2,000-mile-long U.S.–Mexico border from California to Texas to combat illegal immigration.

The Republican majority in the Texas legislative and executive branches have issued repeated calls for getting tough on undocumented immigrants. Yet they have failed to repeal the Texas DREAM Act. In fact, Governor Perry

undocumented immigrant
A person who enters the United States in violation of federal immigration law and thus lacks proper documentation and identification.

defended the act repeatedly during his unsuccessful run for the Republican presidential nomination in 2012.

Texas politicians often face the difficult task of balancing constituents' demands for increased border security against the demands of a growing Latino constituency and a politically active business community pushing for immigration reforms. More than 30 bills addressing immigration were filed in the Texas legislature in 2011, most of them labeled as anti-immigrant by civil rights groups. Although these bills received considerable support from Texas Tea Party activists, after months of intense debate, none passed.[72] With Republicans increasingly concerned about the growth of a pro-Democratic Latino vote, the tone changed in the 2013 session of the legislature, with fewer than 10 immigration bills being filed, and Governor Perry's avoiding the word "immigration" in his State of the State speech altogether.[73] Still, in the 2014 elections many Republican candidates jockeyed for recognition as "tough on immigration" and called for reform or repeal of the Texas DREAM Act. Within days of winning the Republican nomination some of these same candidates moved away from their more divisive language. Meanwhile, Democratic candidates sought to attract and mobilize Latino voters.[74]

 **Students**  **in Action**

From Tehran to Texas

"Civic engagement is a fulfilling experience; it's an opportunity to make a difference and contribute to society. It also builds character and is a valuable learning experience."

—Shirin Tavakoli

Shirin's Journey to Texas

Shirin Tavakoli was born and raised in Iran, where she saw the government violate the rights of the people around her. From an early age, she aspired to involve herself in politics and advocate for human rights. Yet, the strict laws of Iran's Islamic Republic presented what seemed an impassable roadblock to her dream. The opportunity to move to what she'd come to know as the "Dream Land" of America came in 2008 when the U.S. Embassy in Abu Dhabi contacted her for an interview. Her father had initiated Shirin's long, difficult, and expensive immigration process in 2003 by applying for her to become a permanent U.S. resident. She was disappointed when she was denied a visa; but, inspired by her dream of becoming a successful human rights advocate, she refused to lose hope. She persevered through another interview and a small mountain of paperwork, and was eventually granted a visa. Shirin moved to Texas in 2008, leaving her family and friends behind for the opportunities she would never have in her country.

Becoming an Asset to Her New Home

Moving to Texas was harder than Shirin anticipated. Without her support network of family and friends, she struggled to adapt to a new culture and learn a new language. Determined to integrate into her new home, it was ultimately her passion for civic engagement that sustained her during the difficult transition. She excelled in her classes and threw herself fully into campus life. In 2009, her peers at Collin College elected her president of the Student Government Association (SGA), and she became their advocate. Her experience in SGA motivated her to get involved in politics on a broader level; and in the summer of 2009, she began an internship in the office of State Representative Allen Vaught (D-Dallas).

A year later, Shirin's hard work and determination landed her a full tuition scholarship at Southern Methodist University, where she served as president of the campus chapter of Amnesty International, editor-in-chief of the human rights publication *Human Writes*, and founder and president of The Innocence Project of Texas at SMU. After obtaining degrees in political science, international studies, and human rights, she took a job serving the people of Texas as a constituent services liaison for U.S. Congresswoman Eddie Bernice Johnson (D-Texas), working to resolve citizens' issues with federal agencies. In August 2014, Shirin started law school to fulfill her dream of becoming a human rights attorney.

Shirin uses the example of those around the world fighting and dying for a chance to be involved in political life to inspire other young people to get civically engaged. She believes that she never could have come so far without the countless opportunities for civic engagement in this country. She hopes people her age will not take such opportunities for granted. Reflecting on her journey, Shirin is proud to be part of a nation founded and built by immigrants. She understands their struggles and their role in building our society. Her hope is that her fellow Texans will see immigrants not as a threat but as people who have overcome great challenges to contribute to American life.

© Andresr/Shutterstock.com

Water

After a devastating drought in the 1950s, the Texas legislature created the Texas Water Development Board (TWDB) in 1957 and mandated statewide water planning. Since then, the TWDB and the Texas Board of Water Engineers have prepared and adopted nine state water plans, including *Water for Texas–2012*. This plan makes several recommendations for the development, management, and conservation of water resources and for better preparation for and response to drought conditions so that sufficient water will be available for the foreseeable future.[75]

With the state's population expected to double by the middle of the 21st century, assuring all Texans adequate water will be a formidable challenge.[76] In 2012, the Office of the Comptroller issued a report, "The Impact of the 2011 Drought and Beyond," which projected that demand for water will rise by 22 percent by 2060, while the state's current dependable water supply will meet only about 65 percent of that projected demand. Susan Combs, then comptroller of public accounts, declared that "planning for and managing our water use is perhaps the most important task facing Texas policymakers in the 21st century."[77]

As urbanization continues, cities will increasingly compete with small towns, agricultural interests, and the oil and gas industry for the same water. These problems are especially visible along the I-35 corridor and around fast-growing cities like Dallas, Fort Worth, Austin, and San Antonio.[78] In 2011, nearly 26.5 billion gallons of water were used for fracking in Texas. That amount is likely to reach 41 billion gallons by 2020.[79] Texas's water supply was severely depleted by the 2011 drought, when the 30 aquifers that supply about 60 percent of the state's water declined to levels predating the levels of the 1950s drought. Scientists project that it could take years to recover from this low level.[80] TWDB chair Edward Vaughn explained that the message of *Water for Texas—2012* is simple: "During serious drought conditions, Texas does not and will not have enough water to meet the needs of its people, its businesses, and its agricultural enterprises."[81]

In November 2011, voters ratified a constitutional amendment authorizing up to $6 billion in bonds to make loans to local governments for water, wastewater, and flood control projects and in that same election defeated a proposal to provide tax incentives for water conservation on agricultural land.[82] Then in 2012, Spicewood Beach became the first Texas town to have its wells run dry, followed by the town of Robert Lee.[83] In 2013 the city of Barnhart ran dry, and the list maintained by the Texas Council on Environmental Quality of communities that may soon have no water reached 46.[84] That year, the state announced that it would fully fund the State Water Plan for the first time. The 83rd Texas Legislature proposed, and 73 percent of Texas voters ratified, a constitutional amendment to use $2 billion of the "rainy day" fund, the state's savings account, to finance priority projects under the state water plan.

Environmental Protection

Poor air quality and impure water cause serious health problems for many Texans. The Lone Star State leads the nation in hazardous waste generated, carbon dioxide emissions, volatile organic compounds that are recognized carcinogens, and toxic chemicals released into the air and into the groundwater.[85] Coal-fired power plants and oil refineries in Texas annually generate approximately 294 million tons of carbon dioxide and heat-trapping gases, more than the next two states (Pennsylvania and Florida) combined.

The government of Texas routinely clashes with the federal government as the state fights for reduced federal regulation. Between 2009 and 2014, Texas filed 28 lawsuits against the federal government, including 14 against the Environmental Protection Agency (EPA). In 2011, the EPA ruled that coal-fired power plants in Texas and 26 other states must be upgraded with equipment to reduce toxic emissions. Texas led several states in a legal challenge to those regulations. Governor Rick Perry frequently criticized EPA mandates as "overreaching regulation," stating that they have led to a loss of more than 500 jobs in the Lone Star State. In 2014, the U.S. Supreme

Point/Counterpoint

THE ISSUE The process of hydraulic fracturing of underground rock formations to release the flow of natural gas and oil is also known as "fracking." Recent technological developments have increased the use of this practice, creating both opportunities and dangers.

Should Oil and Gas Drillers Use Hydraulic "Fracking"?

Arguments For Fracking

1. The oil and gas industry in the Lone Star State is experiencing large profits at a time when other sectors have not performed as well. This production has created an economic boom in many parts of Texas, contributing to a state economy that is stronger than the national economy. Unemployment is low, and taxes are generated from increased revenue as a result of fracking.

2. As conventional supplies of oil and gas have dwindled in Texas, the process of fracking has allowed industry to unlock large reserves of gas found in shale and other rock formations. Releasing gas though fracking provides another valuable energy resource, reducing Texas's (and the country's) dependence on oil.

3. There is no conclusive proof that fracking causes earthquakes. A report released by the National Research Council in mid-2012 revealed that fracking does not pose a high risk for triggering earthquakes large enough to feel.

Arguments Against Fracking

1. Fracking poses higher environmental risks than does conventional drilling. The equipment used in fracking emits pollutants into the air. Fracking fluid contains hazardous chemicals that will ultimately return to the surface. Pipes may leak, causing groundwater contamination. Texas already leads the nation in recognized carcinogens released into the air and toxic chemicals released into its groundwater. Fracking adds to these pollutants.

2. Fracking requires between 50,000 gallons and 4 million gallons of water to fracture a single well. This resource is too valuable to use in such quantities at this time. The agriculture and timber industries have been gravely affected by record drought conditions and need available water.

3. Fracturing rock may cause geological instability, leading to earthquakes. Geologists made direct links between fracking and earthquakes in Ohio and Oklahoma in 2011 and 2013. As the petroleum industry continues to expand the process of fracking, more earthquakes may be expected.

This "Point/Counterpoint" is based on Debra Black, "Fracking Fracas: Pros and Cons of Controversial Gas Extraction Process," *The Toronto Star*, February 5, 2012; and *Induced Seismicity Potential in Energy Technologies*, Report of the National Research Council, June 15, 2012.

For peer-reviewed scientific studies establishing the link between fracking and earthquakes, see W.-Y. Kim, "Induced Seismicity Associated with Fluid Injection into a Deep Well in Youngstown, Ohio," *Journal of Geophysical Research Solid Earth* 118 (2013), 3506–3518, doi:10.1002/jgrb.50247. See also K. Keranen, H. Savage, G. Abers, and E. Cochran, "Potentially Induced Earthquakes in Oklahoma, USA: Links Between Wastewater Injection and the 2011 Mw 5.7 Earthquake Sequence," *Geology*, March 26, 2013.

Court ruled in favor of the EPA, bolstering its authority to regulate carbon pollution and use the Clean Air Act to fight global climate change.[86] Environmental organizations like the Sierra Club argue the state does too little to protect the environment and have filed several citizen lawsuits against companies accused of violating antipollution laws.

Pollution also hurts fish and wildlife populations. Texas leads all states in the number of endangered fish and wildlife species. Industries in Texas, other gulf states, and Mexico release toxic chemicals directly into the Gulf of Mexico or rivers that flow into it. Also contributing greatly to the gulf's environmental problems is the flow of rivers drawing water from the chemically fertilized farms of rural areas and the lawns and gardens of cities large and small. Catches of fish, shrimp, and oysters from gulf waters are declining. Texans must either do with less seafood, import it from abroad at high prices, or enact environmental protection measures to clean up the Gulf of Mexico and restore its productivity.[87]

Education

Of the 50 states, Texas ranked 44th in high school graduation rate, 47th in average SAT scores, and last in the percentage of the population over 25 with a high school diploma in 2013.[88] Economic performance depends on a well-educated Texas workforce. College educators complain of students poorly prepared for higher education, and employers are particularly concerned that one of every three Texans cannot read and write well enough to fill out a simple job application. Moreover, the state loses many billions of dollars annually because most illiterate Texans are doomed to unemployment or low-paying jobs and thus generate little or no tax revenue.

Teachers are the key element in any educational system, but from year to year, the Lone Star State confronts shortages of certified personnel to instruct its 4 million elementary and secondary school students, a half million of whom have limited English proficiency. Although estimates of the teacher shortage vary, the Texas Education Agency reports that approximately one-fifth of the state's 250,000 teachers quit teaching each year. Some retire, but most of them leave their profession for reasons that include inadequate pay and benefits (Texas ranks 31st in public school teacher pay), low prestige, conflicts with parents, and increasing time-consuming chores that often must be done at night and on weekends. Contributing to their decision to seek other careers is stress over classroom problems affected by the poverty and troubled home lives of many students and burdensome government-mandated assessment and accountability measures.

Early in 2010, Governor Perry announced that Texas would not compete for a federal education grant that could have provided as much as $700 million for the state. Criticizing a goal of the Race to the Top grant in establishing national curriculum standards for math and English as a "federal takeover of public schools," Perry rejected the program. Texas was one of only two states in the nation (the other was Alaska) not to participate in the common standards effort.[89] The governor and legislature reduced funding for higher education, student financial aid, and public schools in 2011 to balance the state budget. The cuts to public education resulted in the elimination of more than 10,000 teaching positions and almost 1,000 support staff jobs.[90] Texas courts have repeatedly intervened to require the state to increase funding as well as provide more equitable financing for public schools. (For a discussion of this issue, see Chapter 13, "Finance and Fiscal Policy.") As of 2014, Texas ranked 43rd among the 50 states in spending per student.[91]

Poverty and Social Problems

The Lone Star State has alarming numbers of children living in poverty and in single parent homes. Births to unwed teenagers, juvenile arrests, and violent acts committed by teenagers and preadolescents also signal some of the social dysfunctionality associated with poverty. Child poverty in Texas increased 47 percent from 2000 to 2011, and by 2014 more than one of every four children here was living in poverty.[92] Many children at all levels of society suffer from abuse and neglect. Estimates of the number of homeless people (including many children) vary widely, but at least 100,000—and perhaps more than 200,000—Texans cannot provide themselves with shelter in a house or apartment. At the same time, 18.5 percent of Texans earn less than $22,113 a year, well below the federal poverty level.[93]

With almost one-fifth of its population below the poverty line, health care is a major issue for Texas. Of the 50 states, Texas has the highest percentage of uninsured residents. In 2013, approximately 6.2 million people were without health insurance, almost a quarter of the state's population.[94] After implementation of the federal Affordable Care Act (also known as "Obamacare") that year, the uninsured rate in Texas dipped slightly from 24.8 percent to 23.5 percent in 2014. Texas, however, is one of 21 states refusing federal funds to expand Medicaid coverage for adults under Obamacare.[95] Some Texans argue that any public assistance for the poor is too much and encourages dependence instead of self-reliance. Other Texans advocate for increased government spending for social service programs, noting that government support increases spending in impoverished communities, keeping local businesses open. Between these extremes are Texans who support a limited role for government in meeting human needs but who call for nongovernmental organizations to play a more active role in dealing with social problems. Texas voters, however, tend to support candidates for public office who promise lower taxes, less government spending, fewer public employees, and a reduction or elimination of social services. As a result, the Lone Star State continues to rank near the bottom of the 50 states in governmental responses to poverty and social problems.

✓ **1.5 Learning Check**

1. True or False: If current trends persist, demand for water will rise by 10 percent by 2060, and the state's current dependable water supply will meet that projected demand.
2. True or False: More than one-third of Texas workers are earning wages below the federal poverty level.

Answers on p. 40.

Selected Reading

Report: Immigrants' Economic Strength Increases

Julián Aguilar

This reading appeared in the May 30, 2013, edition of the Texas Tribune *and discusses the economic impact of immigration in Texas. The full story is available at http://www.texastribune.org/2013/05/30/report-immigrants-economic-strength-increases/.*

Since the 2010 U.S. census, the number of naturalized citizens has increased substantially in Texas, and the state's immigrants account for significant purchasing power and economic output, according to an analysis by a Washington-based think tank urging immigration reform. Immigrants make up more than 20 percent of the Texas workforce, and the state's number of naturalized citizens increased by more than 68,000 in 2011 when compared with 2010, according to a compilation of immigration data by the Immigration Policy Center. The purchasing power of Hispanics and Asians in Texas—whether native born or immigrants—increased to $265 billion in 2012, an increase of $55 billion from 2010.

The study comes as the U.S. Senate is just weeks out from voting on the first comprehensive immigration-reform legislation to come before the chamber since 2007. The policy center's report also says that mass deportation from the state, which has an estimated 1.6 million undocumented immigrants, would cost billions of dollars. "If all unauthorized immigrants were removed from Texas, the state would lose $69.3 billion in economic activity, $30.8 billion in gross state product, and approximately 403,174 jobs, even accounting for adequate market adjustment time," the study says, citing analysis from the Texas-based Perryman Group.

But the Federation for American Immigration Reform, a nonpartisan group that advocates for increased border security and limited legal immigration, said the report doesn't include the costs to provide undocumented immigrants with health care, education and other entitlements. The data is necessary to paint a clearer picture of how illegal immigration affects the state, said Ira Mehlman, a FAIR national spokesman. All people, legal or otherwise, contribute to the economy when they make a purchase or pay rent and sales tax, Mehlman said. But he added that is only one part of the equation. "The question is, does the economic contribution offset the cost of having you here? That's No. 1," he said. "And what impact does it have on other people's ability to contribute economically to their maximum potential? That's the reason we have immigration laws."

The most recent state examination of the give-and-take in Texas was performed in 2006 by then-Comptroller Carole Keeton Strayhorn. That analysis said that if Texas went without the estimated 1.4 million undocumented immigrants living in Texas in 2005, it would have resulted in a net loss of about $17.7 billion in gross domestic product that year. Undocumented immigrants also produced more in-state revenue, $1.58 billion, than what they cost in state services, $1.16 billion, the 2006 report said. Local governments lost about $1.44 billion in health-care and law-enforcement costs that were not reimbursed by the state, however. The office of current Comptroller Susan Combs, who announced this week that she would retire from public office when her term ends in 2015, has said there are no immediate plans to update the 2006 study.

The economic gains have been the focus of various pro-reform groups whose members include elected officials and business leaders. The American Action Forum recently sent a letter signed by more than 100 conservative economists to Congress urging reform and the Partnership for a New American Economy, whose members include New York Mayor Michael Bloomberg, San Antonio Mayor Julián Castro and El Paso Mayor John Cook, have spearheaded traditional and online campaigns urging elected officials to create a path to legal status or citizenship for the country's estimated 11 million undocumented immigrants.

But FAIR's Mehlman said groups that promote an overhaul and stress the need for a legitimate workforce fuel a battle between the "elite and the ordinary." "Illegal immigration amounts to a labor subsidy for them," he said. "They get away with hiring people at low wages and ask everybody else to pick up the cost of education, health care all the things that they don't supply. The practice leads to depressing wages and making those jobs too low-paying to attract native workers. Many of the jobs would be done by native workers at higher wages, therefore paying more in taxes and contributing more in just general economic output and purchasing power," he said.

The 68,000-person increase in the Texas naturalized citizen population means that demographic represents about 33 percent of the state's immigrants. Naturalized citizens are also becoming more educated, with about 29 percent of the group earning at least a bachelor's degree by 2011, compared with 15 percent of noncitizens.

✓ Selected Reading Learning Check

1. True or False: According to the Texas comptroller's analysis, undocumented immigrants produce more revenue for the state than they cost in services.
2. True or False: The mayors of San Antonio and El Paso have tried to prevent undocumented immigrants from gaining legal status or citizenship.

Answers on p. 40.

Conclusion

With changing demographic, economic, social, and environmental conditions in the Lone Star State, Texas policymakers face several challenges. The diversity of the state both demographically and geographically presents myriad opportunities and problems. While the state's economy flourishes, many Texans live in poverty. Both ordinary citizens and public officials must realize that their ability to cope with public problems now and in the years ahead depends largely on how well homes and schools prepare young Texans to meet the crises and demands of an ever-changing state, nation, and world.

Chapter Summary

LO 1.1 **Describe how political culture has shaped Texas's politics, government, and public policy.** The political culture of Texas is dominated by the individualistic and traditionalistic subcultures. The individualistic culture is rooted in the state's frontier experience and is reflected in its constitutionally weak government and low spending on programs. The traditionalistic culture grew out of the Old South, where policies were designed to preserve the social order and the poor and minorities were often disenfranchised (not allowed to vote). With an increasingly diverse population, Texas may be shifting toward an increase in the moralistic subculture, which values government as a way to improve society.

LO 1.2 **Explain the differences among the geographic regions of Texas.** With more than 267,000 square miles of territory, Texas ranks second in size to Alaska among the 50 states. Infrastructure is therefore a major government issue. The cost of political campaigns in such a geographically large state and the necessary fundraising are major political issues. Each of the six major regions in Texas is different in its economic and political climate.

LO 1.3 **Analyze the relationship between the social history of Texas and the political characteristics of the state's diverse population.** Texas has a population of more than 25 million. Over 80 percent of all Texans live in the state's most highly urbanized counties. Texas's past was riddled with intergroup conflict, but the state has increasingly moved toward integration and cooperation. The three largest groups today are Anglos, Latinos (the fastest growing group by number), and African Americans. Texas has a small but growing population of Asian Americans and fewer than 170,000 Native Americans.

LO 1.4 **Describe both the four land-based industries that formed the historic basis for the Texas economy and the diversification of the modern Texas economy**. The Texas economy historically relied on cattle, cotton, timber, and oil and gas. Although each is still important, the Texas economy is now very diverse and includes many businesses that work in renewable energy sources, high technology, the service sector, a variety of forms of agriculture, and international trade. Service jobs make up the bulk of the increase in employment, but most such jobs pay little and offer few benefits.

LO 1.5 **Identify five major policy challenges Texas faces in the 21st century**. Challenges that face Texas include the need to more effectively address immigration, manage the state's water supply, protect the environment, develop educational programs to meet the demands of an industrial and postindustrial society, and formulate policies for combating poverty and social problems. Each of these areas affects the lives of real people. Addressing the issues each raises will cost taxpayers money. The future of Texas depends on Texans' abilities to resolve problems and capitalize on its human resources.

Key Terms

government, p. 3
public policy, p. 3
politics, p. 4
political culture, p. 4
moralistic culture, p. 4
individualistic culture, p. 4
traditionalistic culture, p. 4
progressive, p. 5
African American, p. 5
Latino, p. 5

Jim Crow laws, p. 7
patrón system, p. 7
right to work laws, p. 7
eminent domain, p. 7
social media, p. 9
Protestant fundamentalism, p. 9
North American Free Trade
   Agreement (NAFTA), p. 10
redlining, p. 13
urban renewal, p. 13

exclusionary zoning, p. 13
racial covenants, p. 13
metropolitanization, p. 13
Anglo, p. 14
Asian American, p. 14
Native American, p. 14
biotechnology, p. 25
maquiladora, p. 27
undocumented
   immigrant, p. 29

Learning Check Answers

1.1 1. True. Public policy aims to encourage, discourage, or modify behavior.
   2. Texas has historically been dominated by the individualistic culture and the traditionalistic culture.

1.2 1. Texas is the second largest state in geographical size, making infrastructure a major issue for government and financing campaigns fundraising a major issue for politicians.
   2. False. The regions of Texas are quite different from one another in economy, culture, and politics.

1.3 1. True. Metropolitan Statistical Areas (MSA) are the fastest-growing areas in Texas.
2. Latinos are the fastest-growing ethnic population in Texas, with higher immigration and birthrates than any other group in the state. Along with this growth has come increased political influence.

1.4 1. Cattle, cotton, timber, and oil and gas were most important to the Texas economy in the past.
2. The service sector is currently creating the most jobs for Texans.

1.5 1. False. Demand for water will rise by 22 percent by 2060, and the state's current dependable water supply will meet only about 65 percent of that projected demand.
2. True. In 2010, more than one-third of Texas workers were earning less than $20,000 a year, which was below the federal poverty level for food stamps for a family of four.

Selected Reading Learning Check

1. True. The Comptroller's Office found that undocumented immigrants produced $1.58 billion of in-state revenue and only cost the state $1.16 billion in services.
2. False. The mayors of San Antonio and El Paso have joined Partnership for a New American Economy, which has lobbied elected officials to create a path to legal status or citizenship for the country's undocumented immigrants.

2

Federalism and the Texas Constitution

IN SEARCH OF THE TEXAS CONSTITUTION...

Waco/Tribune-Herald/Herschberger/Herschberger Cartoon Service

CRITICAL THINKING

Take a closer look at the cartoon. What do you think? Is it time to undertake a wholesale revision of our Texas Constitution?

Learning Objectives

2.1 Summarize and analyze federalism and the powers of the state in a constitutional context.

2.2 Summarize how each of the state's previous constitutions shaped its content and the characteristics of the present-day Texas Constitution.

2.3 Analyze the amendment process, focusing on recent constitutional amendment elections as well as attempts to revise the Texas Constitution.

2.4 Explain and analyze the basic sections of the Texas Constitution.

The Texas Constitution, adopted in 1876, serves as the Lone Star State's fundamental law. This document outlines the structure of Texas's state government, authorizes the creation of counties and cities, and establishes basic rules for governing. It has been amended frequently over the course of nearly 14 decades (as illustrated by the cartoon at the beginning of this chapter). Lawyers, newspaper editors, political scientists, government officials, and others who consult the state constitution tend to criticize it for being too long and for lacking organization. Yet despite criticism, Texans have expressed strong opposition to, or complete lack of interest in, proposals for wholesale constitutional revision.

The Texas Constitution is the primary source of the state government's policymaking power. The other major source of its power is membership in the federal Union. Sometimes, tensions between the federal government and Texas may erupt, as when former Governor Perry challenged the passage and implementation of the Affordable Health Care Act (Obamacare). Within the federal system, state constitutions are subject to the U.S. Constitution.

The American Federal Structure

LO2.1 Summarize and analyze federalism and the powers of the state in a constitutional context.

Federalism can be defined as a structure of government characterized by the division of powers between a national government and associated regional governments. The heart of the American federal system lies in the relationship between the U.S. government (with Washington, D.C., as the national capital) and the governments of the 50 states. Since 1789, the U.S. Constitution has prescribed a federal system of government for the nation, and since 1846, the state of Texas has been a part of that system.

Political scientist David Walker emphasizes the important role that states play in federalism: "The states' strategically crucial role in the administration, financing, and planning of intergovernmental programs and regulations—both federal and their own—and their perennial key position in practically all areas of local governance have made them the pivotal middlemen in the realm of functional federalism."[1]

Described by North Carolina's former governor Terry Sanford as "a system of states within a state," American federalism has survived more than two centuries of stresses and strains. Among the most serious threats were the Civil War from 1861 to 1865, which almost destroyed the Union, and economic crises such as the Great Depression, which followed the stock market crash of 1929.

Distribution of Constitutional Powers

Division of powers and functions between the national government and the state governments was originally accomplished by listing the powers of the national government in the U.S. Constitution and by adding the **Tenth Amendment**. The latter asserts that "the powers not delegated to the

Tenth Amendment
The Tenth Amendment to the U.S. Constitution declares that "the powers not delegated by the Constitution, nor prohibited by it to the States, are reserved to the States, respectively, or to the people."

United States by the Constitution, nor prohibited by it to the States, are reserved to the States, respectively, or to the People." Although the Tenth Amendment may seem to endow the states with powers comparable to those delegated to the national government, Article VI of the U.S. Constitution contains the following clarification: "This Constitution, and the laws of the United States which shall be made in pursuance thereof; and all treaties made, or which shall be made, under the authority of the United States, shall be the supreme law of the land; and the judges in every State shall be bound thereby, anything in the Constitution or laws of any State to the contrary notwithstanding." Referred to as the **national supremacy clause**, this article emphasizes that the U.S. Constitution and acts of Congress, as well as U.S. treaties, must prevail over state constitutions and laws enacted by state legislatures.

Powers of the National Government Article I, Section 8, of the U.S. Constitution lists powers that are specifically delegated to the national government. Included are powers to regulate interstate and foreign commerce, borrow and coin money, establish post offices and post roads, declare war, raise and support armies, provide and maintain a navy, levy and collect taxes, and establish uniform rules of naturalization. Added to these **delegated powers** is a clause that gives the national government the power "to make all laws which shall be necessary and proper for carrying into execution the foregoing powers, and all other powers vested by this Constitution in the government of the United States, or in any department or officer thereof." Since 1789, Congress and the federal courts have used this grant of **implied powers** to expand the national government's authority.[2] Another way in which the federal government has expanded its powers is through the commerce clause in Article I, Section 8 of the U.S. Constitution. For instance, the U.S. Supreme Court, in a case originating in Texas, gave significant leeway to Congress under the commerce clause to legislate in matters traditionally reserved for the states. In this case, the Court allowed Congress to set a minimum wage for employees of local governments.[3]

Guarantees to the States The U.S. Constitution provides all states with an imposing list of **constitutional guarantees**, which include the following:

- A state may be neither divided nor combined with another state without the consent of Congress and the state legislatures involved. (Texas, however, did retain power to divide itself into as many as five states under the terms of its annexation to the United States.)
- Each state is guaranteed a republican form of government (that is, a representative government with elected lawmakers).
- Each state is guaranteed two senators in the U.S. Senate and at least one member in the U.S. House of Representatives.
- All states participate in presidential elections through the electoral college. Each state has a number of electoral college votes equal to the total number of U.S. senators and U.S. representatives from that state. (As of 2015, Texas has 38 electoral college votes.)

national supremacy clause
Article VI of the U.S. Constitution states, "This Constitution, and the laws of the United States which shall be made in pursuance thereof; and all treaties made, or which shall be made, under the authority of the United States, shall be the supreme law of the land."

delegated powers
Specific powers entrusted to the national government by Article I, Section 8, of the U.S. Constitution (e.g., regulate interstate commerce, borrow money, and declare war).

implied powers
Powers inferred by the constitutional authority of the U.S. Congress "to make all laws which shall be necessary and proper for carrying into execution the foregoing [delegated] powers, and all other powers vested by this Constitution in the government of the United States, or in any department or officer thereof."

constitutional guarantees
Rights and protections assured under the U.S. Constitution. For example, among the guarantees to members of the Union include protection against invasion and domestic uprisings, territorial integrity, a republican form of government, and representation by two senators and at least one representative for each state.

- All states participate equally in approving or rejecting proposed amendments to the U.S. Constitution. Approval requires ratification either by three-fourths of the state legislatures (used for all but the Twenty-First Amendment, which repealed Prohibition) or by conventions called in three-fourths of the states.
- Each state is entitled to protection by the U.S. government against invasion and domestic violence, although Texas has its own Army National Guard, Air National Guard, and State Guard units. For more information on the state's military forces, see Chapter 9, "The Executive Branch."
- Texas is assured that trials by federal courts for crimes committed in Texas will be conducted in Texas.

Limitations on the States As members of the federal Union, Texas and other states are constrained by limitations imposed by Article I, Section 10, of the U.S. Constitution. For example, they may not enter into treaties, alliances, or confederations or, without the consent of Congress, make compacts or agreements with other state or foreign governments. Furthermore, they are forbidden to levy import duties (taxes) on another state's products. From the outcome of the Civil War and the U.S. Supreme Court's landmark ruling in *Texas v. White* 74 U.S. 700 (1869), Texans learned that states cannot secede from the Union. In the *White* case, the Court ruled that the national Constitution "looks to an indestructible union, composed of indestructible states." In subsequent cases, the U.S. Supreme Court further restricted state power. For instance, a state legislature cannot limit the number of terms for members of the state's congressional delegation. The U.S. Supreme Court held that term limits for members of Congress could be constitutionally imposed only if authorized by an amendment to the U.S. Constitution.[4]

Other provisions in the U.S. Constitution prohibit states from denying anyone the right to vote because of race, gender, failure to pay a poll tax (a tax paid for the privilege of voting), or age (if the person is 18 years of age or older). The Fourteenth Amendment forbids states from denying to any persons the equal protection of the laws. For example, in a 1950 Supreme Court case (prior to the Thelma White case highlighted in the "Students in Action" segment), segregation on the basis of race at the University of Texas law school was held to be in violation of the Fourteenth Amendment's equal protection clause.

The Fourteenth Amendment also provides that no state may deprive persons of life, liberty, or property without due process of law. These protections include those rights covered in the U.S. Constitution's Bill of Rights. This expansion to the states has occurred primarily through a series of cases heard by the U.S. Supreme Court. Using a principle known as the incorporation theory, federal courts have applied portions of the Bill of Rights to the states by virtue of the Fourteenth Amendment's due process clause. In effect, states are obligated to protect the provisions covered in the Bill of Rights. To ensure these protections, Congress has enforcement powers under the Fourteenth Amendment.

Students in Action

Thelma White Case Forced College Integration

"In his court order no. 1616 issued July 25, 1955, Judge Robert E. Thomason prohibited Texas Western College from denying Thelma White 'or any member of the class of persons she represents, the right or privilege of matriculating or registering … because of their race or color.'"

—Veronica Herrera and Alan A. Johnson

How It All Began

On March 30, 1955, Thelma White filed suit in a U.S. District Court challenging the denial of her admission to Texas Western College (TWC; now University of Texas at El Paso [UTEP]). When she applied at TWC, officials rejected her application because of her race. The college was forced to obey the state's segregation law. Black students could attend only two public colleges in Texas: Prairie View A&M or Texas Southern University, both considerable distances from El Paso.

Winning Her Case

While waiting for her lawsuit to go to court, White enrolled at New Mexico A&M (later New Mexico State University), where she continued her education. Before the case went to judgment, the University of Texas System decided that TWC could admit black students. [U.S. District] Judge R. E. Thomason [for the Western District of Texas] ruled that the state laws requiring segregation were invalid, that White must be admitted, and that the entire University of Texas System must admit black students to its undergraduate programs. Before this case, the law and medical schools as well as several graduate programs had been opened to blacks, but all undergraduate schools had remained closed.

Fighting for Educational Rights

White felt that she and other black students were being denied their educational rights. TWC admitted White and 12 other black students for the 1955 fall semester. White's victory opened the door for the students, although she remained at New Mexico A&M. The next year several more black students came to TWC.

Leaving a Legacy

White's legacy lives on at UTEP to this day. In her memory, UTEP founded the Thelma White Network for Community and Academic Development. The network's single purpose is to assist black students with social and academic development at UTEP. Today, African American students are enrolled in virtually every academic program at UTEP, a fact made possible by White and her pioneering efforts to change the educational system in El Paso.

Edited excerpt from Veronica Herrera and Alan A. Johnson, "Thelma White Case Forced College Integration," *Borderlands* 14 (Spring 1996); abridged and reprinted by permission of the authors (Note: the original text and terminology were retained.) *Borderlands* is a collection of student-written articles on the history and culture of the El Paso–Juárez–Las Cruces border region. It is published annually by El Paso Community College. The website for this publication is http://epcc.libguides.com/borderlands.

© Andresr/Shutterstock.com

Interstate Relations and State Immunities

Two provisions of the U.S. Constitution specifically affect relations between the states and between citizens of one state and another state. These provisions are Article IV and the Eleventh Amendment. Article IV of the U.S. Constitution provides that "citizens of each state shall be entitled to all privileges and immunities of citizens in the several states." This means that citizens of Texas who visit another state are entitled to all the **privileges and immunities** of citizens of that state. It does not mean, however, that such visiting Texans are entitled to all the privileges and immunities to which they are entitled in their home state. More than 200 years ago, the U.S. Supreme Court broadly defined "privileges and immunities" as follows: protection by government, enjoyment of life and liberty, right to acquire and possess property, right to leave and enter any state, and right to the use of courts.

Article IV also states that "full faith and credit shall be given in each State to the public acts, records, and judicial proceedings of every other State." The **full faith and credit clause** means that any legislative enactment, state constitution, deed, will, marriage, divorce, or civil court judgment of one state must be officially recognized and honored in every other state. This clause does not apply to criminal cases. For example, a person convicted in Texas for a crime committed in Texas is not punished in another state to which he or she has fled. Instead, such cases are handled through extradition, whereby the fugitive would be returned to the Lone Star State at the request of the governor of Texas. Furthermore, for some felonies, the U.S. Congress has made it a federal offense to flee from one state to another for the purpose of avoiding arrest.

A continuing controversy regarding the full faith and credit clause revolves around whether states must recognize same-sex marriages. In 1996, during President Bill Clinton's administration, Congress passed the Defense of Marriage Act (DOMA), prohibiting the national government from recognizing same-sex marriages and allowing states or political subdivisions (such as cities) to deny any marriage between persons of the same sex recognized in another state. In 2003, The Texas legislature passed a law prohibiting the state or any agency or political subdivision (such as a county or city) from recognizing a same-sex marriage or civil union formed in Texas or elsewhere. In February 2004, the leadership of the state legislature, as well as Governor Rick Perry, expressed support of President George W. Bush's call for a proposed U.S. constitutional amendment that would ban gay marriage. Then, in November 2005, Texas joined 15 other states in adopting a constitutional amendment that banned same-sex marriage and defined marriage as "only the union of one man and one woman."[5] Many opponents believe the constitutional amendment was unnecessary, given the existing state law; supporters of the amendment contend that it was necessary to amend the constitution to preempt any constitutional challenges to state law. According to the National Conference of State Legislatures, 33 states have similar bans, either in their constitutions or by statutory law, as of 2015.

privileges and immunities
Article IV of the U.S. Constitution guarantees that "citizens of each state shall be entitled to the privileges and immunities of citizens of the several states." According to the U.S. Supreme Court, this provision means that citizens are guaranteed protection by government, enjoyment of life and liberty, the right to acquire and possess property, the right to leave and enter any state, and the right to use state courts.

full faith and credit clause
Most government actions of another state must be officially recognized by public officials in Texas.

Although several challenges to the constitutionality of these state laws have been presented to the U.S. Supreme Court, the Court was reluctant to review any such cases until 2012. In the 2013 case, *U.S. v. Windsor*, the U.S. Supreme Court struck down a provision of the Defense of Marriage Act that denied more than 1,000 federal benefits for married couples to married same-sex couples, concluding that the provision infringed on the liberty protected by the due process clause of the Fifth Amendment for those couples.[6] Although the decision applied to federal laws and directives affecting legally recognized same-sex marriages performed in 17 states at the time, it left unclear whether states must recognize same-sex marriages legally sanctioned in other states. In exercising its state's rights, Texas chose to refuse national directives in this area of law. For instance, the Texas National Guard initially refused to provide federal spousal benefits for same-sex couples despite a mandate by the U.S. Department of Defense. As of February 2014, at least three federal lawsuits had been filed as challenges to Texas's ban on same-sex marriage, claiming that the law subjects gay couples to unequal treatment in violation of the U.S. Constitution. In that same month, U.S. District Judge Orlando L. Garcia of the Western District in San Antonio struck down the Texas ban, ruling it did not have a "legitimate government purpose."

The Eleventh Amendment also affects relations between citizens of one state and the government of another state. It provides, in part, that "The Judicial power of the United States shall not be construed to extend to any suit in law or equity, commenced or prosecuted against one of the United States by citizens of another state." U.S. Supreme Court rulings have ensured that a state may not be sued by its own citizens, or those of another state, without the defendant state's consent, nor can state employees sue the state for violating federal law.[7] This law, otherwise known as sovereign immunity, gives a tremendous shield to the government. Yet this power is not absolute. For example, in 1993, several families whose children were eligible for Medicaid sued the state of Texas for its failure to provide these programs. The lower federal courts ordered the state to correct the problem after the plaintiffs and state officials agreed to a consent decree (an agreement of both parties to avoid further litigation). Texas appealed to the U.S. Supreme Court, arguing that sovereign immunity did not allow federal courts to enforce the consent decree. The Supreme Court ultimately held that this was not a sovereign immunity case because the suit was not against the state but against state officials who had acted in violation of federal law. The Eleventh Amendment does not prohibit enforcement of a consent decree; enforcement by the federal courts is permitted to ensure observance of federal law.[8]

State Powers

Nowhere in the U.S. Constitution is there a list of state powers. As mentioned, the Tenth Amendment simply states that all powers not specifically delegated to the national government, nor prohibited to the states, are reserved to the states or to the people. The **reserved powers** of the states are, therefore, undefined and often very difficult to specify, especially when the powers are concurrent with those of the national government, such as the taxing power. Political scientists, however, view reserved powers in several broad categories.

- Police power: protection of the health, morals, safety, and convenience of citizens, and provision for the general welfare
- Taxing power: raising revenue to pay salaries of state employees, meet other costs of government, and repay borrowed money
- Proprietary power: public ownership of property, such as airports, energy-producing utilities, and parks
- Power of eminent domain: taking private property at a fair price for various kinds of public projects, such as highway construction

Needless to say, states today have broad powers, responsibilities, and duties. They are, for example, responsible for the nation's public elections—national, state, and local—because there are no nationally operated election facilities. State courts conduct most trials (both criminal and civil). States operate public schools (elementary and secondary) and public institutions of higher education (colleges and universities), and they maintain most of the country's prisons.

One broad state power that has raised controversy is the power of eminent domain. Customarily, government entities have used the power of eminent domain to appropriate private property for public projects, such as highways, parks, and schools, as long as the property owners are paid a just compensation. In 2005, the U.S. Supreme Court expanded this power under the Fifth Amendment, allowing local governments to seize private homes for private development; the Supreme Court, however, left the door open for states to set their own rules.[9] Governor Rick Perry responded by calling a special legislative session in the summer of that year. As a result, statutory limits were imposed on government entities condemning private property where the primary purpose is for economic development. Exceptions were made, however, for public projects and to protect the city of Arlington's plan to build the Cowboys Stadium, home of the Dallas Cowboys National Football League team. To ensure constitutional protection of private property rights against abuses by governments, an amendment to the Texas Constitution was proposed and adopted in 2009. More recently, controversy surrounding a proposed cross-border pipeline, known as the Keystone Pipeline, to transport oil from Canada to Texas has brought renewed attention to the use of private property for national interests. TransCanada, a Canadian company, began transporting oil in 2014 in the southern stretch of the pipeline from Oklahoma to refineries in the Houston area.

Although most state powers are recognizable, identifying a clear boundary line between state and national powers often remains complicated. Once again, the U.S. Supreme Court has played a critical role in defining this balance of power. Take, for example, the constitutional provision of interstate commerce in the U.S. Constitution. Not until *United States v. Lopez* (1999), a case that originated in Texas, did the U.S. Supreme Court

reserved powers
Reserved powers are derived from the Tenth Amendment of the U.S. Constitution. Although not spelled out in the U.S. Constitution, these reserved powers to the states include police power, taxing power, proprietary power, and power of eminent domain.

indicate that the U.S. Congress had exceeded its powers to regulate interstate commerce when it attempted to ban guns in public schools. Operation of public schools has traditionally been considered a power of state and local governments, and the Supreme Court has used the *Lopez* case, as well as other recent rulings, to rein in the federal government's power.[10] States have also become more willing to make claims of state sovereignty over federal authority in these cases. In 2005, however, in another interstate commerce case, the Supreme Court drew a line on state sovereignty when it came to regulating the use of a class of products—specifically, marijuana for medical treatment of terminally ill patients. In *Gonzales v. Raich* (2005), the Court struck down a California initiative that made an exception to the illegalization of marijuana. It ruled that Congress has the sole power to regulate local and state activities that substantially affect interstate commerce.[11] Although the California measure would have protected noncommercial cultivation and use of marijuana that did not cross state lines, the federal government contended that it would handicap enforcement of federal drug laws. In this regard, the Court ruled that the federal government is primarily responsible for regulating narcotics and other controlled substances. Nevertheless, federal officers have not fully enforced the U.S. restriction on marijuana in California. Since then, California and other states have legalized the medical use of marijuana, and some states, such as Colorado and Washington, have legalized its recreational use. In effect, these states have ignored a limited area of national law.

As of 2013, Texas had 27 lawsuits against the federal government and the Obama administration in its continuing fight for states' rights and a broad interpretation of state power under the Tenth Amendment. These suits, led by Attorney General Greg Abbott, Abbott (a Republican who was elected governor in 2014) have covered a variety of issues, including environmental standards, funding for women's health programs, and health care reform. For instance, in 2013, Abbott sued after the federal government announced that Texas would no longer be eligible for further funding of its Medicaid Women's Health Clinic Program if the state refused to partially fund health clinics affiliated with Planned Parenthood. The Medicaid Women's Health Care Program, which services low-income women, was jointly financed by the federal government (which provided 90 percent of funding) and the State of Texas (which provided the remaining 10 percent). The controversy originated with the passage of Senate Bill (SB) 7, which prohibited spending state money "to contract with entities … that affiliate with entities that perform or promote elective abortions." This provision targeted Planned Parenthood, an organization that offers family planning and other women's health care services. Some, though not all, Planned Parenthood clinics provide abortion services; they do not receive any taxpayer funding but operate as corporations separate from the health care clinics. In February 2012, the Texas Department of Health and Human Services adopted a rule, consistent with SB 7, making Planned Parenthood health clinics ineligible for further funding by the state. In response to Texas's decision, the federal government announced that Texas was ineligible for further funding for the Medicaid Women's Health

Care Program. The state sued the federal government, arguing that the national government was interfering with states' rights. Some Planned Parenthood health clinics were forced to shut down in Texas. Many women's health care providers, including some Planned Parenthood clinics, were able to remain open because of funding through a federal grant awarded to the Women's Health and Family Planning Association of Texas.

In another area of law, Texas was one of 26 states led by Republican attorneys general and governors to challenge the constitutionality of the Patient Protection and Affordable Care Act of 2010 (federal health care reform referred to as Obamacare). The contested provisions included congressional mandates requiring states to expand coverage and eligibility for Medicaid programs, as well as requiring that individuals purchase health insurance or face a penalty. Relying on the same interpretation of the interstate commerce clause as the *Raich* decision discussed above, the national government argued that Congress had the authority to require citizens to purchase health insurance because their failure to do so affected commerce. The states maintained the mandate exceeded congressional authority.[12]

The U.S. Supreme Court ultimately heard the case, concluding that it was within the Congress's taxing power to impose a penalty on individuals who failed to obtain health insurance, but that Congress could not withdraw existing Medicaid funding from states that failed to comply with the expanded coverage requirements for adults.[13] In response, Texas remained one of several states that did not expand Medicaid coverage. Senator Ted Cruz, who staged a failed "marathon speech" in the Senate in 2013, and Governor Perry were especially vocal in opposition to President Obama and the federal law.

Federal-State Relations: An Evolving Process

Since the establishment of the American federal system, states have operated within a constitutional context modified to meet changing conditions. At the same time, the framers of the U.S. Constitution sought to provide a workable balance of power between national and state governments that would sustain the nation indefinitely. This balance of power between federal and state governments has evolved over the years, with certain periods reflecting an expansion or decline of the federal government, while also affecting Texas's resistance to national control over state power.

From 1865 until about 1930, Congress acted vigorously to regulate railroads and interstate commerce within and among states. In addition, with the onset of the Great Depression of the 1930s, the federal government extended its jurisdiction to areas traditionally within the realm of state and local governments, such as regulating the workplace. For example, expansion of federal law extended to worker safety, minimum wages, and maximum hours. This expansion occurred principally through broad interpretation of the interstate commerce clause by the U.S. Supreme Court, which, in a series of cases, expanded the national government's power to include these matters.

Point/Counterpoint

THE ISSUE In 2010, under the Obama administration, Congress passed the Patient Protection and Affordable Care Act providing increased access to health care coverage for more people. Opponents and proponents of the law continued to debate the merits of the newly enacted law even after the U.S. Supreme Court upheld it. Opponents such as Governor Perry continued to argue that this was an overstepping of federal authority; proponents argued that now, more than ever, health care is a necessity for all Texans.

Should Texas Support the Affordable Care Act?

Arguments Against the Affordable Care Act

1. The act is an intrusion on state sovereignty in an area of policy that has traditionally been a state power.
2. A federal mandate is placed on states for the expansion of Medicaid.
3. The law increases taxes and imposes a burden on the state's economy.

Arguments For the Affordable Care Act

1. Expanding Medicaid would provide necessary health care for the state's low-income adults. This expansion is cost-effective for Texas because the federal government will cover 100 percent in the first few years and 90 percent thereafter.
2. Texas will lose billions in federal funding if it opts out of the Medicaid expansion.
3. When fewer people are covered under health insurance, state and local governments will spend more on uncompensated medical care.

Grants of money to the states from the federal government have also been used to influence state policymaking. The number and size of **federal grants-in-aid** grew while Congress gave states more financial assistance. As federally initiated programs multiplied, the national government's influence on state policymaking widened, and the states' control lessened in many areas. However, beginning in the 1980s, and continuing through the administration of George W. Bush, state and local governments gained more freedom to spend federal funds as they chose. In some areas, however, such as public assistance programs, they were granted less money to spend.

The decline in national control over state governments has often been identified as another development in federal-state relations, called devolution. The underlying concept of devolution is to bring about a reduction in the size and influence of the national government by reducing federal taxes and expenditures and by shifting many federal responsibilities to the states. Because one feature of devolution involves sharp reductions in federal aid, states are compelled to assume important new responsibilities with substantially less revenue to finance them. Texas and other states have been forced to assume more responsibility for formulating and funding their own programs in education, highways, mental health, public assistance (welfare),

federal grants-in-aid
Money appropriated by the U.S. Congress to help states and local governments provide needed facilities and services.

and other areas. In some cases, federal programs are shared; the states must match federal monies to benefit from a program, such as the Children's Health Insurance Program (CHIP), or risk losing the funds. (See Chapter 13, "Finance and Fiscal Policy," for a discussion of CHIP funding.)

An important feature of devolution is Congress's use of **block grants** to distribute money to state and local governments. Block grants are fixed sums of money awarded according to an automatic formula determined by Congress. Thus, states that receive block grants have greater flexibility in spending. Welfare policy is an excellent case. Welfare programs became primarily a federal responsibility during the Great Depression and the administration of Franklin D. Roosevelt (1933–1945). Other federal responses to unemployment and poverty included programs such as food stamps and medical assistance for the poor as part of President Lyndon B. Johnson's Great Society. The Clinton administration (1993–2001) and a Republican-controlled Congress, however, eventually forced states to assume more responsibility for welfare programs and supplied federal funding in the form of block grants.[14] President George W. Bush continued these trends and added a new twist to devolution by giving federal financial assistance to faith-based organizations that provide social services to the poor.

Despite the focus on devolution from 2001 to 2009, federal laws such as the No Child Left Behind Act of 2001 suggest that the Republican Congress and Republican President George W. Bush's administration aggressively pursued policies that once again expanded the federal government's role. No Child Left Behind, which among other things requires participating states to administer accountability tests (selected by the state) in public schools, expands the national government's reach into a traditional area of state and local responsibility. In response to compliance pressures, the National Education Association and various school districts from three states, including Texas, sued the U.S. Department of Education for failing to provide adequate money to comply with the initiative and for forcing states and local school districts to incur the unfunded costs. A federal judge dismissed the suit, stating that Congress had allocated significant funding and that the federal government had the power to require states to meet educational standards in exchange for funds.[15]

In 2009, under the Democratic Congress and Democratic President Barack Obama, federal-state relations evolved once again. Responding to the economic downturn that began in 2008, the Obama administration poured billions of dollars into state and local governments to stimulate the economy. For some observers, this action indicated another wave of national authority. As mentioned, Texas has challenged federal authority through lawsuits. Texas has also refused federal funds for unemployment benefits, Medicaid expansion, and public school funding because these funds require the adoption of national standards for state-run programs. The 2009 legislative session took another bold approach. Representative Brandon Creighton (R-Conroe) introduced House Concurrent Resolution (HCR) 50, which demanded that the federal government cease and desist mandates beyond constitutionally delegated powers. Creighton's resolution was similar to

block grant
Congressional grant of money that allows the state considerable flexibility in spending for a program, such as providing welfare services.

other state legislative actions or declarations that are part of the State Sovereignty Movement. This movement, which began gaining momentum in 2009, claims sovereignty under the Tenth Amendment against all powers not otherwise enumerated or granted to the federal government in the U.S. Constitution. In the end, the House adopted the resolution, but time did not permit action in the Senate. Similar bills were proposed in the House during the 2011 legislative session, such as HB 3706 that was assigned to the Select Committee on State Sovereignty, but none made it to the floor. For some observers, these actions symbolize the increasing polarization of national-state politics.

Governor Perry also received national attention when, in 2009, he hinted at the possibility of secession and expressed an initial willingness to refuse federal stimulus funds because he was concerned there would be too many strings attached. Under tremendous pressure, the state, its universities, and local governments ultimately accepted approximately $25 billion through 2014 in stimulus monies. Perry did reject $555 million for the state's unemployment insurance program. During his 2012 presidential bid, Governor Perry positioned himself as a champion of states' rights and described the fight to defend the Tenth Amendment as the "battle for the soul of America." In his 2010 book, *Fed Up! Our Fight to Save America from Washington*, he stated that "the spirit and intent of the Tenth Amendment … is under assault and has been for some time. The result is that today we face unprecedented federal intrusion into numerous facets of our lives."[16] Talk of secession was even more pertinent in 2011 during the 150th anniversary of Texas's attempted secession from the Union at the onset of the Civil War.

✔ **2.1 Learning Check**

1. True or False: The Tenth Amendment specifically identifies states' powers.
2. Does devolution give states more or less freedom to make decisions?

Answers on p. 76.

The Texas Constitution: Politics of Policymaking

······★ **LO2.2** Summarize how each of the state's previous constitutions shaped its content and the characteristics of the present-day Texas Constitution.

As already mentioned, the current Texas Constitution is the main source of power for the Texas state government. Surviving for close to 140 years, this constitution establishes the state's government, defines governing powers and imposes limitations, and identifies Texans' civil liberties and civil rights. Political scientists and legal scholars generally believe that a constitution should indicate the process by which problems will be solved, both in the present and in the future, and should not attempt to solve specific problems. Presumably, if this principle is followed, later generations will not need to adopt numerous amendments. In many areas, however, the Texas Constitution mandates specific policies in great detail, which has required frequent amendments.

The preamble to the Texas Constitution states, "Humbly invoking the blessings of Almighty God, the people of the state of Texas do ordain and establish this Constitution." These words begin the 28,600-word document that became Texas's seventh constitution in 1876. By the closing of 2014, that same document had been changed by no fewer than 483 amendments and contained about 87,000 words.

The constitution's framers spelled out policymaking powers and limitations in minute detail. This specificity, in turn, made frequent amendments inevitable as constitutional provisions were altered to fit changing times and conditions. For more than a century, the length of the Texas Constitution has increased through an accumulation of amendments, most of which are essentially statutory (resembling laws made by the legislature). The resulting document more closely resembles a code of laws than a fundamental instrument of government. To fully understand the present-day Texas Constitution, we will examine the historical factors surrounding its adoption, as well as previous historical periods and constitutions.

Historical Developments

The Texas Constitution provides the legal basis on which the state functions as an integral part of the federal Union. In addition, the document is a product of history and an expression of the dominant political philosophy of Texans living at the time of its adoption.

In general, constitution drafters have been pragmatic people performing an important task. Despite the idealistic sentiment commonly attached to constitutions in the United States, the art of drafting and amending them is essentially political in nature. In other words, these documents reflect the drafters' views and political interests, as well as the political environment of their time. With the passing of years, the Texas Constitution reflects the political ideas of new generations of people who amend or change it.

The constitutional history of Texas began with promulgation of the Constitution of Coahuila y Tejas within the Mexican federal system in 1827 and the Constitution of the Texas Republic in 1836. Texas has since been governed under its state constitutions of 1845, 1861, 1866, 1869, and 1876. Each of these seven constitutions has reflected the political situation that existed when the specific document was drafted.[17] In this section, we will see the political process at work as we examine the origins of these constitutions and note the efforts to revise and amend the current Texas Constitution.

The First Six Texas Constitutions

In 1824, three years after Mexico gained independence from Spain, Mexican liberals established a republic with a federal constitution. Within that federal system, the former Spanish provinces of Coahuila and Tejas became a single Mexican state that adopted its own constitution. Thus, the Constitution of Coahuila y Tejas, promulgated in 1827, marked Texas's first experience with a state constitution.

Political unrest among Anglo Texans, who had settled in Mexico's northeastern area, arose almost immediately. Factors that led Texians (as

How Do We Compare…in State Constitutions?

Year of Adoption, Length of State Constitutions and # of Amendments (2014)

Most Populous U.S. States	Year of Adoption	Approximate No. of Words and # of Amendments	U.S. States Bordering Texas	Year of Adoption	Approximate No. of Words and # of Amendments
California	1879	67,000 (527)	Arkansas	1874	59,000 (99)
Florida	1968	57,000 (121)	Louisiana	1974	70,000 (176)
New York	1894	44,000 (220)	New Mexico	1911	33,000 (165)
Texas	1876	87,000 (483)	Oklahoma	1907	81,000 (193)

Source: The Book of States, 2013, **http://knowledgecenter.csg.org/kc/content/book-states-2013-chapter-1-state-constitutions**

CRITICAL THINKING

➤ Analyze this chart. What are your initial impressions regarding the number of words and number of amendments in the state of Texas in comparison to other state constitutions? In your opinion, should the Texas Constitution be rewritten? If so, what recommendations would you offer for revision of the Texas Constitution?

Texans called themselves at the time) to declare independence from Mexico included, among others, their desire for unrestricted trade with the United States, Anglo attitudes of racial superiority, anger over Mexico's abolition of slavery, increasing numbers of immigrant settlers, insufficient Anglo representation in the 12-member Coahuila y Tejas legislature, and Mexico's failure to provide greater access to government in the English language.[18]

On March 2, 1836, at Washington-on-the-Brazos (between present-day Brenham and Navasota), a delegate convention of 59 Texians and Tejanos issued a declaration of independence from Mexico. Mexicans in Texas who also wanted independence and who fought for a free Texas state referred to themselves as Tejanos. Three Tejanos in particular served as delegates at the convention: Lorenzo de Zavala (representing Harrisburg), Francisco Ruiz, and José Antonio Navarro (both representing Béxar). (Selected Reading, "500 Years in the Making: The Tejano Monument" addresses the official recognition by the state of the contributions of Tejanos, or Texans of Mexican and/or Spanish descent, in the state's development.) The delegates drafted the Constitution of the Republic of Texas, modeled largely after the U.S. Constitution.

During this same period, in an effort to retain Mexican sovereignty, General Antonio López de Santa Anna defeated the Texians (many of whom were not even from Texas) and some Tejanos in San Antonio in the siege of the Alamo, which ended on March 6, 1836. Shortly afterward, Sam Houston's troops, including a company of Tejanos who were recruited by Captain Juan N. Seguín, crushed the Mexican forces in the Battle of San Jacinto on April 21, 1836. Part of Texas's unique history in the United States is its existence as an independent nation for close to 10 years.

After Houston's victory over Santa Anna, Texas voters elected Houston as president of their new republic; they also voted to seek admission to the

Union. Not until 1845, however, was annexation authorized by a joint resolution of the U.S. Congress. Earlier attempts to become part of the United States by treaty had failed. Texas's status as another slave state, as well as concerns that annexation would lead to war with Mexico, stalled the earlier efforts. Texas president Anson Jones ultimately called a constitutional convention whose delegates drew up a new state constitution and agreed to accept the invitation to join the Union. In October 1845, after Texas voters ratified both actions of the constitutional convention, Texas obtained its third constitution and on December 29 became the 28th member of the United States.

These events, however, set the stage for war between Mexico and the United States (1846–1848), especially with regard to where the boundary lines between the two countries would be drawn. Historians argue that U.S. expansionist politicians and business interests actively sought this war. When the Treaty of Guadalupe Hidalgo between Mexico and the United States was signed in 1848, Mexico lost more than half its territory and recognized the Rio Grande as Texas's southern boundary. Negotiations also addressed the rights of Mexicans left behind in Texas, many of whom owned land in the region. Under the treaty, Mexicans had one year to choose to return to Mexico or to remain in the newly annexed part of the United States; it also guaranteed Mexicans all the rights of citizenship. For all intents and purposes, these residents became the first Mexican Americans of Texas and the United States. Many Mexican Americans, however, were soon deprived of most of their rights, especially their property rights.

The Texas Constitution of 1845 lasted until the Civil War began. When Texas voted to secede from the Union in 1861, it joined with other southern states to form the Confederate States of America. At the time, secessionists argued that the U.S. Constitution created a compact among the states, and that each state had a right to secede. During this period, Texas adopted its Constitution of 1861, with the aim of making as few changes as possible in government structure and powers. The new constitution included changes necessary to equip the government for separation from the United States, as well as the maintenance of slavery. After the Confederacy's defeat, however, the Constitution of 1866 was drafted amid a different set of conditions during Reconstruction. For this constitution, the framers sought to restore Texas to the Union with minimal changes in existing social, economic, and political institutions. Although the Constitution of 1866 was based on the Constitution of 1845, it nevertheless recognized the right of former slaves to sue in the state's courts, to enter into contracts, to obtain and transfer property, and to testify in court actions involving black citizens (but not in court actions involving white citizens). Although the Constitution of 1866 protected the personal property of African American Texans, it did not permit them to vote, hold public office, or serve as jurors.

The relatively uncomplicated reinstatement of Texas into the Union ended abruptly when the Radical Republicans gained control of the U.S. Congress after the election of November 1866. Refusing to seat Texas's two senators and three representatives, Congress set aside the state's reconstructed government, enfranchised former slaves, disenfranchised prominent whites, and imposed military rule across the state. U.S. Army officers replaced civil authorities. As in other southern states, Texas functioned under a military government.

Under these conditions, delegates to a constitutional convention met in intermittent sessions from June 1868 to February 1869 and drafted yet another state constitution. Among other provisions, the new constitution centralized more power in state government, provided compulsory school attendance, and guaranteed a full range of rights for former slaves. This document was ratified in 1869. Then, with elections supervised by federal soldiers, Radical Republicans gained control of the Texas legislature. At the same time, Edmund Jackson Davis (commonly identified as E. J. Davis), a former Union army general, was elected as the first Republican governor of Texas. Some historians (such as Charles William Ramsdell and T. R. Fehrenbach) described the Davis administration (January 1870–January 1874) as one of the most corrupt in Texas history.[19] In recent years, however, revisionist historians (such as Patrick G. Williams, Carl H. Moneyhon, and Barry A. Crouch) have made more positive assessments of Davis and his administration.[20]

White Texans during the Davis administration tended to react negatively and with hostility to the freedom of former black slaves and to the political influence, albeit quite limited, that these freedmen exercised when they became voters. Violence and lawlessness were serious problems at the time. Thus, Governor Davis imposed martial law in some places and used police methods to enforce his decrees. Opponents of the Davis administration claimed that it was characterized by extravagant public spending, property

E. J. Davis and some of the Constitutional Convention delegates of 1875

Source: Left: The State Preservation Board, Austin, Texas; Right: Texas State Library and Archives Commission

CRITICAL THINKING

Reflect on these photos. How do Texas's constitutional history and the administration of Governor E. J. Davis continue to influence the state's present-day constitution and government?

tax increases to the point of confiscation, gifts of public funds to private interests, intimidation of newspaper editors, and control of voter registration by the military. In addition, hundreds of appointments to various state and local offices were filled with Davis's supporters.

Although the Constitution of 1869 is associated with the Reconstruction era and the unpopular (with most whites) administration of Governor Davis, the machinery of government created by this document was quite modern. The new fundamental law called for annual sessions of the legislature, a four-year term for the governor and other executive officers, and gubernatorial appointment (rather than popular election) of judges. It abolished county courts and raised the salaries of government officials. These changes centralized more governmental power in Austin and weakened local government.

During the Davis administration, Democrats gained control of the legislature in 1872. In December 1873, Governor Davis (with 42,633 votes) was badly defeated by Democrat Richard Coke from Waco (with 85,549 votes). When Davis refused to leave his office on the ground floor of the Capitol, Democratic lawmakers and Governor-elect Coke are reported to have climbed ladders to the Capitol's second story where the legislature convened. When President Ulysses S. Grant refused to send troops to protect him, Davis left the Capitol under protest in January 1874. In that same year, Democrats wrested control of the state courts from Republicans. The next step was to rewrite the Texas Constitution.

Drafting the Constitution of 1876 In the summer of 1875, Texans elected 75 Democrats and 15 Republicans (six of whom were African Americans) as delegates to a constitutional convention; however, only 83 attended the gathering in Austin. The majority of the delegates were not native Texans. More than 40 percent of the delegates were members of the **Texas Grange** (the Patrons of Husbandry), a farmers' organization committed to strict economy in government (reduced spending) and limited governmental powers. Its slogan of "retrenchment and reform" became a major goal of the convention.[21] So strong was the spirit of strict economy among delegates that they refused to hire a stenographer or to allow publication of the convention proceedings. As a result, no official record was ever made of the convention that gave Texas its most enduring constitution.

In their zeal to undo the policies of the Davis administration, the delegates on occasion overreacted. Striking at Reconstruction measures that had given Governor Davis control over voter registration, the overwrought delegates inserted a statement providing that "no law shall ever be enacted requiring a registration of voters of this state." Within two decades, however, the statement had been amended to permit voter registration laws.

As they continued to dismantle the machinery of the Davis administration, the delegates restricted the powers of the three branches of state government. They reduced the governor's salary, powers, and term (from four years to two); made all executive offices (except that of secretary of state) elective for two-year terms; and tied the hands of legislators with biennial (once every two years) sessions, low salaries, and limited legislative powers. All judgeships became popularly elected for relatively short terms of office. Justice of the

Texas Grange
A farmers' organization, also known as the Patrons of Husbandry, committed to low levels of government spending and limited governmental powers; a major influence on the Constitution of 1876.

peace courts, county courts, and district courts—all with popularly elected judges—were established. In addition, public services were trimmed to the bone. The framers of the new constitution limited the public debt and severely curbed the legislature's taxing and spending powers. They also inserted specific policy provisions. For example, they reinstated racially segregated public education and repealed the compulsory school attendance law, restored precinct elections, and allowed only taxpayers to vote on local bond issues.

Texas's proposed constitution was put to a popular vote in 1876 and was approved by a more than two-to-one majority. Although Texans in the state's largest cities—Houston, Dallas, San Antonio, and Galveston—voted against it, the much larger rural population voted for approval.

Distrust of Government and Its Legacy Sharing in the prevailing popular distrust of, and hostility toward, government, the framers of the Texas Constitution of 1876 sought with a vengeance to limit, and thus control, policymaking by placing many restrictions in the state's fundamental law. The general consensus of the time held that a state government could exercise only those powers listed in the state constitution. Therefore, instead of being permitted to exercise powers not denied by the U.S. Constitution, Texas lawmakers are limited to powers spelled out in the state's constitution. In addition, the 19th-century Texas Constitution (even with amendments) provides only limited powers for the governor's office in the 21st century. It is considered one of the weakest gubernatorial offices in the nation. (See Chapter 9, "The Executive Branch," for a discussion of the governor's office.)

Today: After More Than a Century of Usage

The structural disarray and confusion of the Constitution of 1876 compound the disadvantages of its excessive length and detail. Unlike the Texas Constitution, the U.S. Constitution has only 4,400 words and merely 27 constitutional amendments. Yet with all its shortcomings, the **Texas Constitution of 1876** has lasted for nearly 140 years. For one observer, the virtues of the constitution are "its democratic impulses of restraining power and empowering voters." It is a "document of history as much as it is a charter of governance."[22]

Filling the Texas Constitution with many details and creating a state government with restricted powers would inevitably lead to constitutional amendments. In fact, many substantive changes in Texas government require an amendment. For example, an amendment is needed to change the way the state pays bills, to abolish certain unneeded state and county offices, or to authorize a bond issue pledging state revenues. Urbanization, industrialization, technological innovations, population growth, demands for programs and services, and countless social changes contribute to pressures for frequent constitutional change.

Most amendments apply to matters that should be resolved by statutes enacted by the Texas legislature. Instead, an often uninformed and usually apathetic electorate must decide the fate of many complex policy issues. In this context, special interests represented by well-financed lobbyists and the

Texas Constitution of 1876
The lengthy, much-amended state constitution, a product of the post-Reconstruction era that remains in effect today.

media often play influential roles in constitutional policymaking. They are also likely to influence the success or defeat of proposed amendments.

Governor Rick Perry, for instance, played a pivotal role in advocating for specific constitutional amendment proposals. As the most visible policymaker in Texas, his public support or nonsupport of key propositions swayed voters. In 2005, for example, Governor Perry supported Proposition 2, which signified a new direction in the substantive nature of constitutional amendment proposals on the ballot. The controversial nature of Proposition 2, which sought to ban same-sex marriage, produced unprecedented media coverage and interest group activity. As mentioned previously, the amendment proposal defined marriage as consisting only in the "union of one man and one woman." It also prohibited the state and all political subdivisions from "creating or recognizing any legal status identical or similar to marriage." The measure overwhelmingly passed with 76 percent of the voters (more than 1.7 million) supporting it and 24 percent (more than 500,000) opposing it.[23]

Often, Texas voters are expected to evaluate numerous constitutional amendments. (Table 2.1 provides data on number of amendments proposed and adopted from 1876 through 2014.) Of the 666 constitutional amendment proposals presented to voters, 484 have been approved and 182 have been defeated. According to the Texas Legislative Council, 73 percent of the proposals were approved from 1876 to 2011. From 2003 to 2014, voters were presented with 79 constitutional amendment proposals, with as many as 22 in 2003, and voters approved 94 percent of these proposals. So, unless there is strong and vocal opposition, constitutional amendment proposals will likely be approved.

In 2009, voters were presented with 11 constitutional proposals, all of which passed with comfortable majorities. One proposal that received special attention by graduate students and faculty at four-year universities was Proposition 4. It allowed Texas's seven public "emerging research universities," including the University of Houston, University of Texas at El Paso, Texas Tech, and Texas State University, to compete for research money from the state's National Research University Fund. The objective was to raise the status of these schools to what are referred to as "Tier One" research institutions. As of 2014, only two of Texas's public institutions (the University of Texas at Austin and Texas A&M University) and one private institution (Rice University) were ranked as Tier One by all ranking authorities.[24] (See Chapter 10, "Public Policy and Administration," for a discussion of higher education.)

In 2011, voters considered 10 constitutional amendment proposals, but only 7 were adopted. One proposal in particular that affected college students dealt with authorizing the Texas Higher Education Coordinating Board to expand the state's ability to create bonds for the College Access Loan program. This program provides low-interest loans to college students, irrespective of financial need. Private colleges and universities strongly supported this proposal because of the high cost of tuition. The proposition came as lawmakers were making cuts in educational funding sources for students, specifically the Texas Grants Program and the Texas Equalization Program. (See Chapter 13, "Finance and Fiscal Policy," for a discussion of higher education funding.) Two of the three proposals that were defeated addressed the powers

Table 2.1	Texas Constitution of 1876: Amendments Proposed and Adopted, 1879–2014				
Year Proposed	**Number Proposed**	**Number Adopted**	**Year Proposed**	**Number Proposed**	**Number Adopted**
1879	1	1	1951	7	3
1881	2	0	1953	11	11
1883	5	5	1955	9	9
1887	6	0	1957	12	10
1889	2	2	1959	4	4
1891	5	5	1961	14	10
1893	2	2	1963	7	4
1895	2	1	1965	27	20
1897	5	1	1967	20	13
1899	1	0	1969	16	9
1901	1	1	1971	18	12
1903	3	3	1973	9	6
1905	3	2	1975	12	3
1907	9	1	1977	15	11
1909	4	4	1978	1	1
1911	5	4	1979	12	9
1913	8	0	1981	10	8
1915	7	0	1982	3	3
1917	3	3	1983	19	16
1919	13	3	1985	17	17
1921	5	1	1986	1	1
1923	2	1	1987	28	20
1925	4	4	1989	21	19
1927	8	4	1990	1	1
1929	7	5	1991	15	12
1931	9	9	1993	19	14
1933	12	4	1995	14	11
1935	13	10	1997	15	13
1937	7	6	1999	17	13
1939	4	3	2001	20	20
1941	5	1	2003	22	22
1943	3	3	2005	9	7
1945	8	7	2007	17	17
1947	9	9	2009	11	11
1949	10	2	2011	10	7
			2013	9	9
			2014	1	1
			Totals	666	484

Source: Research Division, Texas Legislative Council, *Amendments to the Texas Constitution Since 1876, http://www.tlc.state.tx.us/pubsconamend/constamend1876.pdf.*

CRITICAL THINKING

Examine this table, what are your initial impressions of the number of constitutional amendments proposed by the Texas legislature and approved by the voters? Should voters be deciding so many constitutional amendments every two years, especially when you consider the nature of some of these proposals?

of county governments: one would have allowed them to use bonds to finance redevelopment projects, especially in deteriorating areas; the other would have allowed El Paso County to create conservation districts to develop and finance parks and recreation areas. Although the second measure was approved by voters in El Paso County, the vote in other areas of the state was sufficient to defeat it. The third proposal would have provided additional tax breaks to landowners who use their property for agriculture or the protection of wildlife, if they also practice water conservation.[25]

In 2013, voters considered and approved another nine constitutional proposals. The subjects included property tax exemptions for the surviving spouse of a member of the armed services killed in action, senior citizens' eligibility for reverse mortgages for a home purchase, and authorization for a home rule municipality to revise its charter with procedures to fill a vacancy for an unexpired term. One proposal that received strong support from Governor Perry, as well as House Speaker Joe Straus, allowed the state legislature to pull $2 billion from the Rainy Day Fund for specially created accounts to make low interest loans for water infrastructure and conservation projects.[26] Organizations such as H2O4Texas.org and stateimpact.npr.org of Texas (a collaboration of local public radio stations) integrated social media sites to inform voters about the proposal and water issues.[27] Facebook pages, such as txwaterprop6yes.org, were created to gain support for the proposal. Voters were also presented with a single constitutional amendment proposal in November 2014, diverting money from the "rainy day" fund (the state's savings account) to the State Highway Fund to pay for road construction and maintenance. It was approved.

✔ 2.2 Learning Check

1. How many different constitutions has Texas had throughout its history?
2. True or False: Texas's present-day constitution has been amended just under 100 times.

Answers on p. 76.

Constitutional Amendments and Revision

LO2.3   Analyze the amendment process, focusing on recent constitutional amendment elections as well as attempts to revise the Texas Constitution.

Each of the 50 American state constitutions provides the means for changing the powers and functions of government. Without a provision for change, few constitutions would survive long. A revision may produce a totally new constitution to replace an old one. Also, courts may alter constitutions by interpreting the wording of these documents in new and different ways. Finally, constitutions may be changed by formal amendment, which is the chief method by which the Texas Constitution has been altered.

Because Texas's registered voters have an opportunity to vote on one or more proposed amendments every two years—and sometimes each year—an understanding of the steps in the **constitutional amendment process** is important. Article XVII, Section 1, provides a relatively simple procedure for amending the Texas Constitution. The basic steps in that process are as follows:

constitutional amendment process
Process for changing the Texas Constitution in which an amendment is proposed by a two-thirds vote of each chamber of the legislature and approved by a simple majority of voters in a general or special election.

- A joint resolution proposing an amendment is introduced in the House or in the Senate during a regular session or during a special session called by the governor
- Two-thirds of the members in each chamber must adopt the resolution
- The secretary of state prepares an explanatory statement that briefly describes the proposed amendment, and the attorney general approves this statement
- The explanatory statement is published twice in Texas newspapers that print official state notices
- A copy of the proposed amendment is posted in each county courthouse at least 30 days before the election
- The voters must approve the proposed amendment by a simple majority vote in a regular or special election
- The governor, who has no veto power in the process, proclaims the amendment

For a constitutional amendment to be considered by Texas voters, the legislature must adopt a joint resolution by a two-thirds vote in each chamber. Hundreds of constitutional amendment resolutions are considered every legislative session. The following were among some of the resolutions introduced, but not passed, by the 83rd legislature's regular session in 2013:

- Repealing the state constitutional provision defining marriage as consisting only of the union of one man and one woman
- Creating a constitutional right to hunt and fish in accordance with state law
- Mandating the legislature to require candidates for public elective office to undergo drug screening
- Changing Senate terms of office to six years and House terms to four years

The Texas legislature decides whether a proposed amendment will be submitted to the voters in a **constitutional amendment election**, typically in November of an odd-numbered year. In some cases, a proposed amendment will be presented to voters in a special election scheduled for an earlier date. For instance, of the 17 amendments proposed in 2007, only one was presented to voters in May; the other proposals were presented in November of that same year. In 2014, voters were presented with one proposal in the general election in November. Part of the problem with frequent constitutional amendment elections is the typically low voter turnout in odd-numbered years, when no statewide offices are up for election. As mentioned earlier, most constitutional amendment proposals are approved by a relatively small percentage of the voting population. Constitutional amendment elections turnout is typically less than 10 percent. Turnout in 2011 was at an all-time low (less than 5 percent) and rose just slightly to 6 percent in 2013. The 2013 constitutional election was also the first statewide election that the new voter photo ID law was implemented. (For more on the new voter law, see Chapter 5, "Campaigns and Elections.")

Unlike voters in other states, Texans do not have the power of **initiative** at the state level; however, this power is exercised under some local governments.

constitutional amendment election
Election, typically in November of an odd-numbered year, in which voters are asked to approve one or more proposed constitutional amendments. An amendment must receive a majority of the popular vote to be approved.

initiative
A citizen-drafted measure proposed by a specific number or percentage of qualified voters that becomes law if approved by popular vote. In Texas, this process occurs only at the local level, not at the state level.

(See Chapter 3, "Local Governments," for a discussion of how these powers work locally.) If adopted, the initiative process would bypass the legislature and allow individual Texans or interest groups to gather the signatures required to submit proposed constitutional amendments and statutes (ordinary laws) for direct popular vote. According to the Council of State Governments, 18 states have some form of constitutional amendment procedure by initiative.[28] In recent years, no serious legislative efforts to amend the Texas Constitution to authorize the initiative process at the state level have emerged.

Constitutional Revision

Attempts to revise Texas's Constitution of 1876 began soon after its adoption. A legislative resolution calling for a constitutional revision convention was introduced in 1887 and was followed by others. Limited success came in 1969, when an amendment removed 56 obsolete constitutional provisions.

The only comprehensive movement to achieve wholesale **constitutional revision** began in 1971. In that year, the 62nd Legislature adopted a joint resolution proposing an amendment authorizing the appointment of a study commission and naming the members of the 63rd Legislature as delegates to a constitutional convention. Except for the state Bill of Rights, any part of the Texas Constitution of 1876 could be changed or deleted. Submitted to the voters in 1972 as a proposed constitutional amendment, the resolution was approved by a margin of more than half a million votes (1,549,982 in favor to 985,282 against).

A six-member committee (composed of the governor, the lieutenant governor, the speaker of the House, the attorney general, the chief justice of the Texas Supreme Court, and the presiding judge of the Court of Criminal Appeals) selected 37 persons to serve as members of the Constitutional Revision Commission. The commission prepared a draft constitution on the basis of opinions and information gathered at public hearings conducted throughout the state and from various authorities on constitutional revision. One-fourth the length of the present constitution, the completed draft was submitted to the legislature on November 1, 1973.

On January 8, 1974, all 181 members of both chambers of the Texas legislature met in Austin at a **constitutional revision convention**. Previous Texas constitutions had been drafted by convention delegates popularly elected for that purpose. When the finished document was put to a vote, the result was 118 for and 62 against, three votes short of the two-thirds majority of the total membership needed for final approval. (Approval required a total of at least 121 votes.) Attempts to reach compromises on controversial issues proved futile.

The Constitutional Convention of 1974 provided perhaps the best demonstration of the politics surrounding Texas's constitution making. First, the convention was hampered by a lack of positive political leadership. Governor Dolph Briscoe maintained a hands-off policy throughout the convention. Lieutenant Governor Bill Hobby similarly failed to provide needed political leadership, and the retiring speaker of the House, Price Daniel Jr., pursued a nonintervention course. Other members of the legislature were distracted by their need to campaign for reelection.

constitutional revision
Extensive or complete rewriting of a constitution.

constitutional revision convention
A body of delegates who meet to make extensive changes in a constitution or to draft a new constitution.

The primary reason that the convention failed to agree on a proposed constitution was the phantom "nonissue" of a right-to-work provision. A statutory ban on union shop labor contracts was already in effect. Adding this prohibition to the constitution would not have strengthened the legal hand of employers to any significant degree. Nevertheless, conservative, anti-labor forces insisted on this provision, and a pro-labor minority vigorously opposed it. The controversy aroused much emotion and at times produced loud and bitter name-calling among delegates on the floor and spectators in the galleries.[29] Stung by widespread public criticism of the 1974 convention's failure to produce a proposed constitution for public approval or rejection, the 64th Legislature resolved to submit a proposal to Texas voters. In 1975, both houses of the legislature agreed on a constitutional revision resolution comprising 10 articles in eight sections to be submitted to the Texas electorate in November of that year. The content of the articles was essentially the same as that of the final resolution of the unsuccessful 1974 convention.

The revision proposed in 1975 represented years of work by men and women well informed about constitution making. Recognized constitutional authorities evaluated the concise and orderly document as one of the best-drafted state constitutions ever submitted to American voters. Although new and innovative in many respects, the proposal did not discard all of the old provisions. In addition to retaining the Bill of Rights, the proposed constitution incorporated such basic principles as limited government, separation of powers, and bicameralism (a two-house legislature).

Nevertheless, Texas voters demonstrated a strong preference for the status quo by rejecting each proposition. Voters in 250 of the state's 254 counties rejected all eight proposals. A mere 23 percent of the estimated 5.9 million registered voters cast ballots, meaning that only about 10 percent of the state's voting-age population participated in this important referendum. When asked to explain the resounding defeat of the eight propositions, Bill Hobby, then lieutenant governor, responded, "There's not enough of the body left for an autopsy."

More Revision Attempts

After the revision debacle of 1975, two decades passed before the next attempt to revise the constitution. In 1995, Senator John Montford (D-Lubbock) drafted a streamlined constitution that incorporated many of the concepts contained in the failed 1975 proposal. Montford's plan also called for a voter referendum every 30 years (without legislative approval) on the question of calling a constitutional revision convention. But Montford resigned from the Texas Senate to become chancellor of the Texas Tech University System in 1996. With such issues as tax changes, welfare reform, and educational finance pressing for attention, the 75th Legislature did not seriously consider constitutional revision in 1997.

In 1998, Senator Bill Ratliff (R-Mount Pleasant) and Representative Rob Junell (D-San Angelo) launched another attempt to revise the constitution.[30] With assistance from Angelo State University students and others, they prepared a complete rewrite of the much-amended 1876 document. Subsequently, Ratliff and Junell introduced another draft for consideration by the 76th Legislature in 1999. It failed to muster enough support for serious consideration in committee and never received a floor vote in either legislative chamber.[31] This proposal would have cut the then 80,000-word document to approximately 19,000 words. Significant changes included expanding the powers of the governor, repealing the current partisan election method of selecting state judges, and increasing salaries of the House speaker and the lieutenant governor.

One proposal that the legislature may consider in future sessions was created by a bipartisan team led by Roy Walthall (a semiretired instructor at McLennan Community College in Waco). In 2010, the team set out to reorganize the constitution. Rather than make substantive changes, which would provoke political opposition, their proposal included changes to make the document more readable and usable. The team claims that they did not change the content or legal meaning. According to Walthall, the bulk of their work was rearranging many of the existing provisions into more logical sections. The governor would have to appoint a commission to study the reorganized constitution, and it could take several legislative sessions before the constitutional proposal would be presented to the state's voters. If approved, a new state constitution would enable Texas to join the other 49 states that have updated their constitutions since the beginning of the 20th century.

During the 21st century, the legislature has ignored or delayed the issue of constitutional revision. A series of budget crises, redistricting issues, and school funding has dominated the legislative agenda. As a result, large-scale constitutional reform remains an unaddressed problem. However, certain individuals in the legislature want to keep the subject on the agenda. At the end of the regular legislative session in 2011, Representative Charles Anderson (R-Waco) introduced a resolution asking the leadership in the legislature to create a joint study committee to examine a reorganization of the state constitution, similar to Walthall's proposal, prior to the 2013 session. The request was never brought up for a vote in the legislature. During the 2013 legislative session, Representative Anderson introduced a similar resolution, HCR 88. It was referred to the House Committee on Government Efficiency and Reform, where it received a public hearing, and Walthall provided testimony. The bill, however, never reached the House floor as the session was coming to a close.[32]

Piecemeal Revision

Because extensive constitutional reform has proved futile, Texas legislators have sought to achieve some measure of government reform by other means, including legislative enactments and piecemeal constitutional amendments. In 1977, for example, the 65th Legislature enacted into law two parts of the 1975 propositions defeated at the polls. One established a procedure for reviewing state administrative agencies; the other created a planning agency within the Office of the Governor. In 1979, the 66th Legislature proposed six amendments designed to implement parts of the constitutional revision package rejected in 1975. Three were adopted by the voters and added to the Texas Constitution. They accomplished the following:

- Established a single property tax appraisal district in each county (discussed in Chapter 3, "Local Governments")
- Gave criminal appellate jurisdiction to 14 courts of appeals that formerly had exercised civil jurisdiction only
- Allowed the governor restricted removal power over appointed statewide officials[33]

Proposals for important constitutional changes have been unsuccessful in the House and the Senate. For example, during the regular session of the 77th Legislature in 2001, Representative Rob Junell (D-San Angelo) submitted a proposal that was considered and approved by the House Select Committee on Constitutional Revision. Among other items, the proposal would have changed the terms of office for state senators and House members. It also would have created a Texas Salary Commission to set salaries for elected and appointed officials of the executive, judicial, and legislative branches. This proposal, however, was never brought up for a floor vote in the legislature.[34]

To modernize the Texas Constitution, one constitutional amendment (adopted in 1999) authorized elimination of certain "duplicative, executed, obsolete, archaic and ineffective provisions of the Texas Constitution." Among resulting deletions were references to the abolished poll tax and the governor's authority "to protect the frontier from hostile incursions by Indians." In November 2007, voters also eliminated the constitutional county office of inspector of hides and animals, which had been created in the 1880s. Nevertheless, the Texas Constitution still has problems.

The Texas Constitution: A Summary

★ **LO2.4** Explain and analyze the basic sections of the Texas Constitution.

Chiefly because of its length, complete printed copies of the Texas Constitution are not readily available to the public. Until publication of its Millennium Edition (2000–2001), the *Texas Almanac* was the most widely used source for the text of this document. That edition and subsequent editions, however, now refer persons seeking the text of the Texas Constitution to the Internet.

Although *Practicing Texas Politics* does not include the entire text of the Texas Constitution, each chapter looks to Texas's basic law for its content. The rest of this chapter presents a brief synopsis of the document's 17 articles.[35]

The Bill of Rights

We begin by examining Article I, the Texas Constitution's Bill of Rights. The **Texas Bill of Rights** is similar to the one found in the U.S. Constitution. Composed of 30 sections, it guarantees protections for people and their property against arbitrary actions by state and local governments. Included among these rights are freedom of speech, press, religion, assembly, and petition; the rights of accused and convicted criminals and victims of crime; and equal rights for women. Article I also includes philosophical observations that have no direct force of law.

✔ **2.3 Learning Check**

1. When was the last time voters were presented with a wholesale constitutional revision proposal from the state legislature?
2. True or False: Amending the Texas Constitution requires two-thirds of the members of each chamber of the state legislature voting for a proposed amendment and three-fourths of the voters approving it in a constitutional amendment election.

Answers on p. 76.

Texas Bill of Rights
Article I of the Texas Constitution, which guarantees protections for people and their property against arbitrary actions by state and local governments. Protected rights include freedom of speech, press, religion, assembly, and petition.

Constitutional Rights Against Arbitrary Governmental Actions

Eleven of Article I's sections provide protections for people and property against arbitrary governmental actions. Guarantees such as freedom of speech, press, religion, assembly, and petition are included. The right to keep and bear arms, prohibitions against the taking of property by government action without just compensation, and protection of contracts are also incorporated. Most of these rights found in the Texas Constitution are also protected under the U.S. Constitution. Thus, with their basic rights guaranteed in both national and state constitutions, Texans, like people in other states, have a double safeguard against arbitrary governmental actions.

One of these constitutional rights, protected for Texans by both state and federal constitutions, centers on freedom of religion. A constitutional right to freedom of religion is essentially the same in both the Texas Constitution and the U.S. Constitution. Yet when one examines the actual wording, it is different. The Texas Bill of Rights, Section 6, states, "All men have a natural and indefeasible right to worship Almighty God according to the dictates of their own conscience. No man shall be compelled to attend, erect or support any place of worship, or to maintain any ministry against his consent ... and no preference shall ever be given to any religious society or mode of worship." Under the U.S. Constitution, the First Amendment (as applied to the states under the Fourteenth Amendment) provides that states "shall make no law respecting an establishment of religion, or prohibiting the free exercise thereof."

Cases on religious freedom stemming from the U.S. Constitution have gone from Texas all the way to the U.S. Supreme Court. Included among these are two cases that yielded different results: one centered on student-led prayer before a school football game; the other involved a Ten Commandments monument placed on the Texas state Capitol grounds. The U.S. Supreme Court, interpreting the establishment clause of the U.S. Constitution to require a separation of church and state, struck down school prayer before public school football games, contending that the message conveyed amounted to an endorsement of religion on school grounds.[36] In contrast, the U.S. Supreme Court upheld the Ten Commandments display, concluding that it is a historical monument among other historical monuments on state grounds.[37]

Rights of Criminals and Victims

Thirteen sections of the Texas Constitution's Bill of Rights relate to the rights of persons accused of crimes and to the rights of individuals who have been convicted of crimes. For example, one section concerns the right to release on bail, another prohibits unreasonable searches and seizures, and a third declares that "the right to trial by jury shall remain inviolate." These provisions relate closely to similar language in the national Bill of Rights.

The Texas Constitution is even more protective of certain rights than is the U.S. Constitution. An additional set of rights added by constitutional amendment in 1989 protects crime victims. This provision was developed in the early 1980s in response to findings of a presidential task force that explored the inequality of rights for crime victims. In general, the state constitution now gives victims rights to restitution, information about the accused (conviction, sentence, release, etc.), protection from the accused throughout the criminal justice process, and respect for the victim's privacy.

Equal Rights for Women Another example of the Texas Constitution's providing more protection than the U.S. Constitution relates to equal rights for women. Attempts nationwide to add a proposed Equal Rights Amendment (ERA) to the U.S. Constitution failed between 1972 and 1982 (even though the amendment was approved by the Texas legislature). Nevertheless, the **Texas Equal Legal Rights Amendment (ELRA)** was added to Article I, Section 3, of the Texas Constitution in 1972. It states: "Equality under the law shall not be denied or abridged because of sex, race, color, creed, or national origin." This constitutional amendment was proposed and adopted after several unsuccessful attempts dating back to the 1950s.[38] Interestingly, the Texas Constitution still has the provision that states, "All free men have equal rights."

Additional Protections Additional protections in the Texas Constitution include prohibitions against imprisonment for debt, outlawry (putting a convicted person outside the protection of the law), and transportation (punishing a convicted citizen by banishment from the state). Monopolies are prohibited by a provision of the Texas Bill of Rights, but not by the U.S. Constitution.

Interpretation of the Texas Constitution by the Texas Supreme Court has also provided additional rights, such as the court's interpretation of Article VII, Section 1, which requires the state legislature to provide support and maintenance for "an efficient system of free public schools." In 1989, the high court first held that the state legislature had a constitutional requirement to create a more equitable public school finance system. The Texas Supreme Court revisited school finance in 2005 and declared the school finance system unconstitutional. Rather than focusing on the system's continued and persistent inequities, however, the court focused on whether the state-imposed property tax cap amounted to a statewide property tax, which the Texas Constitution forbids. (Property taxes can be collected only at the local level.) Because more than 80 percent of all school districts had reached this cap and state funding had continued to decline, the court held that school boards had effectively lost control of tax rates. Equally important, the court rejected district court judge John Dietz's 2004 ruling that more money in the system was necessary to comply with the Texas Constitution's requirement to provide for the "general diffusion of knowledge."[39] Challenges to school funding in the courts continued. In 2014, Judge Dietz considered more evidence in the case after the 83rd Legislature increased funding amounts for public education. (For more on school finance, see Chapter 13, "Finance and Fiscal Policy.")

Philosophical Observations Three sections of the Texas Bill of Rights contain philosophical observations that have no direct force of law. Still stinging from what they saw as the "bondage" years of Reconstruction, the angry delegates to the constitutional convention of 1875 began their work by inserting this statement: "Texas is a free and independent state, subject only to the Constitution of the United States." They also asserted that all political power resides with the people and is legitimately exercised only on their behalf and

Texas Equal Legal Rights Amendment (ELRA)
Added to Article I, Section 3, of the Texas Constitution, it guarantees that "equality under the law shall not be denied or abridged because of sex, race, color, creed, or national origin."

that the people may at any time "alter, reform, or abolish their government." To guard against the possibility that any of the rights guaranteed in the other 28 sections would be eliminated or altered by the government, Section 29 proclaims that "everything in this 'Bill of Rights' is excepted out of the general powers of government, and shall forever remain inviolate."

The Powers of Government and Separation of Powers

Holding fast to the principle of limited government and a balance of power, the framers of the Constitution of 1876 firmly embedded in the state's fundamental law the familiar doctrine of **separation of powers**. In Article II, they assigned the lawmaking, law-enforcing, and law-adjudicating powers of government to three separate branches, identified as the legislative, executive, and judicial departments, respectively.

Article III is titled "Legislative Department." Legislative powers are vested in a bicameral legislature, composed of the House of Representatives with 150 members and the Senate with 31 members. A patchwork of more than 60 sections, this article provides vivid testimony of the many decades of amendments directly affecting the legislative branch. For example, in 1936, an amendment added a section granting the Texas legislature the authority to levy taxes to fund a retirement system for public school, college, and university teachers. Today, public school teachers and personnel employed by public universities and community colleges benefit from pension programs provided by the state.

Article IV, "Executive Department," states unequivocally that the governor "shall be the Chief Executive Officer of the State" but then shares executive power with four other popularly elected officers independent of the governor: the lieutenant governor, the attorney general, the comptroller of public accounts, and the commissioner of the General Land Office. (A state treasurer was originally included in this list, but a constitutional amendment abolished the office.) With this and other provisions for division of executive power, some observers consider the Texas governor no more than first among equals in the executive branch of state government.

Through Article V, "Judicial Department," Texas joins Oklahoma as one of only two states in the country with a bifurcated court system that includes two courts of final appeal: one for civil cases (the Supreme Court of Texas) and one for criminal cases (the Court of Criminal Appeals). Below these two supreme appellate courts are the courts authorized by the Texas Constitution and created by the legislature: the intermediate appellate courts (14 courts of appeals) and more than 1,800 courts of original jurisdiction (district courts, statutory county courts, and justice of the peace courts).

Suffrage

Article VI, titled "**Suffrage**" (the right to vote), is one of the shortest articles in the Texas Constitution. Before 1870, states had the definitive power to conduct elections. Since that time, amendments to the U.S. Constitution, acts of Congress such as the Voting Rights Act of 1965, and U.S. Supreme Court rulings have vastly diminished this power. In addition, amendments to the Voting Rights Act

separation of powers
The assignment of lawmaking, law-enforcing, and law-interpreting functions to separate branches of government.

of 1975 require Texas to provide bilingual ballots. For more than 35 years, Texas had to receive federal preclearance for any changes to voting laws or district boundary lines for elected officials. In 2013, however, mandatory preclearance was eliminated when the U.S. Supreme Court found the requirement unconstitutional in a case originating in Alabama, *Shelby County v. Holder* 570 U.S. __ (2013). Although the U.S. Justice Department has since filed suit against the state to have voter ID laws approved by the 82nd Legislature (2011) declared in violation of the Voting Rights Act for discriminating against minority voters, Attorney General Gregg Abbott interpreted the Shelby decision to allow the immediate implementation of the voter ID photo requirement beginning with the constitutional amendment election in 2013. Through 2014, the state continued to require voters to provide a picture ID to be able to vote.

Within the scope of current federal parameters, the Texas Constitution establishes qualifications for voters, provides for citizen voter registration, and governs the conduct of elections. In response to federal-level changes, this article has been amended to abolish the payment of a poll tax or any form of property qualification for voting in the state's elections and to change the minimum voting age from 21 to 18.

Local Governments

The most disorganized part of the Texas Constitution concerns units of **local government**: counties, municipalities (cities), school districts, and other special districts. Although Article IX is titled "Counties," the provisions concerning county government are scattered through four other articles. Moreover, the basic

suffrage
The right to vote.

Attorney General Greg Abbott making a statement implementing a Voter ID law following the Shelby decision in 2013.

AP Images/Tony Gutierrez

CRITICAL THINKING

Do you think requiring a voter ID photo is a good or bad idea?

structure of county government is defined not in Article IX on counties but in Article V on the judiciary. Article XI on municipalities is equally disorganized and inadequate. Only four of the sections of this article relate exclusively to municipal government. Other sections concern county government, taxation, public indebtedness, and forced sale of public property.

Along with counties and municipalities, the original text of the Constitution of 1876 referred to school districts but not to other types of special districts. Authorization for special districts, however, crept into the Texas Constitution with a 1904 amendment that authorized the borrowing of money for water development and road construction by a county "or any defined district." Since then, special districts have been created to provide myriad services, such as drainage, conservation, urban renewal, public housing, hospitals, and airports.

Other Articles

The nine remaining articles also reflect a strong devotion to constitutional minutiae: Education, Taxation and Revenue, Railroads, Private Corporations, Spanish and Mexican Land Titles, Public Lands and Land Office, Impeachment, General Provisions, and Mode of Amendment. The shortest is Article XIII, "Spanish and Mexican Land Titles." The entire text was deleted by amendment in 1969 because its provisions were deemed obsolete. The longest article is Article XVI, "General Provisions." Among other provisions, it prohibits the bribing of public officials and authorizes the legislature to regulate the manufacture and sale of intoxicants.

local government
Counties, municipalities, school districts, and other special districts that provide a range of services, including rural roads, city streets, public education, and protection of persons and property.

2.4 Learning Check

1. True or False: The Texas Constitution contains constitutional rights not found in the U.S. Constitution.
2. Article II of the Texas Constitution assigns powers to which branches of government?

Answers on p. 76.

Tejano Monument on the Texas Capitol grounds.

Marjorie Kamys Cotera/Bob Daemmrich Photography/Alamy

CRITICAL THINKING

Reflect on this photo. What are your impressions of the Tejano Monument and the images it represents?

Selected Reading

Five Hundred Years in the Making: The Tejano Monument

Cindy Casares

This article appeared in the February 12, 2012, edition of the Texas Observer *and discusses the significance of the Tejano Monument on the grounds of the Texas Capitol.*

On Jan. 13 [2012], workers finally broke ground on the Texas Capitol site where a 525-square-foot statuary honoring the legacy of Tejanos, or Texans of Mexican and Spanish descent, will be dedicated March 29 [2012]. Though the monument is the result of a grassroots effort that began in 2001, the official recognition of Tejanos in this state has taken much longer.

"[N]early 500 years after the mapping of the Texas coast by Alonzo Alvarez de Pineda in 1519, and 175 years after Tejanos José Francisco Ruiz, José Antonio Navarro and Lorenzo de Zavala signed the Texas Declaration of Independence in 1836, the Tejano culture and its contributions to Texas' evolution are being officially recognized by the state," Renato Ramirez, vice president of the Tejano Monument Board, wrote in a December article published on the Latino news site *News Taco.*

For the monument to become a reality at this point in history seems almost fated. It's 2012, an election year, and the first one since the 2010 census let the world know that the future of Texas officially lies with Latinos. Now the world will know that Texas' past lies with Latinos, too.

Most historians agree that the story of Texas taught in schools, beginning in the 1830s and portraying Anglo-Americans as the state's first settlers, leaves out a lot. If I had a dollar for every person in New York City who's asked me where in Mexico my family hails from, I'd be one rich Tejana. In Virginia, my fellow graduate students had no idea most cowboy words are Spanish.

They thought white Texans had invented the industry.

"In 1830," Ramirez said during a recent appearance on a San Antonio radio show, "the Davy Crocketts and Jim Bowies and those guys … they came in illegally and, seven days after they came in illegally, they earned the right to be called Texans. I have not earned that right after 500 years of my family being here. I'm still a Mexican. I want to make it clear that I'm a Tejano."

In reality, 1,000 Tejanos died fighting for independence from Mexico at the Battle of Medina in 1813. Twenty-five years later, 188 Anglo-Americans died at the Alamo. Though the Alamo is perhaps the state's most cherished historical treasure, to this day we don't know the exact location of the Battle of Medina. In 2001, when a McAllen physician named Cayetano Barrera visited the Texas Capitol, he realized that, of the 18 monuments on the grounds, not one portrayed Tejanos in a positive light.

Barrera returned to McAllen and enlisted a group of educators and businesspeople to campaign for a monument.

The group, now a nonprofit called Tejano Monument Inc., had to push three bills through the Texas Legislature to get the monument on the south lawn—the front yard—of the Capitol grounds. "The first comment was that the contribution of Hispanics does not merit being on the south lawn," Ramirez recalls.

So, in 2001, while lawmakers agreed there should be a Tejano monument, its location had yet to be determined. Six years later, in 2007, the state agreed to contribute $1 million to the project's estimated $1.8 million cost. The other $800,000 was raised through private donations.

Then, in 2009, the 81st Legislature passed House Bill 4114 by Trey Martinez-Fischer, D-San Antonio, authorizing placement of the Tejano Monument on the Historic South Grounds—the coveted front lawn. Gov. Rick Perry later signed the bill.

Twelve pieces by Laredo sculptor Armando Hinojosa will tell the Tejano story from the 1500s to the 1800s. That depth of history and context is more important now than ever, given that Mexican-American history is elsewhere being literally removed from the classroom. The same week that ground was broken on Texas' Tejano Monument, Arizona's state superintendent of education, utilizing power granted him by a controversial new state law, ordered public schools in Tucson to stop offering Mexican-American Studies classes.

In contrast, at the Tejano Monument groundbreaking in Austin, the Walmart Foundation announced its $100,000 donation toward a one-year curriculum-development project to improve the understanding of Tejano history in elementary schools. The curriculum is being developed by University of Texas professors and will start in Austin schools, with the hope that it will be replicated statewide.

For Latinos in Texas, there's a lot to be hopeful for this year.

✔ Selected Reading Learning Check

1. True or False: Tejanos are named after people who are Texans of Mexican and Spanish descent.
2. Give one reason why the Tejano Monument is significant.

Answers on p. 76.

Source: Texas Observer, February 10, 2012, http://www.texasobserver.org/five-hundred-years-in-the-making-the-tejano-monument. Reprinted by permission. Cindy Casares is a columnist for the *Texas Observer* and is the founding editor of *Guanabee Media*, an English-language, pop culture blog network about Latinos established in 2007. She has a master's degree in mass communications from Virginia Commonwealth University Brandcenter. Prior to her career in journalism, she spent 10 years in New York City as an advertising copywriter. In her undergraduate years at the University of Texas at Austin, she served under Governor Ann Richards as a Senate messenger during the 72nd Texas Legislature.

For further resources, please visit www.cengagebrain.com.

Conclusion

As a member of the United States, Texas is provided with certain constitutional guarantees as well as limitations on its powers. The U.S. Constitution plays a significant role in defining federal-state relations. This balance of power between the federal government and the state government is constantly evolving. The Texas government derives most of its powers from the Texas Constitution. Understanding Texas's constitutional history explains to a large degree the characteristics of its present-day constitution. Amending the Texas Constitution occurs frequently through constitutional amendment elections, but recent attempts to revise the constitution have not been successful. As a result, the structure of the Constitution of 1876 remains essentially unchanged.

Chapter Summary

LO 2.1 **Summarize and analyze federalism and the powers of the state in a constitutional context**. The American federal system features a division of powers between a national government and 50 state governments. As members of the Union, Texas has certain constitutional guarantees and limitations. Several constitutional provisions in the U.S. Constitution affect interstate relations and state immunity. Controversy may arise when uniformity in certain areas of policy among the states does not exist. Powers not delegated (nor implied, as interpreted by federal courts) to the federal government are reserved to the states or to the people under the Tenth Amendment. These state powers have largely formed around several broad categories, and identifying a clear boundary between state and national powers (or responsibilities) is often complicated. Striking a balance of power between the national and state governments is constantly shifting and evolving over time.

LO 2.2 **Summarize how each of the state's previous constitutions shaped its content and the characteristics of the present-day Texas Constitution**. Today's Texas Constitution is the country's second longest and, by 2014, had 483 amendments. Most amendments are statutory in nature, so the document resembles a code of laws. Texas has had seven constitutions, each reflecting the political situation that existed when the specific document was drafted. The Constitution of 1876 has endured, despite its excessive length, confusion, and statutory detail.

LO 2.3 **Analyze the amendment process, focusing on recent constitutional amendment elections as well as attempts to revise the Texas Constitution**. Changing the Texas Constitution requires an amendment proposed by a two-thirds majority vote of the members in each legislative chamber and approved by a simple majority of the state's voters in a general or special election. Despite several efforts to conduct a wholesale revision of the Texas Constitution, only piecemeal revisions have occurred.

LO 2.4   **Explain and analyze the basic sections of the Texas Constitution**. The Texas Constitution is the fundamental law that sets forth the powers and limitations of the state's government. It is composed of 17 articles. Included are the Bill of Rights, an article on suffrage, articles on the three branches of state government, and provisions concerning the powers of state and local governments.

Key Terms

Tenth Amendment, p. 42

national supremacy clause, p. 43

delegated powers, p. 43

implied powers, p. 43

constitutional guarantees, p. 43

privileges and immunities, p. 46

full faith and credit clause, p. 46

reserved powers, p. 48

federal grants-in-aid, p. 51

block grant, p. 52

Texas Grange, p. 58

Texas Constitution of 1876, p. 59

constitutional amendment process, p. 62

constitutional amendment election, p. 63

initiative, p. 63

constitutional revision, p. 64

constitutional revision convention, p. 64

Texas Bill of Rights, p. 67

Texas Equal Legal Rights Amendment (ELRA), p. 69

separation of powers, p. 70

suffrage, p. 71

local government, p. 72

Learning Check Answers

2.1 1. False. The Tenth Amendment does not specifically identify the powers of the states.
2. Devolution gives the states more freedom to make decisions, especially with funding.

2.2 1. Texas has had seven constitutions throughout its history.
2. False. Our present-day Texas Constitution has been amended more than 400 times.

2.3 1. November 1975 was the last time that voters were presented with a wholesale constitutional revision proposal from the state legislature; more recent attempts have failed.
2. False. Amending the Texas Constitution requires two-thirds of the members of each chamber of the state legislature to vote for a proposed amendment but only a simple majority of the voters to approve it in a constitutional amendment election.

2.4 1. True. The Texas Constitution does contain additional constitutional rights, such as the Equal Legal Rights Amendment, not found in the U.S. Constitution.
2. The Texas Constitution assigns power to the legislative, executive, and judicial branches.

Selected Reading Learning Check

1. True. Tejanos refers to Texans of Mexican and/or Spanish descent who have a long history in Texas.
2. The monument is significant because it officially recognizes the Tejano culture and its contributions to Texas's history and development.

Local Governments

CRITICAL THINKING

How do different levels of local government work together and at times also work against each other?

Learning Objectives

3.1 Explain the relationships that exist between a local government and all other governments, including local, state, and national governments.

3.2 Describe the forms of municipal government organization.

3.3 Identify the rules and social issues that shape local government outcomes.

3.4 Analyze the structure and responsibilities of counties.

3.5 Explain the functions of special districts and their importance to the greater community.

3.6 Discuss the ways that local governments deal with metropolitan-wide and regional issues.

When most Texans think about government, they think about the national or state government, but not about the many local governments. Yet of all three levels of government, local government has the greatest impact on citizens' daily lives. Most people drive every day on city streets or county roads, drink water provided by the city or a special district, attend schools run by the local school district, play in a city or county park, eat in restaurants inspected by city health officials, and live in houses or apartments that required city permits and inspections to build. Many citizens' contacts with local governments are positive. Potholes are filled, trash is picked up regularly, baseball fields are groomed for games—but other experiences are less positive. Streets and freeways are increasingly congested, many schools are overcrowded, and the property taxes to support them seem high. The cartoon that begins this chapter illustrates the complexity of local politics. Because of limited resources, local governments must choose from among competing interests, including sports arenas.

Local governments in Texas, from cities to counties to special districts, have a problem with debt. Harris County, the most populated county in Texas, with a population of more than 4 million residents, has been deemed the state's most indebted county. Harris County has more debt than the combined total of the next nine largest Texas counties, which have a population of more than 10 million people. Local governments have argued that the state has refused to fund necessary projects, thereby forcing them to assume increasing debt. Through a bond election in 2013, Harris County asked its voters to allow the county to borrow almost $300 million. The first bond proposal was for $217 million to renovate and restore the Astrodome; this borrowing would have required higher property taxes. Additionally, Harris County wanted $70 million in bond money to establish a city-county jail processing center. The Astrodome bond issue failed, whereas the jail processing center passed. As of 2014, Harris County has higher per capita property taxes than any other county in Texas.

To confront problems and make local governments more responsive to citizens' needs and wishes, people have to understand how those governments are organized and what they do. Local government comes in many forms. Texas has municipalities (approximately 1,200 city and town governments), counties (254), and special districts (more than 3,000). The special district that most students know best is the school district, but there are also special districts for water, hospitals, conservation, housing, and a multitude of other services. Each local government covers a certain geographic area and has legal authority to carry out one or more government functions. Most collect revenue such as taxes or fees, spend money while providing services, and are controlled by officials ultimately responsible to voters. These local, or grassroots, governments affect our lives directly.

Local Politics in Context

★ **LO3.1**   Explain the relationships that exist between a local government and all other governments, including local, state, and national governments.

Who are the policymakers for **grassroots** governments? How do they make decisions? What challenges do they face daily? Putting local politics in context first requires an understanding of the place of local government in American federalism.

Local Governments and Federalism

In the 19th century, two opposing views emerged concerning the powers of local governments. **Dillon's Rule**, named after federal judge John F. Dillon and still followed in most states (including Texas), dictates that local governments have only those powers granted by the state government, those powers implied in the state grant, and those powers indispensable to their functioning.[1] The opposing Cooley Doctrine, named after Michigan judge Thomas M. Cooley and followed in 10 states, says "Local Government is a matter of absolute right; and the state may not take it away."[2]

Texas's local governments, like those of other states, are at the bottom rung of the governmental ladder, which makes them politically and legally weaker than the state and federal governments. In addition, Texas is among those states that more strictly follow Dillon's Rule.[3] Cities, counties, and special district governments are creatures of the State of Texas. They are created through state laws and the Texas Constitution, and they make decisions permitted or required by the state. Local governments may receive part of their money from the state or national government, and they must obey the laws and constitutions of both. States often complain about unfunded mandates (requirements placed on states by the federal government without federal money to pay the costs). Local governments face mandates from both the national and state governments. Some of these mandates are funded by the higher levels of government, but some are not. Examples of mandates at the local level are as diverse as improving the quality of the air, meeting state jail standards, providing access for the disabled, and meeting both federal and state educational standards.

At the local level, federalism is more than just dealing with the state and national governments. Local governments have to deal with each other as well. Texas has almost 5,000 local governments. Bexar County (home of San Antonio) has 62 local governments, Dallas County has 61, and Travis County (Austin) has 121. The territories of local governments often overlap. Your home, for example, may be in a county, a municipality, a school district, a community college district, and a hospital district—all of which collect taxes, provide services, and hold elections.

Local governments generally treat each other as friends but occasionally behave as adversaries. For example, the City of Houston and Harris County worked with each other, as well as with state and national officials, to

grassroots
Local (as in grassroots government or grassroots politics).

Dillon's Rule
A legal principle, still followed in the majority of states including Texas, that local governments have only those powers granted by their state government.

coordinate the response to Hurricanes Katrina, Rita, and Ike. On the other hand, a small city along the border, La Villa, has been in a dispute with the school district over high water rates. In 2014, the city shut off the school district's water after they refused to pay their bill, impacting over 600 students.[4] Clearly, federalism and the resulting relationships between and among governments (**intergovernmental relations**) are important to how local governments work. (For more on federalism, see Chapter 2, "Federalism and the Texas Constitution.")

Grassroots Challenges

When studying local governments, it is important to keep in mind the challenges these governments face daily. More than 80 percent of all Texans reside in cities, and residents have immediate concerns they want addressed: fear of crime; decaying infrastructures, such as streets, roads, and bridges; controversies over public schools; and the threat of terrorism. Residents' concerns can be addressed in part through communication between government and citizens. For example, the City of Austin has created several Internet websites to inform and engage its citizens on issues. SpeakupAustin! is an online social media portal that was developed with the younger residents of the city in mind. The site gives information on city projects, has a forum for different political and social topics, and allows users to vote and share their opinions on issues. The city has a website, austintexas.gov, that provides resources for all areas of city government, including paying city service bills, business updates, city council emails, and more.

Texas cities are also becoming increasingly diverse, with many African American and Latino Texans seeking access to public services and local power structures long dominated by Anglos. Making sure that all communities receive equal access to public services is a key challenge for grassroots-level policymakers, community activists, and political scientists. Opportunities to participate in local politics begin with registering and then voting in local elections. (See Chapter 5, "Campaigns and Elections," for voter qualifications and registration requirements under Texas law.) Some citizens may even seek election to a city council, county commissioners court, school board, or another policymaking body. Additional opportunities to be politically active include homeowners' associations, neighborhood associations, community or issue-oriented organizations, voter registration drives, and election campaigns of candidates seeking local offices. By gaining influence in city halls, county courthouses, and special district offices, individuals and groups may address grassroots problems through the democratic process.

Grassroots government faces the challenge of widespread voter apathy. Many times, fewer than 10 percent of a community's qualified voters participate in a local election. The good news is that voter interest increases when people understand that they can solve grassroots problems in Texas through political participation.

intergovernmental relations
Relationships between and among different governments that are on the same or different levels.

✓ 3.1 Learning Check

1. Do local governments have more flexibility to make their own decisions under Dillon's Rule or the Cooley Doctrine? Which one does Texas follow?

2. Are intergovernmental relations marked by conflict, cooperation, or both?

Answers on p. 119.

Municipal Governments

★ **LO3.2**   Describe the forms of municipal government organization.

Perhaps no level of government influences the daily lives of citizens more than **municipal (city) government**. Whether taxing residents, arresting criminals, collecting garbage, providing public libraries, or repairing streets, municipalities determine how millions of Texans live. Knowing how and why public policies are made at city hall requires an understanding of the organizational and legal framework within which municipalities function.

Legal Status of Municipalities

City government powers are outlined and restricted by municipal charters, state and national constitutions, and statutes (laws). Texas has two legal classifications of cities: **general-law cities** and **home-rule cities**. A community with a population of 201 or more may become a general-law city by adopting a charter prescribed by a general law enacted by the Texas legislature.[5] A city of more than 5,000 people may be incorporated as a home-rule city, with a locally drafted charter adopted, amended, or repealed by majority vote in a citywide election. Once chartered, a general-law city does not automatically become a home-rule city just because its population increases to greater than 5,000 people. Citizens must vote to become a home-rule city, but that status does not change even if the municipality's population decreases to 5,000 or fewer people.

Texas has almost 900 general-law cities, most of which are fairly small in population. Although some of the more than 350 home-rule cities are small, most larger cities tend to have home-rule charters. The principal advantage of home-rule cities is greater flexibility in determining their organizational structure and how they operate. Citizens draft, adopt, and revise their city's charter through citywide elections. The charter establishes the powers of municipal officers; sets salaries and terms of offices for council members and mayors; and spells out procedures for passing, repealing, or amending **ordinances** (city laws). ✳

Home-rule cities may exercise three powers not held by the state government or general-law cities: recall, initiative, and referendum. **Recall** provides a process for removing elected officials through a popular vote. In November 2013, two members of the city council for Cibolo City, outside of San Antonio, were recalled by voters. The recall was initiated by citizens who opposed the council members' approval of plans for a Walmart to be built in the community. Recall elections in Texas have become more common and can cost a community many thousands of dollars.[6] An **initiative** is a citizen-drafted measure proposed by a specified number or percentage of qualified voters. If approved by popular vote, an initiative becomes law without city council approval, whereas a **referendum** approves or repeals an existing ordinance. Ballot referenda and initiatives require voter approval and, depending on city charter provisions, may be binding or nonbinding on municipal governments.

municipal (city) government
A local government for an incorporated community established by law as a city.

general-law city
A municipality with a charter prescribed by the legislature.

home-rule city
A municipality with a locally drafted charter.

ordinance
A local law enacted by a city council or approved by popular vote in a referendum or initiative election.

recall
A process for removing elected officials through a popular vote. In Texas, this power is available only for home-rule cities.

initiative
A citizen-drafted measure proposed by a specific number or percentage of qualified voters, which becomes law if approved by popular vote. In Texas, this process occurs only in home-rule cities.

referendum
A process by which issues are referred to the voters to accept or reject. Voters may also petition for a vote to repeal an existing ordinance. In Texas, this process occurs at the local level in home-rule cities. At the state level, bonds secured by taxes and state constitutional amendments must be approved by the voters.

Initiatives and referenda can be contentious. For example, in November 2012, Austin voters passed an initiative to change the election system for city council members from a place system, in which council members were elected at large (voted on by all citizens), to single-member districts (voted on by citizens from within a specific geographic area). One controversy resulting from the new election system is the concern that council members will focus more on issues in their districts and less on citywide issues. Austin's mayor, elected at large, will need to draw some consensus among council members to help Austin continue to grow and move forward. On occasion, implementation of voters' decisions may be slow or blocked.

Red-light cameras installed by various cities to reduce the number of accidents (and, according to critics, produce more municipal revenue) brought popular votes over repeal in some communities. In College Station and Baytown, city councils responded to the citizens' rejection of the cameras by turning them off promptly. Voters in Houston rejected the cameras in 2010, but because of legal issues the cameras were not turned off definitively until more than a year after the election. A suit by the company administering the program for the city was not settled until 2012. In Sugar Land, a suburb of Houston, residents petitioned the city to put the red-light camera system on their November 2013 ballot, but the city council tossed out the petition. The city cited technicalities, stating that the petition did not include some names and addresses of petitioners and was not submitted by the required deadline.

Forms of Municipal Government

The four principal forms of municipal government used in the United States and Texas—strong mayor-council, weak mayor-council, council-manager, and commission—have many variations. The council-manager form prevails in almost 90 percent of Texas's home-rule cities, and variations of the two mayor-council systems operate in many general-law cities. Citizens often ask, "How do you explain the structure of municipal government in my town? None of the four models accurately depicts our government." The answer lies in home-rule flexibility. Various combinations of the forms discussed in the following sections are permissible under a home-rule charter, depending on community preference, as long as they do not conflict with state law. Informal practice also may make it hard to define a city's form. For example, the council-manager form may work like a strong mayor-council form if the mayor has a strong personality and the city manager is timid.

Strong Mayor-Council Among larger American cities, the **strong mayor-council form** continues as the predominant governmental structure. Among the nation's 10 largest cities, only Dallas, San Antonio, and San Jose, California, operate with a structure (council-manager) other than some variation of the strong mayor-council system. In New York City, Los Angeles, Chicago, and Philadelphia, the mayor is the chief administrator and the political head of the city. Of Texas's 25 largest cities, however, only Houston

strong mayor-council form
A type of municipal government with a separately elected legislative body (council) and an executive head (mayor) elected in a citywide election with veto, appointment, and removal powers.

and Pasadena still have the strong mayor-council form of government. Many people see the strong mayor-council system as the best form for large cities because it provides strong leadership and is more likely than the council-manager form to be responsive to the full range of the community. In the early 20th century, however, the strong mayor-council form began to fall out of favor in many places, including Texas, because of its association with the corrupt political party machines that once dominated many cities. Now, most of Texas's home-rule cities have chosen the council-manager form.

In Texas, cities operating with the strong mayor-council form have the following characteristics:

- A council traditionally elected from single-member districts, although many now have a mix of at-large and single-member district elections
- A mayor elected at large (by the whole city), with the power to appoint and remove department heads
- Budgetary power (for example, preparation and execution of a plan for raising and spending city money) exercised by the mayor, subject to council approval before the budget may be implemented
- A mayor with the power to veto council actions

Houston's variation of the strong mayor-council form features a powerful mayor aided by a strong appointed chief of staff and an elected controller with budgetary powers (see Figure 3.1). Most Houston mayors have delegated administrative details to the chief of staff, leaving the mayor free to focus on the larger picture. Duties of the chief of staff, however, vary widely depending on the mayor currently in office.

Weak Mayor-Council As the term **weak mayor-council form** implies, this model of local government gives the mayor limited administrative powers. The mayor's position is weak because the office shares appointive and removal powers over municipal government personnel with the city council. Instead of being a chief executive, the mayor is merely one of several elected officials responsible to the electorate. In popular elections, voters choose members of the city council, some department heads, and other municipal officials. The city council has the power to override the mayor's veto.

The current trend is away from this form. None of the largest cities in Texas has the weak mayor-council form, though some small general-law and home-rule cities in Texas and other parts of the country use it. For example, Conroe, a city with a population of more than 55,000 in Montgomery County (north of Houston), describes itself on its website as having a mayor-council form of government. The mayor's powers are limited, and the city administrator manages city departments on a day-to-day basis. The mayor, however, maintains enough status to serve as a political leader.

Council-Manager When the cities of Amarillo and Terrell adopted the **council-manager form** in 1913, a new era in Texas municipal administration began. Today, most of Texas's almost 350 home-rule cities follow the council-manager form (sometimes termed the commission-manager form).

weak mayor-council form
A type of municipal government with a separately elected mayor and council, but the mayor shares appointive and removal powers with the council, which can override the mayor's veto.

council-manager form
A system of municipal government in which an elected city council hires a manager to coordinate budgetary matters and supervise administrative departments.

City of Houston

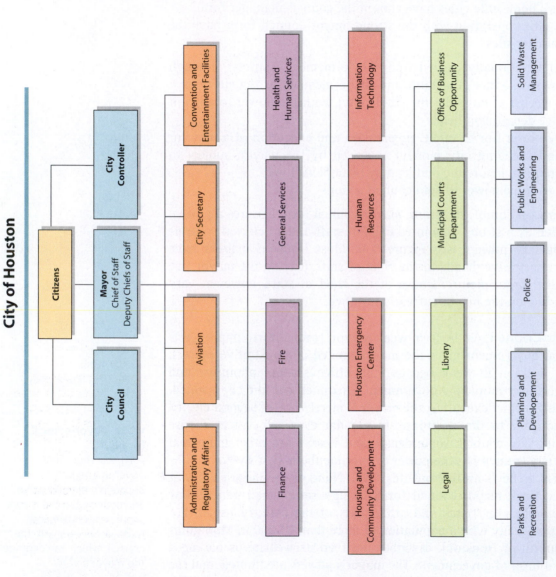

Figure 3.1 Strong Mayor-Council Form of Municipal Government: City of Houston

http://www.houstontx.gov/budget/11budadopt/orgchrt.pdf.

What is the difference between the strong mayor-council and weak mayor-council form of government?

Figure 3.2 illustrates how this form is used in San Antonio. The council-manager form has the following characteristics:

- A mayor, elected at large, who is the presiding member of the council but who generally has few formal administrative powers
- City council or commission members elected at large or in single-member districts to make general policy for the city
- A city manager who is appointed by the council (and can be removed by the council) and who is responsible for carrying out council decisions and managing the city's departments

Under the council-manager form, the mayor and city council make decisions after debate on policy issues, such as taxation, budgeting, annexation, and services. The city manager's actual role varies considerably; however, most city managers exert strong influence. City councils generally rely on their managers for the preparation of annual budgets and policy recommendations. Once a policy is made, the city manager's office directs an appropriate department to implement it. Typically, city councils hire professionally trained managers. Successful applicants usually possess graduate degrees in public administration and can earn competitive salaries. In 2014, city managers for Texas's five largest cities earned $233,000 to $400,000 annually, plus bonuses. Dallas pays its city manager $400,000, the highest salary in the country, plus benefits.[7] Obviously, a delicate relationship exists between appointed managers and elected council members. In theory, the council-manager system has a weak mayor and attempts to separate policymaking from administration. Councils and mayors are not supposed to "micromanage" departments. However, in practice, elected leaders sometimes experience difficulties in determining where to draw the line between administrative oversight and meddling in departmental affairs.

A common major weakness of the council-manager form of government is the lack of a leader to whom citizens can bring demands and concerns. The mayor is weak; the city council is composed of a number of members (anywhere from 4 to 16 individuals, with an average of 7, among the 25 largest cities in Texas); and the city manager is supposed to "stay out of politics." Thus, council-manager cities tend to respond more to elite and **middle-class** concerns than to those of the **working class** and ethnic minorities. (The business elite and the middle class have more organizations and leaders who have access to city government and know how to work the system.) Only a minority of council-manager cities have mayors who regularly provide strong political and policy leadership. One of these exceptions is San Antonio, where mayors, due to personality, generally are strong leaders. The council-manager form seems to work well in cities where most people are of the same ethnic group and social class and, thus, share many common goals. Obviously, few central cities fit this description, but many suburbs do.

Commission   Today, none of Texas's cities operates under a pure **commission form** of municipal government. First approved by the Texas legislature for Galveston after a hurricane demolished the city in 1900, this form lacks a single executive, relying instead on elected commissioners that form a policymaking board.

middle class
Social scientists identify the middle class as those people with white-collar occupations (such as professionals and small business workers).

working class
Social scientists identify the working class as those people with blue-collar (manual) occupations.

commission form
A type of municipal government in which each elected commissioner is a member of the city's policymaking body, but also heads an administrative department (e.g., public safety with police and fire divisions).

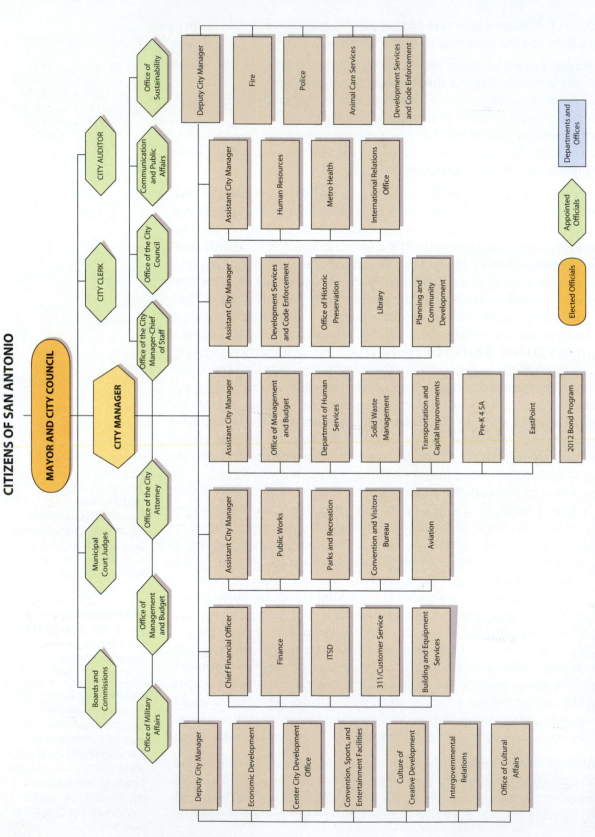

Figure 3.2 Council-Manager Form of Government: City of San Antonio (2014)

http://www.sanantonio.gov/Portals/0/Files/manager/jan2014.pdf

In the commission form, each department (for example, public safety, finance, public works, welfare, or legal) is the responsibility of a single commissioner. Most students of municipal government criticize this form's dispersed administrative structure and lack of a chief executive. The few Texas municipalities that have a variation of the commission form operate more like the mayor-council form and designate a city secretary or another official to coordinate departmental work.

Municipal Politics

★ **LO3.3**   Identify the rules and social issues that shape local government outcomes.

Election rules and socioeconomic change make a difference in who wins and what policies are more likely to be adopted. This section examines several election rules that affect local politics. It then looks at social changes that affect the nature of local politics in Texas.

Rules Make a Difference

All city and special district elections in Texas are **nonpartisan elections**. That is, candidates are listed on the ballot without party labels in order to reduce the role of political parties in local politics. This system succeeded for a long time. However, party politics is again becoming important in some city elections, such as those in the Houston and Dallas metropolitan areas.

Nonpartisan elections have at least two negative consequences. First, without political parties to stir up excitement, voter turnout tends to be low compared with state and national elections. Studies of voting patterns in the United States suggest that voters are racially polarized (that is, people tend to vote for candidates of their own race or ethnicity).[8] Because those who do vote are more likely to be Anglos and middle class, the representation of ethnic minorities and the working class is reduced. San Antonio, for example, has a majority Latino population, but the greater Anglo voter turnout has meant that most San Antonio mayors have been Anglo. The three recent exceptions have been Mexican Americans who have appealed to both Anglos and Latinos (Henry Cisneros, Edward Garza, and Julián Castro). A second problem is that nonpartisan elections tend to be more personal and less issue oriented. Thus, voters tend to vote for personalities, not issues. In smaller cities and towns, local elections are often decided by who has more friends and neighbors.

The two most common ways of organizing municipal elections are the **at-large election**, in which council members are elected on a citywide basis, and the **single-member district election**, in which voters cast a ballot only for a candidate who resides within their district. Texas municipalities have long used at-large elections. However, this system was challenged because it tended to overrepresent the majority Anglo population and underrepresent ethnic minorities. In at-large elections, the city's majority ethnic group tends to be the majority in each electoral contest. This electoral structure works to the disadvantage of ethnic minorities.

✔ **3.2 Learning Check**

1. Name the two legal classifications of cities in Texas and indicate which has more flexibility in deciding its form and the way it operates.
2. Which form of municipal government is most common in Texas's larger home-rule cities? In smaller cities?

Answers on p. 119.

nonpartisan election
An election in which candidates are not identified on the ballot by party label.

at-large election
Members of a policymaking body, such as some city councils, are elected on a citywide basis rather than from single-member districts.

single-member district election
Voters in an area (commonly called a district, ward, or precinct) elect one representative to serve on a policymaking body (e.g., city council, county commissioners court, state House and Senate).

Throughout the country, representative bodies whose members are elected from districts (such as the state legislature and city councils) must **redistrict** (redraw their districts) after every 10-year census. (As we will see later, this also applies to county commissioners courts and some school boards.) After the 2010 census, Texas's city council districts had to be redrawn because of shifts in population within cities and between districts. In 1975, because of its history of racial discrimination, Texas was placed under a provision of the federal Voting Rights Act that required governments to receive clearance from the U.S. attorney general or the Federal District Court for the District of Columbia for rule changes in voting. However, the Supreme Court case of *Shelby v. Holder* (2013) altered preclearance. The Court ruled Section 4 of the Voting Rights Act, which set the formula for determining which states and local governments required preclearance, unconstitutional. Section 5 still allows preclearance, but the Supreme Court's holding now requires new lawsuits for a voting jurisdiction to be brought back under Section 5 through a process called "bailing in." As of 2014, "bailing in" lawsuits had been filed against Texas and the cities of Galveston and Beaumont. In January 2014, several members of the U.S. Congress proposed the Voting Rights Amendment Act of 2014 to reassert federal oversight of voting in Texas and three other states (Georgia, Louisiana, and Mississippi). Despite calls for action from religious groups and civil rights organizations, Congress did not vote on the bill.

In recent decades, the major controversy over redistricting at the local level has been the issue of the representation of Texas's major ethnic groups—particularly Latinos, who were the main source of the state's population growth in the 2010 census. Expansion of the Latino population in urban areas has increased the number of districts in which Latino candidates have a better chance of winning. Low Latino turnout, however, has limited the number of Latino council members who are actually elected.

In 2011, Houston struggled with increasing Latino representation while also providing representation of African Americans, Asian Americans, and Anglos. The final 2011 redistricting plan included four majority Hispanic districts, two majority African American districts, three majority Anglo districts, and two without a majority of one group. (A Latino opportunity district, for example, is one in which there is a large enough population of Latinos to give a Latino candidate a good chance of winning.)[9] Asian Americans were 18 percent of one of the districts with no single ethnic majority. (There were also five at-large positions elected by the whole city.) In the elections that year, two of the Hispanic majority districts were won by Hispanics, two by Anglos. Blacks won the two African American majority districts and one in which there was no ethnic majority. An Asian American won the other district without an ethnic majority. Anglos won all three Anglo majority districts. In 2013, of the 16 positions on the Houston City Council, four were won by African Americans, two by Latinos, one by an Asian American, and the remaining nine by Anglos.

Dividing a city into single-member districts tends to create some districts with a majority of historically excluded ethnic minorities, thereby increasing the chance of electing a Latino, African American, or Asian American

redistricting
Redrawing of boundaries after the federal decennial census to create districts with approximately equal population (e.g., legislative, congressional, commissioners court, and city council districts in Texas).

candidate to the city council. Prompted by lawsuits and ethnic conflict, 20 of Texas's 25 largest cities have adopted single-member districts or a mixed system of at-large and single-member districts. Houston, for example, has 5 council members elected at large (citywide) and 11 elected from single-member districts. Increased use of single-member districts has led to more ethnically and racially diverse city councils.[10] Low voter turnout by an ethnic group, however, can reduce the effect of single-member districts, as happened in Houston in 2011.

Approximately 50 Texas local governments (including 40 school districts) use **cumulative voting** to increase minority representation. In this election system, voters cast a number of votes equal to the positions available and may cast them for one or more candidates in any combination. For example, if eight candidates vie for four positions on the city council, a voter may cast two votes for Candidate A, two votes for Candidate B, and no votes for the other candidates. By the same token, a voter may cast all four votes for Candidate A. In the end, the candidates with the most votes are elected to fill the four positions.

Where racial minority voters are a numerical minority, cumulative voting increases the chances that they will have some representation. The largest government entity in the country to use cumulative voting is the Amarillo Independent School District, which adopted the system in 1999 in response to a federal Voting Rights Act lawsuit. The district was 30 percent minority but had no minority board members for two decades. With the adoption of cumulative voting, African American and Latino board members were elected.

Home-rule cities may also determine whether to institute **term limits** for their elected officials. Beginning in the 1990s, many cities, including San Antonio and Houston, amended their charters to institute term limits for their mayor and city council members. Houston has a limit of three two-year terms for its mayor. Although Houston's popular mayor, Bill White, won election in 2003 with 63 percent of the vote and was reelected twice with 91 and 86 percent of the vote, he could not run again in 2009. (In 2010, he was the unsuccessful Democratic nominee for governor.) In 2008, San Antonio changed its limits from two to four two-year terms for its mayor and city council members, a move expected to make it easier for Latino city council members to build the support necessary to run for mayor. Both supporters and opponents feel strongly about term limits. U.S. Term Limits (USTL) is a non-profit organization that lobbies for term limits in Texas and throughout the country.

Socioeconomic and Demographic Changes

It should be clear, then, that election rules make a difference in who is elected. Historical, social, and economic factors make a difference as well. Texas's increasing levels of urbanization, education, and economic development have made the state more economically, culturally, and politically diverse (or more pluralist). Local politics reflect these changes. Many Texas city governments

cumulative voting
When multiple seats are contested in an at-large election, voters cast one or more of the specified number of votes for one or more candidates in any combination. It is designed to increase representation of historically underrepresented ethnic minority groups.

term limit
A restriction on the number of terms officials can serve in a public office.

Point/Counterpoint

THE ISSUE The council-manager form of government is popular in the United States, and the same is true for many Texas cities. Yet most major cities in the United States, including New York, Boston, Los Angeles, and Houston, use the strong mayor-council form of government. Home-rule cities in Texas, which have a population of more than 5,000, can choose their form of local government. The following are arguments for and against the council-manager form of municipal government.

Should Cities Adopt a Council-Manager Form of Government?

Arguments For a Council-Manager Form

1. This form of government promotes teamwork and a cooperative relationship because the city council hires and fires the city manager. The council provides political control and the city manager directs the administration of the municipality.

2. Because the city manager is not accountable to voters he/she looks at decisions from a business perspective rather than political interest, which provides for more efficient and cost-effective decisions.

3. Major cities have complicated day-to-day operations. City managers are administrative experts professionally trained in public administration or urban studies, but elected officials may not have such training.

Arguments Against a Council-Manager Form

1. In this form of government the mayor is weak; city governments need strong leadership. A strong mayor can lead the city on policy decisions, budget issues, and the day-to-day business of the city.

2. A mayor directly elected by voters is more accountable to voters than an appointed city manager. City managers are more interested in meeting business community needs rather than voter concerns.

3. The city manager may be an "outsider," not from the area, and thereby unfamiliar with the needs of the city.

were long dominated by elite business organizations, such as the Dallas Citizens Council and the San Antonio Good Government League. But greater pluralism and changes in election rules have given a say to a wider range of Texans in how their local governments function. Racial and ethnic conflict remains a problem in Texas, but communities are working to resolve their issues, albeit in differing ways and to different degrees. Growth in the population's size, amount of citizen organization, and income tend to increase the demands on local government and produce higher public spending.

Houston has long been Texas's most diverse local political system. It has a strong business community, many labor union members, an African American community with more than 80 years' experience in fighting for its views and interests, a growing and increasingly organized Latino community, an expanding Asian American community that is becoming more active, and an activist gay community. Multiethnic coalitions have been the norm in

Houston's mayoral races for decades, and nonbusiness interests have significant, if variable, access to city hall.

Dallas has long had serious black-white racial tensions. Although these conflicts have not been resolved, changes in election rules have increased the number of racial minorities on the city council. In 1995, Dallas's Ron Kirk became the first African American in modern times elected mayor of a major Texas city.

In 1991, Austin elected its first Latino mayor, Gus Garcia; in 1998, Laredo elected its first Latina mayor, Betty Flores; and in 2009, San Antonio elected Julián Castro, the youngest mayor (at age 34) of a major U.S. city. Castro was reelected twice, but in 2014 he was appointed by President Obama to head the U.S. Department of Housing and Urban Development. Today, there are more Latino elected officials in Texas than in any other state, with most of them serving at the local level.[11]

Since the 1970s, South Texas's majority Latino population has elected Latino (and some non-Latino) leaders at all levels. In the rest of the state, central cities and some near-in suburbs tend to have a majority of Latinos, African Americans, and Asian Americans, which gives these groups more electoral clout. Suburbs farther from the center tend to be predominantly Anglo and often heavily middle class, which produces more middle-class Anglo leaders. In Texas, as throughout the United States, an increasing number of ethnic and racial minority populations are moving to the suburbs. Clearly, the face of local government has changed as a result of increased use of single-member districts; greater pluralism in the state; and the growing number, organization, and political activity of minority Texans.

Municipal Services

Most citizens and city officials believe city government's major job is to provide basic services that affect people's day-to-day lives: police and fire protection, streets, water, sewer and sanitation, and perhaps parks and recreation. These basic services tend to be cities' largest expenditures, though the amounts spent vary from city to city. Municipalities also regulate important aspects of Texans' lives, notably zoning, construction, food service, and sanitation.

Zoning ordinances regulate the use of land, for instance, by separating commercial and residential zones, because bringing businesses into residential areas often increases traffic and crime. Zoning has received more opposition in Texas than in most other states, although its use is growing. Among Texas's 10 largest municipalities, only Houston has no zoning authority, though the city does help enforce deed restrictions that protect neighborhoods and uses its control of access to utilities to control and direct growth. Developers in Houston use private covenants and deed restrictions in place of city zoning laws. Citizens with complaints about deed restrictions may receive help from the city in resolving issues. Although there are no zoning laws, development is governed by city codes that address how property can be subdivided. For example, there are requirements on lot size and minimum parking.

Students  in Action

Service in the Community

''Working within the community provided an experience in government that I could not have learned in a classroom. It truly exposes the individual needs of those within the community and gives you the sense that you can actually make a difference.''

—Kaitlin Piraro

Kaitlin Piraro worked for the City of Austin part-time at the Dittmar Recreation Center from the spring of 2011 through fall 2012. As a counselor, she worked one-on-one with children aged 5 to 11 in the recreation center's after-school program. Her primary responsibility was to keep the youth, who were from local neighborhoods, focused on positive after-school activities. Kaitlin soon volunteered to work on the teen art project at the center. She provided specific classes for the students in art, cooking, sculpture, painting, and film. She found that introducing new projects to the students was rewarding and they were excited to be involved in interactive learning. Selected art projects were shown at local galleries in Austin. At the end of the semester, Kaitlin worked with others at the center to create an awards ceremony to recognize the students' hard work. She learned how to work with young students, coordinate projects, and communicate with parents and others in the community.

This experience opened Kaitlin's eyes to local bureaucracy, how it works, and how it helps communities. Her hope is to someday work again with city government. She believes that opportunities to work in community projects, as a volunteer, intern, or paid employee, are a great way to learn firsthand about government. Her advice to other students is to explore all possible community projects, so that they can give back and learn more about the needs of their community.

Interview with Kaitlin Piraro on February 24, 2014

© Andresr/Shutterstock.com

Over time, many Texas cities have added libraries, airports, hospitals, community development, and housing to their list of services. Scarce resources (particularly money) of local governments increase competition between traditional services and newer services demanded by citizens or the state and national governments, such as protection of the homeless, providing elder services and job training, fighting air pollution, and delinquency prevention. These competing demands for municipal spending often result in controversy, thus requiring elected officials to make difficult decisions.

The Denton City Council discusses a grassroots petition to ban hydraulic fracking.

AP Images/Tony Gutierrez

CRITICAL THINKING

What are the political and economic ramifications for Texas if cities passed ordinances to ban hydraulic fracturing?

Municipal Government Revenue

Most city governments in Texas and the nation face a serious financial dilemma: they barely have enough money to provide basic services and thus must reject or shortchange new services. Cities' two largest tax sources—sales and property taxes—are limited by state law. These taxes produce inadequate increases in revenue as the population grows, and they are regressive (that is, they put a heavier burden on those who make less money). Moreover, Texas voters are increasingly hostile to higher property taxes. Adding to the problem are low levels of state assistance to Texas cities as compared with the pattern exhibited in many other states. As a result, Texas cities are relying more heavily on fees (such as liquor licenses, franchise fees for cable television companies, and water rates) and are going into debt. Per capita local government debt in Texas, for example, was nearly five times greater than state government debt for the whole country as of 2013.[12]

Local governments were hurt by the recent "Great Recession," particularly the decrease in property values (which are the basis of property taxes) and the slowing of sales tax receipts. The 2009 federal stimulus bill provided $16.8 billion to Texas, but most of that money went to the state rather than to local governments. The major revenue sources for local government, property and sales tax receipts, have grown in counties and municipalities with oil and gas development. Nevertheless, local governments must contend with the costs of growth due to oil and gas exploration and production, including road repairs and sewer and water infrastructure. In 2013, the legislature passed a bill to allocate roughly $225 million to counties to assist with cost of road repairs due to oil and gas activity. This legislative action shows state government's willingness to provide limited assistance for local governments.[13]

Taxes The state of Texas allows municipalities to levy taxes based on the value of property (**property tax**). The tax rate is generally expressed in terms of the amount of tax per $100 of the property's value. This rate varies greatly from one city to another. In 2012 (the most recent year for comprehensive data), rates varied from 5 cents per $100 valuation to $1.52, with an average of 52 cents.[14] A problem with property taxes is that poorer cities with low property values must charge a high rate to provide minimum services. In the Dallas area, for example, in 2012 Highland Park had an annual median family income of $247,000 and set a property tax rate of 22 cents per $100 in valuation. Wylie (north of Dallas) had an annual median family income of $82,000 and set its tax rate at 90 cents per $100 in valuation.

The other major source of city tax revenue is the optional 1¼–2 percent sales tax that is collected along with the state sales tax. Local governments are in competition for sales tax dollars. The sum of city, county, and special district government sales taxes cannot exceed 2 percent. So, for example, a city might assess 1 percent; the county, 0.5 percent; and a special district, 0.5 percent. In order to prevent going over the cap of 2 percent, state law sets up the order in which sales taxes are required to be collected. First to collect is the city, then the county, and third are special districts. Further, voters must approve the imposition of a local sales tax within their jurisdiction. An additional problem is that sales tax revenues fluctuate with the local economy, making it difficult to plan how much money will be available. The hotel occupancy tax is another significant source of revenue for cities with tourism or major sports events, such as the NFL Super Bowl or the NCAA Final Four.

Fees Lacking adequate tax revenues to meet the demands placed on them, Texas municipalities have come to rely more heavily on fees (charges for services and payments required by an agency upon those subject to its regulation). Cities levy fees for such things as beer and liquor licenses and building permits. They collect traffic fines and may charge franchise fees based on gross receipts of public utilities (for example, telephone and cable television companies). Texas municipalities are authorized to own and operate water, electric, and gas utility systems that may generate a profit for the city. Charges also are levied for such services as sewage treatment, garbage collection, hospital care, and use of city recreation facilities. User fees may allow a city to provide certain services with only a small subsidy from its general revenue fund or perhaps no subsidy at all.

property tax
A tax that property owners pay according to the value of real estate and other tangible property. At the local level, property owners pay this tax to the city, the county, the school district, and often other special districts.

Bonds and Certificates of Obligation Taxes and fees normally produce enough revenue to allow Texas cities to cover day-to-day operating expenses. Money for capital improvements (such as construction of city buildings or parks) and emergencies (such as flood or hurricane damage) often must be obtained through the sale of municipal **bonds**, which may be redeemed over periods of 1 to 30 years. The Texas Constitution allows cities to issue bonds, but any bond issue to be repaid from taxes must be approved by the voters. During the recent recession, local governments made more use of certificates of obligation, which do not require voter approval and typically reach maturity in 15 to 20 years. The certificates traditionally have been used for smaller amounts and short-term financing.

Property Taxes and Tax Exemptions Property owners pay taxes on the value of their homes and businesses not just to the city but also to the county, the school district, and often other special districts. When property values or tax rates go up, the total tax bill goes up as well. To offset the burden of higher taxes resulting from reappraisals of property values, local governments (including cities) may grant homeowners up to a 20 percent homestead exemption on the assessed value of their homes. Cities may also provide an additional homestead exemption for disabled veterans and their surviving spouses, for homeowners 65 years of age or older, or for other reasons such as adding pollution controls.

Cities, counties, and community college districts may also freeze property taxes for senior citizens and the disabled. Property tax caps (or ceilings) can be implemented by city council action or by voter approval. The dilemma is that cities can help their disadvantaged citizens, but doing so costs the city revenue. In 2013, exemptions cost Texas cities an estimated $43.9 billion in revenue. As baby boomers reach retirement age, exemptions and property tax caps will reduce revenue even further. Table 3.1 illustrates property taxes from different local governments and the consequences of exemptions and caps.

The Bottom Line Because of pressure against increasing property tax rates, municipal governments sometimes refrain from increased spending, cut services or programs, or find new revenue sources. Typically, city councils are forced to opt for one or more of the following actions:

- Create new fees or raise fees on services such as garbage collection
- Impose hiring and wage freezes for municipal employees
- Cut services (such as emergency rooms) that are especially important for inner-city populations
- Contract with private firms for service delivery
- Improve productivity, especially by investing in technology

Generating Revenue for Economic Development

State and federal appropriations to assist cities are shrinking, especially for economic development. Inner cities face the challenge of dilapidated housing, abandoned buildings, and poorly maintained infrastructure (such as

bond
A mechanism by which governments borrow money. General obligation bonds (redeemed from general revenue) and revenue bonds (redeemed from revenue obtained from the property or activity financed by the sale of the bonds) are authorized under Texas law.

Table 3.1 One Home but Property Taxes from Four Governments (An Example from Walker County on a Home with an Appraised Value of $120,220; Taxes Paid in January 2014)

Taxing Unit	Exemption Amount* Homestead	Exemption Amount* Over Age 65	Taxable Value	Tax Rate Per $100 of Taxable Value	Nominal Tax**	Ceiling***	Actual Tax***
Huntsville ISD	$15,000	$16,000	$ 89,220	$1.2100	$1,080	$595	$ 595
Walker County	0	$12,000	$108,220	$0.6778	$ 734	$455	$ 455
City of Huntsville	0	$12,000	$108,220	$0.4206	$ 455	$319	$ 319
Walker County Hospital District	0	$12,000	$108,220	$0.1590	$ 172	—	$ 172
Total					$2,441		$1,541

Explanation: A county appraisal district decides the value of each property, and each local government sets its tax rate and the amount of the exemption it will give for special circumstances such as living in a home you own (homestead exemption), being 65 or older, or being disabled—all within the limits of state law. The local government does not collect taxes on the exemption amount. Also, sales tax revenue can effectively reduce property tax rates—in this case, rates for the city and county. The property owner in this case pays a total of $1,541 in property taxes to four different local governments.

*The Exemption Amount is deducted from the Appraised Value ($120,220 for each government entity).
**The Nominal Tax is the Taxable Value multiplied by the Tax Rate.
***The Actual Tax may be less than the Nominal Tax because an entity may place a ''ceiling'' on the taxes of those 65 and over and the disabled. As long as the person owns and lives in their residence, the tax from that entity will not go up. Note that three of the four entities use the ceiling, saving this taxpayer $900.

Sources: Calculated by the author from data and rules provided by Walker County Appraisal District, http://www.walkercountyappraisal.com, and Texas Comptroller, http://www.window.state.tx.us/taxes.

CRITICAL THINKING

Would it be fair for local governments to give further exemptions to those in need, or is it unfair to shift the burden to other homeowners?

How Do We Compare…in Funding Services at State and Local Levels?

Texas Expenditures (in millions of dollars)

Type of Government	Number	Total Spent	Hospitals	Public Education	Highways	Police and Corrections
State	1	$ 90,853	$3,353	$14,634	$7,979	$3,783
County	254	$ 14,494	$4,262	$ 51	$1,337	$2,660
Municipality	1214	$ 30,914	$ 39	$ 48	$2,115	$3,522
School district	1079	$ 47,863		$44,245		
Other special districts	2600	$ 10,861	$1,892		$ 241	$ 4
Total for all local governments	**5147**	**$103,719**	**$6,193**	**$44,344**	**$3,693**	**$6,186**

Source: U.S. Census of Governments, 2007, Revised October 24, 2011, http://www.census.gov. A Census of Governments was conducted in 2012, but results will be released over several years. More recent total expenditure data are available for the state and all local governments taken together, but the Census of Governments provides the breakdown for each form of local government. Expenditures are Direct General Expenditures for the function. Totals may vary because of rounding.

sewers and streets). This neglect blights neighborhoods and contributes to social problems such as crime and strained racial relations. Texas cities do have the local option of a half-cent sales tax for infrastructure upgrades, such as repaving streets and improving sewage disposal. The increased sales tax, however, must stay within the 2 percent limit the state imposes on local governments. Following a national trend, some Texas cities are trying to spur development by attracting businesses through tax incentives. The Texas legislature authorizes municipalities to create **tax reinvestment zones** (TRZs) to use innovative tax breaks to attract investment in blighted inner cities and other areas needing development. Major cities using TRZs include Houston, Dallas, Fort Worth, Austin, San Antonio, and El Paso. Smaller cities also have used TRZs. Whether such plans work is controversial. Many observers of similar plans argue that companies attracted by tax breaks often make minimal actual investments and leave as soon as they have realized a profit from tax subsidies. Yet, because TRZs sometimes work, many cities starved for the monetary resources to combat decay are willing to take the gamble.

Counties

★ **LO3.4**   Analyze the structure and responsibilities of counties.

Texas **counties** present an interesting set of contradictions. They are technically an arm of the state, created to serve its needs, but both county officials and county residents see them as locally controlled governments and resent any state "interference." Counties collect taxes on both urban and rural property but focus more on the needs of rural residents and people living in unincorporated suburbs, who do not have city governments to provide services. This form of county government, out of the 19th century, serves 21st-century Texans.

Texas is divided into 254 counties, the most of any state in the nation. The basic form of Texas counties is set by the state constitution, though their activities are heavily shaped by whether they are in rural or metropolitan areas. As an agent of the state, each county issues state automobile licenses, enforces state laws, registers voters, conducts elections, collects certain state taxes, and helps administer justice. In conjunction with state and federal governments, the county conducts health and welfare programs, maintains records of vital statistics (such as births and deaths), issues various licenses, collects fees, and provides a host of other public services. Yet state supervision of county operations is minimal. Rural counties generally try to keep taxes low and provide minimal services. They are reluctant to take on new jobs, such as regulating septic systems and residential development. In metropolitan areas, however, counties have been forced by citizen demands and sometimes the state to take on varied urban tasks such as providing ballparks and recreation centers, hospitals, libraries, airports, and museums.[15]

 Bexar County, which includes the city of San Antonio, created a digital library, bexarbibliotech.org. This program is one of the first of its kind in the

✓ 3.3 Learning Check

1. Which of the following election forms tend to increase the representation of minorities in local government: nonpartisan elections, redistricting, at-large elections, single-member district elections, or cumulative voting?

2. What are the two largest tax sources that provide revenue to local governments? Do these taxes usually provide enough revenue for local governments to meet the demands placed on them?

Answers on p. 119.

tax reinvestment zone (TRZ)

An area in which municipal tax incentives are offered to encourage businesses to locate in and contribute to the development of a blighted urban area. Commercial and residential property taxes may be frozen.

county

Texas is divided into 254 counties that serve as an administrative arm of the state and that provide important services at the local level, especially in rural areas.

United States; it's a bookless public library where patrons scan their library cards and then check out or return virtual books. Visitors can download e-books on their tablets or e-readers, or if they don't have their own they may check out one of 600 devices provided by the library. This system allows the library to reduce costs associated with books that are damaged or not returned, plus it introduces residents to e-technology.

Structure and Operation

As required by the state constitution, all Texas counties have the same basic governmental structure, despite wide demographic and economic differences between rural and urban counties. (Contrast Figure 3.3, Harris County, the most populous Texas county with more than 4 million residents in 2010, with Figure 3.4, Loving County, the least populous with 82 residents in that year.)

The Texas Constitution provides for the election of four county commissioners, county and district attorneys, a county sheriff, a county clerk, a district clerk, a county tax assessor-collector, a county treasurer, and constables, as well as judicial officers, including justices of the peace and a county judge. All elected county officials are chosen in partisan elections and serve four-year terms. In practice, Texas counties are usually highly decentralized, or fragmented. No one person has formal authority to supervise or coordinate the county's elected officials, who tend to think of their office as a personal fiefdom and to resent interference by other officials. Sometimes, however, the political leadership of the county judge produces cooperation.

Commissioners Court All elected county officials make policies for their area of responsibility, but the major policymaking body is called the **commissioners court**. Its members are the county judge, who presides, and four elected commissioners. The latter serve staggered four-year terms, so that two commissioners are elected every two years. Each commissioner is elected by voters residing in a commissioner precinct, thus commissioners are elected from single-member districts. Boundary lines for a county's four commissioner precincts are set by its commissioners court. Precincts must be of substantially equal population as mandated by the "one-person, one-vote" ruling of the U.S. Supreme Court in *Avery v. Midland County* 390 U.S. 474 (1968).

Like cities, counties must redistrict every 10 years, following the federal census. After the 2010 census, county redistricting battles centered on political party power in Dallas County, and racial and ethnic representation were major sources of conflict in Harris County (Houston), Galveston County, and Travis County (Austin). In Dallas County, the Democratic-controlled commissioners court added another Democratic seat, and the Republican majority on Harris County's commissioners court was sued over dilution of Latino votes. The Galveston County plan was rejected by the U.S. Department of Justice for diluting minority votes. Bexar County's (San Antonio) redistricting was less controversial than usual and was

commissioners court
A Texas county's policymaking body, with five members: the county judge, who presides, and four commissioners representing single-member precincts.

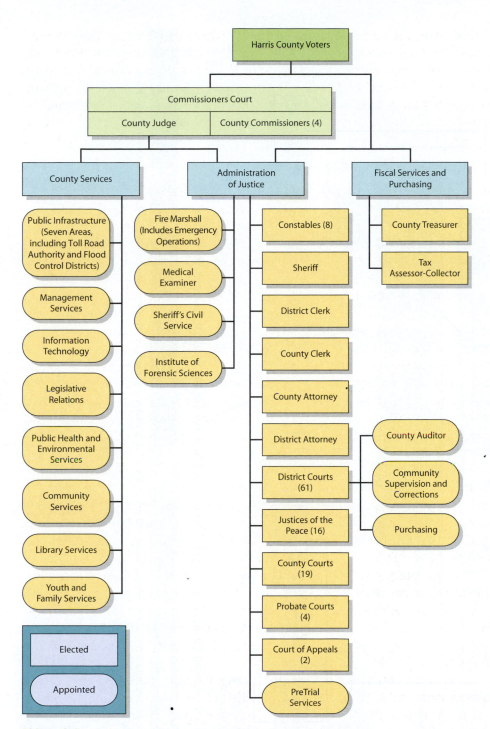

Figure 3.3   Harris County Government (County Seat: Houston).

Compiled by author using FY2014 -2015 Approved Budget, http://www.hctx.net/budget.

CRITICAL THINKING

Do most citizens know the role of their county commissioners court? Why is it important for more citizens to understand its role?

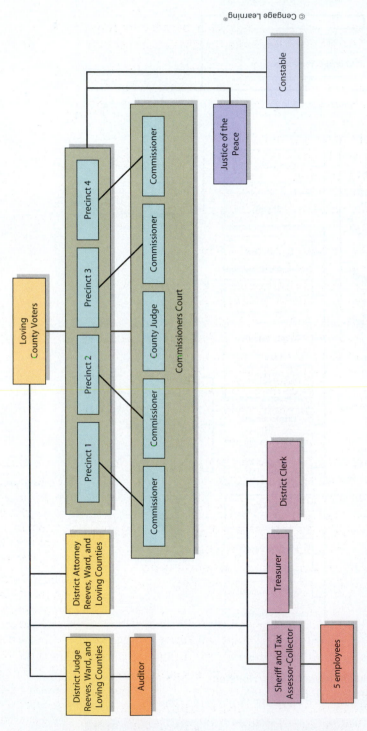

© Cengage Learning®

Figure 3.4   Loving County Government (County Seat: Mentone) Second smallest County in the nation.

CRITICAL THINKING

How does a county's population size change the job of the county commissioners court? Compare Figure 3.3 (Harris County) to Figure 3.4 (Loving County).

overshadowed by the battle over congressional redistricting. (For an in-depth discussion, see the Selected Reading in Chapter 8, "The Legislative Branch.")

The term *commissioners court* is actually a misnomer because its functions are administrative and legislative rather than judicial. The court's major functions include the following:

- Adopting the county budget and setting tax rates, which are the commissioners court's greatest sources of power and influence over other county officials
- Providing a courthouse, jails, and other buildings
- Maintaining county roads and bridges, which is often viewed by rural residents as the major county function
- Administering county health and welfare programs
- Administering and financing elections (general and special elections for the nation, state, and county)

Beyond these functions, a county is free to decide whether to take on other programs authorized, but not required, by the state.

In metropolitan areas, large numbers of people live in unincorporated communities with no city government to provide services such as police protection and water. Within those communities, the county takes on a multitude of functions. In rural areas, counties take on few new tasks, and residents are generally happy not to be "hassled" by too much government. County commissioners may have individual duties in addition to their collective responsibilities. Commissioners in counties that do not have a county engineer, for example, are commonly responsible for the roads and bridges in their respective precincts.

County Judge

The **county judge**, who holds the most prominent job in county government, generally is the most influential county leader. This county officer presides over commissioners court, has administrative responsibility for most county agencies not headed by another elected official, and, in some counties, presides over court cases, but does not need to be a lawyer. Much of the county judge's power or influence comes from his or her leadership skills and from playing a lead role in the commissioners court's budget decisions. The judge has essentially no formal authority over other elected county officials.

County Attorney and District Attorney

The **county attorney** represents the state in civil and criminal cases and advises county officials on legal questions. Nearly 50 counties in Texas do not elect a county attorney because a resident district attorney performs those duties. Other counties elect a county attorney but share the services of a **district attorney** with one or more neighboring counties. Where there are both a county and a district attorney, the district attorney generally specializes in the district court cases, and the county attorney handles lesser matters in county and justice of the peace courts. District attorneys tend to be important figures in the criminal

county judge
A citizen popularly elected to preside over the county commissioners court, and in smaller counties, to hear civil and criminal cases.

county attorney
A citizen elected to represent the county in civil and criminal cases, unless a resident district attorney performs some of these functions.

district attorney
A citizen elected to serve one or more counties who prosecutes criminal cases, gives advisory opinions, and represents the county in civil cases.

justice system because of the leadership they provide to local law enforcement and the discretion they exercise in deciding whether to prosecute cases. The legal advice of the county or district attorney carries considerable weight with other county officials.

If a vacancy occurs during a county attorney's term of office, this office is filled by the commissioners court. Although local voters choose the district attorney, the governor fills a vacancy that occurs between elections. In 2014, Governor Rick Perry was indicted by a Travis County grand jury for abuse of office involving his alleged attempts to force the resignation of Travis County District Attorney Rosemary Lehmberg. A unique responsibility of the Travis County District Attorney's office is overseeing the Public Integrity Unit that is charged with the duty to investigate possible corruption of state-level officials. Complainants suggested that Perry sought Democrat Lehmberg's resignation after she pled guilty to driving while intoxicated, so he could replace her with a Republican district attorney who would be friendlier to Perry's appointees and other Republican elected officials.[16]

County Sheriff   The **county sheriff**, as chief law enforcement officer, is charged with keeping the peace in the county. In this capacity, the sheriff appoints deputies and oversees the county jail and its prisoners. In practice, the sheriff's office commonly focuses on crime in unincorporated areas and leaves law enforcement in cities primarily to the municipal police. In a county with a population of fewer than 10,000, the sheriff may also serve as tax assessor-collector, unless that county's electorate votes to separate the two offices. In a few rural counties, the sheriff may be the county's most influential leader.

Law Enforcement and Judges   Counties have a number of officials associated with the justice system, ranging from sparsely populated Loving County to heavily populated Harris County. The judicial role of the constitutional county judge varies. In counties with a small population, the county judge may exercise important judicial functions such as handling probate matters, small civil cases, and serious misdemeanors. But in counties with a large population, county judges are so involved in their political, administrative, and legislative roles that they have little time for judicial functions. Instead, there are often **statutory county courts** that have lawyers for judges and tend to operate in a more formal manner. In addition to the sheriff and county and district attorneys discussed above, there are the district clerk, justices of the peace, and constables. The **district clerk** maintains records for the district courts.

Each county has from one to eight justice of the peace precincts. The number is decided by the commissioners court. Justice of the peace courts can also be abolished by a commissioners court, as occurred in Brazos County in 2014. **Justices of the peace** (commonly called JPs) handle minor civil and criminal cases, including small claims court cases. Statewide, JPs hear a large volume of legal actions, with traffic cases representing a substantial part of their work. Other duties vary. In most counties, they also

county sheriff
A citizen popularly elected as the county's chief law enforcement officer; the sheriff is also responsible for maintaining the county jail.

statutory county court
Court created by the legislature at the request of a county; may have civil or criminal jurisdiction or both, depending on the legislation creating it.

district clerk
A citizen elected to maintain records for the district courts.

justice of the peace
A judge elected from a justice of the peace precinct who handles minor civil and criminal cases, including small claims court.

serve as coroner (to determine cause of death in certain cases) and as a magistrate (to set bail for arrested persons). Similar to the constitutional county court judge, they do not have to be lawyers but are required to take some legal training. **Constables** assist the justice court by serving subpoenas and other court documents. They and their deputies are peace officers and may carry out security and investigative responsibilities. In some counties, they are an important part of law enforcement, particularly for rural areas of the county. Like other county officials, the judges, justices of the peace, district clerks, and constables are elected in partisan elections for four-year terms.

County Clerk and County Tax Assessor-Collector A county clerk keeps records and handles various paperwork chores for both the county court and the commissioners court. In addition, the county clerk files legal documents (such as deeds, mortgages, and contracts) in the county's public records and maintains the county's vital statistics (birth, death, and marriage records). The county clerk may also administer elections, though counties with larger populations often have an administrator of elections.

A county office that has seen its role decrease over time is the **county tax assessor-collector**. The title is partially a misnomer. Since 1982, the **countywide tax appraisal district** assesses (or determines) property values in the county. The tax assessor-collector, on the other hand, collects county taxes and fees and certain state fees, including the license tag fees for motor vehicles and fees for handicapped parking permits. The office also commonly handles voter registration, although some counties have an elections administrator.

Treasurer and Auditor The **county treasurer** receives and pays out all county funds authorized by the commissioners court. If the office is eliminated by constitutional amendment, the county commissioners assign treasurer duties to another county office. Local voters allowed Tarrant and Bexar Counties to eliminate the office. These counties then authorized the county auditor to deal with responsibilities that were once held by the county treasurer. A county of 10,000 or more people must have a **county auditor**, appointed by the county's district court judges. The auditing function involves checking the account books and records of officials who handle county funds. Some observers worry that allowing the county auditor to perform both jobs of auditor and treasurer eliminates necessary checks and balances in county government.[17]

County Finance

Increasing citizen demands for services and programs impose on most counties an ever-expanding need for money. Just as the structure of county governments is frozen in the Texas Constitution, so is the county's power to tax and, to a lesser extent, its power to spend. Financial problems became even more serious for most counties during the recent Great Recession. As the

constable
A citizen elected to assist the justice of the peace by serving papers and in some cases carrying out security and investigative responsibilities.

county clerk
A citizen elected to perform clerical chores for the county courts and commissioners court, keep public records, maintain vital statistics, and administer public elections, if the county does not have an administrator of elections.

county tax assessor-collector
This elected official no longer assesses property for taxation but does collect taxes and fees and commonly handles voter registration.

countywide tax appraisal district
The district appraises all real estate and commercial property for taxation by units of local government within a county.

county treasurer
An elected official who receives and pays out county money as directed by the commissioners court.

county auditor
A person appointed by the district judge or judges to check the financial books and records of other officials who handle county money.

state's economy strengthened beginning in 2012, so too did financial problems lessen.

Taxation The Texas Constitution authorizes county governments to collect taxes on property, and that is usually their most important revenue source. Although occupations may also be taxed, no county implements that provision. Each year the commissioners court sets the county tax rate. If property tax rate increases exceed an amount that would generate up to 8 percent more than the previous year's revenues, citizens may circulate a petition for an election to roll back (limit) the higher rate. (The other local governments face similar limitations.) Counties may also add 0.5 to 1.5 cents onto the state sales tax, which is 6.25 cents on the dollar. (Remember, however, that the add-on by all local governments may not exceed 2 cents.) Fewer than half of Texas counties (primarily those with relatively small populations) impose a sales tax, and most set the rate at 0.5 cents.

Revenues From Nontax Sources Counties receive small amounts of money from various sources that add up to an important part of their total revenue. All counties may impose fees on the sale of liquor, and they share in state revenue from liquor sales, various motor vehicle taxes and fees, and traffic fines. Like other local governments, counties are eligible for federal grants-in-aid; but over the long term, this source continues to shrink. With voter approval, a county may borrow money through sale of bonds to pay for capital projects such as a new jail or sports stadium. The Texas Constitution limits county indebtedness to 35 percent of a county's total assessed property value.

Tax Incentives and Subsidies Like cities, a commissioners court may grant tax abatements (reductions or suspensions) on taxable property, reimbursements (return of taxes paid), or tax increment financing (TIF; the use of future gains in property value to finance current development projects) to attract or retain businesses. For instance, in 2003, Bexar County offered a $22 million tax abatement for a Toyota factory to be built to produce pickup trucks in San Antonio. The offer was part of a complex incentive package put together by state, county, city, and other officials that totaled an estimated $133 million in tax breaks and infrastructure spending. The plant went into operation in 2006, creating more than 2,000 high-paying jobs and contributing to economic development in the region. From 2008 to 2010, the plant suffered from the national economic downturn, but by 2011 it had returned to full production.[18]

The Bottom Line Despite various revenue sources, Texas counties, like other units of local government, are pressured to increase property taxes or to balance their budgets by eliminating or reducing programs and services. Although administrative costs and demands for expanded public services continue to increase, sources of county revenue are not expanding as quickly as demand.

Expenditures The state restricts county expenditures in certain areas and mandates spending in others. Yet patterns of spending vary considerably from county to county. The biggest variation is between rural and metropolitan counties. The "How Do We Compare" feature in this chapter (p. 96) shows that hospitals and health care, public safety, and roads are the largest expenditures for Texas counties overall. This expenditure pattern holds for Texas's largest counties, which also spend smaller, but still significant, amounts on urban amenities (such as parks) and social services (such as housing and welfare). Rural counties tend to spend a large portion of their budget on public safety and roads but little on social services and urban amenities, which may include music venues or dog parks. Many counties spend little on health and hospitals because they have shifted the costs to a hospital district (a special district).

Although the county judge, auditor, or budget officer prepares the budget, the commissioners court is responsible for final adoption of an annual spending plan. Preparation of the budget generally enhances the commissioners court's power within county government. Counties do not have complete control over their spending because state and federal rules mandate certain county services and regulatory activities. Examples include social services, legal assistance and medical care for poor people, and mental health programs. Over the last decade, counties have made a major effort to pressure the legislature to limit unfunded mandates. An unfunded mandate is a requirement imposed on local governments by the state or a governing agency without providing funding to execute the requirement. Almost all counties have passed resolutions calling for a state constitutional amendment to ban mandates. Through 2014, the Texas legislature had not proposed such an amendment.

County Government Reform

Texas counties experience various problems: rigid structure and duties fixed in the state constitution and statutes, inefficiency related to too many elected officials and the lack of merit systems (hiring people for what they know) for hiring and promoting employees, and too little money. Counties with larger populations may establish merit employment systems, and half of those eligible have done so. One often-suggested reform is county home rule to give counties more ability to organize and operate in accordance with local needs and wishes. Research suggests that although county home rule better meets community demands, it also tends to expand county spending.

Different states allow varying degrees of county home rule. Texas is among the states that are most strongly against home rule.[19] Until 1969, Texas actually had a home-rule provision for counties in the constitution, but it was too difficult to implement. Reviving a workable version today would be hard to achieve. Many (probably most) county officials prefer the present system, as do many people served by counties outside of the metropolitan areas.

Colonias lack infrastructure or utilities.

Lisa Wiltse/Corbis

CRITICAL THINKING

How should county government along the border improve the conditions of colonias? Why?

Border Counties

In recent years, there has been unprecedented population growth in Texas's counties near the Rio Grande because of the North American Free Trade Agreement (NAFTA) and immigration. Unfortunately, population growth has outstripped economic growth, and the traditionally impoverished border region now has even more poor people. Many of the poor live in **colonias** (depressed housing settlements, often without running water or sewage systems). It is estimated that there are currently about 2,300 colonias in Texas, and as many as 400,000 Texans live in substandard conditions in these settlements.[20]

Minimal efforts have been made to deal with problems of the colonias. In 2009, counties were given planning and inspection powers. Additionally, the Texas secretary of state created a plan to provide water and sewage to 32 (of 2,300) colonias; voters approved a constitutional amendment for bonds to fund roads and streets within the colonias; and the federal government provided some aid. However, the state legislature's antitax attitude in recent years has caused actual funding to lag. Advocates for border counties (generally any county within 50 miles of the Texas-Mexico border) fear that the area's serious infrastructure, educational, and medical needs will continue to be neglected.

In recent years, the flow across the border of undocumented immigrants—including those escaping drug-related violence—combined with the sharp increase in drug gangs on the Mexican side of the border, has created great concern and controversy. Sheriffs and police departments have sought and

colonia

A low-income community, typically located in South Texas and especially in counties bordering Mexico, that lacks running water, sewer lines, and other essentials.

obtained federal and state money to increase their law enforcement efforts. The state spent $452 million on border security between 2008 and 2013, and the federal government provided an estimated $15.7 million in aid for 2013. Although the conflict in Mexico occasionally spills over the Rio Grande, the Texas side of the border remains relatively safe. In spite of great growth in population (usually associated with higher crime rates), border cities have lower crime rates than Houston, San Antonio, and Austin. Anecdotal evidence suggests, however, that safety in some rural areas has significantly declined.[21]

The national government's decision to build a physical wall along major portions of the border has created tension in the communities affected. The wall (or border fence) divides communities and separates families and friends from each other. Construction of a permanent wall creates environmental dislocation.

Special Districts

★ **LO3.5** Explain the functions of special districts and their importance to the greater community.

Among local governmental units, the least known and least understood are special district governments, yet they represent the fastest-growing form of government. They fall into two categories: school districts and noneducation special districts. Created by an act of the legislature or, in some cases, by local ordinance (for example, establishing a public housing authority), a **special district** usually has one function and serves a specific group of people in a particular geographic area.

Public School Districts

Citizen concerns over public education cause local school systems to occupy center stage among special district governments. More than 1,000 Texas **independent school districts (ISDs)**, created by the legislature, are governed by popularly elected, nonsalaried boards of trustees. The school board selects the superintendent, who by law and practice makes most major decisions about the district's educational programs and who tends to influence other decisions as well. It is the superintendent who is responsible for the leadership of the school district. Some of the major functions of the superintendent include preparing a budget, administering day-to-day operations, and acting as chief communicator for the district with legislators, media, parents, and others. The board members, generally made up of local businesspeople and professionals, tend to focus on things they know—particularly money issues, such as taxes and budgets. School board elections are generally low-turnout, friends-and-neighbors affairs. When these elections become heated, it is generally because of sharp divisions within the community over volatile cultural issues like sex education or prayer in the schools, racial and ethnic conflict, emphasis on athletic programs (especially football), or differences over taxing and spending decisions.

3.4 Learning Check

1. True or False: Local residents of each county can determine the structure of their own county government.
2. What is the major policymaking body in each Texas county?

Answers on p. 120.

special district
A unit of local government that performs a particular service, such as providing schools, hospitals, or housing, for a particular geographic area.

independent school district (ISD)
Created by the legislature, an independent school district raises tax revenue to support its public schools. Voters within the district elect a board that hires a superintendent, determines salary schedules, selects textbooks, and sets the district's property tax rate.

Texas has traditionally had a highly centralized educational system in which the Texas Education Agency placed significant limitations on local district decisions. Since 1995, however, school boards have been given increased local autonomy over some decisions. National influence has been far more limited and targeted than that of the state. Federal involvement has focused on improving the situation of groups historically neglected or discriminated against in Texas education. Districts must comply with federal regulations in areas such as racial and gender nondiscrimination and treatment of students with disabilities. Money is also a source of influence. In school year 2012-2013, local districts raised an average of 48 percent of their revenue locally (primarily from property taxes), the state contributed 40 percent, and the federal government added 12 percent.[22] Federal aid has particularly targeted the children of the poor and language minorities. Thus, school districts make local educational policy in the context of substantial limits, mandates, and influences from the state and federal governments.

This shared control of public education has been highlighted in recent years by increased state, and now federal, requirements for testing students. Districts have been forced to spend more time and money on preparing students for testing. Supporters say that testing has improved student performance and made local schools more accountable. Critics charge that although students are now better at taking tests, they learn less in other areas.

A second challenge for local education is the increasing ethnic and economic diversity of Texas's schoolchildren. For two decades, traditional minorities have been a majority in Texas schools, and for a decade a majority of Texas students have come from economically disadvantaged families. Meeting their needs is important not only for the children but for the economic health of the entire state.

A third challenge facing Texas education is school finance, which actually has two faces: equity (the quality or ideal of being just, fair, and impartial) and how much should be spent. In 1987, a state district court (later affirmed by the Texas Supreme Court) held that the state's system for school finance violated the Texas Constitution. The basic problem was that poor districts, relying on property taxes, had to tax at a high rate to provide minimum expenditures per pupil. Wealthier districts, on the other hand, could spend considerably more with significantly lower tax rates.

The other school finance issue is the conflict between the increased need for services and the slow growth of funding. Clearly, demands on the schools to do more (and therefore to spend more) have increased. Yet the two major sources of funding for the school districts (state appropriations and the property tax) have expanded more slowly than demand. The proportion of education funding provided by the state has remained under 50 percent, and property tax revenue tends to grow slowly and to fluctuate. In the face of the Great Recession, the 2011 legislature (for the first time in 60 years) reduced the actual amount appropriated for schools. The results were 11,000 teacher layoffs, larger classes, and cuts in programs such as arts and athletics, field trips, support staff, and custodians. Some funding was restored by the 83rd Legislature in 2013.

The property tax is the only local source of tax revenue for Texas public schools. Unlike other local governments, school districts cannot use the sales tax for revenue. Not surprisingly, school districts receive more than 50 percent of property taxes collected in the state. As schools have increased property taxes to pay their bills, many property owners have objected. In response, the legislature required that if a school district increases its tax rate by more than 4 cents per $100 of property value over the previous year's revenue, the district must hold a rollback election, in which voters can decide to keep or roll back the increase. (In the case of other local governments, the increase must exceed 8 percent, and citizens must collect signatures on a petition to force a rollback election.) Forty-four school districts held tax-increase elections in 2011; in 12 cases, voters disapproved the increase.[23] For more detailed discussions of education policy and finance, see Chapter 10, "Public Policy and Administration," and Chapter 13, "Finance and Fiscal Policy."

Junior or Community College Districts

Another example of a special district is the **junior college or community college district**, which offers two-year academic programs beyond high school, as well as various technical and vocational programs. The latter two may be part of the regular degree and certificate programs or special nondegree training programs to meet local worker and employer needs. Each district is governed by an elected board that has the power to set property tax rates within limits established by the state, issue bonds (subject to voter approval), and adopt an annual budget. There are 50 districts, and many have multiple campuses. For example, Austin Community College (ACC) has 11 campuses throughout Austin and the surrounding area. ACC's Hays Campus is in partnership with Texas State University, which allows students to pay community college rates for the first two years of a bachelor's degree program, then transfer to Texas State. Students who are in their first year at ACC Hays are given an option to live in Texas State dormitories. In addition to the community college districts, Lamar University has three two-year units, and the Texas State Technical College System has four campuses. Together, Texas's community colleges enroll almost 790,000 students, which is more than the enrollment of the state's universities. (See Figure 3.5 for the locations of these districts.)

Community colleges, like state universities and technical colleges, are funded by state appropriations, student tuition and fees, and small amounts of federal aid and private donations. Where they differ from public universities is the support that community colleges receive from property taxes raised by the local district. Because of these funds, community colleges were traditionally able to charge lower tuition rates than four-year schools. As a result of the Great Recession, however, community college enrollment increased markedly, while revenues from taxes and the state slowed. Schools increased tuition, and some considered limiting enrollment. By 2012, recovery was under way, but budgets remained difficult through 2014. Studies by both the state comptroller and the Texas Association of Community Colleges found that community colleges stimulate their local economies and are

junior college or community college district
Establishes one or more two-year colleges that offer both academic and vocational programs.

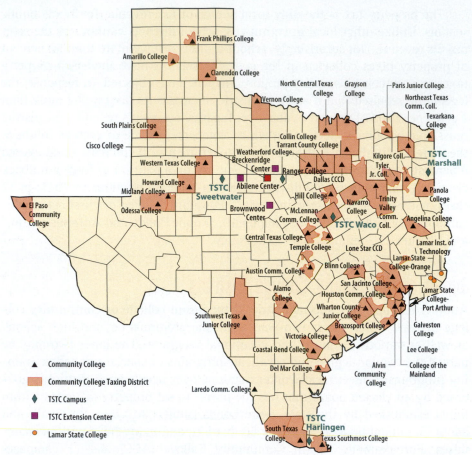

Figure 3.5   Texas Community, Technical, and State Colleges

CRITICAL THINKING

How will tuition increases affect student access to and success in higher education?

critical to a region's economic development. Community colleges were also positively associated with improvements in health and reductions in crime, welfare costs, and unemployment.[24]

Noneducation Special Districts

Texas has almost 2,300 **noneducation special districts** handling a multitude of problems—water supply, sewage, parks, housing, irrigation, and fire protection, to name a few. Among reasons that Texas has so many special districts, three stand out. First, many local needs—such as mass transit, hospitals, and flood protection—cut across the boundaries of cities and counties. Second, in other cases, restrictive state constitutional provisions or the unwillingness of local government leaders make it difficult for an existing government to take on new tasks. And finally, in some cases, individuals create special districts to

noneducation special districts
Special districts, other than school districts or community college districts, such as fire prevention or municipal utility districts, that are units of local government and may cover part of a county, a whole county, or areas in two or more counties.

© 2016 Cengage Learning®

make money for <u>themselves.</u> For example, real estate developers in the Houston area have often developed subdivisions in unincorporated areas through the creation of municipal utility districts. The developer is reimbursed for infrastructure (roads, water and sewage systems) construction costs with bond proceeds. Homeowner property taxes are used to repay bondholders. Therefore, the developer is reimbursed the initial investment costs and homeowners ultimately pay these amounts through property taxes.

One way in which special districts can be manipulated for private gain is illustrated by oilman T. Boone Pickens. In 2007, Pickens created a public water district on eight acres outside of Amarillo. He sold the land at the back of his ranch to five employees. Two of them, the couple who managed his ranch (and the only residents of the eight acres), voted approval of the district. The water district met serious political and legal challenges because it used a public entity for private gain, promoted the unpopular taking of land for rights-of-way, and involved extraction of large amounts of water from the troubled Ogallala Aquifer, which the Panhandle's agriculture and cities depend upon. In 2011, Pickens sold over 200,000 acres of water rights for $103 million to a West Texas-based water supplier. This deal gave nearly half a million West Texans access to water into the next century. Water experts and legislators are increasingly concerned with water shortage, particularly because the state's population is projected to increase to 42 million by 2060.[25]

The structure and powers of special districts vary. Most are governed by a board, collect property taxes and fees, can issue bonds, and spend money to provide one or more services. Mass transit authorities, such as Houston's Metro or Dallas's DART, rely on a 1 percent sales tax. Depending on the board, members may be elected or appointed, or they may automatically sit on the board because of another position they hold. Most special districts are small and hardly noticed by the general public. Only a few, such as the mass transit authorities in the state's largest metropolitan areas, receive continuing public attention.

Special districts will remain an important part of Texas government because they provide many necessary services. But because they are invisible to most voters, they are subject to corruption and abuse of power.

Metropolitan Areas

★ **LO3.6** Discuss the ways that local governments deal with metropolitan-wide and regional issues.

About 88 percent of Texans live in metropolitan areas, mostly central cities surrounded by growing suburbs. People living in a metropolitan area share many problems, such as traffic congestion, crime, pollution, and lack of access to health care. Yet having so many different governments makes it difficult to effectively address problems affecting the whole area. The situation is made worse by differences between central city residents and suburbanites. Most people who live in central cities need and use public facilities, such as public transportation, parks, and medical care, whereas many suburban residents have less interest in public services, particularly public transportation.

✓ **3.5 Learning Check**

1. What are the two categories of special districts in Texas?
2. Why are special districts so important?

Answers on p. 120.

Class and ethnic differences also divide metropolitan communities, particularly the central city from the suburbs.

One way to deal with area-wide problems is **metro government** (consolidation of local governments into one "umbrella" government for the entire metropolitan area). Examples include Miami–Dade County, Florida; Louisville–Jefferson County, Kentucky; and Nashville–Davidson County, Tennessee. In 2013, state Representative Lyle Larson (R-San Antonio) proposed two bills to allow San Antonio and Bexar County governments to consolidate. Bexar County Judge Nelson Wolff and two county commissioners supported consolidation, arguing it was cost effective. San Antonio Mayor Juliàn Castro opposed consolidation. His concerns were twofold: increased government spending and slowed emergency response times for city residents. Both bills died in committee. Instead of consolidation, Texans are likely to continue to rely on councils of governments and annexation.

Councils of Governments

Looking beyond city limits, county lines, and special district boundaries requires expertise from planners who think regionally. In the 1960s, the Texas legislature created the first of 24 regional planning bodies known as **councils of governments (COGs)** or, in some areas, planning/development commissions/councils. (See Figure 3.6.)

COGs are voluntary associations of local governments. Their members perform regional planning activities and provide services requested by member governments or directed by federal and state mandates. Their expertise is particularly useful in implementing state and federally funded programs. Membership may be necessary or helpful in obtaining state or federal grants. COGs also provide a forum where local government leaders can share information with each other and coordinate their efforts.

Municipal Annexation

In an attempt to provide statewide guidelines for home-rule cities grappling with suburban sprawl, the Texas legislature enacted a municipal annexation law in 1963. Under the law, cities have **extraterritorial jurisdiction (ETJ)**, or limited authority outside their city boundaries. Within the ETJ, a home-rule city can regulate some aspects of development and **annex** (make an area a part of the city) contiguous unincorporated areas without a vote by those who live there. How far out an ETJ goes (from one-half mile to five miles) increases with the city's population size, which thus gives central cities an advantage over the suburbs. In most other states, central cities are surrounded by incorporated suburbs and cannot expand. Because of ETJ, however, Texas central cities tend to be much larger in physical size than cities in other states.

The idea of ETJ is to improve order and planning in metropolitan growth. The timing for annexation varies. Houston tends to wait until areas have developed and will provide tax revenue, whereas cities in the Dallas–Fort Worth area tend to annex undeveloped land and oversee its development.

metro government
Consolidation of units of local government within an urban area under a single authority.

council of governments (COG)
A regional planning body composed of governmental units (e.g., cities, counties, special districts); functions include review and comment on proposals by local governments for obtaining state and federal grants.

extraterritorial jurisdiction (ETJ)
The limited authority a city has outside its boundaries. The larger the city's population size, the larger the reach of its ETJ.

annex
To make an outlying area part of a city. Within a home-rule city's extraterritorial jurisdiction, the city can annex unincorporated areas without a vote by those who live there.

1. PRPC (Panhandle Regional Planning Commission)
2. SPAG (South Plains Association of Governments)
3. NORTEX (Nortex Regional Planning Commission)
4. NCTCOG (North Central Texas Council of Governments)
5. ARK-TEX (Ark-Tex Council of Governments)
6. ETCOG (East Texas Council of Governments)
7. WCTCOG (West Central Texas Council of Governments)
8. RGCOG (Rio Grande Council of Governments)
9. PBRPC (Permian Basin Regional Planning Commission)
10. CVCOG (Concho Valley Council of Governments)
11. HOTCOG (Heart of Texas Council of Governments)
12. CAPCOG (Capital Area Council of Governments)
13. BVCOG (Brazos Valley Council of Governments)
14. DETCOG (Deep East Texas Council of Governments)
15. SETRPC (South East Texas Regional Planning Commission)
16. H-GAC (Houston-Galveston Area Council)
17. GCRPC (Golden Crescent Regional Planning Commission)
18. AACOG (Alamo Area Council of Governments)

19. STDC (South Texas Development Council)
20. CBCOG (Coastal Bend Council of Governments)
21. LRGVDC (Lower Rio Grande Valley Development Council)
22. TEXOMA (Texoma Council of Governments)
23. CTCOG (Central Texas Council of Governments)
24. MRGDC (Middle Rio Grande Development Council)

Figure 3.6 Texas Councils of Governments, http://www.txregionalcouncil.org

Source: Reprinted by permission of the Texas Association of Regional Councils

CRITICAL THINKING

Why does Texas have so many levels of government? Are COGs really necessary?

Residents in some areas with few urban services (such as police, fire, and sewer) are happy to be annexed. But, not surprisingly, established suburban communities generally object strenuously to being "gobbled up" without their permission. Examples from the Houston area include Clear Lake City (home of the Johnson Space Center) and Kingwood. In 2006–2007, The Woodlands, a planned community between Houston and Conroe, worked out financial settlements with both cities to avoid annexation. The annexing city is required by law to provide the same level of service to annexed areas that it provides to the remainder of the city, but unincorporated neighborhoods often complain that they had better services than residents of the annexing city.

✔ 3.6 Learning Check

1. What are the two primary ways that Texas deals with problems in metropolitan areas?
2. Which groups want to be annexed? Which do not?

Answers on p. 120.

Selected Reading

Conditions, Health Risks Sicken Colonias Residents

Emily Ramshaw

For years, Texas has had one of the largest proportions of people in poverty in the nation. Among the poorest of Texas's poor are residents of colonias, communities mostly along the border with Mexico that offer few basic services such as water and sewage. Most residents work, but at low-paying jobs. Yet they share the American dream of improving themselves and providing a better life for their children. This story is about health problems facing residents of the colonias.

PHARR — Laura knows what comfort feels like: Before leaving Reynosa, Mexico, for Texas a few years ago, she lived with her in-laws in a house with bedrooms and flushing toilets, with electricity and a leak-free roof. Now, the 23-year-old—since deserted by her husband—pays $187 a month to live in a dirt-floored shack that is part broken-down motor home, part splintered plywood shed. She bathes her five runny-nosed, half-clothed children, all under 10, with water siphoned from a neighbor's garden hose. And she scrubs their diapers and school uniforms in the same sink where she rinses their dinner beans.

As she glanced sheepishly at her feet, Laura, who declined to give her name because of her immigration status, pointed out the family's bathroom: a makeshift outhouse, only yards from the large trash pile her youngest children scale like a mountain. She would return to a better life in Mexico, she said, if she were not sure her children would have a brighter future in the United States. The conditions in which Laura and her children live are common for the roughly half-million people living in Texas' colonias. These impoverished communities are found in all border states, but Texas, with an estimated 2,300 colonias, has the most. First established in the 1950s for migrant workers, many of the colonias (Spanish for neigh-

borhood or community) were created by unscrupulous or predatory developers.

Along the 1,248-mile Texas-Mexico border from El Paso to Brownsville, in communities with names like Agua Dulce and Mexico Chiquito, the overwhelmingly Hispanic residents of these colonias tell identical stories: of migrating with dreams of safety and prosperity, of getting swindled or misled into buying worthless land with no modern infrastructure, of sticking it out so their children—most of them American citizens—will get educated. And of getting sick. At last count, nearly 45,000 people lived in the 350 Texas colonias classified by the state as at the "highest health risk," meaning residents of these often unincorporated subdivisions have no running water, no wastewater treatment, no paved roads or solid waste disposal. Water- and mosquito-borne illnesses are rampant, the result of poor drainage, pooling sewage and water contaminated by leaking septic tanks. Burning garbage, cockroaches, vermin and mold lead to high rates of asthma, rashes and lice infestations. And the poor diet so intrinsically linked to poverty contributes to dental problems, diabetes and other chronic conditions, which residents of the colonias rarely have the health insurance, money or access to regular health care to treat.

"If I see 50 kids, at least 30 of them are very sick," said Dr. Sarojini Bose, a pediatrician and immigrant from India who operates several clinics in the Rio Grande Valley, including a mobile unit. "To see this in the United States, the most powerful country in the world, is heartbreaking." In his 20 years as a border epidemiologist, Dr. Brian Smith, the South Texas regional director for the Department of State Health Services, has seen health trends that mirror the nation's, like the skyrocketing obesity, diabetes and heart disease

linked to high-fat, low-cost diets. But he has also seen the unusual: rates of tuberculosis that are two times the state average and four times the national rate, and the lingering presence of Hansen's disease, or leprosy, almost unheard of in most of the country. There are cases of Dengue fever and Lyme disease carried by mosquitoes and ticks, the result of flooding and non-air-conditioned homes where windows and doors stand open. There is the nagging asthma and bronchitis stemming from the agricultural dust that wafts from nearby sorghum, corn and cotton fields, and the trash burned in the colonias, which often have no waste collection. Public health departments report rates of cholera, hepatitis A, salmonellosis and dysentery in the colonias that far exceed the state average.

Smith and other border health officials have certainly seen improvements. In the last four years alone, the number of residents living in the worst conditions dropped by 17,000, according to state data; 250 more colonias got potable water, paved roads and wastewater systems. And clinic operators and philanthropic physicians have found some creative solutions, including a vaccination program that has dramatically curbed rates of hepatitis A, housing programs that offer window screens to keep out mosquitoes and the installation of street lights to promote recreation. The most successful of them have teamed with so-called "promotoras," Spanish-speaking volunteer nurses who block-walk the colonias offering free medical advice, from notifying residents about public health screenings to teaching new mothers, who get free formula through the state's Women, Infants and Children nutrition program, the value of breast-feeding. "We see the worst of the worst, but we also see rays of light," said Alix Flores, community development director for the Brownsville Community Health Center, which treats nearly 20,000 uninsured people a year.

Despite the progress, the challenges remain immense, and the biggest is access to health care.

In border counties generally, roughly a third of people live in poverty, a fifth have been diagnosed with diabetes and nearly half have no health insurance. In the destitute colonias, the uninsured rate is even higher—up to 80 percent. Despite explosive population growth in the region, Smith said, the capacity of health care providers and community clinics has stayed almost the same. "People just delay care," Smith said, "or else they go without it." While many children and young pregnant women get health care through Medicaid, the joint state-federal health insurer for the poor, and some elderly people qualify for Medicare, the federal insurer of the elderly, border medical providers say many of those between the ages of 19 and 64 fall through the cracks. Even those who do qualify for services often do not take advantage of them, either because of lack of trust, confusion over how to register or fear that any contact with a government program could lead to deportation. According to a report from the Federal Reserve Bank of Dallas, an estimated 64 percent of colonias residents were born in the United States. Eighty-five percent of those under age 18 were born here.

When colonias residents do get treatment, there is little continuity of care. The biggest free health care event for the colonias is Operation Lone Star, a once-a-year medical training exercise run jointly by state agencies, the Texas State Guard and the Army and Air National Guard, where residents wait in line for hours—and often overnight—over the course of two weeks to get basic medical and dental treatment. Community advocates speak, with giant eye-rolls, of state and county vaccination programs, one postponed because health care providers would not work in a building with a broken air conditioner, another largely ineffective because female workers showed up wearing high heels to go door to door in an unpaved colonia. Advocates talk of colonias residents pulling their own teeth because they cannot afford to go to a dentist.

Those lucky enough to schedule a doctor's appointment often struggle to get there: There is little or no public transportation in many far-off colonias, and during the rainy season, the unpaved roads become impassably muddy. Even clinics with the best intentions have run into roadblocks: one promotora recalled a recent case in which a sick woman waited 60 days for an appointment with a doctor who offered pick-ups and drop-offs. But when the van showed up to get her—late, because her colonia had no street signs—there was no room for her young children to ride along with her, forcing her to miss the visit. And then there are the cultural barriers, like the husbands who refuse to let their wives get hysterectomies, even when they are dying from advanced cervical cancer, or the taboo of confessing to a mental health ailment. Shirley Arnolde, head of nursing for Proyecto Desarrollo Humano, a community empowerment group, said she often has to schedule secret appointments with women while their husbands are at work.

Ann Cass, executive director of Proyecto Azteca, a nonprofit affordable-housing organization in the Rio Grande Valley, said that several years ago, some of these burdens were lessened by easy travel into Mexico, where medical bills and prescriptions are far cheaper. But escalating drug violence and a tightening of border security have deterred many from taking cross-border health care trips. The spread of drug violence into the colonias—responsible for at least two murders in the last year [2010], advocates say—has had an impact, too: There is chronic fear, and far less recreation. "People are afraid to walk outside of their homes because of gangs, because of fear of immigration raids," Cass said.

Laura, the young mother in the colonias, lives with a lot of fear—of what would happen to her children if she got deported, of whether they will be able to thrive in school, of how they will grow up to be strong and healthy living in such conditions. For now, the entire family sleeps in the same cramped room, and when someone falls ill—at any given time, one of her "hijitos" has a rib-rattling cough—everyone gets it. When that happens, Laura tries to get a ride to a clinic, where the children are covered by Medicaid. When she gets sick herself, "I just pray," she said. "I'm willing to live like this," Laura said, swatting dust from the laundry she was hanging as toddlers clung to her mud-splattered calves. "For them."

✓ Selected Reading Learning Check

1. What are "promotoras," and what is their role in colonias?
2. What problems on the border caused residents of colonias to avoid traveling to Mexico for medical treatment?

Answers on p. 120.

Source: Emily Ramshaw, "Conditions, Health Risks Sicken Colonias Residents," The Texas Tribune, July 10, 2011. http://www.texastribune.org/2011/07/10/conditions-health-risks-sicken-colonias-residents

Conclusion

Local governments deliver a substantial amount of government services directly to their residents. The success of these governments depends heavily on the actions and cooperation of other local governments and the two levels above them. What local governments do is largely shaped by three forces: formal rules (such as laws, the way governments are organized, and election rules), socioeconomic forces (such as economic power and ethnic/racial cooperation and conflict), and the efforts of individuals and groups. Texas has four kinds of local government with differences in structure and behavior both within each type and among types. Understanding the basic forces at work in local government helps those who want to make a difference apply the general principles of government organization and citizen participation to the issues affecting their own community.

Chapter Summary

LO 3.1 **Explain the relationships that exist between a local government and all other governments, including local, state, and national governments**. Local governments are part of the federal system and thus are affected by decisions made by state, national, and other local governments. Under Texas law and its constitution, local governments are largely limited to what is required or permitted by the state. Although local governments provide the most direct contact between residents and their government, voter apathy at this level remains a problem. This situation is unfortunate because local governments are important to most Texans' day-to-day lives. Election rules for local governments and the way they are organized make a difference in who is elected and who benefits from government.

LO 3.2 **Describe the forms of municipal government organization**. Texas has two legal classifications of municipalities: general-law cities and home-rule cities. Large municipalities have home-rule charters that spell out the structures and powers of individual cities, whereas a smaller municipality is prescribed a charter by the legislature. Texas has four principal forms of municipal government: strong mayor-council, weak mayor-council, council-manager, and commission.

LO 3.3 **Identify the rules and social issues that shape local government outcomes**. Elections for cities and special districts are nonpartisan, and most are organized as either at-large or single-member districts. The increased use of single-member districts; greater pluralism; and the growing number, organization, and political activity of minority Texans are changing the face of local governments. Formal rules and socioeconomic change help shape the way government works, including who wins and who loses. City governments focus primarily on delivering basic services—police and fire protection, streets, water, sewer and sanitation, and often parks and recreation. They also regulate important aspects of our lives, such as construction and food service sanitation. The two major sources of revenue for cities are property taxes and the sales tax. For counties, it is the property tax. Both cities and counties are having a difficult time as they face increasing demands for services from their citizens, the state, and the national government. As a result, local governments are utilizing fees and taking on debt because of limited revenue sources.

LO 3.4 **Analyze the structure and responsibilities of counties**. County governments have fragmented organizational structures and powers restricted by the Texas Constitution. Counties must provide an array of services, conduct elections, and enforce state laws. Actual county activities vary greatly between metropolitan and rural counties. Various county officials are policymakers, but the major policymaker is the commissioners court, comprised of the county judge and four elected commissioners.

LO 3.5 **Explain the functions of special districts and their importance to the greater community**. The many special district governments are separate legal entities providing services that include public schools, community colleges, and noneducation special districts for mass transit and water. Although they are important for the multitude of services they provide, many voters are unaware of this form of government. A lack of public awareness allows smaller and more obscure districts to be subject to fraud and manipulation.

LO 3.6 **Discuss the ways that local governments deal with metropolitan-wide and regional issues**. Dealing with metropolitan-wide problems is a difficult task. To do so, Texas relies heavily on councils of governments, designed to increase cooperation. Annexation remains a controversial process, especially for areas subject to being annexed by home-rule cities without residents' consent.

Key Terms

grassroots, p. 79

Dillon's Rule, p. 79

intergovernmental relations, p. 80

municipal (city) government, p. 81

general-law city, p. 81

home-rule city, p. 81

ordinance, p. 81

recall, p. 81

initiative, p. 81

referendum, p. 81

strong mayor-council form, p. 82

weak mayor-council form, p. 83

council-manager form, p. 83

middle class, p. 85

working class, p. 85

commission form, p. 85

nonpartisan election, p. 87

at-large election, p. 87

single-member district election, p. 87

redistricting, p. 88

cumulative voting, p. 89

term limit, p. 89

property tax, p. 94

bond, p. 95

tax reinvestment zone (TRZ), p. 97

county, p. 97

commissioners court, p. 98

county judge, p. 101

county attorney, p. 101

district attorney, p. 101

county sheriff, p. 102

statutory county court, p. 102

district clerk, p. 102

justice of the peace, p. 102

constable, p. 103

county clerk, p. 103

county tax assessor-collector, p. 103

countywide tax appraisal district, p. 103

county treasurer, p. 103

county auditor, p. 103

colonia, p. 106

special district, p. 107

independent school district (ISD), p. 107

junior college or community college district, p. 109

noneducation special districts, p. 110

metro government, p. 112

council of governments (COG), p. 112

extraterritorial jurisdiction (ETJ), p. 112

annex, p. 112

Learning Check Answers

3.1 1. Local governments have the greatest flexibility under the Cooley Doctrine. Under Dillon's Rule, which is followed closely in Texas, local governments can do only those things permitted by the state.

2. The relations among the three levels of government and among the various local governments are marked by both cooperation and conflict.

3.2 1. The two legal classifications of cities in Texas are general-law and home-rule cities. A home-rule city has more flexibility because it establishes its own charter, which specifies its form and operation. A general-law city adopts a charter set in law by the Texas legislature.

2. The council-manager form is most common in larger home-rule cities, whereas smaller cities are more likely to have a weak mayor-council form of municipal government.

3.3 1. Single-member districts and cumulative voting are most likely to increase the representation of minorities in government. Redistricting may help or hurt, depending on how lines are drawn.

2. Most revenue of local governments comes from property tax and sales tax, but these two sources are frequently inadequate to meet the demands.

3.4 1. False. The structure of county governments is determined by the state constitution.
2. The major policymaking body in each Texas county is the commissioners court.

3.5 1. The two categories of special districts in Texas are school districts and noneducation districts.
2. Many local needs cut across boundaries of cities and counties; and limitations in the state constitution and the unwillingness of some officials to act make it difficult to take on new tasks. Special districts can be a source of abuse of the public interest, however.

3.6 1. The two primary ways Texas deals with problems in metropolitan areas are through councils of government and annexation.
2. Unincorporated communities lacking services such as police and sewers often want to be annexed. Established communities with existing services generally oppose annexation.

Selected Reading Learning Check

1. "Promotoras" are Spanish-speaking volunteer nurses who block-walk the colonias offering free medical advice.
2. Escalating drug violence and tightened border security have deterred residents of colonias from cross-border health care trips to Mexico.

4 ★ Political Parties

Copyright © 2013 BranchToon. All Rights Reserved.

Learning Objectives

4.1 Describe the structure of political parties in Texas, distinguishing between the temporary party structure and the permanent party structure.

4.2 Compare and contrast the different political ideologies found in the Lone Star State.

4.3 Trace the history of political parties in Texas.

4.4 Identify electoral trends in Texas, including the roles of dealigned voters, minor parties, and independent candidates.

CRITICAL THINKING

After reading this chapter and selected reading, do you think that the Democratic Party will return to prominence in Texas in the near future? Why?

Although Texas is a two-party state, the Republican Party has dominated Texas elections and politics for more than two decades. No Democratic candidate has been elected to a statewide office since 1998. Additionally, every Republican presidential nominee has carried the Lone Star State in the last 40 years. Red states are those in which the Republican Party is dominant, whereas Blue states are those in which the Democratic Party prevails. Although Texas is a red state, the Democratic Party believes that it will return to prominence given the Republican Party's platform and nomination of more conservative candidates as well as changing demographics among the state's population and voters. This chapter examines the structure of political parties in Texas, their history, recent electoral trends, voting coalitions, and the effect of the changing demographics of Texas on the political parties in 2014.

Party Structure

LO4.1   Describe the structure of political parties in Texas, distinguishing between the temporary party structure and the permanent party structure.

Although neither the U.S. Constitution nor the Texas Constitution mentions political parties, these organizations are an integral part of the American governmental process. A **political party** can be defined as a combination of people and interests whose primary purpose is to gain control of government by winning elections. Whereas interest groups tend to focus on influencing governmental policies, political parties are chiefly concerned with the recruitment, nomination, and election of citizens to governmental office. (For a discussion of interest groups, see Chapter 7, "The Politics of Interest Groups.") In Texas, as throughout the United States, the Democratic and Republican parties are the two leading political parties. State election laws have contributed to the continuity of the two-party system. These laws not only make the process of getting on the ballot complex for third parties, but they also require that the winner of the general election, held in November of even-numbered years, is the candidate who receives the largest number of votes (a plurality). Third-party candidates have little chance of winning an election by defeating the two major-party nominees.

American political parties exist on four levels: national, state, county, and precinct (the division of an area into smaller units within which voters cast their ballots at the same location). In part, these levels correspond to the organization of the U.S. federal system of government. Whereas a corporation is organized as a hierarchy, with a chain of command that makes each level directly accountable to the level above it, a political party is organized as a **stratarchy**, in which power is diffused among and within levels of the party organization.[1] Each major party is loosely organized so that state and local party organizations are free to decide their positions on party and policy issues. State- and local-level organizations operate within their own spheres

political party
An organization influenced by political ideology whose primary interest is to gain control of government by winning elections.

stratarchy
A political system in which power is diffused among and within levels of party organization.

InflInflInfluencence, separate from one another. Although these levels of the two major parties are encouraged to support national party policies, this effort is not always successful. As mandated by the Texas Election Code, Texas's two major parties are alike in structure. Each has permanent and temporary organizational structures (see Figure 4.1).

Temporary Party Organization

The **temporary party organization** consists of primaries and conventions. These events are temporary because they are not ongoing party activities. Through primaries, members of the major political parties participate in elections to select candidates for public office and local party officers. Primary election voting may involve a second, or runoff, primary.

Conventions elect state-level and senate-district party officers and can be scheduled at precinct, county, state senatorial district, and state levels. Each convention lasts a limited time, from less than an hour to one or two days. At the state level, conventions select party leaders chosen by delegates elected at the local level. Rules of the Texas Democratic and Republican parties mandate that party policy be determined at their conventions. These policy decisions are evidenced by resolutions, passed in both local and state conventions, and by party platforms adopted at the state conventions. A party's **platform** is a document that sets forth the party's position on current issues. In presidential election years, state-level conventions select delegates who attend a party's national convention. Additionally, state delegates nominate a slate of electors to vote in the electoral college if their party's presidential candidate wins a plurality of the general election vote. At the national party convention, candidates are officially chosen to run for president and vice president of the United States. All Texas political conventions must be open to the media, according to state law.

In March 2012, a three-judge federal panel in San Antonio issued an order setting a May primary election date for the Lone Star State—nine days before the Republican state convention and 10 days before the Democratic state convention. The new primary election date significantly affected the Texas Democratic and Republican parties' temporary party organizations and altered their processes for delegate selection. The State Democratic Executive Committee (SDEC) eliminated precinct conventions, and the State Republican Executive Committee (SREC) made them optional. Both parties set April 21 as the date for county and senatorial district conventions.[2] In 2013 under HB3102, the 83rd Legislature provided greater flexibility to the state's political parties by allowing party officials to determine the date, time, and place of all conventions.

Precinct Conventions Precinct conventions in Texas have traditionally occurred every even-numbered year on the first Tuesday in March, which is the day of the first primary. The state executive committees of each party

temporary party organization
Primaries and conventions that function briefly to nominate candidates, pass resolutions, adopt a party platform, and select delegates to party conventions at higher levels.

platform
A document that sets forth a political party's position on issues such as income tax, school vouchers, or public utility regulation.

precinct convention
If a political party decides to conduct a precinct convention, this serves as the lowest level of temporary political party organization. Delegates convene in even-numbered years on a date and at a time and place prescribed by the party's state executive committee to adopt resolutions and to select delegates to a county (or district) convention.

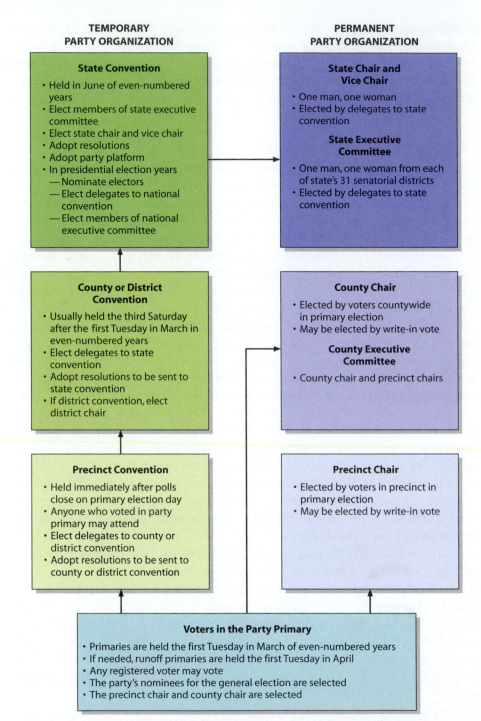

TEMPORARY
PARTY ORGANIZATION

State Convention

- Held in June of even-numbered years
- Elect members of state executive committee
- Elect state chair and vice chair
- Adopt resolutions
- Adopt party platform
- In presidential election years
  — Nominate electors
  — Elect delegates to national convention
  — Elect members of national executive committee

County or District Convention

- Usually held the third Saturday after the first Tuesday in March in even-numbered years
- Elect delegates to state convention
- Adopt resolutions to be sent to state convention
- If district convention, elect district chair

Precinct Convention

- Held immediately after polls close on primary election day
- Anyone who voted in party primary may attend
- Elect delegates to county or district convention
- Adopt resolutions to be sent to county or district convention

PERMANENT
PARTY ORGANIZATION

State Chair and Vice Chair

- One man, one woman
- Elected by delegates to state convention

State Executive Committee

- One man, one woman from each of state's 31 senatorial districts
- Elected by delegates to state convention

County Chair

- Elected by voters countywide in primary election
- May be elected by write-in vote

County Executive Committee

- County chair and precinct chairs

Precinct Chair

- Elected by voters in precinct in primary election
- May be elected by write-in vote

Voters in the Party Primary

- Primaries are held the first Tuesday in March of even-numbered years
- If needed, runoff primaries are held the first Tuesday in April
- Any registered voter may vote
- The party's nominees for the general election are selected
- The precinct chair and county chair are selected

© Cengage Learning®

Figure 4.1   Texas Political Party Organization

CRITICAL THINKING

In what ways does the structure of political parties in Texas encourage participation in partisan politics? In what ways does it discourage participation?

determine the date, time, and place for precinct conventions. In 2014, however, the State Democratic Executive Committee decided not to hold precinct conventions. At the county or senatorial district conventions, those in attendance caucused (met) with other attendees from their precinct. Republican precinct conventions were held at the traditional time after the polls closed on primary election day.

By state law, if a political party decides to conduct a precinct convention, any citizen who voted in the party primary or has completed an oath of affiliation with a political party is permitted to attend and participate in that party's precinct convention as a delegate. Each party's state executive committee may adopt a rule requiring the precinct chair to be the permanent chair of the precinct convention. Otherwise, the precinct chair serves as the temporary chair and the delegates select a chairperson to preside over the convention. Delegates select a secretary to record the proceedings. If a political party holds a precinct convention, it must preregister attendees for the convention by any method the party may adopt by rule. The preregistration requires attendees to affiliate with the party by taking an oath and signing a roster for a primary election that states at the top of each page, "A person commits a criminal offense if the person knowingly votes in a primary election or participates in a convention of a party after having voted in a primary election or participated in a convention of another party during the same voting year."

The main business of the precinct convention is to elect delegates to the county or district convention. Delegates to a party's precinct convention are also allowed to submit and debate resolutions. These resolutions express the positions of precinct convention participants on any number of issues, ranging from immigration and abortion to the national debt. If adopted, a resolution will be submitted to a county or district convention for consideration.

Political parties often place several nonbinding resolutions on the primary ballot for voters to decide upon. These proposals are used to express party primary voters' opinions and have no legal effect. In 2014, the SREC placed six propositions on the Texas Republican primary ballot, each of which was approved by the percentage of voters indicated below.

- Religious Freedom: Texans should be free to express their religious beliefs, including prayer, in public places. (97 percent)
- Second Amendment: Texas should support Second Amendment liberties by expanding locations where concealed handgun license holders may legally carry. (87 percent)
- Franchise Tax: Texas should abolish the state franchise tax, also known as the margins tax, to encourage business growth. (88 percent)
- Welfare Reform: Texas recipients of taxpayer-funded public assistance should be subject to random drug testing as a condition of receiving benefits. (95 percent)
- No Lawmaker Exceptions: All elected officials and their staffs should be subject to the same laws, rules, regulations, and ordinances as their constituents. (99 percent)

- Obamacare: The Affordable Care Act, also known as "Obamacare," should be repealed. (93 percent)

The following four propositions appeared on the 2014 Democratic ballot and were approved by the percentages indicated:

- On Immigration Reform: The United States Congress must pass immigration reform, including an earned path to citizenship for those individuals contributing to the economy and the dependents of those individuals (86 percent)
- A Living Wage for All Texans: Congress should pass legislation raising the federal minimum wage to at least 110% of the federal poverty level for a family of four without exception (89 percent)
- Medicaid Expansion: The Governor and the Texas Legislature should accept federal funds, as provided in the Patient Protection and Affordable Care Act of 2010, for the expansion of Medicaid to provide coverage to millions of uninsured and underinsured Texans (89 percent)
- On Non-Discrimination Legislation: The Congress and the Texas Legislature should adopt legislation that expands protections against discriminations in employment, housing, and public accommodations based upon sexual orientation and gender identity (88 percent)[3]

County and District Conventions State law requires that **county conventions** and **district conventions** occur on the date selected by the party's state executive committee, provided that it does not occur during Passover or Easter weekend. In 2014, Republican and Democratic county and district conventions occurred the third Saturday after the primary elections, or 11 days after the elections. District conventions, rather than a single-county convention, are held in heavily populated counties (such as Harris, Dallas, and Bexar) that have more than one state senatorial district. Each party's state executive committee may adopt a rule requiring the county chair to be the permanent chair of the county convention and requiring the senatorial district executive committee member or chair of the district executive committee, as applicable, to be the permanent chair of the senatorial district convention. Otherwise, the county chair serves as the temporary chair of the county convention and the senatorial district executive committee member or chair of the district executive committee, as applicable, serves as the chair of the senatorial district convention, and the delegates elect a chairperson to preside over the respective convention. Delegates select a secretary to record the proceedings. The main business of county and district conventions is to elect delegates to the state convention. Delegates may also submit proposed resolutions for consideration by the convention.

Under the rules for each party, county and district conventions may select one delegate to the state convention for every 300 votes cast in the county or district for the party's gubernatorial nominee in the most recent general election. Under Republican Party rules, all delegate candidates are submitted by the county or district convention's committee on nominations for approval by convention participants. Rules of the Democratic Party allow state delegates to be selected by precinct delegations. Additionally, in selecting delegates and alternates at all levels, rules of the Democratic Party require delegations to

county convention
A party meeting of delegates held in even-numbered years on a date and at a time and place prescribed by the party's state executive committee to adopt resolutions and to select delegates and alternates to the party's state convention.

district convention
Held in even-numbered years on a date and at a time and place prescribed by the party's state executive committee in counties that have more than one state senatorial district. Participants select delegates and alternates to the party's state convention.

reasonably reflect the presidential preferences (in presidential years), to include young people and people with disabilities, and to reflect diversity in race, sex, gender identity, ethnicity, and sexual orientation. Delegates attending the state or district convention also consider resolutions. These resolutions then go to the party's state convention for consideration.

State Conventions In accordance with the Texas Election Code, in June of even-numbered years, each political party must hold a biennial **state convention** to conduct party business. State conventions occur during a two-day period. Each party's state executive committee may adopt a rule requiring the state chair to be the permanent chair of the state convention. Otherwise, the state chair serves as the temporary chair and the delegates select a chairperson to preside over the convention. Delegates select a secretary to record the proceedings. In addition, delegates conduct the following tasks:

- Certify to the secretary of state the names of party members nominated in the March and April primaries for Texas elective offices (or by convention if no primary was held)[4]
- Write the rules that will govern the party
- Draft and adopt a party platform
- Adopt resolutions regarding issues too specific to be included in the party platform
- Select members of the party's state executive committee

In presidential election years, state convention delegates also perform the following three functions:

- Elect delegates to the national presidential nominating convention (the total number for Texas is calculated under national party rules)
- Elect members from Texas to serve on the party's national committee
- Elect a slate of potential presidential electors to cast Texas's electoral votes if the party's ticket wins a plurality of the state's popular presidential vote

Texas casts 38 electoral votes. A state's electoral vote equals the number of its members in the U.S. Congress (2 senators and, for Texas, 36 representatives apportioned according to the state's population based on the 2010 census). However, in accordance with Article II, Section 1 of the United States Constitution, "no Senator or Representative, or Person holding an Office of Trust or Profit under the United States, shall be appointed an Elector."

Both the Texas Democratic Party and Texas Republican Party used Facebook and Twitter to post minute-by-minute happenings at their respective state conventions in 2014. Additionally, delegates to each party's convention used these forms of social media to communicate their experiences as they occurred.

Selection of National Convention Delegates

Selection of delegates to a national party convention depends on the delegates' support of particular candidates for the party's presidential nomination. In a **presidential preference primary**, rank-and-file party members can vote directly for the presidential candidates of their choice. Primary voting is by

state convention
Convenes every even-numbered year to make rules for a political party, adopt a party platform and resolutions, and select members of the state executive committee; in a presidential election year, it elects delegates to the national convention, names members to serve on the national committee, and elects potential electors to vote if the party's presidential candidate receives a plurality of the popular vote in the general election.

presidential preference primary
A primary in which the voters indicate their preference for a person seeking nomination as the party's presidential candidate.

precinct. Delegates to the party's national convention are usually chosen according to the results of the primary vote. The respective national conventions nominate the parties' candidates for president and vice president.

In many states, parties select delegates to a national convention in **caucuses**. Party members assemble in caucuses at the respective precinct, county, and state levels. Here, they choose national convention delegates who either are pledged to support a particular presidential candidate or are uncommitted.

Democratic Selection In recent years, Texas Democrats have combined the two delegate selection plans into a primary-caucus described as the "Texas Two-Step." In presidential election years, participants are asked to identify their presidential preferences at each convention. However, individuals may choose not to pledge their support to any candidate. Instead, they may indicate that they are uncommitted. Presidential candidates are awarded delegates to local and state conventions in proportion to the number of their supporters in attendance. National delegates include approximately one-third who are based on primary results and two-thirds based on the number of supporters in attendance at the state convention. These delegates are selected by state senatorial districts on an at-large basis. Additionally, **superdelegates** (unpledged party and elected officials) are selected. Superdelegates are state party leaders and elected officials who are automatically seated at the party's national convention. Unlike other delegates to the national convention, they are not required to pledge their support for a particular candidate, and may support any candidate for the party's presidential nomination. In 2012, Texas

caucus
A meeting at which members of a political party assemble to select delegates and make other policy recommendations at the precinct, county, or state senatorial district and state levels.

superdelegate
An unpledged party official or elected official who serves as a delegate to a party's national convention.

Texas state senator, Wendy Davis, left, shakes hands with Texas Attorney General, Greg Abbott, after participating in the Rio Grande Valley Gubernatorial Debate in Edinburg, Texas on September 19, 2014. This was the first of two scheduled debates between the two candidates. On November 4, 2014, Abbott won the election.

(AP Images/The McAllen Monitor/Gabe Hernandez)

CRITICAL THINKING

How might a candidate debate persuade voters?

sent 288 (out of a total of 5,555) delegates to the Democratic National Convention. Pledged delegates were chosen proportionally based on the number of delegates to county and senate district conventions who signed in (or registered) favoring a particular candidate.

Republican Selection The Republican Party selects national delegates proportionally from the results of the presidential preference primary. Some Republican delegates are chosen by congressional district caucuses (at least one was chosen from each district in 2012). Others are chosen on an at-large basis by the entire convention. A nominating committee selects all at-large delegates. State convention delegates approve all national delegates. In 2012, Texas sent 155 (out of a total of 2,286) delegates to the Republican National Convention.

Permanent Party Organization

Each major political party in the United States consists of thousands of virtually autonomous executive committees at the local, state, and national levels. These committees are given great latitude in their operating structures. For Democrats and Republicans alike, the executive committees across the nation are linked only nominally. At the highest level, each party has a national committee. In Texas, the precinct chairs, together with the county, district, and state executive committees, make up the permanent organization of the state parties. The role of the **permanent party organization** is to recruit candidates, devise strategies, raise funds, distribute candidate literature and information, register voters, and turn out voters on Election Day.

Precinct Chair In Texas, the basic party official in both the temporary and the permanent party structures is the **precinct chair**, who is elected to a two-year term by precinct voters in the party primaries. A party precinct chair's duties and responsibilities include registering and persuading voters within the precinct, distributing candidate literature and information, operating phone banks within the precinct on behalf of the party and its candidates, and getting people to the polls. If both parties are evenly matched in strength at the polls, the precinct chairs become more vital in turning people out to vote. A precinct chair is an unpaid party official who also arranges for the precinct convention (in the Republican Party) and serves on the county executive committee. Many of these positions go unfilled in more populous counties (those that have 100 or more precincts) and in counties where one party dominates the other in numbers of voters. In 2014, for instance, out of approximately 700 precincts in Dallas County, neither Democrats nor Republicans filled chairs in more than 400 precincts. Likewise, Democrats and Republicans each filled chairs in only slightly more than half of the 1,000 precincts in Harris County that year.

County and District Executive Committees A **county executive committee** comprises all the precinct chairs and the county chair, who are elected by county party members in the primaries. The county chair heads

permanent party organization
In Texas, the precinct chairs, county and district executive committees, and the state executive committee form the permanent organization of a political party.

precinct chair
The party official responsible for the interests and activities of a political party in a voting district; typical duties include encouraging voter registration, distributing campaign literature, operating phone banks, and getting out the vote on Election Day.

county executive committee
Composed of a party's precinct chairs and the elected county chair, the county executive committee conducts primaries and makes arrangements for holding county conventions.

the party's countywide organization. County executive committees conduct primaries and arrange for county conventions. At the local level, the **county chair** is the key party official and serves as the party's chief strategist within that county. Duties of the county chair include recruiting local candidates for office, raising funds, establishing and staffing the party's campaign headquarters within the county, and serving as the local spokesperson for the party. The Texas Election Code also provides for a **district executive committee**, which is composed of the county chairs from each county in a given district (senatorial, representative, or judicial). District executive committees rarely meet except to nominate candidates to fill a district vacancy, when one occurs.

State Executive Committee For each major political party, the highest permanent party organization in the state is the **state executive committee.** As mandated by state law, an executive committee is composed of one man and one woman from each of the 31 state senatorial districts, plus a chair and a vice chair, one of whom must be a woman and the other a man. For both the Democratic and Republican parties, a state executive committee with 64 members is elected at the party's state convention. On that occasion, delegates from each of the 31 senatorial districts choose two members from their district and place these names before the convention for its approval. At the same time, convention delegates choose the chair and vice chair at large. The party's state chair serves as its key strategist and chief spokesperson. The role of vice chair has traditionally been more honorary in nature. In addition to the 64 statutory members of the party's state executive committee, party rules may allow "add-on" members. An add-on member may represent recognized statewide auxiliary organizations that have voting power within the party, such as women's groups (e.g., Texas Democratic Women, Texas Federation of Republican Women), racial groups (Texas Coalition of Black Democrats, Hispanic Caucus, Republican National Hispanic Assembly), House and Senate caucus chairs, youth groups (Texas Young Democrats, Texas College Republicans), and county chairs associations (e.g., Texas Democratic County Chairs Association and the Texas Republican County Chairmen's Association).

The party's state chair works with the party's state executive committee to recruit candidates for statewide and district offices, plan statewide strategies, and raise funds for the party at the state level. The importance of the state party chair's role as chief fundraiser was emphasized in the 2010 ouster of the incumbent chair of the Republican Party of Texas. Steve Munisteri, a retired Houston attorney, argued that then-chair Cathie Adams lacked both administrative skills and fundraising abilities in his successful attempt to unseat her. Noting that the state party's debts exceeded its assets by more than $300,000 and that the party continued to lose money every month, Munisteri vowed that he would not take a break "until the debt [was] 100 percent retired."[5] Under Munisteri's leadership, the Republican Party retired its debt by November of that year. Munisteri was reelected state party chair in 2012 and again in 2014 at the Republican state convention in Forth Worth in June of that year.

county chair
Elected by county party members in the primaries, this key party official heads the county executive committee.

district executive committee
Composed of county chairs within a district that elects a state senator, U.S. or state representative, or district judge, this body fills a vacancy created by the death, resignation, or disqualification of a nominated candidate.

state executive committee
Composed of a chair, vice chair, and two members from each senatorial district, this body is part of a party's permanent organization.

At its 2012 state convention, the Democratic Party chose the first Latino chair of a major political party in Texas when it selected Rio Grande Valley native and former court of appeals judge Gilberto Hinojosa as its state chair. Hinojosa was reelected state party chair in 2014 at the Democratic state convention in June of that year. The state executive committee of each party must also canvass (or count) statewide primary returns and certify the nomination of party candidates. It also conducts the state convention, promotes party unity and strength, maintains relations with the party's national committee, and raises some campaign money for party candidates (though most campaign funds are raised by the candidates themselves).

✓ **4.1 Learning Check**

1. What is the difference between a party's permanent organization and its temporary organization?
2. True or False: A political party's state chair is chosen by the temporary organization.

Answers on p. 156.

Political Ideology

★ **LO4.2** Compare and contrast the different political ideologies found in the Lone Star State.

Today's politics in the Lone Star State reflect Texas's political history. Traditions that have been determined by centuries of political experience and culture influence current attitudes toward parties, candidates, and issues. Nevertheless, Texans' changing demands and expectations have forced revisions in party platforms and have affected the campaigns of candidates for public office. Political parties cannot remain static and survive, nor can politicians win elections unless they are in step with the opinions of a large percentage of voters.

Since the 1930s, the terms *liberal* and *conservative* have meant more to many Texas voters than have the actual names of political parties. In view of long-standing ideological differences between liberals and conservatives, this terminology must be explained. These ideological labels almost defy definition, however, because meanings change with time and circumstances. Furthermore, each label has varying shades of meaning for different people. In Texas, because of the dominant influences of the individualistic and traditionalistic political cultures and the lesser influence of the moralistic culture, both Democrats and Republicans tend to be more conservative than members of their respective parties nationally. Whereas the Republican Party tends to be dominated by right-wing social conservatives, the Democratic Party is influenced (but not dominated) by left-wing liberals.

The origins of the terms *left* and *right* to refer to political affiliation can be traced back to the time of the French Revolution, when monarchists sat to the right side of the president in the French National Assembly and supporters of a republic sat to his left. The assignment of seats in legislative bodies determined by political affiliation or ideology continues in many countries today. Despite the use of right-left terminology throughout the United States, the Texas legislature has not traditionally used partisan or ideological criteria for assigning floor seats on the right and left sides of House and Senate chambers.

Conservatism

In its purest form, modern conservative doctrine envisions ideal social and economic orders that would be largely untouched by government. According to this philosophy, if all individuals were left alone (the doctrine of laissez-faire) to pursue their self-interests, both social and economic systems would benefit, and the cost of government would be low. **Conservatives**, therefore, are generally opposed to government-managed or government-subsidized programs, such as assistance to poor families with dependent children, unemployment insurance, and the Affordable Care Act ("Obamacare"). Conservatives are further divided between fiscal conservatives and social conservatives. Today's fiscal conservatives give the highest priority to reduced taxing and spending; whereas social conservatives (such as those associated with the Christian Coalition or Christian Citizens) stress the importance of their family values, including opposition to abortion and homosexuality. Social conservatives support school vouchers that would provide government-funded assistance to parents who choose to send their children to private schools, especially church-affiliated schools.[6] In the 2014 Republican run-off for lieutenant governor, state senator Dan Patrick easily defeated incumbent David Dewhurst largely by drawing upon the support of social conservatives. Patrick received endorsements from many social conservative groups including the Texas Conservative Review, the Texas Coalition of Christian Candidates, and several prominent Tea Party affiliated organizations. On his website, Patrick identified two pieces of legislation he was most proud of in passing: placing "In God We Trust" permanently in the Senate chamber and placing "Under God" in the state pledge.

Attempting to distance himself from more extreme conservative Republicans, President George W. Bush used the phrase "compassionate conservatism" to describe his political philosophy. Bush insisted that he was "a conservative who puts a compassionate face on a conservative philosophy."[7] His ideology is sometimes described as **neoconservatism**, in part because it is fiscally conservative while also allowing for a limited governmental role in solving social problems.

In 2009, some conservatives within the Republican Party formed the Tea Party movement. Taking their name from the Boston Tea Party, an event that led to the American Revolution, Tea Party activists have argued that the size and scope of government have grown out of control. Although the Tea Party actually consists of thousands of separate, autonomous groups, the "Tea Party Patriots" is a national umbrella group that has affiliations with approximately 3,400 local groups, according to the organization's estimates. The national website includes discussion forums and information about local organizations. Of the approximately 25 groups listed for Texas, almost all are in suburban areas of the state. Former Governor Perry actively courted the support of Tea Party sympathizers, stating that he did not regard Tea Party activists as

conservative
A person who advocates minimal intervention by government in social and economic matters and who gives a high priority to reducing taxes and curbing public spending.

neoconservatism
A political ideology that reflects fiscal conservatism but accepts a limited governmental role in solving social problems.

extremists and then adding "but if you are, I'm with you."[8] In the 2012 Republican primary runoff, Ted Cruz defeated David Dewhurst for the U.S. Senate nomination due in large part to his support from members of the Tea Party. In 2014, several candidates in the Republican primary aligned themselves with the Tea Party, with mixed success. U.S. Senator John Cornyn and U.S. Representative Pete Sessions easily defeated their Tea Party–backed opponents in the March primary. However in the May Republican primary run-off, Tea Party–backed candidates Dan Patrick and Ken Paxton just as easily won their party's nomination. In the race for lieutenant governor, state senator Dan Patrick defeated three–term incumbent David Dewhurst 65 percent to 35 percent, and in the race for attorney general, state senator Ken Paxton defeated state representative Dan Branch 64 percent to 36 percent.

Liberalism

Liberals favor government regulation of the economy to achieve a more equitable distribution of wealth. Only government, liberals insist, is capable of guarding against air, water, and soil pollution by corporations and individuals. Liberals claim that government is obligated to aid the unemployed, alleviate poverty (especially for the benefit of children), and guarantee equal rights for minorities and women. Liberalism seeks a limited role for government involvement with regard to other social issues, especially those related to morality or religion. Liberals are more likely to oppose prayer in public schools, government subsidies for religious institutions, and any church involvement in secular politics. Many Texas Democrats have a **neoliberal** ideology. This position incorporates a philosophy of less government regulation of business and the economy while adopting a more liberal view of greater government involvement in social programs.

Both Texas liberals and conservatives are often ideologically inconsistent. A conservative may oppose government subsidies, such as welfare assistance for citizens, but support similar payments to corporations. Liberals may oppose laws that force schools to post the Ten Commandments regardless of students' religious beliefs but favor laws that require employers to provide employee health insurance that includes family planning services, even though some practices might be inconsistent with the employer's religious beliefs. Frequently, individuals who have extreme conservative or liberal ideologies accuse individuals with more moderate views of being ideologically inconsistent.

An Overview of Texas Political History

LO4.3 Trace the history of political parties in Texas.

From the time political parties developed in Texas through the 1960s, the Lone Star State was dominated primarily by one political party: the Democratic Party. In the 1970s and 1980s, Texas moved toward a competitive two-party

4.2 Learning Check

1. What is the primary difference between social conservatives and fiscal conservatives?
2. True or False: All Texas Democrats generally have a liberal political ideology.

Answers on p. 156.

liberal
A person who advocates government support in social and economic matters and who favors political reforms that extend democracy, achieve a more equitable distribution of wealth, and protect individual freedoms and rights.

neoliberal
A political ideology that advocates less government regulation of business but supports more governmental involvement in social matters.

structure. By the 1990s and into the 21st century, however, the state had seemingly become a one-party state with the Republican Party in control. Changing demographics, in particular a rapidly growing Latino population, has given Democrats hope that they will be competitive and regain a majority status.

1840s to 1870s: The Origin of the Party System

Before Texas's admission into the Union in 1845, its political parties had not fully developed. Political factions during the years that Texas was an independent republic tended to coalesce around personalities. The two dominant factions were the pro–(Sam) Houston and the anti-Houston groups. Even after the Lone Star State's admission into the Union, these two factions remained. By the 1850s, the pro-Houston faction began referring to itself as the Jackson Democrats (Unionists), whereas the anti-Houston faction called themselves the Calhoun Democrats (after South Carolina senator John C. Calhoun, a states' rights and proslavery advocate). In the course of the Civil War, after Texas seceded from the Union, politics became firmly aligned with the Democratic Party among Anglo Texans.

During the period of Reconstruction (1865–1873) that followed the Civil War, the Republican Party controlled Texas politics. The Reconstruction acts passed by the U.S. Congress purged all officeholders with a Confederate past. Congress also disenfranchised all southerners who had ever held a state or federal office before secession and who later supported the Confederacy. In Texas, any man who had ever been a mayor, a school trustee, a clerk, or even a public weigher (a position originally created to weigh all cotton, wool, hides, and other staples offered for sale, but today a position whose functions are largely obsolete) was denied the right to vote.[9] Republican governor Edmund J. Davis, a former Union army general, was elected in 1869 during this period of Radical Reconstruction. The Davis administration quickly became unpopular with Texas's Anglo majority. During his tenure in office, Davis took control of voter registration and appointed more than 8,000 public officials. From Texas Supreme Court justices to state police to city officials, Davis placed Republicans (including some African Americans) in office throughout the state. Opposed by former Confederates, Davis's administration was condemned by most Anglo Texans for corruption, graft, and high taxation.[10] After Davis's defeat for reelection in 1873 by a newly enfranchised electorate, Texas voters did not elect another Republican governor for more than 100 years.

1870s to 1970s: A One-Party Dominant System

From the end of Reconstruction until the 1970s, Texas and other former Confederate states had a one-party identity in which the Democratic Party was strong and the Republican Party weak. During those years (when a gubernatorial term in Texas was two years), Democratic candidates won 52 consecutive gubernatorial elections, and Democratic presidential nominees carried the state in all but 3 of the 25 presidential elections.

Point/Counterpoint

THE ISSUE The two major parties, as identified in their platforms, differ substantially on many social and economic issues. The following excerpts, taken from each party platform as adopted at their respective state conventions in 2014, illustrate several of these different points of view. The complete texts of the parties' platforms are available on their websites.

What Are the Positions of the Two Major Political Parties on Key Issues?

The Texas Republican Party

Abortion
- Is resolute in the support of the reversal of *Roe v. Wade*.
- Supports the elimination of public funding or the use of public facilities to advocate, perform, or support elective abortions.
- Believes the Republican Party should provide financial support to only those candidates who support the right-to-life planks.

Education
- Supports reducing taxpayer funding to all levels of educational institutions.
- Believes the U.S. Department of Education (DOE) should be abolished and would prohibit the transfer of any of its functions to any other federal agency.
- Believes theories such as life origins and environmental change should be taught as challengeable scientific theories subject to change as new data are produced.
- Encourages non-English-speaking students to transition to English within three years.
- Believes that parents are best suited to train their children in their early development and opposes mandatory pre-school and kindergarten.
- Supports school subjects with emphasis on the Judeo-Christian principles upon which America was founded and that form the basis of America's legal, political, and economic systems.
- Opposes any sex education other than the biology of reproduction and abstinence until marriage.

The Texas Democratic Party

Abortion
- Trusts women to make personal and responsible decisions about when and whether to bear children, in consultation with their family, their physician, and their God, rather than having these personal decisions made by politicians.
- Supports prevention measures that have proven effective at reducing unintended pregnancies.

Education
- Believes the state should establish a 100 percent equitable school finance system with sufficient state revenue to allow every district to offer an exemplary program.
- Believes the state should provide environmental education programs for children and adults.
- Rejects efforts to destroy bilingual education. Believes the state should promote multilanguage instruction, beginning in elementary school, to make all students fluent in English and at least one other language.
- Believes the state should support expanded access to early childhood education, targeting at-risk students.
- Believes all children should have access to an exemplary educational program that values and encourages critical thinking and creativity.

The Texas Republican Party

Capital Punishment

- Believes that properly applied capital punishment is legitimate, is an effective deterrent, and should be swift and unencumbered.

Energy

- Urges development of a comprehensive Texas energy plan to ensure development of domestic energy sources and reduce or eventually eliminate need for foreign energy and ensure export of compressed natural gas and distillates with elimination of onerous environmental regulations.
- Recommends development of coal energy resources and completion of the Keystone Pipeline Project.
- Supports land drilling and production operations including hydraulic fracturing.
- Supports the elimination of the Department of Energy.

Environment

- Believes that changes in climate that we have observed are simply part of the ongoing natural planetary cycle.
- Rejects the use of this natural process to promote more government regulation of the private economy.
- Opposes all efforts of the extreme environmental groups that stymie legitimate business interests and private property use.
- Believes the Environmental Protection Agency should be abolished.

Fire Arms

- Strongly opposes all laws that infringe on the right to bear arms.
- Opposes the monitoring of gun ownership and the taxation and regulation of guns, ammunition, and gun magazines.
- Urges the legislature to pass "constitutional carry" legislation whereby law-abiding citizens that possess firearms can legally exercise their God-given right to carry firearms as well.
- Urges the state to reintroduce and pass laws easing current restrictions on firearms such as open carry and campus carry.

Homosexuality

- Believes that homosexuality must not be presented as an accepted alternative lifestyle in public policy, nor

The Texas Democratic Party

Capital Punishment

- Calls for the passage of legislation that would abolish the death penalty in Texas and replace it with the punishment of life in prison without parole.

Energy

- Supports increased development of renewable energy technologies that spur the economy, protect the environment, create high-paying jobs, and reduce reliance and dependence on foreign oil.
- Supports a transportation policy that encourages the development of affordable, fuel-efficient vehicles that can run on alternative fuels.
- Supports tax incentives for both homeowners and landlords to invest in conservation and energy efficiency.

Environment

- Believes that environmental protection, regulation, and enforcement are essential to preserve the health of people, the quality of life, and to secure long-term economic growth.
- Supports the enactment of state policy that allows local governments to protect air and water quality, public safety, historical sites, and health from actions that adversely affect communities.
- Supports open space acquisition to protect Texas aquifers and watersheds that provide the sole source of drinking water for millions of Texans.
- Supports the adoption, immediate implementation, and strong enforcement of clean air plans by state officials.

Health Care

- Supports guaranteed access to affordable, comprehensive, single-payer health care for all U.S. citizens and legal residents.
- Supports creation of a Texas universal health care plan, as permitted under the Affordable Care Act, to ensure that every Texas resident has health insurance that

The Texas Republican Party

should family be redefined to include homosexual couples.

- Opposes any criminal or civil penalties against those who oppose homosexuality out of faith, conviction, or belief in traditional values.
- Recognizes the legitimacy and value of counseling that offers reparative therapy and treatment to patients who are seeking escape from the homosexual lifestyle.

Health Care

- Believes health care decisions should be between a patient and health care professional/s and should be protected from government intrusion. Abortion is not health care.
- Demands the immediate repeal of the Patient Protection and Affordable Care Act.

Immigration

- Demands the federal government immediately secure the borders and bring safety and security for all Americans.
- Urges Congress to enact a visa program that does not provide amnesty, does not cause mass deportation, and does not provide a pathway to citizenship but does not preclude existing pathways.

Minimum Wage

- Believes the Minimum Wage Law should be repealed.

Voter Registration

- Supports the repeal of all motor-voter laws.
- Supports re-registering voters every four years.
- Supports requiring photo identification of all registrants.
- Supports proof of residency and citizenship as part of the voter registration application.
- Urges that the Voter Rights Act of 1965 codified and updated in 1973 be repealed and not reauthorized.

The Texas Democratic Party

covers medical, vision, and dental care, full reproductive health services, preventive services, prescription drugs, and mental health counseling and treatment.

School Vouchers

- Opposes private school vouchers in all forms, including tax breaks for people or corporations.

Social Security

- Believes Social Security should continue to be the foundation of income security for working Americans and that Social Security is an insurance program placed in the trust of the federal government and not a public welfare cost of government.
- Opposes privatization of the Social Security program as fiscally irresponsible, and considers the use of tax dollars as capital to invest in the stock market as a threat to the income security of working Americans.

Voter Registration

- Believes voter registration should be a lifetime status for all qualified, non-felon Texas citizens, requiring only change of address documentation in person or online.
- Supports efforts to defeat restrictive voter identification and proof of citizenship legislation that would serve only to reduce turnout among the elderly, poor, and people of color.
- Supports expansion of the types of legal identification that can be used to verify residence when a voter does not have a voter registration card at the polling place.
- Supports stronger penalties and stricter enforcement to prevent vote suppression.

In the latter part of the 19th century, Democrats faced a greater challenge from the Populist Party than they did from Republicans. The Populist (or People's) Party formed in Texas as an agrarian-based party, winning local elections throughout the state. From 1892 to 1898, its gubernatorial nominees received more votes than did Republicans. Although its ideas remained influential in Texas (for example, protection of common people by government regulation of railroads and banks), the Populist Party became less important after 1898. In large measure, the Populist Party declined because the Democratic Party adopted Populist issues, such as government regulation of railroads. Rural Texans continued to be active in politics, but most farmers and others who had been Populists shifted their support to Democratic candidates.[11]

In the early 20th century, the Democratic Party strengthened its control over state politics. Having adopted Populist issues, Democratic candidates faced no opposition from Populist candidates. During the next five decades, two factions emerged within the Democratic Party: conservatives and liberals. Fighting between these two factions was often as fierce as between two separate political parties. By the late 1940s and early 1950s, Republican presidential candidates began enjoying greater support from the Texas electorate. With the backing of conservative Democratic governor Alan Shivers, Republican presidential nominee Dwight D. Eisenhower successfully carried Texas in 1952 and 1956. Evidence of the growing strength of the Texas GOP (Grand Old Party, a nickname that the Republican Party adopted in the 1870s) was sharply revealed in 1961, with the election to the U.S. Senate of Texas Republican John Tower, a political science professor at Midwestern State University in Wichita Falls. Originally elected to fill the vacancy created when Lyndon Johnson left the Senate to become vice president of the United States, Tower was the first Republican to win statewide office in Texas since 1869; he won successive elections until his retirement in 1984.

1970s to 1990s: An Emerging Two-Party System

By the late 1970s the winner in a Democratic primary was no longer assured of victory in the general election contest in November. When Bill Clements was elected governor of the Lone Star State in 1978, he became the first Republican to hold that office since Reconstruction. In the 1980s, GOP voters elected growing numbers of candidates to the U.S. Congress, the Texas legislature, and county courthouse offices. Moreover, GOP elected officials began to dominate local politics in suburban areas around the state (Table 4.1).

The Republican Party continued to make substantial gains throughout the 1990s. The Republican victory of U.S. senatorial candidate Kay Bailey Hutchison in 1993 signalled a series of "firsts" for the Texas GOP: the first woman to represent Texas in the U.S. Senate, and the first representation of Texas by two Republican U.S. senators since Reconstruction.

The election of 1994 was a preview of future elections. This election was the last one in which any Democrat won a statewide office. Republican George W. Bush defeated Ann Richards, and Rick Perry was reelected agriculture commissioner. Democrats won only four executive offices: lieutenant governor, attorney general, comptroller of public accounts, and commissioner of the general land office. All other positions, including those on the Texas Supreme Court, the Texas Court of Criminal Appeals, and the Texas Railroad Commission, were won by Republicans. For the first time, Republicans also gained control of the 15-member State Board of Education. Active support by members of the Christian Coalition resulted in Republican victories in three of the six contested races for seats on this board.

In 1996, for the first time since the primary system was established, Republican primaries were conducted in all 254 Texas counties. More of the Lone Star State's voters participated in the Republican primary than in the Democratic primary. In the November general election, Republicans won contests for all statewide offices and gained a Texas Senate majority. Republican presidential candidate Bob Dole carried the state over President Bill Clinton. By 1996, Clinton was certain that he could be elected without Texas's electoral votes, so his campaign effort focused on closely contested states where he was more likely to win. This decision demonstrated the acceptance by national Democratic candidates that Texas was a Republican state and that its electoral votes were not needed for a Democratic presidential victory.

The 1998 elections gave Republicans control of all statewide offices but one. Texas Supreme Court Justice Raul Gonzalez was the lone Democrat in statewide office when he announced his retirement in December 1998. The GOP sweep was complete when Governor George W. Bush appointed a Republican to replace Gonzalez. In 1998, Bush was so popular that he received endorsements from more than 100 elected Democratic officials and almost 70 percent of the vote in the gubernatorial election. Republicans retained control of the Texas Senate and increased their representation in the state House of Representatives, although they did not gain control of the latter chamber.

2000 to 2014: Republican Dominance

After their party's statewide success in 1998, Texas Republicans focused attention on the 2000 national elections. Governor Bush's candidacy for the presidency was enhanced by his ability to maintain the backing of social conservatives within his party while gaining support from minority voters, women, and some Democrats. National Republican leaders seeking an electable candidate found Bush's 1998 gubernatorial victory and his inclusive strategy appealing. Although Bush did not announce that he would seek the Republican presidential nomination until after the Texas legislature completed its 1999 regular session, Republican leaders streamed to Austin during the session. More than one-fourth of Texas Democrats told pollsters they would vote for Bush for president.

In the closest presidential election of modern times, Governor Bush defeated Democratic nominee Al Gore by four electoral votes (271 to 267) in 2000. After controversial recounts and protracted court battles over Florida's 25 electoral votes, George W. Bush was ultimately declared the victor in mid-December 2000 after a 5–4 ruling by the U.S. Supreme Court. Bush's election made lieutenant

Students in Action

"I only hope that the Republican Party is up to the challenge and will make a serious investment in reaching out to Latinos, specifically young Latinos, who are ready to hear something new and positive about our future."

—Fernando Trevino, Jr.

About Fernando Trevino

Fernando Trevino Jr. attended the Mays School of Business at Texas A&M University. He was born in Del Rio, Texas, and later moved to Brownsville. Fernando's interest in politics and public service began very early in life, but was not fully realized until the 2008 Democratic presidential primary. Before this time, he considered himself a "liberal" Democrat. However, it was at this point that he realized the correlations between Latino beliefs and the principles of conservatism and the Republican Party.

What Is It About the Republican Party That Attracted Him to It?

Fernando's parents raised him very conservatively, teaching him never to abandon faith and to be fiscally responsible. He was also always taught that we must cherish and respect our differences. These are traits that he feels make up the essence of the Republican Party: faith, fiscal responsibility, and the power of the individual.

What Is He Doing Now to Share His Beliefs and Encourage Action?

Fernando began his involvement as a congressional intern at the district office of

U.S. Congressman Solomon P. Ortiz (D-Corpus Christi). After leaving the office, Fernando cofounded a Republican club at his high school as well as a political blog: Write for the Right. He then went on to co-organize a Tea Party protest in Brownsville. Fernando has been on talk radio shows in the Rio Grande Valley and on "Canto Talk" on Blog Talk Radio. In 2011, Governor Rick Perry appointed Fernando to a one-year term as a student regent of the Texas A&M University System. When Fernando's term expired, he was appointed to the Texas Guaranteed Student Loan Corporation's Board of Directors and later became Communications Coordinator at the Office of the Lieutenant Governor. In 2014, he served as Deputy Executive Director at Hispanic Republicans of Texas, a political action committee.

© Andresr/Shutterstock.com

governor Rick Perry governor. For the third straight election, all statewide Republican candidates won; Democrats did not even have candidates in most statewide contests or in many local races. In fact, in 2000, the Libertarian Party and Green Party, minor parties with limited support among voters, each had more candidates for statewide office than did the Democratic Party. Of the nine statewide offices up for election in that year, the Democratic Party fielded candidates in only three contests. By contrast, the Libertarian Party ran candidates in seven of the nine races, and the Green Party had candidates in five.

In 2002, Democrats selected what was dubbed the "dream team" for the three highest statewide offices: Laredo businessman Tony Sanchez, a Latino, for governor; former Dallas mayor Ron Kirk, an African American, for U.S. senator; and former state comptroller John Sharp, an Anglo, for lieutenant governor. The expectation was that the multiracial Democratic ticket would encourage higher levels of voter participation by members of historical minority groups. Texas Democrats ran with a full slate of candidates for other statewide offices. On election night, however, the dream quickly turned into a nightmare as the GOP swept all statewide races. The 2002 election increased Republican control over the Texas Senate from a one-seat majority to a seven-seat majority (19 to 12). For the first time since Reconstruction, the GOP gained control of the Texas House of Representatives, winning 88 of 150 seats. The stage was set to elect a Republican speaker of the Texas House in the 78th regular legislative session in January 2003.

Because of redistricting efforts orchestrated by then-majority leader of the U.S. House of Representatives, Tom DeLay, the Texas congressional

Table 4.1		Number of Selected Republican Officeholders, 1974–2014					
Year	U.S. Senate	Other Statewide Offices	U.S. House	Texas Senate	Texas House	S.B.O.E.*	Total
1974	1	0	2	3	16	—	22
1976	1	0	2	3	19	—	25
1978	1	1	4	4	22	—	32
1980	1	1	5	7	35	—	49
1982	1	0	5	5	36	—	47
1984	1	0	10	6	52	—	69
1986	1	1	10	6	56	—	74
1988	1	5	8	8	57	5	84
1990	1	6	8	8	57	5	85
1992	1	8	9	13	58	5	94
1994	2	13	11	14	61	8	109
1996	2	18	13	17	68	9	127
1998	2	27	13	16	72	9	137
2000	2	27	13	16	72	10	140
2002	2	27	15	19	88	10	161
2004	2	27	21	19	87	10	166**
2006	2	27	21	20	79	10	159***
2008	2	27	20	19	77	10	155***
2010	2	27	20	19	77	10	155***
2012	2	27	23	19	101	10	182***
2014	2	27	25	20	98	10	182

*State Board of Education.
**Data for 1974–2004 reprinted by permission of the Republican Party of Texas.
***Data for 2006–2014 were compiled by the authors.

delegation has been majority Republican since 2004. In addition to gaining a majority of Texas congressional seats in the 2004 general election (21 of 32 positions), Republicans won all statewide elections, maintained control of the Texas Senate and the Texas House, and picked up approximately 200 more county- and district-level offices. Benefiting many of the Republican candidates was the fact that at the top of the ballot, President Bush carried the state with more than 61 percent of the popular vote, compared with Senator John Kerry's 38 percent. Inevitably, Republican candidates down the ballot were assisted by the president's coattails.

In 2006, Democrats fielded candidates in only 9 of 15 statewide races; all of them lost. However, Democrats won all countywide races in Dallas County (a Republican stronghold throughout the 1980s and 1990s) and narrowed the margin of Republican control in Harris County. In the gubernatorial election, Republican incumbent Rick Perry defeated Democratic challenger Chris Bell by 1,716,792 votes to 1,310,337 votes. Due in part to the strength of independent candidates Carole Keeton Strayhorn and Richard S. "Kinky" Friedman, Perry became the first gubernatorial candidate of a political party to be elected with less than 40 percent of the vote (39.02 percent). In 1861, following Texas's secession from the Union, F. R. Lubbock was elected governor with 38.05 percent of the vote. Both Perry and Lubbock were able to win because Texas general elections are won by plurality (the highest percent) rather than majority (more than 50 percent).

In the presidential election of 2008, Barack Obama became the second Democratic presidential candidate in history to be elected without winning Texas. Republican nominee John McCain carried the state with almost 1 million more popular votes than Obama (4,479,328 to 3,528,633). Although Obama did not win the state, Democrats could point to gains in several areas. The 2008 election marked the first presidential election in more than a quarter of a century in which the Democratic nominee carried at least four of the state's five most populous counties. One reason Obama fared so well in these counties was the support he received from Latino and African American voters. Democratic candidates also won a majority of countywide offices in Harris County for the first time in more than 20 years. In addition, for the third straight general election cycle, Democrats gained seats in the Texas House of Representatives. In the 2010 Republican primary, incumbent Rick Perry's victory over U.S. Senator Kay Bailey Hutchison and Tea Party activist Debra Medina set up a general election showdown with popular three-term Houston mayor and former Texas Democratic Party chair Bill White. Many believed White to be the most viable Democratic gubernatorial nominee since Ann Richards in 1990. In the general election, however, White lost to Perry, receiving 42 percent of the vote to Perry's 55 percent. Following his reelection to an unprecedented third term, Perry embarked on a national tour promoting his book, *Fed Up! Our Fight to Save America from Washington*, further confirming the belief that he intended to seek higher office.

In 2010, Republican candidates were once again elected to all statewide offices and gained three additional seats in the Texas delegation to the U.S. House of Representatives, with 23 Republicans and 9 Democrats elected.

The Republican Party continued to maintain its majority in the Texas Senate (19 Republicans to 12 Democrats) and extended its majority in the Texas House of Representatives, winning 99 seats (to the Democrats' 51 seats). The Republican Party increased its membership in the Texas House of Representatives to 101 when two Democratic state representatives switched to the Republican Party after the November election. With more than two-thirds of the membership in the Texas House of Representatives, Republicans enjoyed a "supermajority" for the first time since Reconstruction. Supermajority status allowed Republican representatives to regularly suspend the rules of the Texas House of Representatives and push their legislative agenda though the 2011 session with limited opposition from Democratic representatives.

In the presidential election of 2012, Barack Obama was reelected president without carrying the Lone Star State. Republican nominee Mitt Romney won Texas by 57 percent to Obama's 41 percent and received over 1.2 million votes more than the president (4,569,843 to 3,308,124). Although President Obama received fewer votes in 2012 than he had in 2008, he again carried four of the state's five most populous counties (Harris, Dallas, Bexar, and Travis) (see Figure 4.2). As a result of Obama's success with Latino voters in the state, the national Democratic Party began to organize in the state in an effort called "Turn Texas Blue." Several fomer presidential campaign staff members relocated to Texas to develop a voter registration and voter turnout drive using methods refined by the Obama campaign during the 2012 presidential election. Even though most observers believe Democrats will not be competitive in Texas until 2024 at the earliest, by May 2014, Battleground Texas, the organizing group for this effort, claimed 16,000 volunteers. (See the Selected Reading for this chapter for more information on this effort.) Following the 2012 general election, the Republican Party remained firmly in control of all three branches of state government. Although the GOP lost "supermajority" status in the Texas House of Representatives, providing Democrats with more input on proposed legislation, Republicans still held 95 (out of 150) seats in the House, 19 (out of 31) seats in the Senate, and all statewide offices.

In July 2013, Governor Rick Perry announced that he would not seek reelection in 2014. With Perry not running, 2014 marked the first gubernatorial election in 24 years in which an incumbent was not on the general election ballot. In December of that year, Texas Court of Criminal Appeals Judge Larry Meyers, a longtime Republican, switched parties and filed as a Democrat in the special election for Texas Supreme Court, Place 6, against Republican Justice Jeff Brown, who was appointed in 2013. Because Meyers was not required to resign from the Texas Court of Criminal Appeals to run for the Texas Supreme Court, his switch gave Democrats their first incumbent statewide officeholder since 1998. His term on the Court of Criminal Appeals does not expire until January 2017.

In 2014, more than 1.33 million voters participated in the Republican primary compared to more than 540,000 voters in the Democratic primary. This marked the third consecutive primary in which more people voted in the Republican primary than in the Democratic primary. In the race for governor, Attorney General Greg Abbott easily defeated three other candidates

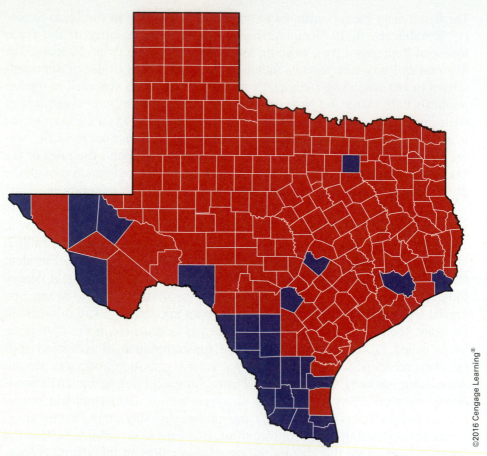

©2016 Cengage Learning®

Figure 4.2   Texas Counties Obama Won (in blue) and Romney Won (in red) in 2012
Presidential Election

Source: www.politico.com

CRITICAL THINKING

How does Democratic presidential candidate Barack Obama's success in four of largest (or
urban) counties in 2012 reflect the changing demographic nature of the state? What implications might this have for the two major parties?

to win the Republican primary, receiving more than 91 percent of the vote.
State Senator Wendy Davis won the Democratic primary with more than 79
percent of the vote.

More than 4.7 million voters cast their ballots in the 2014 general election. This represented a turnout of approximately 35 percent of the 14 million registered voters at that time. Following the election, the Republican

Texas GOP primary candidates for lieutenant governor—Land Commissioner Jerry Patterson, State Sen. Dan Patrick, Agricultural Commissioner Todd Staples, and incumbent Lieutenant Governor David Dewhurst—are shown during a debate at the KERA Channel 13 studios in downtown Dallas in February 2014.

(AP Images/LM Otero).

CRITICAL THINKING

What has been the impact of strong one-party (Republican) dominance on Texas primary elections?

Party retained control of all three branches of government. Republican nominee Greg Abbott defeated Democratic nominee Wendy Davis by more than 950,000 votes (2,790,227 to 1,832,254). Abbott won 59 percent of the vote compared to Davis's 39 percent (the remaining 2 percent was split among the Libertarian Party, Green Party, and write-in candidates). Republicans held on to all 27 statewide offices, with no candidate receiving less than 58 percent of the vote. In legislative races, the Republican Party extended its margin of control in the Texas Senate, by picking up a seat previously held by a Democrat and held 20 (out of 31) seats in the Texas Senate. Although it was unable to regain the "supermajority" status that it had held in the Texas House of Representatives four years earlier, the Republican Party won 98 (out of 150) seats.

✓ **4.3 Learning Check**

1. True or False: In 2012, Democratic presidential candidate Barack Obama received the majority of popular votes in Texas.
2. What has been the impact of Latino and African American support in urban counties?

Answers on p. 156.

Electoral Trends

★ **LO4.4** Identify electoral trends in Texas, including the roles of dealigned voters, minor parties, and independent candidates.

During the past 40 years, competition between Texas's Democratic and Republican parties has brought more women, Latinos, and African Americans into the state's political system. As a result, party politics has become more competitive and more nationalized. Compared with the politics of earlier years, Texas politics today is more partisan (party centered). However, both the Democratic and the Republican parties experience internal feuding (factionalism) among competing groups.

Some political scientists interpret recent polling and election results as evidence of a **dealignment** of Texas voters. These scholars explain that the large percentage of Texans who claim to be independent voters have no allegiance to a political party. According to a 2014 University of Texas/*Texas Tribune* poll, 10 percent of Texas residents identified themselves as independents. Nonetheless, many self-identified independent voters tend to vote for Republican candidates. Other political scientists assert that the rising tide of Republican electoral victories throughout the 1990s and into the 21st century demonstrates that many Texans who were previously Democrats have switched their political affiliation and loyalty to the Republican Party in a **realignment** of voters.

Republican candidates carried Texas in 12 of the 16 presidential elections between 1952 and 2012, including the last nine elections in that period. Republican candidates also won seven of nine gubernatorial elections between 1978 and 2014. As the GOP's dominance of statewide elections increased, so did intraparty competition, just as occurred for the Democrats before them. Texas GOP strongholds are in West Texas; the Panhandle–South Plains; some small towns and rural areas in East Texas; and the suburbs of Dallas, Fort Worth, Houston, San Antonio, and Austin. With the exception of Democratic El Paso, West Texas Republicanism is predominant from the Permian Basin (Midland–Odessa) through the Davis Mountains and the German Hill Country. This West Texas region, like the Panhandle–South Plains area to the north, is populated primarily by conservative farmers and ranchers, as well as people connected with the oil and gas industry in Midland–Odessa and other parts of the Permian Basin.

Although the Democratic Party has been unsuccessful in statewide election contests in recent years, it still controls many county offices. Democratic voting strength is concentrated in El Paso, South Texas, the Golden Triangle (Beaumont, Port Arthur, and Orange), portions of the diverse Central Texas region, and the lower-income neighborhoods of larger cities. **Straight-ticket voting** for all Democratic candidates on the general election ballot has declined, however, as fewer Texans (especially those in rural East Texas) choose to remain "yellow-dog Democrats." This term has been applied to people whose party loyalty is said to be so strong that they would vote for a yellow dog if it were a Democratic candidate for public office. Republican expansion has diminished the intensity of factional politics within the Democratic Party. Nevertheless, Democrats are divided by many interests and issues, and factionalism within Republican ranks has increased greatly with the rise of the Tea Party movement.

Third Parties

Americans commonly apply the term **third party** (or minor party) to any political party other than the Democratic or Republican party. Throughout the United States, third parties have never enjoyed the same success as the two

dealignment
Occurs when citizens have no allegiance to a political party and become independent voters.

realignment
Occurs when members of one party shift their affiliation to another party.

straight-ticket voting
Voting for all the candidates of one party.

third party
A party other than the Democratic Party or the Republican Party. Sometimes called a "minor party" because of limited membership and voter support.

principal parties. A major party's success is measured by its ability to win elections. By this measure, minor parties are unsuccessful. Instead, third parties' successes can be better measured by their ability to make the public aware of their issues, persuade the major parties to adopt those issues, or force the major parties to bring those issues into a coalition. When judged by these measures, third parties in Texas have enjoyed modest success. Lacking the financial resources of the two major parties to purchase expensive airtime on a television or radio station, third parties and third party candidates have often relied on social media (e.g., Facebook or Twitter) to share their messages.

During the 1890s, the Populist Party successfully promoted agricultural issues and displaced the Republicans as the "second" party in Texas.[12] In the 1970s, La Raza Unida elected a few candidates to local offices in South Texas (principally Crystal City, Zavala County, and school board offices) and forced the Democratic Party to begin to address Latino concerns. In the 1990s, Ross Perot's Reform Party had organizations in many areas of the state. During the past 30 years, the Libertarian Party (a party that advocates minimizing government involvement at all levels while maximizing individual freedom and rights) has nominated candidates for national, state, and local offices throughout Texas. In 1988, the Libertarian Party nominated former Texas congressman and longtime advocate of limited government Ron Paul for president. When Paul ran for president in 2008 and 2012, he maintained his

2014 Libertarian gubernatorial nominee, Kathie Glass, campaigning in Midland, Texas.

AP Images/Reporter-Telegram/James Durbin

CRITICAL THINKING

In what ways has the Texas Libertarian Party been successful? In what ways has it been unsuccessful?

advocacy of limited government. In those two presidential campaigns, however, he did so as a candidate for the Republican nomination. As of mid-2014, four Libertarians held local elective offices in the Lone Star State.

Other parties have nominated candidates and increased public awareness of their issues: the Greenback Party (late 19th century), the Prohibition Party (late 19th and early 20th centuries), the Socialist and Socialist Labor parties (early 20th century), the Progressive Party (early to mid-20th century), and the Green Party (late 20th century to early 21st century). The Green Party has advocated environmental protection and government reform policies. In 2000, Green Party presidential candidate Ralph Nader received 2.2 percent of the popular vote in Texas. Two years later, the Green Party fielded candidates for U.S. senator, governor, lieutenant governor, attorney general, comptroller, land commissioner, agriculture commissioner, railroad commissioner, and several statewide judgeships and congressional seats. However, Green candidates (like Libertarians) won no elections and rarely received more than 3 percent of the vote. In 2010, with a gubernatorial nominee for the first time in eight years, a Green Party candidate was on the general election ballot in Texas. That gubernatorial candidate, however, received less than 0.4 percent of the vote. In 2014, the Green Party nominated Brandon Parmer as their gubernatorial candidate and the Libertarians chose Kathie Glass as their nominee.

independent
A candidate who runs in a general election without party endorsement or selection.

Independents

The term **independent** applies to candidates who have no party affiliation. Their success is less likely because they usually lack a ready-made campaign organization and fundraising abilities. In addition, they have difficulty in

How Do We Compare…Which Party Controls the Statehouses in 2015?

Most Populous U.S. States	Governor/Senate/House	U.S. States Bordering Texas	Governor/Senate/House
California	Democrat/Democrat/Democrat	Arkansas	Democrat/Republican/Republican
Florida	Republican/Republican/Republican	Louisiana	Republican/Republican/Republican
New York	Democrat/Democrat/Democrat	New Mexico	Republican/Democrat/Democrat
Texas	**Republican/Republican/Republican**	Oklahoma	Republican/Republican/Republican

Source: http://www.ncsl.org/legislatures-elections/elections/statevote-2012-election-night-results-map.aspx

gaining ballot access. For instance, the Texas Election Code requires independent candidates to file by gathering signatures on a petition. The number of signatures required for a statewide office is "one percent of the total vote received by all candidates for governor in the most recent gubernatorial general election."[13] Based on this criterion, to qualify for statewide ballot access in 2014, an independent candidate was required to gather 49,798 signatures from registered voters who had not voted in either the Democratic or Republican primary elections or the primary runoff elections and who had not signed another candidate's petition for that office that year.

In 1859, Sam Houston was elected governor of Texas as an independent candidate. No one has succeeded in winning the governorship without affiliation with one of the two major political parties since that election. In 2006, songwriter, author, and humorist Richard S. "Kinky" Friedman and former state comptroller Carol Keeton Strayhorn ran for governor as independents. Despite Friedman's celebrity and Strayhorn's previous electoral success on a statewide basis as a Republican, their election experience was the same as that of most independent candidates: they lost. In the general election, Strayhorn received slightly more than 18 percent of the vote, and Friedman garnered a little more than 14 percent. Strayhorn retired from seeking elective office. In 2010 and 2014, Friedman filed as a candidate in the Democratic primary but was unsuccessful in both years.

4.4 Learning Check

1. Who was the last independent candidate to be elected governor of Texas?
2. True or False: Third parties' success comes more often in the form of their ability to make the public aware of the issues than in the number of their candidates elected to office.

Answers on p. 156.

What Must Happen for Texas to Turn Blue?

Forrest Wilder

As of 2014, no Democratic presidential nominee had carried Texas since 1976 and no Democratic candidate had been elected to a statewide office since 1998. However, with changing demographic patterns and the creation of Battleground Texas, Democrats remained hopeful that their party would return to power in the Lone Star State. This article, which appeared in the May 23, 2013, issue of the Texas Observer, explores what must happen for Texas to turn blue. The article is available at http://www.texasobserver.org/what-must-happen-for-texas-to-turn-blue/.

You hear the question often: Is Texas becoming a blue state? Since President Obama won reelection in November with an emerging Democratic coalition of African-Americans, Latinos, women and young voters, political pundits have been talking incessantly about the potential of Texas going Democratic. MSNBC has made it an obsession.

The creation of Battleground Texas—a group formed by former Obama campaign staffers to make the Lone Star State competitive—has only fueled national media speculation that Texas is going blue. On the ground, however, Texas remains as Republican as it gets. The GOP boasts comfortable majorities in both chambers of the Legislature and controls every statewide office; in fact, Democrats haven't won a statewide race in Texas since 1994, a 19-year losing streak that spans 101 defeats.

What has Democrats hoping they can reverse that trend is the state's shifting demographics. Namely, the state's Latino population is booming. Latinos tend to vote Democratic. Therefore, the theory goes, given enough time, Democrats could start winning statewide office again. (Some say 2014, others 2016, 2018, 2020. Some say it will

never happen.) The flaw in the theory, as many Democratic strategists and progressive organizers will acknowledge, is that you should never assume any group of voters will stick with you indefinitely. Another problem is that Texas Latinos go to the polls at a very low rate, compared to Anglo and African-American voters, and compared to Latino voters in other states. If Democrats don't increase the voter turnout rate among Latinos, they might be waiting a long time for the demographics changes to deliver them the state.

Then there's the Republican Party, which isn't going to sit idly by and let the state go Democratic. The state GOP and independent group Hispanic Republicans of Texas have been working for several years to attract more Latino candidates and voters to the party. So what must happen for Democrats to break the GOP's hold on Texas? Increasing Latino turnout is a must, especially in the Houston area. But there's more to it. As polling commissioned by the Democratic group Back to Basics PAC in Harris County during the 2012 election shows, Democrats have no lock on the Latino vote. In fact future control of Texas may hinge on which Latino voters show up at the polls.

For Texas to ever become competitive for them, Democrats will need to lock down Harris County. Home to 4.2 million Texans, almost 70 percent of whom are non-white, Houston is the present and future face of Texas. Former state demographer Steve Murdock has estimated that by 2040, Harris County will have 516,000 fewer Anglos than in 2000 while the number of Latinos will surge by 2.5 million. As Houston goes, so goes Texas. Given that Anglos are already a minority of Harris County's population, you would

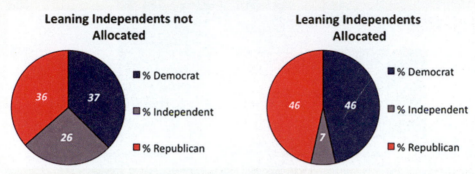

Leaning Independents not Allocated

- % Democrat
- % Independent
- % Republican

36 37 26

Leaning Independents Allocated

- % Democrat
- % Independent
- % Republican

46 46 7

Harris County Electorate Split Evenly Along Partisan Lines

think the Houston area would be ripe for Democratic success. Yet the county has proved an elusive prize. In recent elections, Harris County has been evenly divided.

In 2008, Barack Obama won the county by a little more than 19,000 votes. In 2012, he did slightly worse, beating Mitt Romney by just 971 votes. Latinos, despite representing 40 percent of the population of the county, constitute only 15 percent or so of the electorate. Partly that's due to how young the Latino community is and the presence of many non-citizens. But it's also due to an abysmal turnout rate that's hampering Democratic efforts to turn Houston—and by extension, Texas—blue.

So if you're looking for signs that Democrats are making any progress in Texas, you need to look at Houston. More specifically, you need to see if Democrats are harnessing the booming Latino population there. But hidden in the 2012 election data were trends that should have Democrats worried. In Harris County at least, Republicans showed surprising strength among some Latinos. The Latino community is hardly monolithic. In fact, the Back to Basics post-election survey of Harris County identified "two Hispanic worlds"—one that votes often and splits its vote between Republicans and Democrats, and another that

overwhelmingly favors Democrats but tends not to vote.

The survey found that Latinos who are less likely to vote—and who tend to be working class and less educated—overwhelmingly favored Obama in 2012. Eighty-four percent of these "low-propensity" voters said they favored Obama versus just 15 percent for Romney, according to the polling obtained by the *Observer*. The obvious conclusion is that getting these voters to the polls can do wonders for Democrats, said Jeff Rotkoff, who heads the PAC.

But the remainder of the Latino community in Houston was almost evenly split between Obama and Romney. Perhaps more troubling for Democrats thinking of running for governor or other statewide office is that the survey of Latino voters found significant defections to tea partier Ted Cruz. While Obama carried Harris County Latinos 59–40 overall, the Democratic candidate for U.S. Senate, Paul Sadler, took only 53 percent to Cruz's 46 percent share. Not only did Sadler run behind Obama among Harris County Latinos, but among "high propensity" Latinos—those most likely to vote—Cruz bested Sadler 53–44 percent. That's worth repeating: Among Latinos most likely to vote, Ted Cruz won a majority in Harris County.

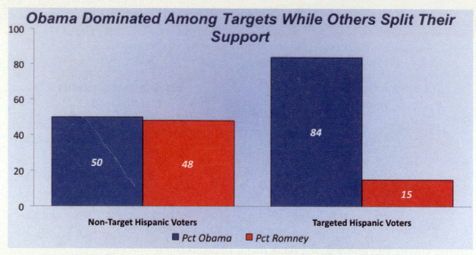

Obama Dominated Among Targets While Others Split Their Support

Non-Target Hispanic Voters: Pct Obama 50, Pct Romney 48
Targeted Hispanic Voters: Pct Obama 84, Pct Romney 15

■ Pct Obama   ■ Pct Romney

Two Hispanic Worlds: Low Propensity Targets vs. All Others

	Presidential Race Pct Obama – Pct Romney	U.S. Senate Race Pct Sadler – Pct Cruz	Sheriff Race Pct Garcia – Pct Guthrie
Total	49 – 49 (0)	48 – 50 (-2)	53 - 45 (+8)
Total Hispanics	59 – 40 (+20)	53 – 46 (+7)	65 – 32 (+33)
Hispanic Targets	84 – 15 (+68)	77 – 23 (+54)	88 – 10 (+79)
Hispanic Non-Targets	50 – 48 (+2)	44 – 53 (-9)	57 – 40 (+18)

Significant defections to Cruz among Hispanics across the board

Two Hispanic Worlds in Harris County: *Base Motivation Targets vs. Non-Targets*

On the other hand, popular Harris County Sheriff Adrian Garcia outperformed Obama among Latinos significantly, beating his Republican opponent 65 percent to 32 percent. The lesson is that Latinos are a diverse bunch and that many—the ones who tend to vote at higher rates—are willing to vote for the right Republican. In short, the 2012 election returns in Harris County add a wrinkle to the conventional wisdom that increased Latino turnout will aid Democrats. If the polling is correct, Democrats will take over Harris County and Texas only if they can turn out the "low propensity" voters most likely to support Democrats. Otherwise, Republicans have shown they can win over enough "high propensity" Latinos to make a Democrat winning statewide in Texas difficult.

Some Texas progressives say they're already making significant gains in Harris County due to efforts organizing and mobilizing in minority communities with traditionally low voter-turnout rates. In four out of five heavily Latino legislative districts

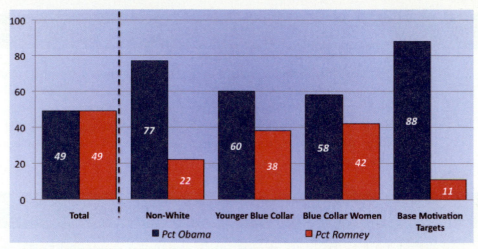

Keys to the Democratic Coalition

targeted by Texas Organizing Project, a group trying to mobilize and engage Latinos, as well as more partisan Democratic outfits, turnout increased in largely Latino districts—by 1.6 percent in Senate District 6 (Sen. Sylvia Garcia) to 10 percent in House District 143, represented by Democratic Rep. Ana Hernandez Luna. Texas Organizing Project (TOP) specifically targeted minority communities with the highest concentrations of "low-propensity" voters, from Pasadena to Katy to the East End and the north side of Houston. The group's goal was to talk to voters five times by knocking on doors three times and calling twice. Texans for America's Future, a super PAC supporting Obama, also targeted low-propensity voters in Harris County, said Rotkoff, the group's founder.

The PAC's post-election survey points to the coalition the Democrats need to build: an amalgam of women, working class folks and minorities.

Many Texas Democrats insist that they've got the message, and are serious about civic engagement and turnout. "The reality is you don't win new voters and get them into the process by ignoring them 18 months every two years," says Matt Glazer, executive director of the progressive group Progress Texas. "The proof of concept is happening and now people are working in an unprecedented way." He points to the 2012 results in Houston as the first fruits of their labor. "The beast has been stirred a little bit."

✓ Selected Reading Learning Check

1. True or False: One of the reasons that President Obama carried Harris County in 2012 was because Latinos comprised a majority of the population and of the electorate.
2. What strategies have groups such as Texas Organizing Project (TOP) and Texans for America's Future used to gain support for Democratic candidates?

Answers on p. 156.

Answers on p. 156.

. . . .

Source: Reprinted with permission from Texas Observer.

Conclusion

Historically, Texas politics has been characterized by prolonged periods of one-party domination—first the Democrats and later the Republicans. With changing demographic patterns, however, the nature of partisan politics in Texas and the struggle for control of public office by political parties continue to evolve. Shifts in voting alignments will change how both parties develop campaign strategies and target groups of voters.

Chapter Summary

LO 4.1   **Describe the structure of political parties in Texas, distinguishing between the temporary party structure and the permanent party structure**. Political parties are organized as stratarchies, in which power is diffused among and within levels of the party organization. The temporary party organization consists of primaries and conventions. Through primaries, members of the major political parties participate in elections to select candidates for public office and local party officers. Primary election voting may involve a second, or run-off, primary. Conventions elect state-level and senate-district party officers and are scheduled at precinct, county/state senatorial district, and state levels. At the state level, conventions also write party rules, adopt party platforms, and (in presidential election years) select delegates to national conventions and presidential electors.

LO 4.2   **Compare and contrast the different political ideologies found in the Lone Star State**. Texas voters and political parties represent various political ideologies, including conservatism and liberalism. Conservatives generally oppose government-managed or government-subsidized programs. However, they are further divided between fiscal conservatives and social conservatives. Fiscal conservatives tend to give the highest priority to reduced taxing and spending. Some fiscal conservatives consider themselves neoconservatives, accepting a limited governmental role in solving social problems. Social conservatives support greater government intervention into social issues (e.g., laws against abortion, laws against same-sex marriage) to support their family values. Liberals generally favor government regulation of the economy to achieve a more equitable distribution of wealth. In Texas, many Democrats have a neoliberal ideology, which incorporates a philosophy of less government regulation of business and the economy while adopting a more liberal view of greater government involvement in social programs.

LO 4.3   **Trace the history of political parties in Texas**. Before Texas's admission into the Union in 1845, its political parties had not fully developed and political factions tended to form around personalities. During the Civil War, as Texas seceded from the Union, politics became firmly aligned with the Democratic Party. However, during the period of Reconstruction (1865–1873) after the Civil War, the Republican Party controlled Texas politics. From the end of Reconstruction until the 1970s, Texas was dominated primarily by one political party: the Democratic Party. In the 1970s and 1980s, Texas moved toward a competitive two-party structure. By the 1990s and into the 21st century, the Lone Star State had seemingly become a one-party state with the Republican Party in control. An increase in the Latino population resulted in efforts in 2014 by the Democratic Party to register and turn out more Latino voters who they believed would vote Democratic.

LO 4.4 **Identify electoral trends in Texas, including the roles of dealigned voters, minor parties, and independent candidates**. Beginning in the late 1970s, competition between Texas's Democratic and Republican parties has brought more women, Latinos, and African Americans into the state's political system. As a result, party politics has become increasingly competitive and nationalized. Compared with the politics of earlier years, Texas politics today is more partisan (party centered). However, both the Democratic and the Republican parties experience internal feuding (factionalism) among competing groups. Some political scientists interpret recent polling and election results as evidence of a dealignment of Texas voters, in that they have little or no allegiance to a political party and have become increasingly independent. However, other political scientists assert that the success of the Republican Party throughout the 1990s and into the 21st century demonstrates that many Texans who were previously Democrats have switched their political affiliation and loyalty to the Republican Party in a realignment of voters. Minor (or third) parties and independents have never enjoyed the same success as the two principal parties. Their victories are generally limited to their ability to make the public aware of their issues or persuade the major parties to adopt those issues.

Key Terms

political party, p. 122

stratarchy, p. 122

temporary party organization, p. 123

platform, p. 123

precinct convention, p. 123

county convention, p. 126

district convention, p. 126

state convention, p. 127

presidential preference primary, p. 127

caucus, p. 128

superdelegate, p. 128

permanent party organization, p. 129

precinct chair, p. 129

county executive committee, p. 129

county chair, p. 130

district executive committee, p. 130

state executive committee, p. 130

conservative, p. 132

neoconservatism, p. 132

liberal, p. 133

neoliberal, p. 133

dealignment, p. 146

realignment, p. 146

straight-ticket voting, p. 146

third party, p. 146

independent, p. 148

Learning Check Answers

4.1   1. The role of the permanent party organization is to recruit candidates, devise strategies, raise funds, distribute candidate literature and information, register voters, and turn out voters on Election Day. The temporary party organization consists of primaries and conventions in which members of the major political parties select candidates for public office.

2. True. Although the state chair presides over the party's permanent organization at the state level, he or she is selected by delegates to the party's state convention, which is its temporary organization at the state level.

4.2   1. Conservatives are generally opposed to government-managed or government-subsidized programs, whereas neoconservatives allow for a limited governmental role in solving social problems.

2. False. Many Texas Democrats have a neoliberal ideology that incorporates a philosophy of less government regulation of business and the economy while adopting a more liberal view of greater government involvement in social programs.

4.3   1. False. In 2012, Mitt Romney won the majority of the popular vote in Texas.

2. One reason Democratic candidates are faring better, especially in urban counties, is the support received from Latino and African American voters.

4.4   1. Sam Houston was the last independent candidate to be elected governor of Texas.

2. True. Rather than judging their success on the basis of elections won, third parties' success can be better measured by their ability to make the public aware of the issues, persuade the major parties to adopt those issues, and/or force the major parties to bring those issues into a coalition.

Selected Reading Learning Check

1. False. Although President Obama carried Harris County in 2012 with the help of Latino support, Latinos comprised only 40 percent of the population and 15 percent of the electorate.

2. Texas Organizing Project (TOP) and Texans for America's Future have targeted minority communities with the highest concentrations of "low-propensity" voters most likely to support Democrats.

5

Campaigns and Elections

Learning Objectives

5.1 Analyze the components of a political campaign, specifically how the process of running and financing a campaign has changed over the years.

5.2 Describe the role that race and ethnicity play in politics, focusing on the importance of minority voters.

5.3 Describe the role that women have played in Texas politics and how that role has evolved.

5.4 Explain the complexities of voting and how the voting process promotes, and inhibits, voter participation.

5.5 Identify the differences among primary, general, and special elections.

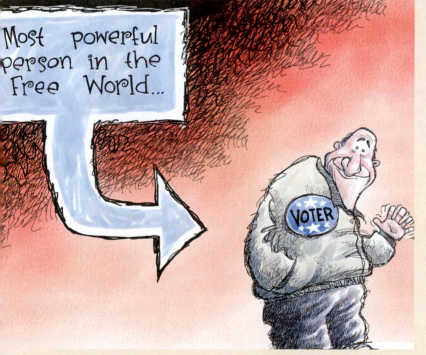

Nick Anderson Editorial Cartoon used with the permission of Nick Anderson, the Washington Post Writers Group and the Cartoonist Group. All rights reserved.

CRITICAL THINKING

How might a voter be considered the most powerful person in the free world?

The fundamental principle on which every representative democracy is based is citizen participation in the political process. As Nick Anderson's cartoon depicts, voters are considered to be the most powerful people in the free world. Yet in Texas, even as the right to vote was extended to almost every citizen 18 years of age or older, participation declined throughout the 20th century's final decades and into the 21st century. This chapter focuses on campaigns and the role that media and money play in our electoral system. Citizen participation through elections and the impact of that participation are additional subjects of our study.

Political Campaigns

LO5.1 Analyze the components of a political campaign, specifically how the process of running and financing a campaign has changed over the years.

Elections in Texas allow voters to choose officials to fill national, state, county, city, and special district offices. With so many electoral contests, citizens are frequently besieged by candidates seeking votes and asking for money to finance election campaigns. The democratic election process, however, gives Texans an opportunity to influence public policymaking by expressing preferences for candidates and issues when they vote.

Conducting Campaigns in the 21st Century

Campaigns are no longer limited to speeches by candidates on a courthouse lawn or from the rear platform of a campaign train. Today, prospective voters are more likely to be harried by a barrage of campaign publicity involving television and radio broadcasting, targeted emails designed to encourage likely supporters to vote and give money, yard signs, bumper stickers, newspapers, and billboards. Moreover, voters will probably receive campaign information by electronic mail, be solicited for donations to pay for campaign expenses, encounter door-to-door canvassers, receive political information in the U.S. mail, receive requests to post candidate "likes" on Facebook pages and other social media sites, and be asked to answer telephone inquiries from professional pollsters or locally hired telephone bank callers. In recent years, the Internet and the array of available social media tools have altered political campaigns in Texas and other states. Politicians set up Facebook pages inviting voters to friend them. Other campaigners "tweet" their supporters on Twitter to announce important events and decisions. To the dismay of some politicians, YouTube videos provide a permanent record of misstatements and misdeeds. Private and public lives of candidates remain open 24/7 for review and comment.

Despite increasing technological access to information about candidates and issues, a minority of Texans, and indeed other Americans, are actively concerned with politics. To most voters, character and political style have become more important than issues. A candidate's physical appearance and personality are increasingly important because television has become a primary mode of campaign communication.

Importance of the Media　Since the days of W. Lee "Pappy" O'Daniel, the media have played an important role in Texas politics. In the 1930s, O'Daniel gained fame as a radio host for Light Crust Flour and later his own Hillbilly Flour Company. On his weekly broadcast show, the slogan "Pass the biscuits, Pappy" made O'Daniel a household name throughout the state. In 1938, urged by his radio fans, O'Daniel ran for governor and attracted huge crowds. With a platform featuring the Ten Commandments and the Golden Rule, he won the election by a landslide.[1] In an attempt to duplicate O'Daniel's feat, Kinky Friedman (a singer, author, and humorist with a cult following) ran unsuccessfully as an **independent candidate** for governor in 2006, using TV appearances the way O'Daniel used the radio. In 2014, Friedman ran unsuccessfully for the Democratic nomination for agriculture commissioner.

By the 1970s, television and radio ads had become a regular part of every gubernatorial and U.S. senatorial candidate's campaign budget. Radio became the medium of choice for many "middle-of-the-ballot" (statewide and regional candidates for offices other than governor or senator) and local candidates. The prohibitive cost of television time, with the exception of smaller media markets and local cable providers, forced the use of radio to communicate with large numbers of potential voters. Today, with more than 13 million potential voters in 254 counties, Texas is, by necessity, a media state for political campaigning. To visit every county personally during a primary campaign, a candidate would need to go into four counties per day, five days a week, from the filing deadline in January to the March primary (the usual month for party primaries). Such extensive travel would leave little time for speechmaking, fundraising, and other campaign activities. Although some candidates for statewide office in recent years have traveled to each county in the state, none has won an election. Therefore, Texas campaigners must rely more heavily on television, radio, and social media exposure than do candidates in other states.

Most Texas voters learn about candidates through television commercials that range in length from 10 seconds for a **sound bite** (a brief statement of a candidate's campaign theme) to a full minute. Television advertisements allow candidates to structure their messages carefully and avoid the risk of a possible misstatement that might occur in a political debate. Therefore, the more money a candidate's campaign has, the less interest the candidate has in debating an opponent. Usually, the candidate who is the underdog (the one who is behind in the polls) wants to debate.

 Candidates also rely increasingly on social media to communicate with voters. The benefit of low cost must be balanced against problems unique to the medium of websites and email. Issues with using social media include limited use and understanding of this type of media by the older (over 65) voting population. Additional complexities include access to and use of

independent candidate
A candidate who runs in a general election without party endorsement or selection.

sound bite
A brief statement of a candidate's theme communicated by radio or television in a few seconds.

computers by older voters, consumer resistance to "spam" (electronic junk mail), hyperlinks to inappropriate websites, and "cybersquatting" (individuals other than the candidate purchasing domain names similar to the candidate's name and then selling the domain name to the highest bidder). In his 2010 general election campaign, Jim Prindle, a Libertarian, purchased rights to RalphHall.org in his bid to defeat U.S. Representative Ralph Hall (R-Rockwall). This site rerouted viewers to Prindle's campaign site. Although he was unsuccessful in his bid to unseat the 15-term incumbent, Prindle said that he had "explored many strategies in marketing and campaigning to help bridge the advantage that incumbents share."[2] Hall failed to win the GOP nomination for a 17th term in 2014.

Mudslide Campaigns Following gubernatorial candidate Ann Richards's victory over Jim Mattox in the Democratic runoff primary of April 1990, one journalist reported that Richards had "won by a mudslide." This expression suggests the reaction of many citizens who were disappointed, if not infuriated, by the candidates' generally low ethical level of campaigning and by their avoidance of critical public issues. Nevertheless, as character became more important as a voting consideration in the 1990s and early 21st century, negative campaigning has become even more prominent.

The 2014 gubernatorial election was particularly acrimonious. In an ad titled "Justice," Democratic gubernatorial nominee Wendy Davis's campaign attempted to demonstrate how Republican gubernatorial nominee Greg Abbott was a hypocrite as both a judge and as attorney general by restricting victims' access to the courts despite his award of over $10 million in 1984 after a tree fell on him and left him paralyzed. The ad showed an empty wheelchair with a narrator saying, "A tree fell on Greg Abbott. He sued and got millions. Since then, he's spent his career working against other victims. Abbott argued a woman whose leg was amputated was not disabled because she had an artificial limb. He ruled against a rape victim who sued a corporation for failing to do a background check on a sexual predator. He sided with a hospital that failed to stop a dangerous surgeon who paralyzed patients. Greg Abbott, he's not for you." Several conservative commentators criticized the ad, and a representative from Abbott's campaign called it "disgusting." In a press release issued by Greg Abbott's campaign, titled, "Sen. Davis Has A Lot To Answer For," Abbot claimed that Davis once raised money for a U.S. House Democrat who is a member of a Democratic socialists group. This statement earned a "Pants on Fire" rating from the Austin American Statesmen's PolitiFact Truth-O-Meter as unconfirmed and ridiculous.

Campaign Reform

Concern over the shortcomings of American election campaigns has given rise to organized efforts toward improvement at all levels of government. Reformers range from single citizens to members of the U.S. Congress and large lobby groups. Reform issues include eliminating negative campaigning, increasing free media access for candidates, and regulating campaign finance.

Eliminating Negative Campaigning Almost 25 years ago, the Markle Commission on the Media and the Electorate concluded that candidates, the media, consultants, and the electorate were all blameworthy for the increase in negative campaigns. Candidates and consultants, wishing to win at any cost, employ negative advertising and make exaggerated claims. The media emphasize poll results and the horserace appearance of a contest, rather than basic issues and candidate personalities that relate to leadership potential. In 2010, another study tested the effectiveness of "comparative" ads run during the Texas governor's race to see if they persuaded voters. Research findings showed that negative commercials influenced voters (especially undecided voters), drawing their preference away from the candidate being attacked.[3]

The 2014 Republican runoff primary for lieutenant governor featured several negative commercials and other attacks between the incumbent lieutenant governor, David Dewhurst, and his opponent and eventual nominee, state senator Dan Patrick. One Dewhurst commercial showed a shirtless Dan Patrick and claimed that Patrick was caught pocketing employees' federal income tax withholdings, not paying his taxes 28 times, hiding assets from creditors and sticking them with $800,000, knowingly employing illegal immigrants, and changing his name from Dannie Goeb to Dan Patrick. A Patrick ad claimed that under Dewhurst's leadership, the Texas Senate passed an expansion of in-state tuition and free health care to illegal immigrants, and that Dewhurst's record was more taxpayer-funded benefits for illegal immigrants.

Increasing Free Media Access Certainly a candidate for statewide office in Texas cannot win without first communicating with a large percentage of the state's voting population. As noted previously, television is the most important, and the most expensive, communication tool. One group supporting media access reform is the Campaign Legal Center. Although initially they sought to increase requirements for broadcasters to make the air waves more available at no cost to political candidates, more recent efforts have focused on campaign finance reform. As long as paid media advertising is a necessary part of political campaigns and media outlets generate a significant source of revenue from political campaigns, fundraising will remain important to electoral success.

By the early 21st century, many political campaigns used social networking resources to get their message out to a larger voter base. Twitter, Facebook, and YouTube became commonly used tools for candidates to reach potential voters. In 2008, Barack Obama used cell phone text messaging as one means of announcing his vice presidential selection (U.S. Senator Joe Biden). That year, Obama also became the first presidential candidate to provide a free iPhone application (Obama '08). Users could get current updates about the campaign and network with other users. Relaying campaign information by phone also provided the Obama campaign with millions of cell phone numbers. These strategies became common practice in both the Obama and Romney presidential campaigns in 2012. This shift, however, was not limited to presidential campaigns.

In 2014, most candidates for statewide office in Texas regularly used social media sites such as Twitter, Facebook, Flickr, LinkedIn, YouTube, Vimeo, and Pinterest to reach potential voters and provide forums for comment and feedback. Because of the open nature of these media and the ability of the public to post comments, campaigns often set strict guidelines for posting comments on candidates' social media sites. However, such guidelines do not always prevent inappropriate comments from appearing or prevent candidates from becoming involved in controversies that arise from such comments. In late 2013, the eventual Republican gubernatorial nominee, Greg Abbott, was criticized for the following exchange:

> "@GregAbbott_TX would absolutely demolish idiot @WendyDavisTexas in Gov race – run Wendy run! Retard Barbie to learn life lesson. #TGDN @tcot"
>
> —Jeff Rutledge (@jefflegal) August 17, 2013

> "Jeff, thanks for your support."
>
> —Greg Abbott (@GregAbbott_TX) August 17, 2013

After the post went viral and Democratic party leaders labeled Abbott insensitive and disrespectful of women, the gubernatorial candidate tweeted that he did "not endorse anyone's offensive language."

(For a detailed discussion about the 2014 gubernatorial candidates' use of social media, as well as challenges they encountered with inappropriate postings on their websites, see this chapter's Selected Reading, "Campaigns Contend with Vitriol on Social Media.")

Campaign Finance

On more than one occasion, President Lyndon Johnson bluntly summarized the relationship between politics and finance: "Money makes the mare go." Although most political scientists would state this fact differently, it is obvious that candidates need money to pay the expenses of election campaigns. Texas's 1990 gubernatorial campaign established a record of $45 million spent on the primary and general election races combined, including more than $22 million by Midland oilman Clayton Williams. He narrowly lost to Ann Richards, who spent $12 million. The 1990 record, however, was shattered by the 2002 gubernatorial election, in which Tony Sanchez's and

Rick Perry's campaigns spent a combined record of more than $95 million. Sanchez outspent Perry by more than two to one ($67 million to $28 million) in the race for governor. Despite his big spending, however, Sanchez lost by 20 percent.[4] Even though $95 million set a new record for spending in a Texas race, it ranks as only the fifth most expensive gubernatorial race. California's 2010 gubernatorial contest, which cost an estimated $250 million, ranks first, followed by New York's gubernatorial race in 2002 ($148 million) and California's gubernatorial races in 1998 ($130 million) and 2002 ($110 million).

Many Texans are qualified to hold public office, but relatively few can afford to pay their own campaign expenses (as gubernatorial candidates Clayton Williams and Tony Sanchez and lieutenant gubernatorial candidate David Dewhurst did). Others are unwilling to undertake fundraising drives designed to attract significant campaign contributions.

Candidates need to raise large amounts of cash at local, state, and national levels. Successful Houston City Council candidates often require from $150,000 (for district races) to $250,000 (for at-large races), and mayoral candidates may need $2 million or more. In 2003, Houston businessman Bill White spent a record $8.6 million on his mayoral election, including $2.2 million of his own money. Some individuals and **political action committees (PACs)** which are organizations created to collect and distribute contributions to political campaigns, donate because they agree with a candidate's position on the issues. The motivations of others, however, may be questionable. In return for their contributions, big donors receive access to elected officials. Many politicians and contributors assert that access does not mean that donors gain control of officials' policymaking decisions. Yet others, such as former Texas House Speaker Pete Laney, attribute the decline in voter participation to a growing sense that average citizens have no voice in the political process because they cannot afford to make large financial donations to candidates.

Both federal and state laws have been enacted to regulate various aspects of campaign financing. Texas laws on the subject, however, are relatively weak and tend to emphasize reporting of contributions with few limits on the amounts of the donations. Federal laws are more restrictive, featuring both reporting requirements and limits on contributions to a candidate's political campaign by individuals and PACs. In 1989, chicken magnate Lonnie "Bo" Pilgrim handed out $10,000 checks on the Texas Senate floor, leaving the "payable to" lines blank, as legislators debated reforming the state's workers' compensation laws. Many were surprised to find that Texas had no laws at that time prohibiting such an action. Two years later, the Texas legislature passed laws prohibiting political contributions to members of the legislature while they are in session; and in 1993 Texas voters approved a constitutional amendment establishing the **Texas Ethics Commission.** Among its constitutional duties, this commission requires financial disclosure from public officials. Unlike the Federal Election Campaign Act, however, Texas has no laws that limit political contributions.

Further restricting the amount of money that can be contributed to campaigns is another area of possible reform. However, success in this area has been fairly limited. In 2002, the U.S. Congress passed the long-awaited

political action committee (PAC)
An organizational device used by corporations, labor unions, and other organizations to raise money for campaign contributions.

Texas Ethics Commission
A state agency that enforces state standards for lobbyists and public officials, including registration of lobbyists and reporting of political campaign contributions.

Campaign Reform Act, signed into law by President Bush. This federal law prohibited **soft money**; increased the limits on individual **hard money** (or direct) contributions; and restricted corporations' and labor unions' ability to run "electioneering" ads that feature the names or likenesses of candidates close to Election Day.[5]

Plaintiffs, including former Texas Congressman Ron Paul (R-Clute) and others, challenged the constitutionality of this act, claiming it was an unconstitutional restraint on freedom of speech. In a sharply divided decision, the U.S. Supreme Court upheld the constitutionality of the "soft money" ban in *McConnell v. FEC*, 540 U.S. 93 (2003). Seven years later, however, in a 5–4 decision, the U.S. Supreme Court in *Citizens United v. Federal Election Commission*, 558 U.S. 50 (2010), overturned a provision of the act that banned unlimited **independent expenditures** made by corporations, unions, and nonprofit organizations in federal elections. This decision was widely criticized by Democrats and by some members of the Republican Party as judicial activism that would give corporations and unions unlimited power in federal elections. In his 2010 State of the Union address, President Obama admonished the Supreme Court, stating, "Last week, the Supreme Court reversed a century of law to open the floodgates for special interests, including foreign corporations, to spend without limit in our elections. Well, I don't think American elections should be bankrolled by America's most powerful interests, or worse, by foreign entities."

That same year, a nine-judge federal appeals court unanimously ruled in *SpeechNow.org v. Federal Election Commission*, 599 F. 3rd 686 (2010), that campaign contribution limits on independent organizations using the funds only for independent expenditures are unconstitutional. The U.S. Supreme Court refused to hear this case on appeal, letting the lower court's decision stand. Decisions in these cases led to creation of **super PACs**, which are independent expenditure–only committees that may raise unlimited sums of money from corporations, unions, nonprofit organizations, and individuals. Super PACs are then able to spend unlimited sums to openly support or oppose political candidates. By 2012, super PACs had been in existence for less than two years; but 1,310 of these PACs reported having raised more than $828 million and having spent more than $609 million on the 2012 presidential candidates. Some of the better-known, better-funded super PACs of the 2012 presidential election included "Priorities USA Action" (supporting Barack Obama), "Restore Our Future" (supporting Mitt Romney), "American Crossroads" (headed by Republican strategist Karl Rove), and "Make Us Great Again" (supporting Rick Perry). Founded by Perry's former chief of staff, Mike Toomey, "Make Us Great Again" contributors included Dallas businessman Harold Simmons, Dallas tax consultant Brint Ryan, Houston attorney Tony Buzbee, Dallas energy executive Kelcy Warren, and Midland energy executive Javaid Anwar. "Make Us Great Again" spent approximately $4 million on Perry's behalf. In a parody of campaign finance rules, comedian Stephen Colbert formed his own super PAC—"Americans for a Better Tomorrow, Tomorrow," also known as "Stephen Colbert's Super PAC." By mid-2014, there were more than 1,000 organized super PACs.

Campaign Reform Act
Enacted by the U.S. Congress and signed by President George W. Bush in 2002, this law restricts donations of "soft money" and "hard money" for election campaigns, but its effect has been limited by federal court decisions.

soft money
Unregulated political donations made to national political parties or independent expenditures on behalf of a candidate.

hard money
Campaign money donated directly to candidates or political parties and restricted in amount by federal law.

independent expenditures
Expenditures that pay for political campaign communications that expressly advocate the nomination, election, or defeat of a clearly identified candidate but are not given to, or made at the request of, the candidate's campaign.

super PAC
Independent expenditure–only committees that may raise unlimited sums of money from corporations, unions, nonprofit organizations, and individuals.

Although the *Citizens United* decision removed limits on how much money can be given to or spent by outside groups on behalf of federal candidates, it did not address limits on campaign contributions to candidates or committees by individual donors. In another sharply divided decision, the U.S. Supreme Court in *McCutcheon v. FEC*, 572 U.S. ___ (2014), struck down the aggregate limits on the amount an individual may contribute during a two-year period to all federal candidates, parties, and political action committees combined. By a vote of 5–4, the Court ruled that the aggregate limit an individual could donate to candidates for federal office, political parties, and political action committees per election per cycle ($117,000, including a limit of $46,200, in 2012, although amounts are adjusted annually for inflation) was unconstitutional under the First Amendment. The amount that can be donated to a specific candidate, political party, or PAC is limited, however. As with the *Citizens United* decision, several groups criticized this ruling as a further erosion of protections against undue influence in elections by a small portion of the electorate. According to the Center for Responsive Politics, only 591 donors out of an estimated 310 million Americans (approximately .0000019 percent of the population) gave the maximum of $46,200 to federal candidates during the 2012 election cycle.[6]

Texas's state campaign finance laws have focused on making contributor information more easily available to citizens. Restrictions on the amount of donations apply only to some judicial candidates. Treasurers of campaign committees and candidates are required to file periodically with the Texas Ethics Commission. With limited exceptions, these reports must be filed electronically. Sworn statements list all contributions received and expenditures made during designated reporting intervals. Candidates who fail to file these reports are subject to a fine.

In 2003, the Texas legislature passed a law requiring officials of cities with a population of more than 100,000 and trustees of school districts with enrollments of 5,000 or more to disclose the sources of their income, as well as the value of their stocks and their real estate holdings. In addition, candidates for state political offices must identify employers and occupations of people contributing $500 or more to their campaigns and publicly report "cash on hand." The measure also prohibits state legislators from lobbying for clients before state agencies.

Recent court decisions and loopholes in disclosure laws have opened the door for "dark money," money spent on elections by anonymous donors. In 2013, a bill passed by the Texas Legislature that would have required nonprofit organizations that spend $25,000 or more on political campaigns to publicly disclose contributors who donate more than $1,000 was vetoed by Governor Perry. One conservative dark money group, "Empower Texans," filed a federal lawsuit in 2014 to prevent the Texas Ethics Commission from compelling them to disclose their list of donors, asserting a right to keep donors' names confidential.

Federal and state campaign finance laws have largely failed to cope with buying influence through transfers of money in the form of campaign contributions. It may well be that as long as campaigns are funded by private sources, they will remain inadequately regulated.

✔ **5.1 Learning Check**

1. True or False: Most Texas voters learn about candidates through newspaper editorials.
2. Which state commission requires financial disclosure from public officials?

Answers on p. 197.

Racial and Ethnic Politics

LO5.2   Describe the role that race and ethnicity play in politics, focusing on the importance of minority voters.

Racial and ethnic factors are strong influences on Texas politics, and they shape political campaigns. Slightly more than half of Texas's total population is composed of Latinos (chiefly Mexican Americans) and African Americans, making Texas a majority-minority state. Politically, the state's historical ethnic and racial minorities wield enough voting strength to decide any statewide election and determine the outcomes of local contests in areas where their numbers are concentrated. Large majorities of Texas's African American and Latino voters participate in Democratic primaries and vote for Democratic candidates in general elections. However, increasing numbers of African Americans and Latinos claim to be politically independent and do not identify with either the Republican or the Democratic party.

Latinos

Early in the 21st century, candidates for elective office in Texas, and most other parts of the United States, recognized the potential of the Latino vote. Most Anglo candidates use Spanish phrases in their speeches, advertise in Spanish-language media (television, radio, and newspapers), and voice their concern for issues important to the Latino community (such as bilingual education and immigration). In each presidential election since 2000, candidates from both major political parties included appearances in Latino communities and before national Latino organizations, such as the League of United Latin American Citizens (LULAC) and the National Council of La Raza, as a part of their campaign strategy. Such appearances recognize the political clout of Latinos in the Republican and Democratic presidential primaries, as well as in the general election.

Although Mexican Americans played an important role in South Texas politics throughout the 20th century, not until the 1960s and early 1970s did they begin to have a major political impact at the state level. A central turning point was during the late 1960s with the creation of a third-party movement, La Raza Unida Party. Founded in 1969 by José Ángel Gutiérrez of Crystal City and others, La Raza Unida fielded numerous candidates at the local and state levels and mobilized many Mexican Americans who had been politically inactive. It also attracted others who had identified with the Democratic Party but who had grown weary of the party's unresponsiveness to the needs and concerns of the Mexican American community. By the end of the 1970s, however, Raza Unida had disintegrated. According to Ruben Bonilla, former president of LULAC, the main reason Raza Unida did not survive as a meaningful voice for Texas's Mexican American population was "the maturity of the Democratic Party to accept Hispanics."

In the 1980s, Mexican American election strategy became more sophisticated as a new generation of college-educated Latinos sought public office and assumed leadership roles in political organizations. Although Latinos are more likely to vote for Democratic candidates, Republican candidates such as George W. Bush have succeeded in winning the support of many Latino voters, and Republican candidates fare better among Latino voters in Texas than they do nationally. Successful GOP candidates emphasize family issues and target heavily Latino areas for campaign appearances and media advertising. Gubernatorial candidate Greg Abbott's first post-primary ad in 2014 was in Spanish and featured his sister-in-law explaining to other Latinos that Abbott shared their values and beliefs. Coincidentally, the ad highlighted that his wife, Cecilia, would be the first Latina First Lady in Texas history.

In 2003, Governor Perry appointed Victor Carrillo to the Texas Railroad Commission. When Carrillo lost his bid for reelection in the 2010 Republican primary, he blamed his defeat by an unknown and underfinanced candidate on his Hispanic surname and its inability to attract support among Republican voters. Governor Perry also appointed two Latino secretaries of state (Henry Cuellar in 2001 and Esperanza "Hope" Andrade in 2008), one Texas Supreme Court justice (Eva Guzman in 2009), and one judge to the Texas Court of Criminal Appeals (Elsa Alcala in 2011). In 2010, Justice Guzman became the first Latina to win a statewide election.

Many members of the Democratic Party believe it is important to have Latino nominees for high-level statewide offices in order to attract Latino voters to the polls. They argue that because the majority of Latinos are more likely to support Democratic candidates, a higher voter turnout will elect more Democrats to office. Focusing on registering and turning out voters among the increasing Latino population, Democratic strategists hope to turn Texas into a Democratic stronghold again (see Chapter 4 Selected Reading, "What Must Happen for Texas to Turn Blue").

In 2002, Laredo businessman Tony Sanchez Jr. became the first Latino candidate nominated for governor by a major party in Texas. Challenged for the Democratic nomination by former Texas attorney general Dan Morales, on March 1, 2002, the two men held the first Spanish-language gubernatorial campaign debate in U.S. history. Underscoring its strategy to attract more Latino voters, in 2012 the Democratic Party selected the first Latino chair of a major political party in Texas when it chose Gilberto Hinojosa to be its state chair. In 2014, Latino candidates for statewide office included the Democratic nominee for lieutenant governor, Leticia Van De Putte, and the Republican nominee for commissioner of the general land office, George P. Bush (son of former Florida governor Jeb Bush and his Latina wife, nephew of former Texas governor and president George W. Bush, and grandson of former president George H. W. Bush).

By early 2015, a substantial number of Latinos held elected office, including the following:

- Three statewide positions (commissioner of the general land office, one supreme court justice, and one judge on the Court of Criminal Appeals)
- One U.S. senator
- Five U.S. representative seats in Texas's congressional delegation
- 42 legislative seats in the Texas legislature
- More than 2,100 of the remaining 5,200 elected positions in the state

Among the many issues, such as bilingual education and political representation, affecting the Latino community, none is more relevant than immigration reform. The Latino community's political impact was clear in the debate over immigration laws, when millions of Latinos in Texas took part in demonstrations or boycotts in early 2006. In addition, in 2010, an estimated 28,000 people participated in a demonstration in Dallas protesting Arizona's immigration law that gave law enforcement broad authority to inquire about immigration status. A similar bill was defeated in the Texas legislature in 2011. Another piece of legislation, however, that would require people to prove U.S. citizenship or legal residence before they can get or renew a Texas driver's license passed and took effect in 2011.[7] In 2014, Governor Perry ordered 1,000 National Guard troops to the Texas-Mexico Border to limit illegal immigration. As the Latino population continues to grow, the immigration issue will in large part determine many Latinos' party support.

Unlike in the past, Democratic candidates can no longer assume they have Latino voter support in statewide electoral contests. Latinos' voting behavior indicates that they respond to candidates and issues, not to a particular political party. Further divisions occur between socioeconomic levels, with Hispanics who earn more than $50,000 per year more likely to support Republican candidates than Hispanics with annual incomes of less than $50,000. Although both national and state Republican Party platforms discourage bilingual education and urge stricter immigration controls, Republican candidates frequently do not endorse these positions. Often, successful Republican candidates actually distance themselves from their party, especially in the Latino community. For instance, during a Republican presidential candidate debate in 2011, Governor Perry drew criticism from his opponents by defending his support for a state law that allows some undocumented students who graduate from a high school in Texas and are working toward legal status to qualify for in-state tuition at Texas public colleges and universities.[8]

In 2012, the Republican National Committee launched the Growth and Opportunity Project, with a list of recommendations and strategies designed to expand the base of the party and win more elections. Among its recommendations, this report encouraged the Republican Party to focus its messaging, strategy, outreach, and budget efforts to gain new supporters and voters

In an effort to win support among Latino voters, 2014 Republican gubernatorial nominee Greg Abbott launched a website in Spanish.

Source: www.gregabbott.com

CRITICAL THINKING

How might developing a website in Spanish win support among Latino voters?

in the Hispanic community (as well as in other racial/demographic communities including Pacific Islanders, African Americans, Asian Americans, Native Americans, women, and youth). In 2013, in an effort to garner greater support among Latinos, a "figurative memo" (informal agreement) went out to all Texas Republican lawmakers urging them not to introduce bills that would embarrass the party with Latino voters.[9]

The sheer size of the Latino population causes politicians to solicit their support because Latino voters can represent the margin of victory for a successful candidate. Lower levels of political activity than the population at large, however, both in registering to vote and in voting, limit an even greater impact of the Latino electorate.

African Americans

In April 1990, the Texas State Democratic Executive Committee filled a candidate vacancy by nominating Potter County court-at-law judge Morris Overstreet, an African American Democrat, for a seat on the Texas Court of Criminal Appeals. Because the Republican candidate, Louis Sturns, was also African American, this historic action guaranteed the state's voters would elect the first African American to statewide office in Texas. Overstreet won in 1990 and again in 1994. He served until 1998, when he ran unsuccessfully for Texas attorney general. Governor George W. Bush appointed

Republican Michael Williams to the Texas Railroad Commission in 1999. This African American commissioner was elected to a six-year term in 2002 and again in 2008. Williams stepped down from the Texas Railroad Commission in 2011 to make an unsuccessful run for Congress, but in August 2012 he was appointed by Governor Perry as commissioner of education.

The appointment of Justice Wallace Bernard Jefferson to the Texas Supreme Court in 2001 made him the first African American to serve on the court. He and another African American, Dale Wainwright, were elected to that court in 2002 and again in 2008. Jefferson again made history in 2004 when Governor Perry appointed him as chief justice. Both Jefferson and Wainwright resigned their respective offices in 2013. Two Anglo male justices replaced them on the court. In 2002, former Dallas mayor Ron Kirk became the first African American nominated by either major party in Texas as its candidate for U.S. senator. Although unsuccessful in the general election, Kirk's candidacy appeared to many political observers as an important breakthrough for African American politicians. Kirk later was appointed U.S. Trade Representative by President Barack Obama and in 2013 resigned to join a Dallas law firm. In 2014, no African Americans from either party were candidates for statewide office.

Since the 1930s, African American Texans have tended to identify with the Democratic Party. With a voting-age population in excess of 1 million, they constitute roughly 10 percent of the state's potential voters. As demonstrated in recent electoral contests, approximately 80 percent of Texas's African American citizens say they are Democrats, and only 5 percent are declared Republicans. The remainder are independents. In recent years, African American support for the Democratic Party and its candidates has declined slightly. By early 2015, a number of African Americans held elected office, including the following:

- Five U.S. representative seats in Texas's congressional delegation
- 19 seats in the Texas legislature
- More than 500 of the remaining 5,200 elected positions in the state

✔ 5.2 Learning Check

1. Which party have Latinos traditionally supported?
2. True or False: In 2014, no African Americans were holding statewide elected office.

Answers on p. 197.

Women in Politics

LO5.3   Describe the role that women have played in Texas politics and how that role has evolved.

Texas women did not begin to vote and hold public office for three-quarters of a century after Texas joined the Union. Until 1990, only four women had won a statewide office in Texas, including two-term governor Miriam A. ("Ma") Ferguson (1925–1927 and 1933–1935). Ferguson owed her office to supporters of her husband, Jim, who had been impeached and removed from the governorship in 1917. Nevertheless, in 1990, Texas female voters outnumbered male voters, and Ann Richards was elected governor. After 1990, the number of women elected to statewide office increased dramatically.

In the early 1990s, Texas women served as mayors in about 150 of the state's towns and cities, including the top four in terms of population (Houston,

Dallas, San Antonio, and El Paso). Mayor of Dallas Annette Strauss (1988–1991) was fond of greeting out-of-state visitors with this message: "Welcome to Texas, where men are men and women are mayors."

In 2010, when Annise Parker was sworn in as mayor of Houston, she made history as the first openly gay mayor of a major U.S. city. Although Parker had been open about her sexual orientation during her previous elections as the city's comptroller and, before that, as a city council member, her November 2009 election as mayor of the nation's fourth-largest city received national media attention. The impact of women's voting power was also evident in several elections early in the 21st century, when women (U.S. Senator Kay Bailey Hutchison and state comptroller Carole Keeton Rylander) led all candidates on either ticket in votes received. In 2013, Governor Perry appointed Indian American Nandita Berry the 109th Texas secretary of state. The Democratic primary election results in 2014 marked the first election in which female candidates held the top two positions on a party's ticket in Texas. The Democratic Party nominated Wendy Davis for governor and Leticia Van De Putte for lieutenant governor. Republicans had no female nominees for statewide office in 2014.

Female candidates also succeeded in winning an increasing number of seats in legislative bodies. In 1971, no women served in Texas's congressional delegation, and only two served in the Texas legislature. As a result of the 2014 election, in 2015 the number of women in Texas's congressional delegation was 3. The number of women in the Texas legislature was 37 (7 in the Senate and 30 in the House of Representatives), a decline from the 44 women who served in the 81st legislature (2009). The expanded presence of women in public office is changing public policy. For example, increased punishment for family violence and sexual abuse of children, together with a renewed focus on public education, can be attributed in large part to the presence of women in policymaking positions.

Despite their electoral victories in Texas and elsewhere across the nation, fewer women than men seek elective public office. Several reasons account for this situation, chief of which is difficulty in raising money to pay campaign expenses. Other reasons also discourage women from seeking public office. Although women enjoy increasing freedom, they still shoulder more responsibilities for family and home than men do (even in two-career families). Some mothers feel obliged to care for children in the home until their children finish high school. Such parental obligations, together with age-old prejudices, deny women their rightful place in government. Yet as customs, habits, and attitudes change, new opportunities for women in public service are expanding.

> ✓ **5.3 Learning Check**
>
> 1. True or False: Women candidates received the most votes for a single office in some elections early in the 21st century.
> 2. By 2015, how many women had served as governor of Texas?
>
> Answers on p. 197.

Voting

★ **LO5.4** Explain the complexities of voting and how the voting process promotes, and inhibits, voter participation.

The U.S. Supreme Court has declared the right to vote the "preservative" of all other rights.[10] For most Texans, voting is their principal political activity.

For many, it is their only exercise in practicing Texas politics. Casting a ballot brings individuals and their government together for a moment and reminds people anew that they are part of a political system.

Obstacles to Voting

The right to vote has not always been as widespread in the United States as it is today. **Universal suffrage**, by which almost all citizens 18 years of age and older can vote, did not become a reality in Texas until the mid-1960s. Although most devices to prevent people from voting have been abolished, their legacy remains.

Adopted after the Civil War (1861–1865), the Fourteenth and Fifteenth Amendments to the U.S. Constitution were intended to prevent denial of the right to vote based on race. But for the next 100 years, African American citizens in Texas and other states of the former Confederacy, as well as many Latinos, were prevented from voting by one barrier after another—legal or otherwise. For example, the white-robed Ku Klux Klan and other lawless groups used terrorist tactics to keep African Americans from voting. Northeast Texas was the focus of the Klan's operations in the Lone Star State.[11]

Literacy Tests Beginning in the 1870s, as a means to prevent minority people from voting, some southern states (although not Texas) began requiring prospective voters to take a screening test that conditioned **voter registration** on a person's literacy. Individuals who could not pass these **literacy tests** were prohibited from registering. Some states used constitutional interpretation or citizenship knowledge tests to deny voting rights. These tests usually consisted of difficult and abstract questions concerning a person's knowledge of the U.S. Constitution or understanding of issues supposedly related to citizenship. In no way, however, did these questions measure a citizen's ability to cast an informed vote. The federal Voting Rights Act of 1965 made literacy tests illegal.

Grandfather Clause Another device, not used in Texas but enacted by other southern states to deny suffrage to minorities, was the **grandfather clause**. Laws with this clause provided that persons who could exercise the right to vote before 1867, or their descendants, would be exempt from educational, property, or tax requirements for voting. Because African Americans had not been allowed to vote before adoption of the Fifteenth Amendment in 1870, grandfather clauses were used along with literacy tests to prevent African Americans from voting while assuring this right to many impoverished and illiterate whites. The U.S. Supreme Court, in *Guinn v. United States* (1915), declared the grandfather clause unconstitutional because it violated the equal voting rights guaranteed by the Fifteenth Amendment.

Poll Tax Beginning in 1902, Texas required that citizens pay a special tax, called the **poll tax**, to become eligible to vote. The cost was $1.75 ($1.50, plus $0.25 that was optional with each county). For the next 64 years, many Texans—especially low-income persons, including disproportionately large numbers of African Americans and Mexican Americans—failed to pay their poll tax during the designated four-month period from October 1 to January

universal suffrage
Voting is open for virtually all persons 18 years of age or older.

voter registration
A qualified voter must register with the county voting registrar, who compiles lists of qualified voters residing in each voting precinct.

literacy tests
Although not used in Texas as a prerequisite for voter registration, the test was designed and administered in ways intended to prevent African Americans and Latinos from voting.

grandfather clause
Although not used in Texas, the law exempted people from educational, property, or tax requirements for voting if they were qualified to vote before 1867 or were descendents of such persons.

poll tax
A tax levied in Texas from 1902 until voters amended the Texas Constitution in 1966 to eliminate it; failure to pay the annual tax (usually $1.75) made a citizen ineligible to vote in party primaries or in special and general elections.

31. This failure, in turn, disqualified them from voting during the following 12 months in party primaries and in any general or special election. As a result, African American voter participation declined from approximately 100,000 in the 1890s to about 5,000 in 1906. With ratification of the Twenty-Fourth Amendment to the U.S. Constitution in January 1964, the poll tax was abolished as a prerequisite for voting in national elections. Then, in *Harper v. Virginia State Board of Elections*, 383 U.S. 663 (1966), the U.S. Supreme Court invalidated all state laws that made payment of a poll tax a prerequisite for voting in state elections.

All-White Primaries The so-called **white primary**, a product of political and legal maneuvering within the southern states, was designed to deny African Americans and some Latinos access to the Democratic primary.[12] Following Reconstruction, Texas, like most of the South, was predominantly a one-party (Democratic) state. Between 1876 and 1926, the Republican Party held only one statewide primary in Texas. Thus, the Democratic primary was the main election in every even-numbered year.

White Democrats nominated white candidates, who almost always won the general elections. The U.S. Supreme Court had long held that the Fourteenth and Fifteenth Amendments, as well as successive civil rights laws, provided protection against public acts of discrimination, but they did not protect against private acts of discrimination. In 1923, the Texas legislature passed a law explicitly prohibiting African Americans from voting in Democratic primaries. When the U.S. Supreme Court declared this law unconstitutional, the Texas legislature enacted another law giving the executive committee of each party the power to decide who could participate in its primaries. The State Democratic Executive Committee immediately adopted a resolution that limited party membership to whites only, which in effect allowed only whites to vote in Democratic primaries. This practice lasted from 1923 to 1944, when the U.S. Supreme Court declared it unconstitutional in *Smith v. Allwright*, 321 U.S. 649 (1944).[13]

Racial Gerrymandering Gerrymandering is the practice of manipulating legislative district lines to underrepresent persons of a political party or group. "Packing" black voters into a single district or "cracking" them to make black voters a minority in two or more districts both illustrate racial gerrymandering. Although racial gerrymandering that discriminates against minority voters is disallowed, federal law allows **affirmative racial gerrymandering** that results in the creation of "majority-minority" districts (also called minority-opportunity districts) favoring election of more racial and ethnic minority candidates. These districts must be reasonable in their configuration and cannot be based solely on race. In *Shaw v. Reno*, 509 U.S. 630 (1993), the U.S. Supreme Court condemned two extremely odd-shaped African American–minority-opportunity districts in North Carolina.

A controversial redistricting plan adopted by the Texas legislature in 2003 to draw new U.S. congressional districts was challenged both by the Texas Democratic Party and by minority groups, contending it diluted minority voting strength. Although the primary purpose of the plan, as crafted by U.S.

white primary
A nominating system designed to prevent African Americans and some Latinos from participating in Democratic primaries from 1923 to 1944.

gerrymandering
Drawing the boundaries of a district designed to affect representation of a political party or group in a legislative chamber, city council, commissioners court, or other representative body.

affirmative racial gerrymandering
Drawing the boundaries of a district designed to favor representation by a member of a historical minority group (e.g., African Americans) in a legislative chamber, city council, commissioners court, or other representative body.

provided in Spanish throughout the state and in Vietnamese and Chinese in Harris County and Houston.

A bill passed by the Texas legislature in 2011 that required voters to provide photo identification to cast a ballot failed to obtain Department of Justice preclearance in August 2012. Following the U.S. Supreme Court's decision in *Shelby County v. Holder*, Texas Attorney Greg Abbott announced that the state's voter ID law that had been challenged by the U.S. Department of Justice "[would] take effect immediately" and tweeted:

> "Eric Holder can no longer deny #VoterID in #Texas after today's #SCOTUS decision. #txlege #tcot #txgop"
>
> —*Greg Abbott (@GregAbbott_TX) JUNE 25,2013*

For a detailed discussion about the photo identification requirement, see this chapter's Point/Counterpoint feature.

The National Voter Registration Act, or **motor-voter law**, permits registration by mail; at welfare, disability assistance, and motor vehicle licensing agencies; or at military recruitment centers. People can register to vote when they apply for, or renew, driver's licenses or when they visit a public assistance office. Motor vehicle offices and voter registration agencies are required to provide voter registration services to applicants. Using an appropriate state or federal voter registration form, Texas citizens can also apply for voter registration or update their voter registration data by mail. If citizens believe their voting rights have been violated in any way, federal administrative and judicial agencies, such as the U.S. Department of Justice, are available for assistance.

Amendments to the U.S. Constitution have also expanded the American electorate. The Fifteenth Amendment prohibits the denial of voting rights because of race; the Nineteenth Amendment precludes denial of suffrage on the basis of gender; the Twenty-Fourth Amendment prohibits states from requiring payment of a poll tax or any other tax as a condition for voting; and the Twenty-Sixth Amendment forbids setting the minimum voting age above 18 years.

Two Trends in Suffrage From our overview of suffrage in Texas, two trends emerge. First, voting rights have steadily expanded to include virtually all persons, of both genders, who are 18 years of age or older. Second, there has been a movement toward uniformity of voting policies among the 50 states. However, democratization of the ballot has been pressed on the states largely by the U.S. Congress, by federal judges, and by presidents who have enforced voting laws and judicial orders.

Voter Turnout

Now that nearly all legal barriers to the ballot have been swept away, the road to the voting booth seems clear for rich and poor alike; for historical minority groups, as well as for the historical majority; and for individuals of all races, colors, and creeds. But universal suffrage has not resulted in a corresponding increase in voter turnout, either nationally or in Texas.

motor-voter law
Legislation requiring certain government offices (e.g., motor vehicle licensing agencies) to offer voter registration applications to clients.

Voter turnout is the percentage of the voting-age population casting ballots. In Texas, turnout is higher in presidential elections than in nonpresidential elections. Although this pattern reflects the national trend, electoral turnout in Texas tends to be significantly lower than in the nation as a whole. Even with George W. Bush running for reelection in the 2004 presidential election, Texas ranked below the national average in voter turnout, at 46 percent of the voting-age population, compared with the national average of 55 percent. According to the Center for the Study of the American Electorate, national turnout was even lower in 2012. Texas had the fifth lowest turnout in the nation, at 44 percent of the voting-age population, compared with the national average of 54 percent. Texas's lower voter turnout rates can be explained in part by the lower percentage of eligible voters in the state. Researchers at the U.S. Election Project at George Mason University estimated that 14 percent of the Lone Star State's population was ineligible to vote in 2012 because of citizenship status. Another 0.2 percent of Texas's population was ineligible to vote because of their status as convicted felons who had not completed serving their sentences. Therefore, voter turnout in Texas fares better when the voting-eligible population (rather than voting-age population) is considered. According to the United States Election Project, the 2012 statewide general election turnout rate of the voting-eligible population in Texas was slightly under 50 percent compared with a national turnout rate of more than 58 percent.[19]

Due in part to less media attention, voter turnout in state and local elections is usually lower than in presidential elections. For instance, the 2010 Texas gubernatorial election yielded only a 27 percent turnout. Although few citizens believe their vote will determine an election outcome, some races have actually been won by a single vote. In local elections at the city or school district level, a turnout of 20 percent is relatively high. Among the five largest cities conducting city council elections in Texas in 2013, none yielded a turnout greater than 20 percent. These figures illustrate one of the ironies in politics: People are less likely to participate at the level of government where they can potentially have the greatest influence.

Low citizen participation in elections has been attributed to the influence of pollsters and media consultants, voter fatigue resulting from too many elections, negative campaigning by candidates, lack of information about candidates and issues, and feelings of isolation from government. Members of the Texas legislature determined that low voter turnout was caused by governmental entities holding too many elections. To cure "turnout burnout," the legislature passed a law that limits most elections to two uniform election dates each year: the second Saturday in May and the first Tuesday after the first Monday in November. However, this change has failed to yield a higher voter turnout as anticipated. For instance, in 2013, less than 6 percent of the voting-age population participated in the state's constitutional amendment election. Elections specifically exempted by statute that can be held on nonuniform dates include the following:

- Runoff elections
- Local option elections under the Alcoholic Beverage Code

voter turnout
The percentage of the voting-age population casting ballots in an election.

- Bond or tax levy elections for school districts or community college districts
- Emergency elections called for or approved by the governor
- Elections to fill vacancies in the two chambers of the Texas legislature
- Elections to fill vacancies in the Texas delegation to the U.S. House of Representatives
- Recall elections as authorized by city charters[20]

People decide to vote or not to vote in the same way they make most other decisions: on the basis of anticipated consequences. A strong impulse to vote may stem from peer pressure, self-interest, or a sense of duty toward country, state, local community, political party, or interest group. People also decide whether to vote based on costs measured in time, money, experience, information, job, and other resources.

Cultural, socioeconomic, and ethnic or racial factors also contribute to the low voter turnout in the Lone Star State. As identified in Chapter 1, some elements of Texas's political culture place little emphasis on the importance of voting.

Of all the socioeconomic influences on voting, education is by far the strongest. Statistics clearly indicate that as educational level rises, so does the likelihood of voting, assuming all other socioeconomic factors remain constant. Educated people usually have more income and leisure time for voting; moreover, education enhances one's ability to learn about political parties, candidates, and issues. Education also strengthens voter efficacy (the belief that one's vote makes a difference). In addition, income strongly affects voter turnout. According to the U.S. Census Bureau, in 2012 Texas ranked eighth in the nation in poverty, with 17.2 percent of the population living below the poverty level. People of lower income often lack access to the polls, information about the candidates, or opportunities to learn about the system. Income levels and their impact on electoral turnout can be seen in the 2012 general election. For example, Starr County, with a median household income of less than $25,000, had a turnout of slightly over 38 percent of its registered voters. By contrast, Collin County, with a median income of more than $83,000, experienced a turnout of almost 70 percent of its registered voters.

Although far less important than education and income, gender and age also affect voting behavior. In the United States, women are slightly more likely to vote than men. Young people (ages 18–25) have the lowest voter turnout of any age group. Nevertheless, participation by young people has increased in the last 10 years. The highest voter turnout is among middle-aged Americans (ages 40–64).

Race and ethnicity also influence voting behavior. Historically, the turnout rate for African Americans has remained substantially below that for Anglos. African Americans tend to be younger, less educated, and poorer than Anglos. In 2012, however, perhaps because of President Obama's candidacy, the percentage of African Americans who registered to vote and voted exceeded the state average for all races. Although Latino voter turnout rates in Texas are slightly below the state average in both primaries and general elections, findings by scholars indicate that the gap is narrowing. Latino voter registration rates for eligible voters in 2012 was 12 percent below that of Anglos and more than 19 percent below that of African Americans, and their voting rate remained approximately two-thirds of the state average.[21]

Administering Elections

In Texas, as in other states, determining voting procedures is essentially a state responsibility. The Texas Constitution authorizes the legislature to provide for the administration of elections. State lawmakers, in turn, have made the secretary of state the chief elections officer for Texas but have left most details of administering elections to county officials.

All election laws currently in effect in the Lone Star State are compiled into one body of law, the **Texas Election Code**.[22] In administering this legal code, however, state and party officials must protect voting rights guaranteed by federal law.

Qualifications for Voting To be eligible to vote in Texas, a person must meet the following qualifications:

- Be a native-born or naturalized citizen of the United States
- Be at least 18 years of age on Election Day
- Be a resident of the state and county for at least 30 days immediately preceding Election Day
- Be a resident of the area covered by the election on Election Day
- Be a registered voter for at least 30 days immediately preceding Election Day
- Not be a convicted felon (unless sentence, probation, and parole are completed)
- Not be declared mentally incompetent by a court of law[23]

Most adults who live in Texas meet the first four qualifications for voting, but registration is required before a person can vote. Anyone serving a jail sentence as a result of a misdemeanor conviction or not finally convicted of a felony is not disqualified from voting. The Texas Constitution, however, bars from voting anyone who is incarcerated, on parole, or on probation as a result of a felony conviction and anyone who is "mentally incompetent as determined by a court." A convicted felon may vote immediately after completing a sentence or following a full pardon. (For examples of misdemeanors and felonies, see Table 12.1 on page 439.) Voter registration is intended to determine in advance whether prospective voters meet all the qualifications prescribed by law.

Most states, including Texas, use a permanent registration system. Under this plan, voters register once and remain registered unless they change their mailing address and fail to notify the voting registrar within three years or lose their eligibility to register in some other way. However, a story published in the *Houston Chronicle* in 2012 revealed that, as a result of outdated

Texas Election Code
The body of state law concerning parties, primaries, and elections.

computer programs and faulty procedures, more than 1.5 million voters in Texas were purged from the voting rolls. It was reported that the registrations of one out of every 10 Texas voters was currently suspended (one out of every five Texas voters under 30). In Collin County, 70 percent of the voters who were removed from voter registration rolls were actually able to prove their eligibility.[24] Following the voter roll purge controversy, Texas Secretary of State Hope Andrade submitted her resignation to Governor Perry on November 20, 2012.

Because the requirement of voter registration may deter voting, the Texas Election Code provides for voter registration centers in addition to those sites authorized by Congress under the motor-voter law. Thus, Texans may also register at local marriage license offices, in public high schools, with any volunteer deputy registrar, or in person at the office of the county voting registrar. Students away at college may choose to reregister using their college address as their residence if they want to vote locally. Otherwise, they must request an absentee ballot or be in their hometown during early voting or on Election Day if they wish to cast a ballot.

Between November 1 and November 15 of each odd-numbered year, the registrar mails to every registered voter in the county a registration certificate that is effective for the succeeding two voting years. Postal authorities may not forward a certificate mailed to the address indicated on the voter's application form to another address; instead, the certificate must be returned to the registrar. This practice enables the county voting registrar to maintain an accurate list of names and mailing addresses of persons to whom voting certificates have been issued. Registration files are open for public inspection in the voting registrar's office, and a statewide registration file is available in Austin at the Elections Division of the Office of the Secretary of State. Although certificates are normally issued in early November, the issuance of new voter registration certificates in 2011 was delayed because of legal battles surrounding redistricting. In early 2012, an order by the U.S. District Court for the Western District of Texas instructed counties to issue the new certificates no later than April 25 of that year.

The color of voter registration certificates mailed to eligible voters differs from the color of the cards sent two years earlier to distinguish the new cards from the old. The Office of the Secretary of State determines the color of voter registration certificates. In 2014, new voter registration certificates were issued in orange and white. Although voter registration certificates are issued after a person registers to vote, one can legally cast a ballot without a certificate by providing some form of identification (such as a driver's license) and signing an affidavit of registration at the polls. However, under the state's law requiring a voter to show a valid photo identification to cast a ballot, the voter's name on the photo identification must appear exactly as it appears on the elections department's registration list. If the name on the photo ID doesn't match exactly but is "substantially similar" to the name on the registration list, the voter will be permitted to cast a ballot as long as the voter signs an affidavit stating that he or she is the same person as the one on the list of registered voters. For this reason, in 2013, Democratic state senator (and 2014 Democratic gubernatorial nominee) Wendy Davis was required to sign an affidavit to prove her identity when she attempted to vote early in the November constitutional amendment election.[25]

Voting Early Opportunities to vote early in Texas are limited to in-person early voting, voting by mail, and facsimile machine voting (for military personnel and their dependents in hostile fire or combat zones). Texas law allows voters to vote "early"—that is, beginning 17 days preceding a scheduled election or first primary and beginning 12 days preceding a runoff primary held in May and other elections. Early voting ends, however, four days before any election or primary. In less populated rural counties, early voting occurs at the courthouse. In more populous urban areas, the county clerk's office accommodates voters by maintaining branch offices for early voting, including at malls, schools, college campuses, and mobile units. Polling places are generally open for early voting on weekdays during the regular business hours of the official responsible for conducting the election. If requested by 15 registered voters within the county, polling places must also be opened on Saturday or Sunday.

Registered voters who qualify may vote by mail during an early voting period. Voting by mail has been available for decades to elderly Texans and those with physical disabilities. Today, anyone meeting any of the following qualifications can vote by mail-in ballot:

- Will not be in his or her county of residence during the entire early voting period and on Election Day
- Is at least age 65
- Is, or will be, physically disabled on Election Day, including those who expect to be confined for childbirth on Election Day
- Is in jail (but not a convicted felon) during the early voting period and on Election Day
- Is in the military or is a dependent of military personnel and has resided in Texas[26]

Since early voting was first used in 1998, the percentage of early voters has consistently been about 20 percent in the general elections. In 2008, however, the Texas secretary of state reported that some counties (Collin and Fort Bend) had early voter turnout in excess of 50 percent of registered voters. Although such measures make voting easier, at least one study indicates that states with longer early-voting periods have experienced a greater decline in voter turnout than states with more restrictive election laws.[27]

Under Texas law, people on space flights can vote electronically from space on Election Day. Six astronauts have cast ballots from space (three of those in presidential elections). The county clerk of the astronaut's home county sends an electronic ballot to the astronaut-voter through NASA, the astronaut votes, and someone in the county clerk's office then decrypts the ballot so it can be counted.[28]

NASA astronaut Michael Fincke, Expedition 18 commander, sent a message from the International Space Station urging all citizens to vote.

NASA

CRITICAL THINKING

With Texas's new law requiring photo identification to vote, how might this affect astronauts' ability to cast ballots from space?

voting precinct
The basic geographic area for conducting primaries and elections; Texas is divided into more than 8,500 voting precincts.

elections administrator
Person appointed to supervise voter registration and voting.

Voting Precincts The basic geographic area for conducting national, state, district, and county elections is the **voting precinct**. Each precinct usually contains between 100 and approximately 2,000 registered voters. Texas has more than 8,500 voting precincts, drawn by the 254 county commissioners courts (a county judge and four commissioners). When a precinct's population exceeds a number prescribed by the Texas Election Code (3,000, 4,000, or 5,000, depending on the county's population), the commissioners court must draw new boundaries.[29] Citizens vote at polling places within their voting precincts or, if voting precincts have been combined for an election, at a polling place convenient to voters in each of the combined voting precincts. Municipal precincts must follow the boundary lines of county-designed voting precincts adjusted to city boundaries. Subject to this restriction, municipal and special district voting precincts are designated by the governing body of each city and special district, respectively.

Election Officials Various county and political party officials administer federal, state, and county elections. Municipal elections and special district elections are the responsibility of their respective jurisdictions (see Chapter 3, "Local Governments"), although they may contract with the county to administer elections. Whereas party officials conduct primary elections, the county clerk or **elections administrator** prepares general election and special election ballots based on certification of candidates by the appropriate authority (that is, the secretary of state for state and district candidates and the county clerk or elections administrator for county candidates). Some counties have officials whose sole responsibility is election administration. In other counties, election administration is one of many responsibilities of the tax assessor-collector or (if designated by the county commissioners court) the county clerk. In 2012, fewer than 30 percent of the counties in Texas employed a full-time elections administrator. There is also a county election commission, which consists of the county judge, county clerk or elections administrator, sheriff, and the chairs of the two major political parties. Commission responsibilities include selecting polling places, printing ballots, and providing supplies and voting equipment.

Point/Counterpoint

THE ISSUE In 2011, the Texas legislature passed a law requiring voters to present one form of photo identification in order to vote. This law, which went into effect in 2013, enhances the penalties for illegal voting from a third-degree felony to a second-degree felony (2 to 20 years in prison and an optional fine of up to $10,000). Attempted illegal voting is a state jail felony (180 days to two years in a state jail and an optional fine of up to $10,000) instead of a class A misdemeanor. In October 2014, shortly before early voting, a U.S. District Court judge ruled the ID law unconstitutional. Because the election was imminent, the Fifth Circuit Court of Appeals permitted the law to be used in the general election. Upon appeal, the U.S. Supreme Court allowed the general election to proceed with the voter ID law in effect. Acceptable forms of photo identification include a driver's license, passport, military ID card, concealed handgun license, or state-issued ID card from the Department of Motor Vehicles.

Should Photo Identification Be a Requirement to Vote?

Arguments For Requiring Photo Identification to Vote

1. *The election process is strengthened.* Requiring a photo ID deters voter fraud and keeps ineligible voters from voting, while restoring and enhancing public confidence in elections. When deceased or other unqualified individuals are on the voter rolls, illegal votes may be cast, canceling out legitimate votes. Since voters do not need to prove their identities at the polls, anyone can vote with anyone else's voter certificate because these documents include no photo. This lax screening process makes it impossible to know how many ineligible voters slip through the system. Requiring a photo ID boosts confidence in the

Arguments Against Requiring Photo Identification to Vote

1. *Voters are disenfranchised and election procedures become increasingly complicated.* Eligible voters should not be needlessly hassled by the state and discouraged or intimidated from exercising their fundamental right to vote without legitimate justification. There is no proof that this extra requirement to vote is needed at all. This regulation is an extreme, costly solution in search of a problem not proven to exist. Almost all evidence of voter fraud involves mail-in ballots. This requirement, however, addresses only voter impersonation at the polls, not mail-in balloting.

Arguments For Requiring Photo Identification to Vote

election process and may promote higher voter turnout.

2. *The integrity of elections is secured.* Requiring voters to show a government-issued photo ID and increasing the criminal penalty for voter fraud helps ensure the integrity of elections. It guarantees continued access to the polls by providing exceptions for certain disabled voters and by authorizing free election ID certificates for eligible voters lacking a photo ID.

3. *No additional burden is placed on citizens.* Currently, photo identification is commonly required to open bank accounts, board airlines, or purchase some items (alcohol, tobacco, or medications). Such safeguards benefit our society and enhance our security. Furthermore, requiring a photo ID to vote is a common practice throughout the United States. By 2012, some form of photo ID was required for voting by 30 states.

Arguments Against Requiring Photo Identification to Vote

2. *Voting among eligible voters is suppressed.* The process of obtaining a photo ID is cumbersome and cost prohibitive for some citizens, even if the state photo ID cards are free. Requiring a photo ID inhibits voting in rural areas, where citizens may have to travel more than 100 miles to a Department of Public Safety (DPS) office. There is no DPS office in 77 of Texas's 254 counties.

3. *A substantial obstacle to the right to vote is created.* Although citizens must show proof of their identity when boarding an airplane or renting movies, these activities are not constitutional rights. Although other states have voter ID laws, this requirement gives Texas one of the most restrictive voter ID laws in the nation. States such as Indiana, Michigan, and Georgia have less stringent voter ID laws that contain photo ID alternatives, such as student IDs, expired driver's licenses, or valid employee ID cards with photographs.

Source: This Point/Counterpoint is abridged and adapted from Rita Barr, "Requiring Voters to Present Voter ID," in *Major Issues of the 82nd Legislature, Regular Session and First Called Session*, Focus Report No. 82-7 (Austin: House Research Organization, Texas House of Representatives, September 30, 2011), 55–56; Mike Ward, "Top 10 Reasons, Pro and Con, on Voter ID," *Austin American Statesman*, January 25, 2011; and Sari Horwitz, "Texas Voter-ID Law is Blocked," *Washington Post*, August 30, 2012. Reprinted by permission.

election judge
Official appointed by the county commissioners court to administer an election in a voting precinct.

County commissioners courts appoint one **election judge** and one alternate judge, each from different political parties, to administer elections in each precinct for a maximum term of two years. Furthermore, each county's commissioners court canvasses and certifies election results. The election judge selects as many clerks as will be needed to assist in conducting general and special elections in a precinct. Clerks must be selected from different political parties. In city elections, the city secretary appoints election judges. In special district elections, election judges are appointed by the district's governing body.

CRITICAL THINKING

What type of voting system does your county use? Why do you believe your county commissioners selected this system?

Voting Systems In general elections, Texas uses three voting systems: paper ballot; optical scan (similar to a Scantron); and direct recording electronic (DRE), also known as a touch screen. In every county, the county commissioners court determines which system will be used. Each system has advantages and disadvantages in such matters as ballot and equipment costs, ease of use by voters, accuracy of counting, labor cost, and time required to count the votes. For example, paper ballots are relatively cheap and easy to use, but counting is a slow, laborious, and error-prone process. Some sparsely populated counties continue to use paper ballots, which must be counted by hand. Some optical scan and DRE systems automatically count each vote as the ballot is cast. Optical scan and DRE systems require mechanical and electronic voting equipment, which is expensive to purchase and store but can reduce election costs when many voters are involved.

After the controversial 2000 presidential election, in which the State of Florida and the U.S. Supreme Court questioned the accuracy of punch-card ballots, both federal and state elected officials evaluated various voting systems. A study conducted by the Office of the Secretary of State of Texas revealed that the 14 Texas counties that used punch-card ballots (including Harris County [Houston]) had many more overvotes (in which voters selected more than one candidate for the same office) than counties using any other balloting method. Punch-card ballot systems are no longer used.

On ballot forms, a list of parties for straight party ticket voting appears first, followed by lists of candidates for national, state, district, and local offices, in that order. (Figure 5.1 shows a sample ballot used in a recent general election.) A list of all write-in candidates who have filed an appropriate declaration is posted in each polling place on the day of an election. The name of one of these candidates may be written in to indicate the voter's selection in the appropriate contest.

In some instances, candidates for nomination or election to an office may request a recount of ballots if they believe vote tabulations were inaccurate. The Texas Election Code also provides detailed procedures for settling disputed elections. Since the 1960s, several changes in voting procedures by both the federal and state governments have been made to encourage full, informed participation in elections.

As a result of the 1975 extension of the federal Voting Rights Act, registration and election materials used in all Texas counties must be printed in both English and Spanish. As noted above, in Harris County and the City of Houston, materials in Chinese and Vietnamese must also be provided. Texas voters can also take voting guides, newspaper endorsements, and other printed material into the voting booth. Disabled voters are ensured access to polling places and the opportunity to cast a secret ballot.

Primary, General, and Special Elections

LO5.5   Identify the differences among primary, general, and special elections.

The electoral process includes the nomination and election of candidates through primary, general, and special elections. A clear distinction must be made between party primaries and general elections. **Primaries** are party functions that allow party members to select nominees to run against the candidates of opposing parties in a general election. **General elections** determine which candidates will fill government offices. These electoral contests are public and are conducted, financed, and administered by state, county, and municipal governments as well as by special districts. This distinction between party primaries and general elections is valid, even though the U.S. Supreme Court has ruled that primaries are of such importance in the selection of general election candidates that they are subject to government regulation.

Thus, even though the state regulates and largely finances primaries, they serve only as a means for political parties to nominate candidates. The general election ballot also includes the names of independent candidates, space for write-in candidates, and names of candidates nominated by party convention because the law does not require nomination by direct primary.

✔ **5.4 Learning Check**

1. Identify four traditional obstacles used in Texas to limit people's right to vote.
2. True or False: The only people who can vote early are those who will be away from their regular polling place on Election Day.

Answers on p. 197.

---

primary
A preliminary election conducted within the party to select candidates who will run for public office in a subsequent general election.

general election
Held in November of even-numbered years to elect county and state officials from among candidates nominated in primaries or (for small parties) in nominating conventions.

No. 0000

GENERAL ELECTION (ELECCIÓN GENERAL)
(CONDADO DE) SOMEWHERE COUNTY, TEXAS
NOVEMBER 4, 2014 (4 DE NOVIEMBRE DE 2014)
SAMPLE BALLOT (BOLETA DE MUESTRA)

INSTRUCTION NOTE: Vote for the candidate of your choice in each race by placing an "X" in the square beside the candidate's name. You may cast a straight-party vote (that is, cast a vote for all the nominees of one party) by placing an "X" in the square beside the name of the party of your choice. If you cast a straight-party vote for all the nominees of one party and also cast a vote for an opponent of one of that party's nominees, your vote for the opponent will be counted as well as your vote for all the other nominees of the party for which the straight-party vote was cast.
(NOTA DE INSTRUCCION: Vote por el candidato de su preferencia para cada candidatura marcando una "X" en el espacio cuadrado a la izquierda del nombre del candidato. Usted podrá votar por todos los candidatos de un solo partido político ("straight-ticket") marcando una "X" en el espacio cuadrado a la izquierda del nombre de ese partido político. Si usted vota por uno de los partidos políticos y también vota por el contrincante de uno de los candidatos de dicho partido político, se contará su voto por el contrincante tanto como su voto por todos los demás candidatos del partido político de su preferencia.)

Candidate for: (Candidatos para:)	Republican Party □ (Partido Republicano)	Democratic Party □ (Partido Demócrata)	Libertarian Party □ (Partido Libertario)	Green Party □ (Partido Verde)	Independent (Independiente)	Write-In (Voto Escrito)
United States Senator (Senador de los Estados Unidos)	□ John Cornyn	□ David M. Alameel	□ Rebecca Paddock	□ Emily "Spicybrown" Sanchez		
United States Representative, District _____ (Representante de los Estados Unidos, Distrito Núm. _____)						
Governor (Gobernador)	□ Greg Abbott	□ Wendy R. Davis	□ Kathie Glass	□ Brandon Parmer		
Lieutenant Governor (Gobernador Teniente)	□ Dan Patrick	□ Leticia Van de Putte	□ Robert D. Butler	□ Chandrakantha Courtney		
Attorney General (Procurador General)	□ Ken Paxton	□ Sam Houston	□ Jamie Balagia	□ Jamar Osborne		
Comptroller of Public Accounts (Contralor de Cuentas Públicas)	□ Glenn Hegar	□ Mike Collier	□ Ben Sanders	□ Deb Shafto		
Commissioner of the General Land Office (Comisionado de la Oficina General de Tierras)	□ George P. Bush	□ John Cook	□ Justin Knight	□ Valerie Alessi		
Commissioner of Agriculture (Comisionado de Agricultura)	□ Sid Miller	□ Jim Hogan	□ David (Rocky) Palmquist	□ Kenneth Kendrick		
Railroad Commissioner (Comisionado de Ferrocarriles)	□ Ryan Sitton	□ Steve Brown	□ Mark A. Miller	□ Martina Salinas		
Chief Justice, Supreme Court (Juez Presidente, Corte Suprema)	□ Nathan Hecht	□ William Moody	□ Tom Oxford			
Justice, Supreme Court, Place 6, Unexpired Term (Juez, Corte Suprema, Lugar Núm. 6, Duración Restante del Cargo)	□ Jeff Brown	□ Lawrence Edward Meyers	□ Mark Ash			
Justice, Supreme Court, Place 7 (Juez, Corte Suprema, Lugar Núm. 7)	□ Jeff Boyd	□ Gina Benavides	□ Don Fulton	□ Charles E. Waterbury		
Justice, Supreme Court, Place 8 (Juez, Corte Suprema, Lugar Núm. 8)	□ Phil Johnson		□ RS Roberto Koelsch	□ Jim Chisolm		
Judge, Court of Criminal Appeals, Place 3 (Juez, Corte de Apelaciones Criminales, Lugar Núm. 3)	□ Bert Richardson	□ John Granberg	□ Mark W. Bennett			
Judge, Court of Criminal Appeals, Place 4 (Juez, Corte de Apelaciones Criminales, Lugar Núm. 4)	□ Kevin Patrick Yeary		□ Quanah Parker	□ Judith Sanders-Castro		
Judge, Court of Criminal Appeals, Place 9 (Juez, Corte de Apelaciones Criminales, Lugar Núm. 9)	□ David Newell		□ William Bryan Strange, III	□ George Joseph Altgelt		
Criminal District Attorney (Procurador Criminal del Distrito)						

(Note: Continue with county and precinct offices.)

Proposed Constitutional Amendment (Enmienda Propuesta A La Constitución)
Instruction Note: (Nota De Instrucción)
Place an "X" in the square beside the statement indicating the way you wish to vote. (Marque con una "X" en el cuadro al lado de la frase que indica la manera en que quiere usted votar.)

No. 1   □ **For** (A Favor)

□ **Against** (En Contra)

"The constitutional amendment providing for the use and dedication of certain money transferred to the state highway fund to assist in the completion of transportation construction, maintenance, and rehabilitation projects, not to include toll roads."
"La enmienda constitucional que establece el uso y dedicación de ciertos fondos transferidos al Fondo Estatal de Carreteras para ayudar a finalizar la construcción, mantenimiento y rehabilitación en relación con el transporte, no incluye caminos de peaje."

Figure 5.1 Top Portion of Sample General Election Ballot for Travis County, Texas

Source: Travis County, Texas, ballot from The Hart Intercivic eSlate Voting System.

CRITICAL THINKING

How competitive was each party in fielding candidates for each position on the ballot?

Primaries

Political parties conduct primaries to select their nominees for public office. In Texas, party primaries are held every two years. Presidential primaries occur every four years and provide a means for Democrats and Republicans to select delegates to their parties' national conventions, where candidates for president and vice president are nominated. Other primaries occur every two years, when party members go to the polls to choose candidates for the U.S. Congress and for many state, district, and county offices.

Development of Direct Primaries A unique product of American political ingenuity, the **direct primary** was designed to provide a nominating method that would avoid domination by party bosses and allow wider participation by party members. This form of nomination permits party members to choose their candidates directly at the polls. For each office (except president and vice president of the United States and some local officials), party members select by popular vote the person they wish to be their party's candidate in the general election, in which candidates of all parties compete. In Texas, an absolute majority of the vote (more than 50 percent) is required for nomination. If the primary fails to produce such a majority, a **runoff primary** is held the fourth Tuesday in May to allow party members to choose a candidate from the first primary's top two vote-getters.

Four basic forms of the direct primary have evolved in America. Most states use some form of **closed primary**, which requires voters to declare a party affiliation when registering to vote. They must show party identification when voting in a primary election and can vote only in the party primary for which they are registered. Other states use an **open primary**, which does not require party identification of voters. At the polls, voters in an open primary can choose a ballot for any party, regardless of their party affiliation. Texas uses a combination of open and closed primaries.

Some states use a variation of the open primary, called the top-two primary (California, Washington) or **jungle primary** (Louisiana). Here all voters receive the same ballot, on which are printed the names of all candidates. Candidates from all parties run in a single election. If a candidate receives more than 50 percent of the vote, he or she is declared the winner. If no candidate receives more than 50 percent, the top two vote-getters will participate in a runoff election. A criticism of the open primary is that it gives voters of one party an opportunity to sabotage the primary of another party. This can occur when voters who normally affiliate with one party try to nominate a "fringe" candidate from the other who has little chance of victory in the general election. Criticisms of top-two and jungle primaries include that they may produce two candidates from the same party competing for the same office in the general election and they limit the possibility of a third-party or independent candidate's ability to win the nomination.

Texas Primaries Before 1905, various practices had been used to select a party's nominees for public office. With the enactment of the Terrell Election Law in 1905, however, Texas political parties gained the opportunity to conduct primaries. The Texas Democratic Party has held primaries since that year. The Republican Party did not begin conducting primaries until 1926. In 1996, for the first time in Texas history, the Republican Party held primaries in all 254 counties of the state. (If there are no locally contested races, a political party has the option of not conducting a primary election within its county.) In 2014, the Republican Party conducted primaries in 246 (out of 254) counties, whereas the Democratic Party conducted primaries in 231 counties.

direct primary
A nominating system that allows voters to participate directly in the selection of candidates to public office.

runoff primary
Held after the first primary to allow party members to choose a candidate from the first primary's top two vote-getters.

closed primary
A primary in which voters must declare their support for a party before they are permitted to participate in the selection of its candidates.

open primary
A primary in which voters are not required to declare party identification.

jungle primary
A nominating process in which voters indicate their preferences by using a single ballot on which are printed the names and respective party labels of all persons seeking nomination. A candidate who receives more than 50 percent of the vote is elected; otherwise, a runoff between the top two candidates must be held.

Students  in Action

"I have always been passionate from an early age about the state of affairs in Texas and the United States as a whole, voicing my opinions and rallying others to make a difference in their lives and the lives of their neighbors."

—Daniel T.A. Moran

In the March 2014 Democratic Primary, Daniel T.A. Moran was selected as the Democratic nominee for the Texas House of Representatives District 63. At 20 years of age, Daniel was among the youngest candidates to appear on the 2014 general election ballot.

Daniel's activism began online, where he discussed politics and religion in America and later served as a news correspondent on several popular podcasts. Daniel started working on campaigns in 2012 by volunteering for a congressional campaign and managing the campaign's social media. He regularly challenges elected officials he sees as complacent and "out of touch with real Texans." In August 2013, Daniel gained local recognition when he confronted his United States representative at a town hall meeting, asking why he voted against allowing secular chaplains to serve in the United States Armed Forces. This story was covered by several national news sources, including the Raw Story, FOX News, and the Blaze.

In June 2013, Daniel's mother was diagnosed with breast cancer. Although initially viewed as an anomaly, his family attributed it to carcinogens, including benzene, used in hydraulic fracturing (fracking) in North Texas.

Daniel declared, "Many in Texas government fight for the oil and gas industry, leading to little or no accountability at the state level to protect the health and safety of North Texans. I knew the only way I could invoke the changes that were necessary to ensure that the rights of minorities are not trampled on and that people are the priority over corporations was to run for office and give a voice to those not being listened to by their supposed representatives."

Daniel attends the University of North Texas in Denton, majoring in Political Science with an emphasis on constitutional law. He plans to go to law school, where he will prepare to fight for the civil rights and liberties of all Texans. Daniel was unsuccessful in his election bid to win a seat in the Texas House of Representatives.

© Andresr/Shutterstock.com

In Texas, bonds of party loyalty loosen at general election time. Beginning in the early 1950s, it became common practice for Texans to participate in the primaries of the Democratic Party and then legally cross over to vote for Republican candidates in the general election. **Crossover voting** is evidence of a long-term trend toward voter independence of traditional party ties. Historically, Texas Republicans were more likely to engage in

crossover voting
A practice whereby a person participates in the primary of one party, then votes for one or more candidates of another party in the general election.

crossover voting. As the number of Republican candidates increased, however, the number of crossover Republican voters correspondingly declined. Today, Democrats in Republican-dominated counties (such as Collin, Denton, Midland, Montgomery, and Williamson) are likely to participate in crossover voting.

The Texas Election Code requires voters to identify their party affiliation at the time of voting, making Texas a combination of a closed primary state and an open primary state. Voter registration certificates are stamped with the party name when voters participate in a primary. Qualified voters may vote in the primary of any party, as long as they have not already voted in another party's primary or participated in another party's convention in the same year. The primary ballot contains the following restriction: "I am a Republican (Democrat) and understand that I am ineligible to vote or participate in another political party's primary election or convention during this voting year."[30] Violation of a party pledge is a misdemeanor offense punishable by a fine of $500.

Administering Primaries In most states, political parties sponsor and administer their own primaries. The Texas Election Code allocates this responsibility to each party's county executive committee. Political parties whose gubernatorial candidate received 20 percent or more of the vote in the preceding general election must nominate all of their candidates in direct primaries conducted in even-numbered years.

The first primary normally occurs the first Tuesday of March. In 2012, however, legal battles regarding redistricting delayed primary elections. The U.S. District Court for the Western District of Texas, in ordering new legislative districts, also set primary election dates for that year. The first primary election was conducted the last Tuesday in May and the runoff (second) primary was conducted the last Tuesday in July. In 2014, the first primary

How Do We Compare...in Types of Primaries?

Most Populous U.S. States	Primary Type	U.S. States Bordering Texas	Primary Type
California	Top-two primary	Arkansas	Open
Florida	Closed	Louisiana	Jungle
New York	Closed	New Mexico	Closed
Texas	**Combination (open/closed)**	Oklahoma	Closed

Source: Pew Center on the States, http://www.pewstates.org/projects/stateline.

returned to the first Tuesday in March, but the runoff (second) primary was conducted the fourth Tuesday in May.

Individuals who want to run in a direct primary for their party's nomination for a multicounty district office or a statewide office must file the necessary papers with their party's state chair. This party official certifies the names of these persons to each county chair in counties in which the election is administered. Prospective candidates who want their names placed on the primary ballot for a county or precinct office must file with their party's county chair. County executive committees for each political party supervise the printing of primary ballots. If the parties conduct a joint primary, the county elections administrator or the county clerk administers the election. If each party conducts its own primaries, county chairs arrange for voting equipment and polling places in the precincts. With the approval of the county executive committee, the county chair obtains supplies and appoints a presiding judge of elections in each precinct. Together with the state executive committee, the county executive committee determines the order of names of candidates on the ballot and **canvasses** (that is, confirms and certifies) the vote tally for each candidate.

Financing Primaries Major expenses for administering party primaries include renting facilities for polls (the places where voting is conducted), printing ballots and other election materials, and paying election judges and clerks. In recent years, approximately 30 percent of the cost of holding Texas primaries has come from filing fees paid by candidates. The balance of these expenses is usually paid by the State of Texas. For example, candidates for the office of U.S. senator pay $5,000, and candidates for governor and all other statewide offices pay $3,750 in filing fees. Candidates for the Texas Senate and the Texas House of Representatives pay $1,250 and $750, respectively.[31] In 2014, the state of Texas spent approximately $13 million to assist with the financing of party primaries and runoffs.

In lieu of paying a fee, a candidate may file a nominating petition containing a specified number of signatures of people eligible to vote for the office for which that candidate is running. A candidate for statewide office must obtain 5,000 signatures. Candidates for district, county, or precinct office, and for offices of other political subdivisions, must obtain either 500 signatures or the equivalent of 2 percent of the area's votes for all candidates for governor in the last general election, whichever is less. Although second (or runoff) primaries are usually less expensive, the average expenditure per voter is greater because voter turnout tends to be lower.

General and Special Elections

The date prescribed by Article I of the U.S. Constitution for congressional elections is the first Tuesday following the first Monday in November of even-numbered years (for example, November 4, 2014, and November 8, 2016). Presidential elections take place on the same day in November every four years (for example, November 8, 2016, and November 3, 2020).

canvass
To scrutinize the results of an election and then confirm and certify the vote tally for each candidate.

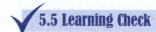

5.5 Learning Check

1. True or False: Political parties are responsible for conducting primary elections.
2. On which day are general elections held?

Answers on p. 197.

In Texas's general elections involving candidates for state, district, and county offices, the candidate who receives a plurality (the largest number of votes) in a contest is the winner. Even if no candidate wins a majority, because of votes received by third-party or independent candidates, the state does not hold a runoff election. Thus, Governor Perry was reelected in 2008 after receiving only 39 percent of the total vote. Elections for governor and other statewide officers serving terms of four years are scheduled in the off year. These **off-year or midterm elections** are held in November of the even-numbered years between presidential elections (for example, November 4, 2014, and November 6, 2018). Along with most other states, Texas follows this schedule to minimize the influence of presidential campaigns on the election of state and local officials. Elections to fill offices for two-year or six-year terms must be conducted in both off years and presidential years.

In addition, **special elections** are called to vote on constitutional amendments and local bond issues, as well as fill interim vacancies in legislative and congressional districts. If no candidate obtains a majority in a special election, a runoff contest between the top two contenders must be conducted to determine a winner. For example, on January 26, 2013, voters participated in a special election to replace District 6 State Senator Mario Gallegos Jr. (D-Houston) following his death in 2012. Because none of the eight candidates running in the special election received a majority of votes, a special runoff election was held on March 2, 2013, in which Democrat Sylvia Garcia defeated Democrat Carol Alvarado for the vacant seat. In addition to participating in special elections to fill vacancies in U.S. congressional and state legislative offices, Texans vote in special elections to act on local bond issues and, occasionally, to elect members of city councils and special district boards. Vacancies in state judicial and executive offices are filled by gubernatorial appointment until the next general election and do not require special elections.

Campaigns Contend With Vitriol on Social Media

Alana Rocha

As candidates and political campaigns increasingly utilize social media sites to reach potential voters, they must also address issues of incivility and inappropriate postings on these sites. Published March 19, 2014, shortly after Republican Attorney General Greg Abbott and Democratic State Senator Wendy Davis won their respective parties' nominations, this article explores how their campaigns addressed some of these issues.

The Texas gubernatorial candidates' Facebook pages and Twitter feeds are prime opportunities for the hopefuls to take their messages directly to supporters and other interested parties, allowing them to showcase their latest announcements and provide forums for comments and feedback. But as the campaigns for Republican Attorney General Greg Abbott and Democratic state Sen. Wendy Davis look to expand the discourse on the issues they consider priorities, they must also contend with the negativity in those forums, including name calling and personal attacks. Commenters have directed such attacks against Davis and Abbott on their respective Facebook pages and elsewhere. At one point, the Abbott campaign alerted the Texas Department of Public Safety about one Facebook comment that appeared to threaten Davis' life.

The campaigns and observers say it's important to take note of the fine line of wanting to engage the electorate while monitoring and potentially censoring input. Dave Carney, Abbott's chief campaign strategist, said it is indeed a tricky job to handle controversial remarks on social media, where commenters are often anonymous. "Things that people say [online], they would never say in person to people," Carney said. "So it's an enabling tool."

This year, a Facebook user commented on Abbott's page saying that if Davis won in November, a ".50 caliber headache was waiting for her." Carney said the Abbott campaign removed the comment from the page after alerting DPS to the post. People wanting to comment on Abbott's online forum, Townhall 254, must adhere to strict guidelines when posting to the page, Carney said. Comments must be civil and about the issue. Comments that do not follow the rules are taken down, he said, adding that it rarely happens because the policy is so detailed. Campaigns largely lose that control in other social media realms, Carney said, "because you get criticized for editing, and stifling people's opinions just makes it worse." The hateful rhetoric has also been directed at Abbott and Republicans, with a commenter on Abbott's Facebook page saying, "When Republicans die, God smiles."

Rebecca Acuňa, a Davis campaign spokeswoman, said in an email that the campaign would not discuss its social media policy or how it handles menacing comments posted on pages, citing security reasons. Acuňa did say that any potential threats are reported to DPS. Regina Lawrence, the director of the Annette Strauss Institute for Civic Life at the University of Texas at Austin, said the campaigns appear to be learning as they go. "They might be one step ahead of the rest of us because they have to figure this out," said Lawrence, who is also a faculty member in UT-Austin's Department of Journalism. It's an issue not confined to campaign forums. News organizations have the same problem with personal attacks in comments. *The Texas Tribune*, [publisher of this article] for example, grapples with it daily, monitoring online comments and deleting those that violate its policy.

With more than seven months until the general election, and plenty of campaign trail still to cover, Lawrence said the online vitriol could grow worse. While she said there is no all-encompassing solution, regular monitoring is key. "It may be a case where we have to take at least a little bit of the bad with the good. And I think campaigns are trying to figure this out as they're working," Lawrence said.

Jay Root contributed to this report.

✓ Selected Reading Learning Check

1. True or False: As Abbott and Davis utilized social media sites to reach potential voters, they also faced issues of incivility and inappropriate postings on these sites.
2. How did Greg Abbott's campaign respond to one posting on his Facebook page that said if Davis won in November a ".50 caliber headache was waiting for her?"

Answers on p. 197.

Alana Rocha is the multimedia reporter for the *Texas Tribune*. *Source:* This article first appeared in the *Texas Tribune*, March 19, 2014, http://www.texastribune.org/2014/03/19/davis-abbott-supporters-lob-attacks-social-media/.

Conclusion

Although most obstacles to voting have been abolished and Texas election laws have extended voting periods and simplified the elections process, many Texans do not exercise their right to vote. In national, state, and local elections, Texans vote at or below the national average. In addition, because education, income, and race and ethnicity are critical factors affecting voter turnout, concern is increasing that decisions are being made by an "elite" minority.

Chapter Summary

LO 5.1 **Analyze the components of a political campaign, specifically how the process of running and financing a campaign has changed over the years**. Political campaigns have evolved from candidate speeches on a courthouse lawn or from the rear platform of a campaign train to sophisticated organizations that utilize media, targeted emails, and social networking resources to win voter support. As a result, political campaigns have become increasingly expensive. Both federal and state laws have been enacted to regulate campaign financing. However, Texas laws are relatively weak, and federal regulations of campaign financing have been limited by judicial decisions and loopholes in disclosure laws.

LO 5.2 **Describe the role that race and ethnicity play in politics, focusing on the importance of minority voters**. Racial and ethnic factors are strong influences on Texas politics, and they shape political campaigns. The increasing size of the Latino population makes Latinos an important factor in elections. However, lower levels of political activity than in the population at large limit an even greater impact of the Latino electorate. A majority of Latino and African American voters participate in Democratic primaries and vote for Democratic candidates in general elections.

LO 5.3 **Describe the role that women have played in Texas politics and how that role has evolved**. Texas women did not begin to vote and hold public office for three-quarters of a century after Texas joined the Union. Before 1990, only four women had won a statewide office in Texas. By the 1990s, the number of women elected to statewide office increased dramatically. Additionally, women served as mayors in about 150 of the state's towns and cities. In several elections early in the 21st century, women led all candidates on either ticket in votes received. In 2014, female candidates held the top two positions on the Democratic Party's ticket. Despite their electoral victories in Texas and elsewhere across the nation, fewer women than men seek elective public office. As customs, habits, and attitudes have changed, opportunities for women in public service expanded; however, the number of women elected to state-level office declined in 2014.

LO 5.4   **Explain the complexities of voting and how the voting process promotes, and inhibits, voter participation**. For most Texans, voting is their principal political activity. Registration is required before a person can vote and is intended to determine in advance whether prospective voters meet all the qualifications prescribed by law. Federal voting rights legislation has expanded the electorate, simplified voter registration, and encouraged voting. Additionally, Texas law extends the early voting period to begin 17 days before an election or 10 days before a primary. However, recent U.S. Supreme Court decisions and Texas's restrictive voter identification law have been criticized for inhibiting voter participation.

LO 5.5   **Identify the differences among primary, general, and special elections**. Primary elections are preliminary elections conducted within a political party to select candidates who will run for public office in a subsequent general election. General elections are conducted in November of even-numbered years to elect county and state officials from among candidates nominated in primary elections (or for small parties, in nominating conventions). Special elections are called by the governor to fill a vacancy (e.g., U.S. congressional or state legislative office) or to vote on a proposed state constitutional amendment or local bond issue.

Key Terms

independent candidate, p. 159

sound bite, p. 159

political action committee (PAC), p. 163

Texas Ethics Commission, p. 163

Campaign Reform Act, p. 164

soft money, p. 164

hard money, p. 164

independent expenditures, p. 164

super PAC, p. 164

universal suffrage, p. 172

voter registration, p. 172

literacy test, p. 172

grandfather clause, p. 172

poll tax, p. 172

white primary, p. 173

gerrymandering, p. 173

affirmative racial gerrymandering, p. 173

at-large majority district, p. 175

early voting, p. 175

motor-voter law, p. 176

voter turnout, p. 177

Texas Election Code, p. 179

voting precinct, p. 182

elections administrator, p. 182

election judge, p. 184

primary, p. 186

general election, p. 186

direct primary, p. 188

runoff primary, p. 188

closed primary, p. 188

open primary, p. 188

jungle primary, p. 188

crossover voting, p. 189

canvass, p. 191

off-year or midterm election, p. 192

special election, p. 192

Learning Check Answers

5.1 1. False. Most Texas voters learn about candidates through television commercials.
2. The Texas Ethics Commission; unlike the Federal Election Campaign Act, however, Texas has no laws to limit political contributions, except for some judicial positions.

5.2 1. Although more Latinos today are likely to split their tickets, traditionally they have supported the Democratic Party.
2. True. In 2014, no African Americans were holding statewide elected positions. Texas Supreme Court justices Wallace Bernard Jefferson and Dale Washington resigned in 2013.

5.3 1. True. With her reelection to the U.S. Senate in 2000, Republican Kay Bailey Hutchison became the first person to receive more than 4 million votes. In 2002, Carole Keeton Rylander (later Strayhorn) received more than 2.8 million votes in her reelection as state comptroller. Hutchison led all candidates on the ticket in 2006 with more than 2.6 million votes received. Several women legislators have been elected.
2. Two: Miriam A. ("Ma") Ferguson (1925–1927 and 1933–1935) and Ann Richards (1991–1995).

5.4 1. Historically, obstacles to voting in Texas included poll taxes, all-white primaries, racial gerrymandering, and diluting minority votes.
2. False. Texas law allows any qualified voter to vote from 17 to 4 days preceding a scheduled election or first primary and from 10 to 4 days preceding a runoff primary.

5.5 1. True. Primary elections are party functions in which party members select nominees to run against the candidates of opposing parties in a general election.
2. General elections are held on the first Tuesday following the first Monday in November of even-numbered years.

Selected Reading Learning Check

1. True. Both candidates had to contend with the negativity in social media forums, including name calling and personal attacks.
2. Abbott's campaign took the post down and alerted the Texas Department of Public Safety about the comment.

The Media and Politics

6

Learning Objectives

6.1 Compare the ways in which Texans get their information today with past patterns.

6.2 Describe the roles of the media in Texas politics.

6.3 Discuss the roles of the media in modern Texas election campaigns.

6.4 Analyze whether there is ideological bias in the Texas media.

6.5 Distinguish how print and electronic media are regulated by government.

6.6 Discuss the positive and negative effects of the changes the media are undergoing in Texas.

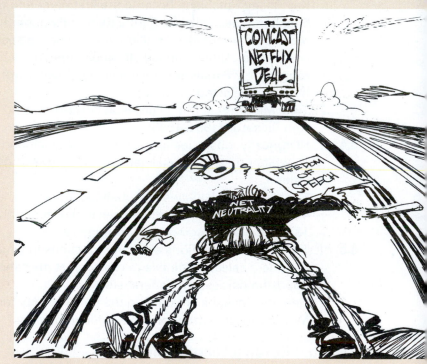

Milt Prigee/Cagle Cartoons

CRITICAL THINKING

Can government protect and promote the individual's needs and the society's interests in the face of great commercial power and rapidly developing communications technology? How? Why?

The media have long had a major impact on politics in Texas and the nation. They play a major role in maintaining our democracy: informing citizens and leaders about what governments and politicians are doing and the debates about those actions, sometimes reporting things officials would rather we didn't know, affecting the set of issues that governments consider seriously, and to some degree shaping public opinion. In carrying out these roles, the media both affect and are affected by the other political actors—government and political leaders, interest groups, and the public. Because of the importance of the media and their diverse nature, there is serious debate about whether and what kinds of bias exist and about the rapidly changing nature of the media (changes such as the decline of newspapers, the growth of the Internet and social media, and the growing concentration of ownership of newspapers, television, and digital media [as illustrated by the cartoon that opens this chapter]). These topics are explored in this chapter.

Please note two points about terminology. First, the word *media* is plural; for example, "The media *have* long had a major impact." Second, there are differences among authors on terminology. The term *print media* is generally accepted for newspapers and newsmagazines. Here, we refer to radio and television as *electronic media* and at times distinguish between broadcast and cable television. The Internet and social media are referred to as *digital media*.

Where Do We Get Our Information?

LO6.1   Compare the ways in which Texans get their information today with past patterns.

Although the simple answer to the question of where we get our information is from newspapers and newsmagazines, television and radio, and the Internet and social media, the answer is more complex. Most people get news from more than one source, and whether they remember the information depends on the trust they have for the source and a number of other factors. Newspapers were once the dominant source of news for individuals. Today, however, newspapers are in decline in both numbers and readership. Television news is widely watched but is thin in content and is gradually being outpaced by the Internet and social media. Although often absent in discussions of sources of news, family and friends are an important source of news for many individuals. The most common way that people (almost three-quarters of all Americans) get news personally is, not surprisingly, from conversations, in person or over the phone. Almost two-thirds of adults follow up the information from family and friends by seeking the story in the news media—traditional or new.[1]

As Table 6.1 shows, television is still the place where the most people get news, but the Internet is second, and newspapers, once first, are now third. The table also shows that many people get their news from more than one source. In the survey reported in Table 6.1, adult Americans were asked to which source they "regularly" turned for news about the 2012 election

Table 6.1 Sources for Campaign News, 2012			
(U.S. adults who regularly turn to each source)			
		January	**October**
TV	Cable News	36%	41%
	Local News	32%	38%
	Network News	26%	31%
	Cable News Talk Shows	15%	18%
	Late Night Comedy Shows	9%	12%
Internet		25%	36%
Print	Local Newspapers	20%	23%
	National Newspapers	8%	13%
Radio	Talk Radio Shows	16%	16%
	NPR	12%	12%
Social Media	Facebook	6%	12%
	YouTube	3%	7%
	Twitter	2%	4%

Note: Numbers do not add to 100% because respondents could answer "regularly" to more than one item.

Source: Pew Research Center's Project for Excellence in Journalism, www.journalism.org/2012/10/25/social-media-doubles-remains-limited/.

CRITICAL THINKING

There are many sources of news. Can you rank them in terms of which are better sources? What are the things you consider in the ranking?

campaign. Respondents could give more than one response, and the total percentages add to more than 260—an average of 2.6 sources regularly consulted. Table 6.2 shows that Texans and the nation have similar patterns of attention to sources of news. Among Texans, television is still the most common source of news, but the other media are not far behind.

Table 6.2 Attention to News Sources in the U.S. and Texas								
	TV News		**Internet News**		**Newspaper News**		**Radio News**	
Attention Paid	**Texas**	**U.S.**	**Texas**	**U.S.**	**Texas**	**U.S.**	**Texas**	**U.S.**
A Great Deal or A Lot	37%	38%	25%	26%	27%	26%	27%	31%
A Moderate Amount	32%	35%	32%	32%	32%	34%	33%	32%
A Little or None	31%	27%	43%	42%	41%	40%	40%	37%
Total	**100%**	100%	**100%**	100%	**100%**	100%	**100%**	100%

Source: 2012 National Election Study Time Series, Survey Documentation and Analysis, University of California, Berkeley, http://sda.berkeley.edu, analyzed by author February 6, 2014.

CRITICAL THINKING

The table shows no major differences in paying attention to the news between the national and Texas samples. Why is this?

Print Media: Newspapers and Newsmagazines

Newspapers were long *the* news media for Americans. Nationally, newspapers began in the colonies in the early 1700s and had become important sources of political news by 1750. After 1800, they grew in number and news content, increasing from 92 newspapers in 1789 (the effective date of the U.S. Constitution) to 1,200 in 1835. The number of U.S. newspapers peaked at just over 2,600 at the beginning of the 20th century and declined to about 1,400 by 2009. Circulation peaked at 37 percent of the population in 1947 and then declined to 15 percent by 2009.[2] From the first newspaper in Texas, the *Gaceta de Texas* (which may have published only one or two editions), to Texas's independence, few newspapers were actually published in the state. By 1860, there were 82. Most ceased publication during the Civil War, but the number increased soon after the war and on into the 20th century.

By 1965, Texas ranked third in the nation in number of daily newspapers, and 80 percent of Texas households subscribed to at least one newspaper. However, competition from television slowed the growth of newspapers, and the advent of the Internet put them into decline. Newspapers have been particularly hurt by the loss of advertising to Internet sites. Loss of classified ads to such sites as Craigslist has been especially damaging to revenue. By 2013, there were 81 dailies in the state, compared to 118 in 1975.[3] Nevertheless, the *Dallas Morning News* ranked 12th nationally in circulation in 2012 (410,000) and the *Houston Chronicle* 14th (326,000). Like others in the state and nation, both newspapers have reduced staff and newspaper size. Nationally, by 2012, newspaper professional employment was down 30 percent since 2000 and below 40,000 for the first time since 1978.[4]

In 2012, Texas had 404 newspapers that were published less often than daily (most commonly weekly).[5] These weeklies tend to provide local social and political news but little state or national news. (Lots of pictures of kids, awards, and weddings help circulation greatly.) They tend to serve small towns and counties, suburban areas, college campuses, and communities with common interests such as business, legal, military, and ethnic groups. One listing shows 46 ethnic newspapers serving African Americans, Latinos, or the major Asian groups (14 in Dallas, 13 in Houston, and 19 in the rest of the state).[6] Decline of the major dailies has given an opening to alternative newspapers in some cities, notably the *Dallas Observer*, *Houston Press*, and *Austin Chronicle*. Availability of print news has been boosted to some extent by the rise of several newspapers to national circulation, particularly the *Wall Street Journal*, *New York Times*, *Washington Post*, *USA Today*, and perhaps the *Los Angeles Times*. These dailies, of course, carry little Texas state and local news.

Newsmagazines have always been fewer in number and read by fewer people. However, such periodicals are quite influential because they tend to be read by elites. Because newsmagazine reporters have more time to gather information and study it, their stories often provide more perspective than those published in newspapers. With its large population, Texas would seem

Office of the weekly *Menard News and Messenger* in Menard, southeast of San Angelo.

Menard News and Messenger

CRITICAL THINKING

Will local newspapers survive the Internet challenge? Why or why not?

a likely candidate for several competing newsmagazines. However, this competition has not emerged. Progressives and liberals have read the *Texas Observer* since 1954, but there is not a comparable conservative newsmagazine. *Texas Monthly*, a slick, well-written magazine, carries some political articles and commentary but focuses more on social and cultural stories. Its article on the best and worst legislators after each biennial session of the Texas legislature is watched with trepidation by legislators up for reelection. As is detailed below, political websites on the Internet have taken up some of the slack from the shortage of state newsmagazines.

The print media have been particularly important sources of political information for at least four reasons. First, compared with television and radio, print media have the space to cover more stories and to develop these stories in greater detail. Although many in the general public are satisfied with only the headlines and highlights, opinion leaders and those actually involved in government and politics need more detail and more complete coverage. Hence the second reason for the importance of newspapers is that they are the major source of news for the elite (the better educated, more affluent population and the political leaders). Third, newspapers remain the largest gatherers of news. The major national newspapers and two wire services (Associated Press [AP] and Reuters) provide much of the national and international news that appears in other newspapers, on television and radio, and in Internet blogs. Newspapers tend to set the news agenda for broadcast news. The print media have more reporters to find the news and are more often the ones who break stories (that is, initially report them). Finally, the major print media today require that stories be vetted for accuracy and attempt to follow standards of objectivity in reporting. Objectivity and vetting are only gradually developing on the Internet and are often problems on the two leading cable news channels, Fox on the right (the conservative side) and MSNBC on the left (the liberal side). (See the section later in this chapter on "Bias?")

Electronic Media: Radio and Television

Commercial radio in the United States began in the 1920s and by the 1930s entered its two-decade "Golden Age." Radio, however, did not penetrate Texas and the rest of the South in the 1930s to the degree that it did elsewhere. In Texas and other states, coverage of the war fronts during World War II enhanced the standing of radio, as did its value as a distraction from the horrors of war. Nationally and in Texas, radio remains pervasive. Ninety-nine percent of American homes have one or more radios receiving broadcasts from more than 11,000 radio stations. In Texas, there are 950 stations, almost double the number of newspapers.[7]

Radio is still an important source of entertainment, particularly music, but it has limited value as a source of political news. Radio stations usually provide five minutes of news on the hour—headlines without much detail. For state and national news, most have at best a small news staff and depend on stories from the news services or feeds from such sources as the Texas State Network or, more recently, Fox News Radio. Local news tends to be light, and politics must compete with local social, cultural, and sports events for the short time available.

Two developments have increased the news impact of radio: the rise of talk radio and the development of radio focused on news. In the 1980s, politically oriented radio call-in talk shows became popular. Two decisions by the federal government had a major impact on this phenomenon. In 1987, the Federal Communications Commission (FCC) abolished the Fairness Doctrine that required stations to provide both sides of controversial topics they chose to air. As a result of the doctrine, both liberals and conservatives had been common in the small world of talk radio. Without the Fairness Doctrine, conservatives quickly outpaced the liberals. The change is rooted in a technical factor. Because of the way radio waves are transmitted, AM radio has a poorer sound quality than FM radio. As a result, since the 1960s AM stations had been losing music listeners (and with them, advertising) to the better sound quality of FM. Talk shows did not require high-quality audio, however, and were welcomed by the AM stations. Nevertheless, since the 1990s, many talk shows have moved from AM to FM.

In a second change, the federal Telecommunications Act of 1996 facilitated the development of large chains of radio stations, which in turn made easier the syndication of popular talk radio programs. This made talk radio available to more stations and their listeners. Clear Channel Communications, headquartered in San Antonio, for example, has become a major national and Texas player in talk radio. It owns 840 stations nationwide, including 58 in Texas of which eight are news and talk radio stations. By 1991, conservative Rush Limbaugh had become the most syndicated talk show host in the United States, followed in the early 2000s by another conservative, Sean Hannity, and many others.

In Texas, nationally syndicated talk show hosts have substantial followings, along with hosts with Texas origins, such as Alex Jones, Michael Berry (husband of Texas Secretary of State Nandita Berry), Neal Boortz, Joe Pagliarulo, and Dan Patrick (who achieved political prominence as a member of the Texas Senate before election as lieutenant governor in 2014). Talk radio has provided an opportunity for its predominantly conservative audience members to air their views and create a sense of community. Studies indicate that talk shows are a mix of news and entertainment, with more than half of listeners simply reinforcing their preexisting views. Nevertheless, research also shows that regular listeners are influenced by the views they hear.[8]

The political role of radio has also been enhanced by the availability of all-news stations—some local, some part of large chains, and some from satellite radio, which provides a variety of news formats. In addition, public radio provides substantial coverage of local, state, and national news. Examples include Austin's KUT, KERA in Dallas, Houston's KUHT, and Texas Public Radio, which operates several stations in San Antonio and the Hill Country. National Public Radio (NPR), the Public Broadcasting System (PBS), and local public radio and TV stations receive a small amount of public financing but raise most of their money from individual and corporate donors. In Austin, KUT's coverage is enriched by a partnership with the online newspaper *The Texas Tribune*. Additionally, several public radio stations in the state have combined resources for reporting on environmental and energy-related issues through a collaboration called StateImpact.

Regularly scheduled television broadcasting in the United States began in 1928. However, Texas did not have commercial television until after World War II, when the industry began to flourish nationally. In 1948 WBAP-TV, the first television station in Texas and the South, was opened by Amon G. Carter, publisher of the *Fort Worth Star-Telegram* and a pioneer in Texas radio. In the 1950s, television flourished in the state. It appears that Texas paralleled the nation in the expansion of television. Nationally, the number of households with television expanded from 9 percent in 1950 to 97 percent in 1975, a percentage that has held steady to the present. Today, 80 percent of households have cable or satellite, although the proportion is declining among younger viewers. As of 2014, there were about 125 television stations in Texas, 12 of which are Public Broadcasting System (PBS) stations, covering 99 percent of the state's population.

As Table 6.1 shows, television news today comes in at least five different formats. From the most to the least used by the public, they are cable news (particularly Fox, MSNBC, and CNN), local news, network news (NBC, CBS, and ABC), news talk shows, and late night comedy shows.

Symbols of the new media: Facebook, Twitter, and the Tumblr site for Texas's online newspaper, *The Texas Tribune*.

Source: www.facebook.com; www.twitter.com; http://texastribune.tumblr.com/

CRITICAL THINKING

How have the Internet and social media influenced the reliability of news?

Digital Media: The Internet and Social Media

In comparison to the other media, the Internet is a recent phenomenon with its roots in the 1960s. The blooming of what we think of as the Internet (sometimes referred to as the Net) and **social media** came in the period 1994–2004. In the last decade, there has been an explosive growth of websites, both in number and function. Not surprisingly, the Net has become a vital part of politics and society. Today, **news websites** and political **blogs** are increasingly important outlets for news. It is now quite rare for a Texas newspaper (including weeklies) or television station not to have a website providing a range of news (some extensive, some not). The connection with social media is also strong. Logos for sites such as Facebook, Twitter, YouTube, Tumblr, Pinterest, Instagram, and Linkedin are commonly found on the state's newspapers, television, and magazines and their Internet sites. (See the three on this page.) These logos encourage readers to join conversations happening on these sites about current issues, and some users prefer to log in through social media to navigate news sites and to post comments.

In addition, since 2009, the *Texas Tribune* has been a high-quality nonprofit online newspaper that reaches a wide range of people, including most of the state's political elite. Texas has long had political newsletters that cover major issues and happenings—generally for a fee. The *Quorum Report*, for example, has been a self-described source of "information and gossip" since 1983 and went online in 1998. One of the more influential political blogs in the state is by *Texas Monthly* senior executive editor Paul Burka (*BurkaBlog*).

The two major political parties, most statewide and some local candidates, and a multitude of interest groups maintain blogs, along with writers on the left and right. Examples of ideological blogs include *Burnt Orange Report* and *Grits for Breakfast* on the left and *North Texas Conservative* and *The Conservative Cloakroom* on the right. In spite (or because) of their minority status in the state, liberals have been more successful in establishing Texas blogs. As Tables 6.1 and 6.2 show, from a fourth to a third of Texans and Americans currently get news from the Internet.

social media
Websites and computer applications that allow users to engage in social networking and create online communities. Social media provide platforms for sharing information and ideas through discussion forums, videos, photos, documents, audio clips, and the like.

news website
An Internet site that provides news. These sites are often affiliated with a newspaper or television station, but many are independent.

blog
A website or web page on which a writer or group of writers record opinions, information, and links to other sites on a regular basis.

Over time, the use of social media has grown considerably among all demographic groups. Today, almost three-fourths of Americans over 18 use social networking sites such as Facebook and Twitter, with small differences in amount of usage based on gender, race/ethnicity, education, income, or residence (urban, suburban, or rural). Only age shows a substantial difference, and even then the oldest generation is not absent. Ninety percent of those 18–29 use social networking sites, compared to 46 percent of those 65 and older.[9] Which site is preferred evolves over time. In the period 2011–2014, Facebook appears to have lost 59 percent of its high school and college users, but numbers for other demographic groups continued to grow.[10]

People get news from social networking sites, but it tends to be incidental to looking for something else. Thus, they have more exposure to news but may disregard or forget the message because it was not their primary focus. Facebook remains the most common networking site (used by almost two-thirds of adults). As Figure 6.1 shows, 30 percent of U.S. adults get news from that site. The range of news topics users find on Facebook is broad. Entertainment news about celebrities is the most common kind of information accessed. News about national government and politics is fourth, and local

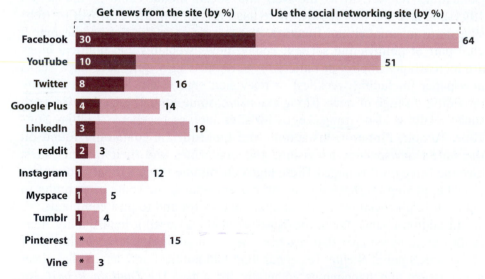

Note: The percent of U.S. adults who get news on Pinterest and Vine is less than one percent each.
Facebook News Survey, Aug. 21-Sept. 2, 2013 (N=5,173)

Figure 6.1   Percent of U.S. Adults Who Get News from Each Social Networking Site and Who Use Each Site

Source: Katerina Eva Matsa and Amy Mitchell, "8 Key Takeaways about Social Media and News," Pew Research Journalism Project, March 26, 2014, http://www.journalism.org/2014/03/26/8-key-takeaways-about-social-media-and-news/.

CRITICAL THINKING

Is the proportion of those getting news from social media likely to increase or decrease? Why?

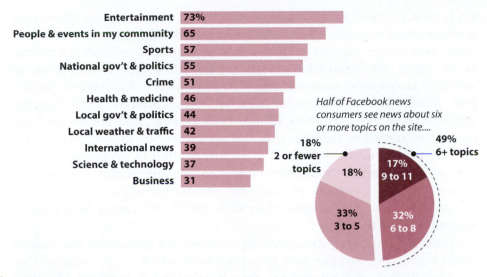

········✕· **Figure 6.2** Percent of Facebook News Consumers Who Regularly See News on Facebook About …

Source: Katerina Eva Matsa and Amy Mitchell, "8 Key Takeaways about Social Media and News," Pew Research Journalism Project, March 26, 2014, http://www.journalism.org/2014/03/26/8-key-takeaways-about-social-media-and-news/.

CRITICAL THINKING

How good are the quantity and quality of news people get on social media?

✔ 6.1 Learning Check

1. From which medium do the most people get their news today?
2. From which medium did most people get their news in the early 20th century?

Answers on p. 236.

government is seventh (see Figure 6.2). Half of social network users have shared the news they gather there with others on the site, and almost half have discussed the information online. A minority also have contributed to news reporting by posting photos or video they took at a news event.[11]

The Media's Roles in Politics

LO6.2   Describe the roles of the media in Texas politics.

The media are commonly said to fill four roles in U.S. and Texas politics: to provide information for the public and decision makers, to help us maintain our democracy, to help shape the public agenda (what government does and doesn't do), and to shape our views.

Providing Information

The first role, providing information, is basic and sounds simple. However, the transfer of information to the public is complex. Most people are not involved in politics and at best care only marginally about what is happening politically. They are more likely to hear and remember ideas and important but unexciting information if it comes from someone they trust. This source may be a trusted newscaster such as Walter Cronkite (1916–2009), the Texan who was anchor for CBS's nightly news program for 19 years, or local news anchors such as Houston's Bill Balleza, Dallas/Fort Worth's Gloria Campos, or San Antonio's Randy Beamer. Bloggers and talk show hosts also may fill this role. Trusted "opinion leaders" are most often friends or relatives who pay close attention to the news on traditional or new media and pass on the information to people they know. Because these leaders are known and trusted, the information they provide is more likely to be heard, remembered, and further explored. A majority of Americans who hear about a story from friends and family follow up by seeking a full news story.[12]

Knowing something about an issue increases the probability that related media stories will be heard and remembered. Members of the political elite are more likely to pay attention to the news and to get more out of it than the general public. They know more initially, and because of their knowledge they feel a greater incentive to become aware of what is happening. Research shows that there is a substantial, long-term difference between ordinary citizens and leaders in understanding the news and in levels of knowledge (remembering and putting it into context). Many scholars see a growing knowledge divide between the informed and the less informed.

An impediment to gaining information for both the interested public and the elite is the softening of the news. Growth in the number and range of alternatives to newspapers and network evening news has produced a sharp increase in competition for advertising dollars, which are closely connected to audience size. To gain more readers/listeners, news providers have increased the amount of entertainment in news broadcasts (often referred to as **soft news**) and decreased the quantity of **hard news**. Local television news in Texas and elsewhere has long focused on accidents, crime, and the reaction of local residents to national events. As a result, although crime has declined in many cities such as Houston and Dallas, regular viewers of local news often believe that crime is increasing. Similarly, followers of talk radio, one of the ideological cable television networks (Fox and MSNBC), or ideological Internet blogs may develop more political knowledge but also come to accept inaccurate or incomplete versions of reality.

Digital media make important contributions to the flow of information to the public. They remove the filters put in place by traditional media and allow the public to communicate directly.[13] The site Reddit (commonly written as reddit), for example, allows users (rather than media professionals) to select the most important stories of the day. Unfortunately, the news role of social media has a fundamental conflict without an easy answer. On the one hand, few people use sites such as reddit (see Figure 6.1), and for those users, entertainment value often trumps substantive value in the news chosen. On the other hand, there is considerable evidence to support the charge that news selection by professional journalists is elitist in nature and does not resonate with a large part of the public.

soft news
News that is more entertaining, sensationalized, covers only the surface, and has little connection to public policy.

hard news
News that focuses on the facts, provides more depth, and commonly has implications for public policy.

Government, interest groups, and the elite want to "get the word out" to the public. This long meant trying to get the print and electronic press to cover their concerns as news. Today, the Internet and social media provide an array of direct outlets for users: advertisements on others' sites; their own Internet sites; blogs; and social media sites like Facebook, Twitter, and Instagram.

Maintaining Democracy

A second task often assigned to the media is protecting democracy. Historically, the media have played a key protective role, but the quality of the protection has varied greatly. The media play a vital informational role for both ordinary citizens and leaders. Without the media reporting what is happening, citizens would be unable to make intelligent decisions in voting and other forms of political participation. We would be dependent on what the government and interest groups tell us. We also rely on the media to investigate and dig out information the government and special interests wish to hide. Over time, the ability of the press to fill these roles has fluctuated.

The Partisan Past Throughout the 19th century, newspapers in Texas and the nation were highly partisan, often scurrilous, and not addicted to the truth. For example, newspapers around the state were strongly divided on the personality of Sam Houston in both the editorial and news pages. When newspapers reemerged after the Civil War, they divided sharply over Reconstruction's Governor Edmund J. Davis. Nevertheless, the "**yellow journalism**" practiced by the Hearst and Pulitzer newspapers at the close of the 19th century laid a foundation for investigative journalism, according to some historians. Others see yellow journalism as the ancestor of today's supermarket tabloids. In any event, the *Galveston News* in the second half of the 19th century began to move away from harsh partisanship, and by the end of the century most Texas newspapers were following suit. Two factors seem to have contributed to this movement toward more evenhanded reporting. One was the growth of news services such as the Associated Press, which meant that newspapers were sharing the same story. The other was the increasing reliance on advertising revenue. Technological changes made possible the publication of large runs of a newspaper, which increased circulation. Publishers had to become more moderate and professional because they could not afford to alienate either advertisers or subscribers. Advertisers then and now look at circulation numbers to determine whether to buy advertising space and how much to pay.

Professionalism and Democracy In the 20th century, **professionalism** gradually became the standard for American and Texas journalists. To be professional, reporting should be objective, neutral, and accurate, not based on partisanship, ideology, or the economic interest of reporters or owners of media outlets. Professional journalism has long been seen as important to democracy. Citizens and leaders gain a fuller and more accurate picture of events, and government and special interests get away with less. However, there are other perspectives. Advocacy journalists strive for accuracy but

yellow journalism
Journalism that is based on sensationalism and exaggeration.

professionalism
Reporting that is objective, neutral, and accurate.

reject objectivity (presenting both sides well). Ideological publications, such as the *Texas Observer,* practice advocacy. In newspapers, the distinction is easier to see. It is on the "news pages" that professionalism—objectivity and neutrality—should apply. Advocacy is practiced on the editorial pages, where editors and columnists give their opinions. In television news, the news and opinion segments tend to be less clearly separated.

Professionalism is, of course, an ideal, and most suppliers of news are judged by how close they come to the ideal, not by whether they are perfect. Several trends have chipped away at the standards of professionalism, and critics have noted that professional journalists tend to see official sources (that is, government officials and other powerful people) as reliable, legitimate, and knowledgeable. Thus, professionals may overreport views of the government and the elite to the neglect of other views. Critics note, for example, that reporters seem to have long taken at face value the bragging by legislative leaders about balancing the Texas state budget when the federal government has not been able to do so. The fuller picture is that the state constitution makes it virtually impossible for the legislature to spend more than the comptroller predicts the state will have available to spend.

Similarly, being objective means presenting multiple perspectives of an issue. However, if there is no debate among the powerful, concerns by ordinary citizens may be neglected. For example, problems at Veterans Affairs hospitals in Texas and the nation were long underreported. Also, there may be two sides to an issue among political leaders but a third side held by the public that may go unreported in the news. For example, in the recent debate over anti-abortion legislation passed by the legislature in 2013, most of the reporting focused on the two extremes—pro-life and pro-choice. However, for years the largest segment of the public has tended to reject the two extremes—no abortion at all or abortion for any reason. Americans are more likely to believe that abortion should be available but only under certain circumstances.[14] The independent nature of Internet and social media interactions give hope that citizen views, not reflected in elite opinion, will also be heard.

In recent years, the national media have become more **adversarial**. Aggressive use of investigations, publicity, and exposure has given them more independence and prominence. There is serious question as to whether the adversarial approach has happened in Texas, at least in the case of the traditional media (print and broadcast). The discussion of media coverage of scandals that follows provides some insight into this issue.

Most observers believe that the national media are more partisan today than during most of the last century. Clearly, some forms of media in Texas are partisan: blogs, social media, and talk radio/television. But the traditional media (newspapers and local television news) tend not to be heavily partisan. In terms of newspapers, differences are more a matter of degree than absolute. The editorial policy of the *Fort Worth Star-Telegram*, for example, is commonly seen as center-left, and its neighbor the *Dallas Morning News* is center-right. The *Morning News*, *Star-Telegram*, *San Antonio Express-News*, *Austin American-Statesman*, and *Houston Chronicle* all endorsed favorite son George W. Bush for president in 2004. In the three

adversarial
Reporting featuring opposition and a combative style. Also called *attack journalism.*

presidential elections from 2004 to 2012, four of the five papers endorsed at least one Republican and one Democrat. Only the Dallas paper was "red" (Republican) in all three elections.

Investigative Journalism Today, we commonly look to the media to help keep our public officials honest by asking hard questions and investigating suspicious actions. Unfortunately, the ability of both the national and state (especially Texas) media to conduct investigations has declined. The reduction in the number of reporters is a major reason. An important tool for the watchdog role of the Texas media is the use of open meetings and open records.

Many government agencies and individual officials in Texas are reluctant to share information about how decisions affecting the public interest are made or the information used in making the decisions. In the past, meetings of school boards and other public boards were often closed to the public. However, during the 1973 session of the legislature, in the aftermath of the Sharpstown scandal (see below), the public interest group Common Cause received strong support from other public interest groups and the media to push through **open meetings** and **open records** legislation. (A weak open meetings act was passed in 1967. The open records act is now officially the Public Information Act.) Today, as these acts have developed, they are among the strongest in the country.

Under open meetings law, government boards must discuss proposals and make their decisions in meetings open to the public. There are a few exceptions, such as personnel matters, contracts, and real property purchases or sales that can be discussed in executive (closed) session, but even then, actual decisions generally must be made in sessions open to the public. Ordinary citizens can, of course, attend, but it is reporting by the media that makes information widely available. Some cities and other government units now stream their meetings and make minutes and other documents available over the Internet.

Most reports, communications, and paperwork generated within executive agencies may be requested by citizens. In 2013, the legislature updated requirements to clarify the inclusion of emails. No reason need be given for the request, and there is no restriction on use of the information. Those most likely to ask for records are the news media, advocacy groups, and activists within the community.

As with open meetings, there are some restrictions as to what can be released, and this limitation can lead to difficulties obtaining information. For example, following the deadly 2013 fertilizer plant explosion in the town of West, the state fire marshal aggressively inspected all 104 ammonium nitrate facilities in the state. When a reporter requested copies of some of the reports, the documents were so heavily redacted (marked through) that they were useless to the reporter. After requesting a state attorney general's opinion, the reporter received more information, although the attorney general's office ordered the fire marshal to redact the names and addresses of the facilities. During 2013-2014, the Texas Attorney General issued a

open meetings
Meetings of public entities that are required by law to be open to the public.

open records
Government documents and records that are required by law to be available to the public.

string of opinions to state agencies ruling that the location of toxic chemi-cals should not be made public because of the danger of terrorism. The opin-ions highlight the conflict between keeping information from those who would do us harm and the public's needing to know where it is safe to live, to go to school, or to work.[15]

The media not only report information they gather from open meetings and open records requests, they also report information obtained by others using data the state requires to be reported. For example, candidates, lobby-ists, and officeholders are required to report financial information such as campaign contributions and expenditures to the Texas Ethics Commission, which places the information online but not always in a readily usable form. Public interest groups such as Texans for Public Justice often compile the information so as to make patterns clearer (for example, their report *Texas' Top Lobbyists* identified lobbyists who received up to $328 million for trying to influence the 2013 legislative session). The online *Texas Tribune* has developed several searchable databases, including salaries of public employees and the *Texas Campaign Finance Database: 2000–2014*.

Scandals and the Media One of the roles often portrayed for the press is investigating wrongdoing by government and its leaders. Texas has a long history of political scandals and conflicts in which the media have played a significant but seldom leading role. The press more commonly spreads the word and keeps the pot boiling, which allows time for concerned citizens and leaders to seek reforms. The classic case is the Sharpstown stock fraud scandal of the early 1970s in which federal prosecutors originated charges that resulted in three convictions (one of which was overturned on appeal). The media gave substantial coverage to the scandal and the subsequent actions of the "Dirty Thirty," a group of legislators who forced public discus-sion of the issues involved. As a result, Governor Preston Smith (named as an unindicted coconspirator), Lieutenant Governor Ben Barnes (who was not a participant in the conspiracy), and a large majority of the legislature were swept from office. A flurry of mild reforms followed.

In three prominent cases, however, the media's investigations uncovered corruption. In the mid-1950s, the managing editor of the *Cuero Record* won a Pulitzer Prize for exposing the defrauding of veterans by the state land commissioner, Bascom Giles, who went to prison. Following up on Sharps-town, in the 1970s, the media and prosecutors found widespread corruption such as illegal hiring of relatives and theft of legislative stamp allotments. In the late 1980s, media investigations produced changes in the membership on the Texas Supreme Court.

Scrutiny of the Texas Supreme Court began when two San Antonio newspapers questioned decisions by justices that favored their campaign contributors. That led to a fuller investigation by *Texas Monthly* and then a national story in 1987 by the investigative television program *60 Minutes*. In a rare move, the Texas Commission on Judicial Conduct publicly repri-manded two justices. Three justices took early retirement. Tenacious report-ing changed personnel on the court and contributed to its moving from all

Democrats to all Republicans. But this did not change the fundamental problem: judges and justices still have to raise money for their election campaigns—$1.5 to $2 million for a single campaign for the Texas Supreme Court. A decade later, in 1998, *60 Minutes* revisited the court and found the same problem. Democratic justices had favored their contributors: plaintiffs' attorneys. Now, Republican justices were favoring their contributors: business and insurance. (For further discussion of this issue, see Chapter 11, "The Judicial Branch.")

In both Sharpstown and the Texas Supreme Court cases, the changes were in personnel, not fundamental changes in the system. Because the system remains unchanged, so too does the likelihood of future abuses. Serious reform is a hard sell in Texas.

Setting the Public Agenda

A third major role of the media is its substantial contribution to setting the public agenda (called **agenda setting**)—that is, influencing which issues are dealt with by government. There are a multitude of problems affecting the public, but if public officials are not aware of them, nothing happens. In addition, officials may be aware of problems but not want to act. For example, low funding for mental health resources in Texas has created major problems for many Texans, but strong resistance to spending the money to increase social services long left Texas in last place among the states in per capita mental health expenditures. Without the public's becoming aware and highly concerned, state leadership can ignore the problem. When a substantial segment of the public or major leaders become aware of issues, action is more likely.

An example of media influence on policy took place in early 2014. The plan of the Texas Department of Transportation (TxDOT) to build a bypass around the town of Snook would have required cutting down several trees and damaging others in a stand of 200- to 300-year-old live oaks. When residents protested in the nearby Bryan/College Station media, TxDOT promised an attempt to save some of the trees but not to save all. A Facebook page and an online petition were created. Then, within days of the story's appearing in a major daily, the *Houston Chronicle*, TxDOT devised a new plan that would move traffic safely, save the trees, and stay within budget.

The Texas media have a limited influence on agenda setting. Competing with the media in setting the public agenda are the governor, legislative leaders, and interest groups, who have more power and resources. In addition, the decline in the number of reporters, the fragmented nature of the state's executive branch, the large number of local governments (particularly the often almost invisible special districts and the fragmented county offices), and reliance on nonlocal and out-of-state collectors of information make it likely that many possible agenda items will be missed. Although the Texas press influences major state-level agenda items and many local issues, it has too few resources to cover, let alone influence, the majority of state agencies, county offices, and special districts.

agenda setting
Affecting the importance given issues by government and public leaders.

Moreover, the elitist nature of the state political system and the power of special interest groups assure plenty of competition for media attention. Grassroots movements such as the Tea Party and the Occupy Movement have learned to use social media combined with traditional methods such as rallies and demonstrations to gain the attention of the public and leaders. However, the ability of ordinary citizens to come together over an issue of concern to them and use the new media sources to add their cause to the public agenda still appears to be in its infancy (but an infancy with possibilities of healthy growth).

Students in Action

A Diverse Career and the Changing Media

Ademide Adedokun was born in London to Nigerian parents and moved to Katy, Texas, when she was nine. At Sam Houston State, she was a double major—history and political science—and active in the university and community. Among other awards, she was selected as the Outstanding Female Student at the university. With a career in public service in mind, she interned with the City of Huntsville and in the office of the local congressman, Kevin Brady.

It is common for congressional staff members to begin as interns, and this was Ademide's route. With the support of Congressman Brady and his chief of staff, she took a staff position with Congressman Pete Olson. In both positions, she worked with constituents. From there, she moved to the staff of the commandant of the Coast Guard in Washington, D.C., where she assisted the communications director in both internal and external messages. In 2012, she received a Master of Public Administration degree from American University in Washington, D.C., and was promoted to speechwriter for the commandant.

Ms. Adedokun was struck by the diversity of the media. "The media has changed," she said, "and that means that we use a variety of methods to transmit messages: internal websites, external websites, speeches, video, and any other method we can think of."

Asked what she learned from being a political science major, she said, "Political science taught me how to write. You cannot enter the professional world without the knowledge of how to write using correct grammar and punctuation. During the course of a workday, no matter what profession you choose, you're going to write e-mails, reports, memos, and every other kind of document."

Source: Interview by R. Mike Yawn.

© Andresr/Shutterstock.com

Shaping Our Views?

A fourth role often attributed to the media is to shape our perceptions of events and issues. Many people believe that the media tell us what to believe—that is, they create opinion. Research finds little evidence for this view. Rather, it finds a much more complex process in which the media play important roles. We have seen that the media are a major source of information. However, this effect is reduced because we are more likely to perceive an issue and its importance if we already know something about the topic or the information comes from a trusted source such as a friend or favorite newscaster. Then, we are more likely to "hear" the news. Similarly, students in an introductory political science class are likely to find the news makes more sense (and therefore remember it) as they learn more background and context from the course.

Personal connection also affects our behavior. In the 2010 national elections, researchers found that putting a reminder that "Today is election day" at the top of Facebook news feeds and a button to click for polling place locations increased turnout by 60,000 voters. However, adding pictures of Facebook friends who voted increased the number by 280,000. That is, invoking people's social networks yielded an additional four voters for every one voter that was directly mobilized.[16]

Do the media change our minds? If we actually have a developed opinion, the answer is "not often." The reason is found in the concept of selective perception and retention. As a general rule, we tend to hear and remember those ideas that support what we already believe and to reject those views that conflict with our own. Consistently, when a group of Republicans and Democrats gather in the same room to listen to their parties' candidates for governor debate the issues, most of the group come away thinking that their candidate made the stronger arguments and won the debate. This tendency means that the media are unlikely to change the minds of those who strongly support candidates or issues, but they may have an effect on marginal supporters. Attack ads are a case in point.

Attack Ads Scurrilously attacking your opponent was a common practice in 18th- and 19th-century politics. Though generally less mean-spirited and less common today, **attack ads** (personal attacks) are still an important part of national and state politics. Advertisements that are negative toward the opponent are quite common and can rise to sharp attacks. A major reason that candidates run attack ads is that they work—on two levels. Negative ads tend to influence the tone and content of news coverage. Said another way, they often generate free media coverage. Second, votes may be won by negative ads. The public tends to accept accurate attacks on the issues, and negativity is often more interesting (and thus more memorable) than positive ads.

People regularly complain about negative campaign ads, but the importance of the political race and the repetition of the ads cause many to "hear" the charges. Already convinced supporters will tend to reject the charges

attack ad
An advertisement meant as a personal attack on an opposing candidate or organization.

made in the ads, but marginal supporters may become less certain and abstain from voting for the candidate. This result seems to be the strongest electoral effect of attack ads. Research shows that as the number of negative ads increases, news coverage tends to become more negative, which lowers participation and trust in government. Although negativity and incivility have always had a role in American politics, research indicates that their audio and visual media presentation increases the likely impact on our emotions and therefore on our view of politics.[17]

A classic example of successful attack ads is the 2002 race for governor between Democrat Tony Sanchez and Republican Rick Perry. Sanchez, a wealthy oilman and banker from the border city of Laredo, was part of the Democrats' "Dream Team," composed of a Mexican American (Sanchez), an African American (Ron Kirk), and a moderately conservative Anglo (John Sharp) running for the top three offices on the ballot. The hope was to energize the Democratic Party's two ethnic bases and to compete with the Republicans for the large conservative Anglo vote. Republicans ran a series of attack ads trying to taint Sanchez with drug money allegedly laundered through his bank. Although the ads appear not to have reduced support from strong Democrats, they probably contributed to the failure of Sanchez's candidacy to mobilize the Latino vote sufficiently to overcome the Republican advantage among Anglo voters.

Priming and Framing Two related concepts are important in understanding the impact of the news on our views: priming and framing. Most issues can be seen in different ways. **Priming** may indicate how important an issue is or which part of a situation is most important. A classic example happened in the 1990 gubernatorial election between liberal Democrat Ann Richards and conservative Republican Clayton Williams. Through much of the campaign, the focus was primarily on the ideological differences between the two. As the conservative candidate in a conservative state, Williams maintained a comfortable lead. But then Williams told a joke to a group of reporters comparing rape to the weather and later refused to shake Richards's hand over charges she had made. As a result, his persona suddenly became the major focus for the press and many voters. (What kind of southern man won't shake a woman's hand, and is he an insensitive sexist?) Poll results began to change, and Richards was narrowly elected. (Cable news, the Internet, and social media greatly speed the spread of news. The impact of the gaffes could have been even larger today.)

Framing provides meaning or defines the central theme. For example, lawsuits against doctors for malpractice, employers for unsafe work conditions, and manufacturers for selling harmful products were long viewed by much of the public as entertaining tidbits or as examples of the little guy/gal striking back at the powerful. However, in the early 1980s, groups of business people, doctors, and conservatives began a series of public relations campaigns lasting more than two decades to reframe the issue as important and costly—to convince the public that frivolous claims and expensive awards from these lawsuits were driving doctors out of the state, raising

priming
The news media indicating how important an issue is or which part of a situation is most important.

framing
The news media providing meaning or defining the central theme of an issue.

prices, and cutting into the economy. The campaigns changed the minds of enough people that the legislature passed legislation in 2003 and the public approved a constitutional amendment to limit the damage awards for these claims. In another example, the 2011 session of the legislature responded to a shortfall of state revenue by cutting a wide range of state services, including $5 billion from public education. Supporters of the cuts framed the issue as fiscal responsibility in hard times, while opponents framed it as damaging education. The dueling frames continued into 2014, even after the 2013 legislature restored a significant amount of the funding.

What Research Finds Our understanding of the influence of the media has undergone substantial change over time. Pundits long suggested a hypodermic model in which the powerful media persuaded the unsophisticated citizenry. However, research found little evidence for this effect. It was followed by a minimal effects model that said the media could only reinforce and activate existing predispositions. Again, the evidence led in a different direction. Today, researchers find considerable evidence for a subtle effects model. The media are not all-powerful but are influential in important ways. In the words of Professors Rosalee Clawson and Zoe Oxley, "This tradition argues that the media influence citizens through agenda setting, priming, and framing; the media influence what citizens think about, which issues or traits citizens bring to bear when evaluating political leaders, and which considerations shape their thinking on political issues."[18]

6.2 Learning Check

1. Are the media today becoming more or less able to investigate government wrongdoing?
2. What does media framing mean?

Answers on p. 236.

Campaigns and Citizen Participation

★ **LO6.3** Discuss the roles of the media in modern Texas election campaigns.

The media play a major role in campaigns for public office and citizen attempts to be heard. With the decline in the ability of political parties to mobilize voters, television and newspapers have long been the major mechanism for candidates to reach potential voters. In a state as large as Texas, this is an extremely expensive undertaking and one that is not always successful. The rise of the Internet and social media has given candidates more ability to reach out directly to voters. The new media have also provided new tools for citizen groups to organize and to try to sell their message.

Campaigns and the Traditional Media

What happens in campaigns casts light on the four major roles of the media just discussed. In the past, candidates relied on rallies and mobilization by local leaders and party organizations. With the advent of television and the decline of political parties, candidates for national, state, and many local offices came to rely on the mass media to get their message out. They seek press coverage of their events, generate situations and issues they hope the media will cover, and buy ads. For years, the ads have made heavy use of television, although by 2008 the Internet was gaining ground. The "How Do We Compare?" table shows 17 media markets in Texas, 6 more than California. As a result, the cost of a traditional media campaign is substantial. For example, in 2010 Democrat Bill White spent $26.3 million trying to unseat Governor Rick Perry. The 2002 gubernatorial campaign cost candidates (and their supporters) a record $95 million. Not surprisingly, candidates seek as much free media coverage as possible. Campaign events are designed more to gain news coverage than to involve those citizens attending, who are often more backdrop than participants.

The relationship between candidates and the press is often testy. Both need each other, but they have different goals. The candidate wants free and friendly coverage; the press wants entertaining news stories—controversy, scandals, and mistakes by the candidate. Candidates at both the state and national level want to control or at least influence the news. In Texas, the news environment makes it easier for the candidates to exercise control.

How Do We Compare...in Media Access?

Most Populous States	Number of Media Markets (2014)	Newspaper Circulation per Capita (2009)	Internet Access (2011)	
			None*	Home & Other*
California	11	0.16	32%	28%
Florida	10	0.14	28%	28%
New York	10	0.31	31%	25%
Texas	**17**	**0.08**	**36%**	**26%**
States Bordering Texas				
Arkansas	3	0.12	39%	20%
Louisiana	7	0.12	34%	25%
New Mexico	1	0.12	40%	21%
Oklahoma	3	0.13	35%	24%

*"None" means no Internet connection available at home or elsewhere. "Home & Other" means Internet connection available through multiple devices at home and elsewhere.
Sources: Television Bureau of Advertising, "Nielson Local Television Market Universe Estimates," http://www.tvb.org/media/file/TVB_Market_Profiles_ Nielsen_TVHH_DMA_Ranks_2013-2014.pdf; U.S. Census Bureau, Statistical Abstract, 2012, Table 1136; and U.S. Census Bureau, 2011 Current Population Survey, reported in Governing the States and Localities, "Internet Connectivity, Usage Statistics for States," http://www.governing.com/gov-data/internet-usage-by-state.html.

CRITICAL THINKING

Texas has the lowest per capita newspaper circulation of all eight states and fares poorly in Internet access compared to the other large states. What factors do you think contribute to this circumstance?

There are fewer reporters; many of them know the candidate; and there is less of a press culture of asking challenging questions. This environment caused problems for Governors George W. Bush and Rick Perry, who went directly from working only in Texas state politics to running for president. They were not used to the rough-and-tumble aspects of national news, and as a result fared poorly in public debates and other encounters with reporters. The opportunities for direct contact with citizens through social media have enhanced the ability of candidates to bypass the traditional media. Facebook and Twitter are now commonly used by campaigns.

One of the complaints about news coverage of campaigns is that it tends to be **horserace journalism**; that is, it focuses more on who is winning than on the issues. Even after officials are elected, stories continue to focus on competition. Will Governor Perry run for governor next time? Will he run for president? Once again, entertainment appears to triumph over content. A strong reason for horserace coverage is that news management wants a large audience and prefers stories that alienate neither side.

Digital Campaigning

The 2008 and 2012 presidential campaigns saw the Internet and social media come of age as a part of campaigning. Mainstream media provided blogs and online news coverage. YouTube, Facebook, and other social media provided outlets for candidates and citizens alike. Candidates began to use the Internet in a major way, putting up high-quality campaign sites and using social media to get out their message. Barack Obama was particularly successful in using the new media in both campaigns. Identifying and microtargeting potential younger voters through their email and social media accounts, his campaign was able to increase support and voter turnout among 18- to 24-year-olds.

In Texas, statewide and many local campaigns now make heavy use of the Internet and social media. In his highly successful 2010 gubernatorial campaign, Governor Perry adapted established campaign practices to modern-day reality, while his primary and general election opponents ran more traditional campaigns. Rather than use direct mail, phone banks, and knocking on the doors of strangers, the Perry campaign asked volunteers to identify 12 friends and turn them out to the polls. Facebook messages to friends were encouraged. Perry refused to meet with newspaper editorial boards (who decide on endorsements) and instead relied on friendly bloggers, social media, and personal appearances. He gave away no yard signs because, his people said, they don't work. (Supporters could buy a sign if they wished.) Social media were used to get Perry's voters organized, connected, and to the polls.[19]

Ted Cruz's upset victory in the 2012 Republican primary for the U.S. Senate was fueled in significant part by skillful use of the Internet and social media. Among other efforts, the campaign advertised and raised funds on a multitude of platforms, targeted people who "liked" those who had endorsed Cruz, manipulated key words for Google searches, and used "promoted Tweets" (paid ads on Twitter that show up first in search results).

horserace journalism
News that focuses on who is ahead in the race (poll results and public perceptions) rather than policy differences.

On the other hand, many traditional national, state, and local candidates were caught unawares by the new media, suffering embarrassment and sometimes defeat. Cell phone pictures and videos of candidates' off-the-cuff remarks and mistakes became common on social media. Some went viral. Other wounds were self-inflicted. Conservative candidate for lieutenant governor Senator Dan Patrick tweeted in February 2014, "MARRIAGE=ONE MAN & ONE MAN. Enough of these activist judges." Even though he quickly changed the tweet, it remains on the Internet and makes "Great Gaffes" listings. (Readers should remember that comments and pictures posted on the Internet are likely to be there forever.) The Internet sometimes encourages or facilitates harsh comments that might not be made face-to-face. In the 2014 gubernatorial campaign, both major party candidates made heavy use of Facebook and Twitter to promote discussion of their issues but had a difficult time limiting negative and scurrilous comments posted about their opponents.

Citizen Participation in the Digital Age

One of the charges against digital media is that use of the Internet and social media contributes to lower **civic engagement** (actions to address issues of public concern). The idea is that because digital communication is not face-to-face, users are not as connected to other people and society. However, research by the Pew Research Internet Project does not support this view. Based on a 2012 survey of Internet users, researchers concluded that there was major growth in political activity on social networking sites during the years 2008–2012. Politics, for most users, is not just a social network activity. Users are frequently active in other aspects of civic life. The study also found a common pattern: lower education and income tend to decrease civic participation. However, among Facebook and Twitter users, education and income had less effect. Finally, the young are as likely as older adults to be engaged in some political activities and are more likely to be politically active on social networking sites.

Studies have consistently shown that Texans are low in civic engagement compared to the rest of the nation. Texas is below the national average in such areas as the proportion of people voting, involved in groups, donating to charity, or volunteering in their community. This lack of engagement is also true online. Both face-to-face and online, Texans are below the national average in discussing political or community issues with friends and family.[20]

Like candidates, citizens on both the left and right have learned to use digital media to increase their influence in the political arena. The Tea Party's success in organizing grassroots campaigns, for example, is commonly attributed to the aggressive use of social media. Similarly, skillful use of the digital media on the last day of the first special session of the 2013 legislature temporarily blocked anti-abortion legislation and boosted State Senator Wendy Davis into the Democratic nomination for governor. Davis filibustered an anti-abortion bill for almost 13 hours, forcing a second

civic engagement
Actions by citizens to address issues of public concern.

special session to be called to pass the bill. The filibuster was streamed live on YouTube to 180,000 viewers. Twitter was used to bring protestors to the state capitol to support Davis, and there were 570,000 tweets about the filibuster that day, including one from President Barack Obama.[21]

✔ **6.3 Learning Check**

1. Why are statewide election campaigns so expensive in Texas?
2. Are campaigns using the Internet and social media more effectively?

Answers on p. 236.

Bias?

★ **LO6.4**   Analyze whether there is ideological bias in the Texas media.

Given the important roles played by the media, it is not surprising that activists of all persuasions often believe the media are biased against them. Until the mid-1980s, the majority of the American public saw the press as relatively unbiased, but since then substantial majorities have come to perceive bias. Research shows that parts of the media have become more partisan and ideological but that much of the "mainstream" media still adheres to standards of objectivity and neutrality. To understand this conclusion will take some explanation.

It is well established by research that over the last 30 years reporters have been more liberal and aligned with the Democratic Party than the general population,[22] while newspaper management has long tended to be more conservative and Republican. Many from both groups do not fit these tendencies, but it is nevertheless a strong and persistent pattern. Owners and publishers tend to be more conservative, possibly because of their greater affluence and business position. Newspapers have traditionally endorsed candidates for public office, and the choices (particularly for the top offices) generally reflect the position of owners and managers. In the 21 presidential elections from 1932 to 2012, Republicans received more newspaper endorsements (17 elections) than Democrats (3 elections). (In 1996, some 70 percent of newspapers made no presidential endorsement!) Texas's pattern is more complex. In the long period of Democratic Party dominance, both parties generally nominated conservative candidates; but in the Democratic primary, there was often a contest between a liberal and one or more conservatives. Texas newspapers, with some variation, generally supported conservatives.

Media Bias and the News

Do personal preferences of reporters and managers affect coverage of the news? The answer is yes in countries with a partisan press, as was the case in the United States until the 20th century. Today, the traditions of professionalism that have come to be the standard for journalists hold that the press should report the facts as they are, not the way journalists want them to be, and that opinion should be clearly separated and identified as such. This view has dominated Texas newspapers and television since the early 1900s with, of course, some exceptions. However, the pattern is changing or at least being challenged at both the national and local levels. Today, the two cable news networks with the largest audiences are Fox and MSNBC, which have, respectively, a conscious bias to the right (conservative) and left (liberal). CNN (Cable News Network), the pioneer in cable news with a tradition of objective reporting, stands third in audience size. In an attempt to keep up with its ideological competitors, it regularly uses ideologues of the left and right to analyze events and issues. In 2012, about 54 percent of CNN's news time was factual reporting, while 46 percent was commentary or opinion. By comparison, Fox spent 55 percent of its time on commentary and opinion and MSNBC 85 percent.[23]

Talk radio has long been dominated by conservatives at both the local and national level. On the Internet, there is a wide range of blogs, making it easy for users to get their information from congenial sources that reinforce the reader's views and entertain them. Texas has popular blogs on both the right and left, with the left tending to be better established. A relatively new phenomenon is the growth in popularity of humorous political talk shows on television—for example, *The Daily Show* with Jon Stewart and *Real Time with Bill Maher*—and the number of people who say they get their political information from these entertainment sources. Unlike talk radio, these programs have tended to be more liberal. The growth of social media increases the role of friends and opinion leaders in originating and framing issues, and the availability of sites such as YouTube and Twitter increases self-selection of what news and views to receive. This practice leads to confirmation bias in which people become more fixed in their beliefs and attitudes because they seek out information that supports their beliefs.[24]

Objective reporting still remains an imperfectly followed standard for the three major television broadcasting networks (CBS, NBC, and ABC), the public networks (NPR, PRI, and PBS), and the major newspapers of Texas. At times, the media deviate from objectivity. When George W. Bush first ran for governor and later for president, he was initially viewed negatively by a large number of the reporters covering him. When he ran for governor, he was seen as uninformed and trading on his father's name. When he ran for president, he was tainted with the negative paintbrush often applied by the national press to Texas politicians such as President Lyndon Johnson and presidential candidate Rick Perry (a rube from the country, unsophisticated, and poorly educated). However, in both campaigns, Bush was able to charm many reporters who warmed to him and gave him more favorable coverage. Another example is the state press's reaction to the 2011 cuts in education funding by the legislature. The issue produced dueling frames. Much of the state press coverage of the issue appeared to accept the view that the actions were based more on anti-public-education and antigovernment ideology than on fiscal responsibility.

What Research Finds

Is there partisan or ideological bias in the media? The findings are clear but nuanced. There is little objective evidence of systematic ideological or partisan bias in the mainstream media.[25] Major newspapers and network television news generally adhere to the standards of objectivity and journalistic professionalism. In the words of media scholar Timothy E. Cook, "Newsmaking is a collective process more influenced by the uncritically accepted routine workings of journalism as an institution than by attitudes of journalists."[26] Reporters and managers tend to act professionally and not let their ideological preferences dictate their choice of stories or direct the tone of their reporting. The ideological divide between reporters and managers probably also tends to reduce ideological or partisan bias. Nevertheless, today there is more debate between the "talking heads" representing differing interpretations on television, and more analysis stories in newspapers. There are many examples of biased coverage of issues and events; however, they balance out over the long run. Where the media have become highly partisan and ideological is in the areas in which consumers can choose their source of information and entertainment—Fox or MSNBC, which blog, which talk show?

Two other forms of bias are also noted in the media: a bias toward the entertaining over the important, and a commercial bias. Both are discussed later in the chapter in the section "Change in the Media."

6.4 Learning Check

1. Do studies find that there is a net bias in the media to the left or right?
2. In which area of the media is there becoming more partisanship?

Answers on p. 236.

Regulation

★ **LO6.5** Distinguish how print and electronic media are regulated by government.

In many countries, the media are owned or heavily regulated by government. In the United States, the First Amendment to the Constitution protects freedom of the press, which has meant little regulation of newspapers. Broadcast media (radio and television) were long regulated to ensure they "serve the public interest, convenience, and necessity" under federal law. In comparison to regulation in other Western nations, the regulation in the United States has been with a light hand.

Regulation of Print and Broadcast Media

U.S. courts have been particularly suspicious of **prior restraint** or censorship before information can be made available to the public. For example, in *New York Times Co. v. United States*, 402 U.S. 713 (1971), the U.S. Supreme Court allowed publication of a highly classified government study of the Vietnam War popularly known as *The Pentagon Papers*. One of the ironies in legal treatment of the media is that the courts have protected the right of the media to criticize government more than is the case in most other countries, while the FCC has regulated obscenity more tightly than have most other Western nations.

The Federal Communications Commission (FCC) is responsible for media regulation. It has a reputation for responding to special interests and being

prior restraint
Suppression of material before it is published, commonly called censorship.

ineffective in protecting the public interest, although it has done better in protecting individuals from unfair publicity. In cable television's early days, broadcast television successfully lobbied for regulations that imposed major and costly restrictions on cable TV. Broadcast television sought to protect its turf through government rules restricting competitive programming and requiring cable to provide new services not required of the broadcasters. It took 20 years to overcome the opposition and see a softening of the rules.

Today, the FCC substantially regulates only television broadcast over the air (technically, "free-to-air" television). Radio and cable television were deregulated in 1996. The media are subject to general laws such as those regulating business practices and monopolies.[27] The Internet has not experienced the degree of regulation faced by the broadcast media and cable but has had to deal with a number of legal issues over time: copyright protection, pornography, cybersecurity, the harvesting of personal information from the Net, and now government spying.

Internet Regulation

Perhaps the biggest regulatory issue facing the Internet today is **net neutrality**, which means that Internet service providers and governments should treat all data on the Internet equally, not discriminating or charging differentially and not blocking content they do not like. The issue came to a head in February 2014 when Comcast, the nation's largest broadband and cable provider, and Netflix, the video streaming site that produces about 30 percent of Internet traffic, announced an agreement. Netflix would pay Comcast for faster and more reliable direct access to its network (and subscribers). Coming only 10 days after Comcast agreed to buy the giant cable TV provider Time Warner Cable, this agreement raised concerns about whether the merger created a monopoly, the bargaining power Comcast's size gave it, and the viability of net neutrality. In January 2014, a federal appeals court had struck down the FCC's net neutrality rules, which might have forbidden the Comcast-Netflix agreement. The FCC then announced it would attempt to reformulate its rules with input from Congress. Debate has centered on whether paying for access could become a norm that could stifle opportunities for startup Internet services and whether reduction in competition will be a long-term consequence. There are loud and articulate voices on both sides of the issues. The cartoon that opens this chapter captures the strong feelings the issue provokes.

State and Local Regulation

State and local governments may regulate the media in areas outside FCC rules. In Texas, regulation has been minimal, although issues over franchises for cable outlets have been a source of considerable conflict. A long-standing free press issue was resolved in 2009 when Texas became the 37th state to pass a **shield law** protecting journalists from having to reveal certain confidential sources. The law, called the Free Flow of Information Act, allows reporters to protect their sources by not having to testify or produce notes in

net neutrality
A legal principle that Internet service providers and governments should treat all data on the Internet equally, not discriminating or charging differentially and not blocking content they do not like.

shield law
A law protecting journalists from having to reveal confidential sources to police or in court.

Texas Tribune **director of technology, Higinio Maycotte (left), and software engineer, Niran Babalola, work in their Austin newsroom. Samples of other national news websites are posted on the walls. The major online nonprofit newspaper,** *The Texas Tribune,* **was founded in 2009.**

Erich Schlegel/Corbis News/Corbis

CRITICAL THINKING

As traditional newspapers decline in Texas, will the digital media gather enough news to keep us well informed?

court. Reporters had argued that they were not able to carry out their investigative role if they could not protect the identity of their sources. Prosecutors long opposed the measure because they believed it impeded evidence gathering. Both sides finally agreed to a compromise that protected sources but required journalists to identify confidential sources in criminal cases if the journalist witnessed a felony.

Change in the Media: More Participation, More Sources, but Less News?

 LO6.6   Discuss the positive and negative effects of the changes the media are undergoing in Texas.

The nature of the media is changing rapidly. From the 19th century, newspapers were the major source of news for Texans. But in the second half of the 20th century, television came to be the dominant source of information for Americans and Texans alike. Now, in the 21st century, the Internet and social

6.5 Learning Check

1. Which medium is most regulated today?
2. Which level of government has traditionally done the most regulating of media?

Answers on p. 236.

media are seriously challenging television news for viewers, particularly among the young. Many see these changes as positive: people now have a wider range of choices for their news and can get it according to their own schedule and wishes. Through the Internet, there is more opportunity for individuals to participate in collection and distribution of news. Others see the changes as fraught with dangers for citizens' level of accurate information.

What do we know? First, newspapers are still the major gatherers of news. Television news and the Internet depend heavily on the major newspapers for originating stories. In the case of Internet news, there is still an ongoing debate as to whether enough people will pay for news on the Net and whether enough advertisers can be obtained to finance the level of news gathering now provided by newspapers. Second, the need to draw audiences by being more entertaining has decreased the amount of hard news across the media. Third, the proliferation of channels on satellite television and blogs on the Internet has led to increased **niche journalism** (also called **narrowcasting**) that appeals to a narrow audience, which often leads to more extreme ideological and partisan views. Finally, the Internet has provided an outlet for a number of sites that check the facts in news stories and politicians' claims, such as PolitiFact, FactCheck, and Snopes.

Concentration of Ownership

Another change profoundly affecting the media is the growing concentration of ownership. Today, just six corporations own most of the national newspapers, newsmagazines, broadcast television networks, and cable news networks, as well as publishing houses, movie studios, telephone companies, Internet service providers, and entertainment firms.[28] The six corporations and some of their media are Time-Warner (CNN, HBO, *Time*); Disney (ABC, ESPN, and several movie studios); Viacom (MTV, Nick Jr., BET, CMT, and Paramount Studios); CBS Corporation (Showtime, NFL.com, and *60 Minutes*); News Corporation Limited (Fox, *Wall Street Journal*, and *New York Post*); and General Electric (Comcast, NBC, and Universal Pictures). The corporations owning the media tend to be conglomerates; that is, they own companies that make or sell a variety of products, not just entertainment and information.

In Texas, local ownership of the media has declined precipitously. Of the major Texas newspapers, only the *Dallas Morning News* is still owned by a Texas company, the A. H. Belo Corporation, which owns a number of newspapers within and outside the state. A spin-off, Belo Corporation, owns television stations in Houston (KHOU), San Antonio (KENS), and Austin (KVUE), as well as out of state. The *Houston Chronicle* and *San Antonio Express-News* are owned by the Hearst chain, the *Fort Worth Star Telegram* by the McClatchy Company, and the *Austin American-Statesman* by Cox Enterprises. Fifty-eight of San Antonio's Clear Channel Communications' 840 radio stations are in Texas.

Homogenization Concentration of media ownership has four consequences that worry critics. The first is **homogenization of news**—the increased

niche journalism (narrowcasting)
A news medium focusing on a narrow audience defined by concern about a particular topic or area.

homogenization of news
Making news uniform regardless of differing locations and cultures.

likelihood that the same stories will be presented in the same way, stories that in the past might have been affected by local and regional culture and concerns. Other critics refer to the *illusion* of choice—many ways to get the same news. Chains tend to provide the same feed to all the radio or television stations they own, for example. The concentration of ownership has combined with the tendency of both newspapers and the electronic media to respond to their limited resources by reducing (or eliminating) the reporters who gather the news and relying on the wire services instead. A quarter of the 952 U.S. television stations that air newscasts do not produce their news programs. Additional stations have sharing arrangements under which much of their content is produced outside their own newsroom.[29]

In a state as large and diverse as Texas, homogenization represents a considerable change. Although the Internet does provide more diversity in the presentation of news, so far the lack of revenue, reporters, and professional standards makes it more reactive and opinion oriented than a reliable source of news with a regional or local focus. A study by the Pew Trust found that 99 percent of the stories covered by blogs originated in the traditional media. Occasionally, the blogosphere does play this new role and forces the traditional media to take notice, but the blogosphere is still a work in progress.

Soft News A second consequence of growing concentration of ownership is the decline in the amount of news and its "softening." Students of news speak of hard news and soft news. Hard news focuses on the facts, provides more depth, and commonly has implications for public policy. Soft news is more entertaining (often sensationalized by focusing on scandal and tragedy), covers only the surface of serious issues, and has little connection to public policy.

Prior to the 1980s, the news departments of the three major television networks (NBC, CBS, and ABC) were substantially shielded from profit expectations, and their evening news broadcasts were *the* national news, most of it hard news. However, in the mid-1980s, new ownership took over the three networks and demanded more advertising revenue from news. In this period, technological change allowed the emergence of competition from cable television. (CNN debuted in 1980, and a wide array of new and entertaining programs and networks soon followed.) Having to compete for audience share, the network news sought more entertainment value in their stories by reducing the amount of hard news and increasing the emphasis on scandal, horserace coverage of campaigns, and controversial sound bites. Eventually, softer coverage of news would come to CNN, NPR, and PBS. Fox and MSNBC, the ideological networks, have made their staple a minimum of hard news, entertaining spin, and drawing in the ideological faithful as viewers.

Less State and Local News In Texas, the national trend toward softer news added to a long-existing pattern of providing minimal and lighter treatment of state and local news. Nonlocal owners of the state's newspapers have tended to show little interest in state and local news, cut staff, and, most important, reduced the size of the **Capitol press corps**. The number of reporters assigned to cover state news in Austin by Texas news outlets dropped from 66 in 1991 to about 50 in 2000 and then to about half that number in 2014. Generally, the Capitol press corps is exclusively print journalists. The decline in full-time reporters covering state government means not just less news about the state but also more reliance on the version of events provided by state agencies and a reduction in the amount of investigative journalism that provides oversight of what our government does and doesn't do. Some observers (such as *Texas Monthly*'s Paul Burka) are less concerned, believing that the Internet will fill the void.[30]

The decline of the traditional Capitol press corps should be seen in perspective. First, it is a phenomenon affecting most other large states. Second, in Texas, it is mitigated to some degree by the emergence of the online non-profit *Texas Tribune* in 2009, the assignment of national correspondents to Austin, and the availability of blogs and high-quality online subscription services. NPR reporter Elise Hu described the Texas press corps, as follows:

> [T]he Texas press corps is unique, political watchers say, because of the shape it's taking amid the state's recent, raging growth. Aside from the *Tribune*, there are influential blogs and newsletters, a regional magazine of national renown, an energetic public radio presence and newly arrived national correspondents stationed in Austin. And that doesn't even count the traditional newspaper and television presence. It doesn't hurt that Texans love reading about Texas—the notion of Texas exceptionalism, it seems, drives demand.[31]

Local television news in Texas and elsewhere is often cited as an example of soft news. Studies regularly show much the same pattern as a Pew Research Center study in 2012. Almost two-thirds of local news coverage dealt with traffic, weather, crime, accidents, and human interest. Houston's KTRK was part of an earlier study and followed the pattern. Soft or not, local television news is watched regularly by about half of Americans, ahead of network news. Perhaps the reason is captured by the Pew researchers' conclusion:

> Local TV news *is* more likely than other media we studied to try to portray regular people from the community and how they feel about things, rather than just officials. The reporting was straightforward and mostly strictly factual, with little of the journalist's opinion thrown in…. Viewers got straight news from their local TV stations, and it was certainly about the community.[32]

Commercial Bias A final concern arising from the growing concentration of media ownership is commercial bias and conflict of interest—that is, favoring the owners' company by presenting favorable stories or ignoring the bad the company does. Traditionally, advertising provides 80 percent of newspaper revenue and subscriptions provide for 20 percent. Highly dependent on advertisers and needing to be responsive to corporate owners, reporters and

Capitol press corps
Reporters assigned to cover state-level news, commonly working in the state capital.

editors face pressure to avoid angering either. Thus, "In a survey of 118 local news directors, more than half report that advertisers try to tell them what to air and not to air—and they say the problem is growing."[33] A third of American newspaper editors responded to a survey that they would not feel free to publish news that might harm their parent company.[34] And for good reason: according to reports, several employees of ABC who had been critical of Disney practices were fired when the company acquired control of ABC. In Texas, Clear Channel has been accused of censoring opinions.[35]

Point/Counterpoint

THE ISSUE For more than a half century, the print media, radio, and television have provided a substantial amount of news in a relatively unbiased, professional manner. However, the Internet and social media are rapidly changing the pattern. Newspapers, the major collectors of news, are in sharp decline, and television news has become softer and in the case of cable news more ideological. Internet news sites are increasing in number, and social media are becoming more diverse and more important sources of news.

The problem is that the greater availability of locations for both news and entertainment has produced greater competition between news and entertainment, in many ways melding the two together. At the same time, this competition has reduced the advertising dollars available to hire people to gather the news. Passionate feelings abound on both sides. Here are some of the serious arguments.

Will the Internet and Social Media Be Able to Replace the Quantity and Quality of News Now Provided by the Traditional Media?

Arguments That the Digital Media Will Fill the Gap

1. Throughout its history, the media have been in constant change. This shift to digital media is simply another step in its evolution.
2. In the long run, the advertising dollars will simply move to Internet news sites, and social media will continue to adapt to meet people's needs.
3. The social media are producing a new approach to news, providing information while entertaining, eliminating the filters that are part of traditional news media, and giving ordinary people the tools to uncover and report the news.

Arguments That the Digital Media Will Fail to Fill the Gap

1. With so many choices, the present trend will continue. People will tend to choose entertaining news over hard and professional news. Soft news will be competing with partisan news.
2. Audience size is key. Advertising dollars will go to entertainment over news and try to censor when it does sponsor news.
3. Amateurs will not be able to produce the quantity and quality of news now provided by professionals even with new tools.

For Good and for Bad: The Rise of the Internet and Social Media

It should be apparent that the traditional media's coverage of government and politics is still dominant but is gradually being supplemented, modified, and replaced by the Internet and social media. Local television news, for example, has seen some long-term decline in viewership but is still regularly watched by almost half the total population. Age, however, plays a major role. Close to three of five persons age 50 and over watch local news, compared to half that proportion for those 18–29.[36] A similar pattern exists for following the news in newspapers. However, traditional media are adapting. Texas television stations and newspapers now commonly have an Internet site and provide varying proportions of their news via the Net. In the words of one executive, "We are not a TV station anymore as much as a provider of news on multiple platforms."[37] One of the major new issues for the traditional media, but particularly major newspapers, is whether to provide news on the Internet for free or by subscription. The issue is still to be resolved. The *Dallas Morning News*, *Fort Worth Star-Telegram*, *Austin American-Statesman*, and *Houston Chronicle* provide some news free but reserve much news to paid subscribers. The online *Texas Tribune* is free and pays its bills through individual contributions, large gifts, corporate sponsorships, and foundation grants. News sites for the major Texas newspapers do not yet match the quality of those of the major national papers.

Some analysts see a major transition happening in the recent rapid expansion of digital newsrooms but acknowledge that it is quite fragile. The decline of newspapers cost more than 16,000 editorial jobs in the 10 years between 2003–2012, and another 38,000 magazine jobs were lost. In the same period, digital newsrooms added 5,000 full-time jobs. Some of the digital sites are flirting with profitability, but most are not yet close.[38] In short, there are prospects that the digital revolution may eventually provide the quantity of news now available from the traditional media, but it is still a work in progress that will see less news in the short run.

The Future?

There is a great deal of debate about the future news role of the Internet and social media, including within the team that wrote this book. Objective observers generally reject the view that citizens and professionals will quickly replace traditional news media with something even better. They also reject the view that news will inevitably degenerate into ideological fiefdoms with no concern for the facts. What do we know, and what are present trends that may continue?

The media will continue to change, as it has for almost three centuries. Newspaper reporters are still the most important gatherers of news. However, economic considerations mean that newspapers and newsmagazines will continue to lose readers and advertising dollars. As they decline, the amount of news collected is likely to decline as well. Television news is also under financial pressure and will not be able to take up the slack. Both the number of people using the Internet and social media and innovations in how they are used will continue to grow.

Two critical questions face the digital media. First, can they take up the slack from the decline of traditional media and provide the quantity of hard news necessary to keep leaders and the public adequately informed? In the short run, objective observers tend to think this may not happen, but in the long run, it is very possible. Blogs and Internet news sites already gather and disseminate news. However, they will need more advertising revenue to hire the reporters to find and report the news. Social media already supplement news gathering, and their output is increasing. However, the way social media are structured means that news gathering tends not to be systematic. There are many sites with many orientations and many individuals whose contributions fluctuate with interest and available time. News also tends to be secondary to entertainment.

Second, will the news provided by the digital media continue journalistic standards of professionalism, or will news become largely partisan and even more negative and serve the interests of the few over the many? One very possible outcome is that the continuing competition between news and entertainment, the greater ability of people to choose their news sources, and the need for advertising revenue to pay for technology will mean a continuation of the present emphasis on soft news and a wide range of partisan venues. Advertisers are already pumping money into the Internet, including social media, and ideological and partisan groups are becoming more sophisticated in pursuing their goals through sites that proclaim lofty goals but simultaneously promote the interests of their sponsors. On the other hand, standards of professionalism are still strong among reporters in both the traditional and new media, and the independent nature of social media may help keep news from tending to one extreme or the other.

Government regulations will play a role. Most new communication technologies face demands for regulations that limit their use, raise costs, and in general limit competition with the established media. Battles over the Internet have already begun in courts, legislative bodies, and regulatory bodies.

Finally, humans and the Internet have shown a remarkable ability to adapt and change. As this chapter shows, the news media have experienced centuries of change. The current transition to digital media is one more step down that path.

✓ 6.6 Learning Check

1. Are the changes in the news media trending toward more or less news gathering?
2. Are people getting news from social media?

Answers on p. 236.

The Faces of Race

Bill Minutaglio

Race and ethnicity have a long and often negative history in Texas. African Americans were subjected to slavery and Jim Crow. Mexican Americans long faced discrimination and economic exploitation. Although both groups are seeing a rising middle class, they are still underrepresented among decision makers and those who influence decisions. In 2012, for example, minorities made up only 12 percent of U.S. newspaper journalists, compared to being more than 36 percent of the population.[†]

Bill Minutaglio is a Texas journalist (18 years at the Dallas Morning News *with articles in leading national magazines), author of three Texas biographies, and an award-winning professor of communications at the University of Texas at Austin. Here he writes about racial diversity in Texas journalism.*

When Charlie Strong was named football coach at the University of Texas on Jan. 5 [2014], many regional and national news accounts duly noted that he is making history as the first African-American head coach of a men's team in UT's 131-year history.

The *Houston Chronicle* mentioned the racial significance of the hire in the second paragraph of its first story. The *Austin American-Statesman* and *San Antonio Express-News* stories referenced it in their fifth paragraphs. *The Dallas Morning News* noted it in the ninth paragraph.

Strong's new job is newsworthy, and his race, given the lack of precedent, is arguably newsworthy as well. What hasn't been widely discussed is

how coverage of the hire highlights the lack of diversity among the state's mainstream media and how that influences coverage. Almost all of the state's newsrooms, *The Texas Observer*'s included, are predominantly white.

It will be interesting in that light to see how the cover of the state's flagship magazine, *Texas Monthly*, responds to the news of Strong's hiring.

In the 1970s' 82 issues, two black people appeared unaccompanied on *Texas Monthly*'s cover: U.S. Congresswoman Barbara Jordan and Cootie Hill, a street hustler from Houston's Fifth Ward. (Two other black faces were featured on the 1970s covers, both as maids attending to white women).

There were no solo black Texans on the covers of the magazine's 120 issues in the 1980s.

Four of *Texas Monthly*'s 120 covers during the 1990s featured stand-alone black Texans: athletes Dennis Rodman, Hakeem Olajuwon, George Foreman and Michael Irvin—the latter depicted with a white-powder moustache. (Carl Lewis was featured on another 1990s cover alongside two white men).

Two stand-alone black Texans graced the 120 covers of the 2000s: quarterback Vince Young and singer Beyoncé. (Others include Michael Irvin and Emmitt Smith flanking white quarterback Troy Aikman).

From 2010 until now, no *Texas Monthly* cover has featured an image of an unaccompanied black person.

They're not alone. The *Observer*, while taking a conceptually different and celebrity-averse approach to cover design, has done little better in representing the state's diversity on its front page.

Why does it matter? According to the *Texas Monthly* website, "The single most important page of a magazine is its cover. It's the one that

....
Source: Bill Minutaglio, "The Faces of Race," *Texas Observer*, February 2014, p. 43.

[†]Emily Guskin, "5 Facts about Ethnic and Gender Diversity in U.S. Newsrooms," Pew Research Center, July 18, 2013, http://www.pewresearch.org/fact-tank/2013/07/18/5-facts-about-ethnic-and-gender-diversity-in-u-s-newsrooms/. By permission.

editors and art directors spend the most time thinking about, arguing over, and tweaking right up until the last minute."

I've worked for three national magazines (*The Sporting News, Talk* and *People*), and the "cover meetings" always had one purely pragmatic aim: to figure out what would sell. Race was always the invisible elephant in the room. I once witnessed an exceedingly awkward debate about why a *People* cover was not being devoted to megastar Beyoncé: because she was, well, not the right person at the moment.

In an increasingly diverse place like Texas—a state still wrestling with bitter racial divisions—every publication needs to do more to mirror the population. Every publication needs more minority writers, more minority news, more minority covers.

I asked Jake Silverstein, the talented and thoughtful editor of *Texas Monthly*, about the challenge:

"Absolutely there is more to be done in terms of diversity at *Texas Monthly*. No question. In the past, the magazine has sometimes struggled to represent the full array of voices in Texas. We have made some strides the past few years but we still have a long way to go.… It's something I take very seriously. What I can say is that this is a problem throughout the magazine industry, and it's my hope that in years to come *Texas Monthly* can be a leader in helping to fix it."

Then I asked *Observer* editor Dave Mann the same question. He, too, recognizes the problem:

"Lack of diversity—both on the cover of our magazine and, especially, in our newsroom—has long been a problem at the *Observer*, and I'm deeply troubled by it. We've worked in recent years to have our magazine better represent the state we cover, and while we've had some successes, our efforts haven't been enough.… We have to do better."

Charlie Strong was hired to make sure the Longhorns perform better on the field. His arrival is as good a reminder as any that Texas media has plenty of room for improvement as well.

✓ **Selected Reading Learning Check**

1. True or false: Minority Texans are underrepresented in newspaper coverage but well represented in Texas magazines.
2. True or false: Texas's major liberal/progressive magazine has extensive coverage of minorities on its covers and in its newsroom.

Answers on p. 236.

Conclusion

In many areas, Texas has patterns that differ significantly from those of the nation, but the media at both levels have remarkably similar histories and patterns. Newspapers were long the major outlet for news and remain important today, particularly as gatherers of news and as the source of the details of the news for the elite. Television is still the source of news for more people, but its content is often soft, and it is being challenged by the Internet and social media. The growth in the number of ways to receive news provides the elite and news junkies a wealth of information. Potentially, the social media provide more opportunity for ordinary Texans to participate in the reporting of news and to select how and what they receive. The concern is that this is making news softer and more ideological. Entertainment value is a driving force.

The media continue to play a number of vital roles, albeit playing some better than others: informing citizens and leaders, helping to maintain democracy, contributing to setting the public agenda, and influencing our views to some degree. Changes in ownership of the media, the availability of better campaign techniques for office seekers and citizen groups, and the movement toward predominance of the Internet and social media portend both challenges and opportunities.

Chapter Summary

LO 6.1 **Compare the ways in which Texans get their information today with past patterns**. The sources of news for Texans are changing. Newspapers were most important in the 1800s and the first half of the 20th century. Today, the interested public gets news from multiple sources. Newspapers are still important, but television is the largest source for most people, and the Internet and social media are growing. A major concern with the changes is the decline in the amount of actual news received by the public.

LO 6.2 **Describe the roles of the media in Texas politics**. There are many platforms from which to receive news, but the content of the news appears to be in decline. Absorbing the news requires some effort and certain conditions, which means that the more interested citizens and leaders are likely to gain much more from the news than the average citizen. Historically, the press was highly partisan and often an unreliable source of accurate information. In the 20th century, it became a more professional provider of information in Texas and the nation, although in recent years the media have become more adversarial. The media have used the state's open meetings and open records acts to provide more information about public policymaking. In Texas and the nation, the ability to investigate is in decline because of lack of money and corporate influence, but the press has generally played a positive role in exposing the state's periodic scandals. The media, together with political leaders and interest groups, participate in setting the agenda of what government will or will not consider. Texas media have worked at this role but face difficulties and are not always successful. The media seldom change people's minds, but they do affect public opinion through priming and framing. They help to shape what we think about and the evaluations we make.

LO 6.3 **Discuss the roles of the media in modern Texas election campaigns**. The media play a large role in campaigns through the ads they run and the coverage they give the candidates. Because the media and the candidates have different goals but need each other, the relationship is often conflictual. Each tries to manipulate the other. Use of the Internet and social media in campaigns has become very important and more sophisticated since 2008.

LO 6.4 **Analyze whether there is ideological bias in the Texas media**. Research indicates that there is not a net bias in the media toward one party or ideology, although many parts of the media—talk shows, the two ideological cable networks, and blogs—have become more partisan. There is evidence of a commercial bias and a strong preference for news that is entertaining, rather than important but boring or difficult to understand.

LO 6.5 **Distinguish how print and electronic media are regulated by government**. The national government has taken primary responsibility for regulation of the media. Newspapers have never faced substantial regulation, and today only broadcast television is still heavily regulated. The major legal issue facing the Internet today is whether and how to apply the idea of net neutrality.

LO 6.6 **Discuss the positive and negative effects of the changes the media are undergoing in Texas**. Newspapers have long been the major gatherers of news. Their decline has meant fewer reporters actually gathering news for the other media to use. The growth of cable news and the increasing role of Internet blogs and social media are giving impetus to softer news and more opportunities for partisanship. The digital media provide more opportunity for citizen participation and innovation and will probably become the dominant news media. How that will affect news is the subject of a major debate.

Key Terms

social media, p. 205
news website, p. 205
blog, p. 205
soft news, p. 208
hard news, p. 208
yellow journalism, p. 209
professionalism, p. 209
adversarial, p. 210

open meetings, p. 211
open records, p. 211
agenda setting, p. 213
attack ad, p. 215
priming, p. 216
framing, p. 216
horserace journalism, p. 219
civic engagement, p. 220

prior restraint, p. 223
net neutrality, p. 224
shield law, p. 224
niche journalism (narrowcasting), p. 226
homogenization of news, p. 226
Capitol press corps, p. 228

Learning Check Answers

6.1 1. More people get their news from television, although digital and social media are becoming more important, particularly for the young.
2. In the early 20th century, most people got their news from newspapers.

6.2 1. With fewer reporters, the media are less able to investigate wrongdoing.
2. Media framing is saying how important an issue is or which part of a situation is most important.

6.3 1. The biggest factor in the high cost of Texas political campaigns is having to advertise in so many markets.
2. Yes, campaigns are using the Internet and social media more effectively.

6.4 1. No, examples of bias tend to balance out.
2. Partisanship tends to appear most consistently in areas in which consumers can choose their preferred ideological presentation.

6.5 1. Broadcast television is the most regulated medium.
2. The federal government has regulated media the most.

6.6 1. With fewer reporters and the decline of newspapers, less news is being gathered.
2. Yes, a wide variety of news is gathered on social media.

Selected Reading Learning Check

1. False. Minorities are underrepresented in Texas magazines as well.
2. False. The need for diversity is recognized but has not arrived.

7

The Politics of Interest Groups

Learning Objectives

7.1 Explain what interest groups are, why they form, and what their essential characteristics are.

7.2 Describe the types of interest groups and analyze the qualities of a powerful interest group.

7.3 Evaluate the kinds of activities that interest groups use to influence Texas government.

7.4 Analyze how interest groups are regulated and evaluate the effectiveness of these laws.

CRITICAL THINKING

Take a closer look at the cartoon. What do you think? Is it time we place stricter restrictions on the role of campaign contributions in Texas elections?

The typical focus of politics is on nomination and election of citizens to public office. There is, however, much more to politics than that. Politics is perhaps best understood as the process of influencing public policy decisions to protect and preserve a group, to achieve the group's goals, and to distribute benefits to the group's members. Organized citizens demand policies that promote their financial security, education, health, welfare, and protection.

Because government makes and enforces public policy decisions, it is not surprising that people try to influence officials who make and apply society's rules or policies, nor is it surprising that one important approach is through group action. History shows that people who organize for political action tend to be more effective in achieving their goals than persons acting alone. This principle is particularly true if a group is well financed. Money plays a big role in state government and state elections, and groups that help politicians finance their campaigns often achieve their goals (as illustrated by the cartoon at the beginning of this chapter).

Interest Groups in the Political Process

★ **LO7.1** Explain what interest groups are, why they form, and what their essential characteristics are.

When people attempt to influence political decisions or the selection of the men and women who make such decisions, they usually turn either to political parties (examined in Chapter 4), the media (examined in Chapter 6), or interest groups (the subject of this chapter).

What Is an Interest Group?

An **interest group** may be identified as a pressure group, a special interest group, or a lobby. It is an organization whose members share common views and objectives. To promote their interests, such groups participate in activities designed to influence government officials and policy decisions for the benefit of group members or their cause. For example, during every regular legislative session, the Independent Colleges and Universities of Texas (ICUT), an organization of more than 40 private colleges and universities, lobbies the legislature against cuts to the Texas Equalization Grants (TEG), a student aid program that provides financial assistance to students who attend these institutions. Another interest group is the Texas Coalition to Abolish the Death Penalty (TCADP), which continues to lobby actively for a moratorium on the death penalty. Parent groups, teacher organizations, and school board associations all actively lobby for more state money for the state's public schools.

Although political parties and interest groups both attempt to influence policy decisions by government officials, they differ in their methods. The

interest group
An organization that seeks to influence government officials and their policies on behalf of members sharing common views and objectives (e.g., labor union or trade association).

principal purpose of party activity is to increase the number of its members who are elected or appointed to public offices, in order to gain control of government and achieve party goals. In contrast, an interest group seeks to influence government officials (regardless of their party affiliation) to the advantage of the group. In general, an interest group wants government to create and implement policies that benefit the group, without necessarily placing its own members in public office.

Part of the purpose of economic groups (for example, the Texas Association of Business) and professional groups (such as the Texas Trial Lawyers Association) is to make their policy preferences known to government officials. Interest groups act as intermediaries for people who share common interests but reside throughout the state; in this way, interest groups add to the formal system of geographic representation used for electing many officeholders. In essence, such organizations serve the interests of their members by providing functional representation within the political system. They offer a form of protection by voicing the interests of such groups as businesspeople, laborers, farmers, religious groups, racial/ethnic groups, teachers, physicians, and college students across the state. These groups are composed of people who have similar interests but who may not constitute a majority in any city, county, legislative district, or state.

The Reasons for Interest Groups

Growth and diversity of interest groups in the United States continue unabated. An increasingly complex society has much to do with the rate of growth of interest groups in the country and within states. Political scientists Allan Cigler and Burnett Loomis contend that these growing numbers, plus high levels of activity, distinguish contemporary interest group politics from previous eras.[1] Interest groups proliferate in Texas and throughout the country for several reasons.

Legal and Cultural Reasons In *NAACP v. Alabama*, 357 U.S. 449 (1958), the U.S. Supreme Court recognized the **right of association** as part of the right of assembly guaranteed by the First Amendment to the U.S. Constitution. This decision greatly facilitated the development of interest groups, ensuring the right of citizens to organize for political, economic, religious, and social purposes.

The nation's political culture has traditionally encouraged citizens to organize themselves into a bewildering array of associations—religious, fraternal, professional, and recreational, among others. Americans have responded by creating literally thousands of such groups. In the 1960s and 1970s, for example, social movements sparked interest group activities on issues involving civil rights, women's rights, student rights, and opposition to the Vietnam War. In Texas, controversies over social issues (e.g., the ban on same-sex marriage), education policy issues (e.g., school finance), and immigration reform have sparked new groups and revitalized existing interest groups. For instance, in 2012, Texans for Real Efficiency and Equity in Education, a new

right of association
The U.S. Supreme Court has ruled that this right is part of the right of assembly guaranteed by the First Amendment to the U.S. Constitution and that it protects the right of people to organize into groups for political purposes.

education group, formed to intervene in the latest round of public school financing lawsuits. Their solution to problems in our current school system is charter schools. In 2013, the Reform Immigration for Texas Alliance (RITA) formed as a statewide network dedicated to building support for comprehensive immigration reform with fair, humane, and sensible policies.

Decentralized Government In a **decentralized government**, power is not concentrated at the highest level. Decentralization is achieved in two principal ways. First, the federal system divides power between the national government and the 50 state governments (as explained in Chapter 2, "Federalism and the Texas Constitution"). In turn, each state shares its power with a variety of local governments, including counties, cities, and special districts. Second, within each level of government, power is separated into three branches, or departments: legislative, executive, and judicial. This separation of powers is especially apparent at the national and state levels.

A decentralized structure increases the opportunities for interest groups to form and influence government. This structure provides different access points for groups to fight their battles at different levels of government and within different branches at each level. For instance, the Texas Bicycle Coalition (now Bike Texas) was unsuccessful in obtaining legislation at the state level to protect bicyclists on Texas roads. Nevertheless, the organization pressed successfully for protective city ordinances, such as in Austin, El Paso, Fort Worth, and San Antonio. Similarly, although Governor Rick Perry vetoed a legislative bill banning texting while driving in 2011, more than 20 Texas cities, including Arlington, Austin, El Paso, Galveston, and San Antonio, passed city ordinances banning texting while driving, especially in school zones. More recently, the American Civil Liberties Union (ACLU) of Texas targeted the Texas Education Commissioner to lobby for a ban on the use of Tasers and pepper spray by security officers against students in schools. Thus, dispersal of power within branches and levels of government enhances an interest group's chance of success.

The Strength of the Party System and Political Ideologies Two other factors have precipitated the influence of interest groups: the strength (or weakness) of the party system and political ideologies. First, the absence of unified and responsible political parties magnifies opportunities for interest group action. A lack of strong, organized political parties can particularly affect policymakers (both state and local). In such cases, public officials are less likely to vote along party lines and therefore are more susceptible to pressure from well-organized interest groups, particularly if candidates rely on interest group campaign contributions. In recent years, the Republican Party has dominated the Texas legislature and other statewide elective and appointive positions. Factions have developed within the Republican Party, however. By 2014, the Texas Tea Party had become a powerful faction within the Texas Republican Party, exercising considerable influence in the party's primaries and its state convention (see Chapter 4, "Political Parties"). These factions weaken party unity. Second, ideologies, or developed systems

decentralized government Decentralization is achieved by dividing power between national and state governments and separating legislative, executive, and judicial branches at both levels.

of political, social, and economic beliefs, have not been strong factors in Texas politics. Instead, public officials rely more on their constituents or on the issues and less on ideology. Public officials are likely to have a stronger commitment to ideological beliefs than most voters, but they remain susceptible to the pressures of interest groups.

Characteristics of Interest Groups

Citizens may join an interest group for a variety of reasons, whether financial, professional, or social. Students who graduate from college often find themselves joining a professional or occupational group (see Table 7.1).

In some cases, people join an interest group simply because they want to be part of a network of like-minded individuals working for a cause. The interest group often provides members with information and benefits and usually tries to involve them in the political process. Such a description suggests that any organization becomes an interest group when it influences or attempts to influence governmental decisions.

There are almost as many **organizational patterns** as there are interest groups. This variety arises from the fact that in addition to lobbying, most interest groups perform nonpolitical functions that are of paramount importance to their members. Texas Impact, for example, is a statewide religious grassroots network representing several faith communities. It emphasizes charitable and spiritual activities but also undertakes interfaith legislative advocacy.

Some interest groups are highly centralized organizations that take the form of a single controlling body. An example of such a centralized group currently operating in Texas is the National Rifle Association. Other groups are decentralized, consisting of loose alliances of local and regional subgroups. Their activities may be directed at either the local, state, or national level. Many trade associations (such as the Texas Mid-Continent Oil and Gas Association) and labor unions (such as those affiliated with the American Federation of Labor–Congress of Industrial Organizations [AFL-CIO]) are examples of decentralized organizations active in Texas politics. Other national organizations, including the National Women's Political Caucus and Common Cause, usually have both state and local chapters in Texas.

Interest groups are composed chiefly of persons from professional and managerial occupations. Members of interest groups tend to have greater resources than most individuals possess. For instance, members are more likely to be homeowners, with high levels of income and formal education, who enjoy a high standard of living. Participation in interest groups, especially active participation, varies. Many citizens are not affiliated with any group, whereas others are members of several. Recent technology provides individuals easier access to interest group membership. For example, the Texas Community College Teachers Association (TCCTA) provides potential members an opportunity to join and register for conferences online. The site includes a number of resources, web links, and access to financial benefits. In addition, TCCTA maintains Facebook and Twitter accounts, a blog, and

organizational pattern
The structure of a special interest group. Some interest groups have a decentralized pattern of organization (e.g., the AFL-CIO, with many local unions). Others are centralized (e.g., the National Rifle Association, which is a national body with a group operating in Texas).

Table 7.1	Texas Professional and Occupational Associations*

Health Related

Texas Dental Association

Texas Health Care Association

Texas Hospital Association

Texas Medical Association

Texas Ophthalmological Association

Texas Nurses Association

Texas Physical Therapy Association

Texas Counseling Association

Law Related

Texas Criminal Defense Lawyers Association

Texas Civil Justice League

Texas Trial Lawyers Association

Mexican American Bar Association of Texas

Texas Women Lawyers

Texas Young Lawyers Association

Texas Association of Consumer Lawyers

Education Related

Texas American Federation of Teachers

Texas Association of College Teachers

Texas Classroom Teachers Association

Texas PTA (Parent Teacher Association)

Texas Community College Teachers Association

Texas State Teachers Association

Texas Library Association

Texas Association of College and University Student Personnel

Texas Faculty Association

Texas School Counselor Association

Texas Association of School Administrators

Miscellaneous

Association of Environmental and Engineering Geologists (AEG) Texas

Texas Society of Architects

Texas Society of Certified Public Accountants

Intelligent Transportation Society (ITS) Texas

*All organizations listed can be found on the Internet.

CRITICAL THINKING

Review Table 7.1 on professional interest groups. Given your professional goals, which interest group might you join? What, do you suppose, would be the advantages of joining a professional interest group?

information on the use of social media in classrooms. Some individuals, however, will not join an interest group—especially when they believe that they still benefit without actually having to join and pay the costs of membership.[2]

An organized group of any size usually comprises an active minority and a passive majority. As a result, decisions are regularly made by relatively few members. These decision makers may range from a few elected officers to a larger body of delegates representing the entire membership. Organizations generally leave decision making and other leadership activities to a few people. Widespread apathy among rank-and-file members and the difficulty of dislodging entrenched leaders probably account for limited participation in most group decisions. Factors that influence **group leadership** include the group's financial resources (members who contribute most heavily usually have greater weight in making decisions), time-consuming leadership duties (only a few people can afford to devote much of their time without compensation), and the personality traits of leaders (some individuals have greater leadership ability and motivation than others).

✔ **7.1 Learning Check**

1. Name at least two factors that motivate interest group formation.
2. True or False: Most interest groups have an active membership.

Answers on p. 272.

Types of Interest Groups

LO7.2 Describe the types of interest groups and analyze the qualities of a powerful interest group.

The increasing diversity of American interest groups at national, state, and local levels of government permits the groups to be classified in several ways. Not only can interest groups be studied by organizational patterns (such as centralized versus decentralized, as discussed earlier), they can also be categorized according to the level or branch of government to which they direct their attention. Some groups exert influence at all levels of government and on legislative, executive (including administrative), and judicial officials. Others may try to spread their views among the general public and may best be classified according to the subject matter they represent. Some groups do not fit readily into any category, whereas others fit into more than one. In this section, we examine various types of interest groups: economic groups, professional and public employee groups, social groups, and public interest groups.

Economic Groups

Many interest groups exist primarily to promote their members' economic self-interest. These organizations are commonly known as **economic interest groups**. Traditionally, many people contribute significant amounts of money and time to obtain the financial benefits of group membership. Thus, some organizations exist to further the economic interests of a broad group, such as trade associations, whereas others seek to protect the interests of a single type of business, such as restaurant associations. The Texas Association of Business (generally known as TAB) is an example of a broader type of interest group,

group leadership
Individuals who guide the decisions of interest groups. Leaders of groups tend to have financial resources that permit them to contribute money and devote time to group affairs.

economic interest group
Interest groups that exist primarily to promote their members' economic self-interest. Trade associations and labor unions are classified as economic interest groups because they are organized to promote policies that will maximize profits and wages.

known as an umbrella organization. There are also individual corporations, such as communications giant AT&T, that use the political process to promote a company's particular economic interests.

Business Groups Businesspeople understand that they have common interests that may be promoted by collective action. They were among the first to organize and press national, state, and local governments to adopt favorable public policies. **Business organizations** typically advocate lower taxes, a lessening or elimination of price and quality controls by government, and minimal concessions to labor unions. At the state level, business organizations most often take the form of trade associations (groups that act on behalf of an industry). The Texas Gaming Association (a group that favors the creation of destination casino resorts in the state) is an interest group that has lobbied the state legislature in recent legislative sessions in support of gambling interests. Two of the many other Texas trade associations are the Texas Association of Builders (a group that focuses on creating a positive environment for the housing industry) and the Texas Good Roads and Transportation Association (a group made up of highway construction contractors, chamber of commerce members, professionals, and transportation experts, among others, dedicated to ensuring efficient transportation and increased funding for highways).

In past legislative sessions, Texas businesses and their representatives succeeded in having many of their policy preferences enacted into law. Some reports indicate that TAB, along with Texans for Lawsuit Reform, contributed more than $2.6 million to support Republican candidates in key legislative races in 2002. Subsequently, the newly GOP-controlled 78th Legislature (2003) passed several "business friendly" bills. One of the more significant bills limited lawsuits against manufacturers, pharmaceutical companies, and retailers.[3] Furthermore, the tobacco industry successfully defeated a statewide ban on smoking in public places, hiring as many as 40 lobbyists in 2009.[4] Big business (such as oil and gas, banking and finance, and insurance) has also been successful in defending tax breaks and subsidies. Small businesses were effective in passing a permanent minimum $1 million deduction to the small business franchise tax exemption in the 2013 legislative session.

Labor Groups Unions representing Texas workers, though relatively active, are not as numerous or powerful as business-related groups. The state's **labor organizations** seek, among other goals, government intervention to increase wages, obtain adequate health insurance coverage, provide unemployment insurance, and promote safe working conditions. Although Texans are traditionally sensitive to the potential political power of organized labor, certain industrial labor organizations are generally regarded as significant in Texas government. These are the Texas affiliates of the AFL-CIO (comprising 1,300 local unions and more than 200,000 members), the Communication Workers of America, and local affiliates of the International Brotherhood of Teamsters. For a highly industrialized state with a large population, union membership in Texas is small compared with that of other states. In 2013, union membership

business organization
An economic interest group, such as a trade association (e.g., Texas Gaming Association), that lobbies for policies favoring business.

labor organization
A union that supports public policies designed to increase wages, obtain adequate health insurance coverage, provide unemployment insurance, promote safe working conditions, and otherwise protect the interests of workers.

Participants in a Texas AFL-CIO "Health Care Can't Wait" rally, held at the Capitol building in Austin in 2013.

Courtesy of Texas AFL-CIO

CRITICAL THINKING

Reflect on this photo. What impact do you think rallies have on lawmakers when passing legislation?

dropped to about 518,000 members in Texas, which is about 4.8 percent of the wage and salary workers, according to the U.S. Bureau of Labor Statistics. With the pending cuts in education, health care, and state jobs in the 2011 legislature, several unions relied on rallies as a means of expressing opposition. The Texas State Employees Union was a leading organizer of the "Save Our State Rally," in which an estimated 6,000 to 7,000 people participated at the steps of the state Capitol. Although the rally brought considerable media attention, the unions were unsuccessful in preventing budgetary cuts made during the legislative session. They held another rally during the 2013 legislative session, but the turnout was not as large.

Professional/Public Employee Groups

Closely related to economic interest groups are groups dedicated to furthering the interests of a profession, such as physicians or attorneys. Public employees have also organized to advance their interests. Teachers have been especially active in their efforts to influence government decisions.

Professional Groups Standards of admission to a profession or an occupation, as well as the licensing of practitioners, concern **professional groups.**

professional group
An organization of physicians, lawyers, accountants, or other professional people that lobbies for policies beneficial to members.

Examples of Texas professional and occupational associations are the State Bar of Texas (attorneys), the Texas Health Care Association, and the Texas Society of Certified Public Accountants. (See Table 7.1 for a list of some of the more important Texas professional and occupational associations.) Professionals are more effective if they organize in groups that advocate for their interests. Physicians won a significant victory in the 76th Legislature in 1999 when Texas became the first state to allow doctors to bargain collectively with health maintenance organizations over fees and policies. The Texas Medical Association (TMA) successfully lobbied for passage of a constitutional amendment, Proposition 12, that authorized the state legislature to impose a $250,000 cap for noneconomic damages in medical malpractice cases. TMA also won approval in the state legislature for a new medical school in the Rio Grande Valley and an increase in the state's cap on student loans for young physicians in order to increase the number of primary care doctors. TMA has sought to improve the Medicaid system by ensuring physician payments, as well as expand Medicaid funding under the Patient Protection and Affordable Care Act so that compensated care is available to more Texas patients.

Public Employee Groups Public officer and employee groups of state and local governments organize to obtain better working conditions, higher wages, more fringe benefits, and better retirement packages. The Texas State Employees Association, which represents government employees, for instance, lobbies for legislation that prevents job cuts and increases pay and health care benefits. Teacher groups were successful in the state legislature when it came to pay raises for every public school teacher, librarian, and registered school nurse in Texas during the 76th legislative session (1999). They also successfully pushed a plan to fully or partially fund state-supported health insurance for public school teachers and other school employees, both active and retired. Teacher organizations have lobbied against cuts in education funding, as well as school finance legislation that they believe provides inadequate new funding and would intrude on local control of school matters. During the 2011 legislative session, teacher associations participated in rallies outside the state Capitol to demand that the legislature use the "rainy day" fund rather than reduce funding for public education. (For more on school finance, see Chapter 13, "Finance and Fiscal Policy.") Teacher organizations have also been vocal with regard to changes in curriculum requirements by the State Board of Education and testing mandates set by the legislature and the Texas Education Agency. (For more on education policy affecting public schools, see Chapter 10, "Public Policy and Administration.")

Among state government employees, the largest group is the Texas Public Employees Association with more than 15,000 members. City government groups include the Texas City Management Association and the Texas City Attorneys Association. Through their organizational activities, these public officer and employee groups resist efforts to reduce the size of state and local governmental bureaucracies (though not always with success). The County Judges and Commissioners Association of Texas and the Justices of the Peace and Constables Association of Texas, for example, have been instrumental in

public officer and employee group
An organization of city managers, county judges, or other public employees or officials that lobbies for public policies that protect group interests.

assuring that measures designed to reform Texas's justice of the peace courts and county courts reflect their members' interests. Two of the state's largest police unions, the Texas Municipal Police Association and the Combined Law Enforcement Associations of Texas, which together represent more than 30,000 officers, joined forces to lobby for police officer rights. Although unsuccessful, the police unions went on record in support of a legislative proposal during the 2011 legislative session that would have banned texting while driving statewide.

Social Groups

Texas also has a wide array of **social interest groups**. These include racial and ethnic organizations, civil rights organizations, gender-based organizations, religion-based organizations, and several public interest groups.

Racial and Ethnic Groups Leaders of Texas's **racial and ethnic groups** recognize that only through effective organizations can they hope to achieve their cherished goals. Examples of these goals include eliminating racial discrimination in employment; improving public schools; increasing educational opportunities; and obtaining greater representation in the state legislature, city councils, school boards, and other policymaking bodies of government.

One formidable group, the National Association for the Advancement of Colored People (NAACP), is an effective racial interest group. According to the Texas State Historical Association, chapters of the Texas NAACP were established during the World War I era, with the first chapter forming in El Paso in 1915. The organization has been successful in influencing public policies relating to school integration and local government redistricting. The NAACP also effectively fought for hate crimes legislation that enhances penalties for crimes on the basis of race, color, disability, religion, national origin, gender, or sexual preference.[5] In addition, the organization continues to advocate strict enforcement against racial profiling. Texas law defines racial profiling as an action by law enforcement personnel on the basis of an individual's race, ethnicity, or national origin as opposed to the individual's behavior or information identifying the individual as being engaged in criminal activity. In 2011, the Texas NAACP actively opposed making a Confederate battle flag image available on specialty Texas license plates. The organization successfully appealed to the Texas Department of Motor Vehicles to prevent legitimizing a symbol that, in their view, represents brutality and fear and that is used by hate groups to promote a racist ideology.[6] The organization, along with Latino groups, strongly advocated against the newly implemented photo voter ID law (for more on this issue, see Chapter 5, "Campaigns and Elections"). Asian Americans in recent years have also formed organizations and PACs such as the Network of Asian American Organizations, which serves the interests of Asian American communities in Central Texas.

In Texas, Latino groups, especially Mexican American organizations, are more numerous than African American interest groups. The oldest Latino group, the League of United Latin American Citizens (LULAC), was

social interest group
Groups concerned primarily with social issues, including organizations devoted to civil rights, racial and ethnic matters, religion, and public interest protection.

racial and ethnic groups
Organizations that seek to influence government decisions that affect a particular racial or ethnic group, such as the National Association for the Advancement of Colored People (NAACP) and the League of United Latin American Citizens (LULAC), which seek to influence government decisions affecting African Americans and Latinos, respectively.

founded in 1929.[7] (See the Selected Reading, "Unsung Hero of Civil Rights," for information on one of LULAC's founders, Alonso S. Perales.) LULAC has worked for equal educational opportunities for Latinos, as well as for full citizenship rights. It continues to advocate for adequate public school funding and bilingual education, as well as higher education policies, like the "Top Ten Percent Rule" and affirmative action, both of which are designed to diversify student populations. In addition, LULAC successfully pressed for state funds to open the school of pharmacy at Texas A&M–Kingsville, which was named after the late state legislator and strong advocate for higher education, Irma Rangel.[8] LULAC has brought attention to the importance of the U.S. Census, as well as to the State Board of Education's unwillingness to incorporate more Hispanic historical figures in public school textbooks.

Another organization, the Mexican American Legal Defense and Education Fund (MALDEF), uses court action in pursuit of political equality, equal education, immigration rights, and representation for Latinos. Both LULAC and MALDEF have been instrumental in addressing redistricting, especially when it comes to voting rights. On behalf of a statewide coalition of Texas Latino organizations called the Texas Latino Redistricting Task Force, among other plaintiffs, MALDEF in 2012 successfully challenged the redistricting plans created by the Texas legislature for the U.S. House of Representatives and the Texas House of Representatives, claiming that the plans did not provide fair representation for Latinos. A three-judge federal court allowed for the creation of two out of the four new congressional seats as Latino-majority districts. The court also created an additional Latino-majority district in the Texas House of Representatives, thus increasing the number of Latino-majority districts to 34. MALDEF also successfully advocated against anti-immigrant legislative proposals, as well as bans on "sanctuary cities" (municipalities that have policies that prohibit local law enforcement officers to inquire into the immigration status of a person or report violations to federal immigration enforcement officials).

Women's Groups   The Texas Women's Political Caucus is an example of a **women's organization** that promotes equal rights and greater participation by women in the political arena. The League of Women Voters of Texas is a nonpartisan organization advocating greater political participation and public understanding of governmental issues. It also assists voters in becoming better informed by publishing *The Texas Voters Guide*, which provides information about elections, candidates, and candidates' positions on various issues.

The Texas Federation of Republican Women, a partisan interest group with more than 160 local clubs, provides resources for women to influence government actions and policies. This organization actively encourages Republican women to run for public office. Another organization that formed in 2003, in response to the dwindling number of Democratic women in the state legislature, is Annie's List. This organization recruits, trains, and supports

women's organization
A women's group, such as the League of Women Voters, that engages in lobbying and educational activities to promote greater political participation by women and others.

progressive female candidates, as well as raises money for these candidates. Among their endorsements in the 2014 statewide races were Democratic candidates Wendy Davis for governor and Leticia Van de Putte for lieutenant governor. The organization provides supporters an opportunity to "Join our Movement" in their website. Annie's List used social media to follow Senator Wendy Davis's 11-hour filibuster against a bill to restrict access to abortions in 2013. Members and supporters live-tweeted from the Capitol during the debate. The hashtag (#standwithwendy) garnered over 500,000 tweets during the course of her speech.

Other interest groups, such as the Hispanic Women's Network of Texas, focus on the concerns and needs of Hispanic women. This organization is a statewide organization dedicated to advancing the interests of Latinas in the public, corporate, and civic arenas. Another organization, Las Comadres Para Las Américas, with its central office in Austin, serves as a network for Latinas and provides training for candidates and public policy advocates. The Texas Latina List, which has its origin in Fort Worth, is a political action committee that recruits and funds Latina candidates at all levels of appointive and elective office.

Religion-Based Groups The Christian Coalition is an example of a **religion-based group**. With millions of Texans identifying themselves as conservative Christians, the organization continues to be one of the state's most influential political forces, though it had more momentum in the 1990s than it does now. This interest group engages in political action, primarily within the Republican Party. Issues that have precipitated the Christian Coalition's entrance on the political scene are abortion, homosexuality, limits on prayer in public schools, and the decline of the traditional nuclear family.[9]

The Texas Freedom Network was formed in the 1990s to oppose the increasing presence of the Christian Coalition. This organization monitors the activities of right-wing conservatives, musters liberal and mainstream voters, and provides an alternative voice on current political issues.[10] The Texas Faith Network, the official blog of the Texas Freedom Network, also formed in the 1990s, monitors religious leaders statewide who represent the religious right and who intend to influence political conservatives (usually Republicans). In recent years, the Texas Freedom Network has worked on several issues such as defending civil liberties, strengthening public schools, and especially protecting religious freedom. The organization is also vocal in its opposition to the social conservatives on the State Board of Education who influence the public school curriculum and the content of textbooks.

Another religion-based organization, the Texas Industrial Areas Foundation, which operates in cities such as Dallas and in the Rio Grande Valley, supports increased funding for parent training, easier access for children to qualify for Medicaid benefits, and increasing Children's Health Insurance Program (CHIP) eligibility to more families.[11] Valley Interfaith, made up primarily of churches and schools, has successfully lobbied the Brownsville school district to increase wages for employees and has indirectly influenced

religion-based group
An interest group, such as the Texas Freedom Network, that lobbies for policies to promote its religious interests.

other public institutions and companies to provide a "living wage" for their workers so they can live above the poverty level. In recent legislative sessions, the organization has actively lobbied the state legislature, demanding restoration of funds cut from CHIP, increases in Medicaid funding, and increases in state funding for public schools, as well as an equitable tax system that does not burden the poor. Sister organizations in San Antonio (Communities Organized for Public Service [COPS], which has been active since the 1970s, and Metro Alliance) successfully lobbied the legislature in the past to allow cities to use sales tax revenue to create job training and early childhood development programs.[12]

Public Interest Groups

Unlike most interest groups, **public interest groups** claim to promote the general interests of society, rather than narrower private or corporate interests. Environmental, political participation, education-related, and public morality (not directly associated with established religion) organizations are often identified as public interest groups.

Public interest organizations pursue diverse goals. Common Cause Texas, for example, focuses primarily on governmental and institutional reform. It advocates open meeting laws, public financing of political campaigns, and stricter financial disclosure laws. Texans for Public Justice supports efforts toward campaign finance reform, such as limitations on campaign contributions by political action committees and individuals. The Texas League of Conservation Voters uses a scorecard to monitor the voting records of state lawmakers who support environment-friendly "green" bills. These public interest organizations also use social media technology, such as Twitter and Facebook, to keep supporters connected. (See Table 7.2 for a partial list of Texas public interest groups.)

Texas Power Groups

Texas legislators readily identify the types of interest groups they consider most powerful: business-oriented trade associations (representing oil, gas, tobacco, chemical manufacturers, insurance, and railroads), professional associations (physicians, lawyers, and teachers), and labor unions. Other groups wielding considerable influence include brewers, truckers, automobile dealers, bankers, and realtors. Some of the most influential interest groups operating not only in Texas but also nationwide are general business organizations (e.g., chambers of commerce), schoolteacher associations, utility companies, insurance companies and associations, hospital and nursing home associations, and bar associations for attorneys.[13]

Interest groups typified as **power groups** have several common traits. For one, these groups maintain strong links with both legislators (whose policy decisions affect group interests) and bureaucrats (whose regulatory authority controls activities of group members). Power groups often are repeat players in Texas politics, meaning they have been influencing politics

public interest group
An organization claiming to represent a broad public interest (environmental, consumer, political participation, and public morality) rather than a narrow private interest.

power group
An effective interest group strongly linked with legislators and bureaucrats for the purpose of influencing decision making and having a continuing presence in Austin as a "repeat player" from session to session.

Table 7.2 Texas Public Interest Groups*

Education Related

Texas Parent PAC

Texans for Education Reform

Texans for Real Efficiency and Equity in Education

Environmental

Texas Campaign for the Environment

Texas Wildlife Association

Environment Texas

Sierra Club, Lone Star Chapter

Public Participation and Social Justice

Texas Association of Community Action Agencies

Communities Organized for Public Service

Public Citizen/Texas

The League of Women Voters of Texas

Equality Texas

Public Morality

Mothers Against Drunk Driving

Texas Right to Life Committee

National Abortion and Reproductive Rights Action League Pro-Choice Texas

*All organizations listed can be found on the Internet.

CRITICAL THINKING

Review Table 7.2, which provides a sample of public interest groups. If given the opportunity, what central issue/concern would you create a public interest group around?

in consecutive legislative sessions for a long time. Another indication of power group influence is having headquarters in Austin. Many business-related associations, for example, own a headquarters building in the capital city. Others lease or rent buildings and office suites there. This proximity to the Texas Capitol and the main offices of state agencies provides regular contact with state officials and gives such associations a path to influence in state government.[14] In some cases, according to watchdog organizations, interest groups have received free use of meeting rooms in the Texas Capitol building for receptions.

One of the most influential power groups is the Texas Medical Association (TMA), formed in 1853. With a well-organized grassroots network, a skilled lobbying team, and more than 47,000 licensed physicians and medical students in Texas, TMA is one of Texas's most powerful professional groups. According to TMA's figures, the group succeeded in passing as much

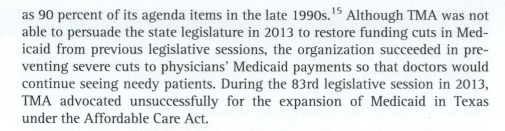

7.2 Learning Check

1. True or False: All interest groups have one objective in common: to promote their self-interest.
2. Which are generally more powerful in Texas, business interest groups or labor groups?

Answers on p. 272.

as 90 percent of its agenda items in the late 1990s.[15] Although TMA was not able to persuade the state legislature in 2013 to restore funding cuts in Medicaid from previous legislative sessions, the organization succeeded in preventing severe cuts to physicians' Medicaid payments so that doctors would continue seeing needy patients. During the 83rd legislative session in 2013, TMA advocated unsuccessfully for the expansion of Medicaid in Texas under the Affordable Care Act.

Interest Group Activities

LO7.3   Evaluate the kinds of activities that interest groups use to influence Texas government.

When interest groups urge their members and others to become actively involved, they encourage people to participate in the political process. In some cases, interest groups even encourage members to consider running for public office. Groups benefit from having their supporters serve in decision-making positions, especially on influential boards and commissions. Local property taxpayers' associations, for example, frequently put forward candidates for public school boards and municipal offices in an effort to keep property taxes low. Likewise, when organizations of real estate agents successfully lobby for the placement of their members in appointed positions on local planning and zoning commissions, they gain a distinct advantage. Because government officials need support for their policies, interest groups seek to mobilize and build that support, particularly for policies that form part of a group's goals and interests. Having the support or opposition of certain interest groups may determine the success or failure of policy decisions.

Interest groups also serve as an outlet for discussions concerning policy issues. In doing so, they shape conflict and consensus in society. Conflict is the more usual outcome because each group is bent on pursuing its own limited ends. This commitment, in turn, leads to clashes with other groups seeking their own ends. Conflict is even more likely when addressing controversial issues, such as school finance, abortion, environmental protection, same-sex marriage, voter identification, redistricting, or immigration reform.

In some cases, however, certain issues may galvanize coalitions among various interest groups. For instance, groups representing teachers, parents, religious organizations, and civil rights organizations have rallied around the need for increased school funding. Even business organizations, such as the Texas Association of Business, joined forces. In 2011, many groups organized rallies called "Save Texas Schools," which were centered on the issue of increased school funding and the necessity to use the "rainy day" fund to cover any budgetary shortfalls. (For more on the "rainy day" fund, see Chapter 13, "Finance and Fiscal Policy.")

Political scientists know that interest groups use a wide range of techniques to influence policy decisions. These **interest group techniques** may be classified as lobbying; personal communication; giving favors and gifts; grassroots activities; electioneering; campaign financing by political action committees; and, in extreme instances, bribery and other illegal or unethical practices.

interest group technique
An action such as lobbying, personal communication, giving favors and gifts, grassroots activities, electioneering, campaign financing by political action committees, and, in extreme instances, bribery and other unethical practices intended to influence government decisions.

Lobbyists wait in the halls of the state Capitol in hope of speaking with state legislators.

Bernie Epstein / Alamy

CRITICAL THINKING

Reflect on this photo. What do you think it takes to be an effective lobbyist? What skills are necessary?

Lobbying

Lobbying is perhaps the oldest, and certainly the best-known, interest group tactic. According to Texans for Public Justice, special interests spent $328 million on lobbying contracts in 2013. Identifying interest groups that hire lobbyists is one way to determine which interests are being represented before the state legislature and which are not. Lobbyists are individuals who attempt to influence government decision makers on behalf of special interests. Lobbying is most often directed at legislators and the lawmaking process, although it is also practiced within state agencies.

Some interest groups, such as the Texas Motorcycle Rights Association, which claims to represent as many as 900,000 licensed motorcycle riders in Texas, will travel to Austin and hold a "lobby day" at the Capitol. On this day, association members meet with lawmakers about preserving bikers' rights. As this chapter's Students in Action feature suggests, even "lobbyists for a day" require a lot of planning and strategy in order to be effective advocates. Another organization, Texas Interfaith Center, provides its members and supporters with information on its website on "faithful participation" and tips for meeting and interacting with legislators.

Not all lobbyists are full-time professionals. Most work for businesses and only occasionally go to Austin to speak to lawmakers about their concerns. Some lobbyists represent cities and counties. Among the most successful lobbyists are former state legislators, legislative aides, and gubernatorial aides. In recent years, Texas has ranked second in the country, after California, in money

lobbying
Communicating with legislators or other government officials on behalf of an interest group for the purpose of influencing decision makers.

spent on lobbying the state government. In previous legislative sessions, lobbyists outnumbered the 181 legislators by a ratio of roughly nine to one. Typically, the number of registered lobbyists increases during an election cycle. During the 83rd legislative session, the number of registered lobbyists stood at 1,706.[16]

Personal Communication One of the main interest group techniques is personal communication by lobbyists. The immediate goal of lobbyists is to inform officials of their group's position on an issue. Because professional lobbyists are often experts in their field (and in some cases are former state officials), their tools of influence are the information and research they convey to public officials. The first task of the lobbyist is to gain access to legislators and other government decision makers. Once the lobbyist has made personal contact with a policymaker and captured the desired attention, he or she may use a variety of techniques to make the government official responsive to the group's demands, preferences, and expectations.

Because the process requires careful strategy, the lobbyist chooses the most appropriate time and place to speak with an official and determines how best to phrase arguments in order to have a positive impact. For maximum effectiveness in using this technique, a lobbyist must select the proper target (e.g., a key legislative committee chair, regulatory agency administrator, county commissioner, or city zoning board member). Successful lobbyists rely heavily on a variety of technology, such as cell phones, iPhones, iPads, Internet communications such as Skype, and other high-tech devices to store and communicate information. In fact, an important early study of interest group politics in Texas concluded that lobbying in the Lone Star State has shifted from an emphasis on personal argument to information-based communications.[17] A former Texas legislator compared lobbyists with pharmaceutical salespeople who explain new medicines to doctors who are too busy to keep up with the latest developments. To perform their jobs effectively, successful lobbyists should clearly indicate the group they represent, define their interests, make clear what they want to do and why, answer questions readily, and provide enough information for politicians to make judgments.

Students in Action

Lobbyist for a Day

Since 2003, at the start of every spring semester in odd-numbered calendar years, a delegation of faculty, staff, and students from St. Mary's University in San Antonio* are recruited and trained on the principles of lobbying. The lobbying team goes to the Capitol for the day to lobby targeted state legislators and senators to try to increase, or at a minimum maintain, funding for Texas Equalization Grants (TEG) funding. This particular source of funding for college students was authorized first in the 1970s to provide the opportunity for low-income students to attend private colleges and universities in Texas.

In 2013, several students were selected to lobby the state legislature for this one-day event. One of the students was Melissa Carrillo, a TEG recipient and biology major who ultimately plans to pursue a career as a medical doctor. What follows are her impressions of this experience.

Student Lobbyist for the Day

In the beginning of the Spring semester of 2013, I was notified that I had been selected for a day of lobbying at our state Capitol in Austin along with a delegation of faculty, staff, and other students from the University. As a biology major, I must admit that I did not fully understand what a day of lobbying meant. Through a series of sessions, we learned processes of lobbying and advocacy. We were also instructed on how we were to target a specific list of state legislators and get their support for TEG funding. As a student who has received this grant, the honor of being selected began to sink in even deeper.

Getting Ready

Preparing for the day at the Capitol was a great learning experience. An alumnus of the University, who lobbies in Austin, taught us that we needed to effectively convey short talking points during our one-on-one sessions with each legislative official. He made it clear that it was more likely that we would meet with a legislative staff member than an actual lawmaker. He also pointed out that staff members are the key mechanisms to ensuring that a specific policy gets through the complex legislative process.

Lobbying at the Capitol

When we arrived in Austin on February 12th, I was surprised that my first meeting was with a senator. In our brief meeting, I expressed to him the personal impact of the TEG in my life, and how much it has made a difference in providing the financial support for my education and future career to become a medical doctor. It was also exhilarating when our university delegation was recognized on the floor of the Texas House of Representatives.

The overall experience deepened my passion to serve as an advocate for educational opportunity and equality. I felt so much pride knowing that I was doing my part in ensuring that the very opportunity that allowed me to attend college would be there for future students. I was also impressed with the importance of civic engagement as a core principle of democracy. It is our civic duty as students and constituents to be active in our community and advocate for important issues that affect us, so that our elected officials can make effective decisions.

*Part of St. Mary's University's mission is dedicated to civic engagement and servant leadership.

Source: Essay written by Melissa Carrillo, April 2, 2014.

© Andresr/Shutterstock.com

Successful lobbyists befriend as many legislators as possible, especially influential legislative leaders such as committee chairs, and they discover their interests and needs. These relationships are formed over time. Lobbyists also put pressure on sympathetic legislators to influence other legislators.

At present, no effective laws prohibit former Texas legislators (including former legislative presiding officers) from becoming lobbyists and immediately lobbying former colleagues. In 2014, according to the National Conference of State Legislatures, at least 31 states required some kind of waiting period, ranging from the conclusion of the legislative session during which the legislator resigns to two years, before a legislator can become a lobbyist.[18] These lobbyists, and the interest groups that contract with them, are more likely to have connections in the state legislature than most other lobbyists. One area that is a target of reform is whether former lawmakers may use surplus campaign funds to launch their lobbying careers. An ethics bill during the 83rd legislative session, vetoed by Governor Rick Perry, would have placed a two-year moratorium on the use of surplus campaign funds by lawmakers-turned-lobbyists for campaign donations to any public official.[19]

Favors and Gifts Another lobbying technique used by interest groups, and especially by lobbyists, involves giving favors and gifts to legislators and other government decision makers. Common favors include arranging daily or weekly luncheon and dinner gatherings; providing free liquor, wine, or beer; furnishing tickets for entertainment events, air transportation, and athletic contests; and giving miscellaneous gifts. Gifts may include flower bouquets and spa treatments for female lawmakers or, for male lawmakers, guns, knives, and deer processing. Free tickets for Cowboys and Texans games, along with free access to some of the biggest collegiate football games across the state, are also commonplace and legal gifts for lawmakers from lobbyists, so long as the value of freebies for any one legislator from an individual lobbyist does not exceed $500 per calendar year. There are limits on the value of "travel gifts" for public officials and candidates, as well as for state agency employees.[20] In addition, public officials must report gifts valued at more than $250 to the Texas Ethics Commission.

Grassroots Activities Yet another influential technique used by interest groups is grassroots lobbying. Interest groups rely heavily on pressure from a grassroots network of organization members and sympathizers. Interest groups attempt to create an image of broad public support for a group's goals, mobilizing support when it is needed. The Internet has emerged as a significant forum for grassroots lobbying. Interest groups are increasingly using social media such as Facebook, Twitter, and blogs. These communication methods are designed to generate information favorable to an interest group's cause and to spread it widely among legislators, other policymakers, and the general public. Special interest groups create Facebook pages to connect with supporters, gather signatures on petitions, or announce events. "Astrotweeting" uses fake social media accounts to provide a false impression of the number of supporters or opponents an issue has. Petition websites are also becoming more common for interest groups to demonstrate support for their positions, although some groups like the Texas Electric Cooperatives argue this approach is much less effective than letters and face-to-face contact with elected officials. The Texas State Teachers Association (TSTA) is very effective at communicating its agenda to its membership through Flickr and Facebook. Another education-related organization, Texans for Education Reform, formed in 2013 to promote charter schools and online "virtual schools," also uses social media such as "tweets" to inform the public and its supporters about issues.

Electioneering

Participating in political campaign activities, or **electioneering**, is widespread among interest groups. These activities usually center on particular candidates, but may also revolve around issue advocacy. If a candidate who favors a group's goals can be elected, the group has a realistic expectation that its interests will be recognized and protected once the candidate takes office. Interest group participation in the election process takes various forms. Publishing or otherwise publicizing the political records of incumbent candidates on their website is one of the simplest and most common forms of interest group participation. Since the 2008 election, an explosion of YouTube videos has provided interest groups an opportunity to disseminate support for candidates or issues. Providing favored candidates with group membership information, mailing lists, and email lists is another valuable contribution that helps candidates solicit money and votes. In addition, groups may allow candidates to speak at their meetings, thus giving them opportunities for direct contact with voters and possible media coverage or Facebook coverage. Public endorsements can also benefit candidates, sending a cue to the group's

electioneering
Active campaigning by an interest group in support of, or in opposition to, a candidate; actions urging the public to act on an issue.

Point/Counterpoint

THE ISSUE Most observers of Texas politics would agree that money plays a big role in political campaigns. Unlike the federal government, except for judicial elections, Texas law does not restrict the amount anyone can contribute to a state political campaign. That campaign donations are unregulated appears to enhance the role of money in elections. Yet the ability to donate money to election campaigns is also a form of political expression and free speech protected by both the Texas Constitution and the U.S. Constitution.

Should Campaign Contributions Be Limited?

Arguments For Limiting Campaign Contributions

1. In states with no campaign contribution limits, it is difficult for anyone to successfully challenge an incumbent.
2. Without a cap on campaign contributions, money controls politics, and wealthy individuals and PACs have tremendous influence in public policymaking.
3. Disclosure of campaign contributions under current laws does not convey a complete picture of the role of money in elections.

Arguments Against Limiting Campaign Contributions

1. Campaign contributions to political candidates are considered a form of freedom of expression protected by the First Amendment of the U.S. Constitution.
2. Campaign contributions to candidates and public officials guarantee only access, not policy outcomes.
3. Limits on campaign contributions has a chilling effect on the right to participate in the democratic process.

Source: Edwin Bender, "Evidencing a Republican Form of Government: The Influence of Campaign Money on State-Level Elections," *Montana Law Review*, 74, no. 1 (2013): 165–82.

membership and other interested voters with regard to which candidates they should support. Facebook pages are also created to generate "likes" for candidates and can facilitate garnering campaign contributions.

Another type of group participation in electioneering involves "Get Out the Vote" (GOTV) campaigns—that is, the favorable vote. Typically, increasing favorable voter turnout entails mailing campaign propaganda, making phone calls to members, registering voters, transporting voters to the polls, and door-to-door canvassing (soliciting votes). Social media, again, provide significant tools for rallying a candidate's base. Texas's controversial abortion bill passed in the 2013 legislative session brought a lot of activity on the Internet from groups on both sides of the issue. As mentioned earlier, Wendy Davis's speech on the Senate floor brought, what some observers called, a "tweet-storming" tactic.

Campaign Financing by Political Action Committees

Because political campaigns are becoming more expensive with each election, contributions from interest group members constitute an important form of participation in both federal and state elections. Although individuals continue

How Do We Compare…in Total Contributions in U.S. Congressional Races?

Most Populous U.S. States	Total Contributions*	Percent Given to Democrats	Percent Given to Republicans	Ranking** to Democrats	Ranking** to Republicans
California	$463,868,029	56.2%	42%	7	44
Florida	$225,697,480	32%	66.3%	31	20
New York	$342,716,194	58.9%	39.4%	4	46
Texas	**$347,239,696**	**25.5%**	**73.3%**	**39**	**10**
U.S. States Bordering Texas					
Arkansas	$18,953,550	28.4%	69.7%	35	16
Louisiana	$32,510,454	19.9%	77.1%	45	8
New Mexico	$19,522,775	51.7%	45.9%	12	39
Oklahoma	$32,554,119	19.7%	78.1%	45	5

*This figure includes PAC contributions to candidates, individual contributions to candidates and parties, and soft money contributions to parties in federal elections. (Soft money contributions are unlimited funds spent independently by supporters to benefit a candidate or by a party to educate voters.)

**Refers to how the state compares with all 50 states. For example, Texas's percentage of contributions to Republicans ranked 10th highest in the nation.

Source: Center for Responsive Politics, "Open Secrets," data reported as of March 25, 2013, http://www.opensecrets.org/states/.

CRITICAL THINKING

Analyze this chart. What are your initial impressions regarding the amount and percentage of monies contributed to Texas congressional candidates for Democrats versus Republicans in comparison to the other states?

to make personal financial contributions to candidates, some campaign funds also come from political action committees (PACs) (see Chapter 5, "Campaigns and Elections"). The Texas Ethics Commission defines a PAC as "a group of persons that has a principal purpose of accepting political contributions or making political contributions." Texas statutes prohibit direct political contributions by corporations and labor unions to individual candidates. These and other groups, however, may form PACs composed of their employees or members.

PACs have the task of raising funds and distributing financial contributions to candidates who are sympathetic to their cause. A PAC may also influence political campaigns involving issues that affect the group's vital interests. Currently, Texas imposes no limits on what PACs (or citizens for that matter) can raise or contribute to candidates running for statewide offices or the legislature, except in judicial races. Proposals to place limits on the amounts that citizens and PACs can contribute to candidates have not been given serious consideration by the legislature, although some limits and deadlines have been placed on campaign contributions to judicial candidates. Additionally, legislators and statewide officeholders cannot accept campaign donations during a legislative session.

PAC activities and their influence continue to increase. According to the Texas Ethics Commission, more than 1,800 active PACs were registered as of 2014.[21] (See Table 7.3 for a list of some of the top Texas contributors.) During the 2012 election cycle, PAC contributions were dominated by interests representing the business sector, ideological (which have partisan affiliations) and single-issue groups, and labor.[22]

During the 2014 gubernatorial primaries, the Republican nominee, Greg Abbott, raised $11.5 million in the second half of 2013 and began 2014 with $27 million in his war chest. In contrast, the Democratic nominee, Wendy Davis, reported having raised $12.5 million. From the period of late February until June of 2014, each candidate raised over $11 million. Yet, Greg Abbott held a $36 million cash advantage over Wendy Davis' $13 million with less than four months before the election.

Perhaps the best indication of power among interest groups is the connection between the election campaign contributions of PACs and lobbying activities. It takes a coordinated effort by an interest group to influence one part of the political process (the campaign) while also affecting policy decisions in other areas (the legislative and executive branches). In this way, interest groups can exercise far greater control over the output of the Texas legislature and other officials than their numbers would indicate.

Bribery and Unethical Practices

Bribery and blackmail, though not common in Texas, nevertheless have occurred in state and local government. For example, in the 1970s, the Sharpstown Bank scandal rocked the legislature. House Speaker Gus Mutscher (D-Brenham) and others were convicted of conspiring to accept bribes for passing deposit insurance bills as requested by Houston banker Frank Sharp. After the scandal, the state legislature passed a law

Table 7.3 Top Texas Contributors, (including PACs) in Spending by Category, 2012 Election

Donor	2011–2012 Spending	Category
1. Texans for Lawsuit Reform	$7,046,000	Focuses on lawsuit restrictions
2. Texas Association of Realtors	$4,840,000	Business group
3. Associated Republicans of Texas	$3,544,000	Supports Republicans
4. Texans for Insurance Reform	$2,896,000	Trial lawyer group
5. Republican State Leadership Committee	$2,726,000	Supports Republicans
6. Annie's List PAC	$2,726,000	Supports Democrat women
7. Republican Party of Texas	$2,564,000	Supports Republicans
8. Border Health PAC	$1,470,000	Focuses on health
9. Valero Energy Corp.	$2,009,000	Business group
10. Texas Democratic Party	$1,745,000	Supports Democrats

Note: List includes interest groups. Period includes the two-year election cycle ending in December 2012. Dollar amounts have been rounded up.

Source: ''Texas Top Contributors,'' 2012 Election Cycle, *Major Reports*, 2013, http://www.tpj.org.

CRITICAL THINKING

Analyze this chart. What are your initial impressions regarding the types of interest groups that are among the top ten donors in Texas elections? In your opinion, do certain interest groups have undue influence in Texas politics?

prohibiting candidates for the office of Speaker of the House of Representatives from giving supportive legislators anything of value for their help or support in a campaign for the speakership. The law requires separate campaign finance committees for election as a representative and for the Speaker's race.

In February 1980, as revealed by an FBI investigation, House Speaker Billy Clayton (D–Springlake) accepted (but did not spend) $5,000 intended to influence the awarding of a state employee insurance contract. Because he had not cashed the checks, a federal district court found Clayton innocent of all bribery charges. In January 1981, he was elected to a fourth term as Speaker of the House. After eight years as Speaker, Clayton left the House to become a lobbyist.

In 1991, five-time Speaker Gib Lewis (D–Fort Worth) was indicted on two misdemeanor ethics charges by a Travis County grand jury. Rather than face the possibility of a trial, subjecting him to a stiffer penalty, Lewis agreed to a plea bargain, was fined $2,000, and announced his decision not to seek reelection to the House of Representatives in 1992. He became a successful lobbyist.

Scrutiny also centered on state Representative Tom Craddick (R-Midland). Although Texas law prohibits a Speaker candidate from donating money to House candidates' elections campaigns, in 2002 Craddick donated $20,000 from his reelection campaign to Campaign for Republican Leadership, a political action committee. In turn, the PAC gave all of its $176,500 to eight GOP House candidates. After Republicans won a majority of House seats, Craddick was elected Speaker in January 2003.[23] Another political action committee, Texans for a Republican Majority (TRMPAC), was organized under the patronage of former U.S. House member Tom DeLay (R-Sugar Land). In 2002, TRMPAC was involved in raising money for GOP candidates seeking seats in the Texas House. Later, in cooperation with DeLay, Speaker Craddick played a major role in the success of a 2003 congressional redistricting effort that resulted in the 2004 election of more Republicans in the Texas delegation to the U.S. House of Representatives.

Craddick was not charged with violation of any law, but DeLay and three associates involved with TRMPAC were indicted in 2005 by a Travis County grand jury for money laundering and conspiracy to launder $190,000 of campaign contributions from corporate contributors.[24] After indictment, DeLay was forced to step down as majority leader in the U.S. House of Representatives. In June 2006, while awaiting trial, DeLay resigned from his congressional seat. Convicted and given a three-year sentence in 2011, DeLay remained free on bond during his appeal. His conviction was overturned in September 2013 by the Third Court of Appeals of Texas. Following this judgment, the Travis County District Attorney's Office announced that it would appeal the decision to the Texas Court of Criminal Appeals, and the appeal was accepted in March 2014. In October 2014, the Texas Court of Criminal Appeals ultimately upheld the Third Court of Appeals' ruling, tossing out the convictions.

7.3 Learning Check

1. Name two techniques lobbyists use to influence legislators.
2. Does Texas place limits on PAC contributions to candidates, as the federal government does?

Answers on p. 272.

Power and Regulation in Interest Group Politics

★ **LO7.4** Analyze how interest groups are regulated and evaluate the effectiveness of these laws.

Clearly, interest groups play a significant role in Texas politics. They have access to a number of strategies and tactics to influence elections and policy decisions. So, how are interest groups regulated? Are these regulations effective? Do interest groups have too much political influence in shaping public policy?

Regulation of Interest Group Politics

Prompted by media reports of big spending by lobbyists and a grand jury investigation into influence peddling, in 1991 the 72nd Legislature proposed a constitutional amendment to create the eight-member **Texas Ethics Commission** to enforce legal standards for lobbyists and public officials. The voters approved the amendment in November of that year, thereby allowing commission members to be appointed by the governor (four members), the lieutenant governor (two members), and the House Speaker (two members).[25] This legislation was initially designed to increase the power of public prosecutors to use evidence that contributions to lawmakers by lobbyists and other individuals are more than mere campaign donations. The legislation also expanded disclosure requirements for lobbyists and legislators, and it put a $500 annual cap on lobbyist-provided food and drink for a lawmaker. The law also bans honoraria (gratuitous payments in recognition of professional services for which there is no legally enforceable obligation to pay) and lobby-paid pleasure trips (unless a legislator makes a speech or participates in a panel discussion). State law also requires public officials to disclose any gifts valued greater than $250 and include a description.

The ethics law defines as illegal any campaign contribution accepted with an agreement to act in the contributor's interest. The problem, however, is the difficulty in proving that a candidate or public official has intentionally accepted a campaign contribution from a particular interest group in exchange for policy benefits. The law also prohibits a candidate or official from receiving a contribution in the Capitol building itself.

Detailed records of political contributions and how this money is spent must be filed with the Texas Ethics Commission between two and seven times each year. These records are open to the public and are available on the commission's website. Candidates for legislative and statewide office are required to file electronic campaign disclosure reports, so that this information can be made instantly available. Current law requires that all candidates file semiannual reports. In contested elections, however, candidates must file itemized contribution and expenditure reports every six months, and 30 days and eight days before the election.

Generally, contributions and expenditures made by candidates in the last two days prior to an election campaign need not be disclosed until the next semiannual report is due. At present, there are no laws in Texas preventing these last-minute contributions by interest groups. Therefore, interest groups can potentially alter the outcome of key races in the few days before the election. It is also not uncommon for special interests to make campaign contributions after the election takes place. Current law prohibits lawmakers and other elected state officials from raising money during the regular legislative session. However, these postelection, or "late train," donations typically take place immediately following the November election until early December.

On its website, the Texas Ethics Commission lists the names of lobbyists and their clients, as well as payments received by each lobbyist. The

Texas Ethics Commission
A state agency that enforces state standards for lobbyists and public officials, including registration of lobbyists and reporting of political campaign contributions.

commission's records, however, do not give a complete picture. Lobbyists do not have to report exact dollar amounts for their contracts; they only need to indicate ranges. For example, compensation from each client is reported as less than $10,000, and then in $15,000 increments up to more than $500,000. For anything over $500,000, the exact amount is required. In addition, lobbyists are required to notify their clients if they represent two or more groups with competing interests, as well as notify the Texas Ethics Commission about any possible conflicts. This information, however, is not made available to the public or lawmakers.

The Texas Ethics Commission is authorized to hear ethics complaints against state officials, candidates for office, and state employees, though its budget and staff are typically very small and allow only a limited number of reviews each year. For the 2013 year, there were 61 sworn ethics complaints.[26] Most infractions center on penalties against campaign and PAC treasurers who failed to file reports; missed filing deadlines; or provided faulty reports on contributions, earnings, or expenditures. Many infractions center on violations of the Texas Election Code. Fines are assessed by the Ethics Commission on any infractions. On rare occasions, the TEC reviews complaints by state officials against organizations. For instance, in 2014, the Texas Ethics Commission, in response to an official complaint by two Republican lawmakers, issued a subpoena to a conservative group, Empower Texas, to release lists of its donors and its communications with lawmakers, when the group refused to register as a lobbyist and abide by ethics rules. The organization filed suit against the TEC claiming that the subpoena violated its First Amendment rights. A federal district judge refused to quash (set aside) the subpoena. Secret money—some observers refer to it as "dark money"—has become increasingly present in campaign contributions by organizations. One of the more contentious legislative proposals during the 2013 session would have required nonprofit organizations that spend money on political campaigns to disclose the names of their donors. Although the legislature passed the bill, Governor Perry vetoed it.[27]

Reform advocates and others contend that staff members with the commission are restricted from investigating complaints because of strict confidentiality rules that expose them to possible criminal prosecution, fines, and jail time. The complaint must be a Texas resident and be able to demonstrate proof of residency. The complaint must be filed on a form provided by the commission and include information about the respondent and the complainant. Once the complaint has been filed, the commission must immediately attempt to contact the respondent.[28] The Texas Ethics Commission is required to dismiss any Election Code complaint if the respondent claims that the violation was a clerical error and corrects the mistake within two weeks. This requirement effectively weakens the ability of the agency to impose fines for most infractions.[29]

Some observers claim that although some ethics laws are in place, they remain ineffective. Questionable connections between lobbyists and legislators are largely unchecked. For instance, when Governor Perry first took office, he issued a "strict" revolving door lobbying policy for his staff, preventing staff members from leaving their employment to become lobbyists. He drew criticism shortly thereafter, however, when he hired senior staff personnel who had been registered as lobbyists during the preceding legislative session. For many observers, special interests had entered the governor's office through a revolving back door.

Although Texas law prohibits corporations and unions from providing campaign contributions directly to candidates, "soft money" can be directed to state Republican and Democratic party coffers for "administrative expenses." In light of the U.S. Supreme Court decision in *Citizens United v. Federal Election Commission* (2009), the Texas Ethics Commission issued an advisory opinion stating that corporations and unions are allowed to make expenditures independent of a political candidate, such as paying for political advertising that calls for the election or defeat of candidates, so long as they do not coordinate with the candidate's campaign. In February 2014, the TEC adopted another rule requiring PACs, before they receive donations from corporations or unions, to provide an affidavit that they intend to "act exclusively as a direct expenditure committee."[30]

As a result of *Citizens United*, a proliferation of super PACs were created, especially at the federal level. In 2014, Texas's prohibition of super PACs for state elections was overturned by the U.S. Fifth Circuit Court of Appeals. Now, just as under federal law, state super PACs can also raise unlimited sums for independent expenditures. Federal law requires the super PAC to report the names of its donors, unless a nonprofit organization is involved. State law requires the disclosure of the names of all donors regardless of the involvement of a nonprofit organization. During the 2012 presidential primary elections, Rick Perry benefited from these super PACs, especially from one called "Make Us Great Again."[31] After withdrawing from the Republican presidential nomination race, Perry received approval from the Federal Election Commission to form his own PAC or super PAC with funds remaining from his presidential campaign, or to transfer these funds to his gubernatorial campaign account.

A powerful relationship continues between campaign contributions and policy decisions. For some observers, little has changed since creation of the Texas Ethics Commission, as the system is still set up to favor incumbents.[32] All attempts to significantly reform campaign finance have been defeated. Proposed reforms have included contribution limits for individuals and PACs in legislative and statewide races, as well as full disclosure laws. As the late journalist Molly Ivins pointed out, "Texas is the Wild Frontier of campaign financing."[33] Campaign contributions are also connected to influential political appointments. During Perry's presidential bid in 2011, media reports revealed that many of his donors received appointments to influential state boards and commissions. Although the regulatory authority of the Texas Ethics Commission was strengthened in 2003 as a part of a review by the Sunset Advisory Commission, many observers argue its powers are inadequate for the job it is intended to perform.[34] (For more information on the Sunset Advisory Commission, see Chapter 10, "Public Policy and Administration.")

Interest Group Power and Public Policy

The political influence of interest groups is determined by several factors. Some observers argue that a group with a sizable membership, above average financial resources, a knowledgeable and dedicated leadership, and a high degree of unity (agreement on and commitment to goals among the membership) will be able to exert virtually limitless pressure on governmental decision makers. Others point out that the more the aims of an interest group are consistent with broad-based public beliefs or stem from issue networks, the more likely the group is to succeed and wield significant power. They also observe that if interest groups are well represented in the structure of the government itself, their power will be enhanced materially. Also, it is noted that a structure of weak governments will ordinarily produce strong interest groups.

From a different point of view, others insist that factors external to the group are also highly relevant. Research indicates that a strong relationship exists between the larger socioeconomic conditions in a state and the power of interest groups. These findings have led some observers to conclude that states with high population levels, advanced industrialization, significant per capita wealth, and high levels of formal education are likely to produce relatively weak interest groups and strong political parties. Interestingly, despite a large population, Texas is among the states with strong interest groups and relatively weak political parties. Compared with other states, scholars rank Texas as one of 26 states where interest groups dominate or fluctuate in power over time.[35] The Center for Public Integrity, in its analysis of transparency and accountability of the 50 state governments, graded Texas a D+, ranking it 27th among all states.[36]

Three circumstances explain why states such as Texas may not fit the expected pattern. First, many Texas interest groups are readily accepted because they identify with free enterprise, self-reliance, and other elements of the state's individualistic political culture. Most Texans are predisposed to distrust government and its agents but to trust interest groups and their lobbyists. Second, the century-long one-party Democratic tradition in Texas and the subsequent one-party Republican trend have rendered interparty competition negligible in many counties and districts. Low levels of political participation, along with the absence of strong parties and meaningful competition between parties, has made Texas government vulnerable to the pressures of strong interest groups and their lobbyists. Finally, the Texas Constitution of 1876 and its many amendments have created state and local governments beset by weak, uncoordinated institutions. Faced with a government lacking sufficient strength to offer any real opposition, interest groups often obtain decisions favorable to their causes.

Pinpointing Political Power

✔ **7.4 Learning Check**

1. True or False: Texas's campaign finance laws often involve public disclosure by public officials and lobbyists.
2. True or False: The Texas Ethics Commission is the primary state agency regulating political contributions and expenditures by lobbyists and public officials.

Answers on p. 272.

Assessing the political power and influence that interest groups have in American government is difficult, and determining the extent of their power in Texas is especially complex. There is no simple top-down or bottom-up arrangement. Rather, political decisions (especially policy decisions) are made by a variety of individuals and groups. Some of these decision makers participate in local ad hoc (specific purpose) organizations; others wield influence through statewide groups. Ascertaining which individuals or groups have the greatest influence often depends on the issue or issues involved.

The political influence of any interest group cannot be fairly calculated by looking at the distribution of only one political asset, whether it be money, status, knowledge, organization, sheer numbers, or in today's world, social media capabilities. Nevertheless, we may safely conclude that organized interest groups in Texas often put the unorganized citizenry at a great disadvantage when public issues are at stake.

Unsung Hero of Civil Rights: "Father of LULAC" a Fading Memory

Hector Saldaña

Mexican American civil rights leader Alonso S. Perales is all but a fading memory for most students of Texas politics. His collected papers, however, are now available to students and researchers.* This reading sheds light on a Texas hero and on efforts to preserve Perales's papers for an archival collection in a university repository.

Though he was once hailed as the "Father of LULAC" and a civil rights giant, Alonso S. Perales today is a historical shadow figure, little more than a name frozen on an elementary school building on the West Side [of San Antonio]. Students pass by his portrait daily without much thought, says Perales Elementary School principal Dolores Mena. "The kids know what he looks like, but they don't know what he's done." "He was a most extraordinary man," recalls retired County Commissioner and Municipal Court Judge Albert Peña, a friend who says he is perplexed why such a historic leader is forgotten to a generation. "But he was very well known when I knew him." That was more than 40 years ago. Perales died in 1960 at the age of 61.

A self-made man, highly educated and erudite, Perales was a prolific writer of position papers and books on the second-class status of Mexican Americans, a newspaper columnist, a spokesman at rallies, a foreign diplomat and shaper of laws. He traveled the globe to promote his culture and to fight for its rights—*En defensa de mi raza.*" "He was the great intellectual of LULAC," says Ed Peña, former LULAC national president in Washington, D.C. "He was our Thomas Jefferson."

....
*The papers of Alonso S. Perales are available in the Hispanic Collections of the M. D. Anderson Library, University of Houston. For an overview, see *Alonso S. Perales Papers, 1898–1991,* http://archon.lib.uh.edu/index.php?p=collections/controlcard&id=436.

In the late 1920s, Perales founded the League of United Latin American Citizens in his image working alongside other activist-philosophers such as J. T. Canales, Ben Garza, M. C. González, Gus García, Carlos Castañeda, George Sánchez, and José Luz Sáenz to shape its goals. Perales delineated that vision in a draft of LULAC bylaws: "To develop within the members of our race the best, purest, and most perfect type of true, loyal citizen of the United States." "We are going to show the world that we have just and legitimate aspirations, that we have self-pride, dignity, and racial pride; that we have a very high concept of our American citizenship; that we have a great love of our country," Perales said in a 1943 radio address.

And as politico Romulo Munguia notes, Perales had the wisdom, guts, and skills to "fight the fight in English." Seventy-five years ago, he declared English "the official language" of LULAC and campaigned for Hispanics to be classified as "white" in the census—actions that rankle modern Latinos, many of whom accuse Perales of elitism in light of today's continuing struggle for equality. But the fiery speaker whose persuasive rhetoric often kept LULAC from splintering also considered certain Anglos the enemy, says one family member. Perales' language in 1929 is blunt: "We shall resist and attack energetically all machinations tending to prevent our social and political unification." He was the voice of calm, however. "We should pity and not despise those who are yet in darkness," Perales wrote. Perales was a bridge builder who never forgot where he came from, say those who knew him. His ideas were born of early struggle and poverty.

A dark-skinned Mexican American, Perales was born in Alice in 1898. Orphaned young, he picked cotton in the fields to earn a living and enlisted in the army during World War I. Through guts and determination, and the belief that education could overcome other handicaps, he graduated with a law degree from George Washington University. He passed the Texas State Bar exam in 1925 and became an early civil rights lawyer in San Antonio.

"He was a poor kid that had nothing and it's hard to visualize how he got from this point to that point. He had a vision; he had a dream. I want to say he was like Martin Luther King—but he preceded Martin Luther King," says Carrizales. To his nephew and namesake, Alonso M. Perales, 77, his uncle was down-to-earth "and a real Tejano."

In 1931, *La Prensa* called Perales the one American [who] defends Mexicans. His early radio speeches made clear that Mexicans were "thirsty for justice" and had a rightful place in the society they labored to support. By the mid-'40s, he had documented more than 150 towns in Texas with establishments that barred service to Hispanics and wrote about it in the book, "*Are We Good Neighbors?*" Throughout the '50s, Perales fought for a living wage for braceros. He opposed restrictive covenants that kept Mexican Americans out of certain neighborhoods; he fought the poll tax. His fight against segregation and for equal rights rivals the work of Martin Luther King, say historians and admirers....

Yet for all his work on behalf of Mexican Americans, Perales has all but faded from collective memory. "We don't know how to take care of our heroes," says Dallas attorney José Ángel Gutiérrez, co-founder of La Raza Unida and a guiding light of the Chicano Movement of the '60s and '70s, about Perales' modern obscurity—which he considers a travesty. "[Perales'] history is there for those who seek it out," Houston attorney Alfred J. Hernandez says. "This is a deep story about *nosotros*." It's a story that can be found in a cache of Perales' personal documents—and that has yet to see the light of day.

Died Too Soon

They say that history belongs to those who write it. Perales' story rests in dozens of moldy boxes once coveted by his widow, a high-strung former opera singer who in later years vacillated between guarding that packaged legacy and threatening to burn the entire lot, says Perales' nephew. The boxes have collected dust since Perales died in 1960. When Marta Perales died a couple of years ago, heirs Raymond Perales and Martha Carrizales—Perales' adopted children—vowed to preserve their father's papers and restore his rightful image. But action has been slow. They eventually asked Henry Cisneros' politically savvy uncle, printer Ruben Munguia, to help sort mountains of pioneering material....

It was Ruben Munguia's last great undertaking, his brother says. He worked meticulously sorting the delicate treasure of documents at his draft table at his Buena Vista Street print shop "because he liked to be around all the action," says Ruben Munguia's daughter Mary Perales. Since his death, the project has languished. Brother and sister do what they can in their spare time. As Carrizales pours over reams of her father's delicate documents, she gushes, "It's like learning about a character in history." Perales' collection is voluminous.... Historian and University of Texas associate professor Emilio Zamora agrees and urged the family to deposit the papers at the Mexican American Library Program at the University of Texas because of its "unmatched historical value." In 2001, he wrote to Carrizales: "I honestly believe that Perales is the most important Mexican American leader of the 20th century." Zamora cites Perales' prominence as an author, diplomat, and LULAC officer, and his ties to Latino organizations, civic service, and civil rights activism. "Not only within the Mexican American community, but I think he's a major civil rights leader of the nation," Zamora says.

That the materials are still out of the hands of researchers is a serious issue, he says.

There is also a fear that the integrity of the collection could be unintentionally undermined and lose research value. "Anyone who's involved in archival collection will tell you that a collection of that immense value has to be deposited somewhere and processed and then made available for researchers," Zamora says. His hope is that the University of Texas gets them ("It's the natural home," he says) because Perales' contemporaries are archived there....

Not Really "Radical"

"My mother was a radical and marched with César Chavez," says Carrizales. "Of course, she could afford that. She was bourgeois. My father wouldn't have agreed with the '60s." Certainly Perales' words from the late '20s–"We shall oppose any radical and violent demonstration which may tend to create conflicts and disturb the peace and tranquility of our country"–had no place in the Chicano Movement. "He was a realist," says Chicano leader Gutiérrez, who notes that the FBI's surveillance of LULAC started because of Perales' overseas activities. "It was very dangerous to be an activist Mexican at that time, very dangerous. You could lose your life, and people did. This was not a time to stand up and be radical, and what he was doing was perceived to be radical."

Zamora argues that Perales' great achievement was taking the cause of Mexican Americans to international forums. Perales spoke at international conferences; he appealed for nations to put pressure on the United States for Mexican American equal rights. Perales participated in founding meetings of the United Nations in 1945. "At that meeting, he again included the Mexican American in the deliberations of human rights," Zamora explains.

"He was an extraordinary man. If we had him today, I'm telling you, he'd be up in front. And he'd be shaking stuff," Zamora says. "He had conservative ideas, but some of his ideas for that time were pretty radical. He had so much

courage and intellect. His stamina and sense of civic responsibility was just tremendous." Many say that the true value of the Perales papers is to put his "conservative" activism in perspective. "It was a very primitive democracy for us," LULAC historian Peña adds. "He was visible when there were very few (Mexican Americans) that were visible." ...

He outlined his views in October 1931 in a position paper, "*El Mexico Americano y la Politica del Sur Texas.*" "If we want to accelerate our political evolution, it's imperative that we change the system," wrote Perales, who argued that self education on issues was more important than party affiliation.

In his eyes, pulling a voting lever blindly was akin to a sin: "It's one thing to vote and know what you're voting for, but it's another thing to do it because someone ordered you to do it and who to vote for," he wrote in Spanish. And though he fought against the poll tax, he urged Latinos to pay it and participate. Former Houston judge Hernandez says that Perales is responsible "for Mexican Americans coming of age" because he was willing to enter *un nido de viboras* (the viper's nest) of an often-racist Texas legal system....

Lost History

It was only in the '70s that major universities became interested in collecting the papers of major Latino figures. In some cases, that was more than 50 years too late. "Man, I could tell you some stories that would make you cry about stuff we've lost," Zamora says from Austin. "We're lacking in the telling of the story because the historical record is not readily available," Zamora adds.

Sociologist and Mexican American studies expert Avelardo Valdez at the University of Houston says that Perales is "part of a constellation of lost figures" in the Mexican American experience. "It's highly significant and important that these kinds of papers are found, and that they be archived and that we have access to them," says Valdez, adding that the find will show "Perales' founding generation was much more progressive than our generation today. It took a lot of guts to be organizing political organizations in the 1920s and '30s in South Texas."

Carrizales says her ultimate dream is that researchers will restore her father's legacy. "He was an activist for human dignity—like César Chavez, like Martin Luther King," Carrizales says. "He needs to be recognized, not glorified, for his efforts. History must do him justice. People need a full cup of information."

✔ **Selected Reading Learning Check**

1. True or False: Perales founded LULAC in the 1920s and is considered the "Father of LULAC."
2. True or False: The purpose of the archival collection is to preserve Perales's personal papers and works in a university repository.

Answers on p. 272.

....

Source: The Houston Chronicle by HOUSTON CHRONICLE PUBLISHING CO.. Reproduced with permission of HOUSTON CHRONICLE PUBLISHING CO. in the format Republish in a book via Copyright Clearance Center.

Conclusion

As we have learned, there are numerous interest groups in Texas. They exert tremendous influence over public decisions at all levels and in all branches of government. Some interest groups, however, have more influence than others. They participate in an assortment of activities and use a variety of techniques to influence government. What's more, few, if any, regulations effectively control the power of interest groups in Texas. These factors suggest that interest groups will continue to play a significant role in Texas politics for years to come.

Chapter Summary

LO 7.1 **Explain what interest groups are, why they form, and what their essential characteristics are.** Interest groups act on behalf of their members to influence policy decisions made by government officials. Various factors foster interest group formation or effectiveness, such as legal and cultural reasons, a decentralized government, and the strength of the party system and political ideologies. Interest group participation influences public policy at all levels and within each branch (legislative, executive, judicial) of Texas government. Involvement in an interest group provides members with information and opportunities to become active in the political process. Interest groups vary by organizational pattern, membership, and leadership.

LO 7.2 **Describe the types of interest groups and analyze the qualities of a powerful interest group.** In general, all interest groups at all levels of government can be classified according to their interests, membership, and the public policies they advocate. Among the types of interest groups that are trying to influence government policies and policymakers are those interested in economic issues, the professions, public employment matters, social issues, and the public good. Some interest groups are more powerful than others when one considers their financial resources and success rates within the legislature.

LO 7.3 **Evaluate the kinds of activities that interest groups use to influence Texas government.** Interest groups are involved in all types and areas of political activity. They serve various functions, which include recruiting candidates for public office, shaping consensus on issues, and providing an outlet for concerned citizens. To influence policy decisions, interest groups use several techniques, including lobbying, personal communication, giving favors and gifts, grassroots activities, electioneering, campaign financing by political action committees (PACs), and, in extreme cases, resorting to bribery and other unethical or illegal practices.

LO 7.4 **Analyze how interest groups are regulated and evaluate the effectiveness of these laws.** An eight-member Texas Ethics Commission is charged with enforcing legal standards for lobbyists and public officials. Although money is a powerful influence over policy decisions, the state only limits campaign contribution amounts for judicial candidates and places few other restrictions on donations. Texas's campaign finance laws are best characterized as involving public disclosure by public officials, lobbyists, and PACs.

Key Terms

interest group, p. 238

right of association, p. 239

decentralized government, p. 240

organizational pattern, p. 241

group leadership, p. 243

economic interest group, p. 243

business organization, p. 244

labor organization, p. 244

professional group, p. 245

public officer and employee group, p. 246

social interest group, p. 247

racial and ethnic groups, p. 247

women's organization, p. 248

religion-based group, p. 249

public interest group, p. 250

power group, p. 250

interest group technique, p. 252

lobbying, p. 253

electioneering, p. 257

Texas Ethics Commission, p. 262

Learning Check Answers

7.1 1. Legal decisions, political culture, a decentralized government, the strength of the party system, and political ideologies are among the factors that contribute to the formation of interest groups.

2. False. Active membership will vary, depending on the organization and leadership of the organization.

7.2 1. False. Unlike most interest groups, public interest groups are interested in promoting the public interest.

2. In Texas, business groups are generally more powerful than labor groups.

7.3 1. Lobbyists use personal communication as well as favors and gifts to influence legislators.

2. Unlike federal law, Texas law does not limit campaign contributions by PACs.

7.4 1. True. Texas's campaign finance laws often involve disclosure by public officials and lobbyists, though critics would argue that current disclosure requirements are not sufficient to reform the system.

2. True. The Texas Ethics Commission is the primary state agency regulating the political contributions and expenditures by lobbyists and public officials.

Selected Reading Learning Check

1. True. LULAC was formed in 1929; it is the oldest Latino-based organization dedicated to civil rights in the United States.

2. True. The importance of the Perales collection is to preserve his papers and works in a university repository for research by students and scholars.

The Legislative Branch

Nick Anderson Editorial Cartoon used with the permission of Nick Anderson, the Washington Post Writers Group and the Cartoonist Group. All rights reserved.

CRITICAL THINKING

Who should decide if concealed handgun licensees can carry their weapons on college campuses—the legislature or the college?

Learning Objectives

8.1 Describe the structure of the Texas legislature.

8.2 Describe the membership of the Texas legislature, including legislators' formal and informal qualifications and compensation.

8.3 Compare the organization of the Texas House of Representatives and the Texas Senate.

8.4 Outline the responsibilities of the Texas legislature.

8.5 Explain the influences on legislators' voting decisions.

In April 2007, a deranged student went on a shooting rampage at Virginia Tech University. In a systematic attack, the student chained and locked entry doors to a classroom building and then moved from room to room killing 32 faculty and students and wounding 17. Virginia Tech did not allow licensed handgun owners to bring their weapons on campus. During the interim of the 80th (2007) legislative session, the Texas House Committee on Law Enforcement studied the impact of laws that banned concealed gun license holders from carrying guns on college campuses. The committee recommended the elimination of this ban. In each session of the Texas legislature since 2009, lawmakers have proposed campus carry laws. Unlike the images in Nick Anderson's cartoon, no one would be able to openly carry a gun, although some gun rights advocates urged lawmakers in the 84th Legislature (2015) to approve this option. Through 2014, all efforts to change Texas law were unsuccessful. A law passed by the 83rd Legislature (2013) allows handgun licensees to store and transport guns in locked, private vehicles while on a college campus. (For a discussion of arguments for and against campus carry laws, see this chapter's Point/Counterpoint feature.)

Lawmaking by any elected representative body is a slow, frustrating, and often disappointing process. Most citizens are impatient with political tactics and procedural delays, even if their policy objectives are eventually achieved. And they often dislike the inevitable compromises involved in the legislative process.

Nevertheless, our legislators perform work of vital importance. They make laws that affect the life, liberty, and property of all persons in the state. After years of research, Professor Alan Rosenthal (1932–2013) of Rutgers University concluded: "[Legislatures] are far from perfect, yet they are the best we have, and preferable to any conceivable alternative. Not only that, they actually work, albeit in rather messy and somewhat mysterious ways—representing, lawmaking, and balancing the power of the executive."[1] After reading this chapter on the Texas legislature, you can decide whether Rosenthal's conclusions apply to the Lone Star State.

Legislative Framework

★ **LO8.1**   Describe the structure of the Texas legislature.

In Texas's Declaration of Independence, delegates complained that the Mexican government "had dissolved, by force of arms, the state Congress of Coahuila and Texas, and obliged our representatives to fly for their lives from the seat of government, thus depriving us of the fundamental right of representation." That fundamental right was subsequently established in the Constitution of the Republic of Texas and in all of Texas's five state constitutions, wherein Texans have entrusted the power to enact bills and adopt resolutions to popularly elected legislators. These powers are the essence of representative government. Other legislative functions include proposing constitutional amendments, adopting budgets for state government, levying taxes, redistricting, and impeaching and removing executive and judicial officials if warranted.

In Texas and 40 other states, the larger chamber of the **bicameral** (two-chamber, or two-house) legislature is called the House of Representatives. Some other states use the terms Assembly, House of Delegates, or General Assembly. Only Nebraska has a **unicameral** (one-chamber, or one-house) legislature, with 49 senators. In the 49 states with bicameral legislatures, the larger chamber ranges in size from 40 members in Alaska to 400 members in New Hampshire. Texas has 150 members in its House of Representatives. The smaller legislative chamber is called the Senate. Alaska has the smallest Senate, with 20 members; Minnesota has the largest, with 67. The Texas Senate has 31 members.

Election and Terms of Office

Voters residing in representative and senatorial districts elect Texas legislators. Representatives are elected for two years. Senators are usually elected for four years. Terms of office for members of both houses begin in January of odd-numbered years.

Legislative redistricting for both the Texas House and the Senate occurs in the first odd-numbered year in a decade based on the results of the decennial census. After the 2010 census, redistricting efforts began in 2011. In each even-numbered year, voters elect a new House of Representatives, as they did in 2012 and 2014. A new Senate was also elected in 2012. Because Senate terms are four years, however, in January of the next odd-numbered year (for example, 2013), senators draw lots by choosing from 31 numbered pieces of paper sealed in envelopes. The 16 who draw odd numbers get four-year terms, and the 15 who draw even numbers get only two-year terms. Thus, in 2014, elections were held for 15 positions in the Senate. Approximately one-half of the senators (that is, 15 or 16) will then be elected in each even-numbered year through 2020.

A legislator may be expelled by a two-thirds majority vote of the membership of the legislator's chamber. If a member of the legislature dies, resigns, or is expelled from office, the vacancy is filled by special election. A legislator called to active military duty for longer than 30 days retains the office if he or she appoints a qualified temporary replacement who is approved by the appropriate chamber. As of 2014, three male representatives had been called to military duty. Each appointed his wife as a temporary replacement.[2]

Sessions

Texas law requires **regular sessions** to begin on the second Tuesday in January of each odd-numbered year (for example, January 13, 2015). In practice, these regular biennial sessions always run for the full 140 days, as authorized by the Texas Constitution (for example, through June 1,

bicameral
A legislature with two houses or chambers, such as Texas's House of Representatives and Senate.

unicameral
A one-house legislature, such as the Nebraska legislature.

regular session
A session of the Texas legislature that is constitutionally mandated and begins on the second Tuesday in January of odd-numbered years and lasts for a maximum of 140 days.

Senator Wendy Davis (D-Ft. Worth) successfully filibusters a bill to reduce the number of abortion providers in Texas during the First Special Session of the 83rd Legislature. The bill had passed in the Texas House of Representatives.

Marjorie Kamys Cotera / Polaris / Newscom

CRITICAL THINKING

Would a unicameral legislature benefit or harm Texas?

special session
A legislative session called by the governor and limited to no more than 30 days.

2015). A beneficiary of these legislative sessions is the Austin economy because legislators and lobbyists spend millions for housing and entertainment during each session.

The governor may also call **special sessions**, lasting no longer than 30 days each, at any time. From 2001 through 2014, Governor Rick Perry called 12 special sessions on a number of matters including congressional and legislative redistricting and imposing limitations on abortion. During special sessions, the legislature may consider only those matters placed before it by the governor. Special sessions are unpopular with legislators and costly to taxpayers. Per diem costs to cover legislators' travel and living expenses equal $27,300 per day and total more than $800,000 for a 30-day session.[3] The three special sessions convened in 2013 cost Texas taxpayers more than $2.5 million.

Districting

Providing equal representation in a legislative chamber involves dividing a state into districts with approximately equal numbers of residents. Population distribution changes constantly as the result of migration, births, and deaths. Therefore, legislative district boundaries must be redrawn periodically to ensure equitable representation. Such redistricting can be politically disadvantageous to a legislator. It may take away areas of constituents who have provided strong voter support; it may add an area of constituents who produce little support and much opposition; or it may produce a new district that includes the residences of two or more representatives or senators, only one of whom can be reelected to represent the district.[4]

In Texas, the first legislative and congressional elections in districts determined by the 2010 census were conducted in November 2012 for offices filled in January 2013. For the previous 10 years, the 2000 census was the basis for legislative and congressional representation.

State Legislative Districts Although the Texas Constitution requires reapportionment and redistricting in the first legislative session after the federal census, in the decades after 1876, the legislature sometimes failed to redivide the state's population and map new districts for legislators. Thus, some districts for state representatives and senators became heavily populated and greatly underrepresented. Others experienced population decline or slow growth, resulting in overrepresentation.

In 1948, legislative districting inequities led to the adoption of a state constitutional amendment designed to pressure the legislature to remedy this situation. The legislature's failure to **redistrict** during the first regular session after a decennial census brings the Legislative Redistricting Board into operation. This board consists of five ex officio (that is, "holding other office") members: the lieutenant governor, Speaker of the House of Representatives, attorney general, comptroller of public accounts, and commissioner of the General Land Office. The board must meet within 90 days after the legislative session and redistrict the state within another 60 days.

Although the legislature drew new legislative districts after the federal censuses of 1950 and 1960, the Texas Constitution's apportionment formulas for the Texas House and Senate discriminated against heavily populated urban counties. These formulas were not changed until the U.S. Supreme Court held in *Reynolds v. Sims*, 377 U.S. 533 (1964) that "the seats in both houses of a bicameral state legislature must be apportioned on a population basis." This "one person, one vote" principle was first applied in Texas by a federal district court in *Kilgarlin v. Martin*, 252 F. Supp. 404 (1965).

Redistricting by the Texas legislature often sparks complaints about **gerrymandering**, a practice that involves drawing legislative districts to include or exclude certain groups of voters in order to favor one group or political party. Usually, gerrymandered districts are oddly shaped rather than compact. The term "gerrymander" originated to describe irregularly shaped districts created under the guidance of Elbridge Gerry, governor of Massachusetts, in 1812. The political party holding the most positions in the legislature often benefits in elections conducted after redistricting. Many state and federal court battles have been fought over the constitutionality of Texas's legislative districting arrangements.

Members of the Texas Senate have always represented **single-member districts**—that is, the voters of each district elect one senator. Redistricting according to the 2010 federal census provided for an ideal population of 811,147 (the total state population of 25,145,561 divided by 31) in each senatorial district. Many of the 31 senatorial districts cover several counties, but a few big-city senatorial districts are formed from the territory of only part of a county (see Figure 8.1).

Until 1971, a Texas county with two or more seats in the House was a **multimember district** in which voters elected representatives at-large to represent the whole county. Voters in these counties voted in all House races in the county. In 1971, however, single-member districts were established in Harris, Dallas, and Bexar counties. Four years later, single-member districting was extended to all counties in which voters elected more than one representative. The change to single-member districts was largely a result of court actions. Election results demonstrate that single-member districts reduce campaign costs and increase the probability that more African American and Latino candidates will be elected. As a result of the 2010 federal census, redistricting provided each state representative district with an ideal population of 167,637 (total state population divided by 150). (See Figure 8.2.)

redistricting
Redrawing of boundaries after the federal decennial census to create districts with approximately equal population (e.g., legislative, congressional, and State Board of Education districts in Texas). Local governments must also redistrict for some positions.

gerrymandering
Drawing the boundaries of a district, such as a state senatorial or representative district, to include or exclude certain groups of voters and thus affect election outcomes.

single-member district
An area that elects only one representative to a policymaking body, such as a state House, state Senate, or U.S. Congress.

multimember district
A district in which all voters participate in the election of two or more representatives to a policymaking body, such as a state House or state Senate.

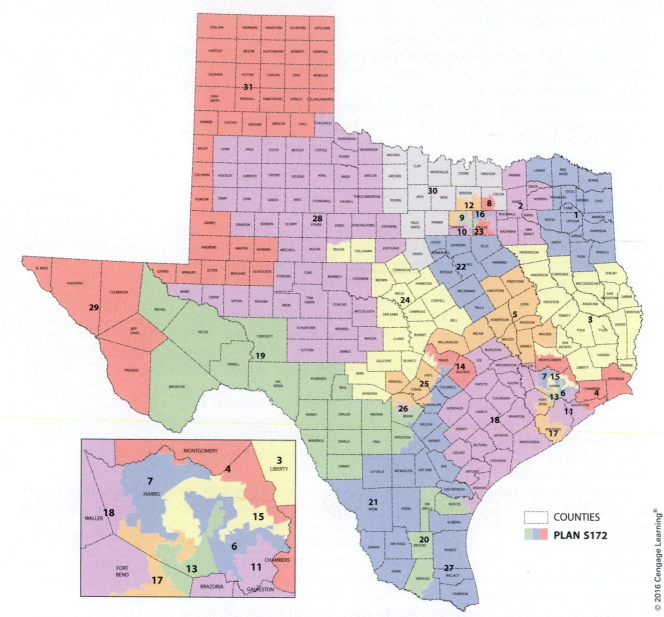

Figure 8.1   Court-Ordered Interim Texas State Senate Districts (for electing state senators in 2012–2014). The accompanying map shows districts wholly or partially within Harris County.

CRITICAL THINKING

Should drawing maps that favor the election of members from a specific political party be illegal?

Because members of the state legislature attempt to gain political advantage for their political party through gerrymandering, redistricting is a complex process that is often resolved in the courts. Redistricting after the 2010 census was no exception. Beginning in 2011, the 82nd Legislature

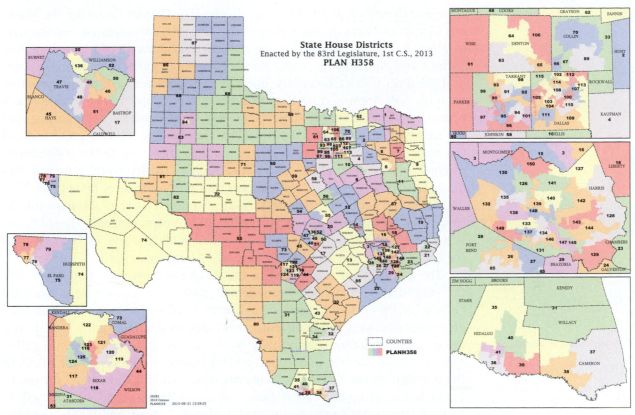

Figure 8.2 Court-Ordered Texas State House Districts (for electing state representatives in 2014). The accompanying maps show districts wholly or partially within urban counties.

CRITICAL THINKING

Should state representatives be elected on a multimember or single-member basis?

passed redistricting bills for Texas House, Senate, and congressional district boundaries. The plans favored the election of Republicans. Because members of historical minority groups, especially African Americans and Latinos, tend to vote for Democratic candidates, the redistricting plans also appeared to reduce the influence of these voters.

Under the provisions of the Voting Rights Act in force in 2011, Texas was required to obtain preclearance from the federal government of any changes in voting laws and voting boundaries. Texas's history of discrimination against minority voters forced this requirement on the state. Changes had to be approved by either the U.S. Department of Justice or the U.S. District Court in Washington, D.C. Attorney General Greg Abbott sent the redistricting plans to the U.S. District Court. All plans were denied preclearance and found to discriminate against minority voters.

Private citizens can also challenge the fairness of redistricting plans. Several members of historical minority groups and organizations that represent these groups filed lawsuits in the U.S. District Court for the Western District of Texas in San Antonio. The lawsuits, consolidated into the case of *Perez v. Perry*, claimed that the redistricting plans discriminated against Latinos and African Americans. Because the 2012 party primaries could not be held until district boundary lines were established, a three-judge panel from the San Antonio district court drew interim maps for use in that year's primaries. The fairness of these maps was challenged by Republicans, and the case was appealed directly to the U.S. Supreme Court. That court ordered the maps redrawn in a way that was more consistent with the legislature's original redistricting plans. The San Antonio district court followed this directive, redrew the maps, and ordered that party primaries be held on May 29, 2012. The San Antonio district court also ordered use of its maps for the November general elections. In November 2012, voters elected 95 Republicans and 55 Democrats to the Texas House, 19 Republicans and 11 Democrats to the Texas Senate, and 24 Republicans and 12 Democrats to the U.S. House.

The court-drawn maps used in the 2012 elections were temporary and the state-drawn maps had been denied preclearance; therefore, the 83rd Legislature (2013) had to produce redistricting plans for legislative and congressional elections. Although legislators failed to accomplish this task during the regular legislative session, they were successful in doing so in a called special session. Senate and congressional boundary lines were identical to those drawn by the San Antonio district court. The map approved for use in Texas House elections varied from the court-drawn map with regard to 14 state representative districts in Dallas, Harris, Tarrant, and Webb counties.

The day before Governor Perry signed both bills into law, in the case of *Shelby County v. Holder*, the U.S. Supreme Court ruled that the automatic preclearance requirements of the Voting Rights Act were no longer applicable. Section 4 of that law provided a formula for determining which states, mostly southern, had histories of voter discrimination that required preclearance. Those complaining that a law or redistricting plan discriminates against racial or ethnic minorities must now file a lawsuit and prove discrimination. The U.S. Department of Justice and the original plaintiffs in *Perez v. Perry* immediately challenged the House and congressional redistricting plans, arguing the new redistricting plans intentionally discriminated against minority voters. The Texas attorney general's office contended that any dilution of minority voting strength was a by-product of the legal practice of partisan gerrymandering that favored Republican candidates. Although the federal district court in San Antonio ordered use of the legislature's 2013 maps for the 2014 primaries and general election, a trial began in July 2014 and continued through autumn.

U.S. Congressional Districts In the year after a federal census, the Texas legislature must draw new boundaries for the state's U.S. congressional districts (from which representatives to the U.S. House of Representatives are elected). As in other districts created for representation purposes, population in the respective districts must be equal. Results of the 2010 federal census indicated that each of Texas's 36 congressional districts should have an ideal population of 698,488.

Redistricting plans for congressional positions faced the same challenges as those for state legislative boundaries. As of 2014, those plans likewise remained under challenge in the courts. For details concerning congressional redistricting politics from 2011 to 2014, see Figure 8.3 as well as this chapter's Selected Reading.

Legislators

......★ **LO8.2** Describe the membership of the Texas legislature, including legislators' formal and informal qualifications and compensation.

Members of the Texas legislature may not hold another government office. Furthermore, they must meet specific state constitutional qualifications concerning citizenship, voter status, state and district residence, and age. Despite such restrictions, millions of Texans possess all of the legal qualifications to serve in the legislature. As is true of the memberships in other state legislatures, however, biographical data for members of recent Texas legislatures suggest many informal qualifications that restrict opportunities for election.

Qualifications and Characteristics

The Texas Constitution specifies the formal qualifications for House and Senate members. Table 8.1 provides a list of qualifications for positions in the two chambers. Age and state residency requirements differ between the Texas House and Senate. If a question arises concerning constitutional qualifications or if a dispute develops over election returns, each legislative chamber determines who will be seated.

✔ **8.1 Learning Check**

1. In which type of legislative session does a governor have more authority: a regular session or a special session?
2. True or False: Gerrymandered districts are illegal.

Answers on p. 316.

Table 8.1   Constitutional Qualifications for Membership in the Texas Legislature

Qualification	House	Senate
Citizenship	U.S. citizen	U.S. citizen
Voter status	Qualified Texas voter	Qualified Texas voter
Residence in district to be represented	One year immediately preceding election	One year immediately preceding election
Texas residence	Two years immediately preceding election	Five years immediately preceding election
Age	21 years	26 years

Source: Constitution of Texas, Art. 3, Secs. 6 and 7.

CRITICAL THINKING

What do longer residency requirements and being older suggest about the role of senators compared to representatives?

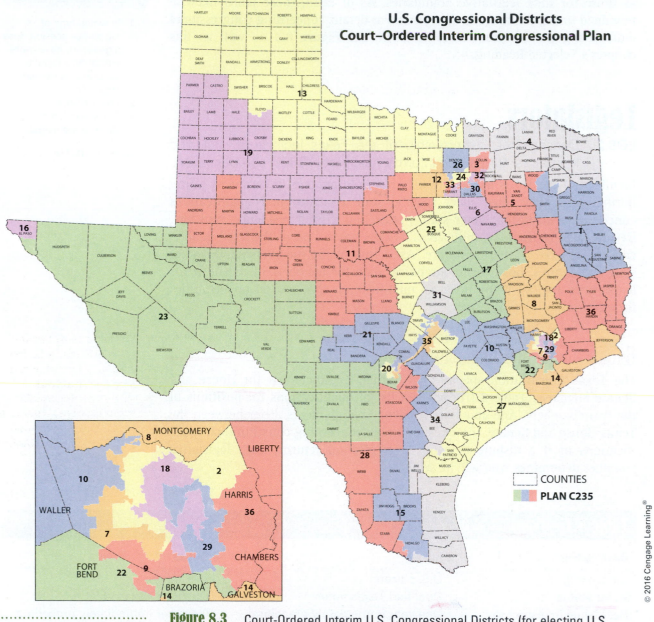

U.S. Congressional Districts
Court–Ordered Interim Congressional Plan

COUNTIES

PLAN C235

Figure 8.3   Court-Ordered Interim U.S. Congressional Districts (for electing U.S. representatives for 2012–2014). Accompanying map shows districts wholly or partially within Harris County.

CRITICAL THINKING

If a particular ethnic or racial group is primarily responsible for an increase in population in a state, should that group be entitled to the possibility of more representation in the U.S. Congress for members from their ethnic or racial group?

In order to be elected, the typical Texas legislator also meets a number of informal qualifications. These informal qualifications include being an Anglo Protestant male between 35 and 50 years of age, a native-born Texan, and an attorney or a businessperson who has served one or more previous terms of office. Although such characteristics do not guarantee any prede-termined reaction to issues and events, legislators tend to be influenced by their experiences and environments. Because these factors can have policy consequences, any study of the legislature must account for the biographical characteristics of legislators. See Table 8.2 for data on political party affilia-tion, racial/ethnic classification, gender of legislators, and turnover from selected legislatures from 1971 to 2015.

Gender and Ethnic Classifications Anglo men dominate the Texas legis-lature, and almost all Anglo men in the legislature are Republicans (only six of the 181 legislators in the 84th legislative session are Anglo male Democrats). As reflected by Table 8.2, over time the legislature has become more diverse, and includes more women and members of historical minority groups in 2015 than

State Senator Leticia Van de Putte, a Latina, mother of six children, and a pharmacist, waves to the crowd before giving remarks at a Planned Parenthood rally at the state Capitol on March 8, 2011.

AP Images/ Austin American-Statesman, Deborah Canon

CRITICAL THINKING

How would increasing the number of women in elected office affect public policy?

Table 8.2 Texas Trends in Legislative Representation for Selected Legislatures (January 1971–January 2015)

Number of regular session	Year of regular session	Political Party		Racial/Ethnic Classification					Gender		Turnover
		Dem.	Rep.	Anglo	Latino	African American	Asian American		Men	Women	
HOUSE OF REPRESENTATIVES: 150 MEMBERS											
62nd	1971	140	10	137	11	2	0		149	1	20.0 %
63rd	1973	133	17	131	11	8	0		145	5	46.7 %
67th	1981	114	36	119	18	13	0		139	11	24.0 %
68th	1983	115	35	117	21	12	0		137	13	27.3 %
72nd	1991	92	58	117	20	13	0		131	19	20.1 %
73rd	1993	91	59	110	26	14	0		125	25	22.8 %
77th	2001	78	72	108	28	14	0		120	30	8.4 %
78th	2003	62	88	105	30	14	1		118	32	24.0 %
82nd	2011	51	89	101	30	17	2		118	32	23.3 %
83rd	2013	55	95	96	33	18	3		119	31	28.7 %
84th	2015	52	98	95	35	17	3		120	30	16.7 %
SENATE: 31 MEMBERS											
62nd	1971	29	2	29	1	1	0		30	1	12.9 %
63rd	1973	28	3	29	2	0	0		30	1	48.4 %
67th	1981	24	7	27	4	0	0		30	1	26.7 %
68th	1983	26	5	26	4	1	0		31	0	32.3 %
72nd	1991	23	8	24	6	2	0		27	4	16.7 %
73rd	1993	18	13	23	6	2	0		27	4	25.8 %
77th	2001	15	16	22	7	2	0		27	4	6.5 %
78th	2003	12	19	22	7	2	0		27	4	22.6 %
82nd	2011	12	19	22	7	2	0		25	6	6.5 %
83rd	2013	12	19	22	7	2	0		25	6	19.4 %
84th	2015	11	20	22	2	7	0		24	7	12.9 %

Source: Texas Legislative Reference Library, Texas Legislative Council, and the unofficial count of the Office of the Secretary of State (November 5, 2014).

CRITICAL THINKING

What do you believe are the most important trends in the membership of the Texas legislature over past decades?

it did in 1971. Although more than 50 percent of the state's population is female, approximately 20 percent of state legislators are women. Reports of male legislators meowing like cats when their female colleagues debate each other, making comments about female legislators' physical attributes, and, according to some, treating women with general disrespect caused one legislator to describe the Texas House and Senate as "the last of the good ol' boys' clubs."[5]

Representation of members of historical racial or ethnic minorities increased substantially from the late 1960s through the early 1990s. Both African Americans and Latinos have been underrepresented in the Texas legislature. Texans elected the first Asian American legislator in the 1960s. Voters did not elect another Asian American for almost 40 years. No Asian American has ever been elected to the Texas Senate.

Political Party Affiliation In 1961, no Republican held a seat in the Texas legislature. When the legislature convened in 1997, the GOP had a Senate majority. By January 2003, Republicans controlled both the Senate and the House. Since that year, each chamber has produced more "party line" votes—that is, all Democrats voting one way on an issue and all Republicans voting the other way.

Throughout the first decade of the 21st century, Republicans increased their strength in both the Texas House of Representatives and the Texas Senate. In 2011, Republicans achieved supermajority status (two-thirds of total membership) in the Texas House of Representatives, with 101 Republican representatives compared to 49 Democrats. Republican representation in the Texas Senate has fluctuated between 19 and 20 of the 31 senate seats since 2007, an insufficient number for Republicans to hold a supermajority. Although most of the increase in Republican strength resulted from elections, between 2009 and 2012, four Democratic representatives switched to the GOP. In the elections of 2012 and 2014, Democrats increased their numbers in the House of Representatives, winning 55 seats in the Texas House in 2012 and 52 in 2014. The numbers remained constant in the Senate, where Democrats won 12 seats in 2012 and 11 in 2014.

Central city residents usually elect African American and Latino Democrats, whereas Republican senators and representatives receive their strongest support from rural and suburban Anglo voters. Residents of Mexican border districts largely elect Latino Democrats.

Education and Occupation In government, as in business, most positions of leadership call for college credentials. Nearly all members of recent Texas legislatures attended one or more institutions of higher education. Most of them could claim a bachelor's degree, and many had graduate or professional degrees (especially in law).

Traditionally, Texas legislators have included many attorneys and business owners or managers. Lesser numbers of real estate and insurance people, as well as some farmers, ranchers, and teachers, also have served. Health care professionals, engineers, and accountants have held few legislative seats, although 3 of the 31 members of the Senate in the 83rd Legislature were physicians, and another was a pharmacist. Laborers have held almost none.

Lawyer-legislators may receive retainers (payments) from corporations and special interest groups, with the understanding that legal services will be performed if needed. Some question whether lawyer-legislators are hired for legal services, to delay a court proceeding with a continuance, or to influence legislation. An attorney who serves in the legislature can obtain a continuance (that is, a postponement) of any case set for trial during a period extending from 30 days before to 30 days after a legislative session. To avoid abuse of this privilege, judges can deny a continuance if a lawyer was hired to assist with a case within 10 days of trial or any related legal proceeding. Payments received for obtaining a continuance must be disclosed. A legislator may not represent paying clients before state agencies. (For a discussion of state agencies, see Chapter 10, "Public Policy and Administration.")

Religious Affiliation The Texas Constitution guarantees freedom of religion and prohibits use of public funds for the benefit of a sect or religious group. Even though Texans recognize separation of church and state, a legislator's religious beliefs may play a critical role in the formulation of public policy. These factors are especially important when considering legislation involving issues related to moral behavior (such as abortion or gambling) and some economic matters (such as state aid to church-related schools). Although the religious affiliation of each legislator is not a matter of record, it does appear that in Texas Catholic senators and representatives are most numerous, followed (in order) by Baptists, Methodists, and Episcopalians.

Legislative Experience In a legislative body, experience is measured in terms of turnover (that is, first-termers replacing experienced members who have retired or lost an election) and tenure (years served in a legislative chamber). For the 10 most recent Texas legislatures (75th–84th), the average turnover in the House was about 17 percent of the membership every two years. In the Senate, it was about 9 percent. Turnover tends to be greater for the first legislature after redistricting. Table 8.2 provides information on the turnover rate for elections immediately preceding and following redistricting.

The average length of service by legislators in the 10 most recent legislatures was more than six years in both the House and the Senate. Many senators served first as representatives. In 2015, for example, 12 of the 31 senators in the 84th Legislature had served as representatives. After a term in office, an incumbent is more likely to win an election than is an inexperienced challenger.

As a general rule, lawmakers become most effective after they have spent two or more years learning procedural rules related to enacting legislation and working with constituents, bureaucrats, lobbyists, fellow legislators, and other elected officials. Several representatives and senators have held their current positions for decades. The most senior member of the House, Tom Craddick (R-Midland), was first elected in 1968; the most senior member of the Senate, John Whitmire (D-Houston), was first elected in 1982. (Senator Whitmire was in the House of Representatives for 10 years prior to his election to the Senate.) Texas is one of 35 states that does not have term limits for legislators. Even though some Democrats and Tea Party

Republicans worked to achieve term limits for state-level officeholders (including legislators) during the 83rd legislative session, these efforts, like several earlier attempts, failed.

Compensation

The lowest-paid state legislators in the nation are from New Hampshire. These elected officials are paid $200 per year with no per diem (compensation to cover expenses). Although New Mexico does not pay members of its legislative bodies any annual salary, they do receive up to $154 per diem for each day the legislature is in session. In contrast, California's annual salary of $90,526 is more than any other state pays its legislators. Texas's state senators and representatives receive low pay, reasonable allowances, and a relatively generous retirement pension after a minimum period of service.

Pay and Per Diem Allowance Originally, Texas legislators' salaries and per diem (daily) personal allowances during a regular or special session were specified by the state constitution and could be changed only by constitutional amendment. Now, as authorized by a constitutional amendment, the Texas Ethics Commission sets the per diem expense allowance. In addition, this commission may recommend salary increases for legislators and even higher salaries for the Speaker and the lieutenant governor; however, Texas voters must approve all such recommendations and therefore make the ultimate decision. The $600 monthly salary ($7,200 per year) has not increased since 1975.

For the 83rd Legislature, which convened in January 2013, the per diem allowance to cover meals, lodging, and other personal expenses was $150 for senators, representatives, and the lieutenant governor. This per diem amounted to a total of $21,000 per official for the 140-day regular session.

Expense Allowances At the beginning of a session, each chamber authorizes contingent expense allowances. For example, during the 83rd regular session, the House authorized every representative's operating account to be credited monthly with $13,250. The monthly allowance for the interim was $11,925. House members use money in this account to cover the cost of official work-related travel within Texas, postage, office operations, and staff salaries. Representatives can also use money from campaign contributions to supplement their assistants' salaries and their own travel allowances. Some legislators use political donations to pay rent for housing in Austin.

From January 2013 to January 2015, each senator in the 83rd Legislature had a maximum monthly allowance of $38,000 for intrastate travel expenses and staff salaries. Other expenses for carrying out official duties (for example, subscriptions, postage, telecommunications, and stationery) were paid from the Senate's contingent expense fund. Like representatives, Senate members can supplement staff salaries with money from campaign contributions.

Staff members assist legislators with office management, research, constituent service, and communication. Although assistance in responding

 to postal mail and email is a staff function, communications via social media, especially Twitter, is of increasing importance for legislators. Many legislators have staff to manage these accounts, but some elected officials prefer to handle their social networking accounts directly. In the 83rd legislative session, more than 80 percent of the state's representatives and senators had active Twitter accounts.

Retirement Pension Under the terms of the Texas State Employees Retirement Act of 1975, legislators contribute 8 percent of their state salaries to a retirement fund. Retirement pay for senators and representatives amounts to 2.3 percent of the state-funded portion of a district judge's annual salary ($140,000 in fiscal years 2014 and 2015) for each year served and cannot exceed the annual salary of state district judges. Representative Tom Craddick, therefore, is eligible for $140,000 in annual retirement benefits.

Legislators with a minimum of 12 years of service may retire at age 50 with an annual pension of $38,640. Those with at least eight years of service may retire at age 60 with a pension of $25,760 per year. In a somewhat complex process, a legislator (and members of the executive branch) may retire as a state employee for previous years of service and receive retirement benefits (based on annual salary). At the same time, the individual continues to serve as an elected official and receives compensation for that position as well. Unless a legislator has previously held a higher-paying position in government, however, the annual benefit would only be about $5,000. Consequently, the option, although attractive to those in the executive branch, is less so for most members of the legislature. Many legislators do not serve long enough to qualify for a pension, but for those who are eligible, payments can begin while they are relatively young.

✔ **8.2 Learning Check**

1. True or False: A formal qualification for a member of the Texas legislature is that she or he must be a practicing Christian.
2. During a legislator's term of office, which will be higher: legislators' salaries or their per diem allowances?

Answers on p. 316.

How Do We Compare...in Salary of Legislators?

Annual Salary of Legislators for the Year of the Last Regular Session

Most Populous U.S. States	Annual Salary	U.S. States Bordering Texas	Annual Salary
California	$ 90,526	Arkansas	$15,869
Florida	$ 29,697	Louisiana	$16,800*
New York	$ 79,500	New Mexico	$ 0**
Texas	**$ 7,200**	Oklahoma	$38,400

*Legislators in Louisiana also receive a $6,000 per year expense allowance.
**Legislators in New Mexico receive mileage and a per diem allowance but no annual salary.
Source: National Council of State Legislatures, "2013 State Legislators Compensation Data," March 15, 2013, http://www.ncsl.org/research/about-state-legislatures/2013-ncsl-legislator-salary-and-per-diem.aspx.

Legislative Organization

····· ★ **LO8.3** Compare the organization of the Texas House of Representatives and the Texas Senate.

Merely bringing legislators together in the Capitol does not ensure the making of laws or any other governmental activity. Gathering people to transact official business requires organized effort. The formal organization of the Texas legislature features a presiding officer and several committees for each chamber. The informal organization involves various caucuses that do not have legal status.

Presiding Officers

The Texas Constitution establishes the offices of president of the Senate and Speaker of the House of Representatives. It designates the lieutenant governor as president of the Senate and provides for the election of a Speaker to preside over the House of Representatives.

President of the Senate: The Lieutenant Governor The most important function of the lieutenant governor of Texas is to serve as **president of the Senate.**[6] Just as the vice president of the United States is empowered to preside over the U.S. Senate but is not a member of that national lawmaking body, so too the lieutenant governor of Texas is not a member of the state Senate. The big difference between them is that the lieutenant governor presides over most sessions and plays a leading role in legislative matters (see Table 8.3 for powers), whereas the vice president seldom presides or becomes involved in the daily business of the U.S. Senate.

Chosen by the people of Texas in a statewide election for a four-year term, the lieutenant governor is first in line of succession in the event of the death, resignation, or removal of the governor. When the governor is absent from the state, the lieutenant governor serves as acting governor and receives the gubernatorial salary, which amounted to more than $400 per day at the beginning of 2015. Ordinarily, however, the lieutenant governor's salary is $600 per month, which amounts to about $20 per day.

Because of the lieutenant governor's powers (most of which have been granted by Senate rules rather than by the Texas Constitution), this official is perhaps the most powerful elected officer in the state, especially when the legislature is in session. If the lieutenant governor dies, resigns, or is elected to another office, the Senate elects one of its members to serve as acting lieutenant governor. At the beginning of each session, the Senate elects a president pro tempore, who presides when the lieutenant governor is absent or disabled.

Speaker of the House The presiding officer of the House of Representatives is the **Speaker of the House**, a representative elected to that office for a two-year term by the House in an open (that is, not secret) vote by the House membership.[7] Proceedings in the House are controlled by the Speaker (see Table 8.3).

president of the Senate
Title of the lieutenant governor in his or her role as presiding officer for the Texas Senate.

Speaker of the House
The state representative elected by House members to serve as the presiding officer for that chamber.

Table 8.3	Comparison of Powers of Presiding Officers

Lieutenant Governor	Speaker of the House
Issues interim charges to standing committees for subjects to be studied in the interim between regular sessions	Issues interim charges to standing committees for subjects to be studied in the interim between regular sessions
Creates and abolishes committees	Creates and abolishes committees
Appoints Senate committee and subcommittee chairs and vice chairs	Appoints House committee and subcommittee chairs and vice chairs
Appoints members of Senate committees and subcommittees	Appoints members of House committees and subcommittees (limited by seniority rules)
Determines the Senate committee to which a bill will be sent after introduction	Determines the House committee to which a bill will be sent after introduction
Recognizes senators who wish to speak on the Senate floor or make a motion	Recognizes members who wish to speak on the House floor or make a motion
Votes only to break a tie vote	Votes (rarely) on bills and resolutions
Serves as joint chair of the Legislative Council, the Legislative Budget Board, and the Legislative Audit Committee	Serves as joint chair of the Legislative Council, the Legislative Budget Board, and the Legislative Audit Committee

CRITICAL THINKING

How is the lieutenant governor more powerful than the Speaker of the House?

House rules authorize the Speaker to name another representative to preside over the chamber temporarily. The Speaker may also name a member of the House to serve as permanent speaker pro tempore for as long as the Speaker desires. A speaker pro tempore performs all the duties of the Speaker when that officer is absent.[8] The Speaker occupies an apartment in the Capitol.

Because of the Speaker's power, filling this House office involves intense political activity. Lobbyists make every effort to ensure the election of a Speaker sympathetic to their respective causes, and potential candidates for the position begin to line up support several months or even years before a Speaker's race begins. Long before this election, anyone aspiring to the office of Speaker will attempt to induce House members to sign cards pledging their support. House rules, however, prohibit soliciting written pledges during a regular session. Once elected, a Speaker usually finds it easier to obtain similar pledges of support for reelection to the speakership.

Speaker candidates must file with the Texas Ethics Commission. No limitations on donations exist. According to judicial decision, any attempts to limit spending are unconstitutional because such restrictions would "significantly chill political speech protected by the First Amendment" of the U.S. Constitution.[9]

Since 2009, Joe Straus (R–San Antonio) has served as Speaker. Straus has had bipartisan support since his original election to the speakership by the 81st Legislature and has maintained that support in subsequent reelections in 2011 and 2013. Tea Party activists within the Republican Party have unsuccessfully challenged Straus, both for reelection to his representative's seat and the speakership.[10]

Committee System

Presiding officers appoint committee chairs and vice chairs and determine the committees to which bills will be referred. (See Table 8.4 for committee titles and the numbers of members for House and Senate committees in the 83rd Legislature.) Because both House and Senate committees play important roles in the fate or fortune of all bills and resolutions, selection of committee members goes a long way toward determining the amount and type of legislative output during a session. Permanent staff members are available to assist legislators with committee work on a continuing basis. Usually, these staff members also work on interim study committees created to examine legislative issues between regular sessions.

House Committees In the Texas House of Representatives, **substantive committees** consider bills and resolutions relating to the subject identified by a committee's name (for example, elections or transportation). Substantive committees sometimes have subcommittees in which a few of the committee's members focus more closely on specific issues under the committee's jurisdiction. Seniority, based on years of service in the House of Representatives, determines a maximum of one-half the membership for substantive committees, excluding the chair and the vice chair. When a regular session begins,

substantive committee Appointed by the House Speaker, this committee considers bills and resolutions related to the subject identified by its name (such as the House Agriculture Committee) and may recommend passage of proposed legislation to the appropriate calendars committee.

| **Table 8.4** | Texas House and Senate Committees, 83rd Legislature, January 2013–January 2015 |

House Committee (number of members)
32 Substantive Committees

Agriculture and Livestock (7)
Appropriations (27)
Business and Industry (7)
Corrections (7)
County Affairs (9)
Criminal Jurisprudence (9)
Culture, Recreation, and Tourism (7)
Defense and Veterans' Affairs (9)
Economic and Small Business Development (9)
   Subcommittee on Manufacturing (5)
Elections (7)
Energy Resources (11)
Environmental Regulation (9)
Government Efficiency and Reform (7)
Higher Education (9)

House Committee (number of members)
6 Procedural Committees

Calendars (15)
General Investigating and Ethics (5)
House Administration (11)
Local and Consent Calendars (13)
Redistricting (9)
Rules and Resolutions (11)

8 House Select Committees

Criminal Procedure Reform (5)
Child Protection (9)
Economic Development Incentives (13)
Federalism and Fiscal Reponsibility (5)
Redistricting (19)
Transparency in State Agency Operations (8)
Transportation Funding (7)
Transportation Funding, Expenditures and Finance (9)

Table 8.4   (Continued)

Homeland Security and Public Safety (9)
Human Services (9)
Insurance (9)
International Trade and Intergovernmental Affairs (7)
Investments and Financial Services (7)
Judiciary and Civil Jurisprudence (9)
Land and Resource Management (9)
Licensing and Administrative Procedures (9)
Natural Resources (11)
Pensions (7)
Public Education (11)
Public Health (11)
Special Purpose Districts (9)
State Affairs (13)
Technology (5)
Transportation (11)
Urban Affairs (7)
Ways and Means (9)

Joint Committee (number of members)
7 Joint Committees (through August 2014)

Review Texas Lottery and Texas Lottery
    Commission (10)
Oversight of Higher Education Governance,
    Excellence and Transparency (16)
Coastal Barrier System (23)
Education for a Skilled Workforce (14)
Effects of Border Wait Times (10)
Human Trafficking (18)
Water Desalination (12)

Senate Committee (number of members)
18 Standing Committees

Administration (6)
Agriculture, Rural Affairs, and Homeland Security (5)
Business and Commerce (9)
Criminal Justice (7)
Economic Development (7)
    Subcommittee on Public Private Partnerships (3)
Education (9)
Finance (14)
    Subcommittee on Fiscal Matters (5)
Government Organization (7)
Health and Human Services (9)
Higher Education (7)
Intergovernmental Relations (5)
Jurisprudence (7)
Natural Resources (11)
Nominations (7)
Open Government (4)
State Affairs (8)
Transportation (9)
Veterans Affairs and Military Installations (5)

2 Senate Select Committees

Redistricting (14)
Transportation Funding, Expenditures and Finance (9)

Source: Texas Legislature Online, including websites for the House (http://www.house.state.tx.us) and Senate (http://www.senate.state.tx.us).

CRITICAL THINKING

How could serving on a specific committee benefit a legislator?

procedural committee
These House committees (such as the Calendars Committee and House Administration Committee) consider bills and resolutions relating primarily to procedural legislative matters.

each representative, in order of seniority, designates three committees in order of preference. A representative is entitled to become a member of the committee of highest preference that has a vacant seniority position. The Speaker appoints other committee members.

Seniority does not apply to membership on **procedural committees**, each of which considers bills and resolutions relating primarily to an internal legislative matter (for example, the Calendars Committee, which determines when a bill will be considered by the full House). The Speaker appoints all members of procedural committees.

Although substantive and procedural committees are established under House rules adopted in each regular session, the Speaker independently creates **select committees** and **interim committees** and appoints all members. A Speaker usually creates select committees during a session to consider legislation that crosses committee jurisdictional lines or during an interim to conduct special studies.

Senate Committees Senate rules provide for **standing committees** (though the rules do not identify them as substantive or procedural committees), select committees, and interim committees. Standing committees sometimes have subcommittees. As president of the Senate, the lieutenant governor appoints all committee members and designates the chair and vice chair of each committee.

Legislative Caucus System

Legislative caucuses are organizations determined on the basis of partisan, philosophical, racial, ethnic, or other special interests. Through the 1980s, Democratic leadership in the Texas House of Representatives and the Senate absorbed potential opponents within their teams and discouraged caucuses. Although increasingly important for legislators and interest groups, legislative caucuses are prohibited from receiving public money. These groups stay connected to voters through Facebook, Twitter, Pinterest, and RSS feeds. Some groups attempt to heighten the impact of their messages by subscribing to services such as ShareThis. Supporters become a distribution network sending press releases and other information through their social networks. Some caucuses do not have web pages. They rely solely on Facebook and other social media platforms to engage voters who share their interests.

Party Caucuses The strengthening of party caucuses in each chamber of the Texas legislature was one indication that Texas was becoming a two-party state. The House Democratic Caucus was organized in 1981. In recent years, all Democratic legislators have been reported as belonging to their party's House or Senate caucuses. Under the leadership of Representative Tom Craddick (R–Midland), the House Republican Caucus was organized in 1989. Although they have no formal organizational role in either chamber, party caucuses take policy positions on some issues and promote unity among their members.

Racial/Ethnic Caucuses Racial and ethnic groups also organize and form voting blocs to maximize their power. Because African Americans and Latinos constitute significant minorities in the Texas legislature, it is not surprising that they have formed caucuses for this purpose. The Legislative Black Caucus concentrates on issues affecting African American Texans, such as hate crimes laws.

The House-based Mexican American Legislative Caucus focuses on issues such as voting rights and providing higher education opportunities in South Texas and along the Mexican border. Members of the caucus led efforts to establish the University of Texas–Rio Grande Valley, a merger of UT Pan American and UT Brownsville. The institution includes a medical

select committee
This committee, created independently by the House Speaker or the lieutenant governor, may consider legislation that crosses committee jurisdictional lines or may conduct special studies.

interim committee
A House or Senate committee appointed by the Speaker or lieutenant governor to study an important policy issue between regular sessions.

standing committee
A Senate committee appointed by the lieutenant governor for the purpose of considering proposed bills and resolutions before possible floor debate and voting by senators.

legislative caucus
An organization of legislators who seek to maximize their influence over issues in which they have a special interest.

school. It receives funding from the Permanent University Fund (PUF), a state endowment financed by oil and gas royalties from state-owned natural resources—funding that was denied under previous law. Both the Mexican American Legislative Caucus and the Senate Hispanic Caucus include a few Anglo and African American members who have large numbers of Latino voters in their districts. In January 2011, nine Republican representatives (six Latino and three Anglo) formed the Hispanic Republican Conference.

Ideological Caucuses

Ideological Caucuses House-based ideological caucuses have also emerged. The Texas Conservative Coalition attracts Republicans and conservative Democrats, whereas the liberal Legislative Study Group appeals to many Democrats (including several who are also members of the Legislative Black Caucus and the Mexican American Legislative Caucus). The conservative and liberal caucuses reflect opposing views on most issues. A few representatives, however, belong to both caucuses.

Although not a typical caucus, the Independent Conservative Republicans of Texas (ICRT) counts nearly all Republican legislators as its "founding members." Launched by Senator Dan Patrick (R-Houston) early in 2010, the ICRT offers an ideological "Contract for Texas," combats the influence of GOP moderates, and reaches out to the Tea Party movement. In December 2010, shortly before the beginning of the 82nd regular legislative session, the Tea

State Senators Dan Patrick (R-Houston) and Leticia Van de Putte (D-San Antonio) discuss an issue during the 82nd Legislature. The two opposed each other in 2014 as nominees for their respective parties in the race for lieutenant governor. Patrick won that election.

Texas Senate Media Services

CRITICAL THINKING

What is the appropriate relationship between elected officials who are members of opposing political parties?

Party Caucus was formed with 49 members. By the 83rd legislative session, the group reported that 63 legislators were members. Working with the caucus is an advisory council composed of Tea Party organizers from across Texas.[11]

Bipartisan Caucuses Some caucuses are framed around specific issues. Because an issue may be important to both Republicans and Democrats, caucus membership is bipartisan. For example, the House Women's Health Caucus supports legislation on issues related to women's health care. In 2013, members of the caucus, including its sole Republican, unsuccessfully opposed setting additional restrictions on abortion clinics.[12] A more inclusive bipartisan caucus is the "farm-to-table" caucus founded by Republican Representative Lois Kolkhurst (R-Brenham) and Democratic Representative Eddie Rodriguez (D-Austin). In the 83rd legislative session, caucus members succeeded in passing bills that eased restrictions on "cottage foods" (foods prepared in home kitchens for commercial sale) and food sampling at cooking demonstrations and farmers' markets.[13]

8.3 Learning Check

1. True or False: The Speaker of the House of Representatives presides over that body but cannot vote on a bill or resolution.
2. In the Texas Senate, who determines the committee to which a bill will be sent after its introduction?

Answers on p. 316.

Legislative Operations

★ **LO8.4** Outline the responsibilities of the Texas legislature.

As the chief agent in making public policy in Texas state government, the legislature must have powers to function. Legislators also need immunity from interference while performing their official duties. Thus, lawmaking is governed by detailed rules of procedure for each legislative chamber.

Powers and Immunities

Although bound by restrictions found in few state constitutions, the legislature is the dominant branch of Texas government and the chief agent in making public policy. Legislators control government spending, which makes state agencies and personnel—and, to some extent, units of local government—dependent upon them. Composed of one or more appropriation bills, the biennial state budget authorizes state spending. The budget is the most important legislation for regular (and, sometimes, special) sessions. To become law, an appropriation bill must pass in both legislative chambers, but it is subject to the governor's veto power (see Chapter 9, "The Executive Branch"). Although appropriation bills may originate in either the House or the Senate, all revenue-producing bills, such as a bill that imposes a state tax, must originate in the House. (For more on taxing and spending, see Chapter 13, "Finance and Fiscal Policy.") Along with their powers, lawmakers have immunities from prosecution designed to allow them to function freely.

Making Public Policy The most typical exercise of legislative power involves making public policy by passing bills and adopting resolutions. All proposed legislation must be introduced by an elected senator or representative in the appropriate chamber; however, private citizens often communicate their desire for new laws to elected officials. Commentators frequently criticize the legislative process, noting that campaign donors and their lobbyists are more likely to gain support for their proposals than the average citizen.

In 2012, however, the House Government Efficiency and Reform Committee launched a wiki site called the Texas Red Tape Challenge in an effort to engage more Texans in the lawmaking process. Like a similar project in Great Britain, the site was intended to allow crowdsourcing for proposed legislation for the 83rd Legislature. Texans were encouraged to submit and comment on ideas regarding licensing, regulations, education, and manufacturing. In its final report, the committee noted that almost 1,000 people participated during the three months the site was open. Unlike Great Britain, which has changed almost 100 laws based on citizen comment, the committee had no recommendations for new legislation.[14]

Each bill or resolution has a distinctive abbreviation that indicates the chamber of origin. Every legislative proposal is given a number indicating the order of introduction. Texas Legislature Online maintains the history, text, analysis, and any fiscal note for each proposed bill or resolution.

A **simple resolution**, abbreviated HR (House Resolution) if introduced in the House and SR (Senate Resolution) if introduced in the Senate, involves action by one chamber only and is not sent to the governor. Adoption requires a simple majority vote (more than one-half) of members present. Matters dealt with by simple resolution affect only the chamber that is voting on the resolution and include rules of the House or Senate, procedures for House or Senate operations, and invitations extended to nonmembers to address a particular chamber.

After adoption by simple majority votes of members present in both the House and the Senate, a **concurrent resolution** (HCR or SCR) is sent to the governor, who has two options: sign it or veto it. Typical examples are resolutions that request action by the U.S. Congress; grant permission to sue the state; or name state icons, such as the state squash (pumpkin) and state musical instrument (guitar). In addition, the chambers adopt a concurrent resolution to adjourn at the end of any legislative session—a measure that does not require approval by the governor.

Adoption of a **joint resolution** (HJR or SJR) requires approval by both houses but no action by the governor. The nature of a joint resolution determines whether a simple majority or a two-thirds vote is required. Proposed amendments to the Texas Constitution are examples of joint resolutions requiring a two-thirds majority vote of the membership of each house. Ratification of proposed U.S. constitutional amendments that require a vote of state legislatures are approved with a joint resolution adopted by simple majority votes of members present in both houses.

Before enactment, a proposed law is known as a **bill** (House bill [HB] or Senate bill [SB]). Each regular session brings forth an avalanche of bills, but fewer than 25 percent became law in 2013. In that year's regular session of the 83rd Legislature, 3,950 bills were introduced in the House and 1,918 in the Senate. Together, both chambers enacted 732 House bills and 705 Senate bills. The governor vetoed 15 House bills and 11 Senate bills.[15]

simple resolution
A resolution that requires action by one legislative chamber only and is not acted on by the governor.

concurrent resolution
A resolution adopted by House and Senate majorities and then approved by the governor (for example, a request for action by Congress or authorization for someone to sue the state).

joint resolution
A resolution that must pass by a majority vote in each house when used to ratify an amendment to the U.S. Constitution. As a proposal for an amendment to the Texas Constitution, a joint resolution requires a two-thirds majority vote in each house.

bill
A proposed law or statute.

For purposes of classification, bills fall into three categories: special, general, and local. A special bill makes an exception to general laws for the benefit of a specific individual, class, or corporation. Of greater importance are general bills, which apply to all people or property in all parts of Texas. To become law, a bill must pass by a simple majority of votes of members present in both the House and the Senate, but a two-thirds majority vote of the membership in each chamber is required to pass an emergency measure that will take effect as soon as the governor signs it. A local bill creates or affects a single unit of local government (for example, a city, county, or special district). Such bills usually pass without opposition if sponsored by all legislators representing the affected area.

Constitutional Amendment Power In addition to exercising their principal powers by passing bills and adopting resolutions, the House and Senate have other important powers. Members of either chamber may introduce a joint resolution to amend the Texas Constitution. A proposal is officially made when the joint resolution is approved by a two-thirds majority vote of the total membership of each house. (The constitutional amendment process is covered in detail in Chapter 2, "Federalism and the Texas Constitution.")

Administrative and Investigative Powers The legislature also defines the responsibilities of state agencies and imposes restrictions on them through appropriation of money for operations and through **oversight** of activities. One form of oversight involves requiring state agencies to make both periodic and special reports to the legislature.

Both the House and the Senate receive information from the state auditor concerning irregular or inefficient use of state funds by administrative agencies. The auditor is appointed by (and serves at the will of) the Legislative Audit Committee. This six-member committee is composed of the Speaker, the chair of the House Appropriations Committee, the chair of the House Ways and Means Committee, the lieutenant governor, the chair of the Senate Finance Committee, and a senator appointed by the lieutenant governor.

Another control over state agencies is the legislature's Sunset Advisory Commission, which makes recommendations to the House and Senate concerning the continuation, merger, division, or abolition of nearly every state agency. Affected agencies are reviewed every 12 years (see Chapter 10, "Public Policy and Administration").

Most of the governor's board and commission appointments to head state agencies must be submitted to the Senate and approved by at least two-thirds of the senators present. Thus, the Senate is in a position to influence the selection of many important officials. The unwritten rule of **senatorial courtesy** requires that the Senate "bust" (reject) an appointment if the appointee is declared "personally objectionable" by the senator representing the district in which the appointee resides. Consequently, a governor will privately seek prior approval by that senator before announcing a selection.

To support its power to exercise oversight of administrative agencies and to investigate problems that may require legislation, the legislature has

oversight
A legislative function that requires reports from state agencies concerning their operations; the state auditor provides information on agencies' use of state funds.

senatorial courtesy
Before making an appointment, the governor is expected to obtain approval from the state senator in whose district the prospective appointee resides; failure to obtain such approval will probably cause the Senate to "bust" the appointee.

the authority to subpoena witnesses, administer oaths, and compel submission of records and documents. Such action may be taken jointly by the two houses as a body, by one house, or by a committee of either house. Refusal to obey a subpoena may result in prosecution for contempt of the legislature, which is a misdemeanor offense punishable by a jail sentence of from 30 days to a year and a fine ranging from $100 to $1,000.

Impeachment and Removal Powers The House of Representatives has the power to **impeach** all elected state judges and justices in Texas. The House may also impeach elected executive officers, such as the governor, and appointed state officials. In 2013, Speaker Joe Straus directed the Select Committee on Transparency in State Agency Operations to investigate University of Texas regent Wallace Hall for possible violations of his duties as a regent. A 2014 report alleged Hall had committed impeachable offenses, including releasing student information and pressuring university officials.[16] Although Hall avoided being the first unelected state official to be impeached, he was publicly reprimanded and censured by the investigatory committee.

Impeachment involves bringing charges by a simple majority vote of House members present. It resembles the indictment process of a grand jury (see Chapter 11, "The Judicial Branch"). Following impeachment, the Senate conducts a proceeding with the Chief Justice of the Texas Supreme Court presiding, after which it renders judgment. Conviction requires a two-thirds majority vote of the Senate membership. The only punishment that the Senate may impose is removal from office and disqualification from holding any other public office under the Texas Constitution. If a crime has been committed, the deposed official may also be prosecuted before an appropriate court.

Immunities In addition to their constitutional powers, state senators and representatives enjoy legislative immunities conferred by the Texas Constitution. They may not be sued for slander or otherwise held accountable for any statements made in a speech or debate during a legislative proceeding. This protection does not extend to remarks made under other circumstances. They may not be arrested while attending a legislative session or while traveling to or from the legislature's meeting place for the purpose of attending, unless charged with "treason, felony, or breach of the peace."

Rules and Procedures

Enacting a law is not the only way to get things done in Austin. Passing bills and adopting resolutions, however, are the principal means whereby members of the Texas legislature participate in making public policy. The legislature conducts its work according to detailed rules of procedure.

To guide legislators in their work, each chamber adopts its own set of rules at the beginning of every regular session. Usually, few changes are made to the rules of the preceding session. Whether a bill is passed or defeated depends heavily on the skills of sponsors and opponents in using House rules and Senate rules. Experienced legislators are more likely to have

impeachment
Process in which the Texas House of Representatives, by a simple majority vote, initiates action (brings charges) leading to possible removal of certain judicial and executive officials (e.g., the governor) by the Senate.

bills approved because of their understanding of the rules and stronger relationships with the leadership.

The lieutenant governor and the Speaker decide questions concerning interpretation of rules in their respective chambers. Because procedural questions may be complex and decisions must be made quickly, each chamber uses a **parliamentarian** to assist its presiding officer. Positioned on the dais immediately to the left of the lieutenant governor or Speaker, this expert on Senate or House rules provides answers to procedural questions.

How a Bill Becomes a Law

The Texas Constitution calls for regular legislative sessions divided into three periods for distinct purposes. The first 30 days are reserved for the introduction of bills and resolutions, action on emergency appropriations, and the confirmation or rejection of recess appointments (appointments made by the governor between sessions). The second 30 days are generally devoted to committee consideration of bills and resolutions. The remainder of the session, which amounts to 80 days, is devoted to floor debate and voting on bills and resolutions. Throughout a session, action may be taken at any time on an emergency matter identified by the governor and incorporated into a bill that is introduced by a legislator. The full process of turning a bill into a law is complex; however, certain basic steps are clearly outlined.

Although most bills can originate in either chamber, the following paragraphs trace the path of a bill from introduction in the House to action by the governor.[17] Figure 8.4 illustrates this procedure.

1. Introduction in the House Any House member may introduce a bill by filing nine copies (or, as required by the Texas Constitution, 11 copies of every bill related to conservation and reclamation districts) with the chief clerk. This staff person supervises legislative administration in the House. Prior to a regular session, members and members-elect (newly elected but not yet having taken the oath of office) may prefile bills as early as the first Monday after the November general election. Members may prefile bills 30 days before the start of a special session. It is common practice for an identical bill, known as a **companion bill**, to be introduced by a senator in the Senate at the same time the bill is introduced in the House. This action allows simultaneous committee action in the two chambers.

2. First Reading (House) and Referral to Committee After receiving a bill, the chief clerk assigns it a number in order of submission, although the first few numbers are reserved for the most important bills, such as the budget. Then the bill is given to the reading clerk for the first reading. The reading clerk reads aloud the caption (a summary of contents) and announces the committee to which the bill has been assigned by the Speaker.

3. House Committee Consideration and Report Before any committee action, the committee staff must distribute a bill analysis that summarizes important provisions of the bill to committee members.[18] The committee

parliamentarian
An expert on rules of order who sits at the left of the presiding officer in the House or Senate and provides advice on procedural questions.

companion bill
Filed in one house but identical or similar to a bill filed in the other chamber; speeds passage of a bill because committee consideration may take place simultaneously in both houses.

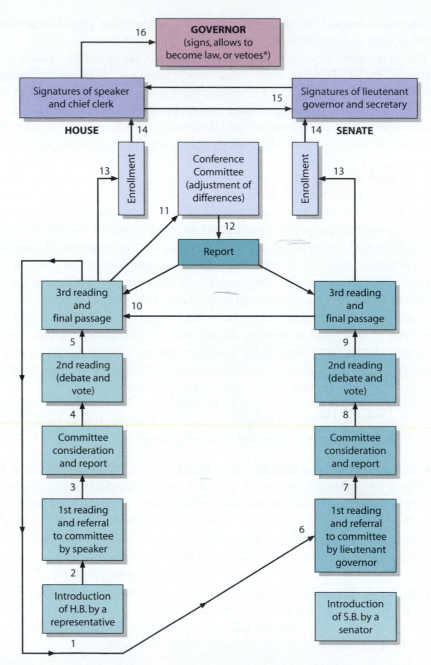

Figure 8.4   Route Followed by a House Bill from Texas Legislature to Governor

*In case of veto while the legislature is still in session, a bill can be passed over the governor's veto by a two-thirds majority of each house.
Source: Prepared with the assistance of Dr. Beryl E. Pettus.

CRITICAL THINKING

Should the process for a bill's becoming a law be simplified or made more complex?

chair decides whether the bill needs a fiscal note (provided by the Legislative Budget Board) projecting the costs of implementing the proposed legislation for five years. The committee chair also decides whether a bill requires the Legislative Budget Board to prepare an impact statement. Among the types of bills requiring an impact statement are those that would change punishment for a felony offense or change the public school finance system.

As a courtesy to sponsoring representatives, most bills receive a committee hearing at which lobbyists and other interested persons have an opportunity to express their views. House rules require public notice of any formal meeting or public hearing. Witnesses may also submit online videos. The committee chair decides whether a bill will go to a subcommittee for a hearing. A subcommittee includes only some members of the full committee. After a hearing, the subcommittee submits a written report to the committee. Recommended changes to proposed bills may be made by amendments, in which event the legislature must vote on each proposed amendment, or by substituting a new bill for the proposed bill.

Two committees determine the order in which bills are cleared for floor action. The Local and Consent Calendars Committee and the Calendars Committee conduct sessions that are open to the public, the press, and all representatives. The Local and Consent Calendars Committee assigns three types of legislative proposals to the Local, Consent, and Resolutions Calendar. The following are examples of these types of bills that were passed in the 83rd regular session in 2013:

- *Local bills* affecting a limited number of localities, districts, counties, or municipalities: HB 3792 by Representative Garnet Coleman (D-Houston), revising the expiration date for authority of Texas Southern University to collect an intercollegiate athletics fee
- *Consent bills* that are uncontested and not likely to face opposition: HB 1272 by Representative Senfronia Thompson (D-Houston), continuing the Human Trafficking Prevention Task Force
- *Noncontroversial resolutions*, other than congratulatory and memorial resolutions: HCR 23 by Representative David Simpson (R-Longview), designating Gregg County as the Balloon Race Capital of Texas

The Calendars Committee places other bills on three daily calendars. The following are examples of these types of bills passed in the 83rd regular session in 2013:

- The *Emergency Calendar*, for bills needing immediate action, as well as all taxing and spending bills: SB 1 by Senator Tommy Williams (R-The Woodlands), the general appropriations bill
- The *Major State Calendar*, for nonemergency bills that change policy in a major field of government activity and that have a major statewide impact: SB 215 by Senator Brian Birdwell (R-Granbury), continuing the Texas Higher Education Coordinating Board and revising the Texas Guaranteed Student Loan Corporation
- The *General State Calendar*, for nonemergency bills having statewide application but limited legal effect and policy impact: HB 29 by Representative Dan Branch (R-Dallas), requiring certain institutions of higher education to offer undergraduates a fixed tuition plan

Within 30 days after receiving a bill, a calendars committee must decide by record vote whether to place the bill on a calendar for floor consideration. After this period expires, any representative may introduce a motion on the House floor to place the bill on an appropriate calendar. If the motion is seconded by five representatives and adopted by a simple majority vote, the House may schedule the bill for floor action without approval of a calendars committee. This procedure is seldom attempted. Because of the authority to decide if a bill will be placed on the calendar, the chair of the Calendars Committee is often identified as the fourth most powerful state government official, only less powerful than the lieutenant governor, the Speaker, and the governor.

4. Second Reading (House) Usually, the second reading is limited to caption only. The author of a bill, the committee member reporting on behalf of the committee, or another designated member has the privilege of beginning and ending floor debate with a speech of not more than 20 minutes. Other speakers are limited to not more than 10 minutes each, unless extra time is granted. A computer on each representative's desk provides easy access to the text of amendments proposed during floor debate. After discussion ends and any amendments are added, a vote is taken on "passage to engrossment" (preparation of an officially inscribed copy). A quorum (the minimum number required to do business) is constituted when at least two-thirds of the House members (100 representatives) are present.

Approval of a bill on second reading requires a simple majority vote. A motion may be made to suspend the rules by a four-fifths majority vote of members present and to give the bill an immediate third reading. Thus, an exception can be made to the constitutional rule that all bills must be read on three separate days, though an exception for the third reading is seldom made in the House.

Provisions of the Texas Constitution, statutes, procedural rules, and practices within the respective chambers govern legislative voting. A record vote usually involves an electronic system. Votes are recorded and tallied as each representative presses the button on a desktop voting machine. This action turns on a light (green, yes; red, no; white, present but not voting) beside the representative's name on the two huge tote boards mounted on the wall behind the House Speaker's podium. House and Senate journals list the record votes of members of the respective chambers. Any House member may call for a record vote. House rules prohibit **ghost voting** (pressing the voting button for another representative) unless a member has given permission for the vote to be cast. When a representative asks for "strict enforcement," the voting machine of an absent member is locked.

Occasionally (especially at the end of a session), representatives engage in lengthy debates on bills they do not oppose (called buffer bills) or on the actual bill they are opposing. Such action is intended to prevent the House from voting on a bill that would probably be approved if brought up for a vote. This delaying action is called **chubbing**. In 2013, House Democrats

ghost voting
A prohibited practice whereby one representative presses the voting button of another House member who is absent.

chubbing
A practice whereby representatives engage in lengthy debate for the purpose of using time and thus preventing a vote on a bill that they oppose.

engaged in chubbing to delay action on a bill that was designed to reduce the number of abortion providers in the state (SB 5). In the last two days of the first special session, Democratic representatives provided procedural challenges to the consideration of a bill on punishment for 17-year-old capital murderers. This tactic, coupled with extensive debate on SB 5 and the proposal of more than 25 amendments, kept the Senate from considering the bill until the final day of the special session. This delay was sufficient to allow for a successful filibuster by State Senator Wendy Davis (D-Ft. Worth) in the Texas Senate. In a second special session, a similar bill passed. Chubbing can be ended if 100 members vote to suspend House rules.

To limit legislative logjams and discourage uninformed voting in the final days of a regular session, House rules contain prohibitions against second and third readings for the following bills:

- Nonlocal House bills during the last 17 days
- Local House bills during the last 10 days
- Senate bills during the last five days

Other detailed restrictions apply to House actions on the 126th to 139th days of a regular session. On the 140th, or final, day, House voting is limited to correcting bills that have passed. The Senate has similar end-of-session restrictions on considering legislation.

5. Third Reading (House) On the third reading, passage of a bill requires a simple majority vote of members present. Amendments may still be added at this stage, but such action requires a two-thirds majority vote. After the addition of an amendment, a copy of the amended bill is made, checked over by the chief clerk, and stamped "Engrossed."

6. First Reading (Senate) After a bill passes on the third reading in the House, the chief clerk adds a statement certifying passage and transmits the bill to the Senate (where the original House number is retained). In the Senate, the secretary of the Senate reads aloud the House bill's caption and announces the committee to which the bill has been assigned by the lieutenant governor. All House bills sent to the Senate must have a Senate sponsor; likewise, all Senate bills sent to the House must have a House sponsor.

7. Senate Committee Consideration and Report Senate procedure differs somewhat from House procedure. A senator may "tag" any bill by filing a request with either the Senate secretary or the committee chair to notify the tagging senator 48 hours before a hearing will be held on the bill. A tag usually kills the bill if done during the last days of a session.

If a majority of the committee members wants a bill to pass, it receives a favorable report. Bills are listed on the Senate's Regular Order of Business in the order in which the secretary of the Senate receives them. Unlike the House, the Senate has no calendar committees to control the flow of bills from standing committees to the Senate floor. At the beginning of each session, however, the Senate Administration Committee "parks" a blocking bill (called a "blocker" or a "rosebush" bill because every rosebush has a thorn)—on which floor action is not intended—at the head of the line. Bills arriving later are designated "out of order," and a vote of two-thirds of senators present and voting is required to suspend the regular order (that is, bypass the blocker bill) and bring the "out-of-order" bill to the Senate floor for debate. In 2013, two blockers were used: SB 234, establishing a county park beautification and improvement program, and SJR 21, allowing the state to receive gifts of historical value. This **two-thirds rule** enhances the power of a party or a bipartisan group that can control more than one-third of the votes (which would be 11 votes if all 31 senators were voting).[19] In recent years some Republican senators led by Senator Dan Patrick (R-Houston) have vigorously opposed the rule, arguing it gives the minority party too much power. Through 2014, the Senate had not abandoned the two-thirds rule, but Patrick's election as lieutenant governor in 2014 made its continuation less certain.

8. Second Reading (Senate) As with second readings in the House, the Senate debates the bill and considers proposed amendments. A computer on the desk of each senator displays the texts of proposed amendments. During the debate, custom permits a senator to speak about a bill as long as physical endurance permits. This delaying tactic is known as **filibustering**. But a filibuster may be stopped if another senator is recognized for the privileged, nondebatable motion to "move the previous question," which means requiring an immediate vote. The motion must be seconded by at least five senators and requires a majority vote of senators present. Another privileged, nondebatable motion that can halt a filibuster is a motion to adjourn or recess. A filibuster is most effective if undertaken toward the end of a session when time is short.

In 2013, for example, Senator Wendy Davis killed an abortion bill (SB 5) during the 83rd Legislature's first special session. Through a series of procedural challenges from both Republicans and Democrats, Republican senators ended the filibuster with less than 15 minutes remaining. An outburst erupted from the crowd observing the Senate from the gallery located above the Senate chamber. The chaos continued so long that a timely vote did not occur. Several prochoice/pro-abortion organizations joined to create a "tweetstorm" of support for Davis's filibuster. Among the 547,000 tweets to #standwithwendy was one from President Barack Obama that was retweeted another 20,000 times. In addition, a livestream of the debate was available online and supporters live-blogged from the Capitol urging followers across the nation to contact local media outlets about the filibuster.[20]

When debate ends, a roll call vote is called by the secretary of the Senate. Unless a senator holds up two fingers to indicate an intention to vote no, the presiding officer usually announces that the chamber unanimously approves the bill after only a few names are called. The vote is recorded only if requested by three senators. A computer-controlled board at the front of the chamber shows how each senator has voted. A vote requires a quorum of 21 senators present. A simple majority of "yea" votes of members present is sufficient to pass a bill.

two-thirds rule
A procedural device to control bringing bills to the Senate floor for debate.

filibustering
A delaying tactic whereby a senator may speak, and thus hold the Senate floor, for as long as physical endurance permits, unless action is taken to end the filibuster.

9. Third Reading (Senate) If passed on the second reading, a bill can have its third reading immediately, assuming the rules have been suspended. This action is routinely taken in the Senate by the required four-fifths majority vote of members present. Amending a bill on the third reading requires a two-thirds majority vote of members present. A simple majority vote is required for passage.

10. Return to the House After passage by the Senate, a House bill returns to the chief clerk of the House, who supervises preparation of a perfect copy of the bill and delivers it to the Speaker. When an amendment has been added in the Senate (as usually happens), the change must be voted on in the House. If the House is not prepared to accept the amended bill, the ordinary procedure is to request a conference. Otherwise, the bill will die unless one of the chambers reverses its position.

11. Conference Committee When the two chambers agree to send the bill to conference, each presiding officer appoints five members to serve on the **conference committee**. Attempts are made to adjust differences and produce a compromise version acceptable to both the House and the Senate. At least three Senate members and three House members must agree before the committee can recommend a course of action in the two houses. The author of the House bill usually serves as the conference committee chair.

12. Conference Committee Report The conference committee's recommended settlement of questions at issue must be fully accepted or rejected by a simple majority vote in each chamber. Most recommendations are accepted. Both chambers, however, may agree to return the report to the committee, or, on request of the House, the Senate may accept a proposal for a new conference.

13. Enrollment After both chambers have accepted a conference report, the chief clerk of the House prepares a perfect copy of the bill and stamps it "Enrolled." The report is then presented to the House.

14. Signatures of the Chief Clerk and Speaker When the House receives the enrolled bill and the conference committee report, the bill is identified by chamber of origin and read by number only. Subsequently, it is signed by the chief clerk, who certifies the vote by which it passed. Then the House Speaker signs the bill.

15. Signatures of the Secretary of the Senate and the Lieutenant Governor Next, the chief clerk of the House takes the bill to the Senate, where it is read by number only. After certifying a passing vote, the secretary of the Senate signs the bill. Then the lieutenant governor does likewise.

16. Action by the Governor While the legislature remains in session, the governor has three options. The governor can sign the bill; allow it to

conference committee
A committee composed of representatives and senators appointed to reach agreement on a disputed bill and recommend changes acceptable to both chambers.

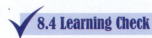

8.4 Learning Check

1. What is the most typical way in which the legislature exercises its legislative power?
2. True or False: Members of the Texas House of Representatives have no way to delay a vote on a bill through debate.

Answers on p. 316.

remain unsigned for 10 days, not including Sundays, after which time it becomes law without the chief executive's signature; or, within the 10-day period, veto the measure by returning it to the House, unsigned, with a message giving a reason for the veto (or to the Senate if a bill originated there). The Texas Constitution requires a vote of "two-thirds of the membership present" in the first chamber that considers a vetoed bill (in this case, the House of Representatives) and a vote of "two-thirds of the members" in the second chamber (in this case, the Senate) to override the governor's veto.[21]

After a session ends, the governor has 20 days, counting Sundays, in which to veto pending legislation and file the rejected bills with the secretary of state. A bill not vetoed by the governor automatically becomes law at the end of the 20-day period. Because the legislature is no longer in session, the governor's postadjournment veto is of special importance because it cannot be overridden. Usually, relatively few bills are vetoed.

Influences Within the Legislative Environment

LO8.5   Explain the influences on legislators' voting decisions.

In theory, elected legislators are influenced primarily, if not exclusively, by their constituents (especially constituents who vote rather than those who make big campaign contributions). In practice, however, many legislators' actions bear little relation to the needs or interests of the "folks back home." Texas senators and representatives are not completely indifferent to voters, but many of them fall short of being genuinely representative.

Large numbers of citizens are uninterested in most governmental affairs and have no opinions about how the legislature should act in making public policy. Others may have opinions but are inarticulate or unable to communicate with their legislators. Therefore, lawmakers are likely to yield not only to the influence of the presiding officers in the House and Senate but also to pressure from the governor. A threatened gubernatorial veto can kill a bill, as occurred with proposed legislation to ban texting while driving during the 83rd legislative session. The chair of the Senate Transportation Committee allowed the bill to die in committee, remarking, "If it is not going to pass in the governor's mansion, why do we need to go through this?"[22] Other powerful political actors include the attorney general and judges who determine the constitutionality of laws; the state comptroller, who estimates state revenue for budgeting purposes; and lobbyists, who seek to win voluntary support or force cooperation for legislation that benefits the special interests they represent.

Events influence the introduction and passage of laws. See the Point/ Counterpoint feature for the effect of "active shooter" incidents on college

Students in Action

An Internship in Texas Government

"Senator [Rodney] Ellis' leadership and determination to help our youth prepared me to become the youngest African-American City Council Member in the history of Georgetown, Texas."

—Shelley P. Davis, former Texas Legislative Intern

If working in government appeals to you, whether as an elected official, political activist, or government employee, you could become a Student in Action through the Texas Legislative Internship Program (TLIP). Established by Senator Rodney Ellis (D-Houston) in 1990, the program is administered by the Office of Government Affairs at Texas Southern University. Internships are available in the spring semester of each academic year. Selected students intern with elected officials, in government offices, and for nonprofit advocacy organizations at the national, state, and local levels. In years in which the legislature is in session, interns who are in Austin have the opportunity to learn the legislative process through their work with more senior members of the legislature or in the offices of the governor and lieutenant governor.

College undergraduates with at least 60 hours of college credit and graduate and law students are eligible to apply for the program. Admission is competitive and requires exceptional writing skills and computer literacy. Through their work in the designated offices, students gain practical experience and assist with research and writing on work-related

projects. Those accepted into the program must negotiate with their colleges to receive between six and 15 college credit hours. Interns receive a $7,000 stipend (as of 2014). Videoed testimonials from student participants are posted on the Texas Senate's TLIP website for each class of interns since 2001. The program also has its own Facebook page. More than 600 students have participated in the program over the past 23 years. Many have remained active in politics, either running for office themselves or working in political campaigns. Three TLIP graduates served in the Texas legislature during the 83rd legislative session: Representatives Ana Hernandez (D-Houston), Armando Walle (D-Houston), and Ron Reynolds (D-Missouri City).

© Andresr/Shutterstock.com

campuses and proposed laws. Additional sources of information and influence include research organizations and the media.

Research Organizations

Policymakers need reliable information. Most Texas legislators depend heavily on information provided by their staffs, by administrative agencies, and by

Point/Counterpoint

THE ISSUE In November 2012, the Texas A&M University student senate approved the "Texas A&M Personal Protection Bill" asking university officials and state legislators to allow concealed handgun license holders (CHLs) to carry handguns into university buildings. In special circumstances, the Texas A&M system allows faculty members or students to carry weapons on campus. Without that permission, and at all other institutions, carrying a concealed handgun on a campus is a third-degree felony. Despite the students' request, the 83rd Legislature did not approve any change to the campus carry law. As of mid-2014, Texas and 20 other states banned licensed individuals from carrying concealed handguns on college campuses. The remaining 29 states allowed at least some licensed permit holders to carry concealed handguns on all or part of a campus.

How Would Authorizing CHLs to Carry Guns on Campuses Increase or Decrease Campus Safety?

Arguments For Banning Concealed Carry on Campus

1. Overall, college campuses are safer from crime than the cities in which they are located.
2. Although homicide is less likely to occur on a campus, suicides are more common. If guns are readily available, one study suggests, the suicide rate increases 32 percent among minors and 6.5 percent among adults.
3. Campus administrators, faculty, police departments, and students oppose allowing those with CHL permits to carry on campus. In one study of 15 midwestern universities, almost 80 percent of surveyed students said they would feel unsafe if faculty and fellow students could carry handguns.
4. Campus law enforcement personnel will be unable to distinguish between the "good guys" and the "bad guys" during an incident and innocent people may be killed.

Arguments Against Banning Concealed Carry on Campus

1. "Active shooter" incidents, in which the gunman shoots into a confined space in an indiscriminant way in an attempt to kill people, have occurred on both rural and urban campuses in recent years. CHL permit holders have a right to defend themselves in these instances.
2. More than 90 percent of suicides occur in the home. CHL permit holders must be over the age of 21 and would likely live off campus. The right to carry handguns on campus would have little to no impact on the suicide rate.
3. Those who oppose the right to carry on campus do not understand that most active shooters are methodical in their movements and shoot at close range. Those with CHL permits must undergo training and would not be shooting wildly but aiming at a stable, nearby target.

Sources: Andrew Roush, "TXEXplainer: Campus-carry Legislation," *Alcalde*, May 7, 2013, http://alcalde .texasexes.org/2013/05/txexplainer-campus-carry-legislation/; Students for Concealed Carry, "Common Arguments," http://concealedcampus.org/common-arguments/.

lobbyists. In addition, legislators obtain information from official research bodies and independent providers of public policy research, sometimes called "think tanks."

The Texas Legislative Council Authorizing special research projects by its staff is one function of the Legislative Council. This council is overseen by the lieutenant governor (joint chair), the Speaker of the House (joint chair), six senators appointed by the lieutenant governor, the chair of the House Administration Committee, and five representatives appointed by the Speaker. The council's employees provide bill drafting, advice for legislators, legislative research and writing, publishing and document distribution, interim study committee research support, demographic and statistical data compilation and analysis, computer mapping and analysis, and other computer services.

The House Research Organization A bipartisan steering committee of 15 representatives—elected by the House membership for staggered four-year terms—governs the House Research Organization (HRO). Although the HRO is an administrative department of the House, it is independent of House leadership. Its annual operating budget is set by the steering committee and the House Administration Committee.

In addition to producing reports on a variety of policy issues and House procedures, the HRO prepares the *Daily Floor Report* for each day the legislature is in session. In this publication, HRO personnel analyze important bills to be considered, providing a summary of bill content and presenting arguments for and against each bill. After a regular session, the HRO staff publishes a report on the session's important bills and resolutions, including some that were defeated.

The Senate Research Center Organized under the secretary of the Senate, the Senate Research Center analyzes bills under consideration by the Senate and conducts research on diverse issues. Primarily, it responds to requests from Senate members for research and information. The lieutenant governor, however, as president of the Senate, also calls on the center's information and expertise. The center's periodic publications range from the semimonthly *Clearinghouse Update*, which presents brief accounts of issues facing Texas and the nation, to *Highlights of the … Legislature*, which summarizes hundreds of bills and joint resolutions for each regular session. Some other publications produced by the center include *The Senate Guide to Ethics and Financial Disclosure* and *Legislative Lexicon*, which defines words, terms, and phrases that form the "legislative lingo" used by legislators and staff.

The Center for Public Policy Priorities Founded in 1985 as an Austin office of the Benedictine Resource Center, the Center for Public Policy Priorities has been operating as an independent nonprofit organization since 1999. Its principal focus is on the problems of low- and moderate-income families in Texas. Legislators and other public officials have used its policy analyses on issues ranging from state taxation and appropriations to public education and health care access. But some critics, like former House Appropriations Committee chair Rob Junell (D-San Angelo), insist that research by staff of "The Center for Too Many P's" is tainted with liberal bias.

The Texas Public Policy Foundation Established in 1989 in San Antonio, the Texas Public Policy Foundation (TPPF) is primarily funded by conservative activists. The foundation focuses its research on issues supporting limited government, free enterprise, private property rights, and individual responsibility. Using policy research and analysis, TPPF seeks to influence Texas government by recommending its findings to legislators and other policymakers, group leaders, media persons, and the general public. An editorial in the liberal *Texas Observer* asserted that "the Texas Public Policy Foundation has become the in-house think tank of the state's current Republican leadership."[23] As evidence of this influence, of the top 25 Twitter accounts accessed by members of the 83rd Legislature, the only research organization on the list was the Texas Public Policy Foundation.[24]

The Media

Without social media, measuring the influence of media on legislators' political decisions was difficult. Identifying the Twitter accounts most frequently accessed by legislators now provides insight into the media sources on which officials rely for information. In 2013, members of the 83rd Legislature most frequently followed the online news site the *Texas Tribune*. Other important media sites included *Quorum Report* (a daily online newsletter that focuses on Texas politics and state government), the *Austin American-Statesman*, *Texas Monthly*, and *Texas Insider* (a site that redistributes press releases and articles from multiple sources).[25] In addition, newsletters and other publications produced for subscribers or members of special interest groups highlight legislators' actions. On some policy issues, lawmakers may be impressed by newspaper editorials and articles, postings by bloggers, and editorial cartoons such as those printed in *Practicing Texas Politics*.[26]

✔ **8.5 Learning Check**

1. True or False: The House Research Organization influences the House through the *Daily Floor Report,* which presents arguments for and against each bill.
2. How do social media provide insight on media sources that are important to legislators?

Answers on p. 317.

Selected Reading

Recent Congressional Redistricting in Texas: Legislation, Litigation, and Jeff Wentworth's Proposal

Charles Jerry Wilkins and Lyle C. Brown

Congressional redistricting in the Lone Star State is a responsibility of the state legislature, but litigation invariably results in districts drawn by federal courts. Such has been the case in the 21st century. Jeff Wentworth, a former Republican legislator from San Antonio, believes that there is a better way.

Legislative and Judicial Actions Since 2001

After redistricting in 2001, Texas Republicans won 88 (59 percent) of the 150 state House seats in 2002 and 19 (61 percent) of the 31 state Senate seats; but GOP candidates won only 15 (47 percent) of the 32 U.S. House seats. Desiring a larger GOP representation in Washington, D.C., then-U.S. House majority leader Tom DeLay (R-Sugar Land) pressured the Texas Legislature to draw new districts in its 78th regular session in 2003. To prevent this action, 51 Democrats broke a House quorum (100 of 150 members) by fleeing to Ardmore, Oklahoma, where they remained until time ran out for action on a redistricting bill.

In the summer of 2003, Governor Rick Perry called three special sessions. During the first session, Senate Democrats invoked a two-thirds rule that prevented consideration of a congressional redistricting bill. Then, when they learned that the president of the Senate would not follow that rule in a second session, 11 of the Senate's 12 Democrats made a quorum-busting flight to Albuquerque, New Mexico, where they remained until Senator John Whitmire caved in and returned to Austin. The redistricting bill that passed in the third special session brought court challenges, but Republicans were elected to 2l (66 percent) of Texas's 32 congressional seats.

As a result of subsequent elections in the first decade of the 21st century, Texas Republicans elected to the U.S. House totaled 19 (59 percent) in 2006, 20 (63 percent) in 2008, and 23 (72 percent) in 2010. Only 2 of the Democrats elected in 2010 were Anglos, while 4 were Latinos and 3 were African Americans. Among Republican representatives, 21 were Anglos, 2 were Latinos, and none was an African American.

Because Texas's population grew from nearly 23 million in 2000 to about 25 million in 2010, the Lone Star State gained four seats (for a total of 36) in the U.S. House of Representatives. Latinos accounted for about 65 percent of the population growth. Consequently, they called for increased representation. For Republicans in control of the Texas Legislature, the problem has been that Latinos tend to vote for Democratic candidates. Therefore, when legislative boundary lines are drawn to favor the election of Republicans, the resulting districts frequently dilute the voting strength of Latinos, an action prohibited by the federal Voting Rights Act.

In 2011, the legislature failed to pass a congressional redistricting bill during its 82nd Regular Session that ended on May 30th. On the following day, however, Governor Perry called a special session; and one item on the agenda was congressional redistricting. SB 4, the congressional redistricting bill, was passed on June 20; but Governor Perry did not sign it until July 18. On the following day, as then required by the federal Voting Rights Act, Texas's Attorney General Greg Abbott "formally" sought preclearance of the Texas congressional district maps (together with district maps for both houses of the Texas Legislature and the State Board of Education) from a three-judge panel of the U.S. District Court in Washington, D.C. Abbott anticipated that this court would be more inclined to grant preclearance than the Voting Rights Division of the Democrat-controlled U.S. Department of Justice. Nevertheless, the attorney general also "informally" submitted the congressional maps to the U.S. Department of Justice.

On September 19, 2011, the U.S. Department of Justice announced that it opposed preclearance for Texas's congressional districts. Two months later, on November 8, 2011, the D.C. court refused to grant summary judgment for preclearance and announced that a full trial would be required. This court did not rule on the preclearance issue until August 28, 2012. One sticking point was the gerrymandering of Representative Lloyd Doggett's District 25. It contained parts of the City of Austin and Travis County, with their large numbers of Democrats.

As Texas's most liberal congressman, Doggett aroused GOP anger by his effort to prevent Texas's receiving $830 million of federal education aid unless Governor Rick Perry guaranteed that the money would be used to increase state spending on education. In 2009, the state had used $3.35 billion of federal aid intended to supplement state spending to replace state funding. After nine months of controversy, the "Doggett Amendment" was repealed by Congress in April 2011, while congressional redistricting was being considered in the Texas Legislature.

In 2003, Republican legislators had sought to destroy Doggett politically by dividing Travis County among three districts. They drew Doggett's district to extend southward from Austin through a largely Latino-populated area, but he was reelected from 2004 through 2010. In 2011, Republicans went further in their effort to purge Doggett. The congressional redistricting bill divided Travis County among five districts. Nevertheless, Doggett sought and won the Democratic Party's nomination to represent the newly drawn District 35 stretching from Austin southward to San Antonio with a heavily Latino population.

Even before the D.C. court began considering the preclearance issue, several groups and individuals filed lawsuits contending that the congressional districts adopted by the Texas Legislature had disadvantaged racial and ethnic groups in violation of Section 5 of the Voting Rights Act. On July 27, 2011, these suits were consolidated for trial by a three-judge panel of the U.S. District Court for the Western District of Texas in San Antonio. The trial was conducted from September 6 through September 17. Deciding that temporary redistricting was needed before the 2012 primaries could be held, the San Antonio court produced interim maps on November 26.

Responding to Republican complaints that these maps favored Latinos and Democrats, Attorney General Abbott petitioned the U.S. Supreme Court to block use of the maps. In a per curia opinion dated January 20, 2012, that court ruled against the interim maps and directed the district court in San Antonio to use the legislature's maps as a "starting point" for creating new maps.

In response to this directive, the San Antonio court instructed parties to the lawsuit to seek agreement on drawing new congressional districts. Nevertheless, Attorney General Abbott insisted that there could be no compromise concerning District 25 because its population had an Anglo majority and thus was not protected against racial gerrymandering. Negotiation, however, did produce an agreement between Abbott and the Texas Latino Redistricting Task Force influenced largely by the Mexican American Legal Defense and Education Fund, Texas LULAC, the Southwest Voter Registration Education Project, and the GI Forum. But the Mexican American Legislative Caucus, the NAACP, the Legislative Black Caucus, and the Texas Democratic Party rejected the agreement. Nevertheless, on February 28, 2012, the San Antonio court produced maps providing opportunities for minority representation in two of the four new congressional districts: District 33 in the Dallas–Fort Worth area and District 35 in the Austin–San Antonio area. The court set May 29th for the 2012 primaries that should have been conducted on March 6.

On August 28, 2012 (three months after the May primaries), the U.S. District Court for the District of Columbia denied preclearance for all Texas legislative and congressional maps authorized by the Texas Legislature in 2011. Although maps ordered by the U.S. District Court in San Antonio were based on the legislature's maps, on September 19, the U.S. Supreme Court refused to prevent use of the San Antonio court's maps for the general election in November 2012. In that election 24 Republicans (23 Anglos and one Latino) and 12 Democrats (Lloyd Doggett and one other Anglo, 5 Latinos, and 5 African Americans) were elected to the U.S. Congress. That no additional seats were won by Latinos was a disappointment for Latino Democrats.

After the Texas legislature failed to create new congressional districts in its 83rd regular session in 2013, this task was given to a special session called by Governor Perry. The result was passage of Senate Bill 4, which adopted the federal court–drawn map that had been used for the 2012 election. The bill was sent to Governor Perry on June 24, 2013. He signed it on June 26, only one day after the U.S. Supreme Court decided in *Shelby County v. Holder* that the formula in Section 4 of the Voting Rights Act was unconstitutional and could not be used to force jurisdictions such as Texas to seek preclearance. Nevertheless, in *Perez v. Perry*, Texas minority groups and the U.S. Department of Justice challenged Texas's Congressional redistricting plan as violating Section 2 of the Voting Rights Act by discriminating against minority voters and asked the court to subject Texas to preclearance requirements of Section 3 of the Voting Rights Act. Trial was set for July 14, 2014.

Senator Wentworth's Proposal

Frustrated by a redistricting system featuring time-consuming legislative battles, political gerrymandering, and court actions, former Senator Jeff Wentworth proposed redistricting reform in several legislative sessions beginning in 1993. In that year he responded to Democratic gerrymandering in the preceding regular session. His proposals were approved in the Senate in regular sessions in 2005, 2007, and 2011, but did not pass in the House. Wentworth's last effort was passed by the Senate but not the House in the special session of the 82nd legislature that approved the 2011 congressional redistricting bill.

Wentworth's proposal called for a congressional redistricting commission composed of nine members selected for two-year terms as follows:

- 2 members appointed by a majority vote of representatives belonging to the political party with the most members of the House
- 2 members appointed by a majority vote of representatives belonging to the political party with the second-highest number of members of the House
- 2 members appointed by a majority vote of senators belonging to the political party with the most members of the Senate
- 2 members appointed by a majority vote of senators belonging to the political party with the second-highest number of members of the Senate
- 1 nonvoting member to serve as presiding officer, appointed by the affirmative vote of at least 5 of the other members

Each member must be a resident of Texas, and at least one member appointed by the Senate and one member appointed by the House must reside in a county not designated as a metropolitan statistical area. Disqualified from serving on the commission are elected officials; political party officers, other than precinct committee members; registered lobbyists; or persons who have served in any of these capacities within the previous two years. A commission member cannot be a candidate for public office or actively participate in or contribute to the campaign of any candidate for state or federal office. A redistricting plan could be adopted by a vote of at least five commission members.

While many Texans are not enthusiastic about establishing a congressional redistricting commission, redistricting failures and resulting delay of party primaries have caused several of Texas's newspaper editors to conclude that Wentworth's proposal or a similar plan, such as the one used in California, for changing the state's redistricting process is overdue. Wentworth did not serve in the 83rd legislature and no action was taken on the issue during either the regular or called sessions.

What's to Be Done in Texas?

In the aftermath of the census of 2010, the Republican majority in the Texas Legislature (with the blessing of the Republican governor) re-drew Congressional district boundaries to their own advantage. In California, however, a new Citizens Redistricting Commission, formed after voters approved a citizen-proposed initiative, re-drew legislative boundaries in a formally nonpartisan way. District boundaries were not specifically designed to benefit either a particular political party or incumbent. Both the Texas redistricting plan and the California plan were challenged in the courts. All legal challenges to the California plan were dismissed, but as of 2014 Texas redistricting was still in legal limbo. Although the California process has been criticized, it appears to be supported by a strong majority of California voters and very well may stand the test of time.

In response to the partisan and legal bickering in Texas, there have been suggestions that perhaps the state would do well to follow California's example and turn redistricting over to a commission as Wentworth proposed. Even if there is a popular groundswell of support for this approach, however, it will have to be funneled through the Texas legislature, since the Lone Star State, unlike California, does not have a direct initiative process available to its voters.

✔ Selected Reading Learning Check

1. True or False: Republican lawmakers drew boundary lines in a way that favored the reelection of Representative Lloyd Doggett to the U.S. House of Representatives.
2. How many members would be appointed to the congressional redistricting commission proposed by Senator Jeff Wentworth?

Answers on p. 317.

....

Source: Charles Jerry Wilkins is adjunct professor of public affairs at San Diego State University. Lyle C. Brown is professor emeritus of political science at Baylor University. This article is based on a 2012 paper presented by Wilkins and Brown at a meeting of the Southwestern Political Science Association (SWPSA) and a 2014 paper, co-authored by Brown and Wilkins, which Wilkins presented at a SWPSA meeting. The article is reprinted by permission of the authors.

Conclusion

The framework of the Texas legislature reflects public demand for representative government. Legislators are chosen in popular, partisan elections. Much of the work of both the House and the Senate is done in committees, but floor debate and votes on bills and resolutions attract more public attention. Through their control of state taxing and spending, legislators have an immediate impact on the state's economy and the well-being of all Texans.

Chapter Summary

LO 8.1   Describe the structure of the Texas legislature. The Texas legislature is a bicameral legislature composed of 31 senators elected for four-year terms and 150 representatives elected for two-year terms. Biennial regular sessions are limited to 140 days, and special sessions called by the governor are limited to 30 days. New legislative districts are drawn after each federal decennial census.

LO 8.2   Describe the membership of the Texas legislature, including legislators' formal and informal qualifications and compensation. Legislators must be U.S. citizens, qualified Texas voters, and residents of their districts for one year. Minimum Texas residence is one year for representatives and two years for senators. Minimum age is 21 for representatives and 26 for senators. Legislators tend to be white, male, middle-aged Republicans. They are paid $7,200 per year in salary, but they also receive per diem payments when the legislature is in session and generous retirement benefits after several years of service.

LO 8.3   Compare the organization of the Texas House of Representatives and the Texas Senate. The lieutenant governor presides over the Senate, and the Speaker presides over the House. Both appoint committee members and name committee chairs and vice chairs for their respective chambers. Senators and representatives form legislative caucuses, which are groups with common interests. There are party caucuses for Democrats and Republicans, racial/ethnic caucuses for African Americans and Mexican Americans, ideological caucuses for conservatives and liberals, and some bipartisan caucuses organized around specific public policy issues.

LO 8.4   Outline the responsibilities of the Texas legislature. Legislators have primary responsibility for adopting public policy. Additionally they have the ability to check the power of the executive and judicial branches through the use of their investigative and impeachment powers. Constitutional provisions and rules of the House and Senate control the detailed process whereby a bill is passed in both chambers. The governor may sign a bill, allow it to become law without signing, or veto it. A veto kills a bill, unless the veto is overridden by a two-thirds vote in each chamber.

LO 8.5   Explain the influences on legislators' voting decisions. In theory, voters have the most influence over legislators because voters elect them to office. In practice, legislators are influenced by a number of third parties. Among the individuals and entities that influence legislators' policy decisions are the governor and other state officials, lobbyists, research organizations, and the media.

Key Terms

bicameral, p. 275
unicameral, p. 275
regular session, p. 275
special session, p. 276
redistricting, p. 277
gerrymandering, p. 277
single-member district, p. 277
multimember district, p. 277
president of the Senate, p. 289
Speaker of the House, p. 289

substantive committee, p. 291
procedural committee, p. 292
select committee, p. 293
interim committee, p. 293
standing committee, p. 293
legislative caucus, p. 293
simple resolution, p. 296
concurrent resolution, p. 296
joint resolution, p. 296
bill, p. 296

oversight, p. 297
senatorial courtesy, p. 297
impeachment, p. 298
parliamentarian, p. 299
companion bill, p. 299
ghost voting, p. 302
chubbing, p. 302
two-thirds rule, p. 304
filibustering, p. 304
conference committee, p. 305

Learning Check Answers

8.1 1. A governor has more authority in a special session because he sets the legislative agenda and the time for meeting.
2. False. Gerrymandered districts are legal so long as they do not dilute minority voting strength.

8.2 1. False. Although many legislators are practicing Christians, no religious requirements for elected office are included in state law.
2. The legislator's per diem allowance will be higher, at $150 per day during the 83rd legislative session. Legislators receive only $600 per month (or $7,200 per year) in salary.

8.3 1. False. The Speaker of the House of Representatives can vote on bills or resolutions, although he often chooses not to do so.
2. The president of the Senate, who is the lieutenant governor, determines the Senate committee to which a bill will be sent after introduction.

8.4 1. The legislature most frequently exercises its legislative power by passing bills and resolutions.
2. False. Members of the Texas House of Representatives can use chubbing to delay a vote on a bill.

8.5
1. True. The House Research Organization influences the House through the *Daily Floor Report* that provides arguments for and against each bill.
2. Social media sites such as Twitter allow researchers to measure the number of times a legislator accesses a media outlet's account.

Selected Reading Learning Check

1. False. The Republican majority in the Texas House and Senate drew the boundaries of District 25 in a way that attempted to defeat Representative Doggett. In fact, he now represents District 35, extending from Austin to San Antonio.
2. Nine. Eight voting members appointed by the parties with the most representatives in the House and Senate and the parties with the second-most representatives in the House and Senate and a nonvoting presiding officer appointed by the commission's members.

The Executive Branch

9

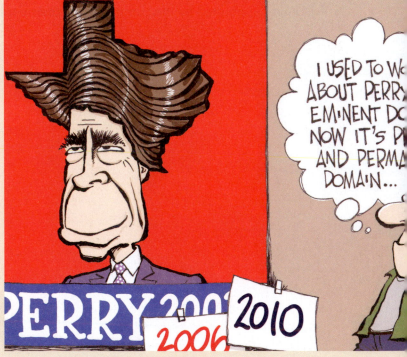

©John Branch/San Antonio Express-News

CRITICAL THINKING

Should the Texas governor be subject to term limits?

On July 14, 2013, Texas Attorney General Greg Abbott announced that he would seek the GOP nomination for governor. He made the announcement on the 29th anniversary of the day that a falling oak tree changed his life forever, breaking his back, damaging his kidneys, and confining him permanently to a wheelchair. Abbott credits the accident with giving him a "spine of steel" and a focus not on the challenges life brings but on his response to challenges. When he overcame Democratic Texas Senator Wendy Davis's challenge in the 2014 gubernatorial election, Abbott's victory marked the end of an era in the Lone Star State. For most young Texans, Rick Perry was the only governor they had ever known, having served a record 14 years in the governor's office.

Because of his long tenure, his run for the Republican Party's nomination for president in 2012, and his activities indicating continued presidential ambition for 2016, Perry is a nationally known figure, often appearing in national and international media. Given the level of attention and media coverage the office receives, you might be surprised to learn that, unlike the president of the United States and the governors of most other states, the position of Texas governor is a relatively weak one with regard to formal powers.

Several of Texas's political traditions and institutions stem from the state's experiences after the Civil War (1861–1865). Even today, the state's executive structure shows the influence of anti-Reconstruction reactions against Governor E. J. Davis's administration (1870–1874). When Davis made aggressive use of state government power in an effort to enfranchise and protect freed slaves, a large majority of Anglo Texans complained that numerous abuses of power occurred, committed by state officials reporting directly to Governor Davis.[1] This piece of Texas history helps explain why, after more than 140 years, many Texans still distrust the "strong" executive model of state government. The U.S. president (with Senate approval) appoints and can independently remove members of a cabinet. In Texas, however, Article IV of the Texas Constitution establishes a multi-headed executive branch, or plural executive, over which the governor has only limited formal powers (see Figure 9.1).

As you learn about the workings of the executive branch of Texas government, consider an observation by Dr. Brian McCall, a former member of the Texas House of Representatives and subsequently chancellor of the Texas State University System. In his book *The Power of the Texas Governor: Connally to Bush*, McCall states: "It is widely reported that the governorship of Texas is by design a weak office. However, the strength of an individual governor's personality can overcome many of the limitations imposed on the office."[2] As you read this chapter, answer the following questions: Is the current head of Texas's executive branch a strong governor? How much power should other elected officials in this branch have?

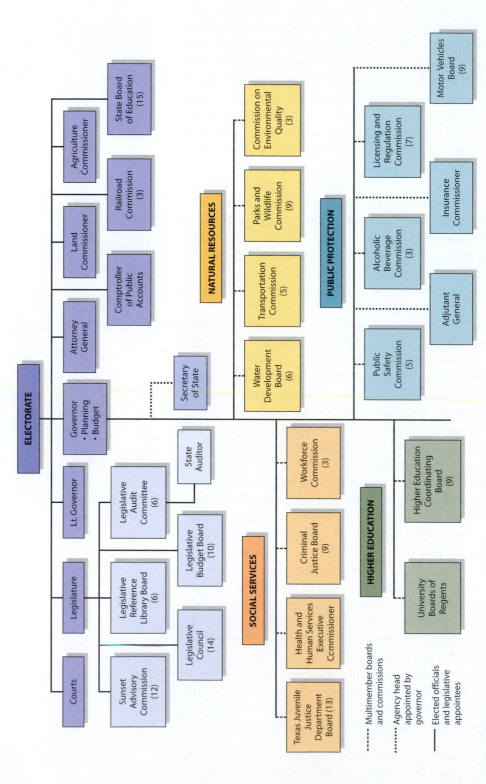

Figure 9.1 The Structure of Texas Government: Important Agencies and Offices (with number of governing body members).

CRITICAL THINKING

What are the advantages and disadvantages of having a plural executive?

Gubernatorial Elections

LO9.1   Analyze gubernatorial elections and the impact of campaign funds on the politics of the governorship.

Bills passed by the Texas legislature and selection of every appointed leader of state agencies, boards, and commissions from 2001 to January 2015 gave Governor Perry more power than earlier governors had held,[3] but Texas still does not have a governor who merits the title "chief executive." Nevertheless, limited executive power does not discourage ambitious gubernatorial candidates who wage multimillion-dollar campaigns in their efforts to win this prestigious office.[4]

Successful gubernatorial candidates must meet constitutional prerequisites, including minimum age (30 years), U.S. citizenship, and Texas residency (for five years immediately preceding the gubernatorial election). According to Section 4 of the Texas Constitution's Bill of Rights, the governor and all other officeholders must also acknowledge the existence of a Supreme Being. There are also numerous extralegal restraints facing those who would become governor. Historically, governors elected after the Reconstruction Era were Democrats with a conservative-moderate political ideology. This mold for successful gubernatorial candidates seemed unbreakable, but William P. ("Bill") Clements Jr. (in 1978 and 1986) and George W. Bush (in 1994 and 1998) broke tradition by becoming Texas's first and second Republican governors, respectively, since E. J. Davis. (See the inside back cover of this text for a listing of Texas governors since 1874.) As conservative businesspeople, Clements and Bush resembled most of their Democratic predecessors in the governor's office; however, their Republicanism, and the fact that they had not previously held elective public office, represented a dramatic departure from the past.[5]

Republican Rick Perry entered the governor's mansion at the end of 2000 without having won a gubernatorial election. He had served as a state legislator, agriculture commissioner, and for two years as lieutenant governor before Governor Bush was elected president of the United States. Although most states place term limits on governors, Texas does not. Therefore, in addition to serving the remainder of Governor Bush's term, Perry was elected three times after that (2002, 2006, and 2010), making him the longest serving governor in Texas history.[6] He served so many years that even some members of his own party are proposing to amend the Texas Constitution to limit the number of terms statewide officeholders may serve.[7] Greg Abbott continued the new tradition of Republican dominance in statewide races when he defeated Wendy Davis in the gubernatorial election of 2014. Abbott combined a career in the private sector as a lawyer with a career in public service, having served on the Texas Supreme Court and as attorney general before becoming governor.

Gubernatorial Politics: Money Matters

Regardless of a candidate's background and qualifications, to be a serious contender for the governor's office, he or she must raise significant money to fund a campaign. Campaign funds allow candidates to buy advertising

Point/Counterpoint

THE ISSUE Rick Perry became governor of Texas for two years after Governor George W. Bush won the presidential election of 2000. Subsequently, Perry was elected to three four-year terms, making his total tenure as governor a record-breaking 14 years. Thirty-six states impose term limits on governors, but Texas and 13 other states do not have such restrictions. In 2013, the Texas legislature considered term limits. The Senate approved the measure, but the House did not.

Should the Texas Constitution Be Amended to Limit Terms Served by the State's Governor?

Arguments For Term Limits

1. Limited terms produce new officeholders with fresh ideas.
2. Election for a limited time causes an officeholder to place the interests of the public above that of a political party or special interests.
3. Shorter tenure results in less corruption and fewer scandals.
4. Each term increases the age of an officeholder and the probability of death while in office; thus the need for a special replacement election.

Arguments Against Term Limits

1. Voters will not reelect someone who is incompetent or corrupt.
2. Representative democracies are based on the principle of popular election, which should not be restricted by reelection control.
3. Longer service provides more experience, which enhances governing skill.
4. A governor constrained by term limits will be disadvantaged when dealing with unelected lobbyists and bureaucrats, and with elected legislators and judges not subject to term limits.

Based on Einer Elhauge, "Are Term Limits Undemocratic?" *University of Chicago Law Review*, 64 (Winter, 1997), 83–201.

time, hire consultants, travel the state, and stage rallies. In politics, money talks (even shouts, screeches, and screams), but it is not always the deciding factor. In 2002, South Texas Democrat Tony Sanchez spent in excess of $67 million of campaign money and received more than 1.8 million votes in an unsuccessful bid for the governorship. Perry raised less than half the amount that Sanchez spent but was returned to office with 2.6 million votes. In 2006 and 2010, Governor Perry outspent and defeated his opponents in primary and general elections, and worked to repay his supporters when elected.

The practice of buying influence with campaign contributions permeates American politics. After pumping millions of dollars into a winning gubernatorial election campaign, donors of large amounts of money are often appointed to key policymaking positions. Texas politics is no exception. A 2010 study by Texans for Public Justice found that 20 percent of the $83 million that Perry raised from January 2001 to February 2010 came from people who then received appointments from him. The top 10 average donations per appointee ranged from $48,342 for the Higher Education Incentives Task Force to $118,488 for the Parks and Wildlife Commission. The average donations from regents appointed to the top four university systems were

Texas A&M, \$113,127; University of Texas, \$83,462; Texas Tech, \$64,343; and University of Houston, \$48,714.[8] Perry rankled his Republican allies in 2013 by appointing Democratic Houston trial attorney and Aggie alumnus Anthony Buzbee to the Texas A&M University System Board of Regents. Though ideologically opposed, Buzbee gave \$250,000 to support Perry's 2012 presidential bid and more than \$73,000 to his state political account. Buzbee explained, "It's not a Democrat or Republican thing. It's an A&M thing."[9] In 2014, Buzbee led Perry's legal team after the governor was indicted.

Candidates also use their fundraising efforts to symbolize the support they hold among the people of Texas, and thus work hard to publicize large totals at filing deadlines. After the January 2014 filing deadline, Greg Abbott's campaign proudly announced \$27 million in donations (sometimes referred to as a "campaign war chest"). This sum was almost twice the amount his Democratic opponent, Wendy Davis, reported. Yet Davis's campaign issued a triumphant statement and tweeted that she had raised more money than he since the last filing deadline, and that this must "scare the tar out of" Abbott. The Abbott campaign countered that 20 percent of her total was not given directly to her campaign but to a group supportive of her efforts, and immediately took to social media to discredit her claims. One ally tweeted, "How gullible some folks are. Can't wait for the facts to embarrass those who take the hook, line and sinker! #FuzzyMath."[10]

Greg Abbott and Wendy Davis on the gubernatorial campaign trail.

AP Images/Tony Gutierrez

CRITICAL THINKING

Should there be legal limits on the size of campaign contributions?

Gubernatorial Politics: Budgetary Influence

In addition to campaign donations, money can also serve as a tool to gain legislators' support for a governor's agenda. Lacking sufficient constitutional powers, a Texas governor must rely heavily on skills in personal relations, competent staff assistance from communications professionals, and talent for both gentle persuasion and forceful arm-twisting. Although arm-twisting is usually done without publicity, this secrecy is not always the case. For example, Governor Perry applied substantial political pressure on legislators from El Paso and South Texas to support his plan to limit medical malpractice claims against physicians and other health care professionals. Early in January 2003, he made public statements about funding a new medical school in El Paso and expanding the Regional Academic Health Center in the Rio Grande Valley. According to a newspaper report, the governor warned that such spending would depend on legislators in those areas supporting his plan to change the state's medical malpractice and liability laws.[11]

Yet arm-twisting has its legal limits. In April 2014, after complaints were filed by Texans for Public Justice, Special District Judge Bert Richardson impaneled a grand jury in Travis County (Austin) to determine whether Perry abused his power in following through on a threat to veto $7.5 million in state funding for public corruption prosecutors. Under state law, the Travis County district attorney's office oversees the state's Public Integrity Unit, which is responsible for investigating and prosecuting state officials for alleged wrongdoing. In April 2013, Travis County District Attorney Rosemary Lehmberg was convicted of drunk driving and filmed berating jail officers while in jail. Perry called for her resignation and threatened to veto funding of the Public Integrity Unit if she refused. When she did not resign, he vetoed the appropriation. Subsequently, Travis County commissioners agreed to provide $1.7 million in funding. However, the Public Integrity Unit struggled to fulfill its mission with the loss of more than half its staff through resignations, retirements, and layoffs.[12]

In August 2014, Perry became only the second Texas governor to be indicted. (The other was James E. "Pa" Ferguson in 1917.) The indictment charged Perry with "abuse of official capacity," a first-degree felony punishable by up to 99 years in prison. It also charged him with "coercion of a public servant," a third-degree felony that can result in up to 10 years in prison.[13] The governor and his supporters sought to spin the indictment in his favor, denying wrong doing and suggesting that the charges were the result of a partisan attack by Democrats.[14] A tweet from Perry's personal account mocked Lehmberg and suggested that she was the one who indicted the governor, despite the fact that she had no hand in the indictment and the special prosecutor was appointed by a Republican judge.[15]

✓ 9.1 Learning Check

1. What are the constitutional requirements for gubernatorial candidates?
2. True or False: Governors often reward campaign donors with appointments to government positions.

Answers on p. 356.

Overview of the Governorship

LO9.2 Summarize how the constitution and laws of Texas provide resources, as well as succession and removal procedures, for the governor.

The constitution and laws of Texas endow the governor with certain benefits and resources. They also provide procedures for removing a governor from office and providing a successor if the governor does not finish an elected term.

Compensation and Benefits

The biennial state budget for fiscal years 2014–2015 set the governor's salary at $150,000 per year, which is the same as salaries for the state's attorney general and comptroller of public accounts. In 2011, Governor Perry stirred controversy when his federal campaign filings forced him to disclose that in addition to his salary of $150,000 per year, he also received retirement benefits from the state worth more than $92,000 per year. In a complex process that did not have to be disclosed under state law, Perry was able to retire as a state employee while continuing to receive pay as an elected official.[16]

State money pays the governor's expenses for official trips but not travel expenses for political campaigning or other nonofficial activities. Nevertheless, the Department of Public Safety provides personnel to protect the governor at all times at state expense. Travel expenses and overtime for Perry's security detail during the 160 days he campaigned for the Republican Party's 2012 presidential nomination cost the state more than $3.6 million.[17] This information caused some Texans to insist that such expenses be covered by campaign funds.[18] The Texas Supreme Court ruled that separating expenses between the governor's campaign and official functions would require the Department of Public Safety to provide a detailed breakdown of how money for the governor's security is spent. To do so, according to the court, compromises a governor's safety and is therefore confidential.[19] Other fringe benefits of the governor's office include staff and maintenance for a personal residence. Whether taxpayers are responsible for a governor's legal expenses resulting from a criminal investigation is unresolved. Although taxpayers paid more than $132,000 for Governor Perry's legal representation prior to indictment, post-indictment he used his campaign funds. Political supporters may also cover the costs of luncheons, dinners, receptions, and other social activities at the governor's residence and elsewhere.[20]

The Texas Constitution forbids the governor and other executive officers (except the lieutenant governor) from holding any other civil or corporate office, and the governor may receive neither compensation nor the promise of pay for other employment after taking office. Nevertheless, governors do own property and make investments while serving. To avoid the appearance of conflict between their personal economic interests and the public's interest, both Governors Bush and Perry placed their assets in blind trusts (a legal arrangement whereby holdings are administered by others and the elected official does not know which assets are in the trust). This action did not prevent Perry from being accused of benefiting from improper real estate deals while in office.[21] In March 2011, he was fined $1,500 by the Texas Ethics Commission for not reporting rental properties and for failing to file information regarding amounts owed on that property.[22]

governor's office
The administrative organization through which the governor of Texas makes appointments, prepares a biennial budget recommendation, administers federal and state grants for crime prevention and law enforcement, and confers full and conditional pardons on recommendation of the Board of Pardons and Paroles.

As public opinion in Texas shifted toward support for decriminalization of marijuana toward the end of his governorship, Perry began making statements indicating openness to such a policy that may provide political cover for other Texas politicians to follow suit. Perry noted in speeches and interviews that he had worked with other Texas policymakers to lower penalties, promote drug courts, and enact sentencing reforms that deemphasized incarceration for low-level, nonviolent offenders. During a speech in Switzerland, Perry remarked, "What I can do as the governor of the second largest state in the nation is to implement policies that start us toward a decriminalization and keeps people from going to prison and destroying their lives, and that's what we've done over the last decade."[31]

Many of the governor's speeches and public appearances reflect his role as chief of state.[32] Of course, a governor cannot accept all invitations to deliver speeches or participate in dedications, banquets, and other public events. Within the limits of time and priorities, however, every governor does attempt to play the role of chief of state. The breadth and depth of this role cannot be fully measured, but its significance should not be underestimated in determining a governor's success. Effective governors must be able to make impressive speeches, to remain at ease while communicating in interviews with newspaper and television reporters, and to communicate directly with Texans by writing (usually with staff assistance) newspaper articles of their own.[33] Debates and interviews present risks that candidates with comfortable leads may choose to avoid when campaigning. Furthermore, research on Governor Perry's 2006 campaign confirmed that he received more positive press from all media and a more lasting benefit with voters when he made personal appearances in an area than when he relied solely on advertising or newspaper endorsements.[34] In the midst of his GOP primary campaign in 2010, Perry opted not to debate opposing candidates[35] and refused to meet with editorial boards in Texas to answer questions concerning his policies and the campaign. (An editorial board usually is composed of the editorial page editor and editorial writers for a newspaper.)[36] Likewise, Greg Abbott refused repeated calls by Republican challenger Tom Pauken for a public debate during his primary run for the GOP's gubernatorial nomination in 2014.[37]

 In his 2010 campaign, Rick Perry recognized and made full use of the potential of social media as a campaign tool, and he continued to use it after the election to enhance his informal powers. He established direct links to his social media accounts through the official web page of the Office of the Governor, on which he also provided links to sign up for email updates, an RSS feed, and podcasts of his speeches. By the end of his time as governor, and with an eye on a potential run for the presidency in 2016, Perry's Facebook, Google+, and Twitter pages were being updated several times a week. The posts highlighted his legislative victories; provided links to videos of his interviews and flattering news stories; and included pictures from his travels, holiday greetings to supporters, and more. He also regularly posted to Flickr, YouTube, Instagram, and LinkedIn. By the end of his term, he had more than 1,116,000 likes on his Facebook page, 253,000 followers on his personal Twitter account, 33,400 followers on his staff account, and more than 22,600 followers on

Google+. Direct communication with the public without the filter of the media allowed Perry to rally support for his causes and campaigns quickly and effectively. Even without the national celebrity status Perry gained through his 2012 presidential campaign, Greg Abbott began his term with more than a third as many likes on his Facebook page (389,000), though with only 37,800 followers on Twitter and 290 followers on Google+. Like Perry, Governor Abbott uses his social media accounts to enhance his informal powers by engaging the public directly and managing his image in the media.[38]

Public involvement of family members may be a source of support for a governor. Laura Bush, for example, enhanced her husband's image as a governor committed to improving education. A former librarian, her First Lady's Family Literacy Initiative Program for Texas and Texas Book Festival promoted literacy and reading. Anita Perry, with bachelor's and master's degrees in nursing and 17 years of experience in various fields of nursing, often spoke on topics such as Alzheimer's disease, breast cancer awareness, and prevention of family violence. In addition, she worked with her husband to host the annual Texas Conference for Women, which addresses issues such as women's health care, personal growth, and professional development. She made history by working as a consultant for the Texas Association Against Sexual Assault. No wife of any earlier governor was employed while her husband was in office.[39] In 2011, Anita Perry encouraged her husband to seek the presidency and played an important role in his effort to obtain the GOP nomination.[40] Perry then published a book, *Fed Up! Our Rights, Our Constitution, Our Fight to Save America from Washington*, and spent more than $20 million in an unsuccessful campaign for the Republican Party's nomination as its presidential candidate in 2012.[41]

In the 2014 gubernatorial race, Greg Abbott often introduced his wife Cecelia by noting that she was poised to become "the first Latina first lady in the history of the great state of Texas," and talking about how marrying the granddaughter of Mexican immigrants gave him an appreciation of Mexican culture. After a campaign stop at a Mexican restaurant in Lubbock, a local Democrat accused him of "piñata politics" and using Hispanics as a "prop." Republicans rushed to paint the statement as an offensive swipe at Abbott's wife. Posting a link to a news story about the incident to Twitter, Abbott tweeted, "Ha! Democrats frustrated about my #Latina wife & growing connection (between) Hispanics & Republicans."[42] Cecilia Abbott, a former teacher, left her job as managing director of community relations for a health care provider focusing on senior citizens to play a larger role in her husband's campaign.[43]

> ## ✔ 9.3 Learning Check
>
> 1. True or False: The governor's informal powers are not based on law.
> 2. True or False: Public involvement of family members may be a source of support for the governor.
>
> Answers on p. 356.

Executive Powers of the Governor

LO9.4 Explain the effect of checks and balances on the executive powers of the governor.

The governor of Texas is inaugurated on the third Tuesday in January of every fourth year, always in the odd-numbered year before a presidential election (for example, January 20, 2015). In the inauguration ceremony, the governor swears "to cause the laws to be faithfully executed."

The governor's executive powers include nominating individuals to fill appointive offices (subject to approval of the Senate) and exercising limited control over state administration as authorized by the Texas Constitution and by statutes enacted by the Texas legislature. These powers are used to do the following:

- Nominate (and in some cases remove) state officials
- Deal with problems caused by civil disorder and natural disasters
- Participate in state budget making and budget management
- Announce policies by issuing executive orders
- Make public proclamations for ceremonial and other purposes
- Promote the economic development of Texas

In some respects, the governor exercises executive powers like those wielded by heads of other large organizations (for example, university presidents, business chief executive officers, union leaders, or the U.S. president), though with obvious differences. Of course, the executive powers of the governor of Texas resemble those of the country's other 49 state governors; however, different state laws and state constitutions give some governors more executive powers and other governors less.

Appointive Power

One of the most significant executive powers of the Texas governor is **appointive power**. The same laws that create administrative agencies allow a governor to nominate friends and political supporters. The governor's ability to nominate citizens for these positions, subject to approval by the Texas Senate, remains both an important political tool and a fundamental management power.

Department heads appointed by the governor include the secretary of state; the adjutant general, who heads the Texas Military Forces; the executive director of the Office of State-Federal Relations; the executive commissioner of health and human services; commissioners of education, insurance, and firefighters' pensions; and the chief administrative law judge of the State Office of Administrative Hearings (SOAH). The governor has the power, "notwithstanding other law," to designate and change the chairs of most state boards and commissions, either by designating a current member or appointing a new member to serve as chair. Not affected by this law are the presiding officers of governing bodies of higher education institutions and systems, along with those who advise or report to statewide elected officials other than the governor. Because he served for so long, Governor Perry managed to appoint allies and supporters to every appointed position available, making him more powerful than perhaps any governor in Texas history. As a result, Governor Abbott entered office with significantly less influence in the executive branch than his predecessor.[44]

Gubernatorial appointive power is not without certain legal and political limitations. The Texas Constitution requires that all appointees (except personal

appointive power
The authority to name a person to a government office. Most gubernatorial appointments require Senate approval by two-thirds of the members present.

staff) be confirmed by the Senate with a two-thirds vote of senators present. This practice is known as "advice and consent," and it applies to the appointees of U.S. presidents and governors in most other states as well. To avoid rejection by the Senate, the governor respects the tradition of senatorial courtesy by obtaining approval of the state senator representing a prospective appointee's senatorial district before sending that person's name forward for Senate confirmation. Political prudence also demands that the appointments director in the governor's office conduct a background check on the appointee to avoid possible embarrassment—as occurred when, for example, Governor Dolph Briscoe appointed a dead man to a state board.

Texas governors may try to circumvent the Senate by making appointments while the Senate is not in session. The Texas Constitution, however, requires that these **recess appointments** be submitted to the Senate for confirmation within 10 days after it convenes for a regular or special session, though confirmation hearings do not have to occur immediately. Failure of the Senate to confirm a recess appointment prevents the governor from reappointing that person to the same position.

Senate approval is not required for appointment of the nonvoting student member on the board of regents for each of the state's university systems, such as the Texas A&M University System, which consists of 10 universities and a health science center. In 2011, however, such an appointment did provoke strong criticism of Perry.

Section 51.355 of the Texas Education Code stipulates that the student government of each general academic teaching institution and medical and dental unit in a university system shall select five applicants for student regent and send their applications to the chancellor of that system. From these applications, the chancellor picks two or more applicants and forwards their applications to the governor. Although the governor may ask to review all applications received by a student government, the code does not authorize appointment of someone who applies directly to the governor. Nevertheless, Perry opted to appoint Fernando Trevino Jr. (the student featured as Chapter 4's "Student in Action"), a conservative activist enrolled at Texas A&M University in College Station, even though he had submitted his application directly to the governor's office. By a vote of nine to five, the Texas A&M student senate adopted a resolution criticizing Perry's appointment, but the governor did not back down.[45] Perry again appointed a University of Texas at Austin student who applied directly to his office in April of 2014, prompting charges from the Senate Higher Education Committee and two private sector lawyers that the governor had violated the law. Since the Education Code does not include penalty provisions that would apply to the governor in this situation, a suit to establish a violation is unlikely, but these incidents may result in legislative action to clarify the law.[46]

One limitation on the governor's appointive power is that the members of most state boards and commissions serve for six years, with overlapping terms of office. Thus, only one-third of the members finish a term every two years. A first-term governor like Greg Abbott must work with carryovers from previous administrations, even if such carryovers are not supportive of the new governor.

recess appointment
An appointment made by the governor when the Texas legislature is not in session.

Diversity of appointees remains a challenge. Data provided by the Office of the Governor on gender classification of Perry's 7,159 appointments as of July 2014 (not including the Interstate Oil and Gas Compact Commission and a few others) showed that 64 percent were men and 36 percent were women. Racial/ethnic classification of the appointees was as follows: Anglo, 75 percent; Latino, 14 percent; African American, 9 percent; and Asian or other, 2 percent.

The appointive power of the governor extends to filling vacancies for elected heads of the executive departments, members of the Railroad Commission, members of the State Board of Education, district attorneys, and judges (except those for county, municipal, and justice of the peace courts). These appointees serve until they are elected or replaced at the next general election. In addition, when a U.S. senator from Texas dies, resigns, or is removed from office before his or her term expires, the governor fills the vacancy with an interim appointee. That appointee serves until a successor is elected in a special election called by the governor. A vacancy in either chamber of the Texas legislature or in the Texas delegation to the U.S. House of Representatives does not result in an interim appointment. Instead, the governor calls a special election to fill the position. The winner of the special election serves until after the next regularly scheduled general election.

Removal Power

In creating numerous boards and commissions, the legislature gives the governor extensive appointive power but no independent **removal power** over most state agencies. This limitation restricts gubernatorial control over the state bureaucracy. The legislature limits the governor's independent removal power to members of the governor's staff and three statutory officials whose offices were created by the legislature: the executive director of the Department of Housing and Community Affairs, the executive commissioner of health and human services, and the insurance commissioner.

Elected department heads and their subordinates are not subject to the governor's removal power. Moreover, the governor cannot directly remove most board and commission officials. The governor may informally pressure an appointee to resign or accept another appointment, but this pressure is not as effective as the power of direct removal. Except for the few positions described previously, governors may not remove someone appointed by a predecessor. They may remove their own appointees with the consent of two-thirds of the state senators present; however, this authority still falls short of independent removal power.

Military Power

Article 4, Section 7, of the Texas Constitution states that the governor "shall be Commander-in-Chief of the military forces of the State, except when they are called into actual service of the United States." Appointed by the governor, the adjutant general commands the three branches of the Texas Military Forces

removal power
Authority to remove an official from office. In Texas, the governor's removal power is limited to staff members, some agency heads, and his or her appointees with the consent of the Senate.

(with approximate personnel numbers): Texas Army National Guard (19,100), the Texas Air National Guard (3,000), and the Texas State Guard (2,000).

The president of the United States can order units of the Army National Guard and Air National Guard to federal service in time of war or national emergency. Pay for National Guard personnel while on active duty and for training periods (usually one weekend each month) is the same as that for regular military personnel of the same rank. Texas State Guard units serve within Texas and support the other two branches of the Texas Military Forces. For the most part, State Guard soldiers are not paid for training activities, but when activated by the governor, they receive full pay.

In June 1943, an African American in Beaumont, Texas, was accused of raping a white woman, sparking a riot in which as many as 4,000 Anglo citizens attacked black neighborhoods and businesses with guns, axes, and hammers. Since all Texas National Guard personnel were in federal service because of World War II, acting governor A. M. Aiken used Texas State Guard units to impose **martial law** (temporary rule by state military forces and suspension of civil authority) on Beaumont.[47] The action was taken according to the constitutional provision that the governor "shall have power to call forth the militia to execute the laws of the State, to suppress insurrections, and to repel invasions." Until the constitution was amended in 1999, this power extended to "protecting the frontier from hostile incursions by Indians or other predatory bands."

As circumstances demand, the governor authorizes the mobilization of Army and Air National Guard personnel to perform relief and rescue service in counties hit by hurricanes, floods, fires, and other natural disasters. In April 2013, Governor Perry mobilized members of the Guard to assist in responding to the fertilizer plant explosion in the city of West, Texas.[48] Governor Perry activated some National Guard personnel to assist with border security along the Texas-Mexico border in 2007. When the number of unaccompanied immigrant children crossing into Texas surged in 2014, Perry deployed 1,000 Guard personnel to the border at state expense after President Obama refused to take this action.[49] The Guard also fights alongside the U.S. Army, Navy, Air Force, and Marines in foreign combat. Since the invasion of Afghanistan in 2001, more than 33,200 Texas Guard personnel have served in Afghanistan, Iraq, and other countries. Despite this service, cuts to federal government spending meant that the Texas Guard lost many of their attack helicopters to active duty branches in 2014.[50]

Law Enforcement Power

In Texas, law enforcement is primarily a responsibility of city police departments and county sheriffs' departments. Nevertheless, the Texas Department of Public Safety (DPS), headed by the Public Safety Commission, is an important law enforcement agency. The governor appoints the commission's five members, subject to Senate approval. The director of public safety is appointed by the commission and oversees more than 8,000 personnel in the

martial law
Temporary rule by military authorities when civil authorities are unable to handle a riot or other civil disorder.

DPS. Included among the department's responsibilities are highway traffic supervision, driver licensing, and criminal law enforcement in cooperation with local and federal agencies.

If circumstances demand swift but limited police action, the governor is empowered to assume command of the Texas Rangers, a division of DPS composed of a small number of highly trained law enforcement personnel operating statewide. As of September 2014, membership in this elite group totaled 159: 156 men (119 Anglo, 29 Latino, 7 African American, 1 Native American) and 3 women (2 Anglo, 1 Latina).

Budgetary Power

Gubernatorial **budgetary power** is subordinated in part to the legislature's prerogative of controlling the state's purse strings. By statutory requirement, the governor (assisted by personnel in the Budget, Planning, and Policy Division of the Governor's Office) and the Legislative Budget Board should prepare separate budgets for consideration by the legislature in regular session. Texas law requires distribution of the governor's budget to each legislator before delivery of the governor's State of the State message. Traditionally, both the House and the Senate have been inclined to give greater respect to the Legislative Budget Board's spending proposals. (For further discussion of the state's budget process, see Chapter 13 "Finance and Fiscal Policy.")

The Texas governor's principal control over state spending comes from the constitutional power to veto an entire appropriations bill or to use the **line-item veto** to eliminate individual budget items. In June 2013, Governor Perry announced 10 line-item vetoes of the 83rd Legislature's appropriations; but 8 were vetoes of **contingency riders** for bills that the legislature had not passed. The other 2 line-item vetoes were for contingency riders for bills that had been passed but were vetoed by the governor.[51] One was the controversial veto of funding for the Public Integrity Unit that led to Governor Perry's indictment for abuse of official capacity and coercion of a public servant.

The line-item veto is an important power even when not used because legislators may avoid including items in the budget that the governor signals he will veto. Governor Perry's decision to oppose Medicaid expansion is an example. Under the Affordable Care Act, the federal government will cover 100 percent of expanded access to the federal health insurance program for low-income citizens until 2017, gradually declining to 90 percent by 2020. Texas has the largest uninsured population in the nation. In the first five years under the expanded program, the state would have received $76 billion to provide health care coverage for poorer citizens. Expansion was strongly supported by the Texas Medical Association, Texas Hospital Association, and many other groups. Yet Perry's opposition was a clear signal to legislators that authorizing the funding would result in a gubernatorial veto. Therefore, expansion and funding were never proposed.[52]

budgetary power
The governor is supposed to submit a state budget to the legislature at the beginning of each regular session. When an appropriation bill is enacted by the legislature and certified by the comptroller of public accounts, the governor may veto the whole document or individual items.

line-item veto
Action by the governor to eliminate an individual budget item while permitting enactment of other parts of an appropriation bill.

contingency rider
Authorization for spending state money to finance provisions of a bill if the bill becomes law.

Executive Orders and Proclamations

Although the Texas Constitution identifies the governor as the "Chief Executive Officer of the State," it does not empower him or her to tell other state officials what they must do unless such action is authorized by the legislature. Nevertheless, governors use executive orders to set policy within the executive branch and to create or abolish task forces, boards, commissions, and councils. Each **executive order** is identified by the governor's initials and is numbered chronologically.

Executive Orders are not used frequently in Texas, with Governor Perry's issuing only one each year in 2012 and 2013 and none in 2014. In 2009, Perry's 73rd executive order (RP73) affected college students and faculty when it directed the Texas Higher Education Coordinating Board, in cooperation with public colleges and universities, to look at "opportunities for achieving cost efficiencies." Subjects under review were state funding for higher education based on courses completed, faculty workload, distance learning, alternatives to new campuses, energy use, and cost of instructional materials. Executive order RP75, issued in August 2011, related to the establishment and support of WGU Texas (a partnership with the Western Governors University), a nonprofit independent university offering "online degrees based on demonstrated competence as opposed to degrees based on credit hours, clock hours or grades."[53]

Another instrument of executive authority is the **proclamation**, an official public announcement often used for ceremonial purposes (for example, naming January 2014 "Crime Stoppers Month"). Some proclamations declare a state of emergency, as in 2014, when extreme winter weather caused a shortage of liquefied petroleum gas and the governor joined several others states in issuing a proclamation waiving certain regulations and requirements in order to deliver gas throughout the region. Others proclaim a region to be a disaster area, as when a 2014 proclamation extended the designation of disaster area for certain Texas counties experiencing exceptional drought. Additional uses of proclamations include calling special sessions of the legislature and special elections, as well as announcing the ratification of amendments to the U.S. Constitution.

Economic Development

The governor's office has direct control over efforts to attract investment and move businesses to Texas from other states and countries. Not only did Governor Perry recruit specific corporations, such as Toyota, to Texas, he also oversaw media and public relations campaigns in other states.[54] While Perry took business-recruiting trips around the country, Texas spent millions of dollars for television and radio ads in states such as California, Illinois, Connecticut, and New York in an effort to lure employers to relocate their businesses to the Lone Star State.[55]

The Texas Enterprise Fund (TEF), originally funded in 2003 with $295 million from the state's "rainy day" fund (an account intended to pay for

executive order
The governor issues executive orders to set policy within the executive branch and to create task forces, councils, and other bodies.

proclamation
A governor's official public announcement (such as calling a special election or declaring a disaster area).

state operations in times of emergency), is used to attract or retain industries. Additional multimillion-dollar appropriations for TEF were made in 2005, 2007, 2009, and 2011. No funding was requested in 2013 when the 83rd Legislature met. Instead the Office of the Governor asked to "retain the rider that allows for the reappropriation of unexpended balances and appropriation of revenue received in order to continue the program that is already in place."[56] To complement TEF money, Perry established TexasOne, a nonprofit, tax-exempt corporation that operates with directors appointed by the governor. Its primary mission is to attract businesses from other states and countries by marketing economic opportunities in Texas. In launching TexasOne, Perry invited major companies and business-related groups to support the fund for three years with a range of annual tax-deductible contributions.[57] To recruit out-of-state companies, prospective contributors were informed that visiting executives would be given "red carpet treatment throughout: flight into Texas, limousine transportation, four-star hotel accommodations, reception on arrival, evening with local and state leadership, … etc."[58]

The Emerging Technology Fund (ETF) is designed to help small to mid-size companies develop new technology for a wide range of high-tech industries. In 2014, the fund generated controversy even among Texas Republicans. Though ETF-funded businesses showed an overall positive return in terms of job creation and tax revenue during the life of the program, 16 recipients had declared bankruptcy. Gubernatorial candidate Greg Abbott repeatedly declared that Texas should not be in the in the business of "picking winners and losers."[59] (For more on ETF, see this chapter's Selected Reading, "High-Tech Investing in Texas After Governor Perry.")

✓ **9.4 Learning Check**

1. True or False: Most gubernatorial appointments must be approved by a two-thirds vote of the House of Representatives.
2. What constitutional power allows the governor to exercise control over state spending?

Answers on p. 356.

Legislative Powers of the Governor

LO9.5 Analyze the shared power of the executive and legislative branches.

Perhaps the most stringent test of a Texas governor's capacity for leadership involves handling legislative matters. The governor has no direct lawmaking authority, but **legislative power** is exercised through four major functions authorized by the Texas Constitution:

- Delivering messages to the legislature
- Signing bills and concurrent resolutions
- Vetoing bills and concurrent resolutions
- Calling special sessions of the legislature

legislative power
A power of the governor exercised through messages delivered to the Texas legislature, vetoes of bills and concurrent resolutions, and calls for special sessions of the legislature.

However, the success of a legislative program depends heavily on a governor's ability to bargain with influential lobbyists and legislative leaders (in particular, the Speaker of the House of Representatives and the lieutenant governor).[60]

Message Power

Article 4, Section 9, of the Texas Constitution requires the governor to deliver a State of the State address at the "commencement" (beginning) of each regular session of the legislature, but this directive is not interpreted to mean the first day of the session. On occasion, the governor may also present other messages, either in person or in writing, to the legislature. A governor's success in using **message power** to promote a harmonious relationship with the legislature depends on such variables as the timing of messages concerning volatile issues, the support of the governor's program by the chairs of legislative committees, and the governor's personal popularity with the public.

Bill Signing Power

While the legislature is in session, the governor indicates approval by signing bills and concurrent resolutions within 10 days (not counting Sundays) after receiving them. Bills and concurrent resolutions that are neither signed nor vetoed by the governor during that period become law anyway. After the legislature adjourns, however, the governor has 20 days (counting Sundays) to veto pending bills and concurrent resolutions.

Most media coverage of signings is the result of "photo ops" staged in Austin or elsewhere weeks or even months after official signings. Defenders

message power
The governor's effectiveness in communicating with legislators via the State of the State address at the "commencement" of a legislative session and other messages delivered in person or in writing.

Governor Rick Perry's ceremonial signing of HB 274, the "Loser Pay" Tort Reform Bill, on May 30, 2011, the last day of the 82nd Legislature. Standing immediately behind Perry (left to right) are Representative Paul D. Workman (R-Austin), Representative Connie Scott (R-Corpus Christi), and Senator Joan Huffman (R-Houston).

Marjorie Kamys Cotera/ Daemmrich Photos/ The Image Works

CRITICAL THINKING

Does the governor exercise too much, too little, or the right amount of influence over legislation?

of these ceremonial re-signings contend that the events help inform Texans about new laws. Critics insist that the principal objective of the signings is to give favorable publicity to the governor, bill sponsors, and others who wish to be identified with the legislation.[61]

Veto Power

The governor's most direct legislative tool is the power to block legislation with a veto. During a legislative session, the governor vetoes a bill by returning it unsigned (with written reasons for not signing) to the chamber in which the bill originated. If the legislature is no longer in session, a vetoed bill is filed with the secretary of state. **Veto power** takes different forms. In addition to general veto authority, the governor has the line-item veto (described earlier in this chapter), which can be used to eliminate one or more specific spending authorizations in an appropriation bill while permitting enactment of the remainder of the budget. Using the line-item veto power to refuse funding for a specific agency, the governor can effectively eliminate that agency. This line-item veto authority places the governor in a powerful bargaining position with individual legislators in the delicate game of **pork-barrel politics**. That is, the governor may strike a bargain with a senator or representative in which the chief executive promises not to deny funding for a lawmaker's pet project (the pork). In return, the legislator agrees to support a bill favored by the governor.

During a session, the governor's veto can be overridden by a two-thirds majority vote in both houses; but overriding a veto has occurred only once since the administration of Governor W. Lee O'Daniel (1939–1941). In 1979, the House and Senate overrode Governor Clements's veto of a bill giving Comal County commissioners power to establish hunting and fishing regulations for the county. The strong veto power that the Texas Constitution gives to the governor and the governor's informal power of threatening to veto a bill are formidable weapons for dealing with legislators.

The governor of Texas may also exercise a **postadjournment veto** by rejecting any pending legislation within 20 days after a session ends. Because most bills pass late in a legislative session, the postadjournment veto allows the governor to veto measures without threat of any challenge.

Throughout most of the 77th Legislature's regular session in 2001, Governor Perry vetoed only a few bills. But in what some critics termed the "Father's Day Massacre," he exercised 78 postadjournment vetoes at 9 P.M. on the last possible day to do so (June 17). Surpassing Governor Clements's 59 vetoes in 1989, Perry's total of 82 vetoes in 2001 set a record. For the following six regular legislative sessions, his veto totals were 48 (78th, 2003), 19 (79th, 2005), 51 (80th, 2007), 35 (81st, 2009), 24 (82nd, 2011), and 26 (83rd, 2013).[62] Among Perry's more controversial vetoes in 2013 was his killing of HB 950. The bill would have allowed women in Texas to sue employers for wage discrimination—a move Perry believed threatened Texas's strong job creation record.[63]

veto power
Authority of the governor to reject a bill or concurrent resolution passed by the legislature.

pork-barrel politics
A legislator's tactic to obtain funding for a pet project, usually designed to be of special benefit for the legislator's district.

postadjournment veto
Rejection by the governor of a pending bill or concurrent resolution during the 20 days after a legislative session ends.

Special Sessions Power

Included among the governor's powers is the authority to call special sessions of the legislature. The Texas Constitution places no restrictions on the number of special sessions a governor may call, but the length of a special session is limited to 30 days. During a special session, the legislature may consider only those matters the governor specifies in the call or subsequently presents to the legislature. The two exceptions to this requirement of gubernatorial approval are confirmation of appointments and impeachment proceedings. The threat of calling a special session is a tool the governor wields to influence the legislature to heed his wishes. For example, Governor Rick Perry threatened a special session in 2013 if legislators failed to include in the budget a $1.8 billion tax cut and $2 billion for major water and infrastructure projects.[64] In the end, the governor called three special sessions. The first drew national and international attention when Senator Wendy Davis (D-Ft. Worth) delivered a marathon filibuster against a bill to restrict access to abortions. (This filibuster and its results are discussed in Chapter 8, "The Legislative Branch.") Although Davis succeeded in keeping the bill from passing, within hours Governor Perry quickly called a second special session. In that session the Texas legislature passed some of the most restrictive abortion laws in the country, along with juvenile justice bills and transportation measures.[65] Because the legislature failed to fully resolve the transportation issues, Perry called a third special session that ended quickly, with only one agenda item—the proposal of a constitutional amendment to provide more funding for transportation infrastructure.[66]

9.5 Learning Check

1. True or False: During a session, the governor's veto can be overridden by a two-thirds majority vote in the House and in the Senate.
2. How can the legislature be convened for a special session?

Answers on p. 356.

Judicial Powers of the Governor

★ **LO9.6** Illustrate powers the governor exercises over the judicial branch of state government.

The governor exercises a few formal judicial powers, including the power to do the following:

- Fill vacancies on state (but not county or city) courts
- Play a limited but outdated role in removing judges and justices
- Perform acts of clemency to undo or reduce sentences given to some convicted criminals

Appointment and Removal of Judges and Justices

More than half of Texas's state judges and justices first serve on district courts and higher appellate courts through gubernatorial appointment to fill a vacancy caused by the creation of a new state court or a judge's death, resignation, or removal from office. The Texas judicial system has been heavily influenced by Governor Perry, whose long tenure allowed him to appoint almost 250 judges. The vast majority of them share Perry's probusiness stance, making it very difficult to win cases against large corporations in Texas.[67] Like other governors, Perry used this power to diversify the state's judicial system. For example, Governor Perry twice made history with his appointments of Wallace B. Jefferson, initially as the first African American to serve on the Texas Supreme Court and then, in 2004, as chief justice of that court. Chief Justice Jefferson returned to the private practice of law in 2013. In 2004, Perry appointed his former general counsel, David Medina, a Latino, to the Texas Supreme Court; and in 2009, he named Justice Eva Guzman as the first Latina to serve on that court. Nearly all his appointees to the Texas Supreme Court won subsequent election.[68]

According to Article XV, Section 8, of the Texas Constitution, the governor may remove any jurist "on address of two-thirds of each house of the Legislature for willful neglect of duty, incompetence, habitual drunkenness, oppression in office, or other reasonable cause which shall not be sufficient ground for impeachment." Governors and the legislature have not used this process for many years. Instead, they have left removal of state jurists to other proceedings and to voters. (See Chapter 11, "The Judicial Branch," for a discussion of the disciplining and removal of judges and justices.)

Acts of Executive Clemency

Until the mid-1930s, Texas governors had extensive powers to undo or lessen punishment for convicted criminals through acts of clemency that set aside or reduced court-imposed penalties. A constitutional amendment adopted in 1936 reduced the clemency powers of the governor and established the Board of Pardons and Paroles, which is now a division of the Texas Department of Criminal Justice.

Release of a prisoner before completion of a sentence on condition of good behavior is called **parole**. The seven-member Board of Pardons and Paroles, along with 14 commissioners appointed by the Chair, grants parole without action by the governor. The governor, however, may perform various acts of executive clemency that set aside or reduce a court-imposed penalty through pardon, reprieve, or commutation of sentence. Only if recommended by the Board of Pardons and Paroles can the governor grant a full pardon or a conditional pardon; however, pardons are rare in Texas. In fiscal year 2013, for example, the board considered 170 requests for full pardon and recommended pardon in 44 of these cases. Governor Perry announced pardons around Christmas each year. In 2013, he granted 14.[69]

A **full pardon** releases a person from all consequences of a criminal act and restores the same rights enjoyed by persons who have not been convicted of crimes. In 2010, Governor Perry granted a full pardon to Timothy Cole after DNA evidence proved he had been wrongfully imprisoned for more than 13 years. Unfortunately, Cole died in prison nine years before the pardon.[70] As attorney general, Greg Abbott subsequently issued an opinion stating that parole could be granted posthumously. Under a **conditional pardon**, the governor may withhold certain rights, such as being licensed to practice a

parole
Supervised release from prison before completion of a sentence, on condition of good behavior.

full pardon
An act of executive clemency, on recommendation of the Board of Pardons and Paroles, that releases a convicted person from all consequences of a criminal act and restores the same rights enjoyed by others who have not been convicted of a crime.

conditional pardon
An act of executive clemency, on recommendation of the Board of Pardons and Paroles, that releases a convicted person from the consequences of his or her crime but does not restore all rights, as in the case of a full pardon.

selected occupation or profession. Acting independently, the governor may revoke a conditional pardon if the terms of that pardon are violated.

The governor may also independently grant one 30-day reprieve in a death sentence case. A **reprieve** temporarily suspends execution of a condemned prisoner, but governors seldom grant reprieves. Rick Perry's decision not to grant a reprieve to Cameron Todd Willingham, who was executed in 2004, subjected the governor to substantial criticism when subsequent evidence suggested that Willingham might have been innocent. In the midst of controversy over the Willingham case, former governor Mark White stated in an interview on National Public Radio that it was time for Texas to reconsider use of the death sentence. White had strongly supported capital punishment while he was governor (1983–1987).[71]

If recommended by the Board of Pardons and Paroles, the governor may reduce a penalty through **commutation of sentence** and may remit (return) forfeitures of money or property surrendered as punishment. Having previously granted only one death penalty commutation, in June 2005 Governor Perry commuted the sentences of 28 death row inmates convicted of crimes committed when they were younger than age 18. He took this action after the U.S. Supreme Court ruled in *Roper v. Simmons*, 543 U.S. 551 (2005), that people cannot be executed if they were minors at the time of the crime. The Court held that execution of these individuals would violate the Eighth Amendment's ban on cruel and unusual punishment.

In 2014, the Texas death penalty had major implications for both federalism and international relations. Edgar Tamayo, a Mexican national, was sentenced to death for killing a Houston police officer. The Mexican government protested that the trial was tainted by a failure to conform to the Vienna Convention on Consular Relations, a 1963 treaty that requires police to inform foreign citizens of their right to assistance from their country's local consul (a representative of the foreign government). The U.S. State Department protested that the case might "impact the way American citizens are treated in other countries." Tamayo's lawyers protested that he was mentally impaired, and thus the death penalty constituted cruel and unusual punishment under the Eighth Amendment to the U.S. Constitution. Governor Perry denied requests for clemency, and Attorney General Greg Abbott opposed any delays. The state executed Tamayo by lethal injection on January 22, 2014.[72]

> ✓ **9.6 Learning Check**
>
> 1. True or False: A vacancy on a Texas district court or higher appellate court is filled by gubernatorial appointment.
> 2. Which Texas official has power to independently grant one 30-day reprieve in a death sentence case?
>
> Answers on p. 356.

The Plural Executive

★ **LO9.7** Describe the powers of the secretary of state and elected department heads.

Politically, the governor is Texas's highest-ranking officer; but the governor and the lieutenant governor share executive power with four elected department heads. These department heads (with annual salaries budgeted by the legislature for the biennial period covering fiscal years 2014–2015) are the attorney general ($150,000), comptroller of public accounts ($150,000), commissioner of the

> **reprieve**
> An act of executive clemency that temporarily suspends execution of a sentence.
>
> **commutation of sentence**
> On the recommendation of the Board of Pardons and Paroles, the reduction of a sentence by the governor.

General Land Office ($137,500), and commissioner of agriculture ($137,500). The secretary of state, with a salary of $125,880 in fiscal years 2014–2015, is appointed by, and serves at the pleasure of, the governor. Positions of governor, lieutenant governor, comptroller of public accounts, and commissioner of the General Land Office are created in Article IV of the Texas Constitution. The commissioner of agriculture holds an office created by statute, now located in the Texas Agriculture Code. These executive officials are referred to collectively as the state's **plural executive**. Also performing executive functions are the three elected members of the Railroad Commission of Texas and the 15 elected members of the State Board of Education. (For information on these two agencies, see Chapter 10, "Public Policy and Administration.")

Elected department heads are largely independent of gubernatorial control. However, with the exception of the office of lieutenant governor, should one of these positions become vacant during an official's term of office, the governor, with Senate approval, appoints a successor until the next general election.

The Lieutenant Governor

Some observers consider the lieutenant governor to be the most powerful Texas official, yet the **lieutenant governor** functions less in the executive branch than in the legislative branch, where he or she serves as president of the Senate. The Texas Constitution requires the Senate to convene within 30 days whenever a vacancy occurs in the lieutenant governor's office. Senators then elect one of their members to fill the office as acting lieutenant governor until the next general election. Thus, the Senate chose Senator Bill Ratliff to replace Lieutenant Governor Rick Perry when Perry succeeded Governor George W. Bush following the 2000 presidential election.

The annual state salary for the office of lieutenant governor is only $7,200, the same as that paid to members of the legislature. Like legislators, the lieutenant governor may also hold a paying job in private business or practice a profession. For example, from 1992 to 1998, Lieutenant Governor Bob Bullock was affiliated with the law firm of Scott, Douglass, & McConnico, LLP, in Austin, from which he received a six-figure annual salary.

Many Texas lobbyists and members of the business community supported John Sharp, a Democrat and former comptroller of public accounts, in the 2002 race for lieutenant governor; but multimillionaire Republican David Dewhurst, the state's commissioner of the General Land Office at that time, won the November general election. To finance his campaign, Dewhurst used more than $10 million of his own money plus $13 million that he borrowed. After his victory, Dewhurst recouped some of this money at fundraising events where Sharp's former supporters "caught the late train" by making postelection contributions to Dewhurst.[73] In 2006 and 2010, Dewhurst was reelected. Dewhurst continued as lieutenant governor in 2012 after Ted Cruz defeated him in a runoff primary contest for nomination as GOP candidate for the office of U.S. senator. After more than a decade in office, Dewhurst lost the Republican nomination for lieutenant

plural executive
The governor, elected department heads, and the secretary of state, as provided by the Texas Constitution and statutes.

lieutenant governor
Popularly elected constitutional official who serves as president of the Senate and is first in the line of succession if the office of governor becomes vacant before the end of a term.

governor to Dan Patrick (R-Houston) in 2014. Following Ted Cruz's defeat of the lieutenant governor, Patrick also successfully portrayed Dewhurst as insufficiently conservative to deserve Republican primary voters' support.[74]

The Attorney General

One of Texas's most visible and powerful officeholders is the **attorney general**. Whether joining lawsuits to overturn federal health care reform, arguing affirmative action questions in court, or trying to resolve redistricting disputes, the state's chief lawyer is a major player in making many important public policy decisions. This officer represents the state in civil litigation and issues advisory opinions on legal questions if requested by state and local authorities. When Attorney General John Cornyn decided to run for a seat in the U.S. Senate in 2002, the Republican Party nominated Supreme Court Justice Greg Abbott for attorney general. In the November election of that year, Abbott defeated Democrat Kirk Watson, a former Austin mayor. Before Abbott began his elected term in January 2003, Governor Perry appointed him to serve for a few weeks in that office following Cornyn's resignation in November 2002. Abbott won a second term in 2006 and was reelected in 2010.

Upon his appointment, Abbott declared that he was "philosophically very committed to open government" and that he would enforce the state's open records laws for the benefit of the public and the media. This statement was welcomed by the press and public interest groups that had complained about lack of access to information concerning government operations.[75] Though Abbott defended his record, his decisions in 2014 to block public access to state information about both lethal injection drugs and the location of dangerous chemicals drew criticism from the media and his political opponents.

With more than 4,000 employees, the Office of the Attorney General gives advice concerning the constitutionality of many pending bills. The governor, heads of state agencies, and local government officials also request opinions from the attorney general on the scope of an agency's or official's jurisdiction and the interpretation of vaguely worded laws. Although neither judges nor other officials are bound by these opinions, the attorney general's rulings are considered authoritative unless overruled by court decisions or new laws. In an advisory opinion in 2013, the attorney general stated that government entities offering health benefits to employees' same-sex partners violated Texas's ban on same-sex marriage.[76]

Another power of the attorney general is to initiate, in a district court, quo warranto proceedings, which challenge an official's right to hold public office. Such action may lead to removal of an officeholder who lacks a qualification set by law or who is judged guilty of official misconduct. Among its many functions, the Office of the Attorney General enforces child support orders issued by state courts and administers the Crime Victims' Compensation Fund.

While campaigning for governor in 2013, Attorney General Greg Abbott described his workday: "I go into the office, I sue the federal government,

attorney general
The constitutional official elected to head the Office of the Attorney General, which represents the state government in lawsuits and provides legal advice to state and local officials.

and then I go home."[77] Between 2002 and 2014, Abbott filed 31 lawsuits against the federal government. Three of the cases were filed while George W. Bush was serving as president. The remaining 28 were filed during the Obama administration. Most frequently, the attorney general sued the Environmental Protection Agency. Additionally, he brought lawsuits challenging the Affordable Care Act (*National Federation of Independent Business v. Sebelius*, 567 U.S. ___ (2012) and asking federal courts to approve Texas's redistricting maps and voter identification law.[78] In the course of the voter ID litigation, Abbott's office erred by releasing about 6.5 million Social Security numbers to lawyers challenging the voter ID law. Luckily, the mistake was detected before any identity damage was done. The Texas law was initially struck down by a federal court as discriminatory, but following the U.S. Supreme Court's decision in *Shelby County v. Holder*, 570 U.S. ___ (2013), to overturn parts of the historic Voting Rights Act, Abbott announced that the voter ID law would be implemented immediately.[79]

The attorney general also submits *amicus curiae* briefs on behalf of the state's efforts to influence the outcome of court cases. In 2014, Abbott garnered further support from opponents of gay rights when he filed amicus curiae briefs arguing that federal courts should not be able to decide challenges to the City of Houston's decision to grant benefits to some same-sex partners of employees.[80]

When Abbott announced he would seek the governorship, he sparked a tight race for his replacement. Ken Paxton defeated fellow GOP legislator Dan Branch in a runoff primary election to replace Abbott. Paxton won the general election in November against challenger Sam Houston.

The Comptroller of Public Accounts

One of the most powerful elected officers in Texas government is the **comptroller of public accounts**, the state's chief accounting officer and tax collector. After a biennial appropriation bill passes by a simple majority vote in the House and Senate, the Texas Constitution requires the comptroller's certification that expected revenue will be collected to cover all of the budgeted expenditures. Otherwise, an appropriation must be approved by a four-fifths majority vote in both houses. One of the comptroller's duties is to designate hundreds of Texas financial institutions (mostly banks, but also a few savings associations and credit unions) to serve as depositories for state-collected funds.

Susan Combs, former commissioner of agriculture, served as comptroller from 2007 to 2015. Among the controversies that arose during her two terms in office was criticism of a security lapse in which personal data of more than 3.5 million Texans were inadvertently released. In 2011, conflict arose between Combs and Governor Perry when the comptroller notified online retailer Amazon.com that it owed Texas $269 million in sales tax. The amount of the claim was based on the value of digital downloads, books, Kindle e-readers, and other merchandise sold to purchasers in Texas from the company's website. Governor Perry criticized Combs's action, but she did not

comptroller of public accounts
An elected constitutional officer responsible for collecting taxes, keeping accounts, estimating revenue, and serving as treasurer for the state.

back down. Although the governor vetoed a bill in 2011 that strengthened Combs's argument for taxes, he ultimately approved similar legislation that was included in the state's biennial budget for 2012–2013. In April 2012, the comptroller negotiated an agreement with Amazon.[81] (For more information on the Amazon affair, see Chapter 13, "Finance and Fiscal Policy.")

In 2014, Glenn Hegar of Katy defeated Democrat Mike Collier to replace Combs, who decided to retire from politics. As the state's comptroller, Hegar supervises about 2,800 employees. The comptroller's office promotes the cause of "transparency in government" by maintaining the "Window on State Government" website. This site allows anyone to see how state tax money is being spent. For example, you can find the amount of money Hegar's department and other state agencies have paid to individual vendors for goods or services or to its employees for official travel expenses. As directed by the legislature, Hegar promotes consistency in accounting methods and standards by all state agencies; he does the same for Texas's counties, cities, and special districts.[82]

The Commissioner of the General Land Office

Although less visible than other elected executives, the **commissioner of the General Land Office** is an important figure in Texas politics. Since the creation of the General Land Office under the Constitution of the Republic of Texas (1836), the commissioner's duties have expanded to include overseeing the state's public lands and thus awarding oil, gas, and sulfur leases for lands owned by the state (including wind rights especially in the Texas tidelands); serving as chair of the Veterans Land Board; and sitting as an ex officio member of other boards responsible for managing state-owned lands. With more than 600 employees, the General Land Office also oversees growth of the Permanent School Fund, which is financed by oil and gas leases, rentals, and royalties and which each year provides hundreds of millions of dollars to benefit the state's public schools. In addition to these responsibilities, the General Land Office maintains an archive of about 35 million documents and historic maps relating to land titles in Texas.

Former lobbyist and state senator Jerry Patterson held this office from 2003 to 2015. A vocal and sometimes controversial advocate for gun rights, as a legislator Patterson sponsored a bill that became Texas's concealed handgun law. As land commissioner, Patterson declined having security guards like those provided to other executive branch officials, instead carrying a .22 Magnum pistol in his left boot and a .380-caliber semiautomatic pistol at the small of his back.[83] In 2007, he scuttled a deal to transfer the Christmas Mountains in West Texas to the National Park Service because of the restrictions on hunting and firearms that would have resulted. Four years later, he decided to transfer the land to the Texas State University System for the study of biology, geology, archaeology, and wildlife management.[84]

Because the General Land Office administers vast landholdings for the state, the commissioner is involved in many legal disputes. Enforcement of Texas's Open Beaches Act, separating private land and public land along the

commissioner of the General Land Office As head of Texas's General Land Office, this elected constitutional officer oversees the state's extensive landholdings and related mineral interests, especially oil and gas leasing, for the benefit of the Permanent School Fund.

Gulf Coast, attracts media attention when controversies arise over construction in the beach area. After the Supreme Court of Texas ruled in *Severence v. Patterson* (2012) that the state's Open Beaches Act does not apply to beachfront areas on Galveston Island, Patterson declared that voters should oust the justices responsible for the decision.[85] Because the land commissioner is tasked both with monitoring the environmental quality of public land and water and with generating revenue from state land, the commissioner is sometimes caught between the interests of Texans who seek to protect the environment and businesses seeking to extract resources. In such disputes, Patterson leaned toward generating income, as when he strongly supported the construction of the Keystone XL Pipeline to transport tar sands oil from Canada through Texas.[86]

In 2014, Patterson failed in an attempt to win the Republican nomination for lieutenant governor. Nomination as Republican candidate for land commissioner was won by a member of the third generation of the Bush family to hold office for Texas—George P. Bush, grandson of former Texas congressman and president of the United States George H. W. Bush, and nephew of former Texas governor and president of the United States George W. Bush. George P. Bush defeated the Democratic Party's candidate, former El Paso mayor John Cook, in the November general election.

The Commissioner of Agriculture

By law, the **commissioner of agriculture** is supposed to be a "practicing farmer." This criterion is vague enough to qualify anyone who owns or rents a piece of agricultural land. Party identification with the state's voters (most of whom live in suburbs or central cities) is the principal requirement for winning the office.

This state officer is responsible for enforcing agricultural laws and for providing service programs to Texas farmers, ranchers, and consumers. Control over the use of often controversial pesticides and herbicides is exercised through the Department of Agriculture's Pesticide Programs Division. This division restricts the use of high-risk chemicals; it licenses dealers, professional applicators, and private applicators who apply dangerous pesticides and herbicides on their own farms and ranches. Other enforcement actions of the department include inspections to determine the accuracy of commercial scales, pumps, and meters. Such inspections protect Texas consumers at grocery store scales, gasoline pumps and other venues.

Todd Staples served as Texas's agriculture commissioner from 2007 to 2015. In May 2008, Staples led a 24-member trade delegation to Cuba to promote the export of Texas agricultural products to that country.[87] In March 2009, he traveled to Iraq as a guest of Texas A&M University's Norman Borlaug Institute for International Agriculture. While there, he promoted the export of Texas agricultural products to Iraq and announced that he had asked President Obama to give priority to lifting the U.S. trade embargo against Cuba.[88]

Under Staples's direction, the Texas Public School Nutrition Policy prohibits schools from serving deep-fried food in cafeterias and from selling soft drinks, candy, and other "foods of minimal nutritional value" until the end of a day's last scheduled class. Moreover, Staples announced that he

commissioner of agriculture
The elected official, whose position is created by statute, who heads Texas's Department of Agriculture, which promotes the sale of agricultural commodities and regulates pesticides, aquaculture, egg quality, weights and measures, and grain warehouses.

Students in Action

The Mickey Leland Environmental Internship Program

What It Is

The Mickey Leland Environmental Internship Program was founded in 1992 at the Texas Water Commission, which was a predecessor to the current Texas Commission on Environmental Quality. While representing Houston districts in the Texas House of Representatives (1973–1979) and the U.S. House of Representatives (1979–1989), Mickey Leland worked to promote a clean and healthy environment, proving to be an effective leader on environmental issues within Texas as well as the entire nation. Congressman Leland was a member of the Subcommittee on Health and Environment and encouraged public awareness in the protection of public health as well as environmental issues. In August 1989, he died in a plane crash while on a mission to visit a camp for Sudanese refugees in Ethiopia. The internship in his honor is designed to continue his work of increasing awareness of environmental issues, encouraging students to consider careers in the environmental field, and promoting the participation of minorities and the disadvantaged in environmental policy development. Learn more at the internship's website, http://www.tceq.texas.gov/adminservices/employ/mickeyleland/index.html.

What You Can Do

Undergraduate students enrolled full-time are eligible to apply for the internship program. Depending on your area of study, the internship offers the opportunity to fit a broad range of interests while providing a hands-on experience within the Texas legislature. Students are involved in the decisions and actions of the legislature, including researching and drafting legislation, as well as attending committee hearings, working on special projects, and assisting in general office operations.

How It Helps

Any internship provides the ever-important real-world experience that businesses and professionals look for upon graduation. The Mickey Leland Internship is no exception and encourages careers in law, political science, communications, psychology, and education, among others.

© Andresr/Shutterstock.com

would fight obesity by taking healthy eating habits into children's homes—that is, from "the lunchroom into the living room."[89]

Staples lost in his attempt to win the Republican nomination for lieutenant governor in the 2014 GOP primary. A number of candidates sought to replace him in the office of agriculture commissioner, including singer, humorist, writer, and tequila salesman Kinky Friedman, who has run repeatedly and unsuccessfully for political office in Texas. Cleburne farmer Jim Hogan defeated Friedman in the Democratic primary runoff. In the Republican primary runoff, a rare endorsement from Governor Perry and ties to rocker Ted Nugent helped Sid Miller defeat Tommy Merritt, his former colleague in the state House of Representatives. Though Friedman attempted to make the primary's main issue the legalization of marijuana, his Democratic opponents stayed focused on traditional forms of agriculture and water problems.[90] In the general election, Republican Sid Miller was elected. Before his term expired, Staples resigned in September 2014 and became president of an interest group, the Texas Oil and Gas Association.

The Secretary of State

The only constitutional executive officer appointed by the governor is the **secretary of state**. This appointment must be confirmed by a two-thirds vote of the Senate. The secretary of state serves a four-year term concurrent with that of the governor. As noted below, however, most secretaries of state serve for only a year or so. The secretary of state oversees a staff of approximately 250 people and is the chief elections officer of Texas. Principal responsibilities of the office include the following:

- Administering state election laws in conjunction with county officials
- Tabulating election returns for state and district offices
- Granting charters (organizational documents) to Texas corporations
- Issuing permits to outside corporations to conduct business within Texas
- Processing requests for extradition of criminals to or from other states for trial and punishment

With these diverse duties, the secretary of state is obviously more than just a record keeper. How the office functions is determined largely by the occupant's relations with the governor. As indicated by the following summary of the eight appointments to the office within the 15 years before 2015, secretaries of state do not remain in office very long.

After Rick Perry became governor at the end of 2000, he appointed Representative Henry Cuellar (D-Laredo) as his first secretary of state. When Cuellar resigned after two years, Perry named Republican Gwyn Shea to that office in January 2002. She resigned in July 2003 and was replaced by a succession of four different Republican men who held the office until Perry appointed Esperanza "Hope" Andrade in July 2008. Early in April 2012, Andrade announced a voter education program titled "Make Your Mark on Texas," and she began touring the state to encourage voting in the primaries and general election of the 2012 election cycle.[91] After voting roll purges in 2012 identified many living voters as deceased and removed them from state voting records (including one state legislator), Andrade resigned. Her replacement, John Steen, oversaw the implementation of the controversial new voter ID law in Texas.

After one year, Steen announced that he would leave the office, and in January 2014 Governor Perry replaced him with Nandita Berry, who immigrated to the United States from India at the age of 21 to pursue a career in law. The 109th secretary of state became the first Indian American to hold the post.[92]

secretary of state
The state's chief elections officer, with other administrative duties, who is appointed by the governor for a term concurrent with that of the governor.

✔ **9.7 Learning Check**

1. True or False: Heads of state agencies may not request opinions from the attorney general concerning the scope of their jurisdiction.
2. What is one important power of the secretary of state for persons desiring to establish a Texas corporation?

Answers on p. 356.

High-Tech Investing in Texas After Governor Perry

Jeff Key

Investing in high-technology ventures in Texas entered a new phase when Governor Rick Perry left office in January 2015. For a decade, Perry used state funds to assist state university researchers and high-tech entrepreneurs in getting their inventions to market. These grants and the way that they are administered have been a source of controversy. Questions about the appearance of politicians picking "winners and losers" and charges of "crony capitalism" have been raised by Republicans and Democrats alike. The future of this practice was in question after the Lone Star State chose a new governor in November 2014.

Under pressure from Governor Rick Perry, the 79th Texas Legislature created the Emerging Technology Fund (ETF) in 2005 with $200 million from the state's Rainy Day Fund. The goal of the ETF is to keep the profits "home-grown" high-tech projects developed by researchers at state universities and private firms in the Lone Star State. Grants from the ETF are intended to help develop and commercialize new products in order to get them out of the lab and into the market. Because venture capital generally is not available to turn discoveries into marketable products, the ETF is designed to fill a critical gap. If a project attracts private investors and the product goes to market, the state's grant becomes equity in the company and the ETF shares in royalties and revenue.

Scandal and Reform of the ETF

Governor Perry's 2010 reelection campaign and short-lived entry into the 2012 Republican presidential primary attracted national attention to his economic development policies. The ETF has been dogged by scandals that have prompted reforms. Problems of poor oversight and lack of transparency raised ethical questions about how the fund was being administered.

Soon after the ETF started issuing grants, members of the state legislature began asking questions about how the fund operated. Regional centers serve as incubators for proposals that are reviewed by a 17-member advisory committee appointed by the governor. The advisory committee makes recommendations on whether or not proposals should be funded. The final step requires the governor, lieutenant governor, and Speaker of the House of Representatives to sign off on each grant. Allegations that projects put forward by those with ties to the governor got preferential treatment led to charges of "crony capitalism." The governor's office could not explain why some projects were approved and others were rejected. This lack of transparency led to calls for stronger ethical guidelines; greater legislative oversight, including audits; reforms in the appointment of the Advisory Committee; and even stripping the governor, lieutenant governor, and Speaker of the House of Representatives of their final approval power over grants.

These concerns were brought into focus in 2009 by a $50 million ETF grant to Texas A&M University to develop pharmaceuticals. Irregularities in the approval process drew particular scrutiny. Governor Perry, Lieutenant Governor David Dewhurst, and Speaker Tom Craddick approved the grant even though the advisory committee had not recommended it. In response to the Texas A&M grant, the 81st Legislature passed HB 2531 requiring the governor's office to submit annual reports to the legislature on how fund money is used. With this minor reform, the Republican-controlled legislature appropriated $203.5 million for ETF grants for the 2010–2011 biennium. Many saw the scandal as just another chapter in the struggle between two great universities, the University of Texas at Austin and Texas A&M University, in which Governor Perry was only advancing the interests of his alma mater. While a student at Texas A&M, Perry had been a yell leader.

In 2010, a more compelling ETF scandal emerged involving possible conflicts of interest among ETF staff and advisory committee members, companies receiving grants, and the governor himself. At the scandal's core was a $4.5 million cancer research grant to Convergen Life-Science, Inc., headed by David Nance, a longtime Perry campaign donor and ETF advisory committee member. The Convergen proposal was rejected by the local review board (the lowest hurdle in the ETF approval process), but Nance appealed directly to the governor's office, the ETF executive director, and the ETF advisory committee chair. Governor Perry, Lieutenant Governor Dewhurst, and Speaker Joe Straus then approved the grant. Adding to the appearance of impropriety, ETF executive director Alan Kirchoff abruptly resigned before the grant contract was signed and went to work as a lobbyist for Nance-owned companies. A subsequent investigation by the Texas Rangers and the Public Integrity Unit of the Travis County district attorney's office did not result in a criminal prosecution. However, the scandal prompted the governor's office to produce the first written ethics policy for the ETF's advisory committee.

These scandals, reports of bankruptcies by grant recipients, and a five-month audit of the fund by state auditor John Keel issued in April 2011 attracted the attention of the 82nd Legislature. House Bill 2457, authored by Representative John Davis (R-Houston), was passed by the legislature in May 2011 and signed by Governor Perry. The bill introduced significant ETF reforms. The governor now appoints only 13 members of the advisory committee, and the lieutenant governor and Speaker each appoint two. The law also prescribes greater openness in the grant process, from initial submission to final authorization. With these reforms, the legislature appropriated $140 million for ETF grants in fiscal years 2012–2013.

Representative Davis sought an even more sweeping reform of the ETF in the 83rd Legislature. His HB 3162, coauthored with Representative Angie Chen Button (R-Garland), passed by a vote of 136–1 on May 7, 2013, and went to the Senate the next day. The bill would have changed the fund's name to the Texas Research Technology Fund and completely transformed the way it operates. The governor, lieutenant governor, and Speaker would have been stripped of their power to approve grants. Bound by state open meetings laws, an independent 15-member board appointed by the governor, the lieutenant governor, and the Speaker would have had final approval authority over grants. However, Lieutenant Governor Dewhurst killed the bill. Exercising his constitutional power over the Senate calendar, he refused to schedule a vote on the bill. Dewhurst explained his actions in a press release stating that he had requested an audit in 2011 and that reforms had been enacted to ensure openness. He argued that this new bill would have been a "step back from those principles." Notably, the 83rd Legislature allocated only $50 million for ETF grants over the next two years.

The ETF After Perry

Rick Perry's decision not to seek a fourth full term as governor created a scramble for statewide offices. Attorney General Greg Abbott, the Republican gubernatorial candidate, declared that Texas needs to "get out of the business of picking winners and losers." This statement suggested that he might not, if elected, continue economic development policies like the ETF. Democratic candidate Wendy Davis similarly decried Perry's policies. Whoever won the governor's race in November 2014, it was unlikely that the governor's office would be "open for business" as it was under Rick Perry. However, the Lone Star State needs to attract investment in the high-tech sector. That challenge awaited the new governor and the 84th Legislature in 2015.

✔ Selected Reading Learning Check

1. What is the goal of the Emerging Technology Fund (ETF)?
2. True or False: The ETF has seen so much success and so few scandals that Texas politicians of both parties support its continuation without change in the future.

Answers on p. 356.

Jeff Key is professor and head of the Department of Political Science at Hardin-Simmons University. This article was written especially for *Practicing Texas Politics, 2015–2016*.

Conclusion

Texas's constitutionally weak governor has grown stronger in recent years, but the term *chief executive* still does not accurately describe the head of the state's executive branch. The state constitution created a plural executive that diffuses power among a variety of independently elected officials. Governor Perry's power was enhanced by his long tenure and subsequent ability to appoint thousands of supporters to government posts, an advantage that can only accrue to Governor Abbott if his ability to raise campaign money and to appeal to voters enables him to win successive elections. Use of executive, legislative, and judicial powers vested in the Texas governor by statutes and the state constitution—when combined with political leadership and informal powers not based on law—enhance the importance of the office.

Chapter Summary

LO 9.1   **Analyze gubernatorial elections and the impact of campaign funds on the politics of the governorship**. Successful gubernatorial candidates must meet the constitutional requirements for the office, including a minimum age of 30, U.S. citizenship, Texas residency, and acknowledgment of a Supreme Being. Historically, conservative-moderate Democrats dominated races for the office, though the trend in recent decades is for conservative Republicans to win decisive victories. Serious candidates must also procure substantial campaign funds. Governors often reward large donors once in office by appointing them to important government positions.

LO 9.2   **Summarize how the constitution and laws of Texas provide resources, as well as succession and removal procedures, for the governor**. The constitution and laws of Texas provide governors financial compensation of $150,000 per year, along with travel and security funds, fringe benefits, and a sizable staff. Succession procedures are in place for those who do not finish their terms because they resign, die, or are removed from office. Governors may be removed by House impeachment and Senate conviction, though this has only happened once.

LO 9.3   **Discuss the informal powers of the governor**. Since 1876, Texas governors have held a weak constitutional office. Governors rely heavily on their informal powers, which derive from their popularity with the public and are based on traditions, symbols, and ceremonies. Modern governors may enhance their informal powers by public appearances, use of traditional and electronic media, and the support of family members.

LO 9.4   **Explain the effect of checks and balances on the executive powers of the governor**. The governor has power to appoint some department heads and members of the state's multiple boards and commissions, but only with approval of the Texas Senate. The legislature and the plural executive limit the governor's removal power. The governor checks the budgetary power of the legislature with strong veto powers, including a line-item veto. The governor may also use proclamations to call the legislature into special sessions.

LO 9.5   **Analyze the shared power of the executive and legislative branches**. To be successful in promoting their favored legislation, governors must bargain with lobbyists and legislators. To do so, they need to make skillful use of their formal legislative powers, which include delivering messages to the legislature, signing or vetoing bills and concurrent resolutions, and calling special sessions of the legislature.

LO 9.6   **Illustrate powers the governor exercises over the judicial branch of state government**. The governor fills vacancies on state courts caused by the creation of a new state court or a judge's death, resignation, or removal from office. Governors may remove judges, but only with direction by two-thirds of each house of the legislature, making it a rare occurrence. The governor may also grant clemency to undo or reduce sentences for some convicted criminals.

LO 9.7   **Describe the powers of the secretary of state and elected department heads**. All governors must share executive power with the lieutenant governor and four elected department heads: the attorney general (who acts as the state's chief lawyer), state comptroller (who acts as the state's chief accounting officer and tax collector), land commissioner (who manages the state's land and the revenue it produces), and agriculture commissioner (who both regulates and promotes Texas agriculture). The only appointed executive department head provided for in the Texas Constitution is the secretary of state, whose responsibilities include administering elections, granting charters and permits to corporations, and processing requests for extradition of criminals.

Key Terms

governor's office, p. 325	line-item veto, p. 336	veto power, p. 340
appointive power, p. 332	contingency rider, p. 336	pork-barrel politics, p. 340
recess appointment, p. 333	executive order, p. 337	postadjournment veto, p. 340
removal power, p. 334	proclamation, p. 337	parole, p. 342
martial law, p. 335	legislative power, p. 338	full pardon, p. 342
budgetary power, p. 336	message power, p. 339	conditional pardon, p. 342

Learning Check Answers

9.1 1. Governors of Texas are constitutionally required to be U.S. citizens, to be Texas residents for five years immediately preceding the gubernatorial election, and to acknowledge the existence of a Supreme Being.

2. True. Major donors to gubernatorial campaigns are frequently appointed to government posts.

9.2 1. False. Although the size of the governor's staff has shrunk in recent years, it is much larger now than earlier in Texas history.

2. The Texas Constitution provides for impeachment by a simple majority vote of the House and conviction by a two-thirds majority vote of the Senate.

9.3 1. True. Informal powers of the governor are not based on law.

2. True. Public involvement of family members may be a source of support for the governor.

9.4 1. False. Most gubernatorial appointments must be approved by a two-thirds vote of the Senate.

2. The governor may veto an entire appropriation bill or use the line-item veto to eliminate individual budget items.

9.5 1. True. During a session, the governor's veto can be overridden by a two-thirds majority vote in the House and in the Senate.

2. The governor can call a special session.

9.6 1. True. A vacancy on a Texas district court or higher appellate court is filled by gubernatorial appointment.

2. The governor can independently grant one 30-day reprieve in a death sentence case.

9.7 1. False. The heads of state agencies, along with the governor and even local government officials, may request opinions from the attorney general on the scope of their jurisdiction.

2. The secretary of state grants charters to Texas corporations.

Selected Reading Learning Check

1. The goal of the ETF is to keep the profits from high-tech projects developed by researchers at state universities and private firms in Texas.

2. False. Scandals and reports of bankruptcies by ETF grant recipients have prompted politicians of both parties to call for reform or abandonment of the program.

10 Public Policy and Administration

Learning Objectives

10.1 Describe the role of bureaucracy in making public policy in Texas.

10.2 Analyze the major challenges faced by the Texas education system.

10.3 Describe the health and human services programs in Texas and discuss how efforts to address the needs of its citizens have been approached.

10.4 Compare the roles of government in generating economic development while maintaining a safe and clean environment for the state's residents.

CRITICAL THINKING

Some groups in Texas are served well by public policy, others poorly. Why?

O ne good way to see what is important in public policy is to follow the money. For many years in Texas, the state government has spent the lion's share of the budget on four areas. For example, in the 2014–2015 biennium (two-year budget cycle), the legislature appropriated $200 billion as follows:

- Education: 37 percent
- Health and human services: 37 percent
- Business and economic development: 13 percent
- Public safety and criminal justice: 6 percent
- Everything else: 7 percent[1]

Although regulation costs the state government little (0.6 percent of the total in 2014–2015), it has profound cost effects on individuals, companies, and local governments. Regulation commonly shifts costs and benefits from one group to another. For example, contaminated air hurts the quality of life and increases medical costs for children with respiratory problems such as asthma, as well as for the elderly, but regulations requiring special equipment to reduce emissions from smokestacks cost businesses money. Not surprisingly, regulatory policy is fraught with controversy.

This chapter examines public policy in Texas through two lenses: (1) the situation and behavior of the agencies and people who implement the policies and (2) the nature of the policies themselves. Covered are the major policy areas of education, health and human services, business and economic development, and the environment. The other big-ticket item in Texas state government—public safety and criminal justice—is covered in Chapter 12, "The Criminal Justice System," and details on state spending are provided in Chapter 13, "Finance and Fiscal Policy."

State Agencies and State Employees

LO10.1 Describe the role of bureaucracy in making public policy in Texas.

Surprisingly, scholars who study public policy have not agreed on a single definition of it. However, many suggest the simple and useful definition utilized in this chapter: **Public policy** is what government does or does not do to and for its citizens.[2] Policy is both action, such as state or local governments raising or lowering speed limits, and inaction, such as Texas state government not accepting federal funds for expansion of Medicaid under the Affordable Care Act (Obamacare).

State government policies profoundly affect the lives of all of us. Services, subsidies, taxes, and regulations affect students from kindergarten through graduate school, the impoverished, the middle class, the wealthy, and small and large businesses. State policies affect our safety and health and the profitability of businesses. The impact of a given policy varies by group. (Who gets a tax cut? Who doesn't?) Thus, public policy is a source of great conflict because groups compete to gain benefits and reduce costs to themselves. As the opening cartoon suggests, some are better positioned than others to win this battle.

public policy
What government does or does not do to and for its citizens.

State Agencies and Public Policy

Public policy is the product of a series of interactions among a variety of groups and institutions. Commonly, an interest groups begins the process by bringing problems to the attention of government and then lobbying for solutions that benefit the members of the group. Political parties and chief executives often select and combine the proposals of interest groups into a manageable number and push them as part of their program or agenda. The legislature then accepts some of the proposals through the passage of laws, the creation or modification of agencies, and the appropriation of money to carry out the policies. Finally, the executive branch implements the policies. At the national level, the president provides rules and instructions for the agencies that actually carry out the policies. In Texas, the more than 200 agencies have substantial independence from the governor, which means that each agency has more latitude and independence than federal agencies in deciding what was meant by the legislature and in applying the law to unforeseen circumstances. Not surprisingly, a great deal of informal interaction (and lobbying) occurs among Texas interest groups, political parties, top executives, legislators, and agencies themselves.

The Institutional Context

The way in which the Texas executive branch is organized has a major effect on public policy. A key reason is that the fragmentation of authority strongly affects who has access to policy decisions, as well as how visible the decision process is to the public. The large number of agencies means they are covered less by the media and, therefore, are less visible to the public. The power of the one state official to whom the public pays attention (the governor) is limited. Special interest groups, on the other hand, have strong incentives (profits) to develop cozy relationships with agency personnel, and most agencies do not have to defend their decisions before a higher authority (such as the governor).

In addition to agencies headed by the elected officials discussed in Chapter 9, "The Executive Branch," more than 200 boards, commissions, and departments implement state laws and programs in Texas. Most boards and commissions are appointed by the governor; however, once citizens are appointed to a board, the governor relies on persuasion and personal or political loyalty to exercise influence. The exceptionally long tenure of Governor Rick Perry meant that he appointed all of the members of most boards and developed a close working relationship with those agencies of special concern to him. For example, Governor Perry had a strong interest in his alma mater, Texas A&M University, and significantly influenced its direction through the policies and hiring decisions made by members of the board of regents of the Texas A&M University System (whom he appointed).

Fragmentation of the state executive into so many largely independent agencies was an intentional move by the framers of the Texas Constitution and later legislatures to avoid centralized power. Administering state programs through boards was also thought to keep partisan politics out of public administration. Unfortunately, this fragmentation simply changes the nature of the politics, making it more difficult to coordinate efforts and hold the agencies responsible to the public.

Boards governing state agencies are not typically full-time; instead, they commonly meet quarterly. In most cases, a full-time board-appointed executive director oversees day-to-day agency operations. Boards usually make general policy decisions and leave the details to the executive director; however, some boards are much more active and involved (for example, the Texas Commission on Environmental Quality). In recent years, the governor's influence has increased through the ability to name a powerful executive commissioner to run two major agencies—the Health and Human Services Commission and the Texas Education Agency. Two important boards—the Railroad Commission of Texas (RRC) (which regulates the oil and gas industry) and the State Board of Education—are elected. Members of both tend to be quite active; however, the State Board of Education is limited by its lack of authority over the commissioner of education, who heads the Texas Education Agency and reports to the governor.

Some agencies were created in the Texas Constitution. Others were created by the legislature, either as directed by the state constitution or independent of it. As problems emerge that elected officials believe government must address, they look to existing state agencies or create new ones to provide solutions. Sometimes, citizen complaints force an agency's creation. For example, citizen outrage at rising utility rates resulted in the creation in 1975 of the Public Utilities Commission (PUC) to review and limit those rates. (Lobbying by special interest groups and the orientation of gubernatorial appointments over time, however, have changed the direction of the PUC's policies to again draw the ire of consumer advocates.) Lobbying by special interest groups to protect their own interests is also important in the creation of agencies. The most famous Texas case was lobbying by the oil and gas industry in the early 20th century to have the Railroad Commission create a system of regulation to reduce economic chaos in the fledgling industry.

The **sunset review process** is an attempt to keep state agencies efficient and responsive to current needs. Each biennium, a group of state agencies is examined by the Sunset Advisory Commission, which recommends to the legislature whether an agency should be abolished, merged, reorganized, or retained. It is the legislature that makes the final decision. At least once every 12 years, each of 130 state agencies must be evaluated. (Universities and courts are not subject to the process.) The Sunset Advisory Commission is composed of 10 legislators (five from each chamber) and two public members. The commission has a staff of 32 employees. In 2014–2015, it reviewed 21 agencies, including the giant Health and Human Services Commission and the University Interscholastic League (UIL, which regulates public school competitions such as athletics), along with lesser known agencies such as the State Office of Administrative Hearings.

A major problem with the sunset review process, according to critics, is that the legislature has little taste for the abolition or major restructuring of

sunset review process
During a cycle of 12 years, each state agency is studied at least once to see if it is needed and efficient, and then the legislature decides whether to abolish, merge, reorganize, or retain that agency.

large agencies. For example, the Sunset Advisory Commission's staff found that the mission and "byzantine" regulations of the Alcoholic Beverage Commission were hopelessly outdated, yet the legislature continued the commission with only minor changes. In the 2013 session, the legislature failed to pass the sunset bills making changes in the Texas Education Agency and the Railroad Commission but did pass bills continuing their existence. It is not surprising that regulated groups (often enjoying close relationships with friendly administrators and legislators) and state employees fighting for their jobs and turf (the agency's size, power, and responsibility) wage vigorous campaigns to preserve agencies and continue business as usual. From the Sunset Advisory Commission's authorization in 1977 through 2013, a total of 437 agencies were reviewed. Eighty-two percent were retained, 8 percent were abolished, and 10 percent were reorganized in major ways (such as combining two or more agencies). Of those agencies retained, some had changes, such as adding public members (people not from the regulated industry) on governing boards, improving procedures, or changing policies. According to the commission, from 1982 through 2013, the sunset process saved the state $946 million, or approximately $25 for every dollar spent in the sunset review process.[3]

State Employees and Public Policy

For most people, the face of state government is the governor, legislators, and other top officials. Certainly, these people are critical decision makers. However, most of the work of Texas state government (called **public administration**) is in the hands of people in agencies headed by elected officials and appointed boards. These **bureaucrats** (public employees), though often the subject of criticism or jokes about inefficiency and "red tape," are responsible for delivering governmental services to the state's residents. The public may see them in action as a clerk taking an application, a supervisor explaining why a request was turned down, or an inspector checking a nursing home.

The nature of bureaucracy is both its strength and its weakness. Large organizations, such as governments and corporations, need many employees doing specialized jobs with sufficient coordination to achieve the organization's goals (profits for a company, service for a government). That means employees must follow set rules and procedures so they can provide relatively uniform results. When a bureaucracy works well, it harnesses individual efforts to achieve the organization's goals. Along the way, however, "red tape" (the rules and procedures that bureaucrats must follow) slows the process and prevents employees from making decisions that go against the rules. State rules should mean the same in Dallas as in Muleshoe, but making decisions may seem slow, and "street level" bureaucrats may not have the authority to make adjustments for differences in local conditions. Thus, bureaucracies are necessary but sometimes frustrating.

Bureaucracy and Public Policy We often think of public administrators as simply implementing the laws passed by the legislature, but the truth is

public administration
The implementation of public policy by government employees.

bureaucrats
Public employees.

that they must make many decisions about situations not clearly foreseen in the law. Not surprisingly, their own views, their bosses' preferences, their agency's culture, and the lobbying they receive make a difference in how they apply laws passed by the legislature. Agencies also want to protect or expand their turf. Lobbyists understand the role of the bureaucracy in making public policy and work just as hard to influence agency decisions as they work to influence legislation.

Public agencies also must build good relations with state leaders (such as the governor), key legislators, and executive and legislative staff members because these people determine how much money and authority the agency receives. Dealing with the legislature often involves close cooperation between state agencies and lobbyists for groups that the agencies serve or regulate. For example, the Texas Good Roads/Transportation Association (mostly trucking companies and road contractors) and the Texas Department of Transportation have long worked closely, and relatively successfully, to lobby the legislature for more highway money.

In Texas, three factors are particularly important in determining agencies' success in achieving their policy goals: the vigor and vision of their leadership, their resources, and the extent to which elites influence implementation (called **elite access**). Many Texas agencies define their jobs narrowly and make decisions on narrow technical grounds, without considering the broader consequences of their actions. Texas environmental agencies have often taken this passive approach, which is one reason for Texas's many environmental problems. For example, a former Texas Commission on Environmental Quality commissioner complained:

> One [issue] that always floored me was the high mercury level in East Texas lakes.... People were eating fish contaminated with levels of mercury that could only be attributed to pollution from nearby coal-fired power plants. Yet when permit applications for new coal plants came before the board, the majority of commissioners refused to consider the impact on area lakes. They said water issues are not relevant to air permits.... The regulators tasked with cleaning up the lake, meanwhile, considered airborne emissions to be beyond their purview. So the issue never gets addressed.[4]

Other agency heads, however, take a proactive approach. Beginning in 1975, for example, three successive activist comptrollers transformed the Texas Comptroller's Office. It became a major player in Texas government, a more aggressive collector of state taxes, a problem solver for other agencies, and, under comptroller Carole Keeton Strayhorn, a focus of controversy. Elected agency heads, such as the comptroller and attorney general, have more clout (and perhaps incentive) to be proactive about their agency's job than do appointed agency heads.

Historically, Texas government agencies have had minimal funds to implement policy. Consider the example of nursing homes, which are big business today and mostly run for profit. A major problem is that almost two-thirds of nursing home residents depend on Medicaid to pay for their care. However,

elite access
The ability of the business elite to deal directly with high-ranking government administrators to avoid full compliance with regulations.

Medicaid rates, set by the state, have not gone up as fast as costs. For at least the last decade, Texas's rates have ranked 49th among the 50 states. Low rates make it increasingly difficult for nursing homes to make a profit. The less scrupulous companies maintain profits by cutting staff and services.[5]

Nursing home residents are generally weak and unable to leave if the service is bad or threatens their well-being. Therefore, residents depend heavily on government inspectors to ensure that they are treated well. Unfortunately, the number of nursing home inspectors in Texas has been like a roller coaster—sometimes up, sometimes down. When the number of inspectors relative to the number of residents decreases, the number of inspections decreases, and abuse tends to increase. Even when there are enough inspectors, connections of nursing home company executives and lobbyists to top agency administrators often ensure that infractions result in a slap on the wrist and a promise to do better. (This process is called elite access.)

One study noted that Texas ranked 10th worst among the states in serious deficiencies per home but in the middle for the amount of average fines. A 2011 Texas State Auditor's report found that the Department of Aging and Disability Services (DADS) "rarely terminates its contracts with nursing facilities that have a pattern of serious deficiencies. In fiscal year 2010, the Department recommended contract termination for 372 nursing facilities. However, it reconsidered or rescinded all but one of those terminations."[6] Over the years, both the Health and Human Services Commission and the state attorney general have been criticized for their lack of fervor in pursuing nursing home violations.

As these reports indicate, elite access and lack of resources make policy less effective and abuse more common in Texas nursing homes. (Also contributing is Texas's shortage of nurses, in major part because of too few state nursing programs.) At least since the 1990s, Texas has had more severe and repeated violations of federal patient care standards than most other states. A study by a nursing home advocacy group ranked Texas the worst nursing home state, failing on six of eight statistical measures. A study by the Commonwealth Fund, the SCAN foundation, and AARP ranked Texas's long-term care system 42nd on quality of care, due largely to poor nursing home ratings. Harm to residents can include neglect, physical and verbal abuse, injury, and death. For-profit nursing homes tend to do more serious and repeated harm to residents than do government and nonprofit homes.[7] Clearly, bureaucrats do greatly affect policy, and their decisions impact people's lives.

Number of State Employees

Governments are Texas's biggest employers. In 2012, the equivalent of 311,000 Texans drew full-time state paychecks. Put another way, Texas had 119 full-time state employees for every 10,000 citizens. Although this number sounds like a lot, Texas ranked 43rd of the 50 states in number of state employees per 10,000 citizens. Texas is following a national pattern. More populated states tend to have fewer employees relative to their population. Thus, as populations grow, most states, including Texas, are hiring proportionately fewer employees. From 1993 to 2012, the number of state employees declined relative to the population in both Texas and the nation. This decline is because of the economies of scale (meaning that as agencies grow, they may require more total employees but not as many relative to the population they serve; for example, as demand increases, many employees may be able to process more cases in the same amount of time). Another reason Texas ranks so low compared to other states is that Texas state government passes a great deal of responsibility to local governments. In 2012, Texas local governments employed 1,105,000 workers, or 424 per 10,000 residents, placing Texas seventh among the 50 states. Moreover, as with local governments in other states, local government employment in Texas is increasing faster than the state's population.

Competence, Pay, and Retention Although most public administrators do a good job, some are less effective than others. Many observers believe that bureaucratic competence improves with a civil service system along with good pay and benefits. In the first century of our nation, many thought that any fool could do a government job, and as a result, many fools worked in government. From local to national levels, government jobs were filled through the **patronage system**, also known as the spoils system. Government officials hired friends and supporters, with little regard for whether they were competent. The idea was that "to the victor belong the spoils." **Merit systems**, on the other hand, require officials to hire, promote, and fire government employees on the basis of objective criteria such as tests, education, experience, and performance. If a merit system works well, it tends to produce a competent bureaucracy. A merit system that provides too much protection, however, makes it difficult to fire the incompetent and gives little incentive for the competent to excel.

Texas has never had a merit system covering all state employees, and the partial state merit system was abolished in 1985. What replaced it was a highly centralized compensation and classification system covering most of the executive branch but not the judicial and legislative branches or higher education. The legislature sets salaries, wage scales, and other benefits. Individual agencies are free to develop their own systems for hiring, promotion, and firing (so long as they comply with federal standards, where applicable). Critics worried that the result would be greater turnover and lower competence. A survey of state human resource directors, however, indicates that agencies have developed more flexible personnel policies that provide some protection for most employees. Moreover, patronage appointments have not become a major problem in state administration. In the words of one observer, "It's not uncommon for state agencies to become repositories for campaign staff or former office-holders.... But there are no wholesale purges" when new officials are elected.[8]

In Texas, most employees (public and private) are "at will"—that is, they can be fired or can quit for good, bad, or no reason. The employment relationship is voluntary. Generally, only those under a contract or union agreement are not "at will" employees. The employer cannot fire a person for illegal reasons, such as race, retaliation for reporting illegal activity, or exercising civil liberties. For example, in a Virginia case, a federal appeals court held that a sheriff violated his employees' free speech rights by firing them for "liking" his opponent's campaign site on Facebook.

patronage system
Hiring friends and supporters of elected officials as government employees without regard to their abilities.

merit system
Hiring, promoting, and firing on the basis of objective criteria such as tests, degrees, experience, and performance.

In recent years, Texas state government employee turnover has been consistently high: 14 to 17 percent in fiscal years 2003–2010. By comparison, in fiscal year 2004, turnover was 9 percent for Texas's local governments and 10 percent for the nation. In that year, turnover cost the state government $345 million, according to the State Auditor's Office. Turnover is highest for workers in social services and criminal justice. Exit surveys (filled out by employees leaving state employment) reveal that the top three reasons for leaving state employment are retirement, desire for higher pay or better benefits, and desire for more satisfactory working conditions. Note in "How Do We Compare … in State Employee Compensation?" that state government salaries in Texas tend to be higher than those of our neighbors but lower than those of other large states. In 2009, the legislature increased the number of state positions with salaries that compare favorably with Texas's private sector from approximately 56 to 83 percent. The higher wages and the recent recession have contributed to holding down turnover.[9]

Other nonfinancial factors help attract state employees. Studies consistently show that large numbers of government employees have a strong sense of service and thus find being a public servant rewarding. Three "perks" also increase the attractiveness of public employment: paid vacations, state holidays, and sick leave.

Another incentive for employment can be equitable treatment. For many years, Texas state government has advertised itself as an "equal opportunity employer," and evidence indicates that it has been, albeit imperfectly. Table 10.1 shows that women make up more than one-half of

How Do We Compare…in State Employee Compensation?

Average Monthly Pay per Full-Time-Equivalent (FTE) Employee, 1993 and 2012

Most Populous U.S. States	1993	2012	U.S. States Bordering Texas	1993	2012
California	$3,644	$6,214	Arkansas	$2,261	$3,847
Florida	$2,266	$3,970	Louisiana	$2,242	$4,220
New York	$3,335	$5,601	New Mexico	$2,223	$4,356
Texas	**$2,426**	**$4,421**	Oklahoma	$1,897	$3,809

Source: Calculations by author based on data from U.S. Census Bureau, *2012 Census of Governments, and 2010 Annual Survey of Public Employment and Payroll,* revised January 2012, http://www.census.gov//govs/apes/historical_data_2010.html.

CRITICAL THINKING

What factors would account for the wide variations in pay shown in the table?

Table 10.1	Texas Minorities and Women in State Government Compared with the Total Civilian State Workforce (in percentage)*					
	African American		**Hispanic American**		**Female**	
Job Category	**Govt.**	**Total Workforce**	**Govt.**	**Total Workforce**	**Govt.**	**Total Workforce**
Official, administrator	10	9	15	20	51	39
Professional	11	11	16	17	56	59
Technical	15	14	24	21	56	42
Administrative support	19	14	31	31	87	66
Skilled craft	8	6	25	47	4	4
Service and maintenance	30	15	26	48	52	41
TOTALS	**17**	**12**	**21**	**33**	**57**	**46**

*State agencies workforce includes executive agencies and higher education for fiscal year 2012; statewide civilian workforce includes both private and public workers and is for calendar year 2011.

Note on interpretation: The first cell indicates that 10 percent of Texas government officials and administrators are African American; the next cell to the right shows that 9 percent of the officials and administrators in the state's total economy are African American.

Source: Compiled from Texas Workforce Commission, Civil Rights Division, January 11, 2013, *Equal Employment Opportunity and Minority Hiring Practices Report, Fiscal Years 2011–2012,* http://www.twc.state.tx.us/news/eeo-minority-hiring-2013.pdf.

CRITICAL THINKING

Where are there larger differences between the government and total workforce? Why?

✔ 10.1 Learning Check

1. True or False: Public administrators simply implement the laws passed by the legislature without making any changes.
2. What three factors are particularly important in determining how successful agencies are in achieving their policy goals?

Answers on p. 402.

state employees and are more likely to hold higher positions (official, administrator) in government than in the private economy. Women and African Americans make up a greater proportion of public than private employment, whereas Latino Texans are more likely to be employed in the private economy. In relation to their numbers in the state's population, Latinos are underrepresented in the top job categories in both the public and private arenas. Data on newly hired state employees indicate that these patterns will probably continue.

Education

LO10.2 Analyze the major challenges faced by the Texas education system.

After a legislative hearing on health problems along the Mexican border, Representative Debbie Riddle (R-Tomball) asked an *El Paso Times* reporter, "Where did this idea come from that everybody deserves free education, free medical care, free whatever? It comes from Moscow, from Russia. It comes straight out of the pit of hell."[10] While this phrasing is extreme, education and social services are controversial in Texas.

Public Schools

Texas's commitment to education began with its 1836 constitution, which required government-owned land to be set aside for establishing public schools and "a University of the first class." Later, framers of the 1876 constitution mandated an "efficient system of public free schools." What continues to perplex state policymakers is how to advance public schools' efficiency while seeking equality of funding for students in districts with varying amounts and values of taxable property. (See Chapter 13, "Finance and Fiscal Policy," for a discussion of school finance issues.) Texas schools are also faced with meeting the needs of a changing student body.

In the 21st century, students have come increasingly from families that are ethnic minorities or economically disadvantaged. According to Texas Education Agency data, in the 2012–2013 academic year, 51 percent of Texas students were Latino, 30 percent Anglo, 13 percent African American, 4 percent Asian, and 2 percent other (multiracial, Native American, and Pacific Islander). In addition, 60 percent of Texas students were economically disadvantaged (those eligible for free or reduced-price lunches). Historically, Texas has not served minority and less affluent students as well as it has Anglo and middle-class students. If this pattern continues, studies project that Texans' average income will decline, while the costs of welfare, prisons, and lost tax revenues will increase. Table 10.2 looks at how Texas's educational efforts and outcomes compare to those of other states.

One indication that the state can do better comes from *U.S. News and World Report*'s ranking of the nation's best high schools (based on criteria such as college readiness and geometry and reading proficiency). Of 1,492 Texas high schools examined, 357 made the 2014 list. Fourteen Texas high schools were ranked among the top 100 in the nation, including the nation's highest ranked school, Dallas's School for the Talented and Gifted. Three schools making the top 100 were located in Donna, Mercedes, and Brownsville, all in South Texas. Of the 14 high-achieving schools, 12 had a non-Anglo majority, and 8 had a majority of economically disadvantaged students.[11]

Today, more than 1,000 independent school districts and about 200 charter operators shoulder primary responsibility for delivery of educational services to 5 million students. (Chapter 3, "Local Governments," discusses the organization and politics of local school districts.) Although local school districts have somewhat more independence than in the past, they are part of a relatively centralized system in which state authorities substantially affect local decisions, from what is taught to how it is financed.

State Board of Education Oversight of Texas education is divided between the elected **State Board of Education (SBOE)** and the commissioner of education, who is appointed by the governor to run the Texas Education Agency. Over the years, the sometimes extreme ideological positions taken by many SBOE members have embarrassed the legislature and caused it to whittle away the board's authority. For several years, the board was even made appointive rather than elective. Today, the greater power over state

State Board of Education (SBOE)
A popularly elected 15-member body with limited authority over Texas's K–12 education system.

education is in the hands of the commissioner of education through control of the Texas Education Agency, but the SBOE remains important and highly controversial.

Among the board's most significant powers are curriculum approval for each subject and grade, textbook review for public schools, and management of investment of the Permanent School Fund.[12] Revenue from the $29 billion fund goes to public schools ($1.9 billion in the 2012–2013 biennium). Among other things, it pays for textbooks and guarantees more than $55 billion in bonds for school districts. (The guarantee allows districts to pay lower interest rates on their bonds.)

Representing districts with approximately equal population (1.8 million), the 15 elected SBOE members serve without salary for overlapping terms of four years. The governor appoints, with Senate confirmation, a sitting SBOE member as chair for a two-year term.

Deep ideological differences divide the board. The ideological split also follows partisan and ethnic lines. The socially conservative members tend to be Anglo Republicans, whereas the moderate and liberal members are commonly African American and Latino Democrats. Openly hostile debates on subjects such as textbook adoption and public criticism of possible conflicts of interest in the selection of investment managers and independent financial consultants for the Permanent School Fund have been common. The clashes have led some legislators to advocate reforming board procedures and others to call for elimination of the SBOE.

Probably the most contentious issue facing the SBOE is its periodic review of textbooks. Books for the foundation curriculum (English, math, science, and social studies) are reviewed at least once every eight years; other textbooks may have a longer cycle. The SBOE places a book on an accepted or rejected list. To be eligible for adoption, instructional materials must cover at least 50 percent of the elements of the Texas Essential Knowledge and Skills (TEKS) for its subject and grade level. Approved books must also meet the SBOE's physical specifications (for example, quality of binding and paper). Recently, the number of electronic books and instructional materials has been increasing, although traditional paper materials still predominate. Books must be free of factual errors. Critics charge that some board members have interpreted this requirement to mean that ideas conflicting with their own views are errors.

A long-standing source of conflict has been the challenge to the theory of evolution by supporters of creationism and intelligent design. The board's debate over the TEKS social studies standards in 2010 was particularly harsh and was described by some as a "culture war."[13] In 2014, in a rare display of compromise, the board responded to a request for Mexican American studies by putting out a request for materials for use in Mexican American studies and courses that highlight contributions from African Americans, Native Americans, and Asian Americans.

Individual school districts make their own textbook adoption decisions. Traditionally, the state paid 100 percent of the cost if local school districts used books on the approved lists but not more than 70 percent for books not

Table 10.2 Effort and Outcomes in Texas Education (Rank Among the 50 States)

Texas Public Schools		Texas Public Higher Education	
State and local expenditure per pupil	39th	Expenditure per full-time student	12th
Average teacher salary	33rd	Average faculty salary	27th
High school graduation rate	44th	Average tuition and fees at public universities	27th
Percent of students scoring Advanced or Proficient in math on NAEP* for 8th graders	8 states higher, 22 lower, 9 similar	Percent of population with a bachelor's degree or higher	30th
Percent of students scoring Advanced or Proficient in reading on NAEP* for 8th graders	29 states higher, 5 lower, 5 similar		
Percentage of high school students who play on a sports team	12th		

*National Assessment of Educational Progress, called the Nation's Report Card.

Source: Legislative Budget Board, *Texas Fact Book, 2012,* http://www.lbb.state.tx.us; Texas Higher Education Coordinating Board, *2012 Texas Public Higher Education Almanac,* http://www.thecb.state.tx.us; and National Center for Education Statistics, *National Assessment of Educational Progress, 2013,* http://www.nationsreportcard.gov/.

CRITICAL THINKING

Education is often said to be important to individuals, the state, and the nation. But how serious are we? Do the numbers above suggest that Texas is seeking or achieving the excellence in education that it could?

on the adoption lists. This rule made SBOE approval very important to the cash-strapped districts. However, in 2011, the legislature created an Instructional Materials Allotment that districts can use to buy books and materials regardless of SBOE approval. This change is reducing the significance of board textbook approval. The change is also of great importance to other states. Texas, California, and Florida purchase huge numbers of textbooks (more than 48 million textbooks a year in Texas). Thus, publishers cater to these markets. Other states have complained that their textbook options are limited to books published for one or more of the three big "state adoption" markets.

Texas Education Agency Which level of government should make educational policy? The local level, according to many Texans. Local officials know local needs, and most parents and citizens believe that they should have a say. However, many public officials and scholars who study education believe that the broader, more professional perspective found at the state or national level encourages higher educational standards. Texas responds to both of these views. Local school boards and superintendents run the schools, but almost all of their decisions are shaped by state and, to a much smaller extent, federal rules and procedures. The U.S. Department of Education provides some financial assistance, requires nondiscrimination in several areas (including race, gender, and disability), and, under the No Child Left Behind and Race to the Top programs, demands extensive testing.

In the Lone Star State, the **Texas Education Agency (TEA)**, headquartered in Austin, has fewer than 700 employees. Created by the legislature in 1949, the TEA today is headed by the **commissioner of education**, appointed by the governor to a four-year term with Senate confirmation. Under Governor Rick Perry, commissioners were closely connected and responsive to the governor. The TEA has the following powers:

- Oversees development of the statewide curriculum
- Accredits and rates schools (during 2012–2014, the rating system was under review)
- Monitors accreditation (whenever a local school district or school fails to meet state academic or financial standards for consecutive years, TEA has a range of sanctions, including changing its leaders and closure)
- Oversees the testing of elementary and secondary school students
- Serves as a fiscal agent for the distribution of state and federal funds (administers about three-fourths of the Permanent School Fund and supervises the Foundation School Program, which allocates state money to independent school districts)
- Monitors compliance with federal guidelines
- Approves new charter schools and supervises existing ones (moved from the SBOE by the legislature in 2013)
- Grants waivers to schools seeking charter status and exemptions from certain state regulations
- Manages the textbook adoption process, assisting the State Board of Education and individual districts
- Administers a data collection system on public school students, staff, and finances, and operates research and information programs
- Handles the administrative functions of the State Board for Educator Certification (placed under TEA in 2005 as part of the sunset review process)

Much of what the TEA does goes unnoticed by the general public, but some decisions receive considerable attention and have effects beyond education. The ratings of schools are advertised to draw home buyers into neighborhoods and subdivisions, and the decision to close a school or school district has profound effects on the community it serves. Thus, TEA has been cautious and taken less drastic steps before closing schools or districts. One of the few districts closed by TEA is the North Forest ISD in northeast Houston. After decades of warnings and interventions, the district was marked for closure in 2011, then given a reprieve, and finally combined with the Houston ISD in 2013.

Charter Schools In 1995, the legislature authorized the SBOE to issue charters to schools that would be less limited by TEA rules. There was hope that with greater flexibility, these schools could deal more effectively with at-risk

Texas Education Agency (TEA)
Administers the state's public school system of more than 1,200 school districts and charter schools.

commissioner of education
The official who heads the TEA.

students. Compared with students at traditional schools, charter school students are more economically disadvantaged, more are African American, slightly more are Latino, and fewer are Anglo. Although charter schools are public schools, they draw students from across district lines, use a variety of teaching strategies, and are exempt from many rules, such as state teacher certification requirements. Charters are granted to nonprofit corporations that, in turn, create a board to govern the school. The particular organization varies from school to school. Charter schools cannot impose taxes but can now issue bonds for new construction. They receive most of their funding from the state, with the rest coming from federal and private sources. Thus, most charter schools have less revenue per pupil than do traditional schools ($1,703 less per student in terms of ADA [Average Daily Attendance] in 2013–2014). In addition, charter schools have to spend part of the state money on facilities (an average of $829 per student).[14] In early 2014, Texas had 552 charter school campuses serving 179,000 students (which is less than 4 percent of all public school students). In 2013, the Texas legislature passed a major revision of charter school regulations, including raising the cap on the number of charters granted from 215 in 2013 to 305 in 2019. The legislation also made the commissioner of education responsible for initial charter approval.

The effectiveness of charter schools in meeting the needs of at-risk students is sharply debated. Some Texas charter schools have "compiled terrific records of propelling minority and low-income kids into college."[15] In the 2014 *U.S. News and World Report* listing of the nation's best high schools, three of the 10 best high schools in Texas were charter schools: Yes Prep North Central in Houston (28th in the nation), IDEA Academy and College Preparatory School in Donna (South Texas, 30th), and Kipp in Austin (63rd). Some other charter schools have been marked by corruption and academic failure. A study by Stanford University researchers found that results varied by state. In Texas, the researchers compared the progress of students of comparable background in charter and traditional schools and found that Latino and African American students tended to do better in traditional schools, whereas students in poverty (including all ethnicities) tended to fare slightly better in charter schools.[16]

Testing Educators and political leaders are sharply divided about how to assess student progress and determine graduation standards. Nevertheless, testing as a major assessment tool is now federal and state policy. Texas first mandated a standardized test in 1980 and began to rely heavily on testing in 1990. An essential component of the state testing program is the **Texas Essential Knowledge and Skills (TEKS)**, a core curriculum that sets out the knowledge students are expected to gain. This curriculum is required by the legislature and is approved by the State Board of Education.

The current testing program is the **State of Texas Assessment of Academic Readiness (STAAR)**. Mandated by the legislature in 2007 and 2009, STAAR went into effect in the spring of 2012. It included a number of key mandates:

- End-of-course examinations in the four high school core subject areas (math, science, English, and social studies).

Texas Essential Knowledge and Skills (TEKS)
A core curriculum (a set of courses and knowledge) setting out what students should learn.

State of Texas Assessment of Academic Readiness (STAAR)
A state program of end-of-course and other examinations begun in 2012.

- A requirement to pass both end-of-course tests and courses in order to graduate.
- For grades 3–8, new tests to assess reading and math for each level, as well as writing, science, and social studies for certain grade levels.
- The new tests and curriculum to be more closely tied to college readiness and preparation for the workplace.
- The new tests to be more rigorous and standards to be gradually raised through 2016.

In the first round of STAAR tests, statewide passing rates for freshmen varied from 55 percent for writing to 87 percent for biology. However, if the 2016 standards had been applied, a majority of students would have failed in each subject. Not surprisingly, the results were met with controversy.

Increasing the number of tests, how much they count, and their level of difficulty caused a strong backlash. In 2013 the legislature decreased the number of end-of-course tests to five and cut testing for high-performing students in grades 3–8. Although testing continues to be a major part of Texas's education policy, the testing program was in a period of transition in 2014, the outcome of which was not clear.[17]

One of the most controversial aspects of the testing programs is that test results are used to evaluate teachers, administrators, and schools. This practice is intended to increase "accountability"—that is, to hold teachers and administrators responsible for increasing student learning. Many educators object to having their pay—and perhaps their job—depend on student performance because student success is so much affected by students' backgrounds and home environments. The use of test results for accountability is continued under STAAR; however, the ratings were temporarily suspended in 2012 to allow development of a new system. For 2014, schools had to meet performance targets on each of four indexes (student achievement, student progress, disadvantaged students closing performance gaps, and postsecondary readiness). Schools were labeled: Met Standard, Met Alternative Standard (both are acceptable), or Improvement Required (unacceptable).

From its beginning, the statewide testing program has drawn cries of protest from many parents and educators. Social conservatives argue that the program tramples on local control of schools, whereas African American and Latino critics charge that the tests are discriminatory. Educational critics complain that "teaching to the test" raises scores on the test but causes neglect of other subjects and skills. Questions are also raised when the federal No Child Left Behind program sometimes produces substantially different evaluations of schools than does the Texas system (because they use different criteria). Supporters of testing argue that the policy holds schools responsible for increasing student learning. As proof, they point to the improved test scores of most groups of students since the program began.

Because test results are so important to both students and their schools, there has been controversy over how high standards should be. Some parents and advocates for disadvantaged students argue that standards are too high. Other critics argue that the previous test (Texas Assessment of Knowledge and Skills, or TAKS) suffered from grade inflation—that is, scores increased because of low standards, not student improvement.[18] In January 2012, education commissioner Robert Scott, who led much of the development of the use of tests as a policy tool, said that testing had become a "perversion." Over the previous decade, he argued, too much reliance had been placed on tests. He wanted test results to be "just one piece of the bottom line, and everything else that happens in a school year is factored into that equation."[19] In August 2012, following Scott's resignation, Governor Perry named former Railroad Commissioner Michael Williams to head the agency.

Some critics believe that national tests such as the National Assessment of Educational Progress (NAEP) are better measures because they are not "taught to." The NAEP shows mixed results for Texas. For example, between 1990 and 2013, math scores on the NAEP for Texas eighth graders improved significantly for each major ethnic group and economic level. The gap in scores between African American and Anglo eighth graders narrowed, as did the gap between the less and more affluent. However, the gap between Latinos and Anglos was not significantly different. On the other hand, on the eighth-grade reading test, the scores over the years were flat, and the score gap did not substantially improve for African American, Latino, or economically disadvantaged students.[20] Table 10.2 compares NAEP scores in·Texas to those of other states. The results are mixed.

Colleges and Universities

Texas has many colleges and universities—103 public and 44 private institutions of higher education serving more than 1.6 million students annually. There is also a growing number of for-profit and nonprofit online institutions. This large and growing number of institutions reflects several factors: the early tradition of locating colleges away from the "evils" of large cities, the demand of communities for schools to serve their needs, the desire to make college education accessible to students, and the growing popularity of online programs. Most potential Texas students live within commuting distance of a campus. Public institutions include 37 universities, nine health-related institutions, 50 community college districts (many with multiple campuses), three two-year state colleges, and four colleges of the Texas State Technical College System. All receive some state funding and, not surprisingly, state regulation.

Texas has three universities widely recognized as being among the prestigious tier-one national research universities: Rice University (private), the University of Texas at Austin (public), and Texas A&M University in College Station (public). All three are ranked by *U.S. News and World Report* among the top 100 national universities, along with three private schools, SMU, Baylor, and TCU. Three other Texas universities made the second 100: UT-Dallas at 142nd, Texas Tech (161st), and University of Houston (190th).[21]

Among public universities, UT-Austin and A&M-College Station are commonly referred to as the state's "flagship" universities; they have traditionally been the most prestigious academically and the most powerful politically.

Most observers believe that Texas needs more flagship universities to serve the increasing number of highly qualified students and to carry out the research necessary to attract new businesses and grow the economy. In 2009, a constitutional amendment gave access to funding through the Texas Research Incentive Program that encourages seven other universities to try to join the list of tier-one universities: the Universities of Texas at Arlington, Dallas, El Paso, and San Antonio; Texas Tech University; University of Houston; and University of North Texas. In 2012, Texas State University–San Marcos was added to the list of emerging research institutions by the Higher Education Coordinating Board. To achieve tier-one status, each school will have to raise more money and produce more research and successful doctoral graduates. There are no universally accepted criteria for tier-one status. Having met some of the common criteria, including a listing by the Carnegie Foundation, the University of Houston advertises itself as a tier-one university.

Most Texas universities are members of a system governed by a board of regents and managed by a chancellor and other administrators. The University of Texas and Texas A&M University have evolved into large systems with multiple campuses spread across the state. Four universities are not members of a system (for example, Texas Woman's University), and the rest are part of four other university systems (for example, the Texas State University System). The *Texas Almanac* lists Texas state and private schools and indicates their systems.[22]

Boards of Regents Texas's public university systems, public universities outside the systems, and the Texas State Technical College System are governed by boards of regents. Regents are appointed by the governor for six-year terms with Senate approval. A board makes general policy, selects each university's president, and provides general supervision of its universities. In the case of systems, the board usually selects a chancellor to handle administration and to provide executive leadership. The president of one of the universities may simultaneously serve as chancellor. Day-to-day operation of the universities is in the hands of the individual school's top officials (commonly the president and the academic vice president, though terminology varies). Governance of community colleges is by local boards, as discussed in Chapter 3, "Local Governments."

Texas Higher Education Coordinating Board The **Texas Higher Education Coordinating Board (THECB)** is not a super board of regents, but it does provide some semblance of statewide direction for all public (not private) community colleges and universities. In the 2013 sunset review process, the legislature significantly changed the agency's focus from regulation of public higher education to coordination. The sunset bill removed significant parts of the agency's authority, including the power to consolidate or eliminate low-producing academic programs and to approve capital projects. Other changes adopted during the sunset process aim to improve the effectiveness of the agency's coordination efforts and its relationship with higher education institutions through paying more attention to their input.

The nine members of the board receive no pay and are appointed by the governor to six-year terms with Senate approval. Gubernatorial power also

Texas Higher Education Coordinating Board (THECB)
An agency that provides some coordination for the state's public community colleges and universities.

extends to designating two board members as chair and vice chair, with neither appointment requiring Senate confirmation. Governors have substantial influence over higher education because they generally have a close relationship with the board. The commissioner of higher education, who runs the agency on a day-to-day basis and plays a significant role in higher education policy, is appointed (and can be removed) by the board.

Students in Action

Booze and Ballots: A Tale of Two Different Times

''We involved a lot of students in the public sphere for the first time, and some continued to be involved. We saved some lives and had a lot of fun.''

—Anonymous

Texas law allows citizens of almost any political entity to vote their area wet (the sale of alcohol is allowed) or dry (the sale of alcohol is prohibited). Walker County, home of Huntsville and Sam Houston State University (Sam), voted dry in 1914 and remained so until 1971. That year, Citizens for a Progressive Huntsville, composed mainly of Sam students and led by two students, circulated a petition for an election to permit alcohol sales within the city. Most of the 916 who signed the petition were thought to be Sam students or faculty. Townspeople were reluctant to sign the petition because others could see their names on the list. When the vote was held by secret ballot, however, all four voting boxes favored a wet community, which won with 62 percent of the votes. An estimated 800 students voted (out of 3,118 total votes).

In 2008, a Sam student ran unsuccessfully for the Huntsville City Council. Although it was not part of his public message, he told fellow students that his major concern was to extend bar hours from 12 midnight to 2 A.M. Even so, he couldn't get his own fraternity brothers out to the polls.

In 1971, in the wet issue, campus activists found a concern that could pull together students of widely varying views. Nearly 40 years later, the presidential election of 2008 produced a larger-than-usual student vote, but there was no local student-led movement to capitalize on the bar hours issue.

What's the Advice to Students?

''Sometimes it takes an issue like booze to get people interested enough to act on other, more important matters.''

Sources: Interviews and archives of the Walker County Clerk, City of Huntsville, and the Huntsville Public Library.

© Andresr/Shutterstock.com

Higher Education Issues Two sets of issues have challenged Texas higher education in recent years: funding and affirmative action. Funding and the sharp increase in tuition rates are discussed in Chapter 13, "Finance and Fiscal Policy," but we address affirmative action in the following paragraphs.

Improving the educational opportunities of Texas's ethnic minorities and the economically disadvantaged is an important but controversial issue, and one with a long history in the state. A 1946 denial of admission to the University of Texas law school on the grounds of race led to the "landmark [U.S. Supreme Court] case, *Sweatt* v. *Painter*, that helped break the back of racism in college admissions" throughout the country.[23] Texas's long history of official and private discrimination still has consequences today. Although many Latinos and African Americans have become middle class since the civil rights changes of the 1960s and 1970s, both groups remain overrepresented in the working class and the ranks of the poor. To overcome this problem, in 2000 the THECB adopted an ambitious program, called Closing the Gaps, to increase college enrollment and graduation rates for all groups by 2015. The program has been quite successful. By 2014, African American enrollment in higher education was on target to double the 2015 goals. Latinos had doubled their enrollment but were at 86 percent of target levels. Anglo participation was down slightly. In terms of graduation or receipt of certificates, both Latinos and African Americans were on track to reach the 2015 goals. Women were enrolled and graduating at significantly higher rates than men.[24]

A study financed by the Bill and Melinda Gates Foundation concluded that if the goals of Closing the Gaps were achieved, "When all public [state and local] and private costs are considered, the annual economic returns per $1 of expenditures by 2030 are estimated to be $24.15 in total spending, $9.60 in gross state product, and $6.01 in personal income."[25]

Texas colleges and universities commonly describe themselves as equal opportunity/affirmative action institutions. **Equal opportunity** simply means that the school takes care that its policies and actions do not produce prohibited discrimination, such as denying admission on the basis of race or sex. **Affirmative action** means that the institution takes positive steps to attract women and minorities. For most schools, this means such noncontroversial steps as making sure that the school catalog has pictures of all groups—Anglos and minorities, men and women—and recruiting in predominantly minority high schools, not just Anglo schools. However, some selective admission universities have actively considered race along with other factors in admissions and aid, and other schools have had scholarships for minorities. This side of affirmative action has created conflct.

Some Anglo applicants denied admission or scholarship benefits challenged these affirmative action programs in the courts. In the case of *University of California v. Bakke* (1978), the U.S. Supreme Court ruled that race could be considered as one factor, along with other criteria, to achieve diversity in higher education enrollment; however, setting aside a specific number of slots for one race was not acceptable.[26] Relying on the *Bakke* decision, the University of Texas Law School created separate admission

equal opportunity
Ensures that policies and actions do not discriminate on factors such as race, gender, ethnicity, religion, or national origin.

affirmative action
Takes positive steps to attract women and members of racial and ethnic minority groups; may include using race in admission or hiring decisions.

pools based on race and ethnicity, a practice the U.S. Fifth Circuit Court of Appeals declared unconstitutional in *Hopwood v. Texas* (1996).[27] In 2003, the U.S. Supreme Court issued two rulings on affirmative action. In the Michigan case of *Grutter v. Bollinger*, the court ruled that race could constitute one factor in an admissions policy designed to achieve student body diversity;[28] on the same day in another Michigan case, *Gratz v. Bollinger*, the court condemned the practice of giving a portion of the points needed for admission to every underrepresented minority applicant.[29]

After the *Hopwood* ruling, Texas schools looked for ways to maintain minority enrollment. In 1997, Texas legislators mandated the **top 10 percent rule**, which provided that the top 10 percent of the graduating class of every accredited public or private Texas high school could be admitted to tax-supported colleges and universities of their choosing, regardless of admission test scores. Thus, the students with the best grades at Texas's high schools, including those that are heavily minority, economically disadvantaged, or in small towns, can gain admission. The top 10 percent rule has helped all three groups. For students not admitted on the basis of class standing, the University of Texas at Austin used a "holistic review" of all academic and personal achievements, which might take into consideration family income, race, and ethnicity (with no specific weight and no quotas). The use of race in the holistic review produced another court challenge (*Fisher v. University of Texas*), which was heard before the U.S. Supreme Court during the fall of 2012.[30] The Court held that a university's use of race must meet a test known as "strict scrutiny," meaning that affirmative action will be constitutional only if it is "narrowly tailored." Courts can no longer simply accept a university's determination that it needs to consider race to have a diverse student body. Instead, courts themselves will need to confirm that the use of race is "necessary." The Supreme Court sent the case back to the Fifth Circuit Court, which in July 2014 upheld the university's use of race in admissions. An appeal was expected.

In fall 2010 through fall 2013, Anglos were a minority of incoming University of Texas at Austin (UT-Austin) freshmen—46 to 48 percent— although they remained a majority of the total student body until 2012. In 2003–2004, Texas A&M University announced that it would not use race in admissions decisions but would increase minority recruiting and provide more scholarships for first-generation, low-income students. (First-generation students are the first in their immediate family to attend college.) A&M also dropped preferences for "legacies" (relatives of alumni), who were predominantly Anglo. A&M's freshmen and transfers were 60 percent Anglo in fall 2013. All Texas institutions of higher education are under mandate from the Higher Education Coordinating Board to actively recruit and retain minority students under its Closing the Gaps initiative.

The top 10 percent rule is controversial, especially among applicants from competitive high schools denied admission to the state's flagship institutions— the University of Texas at Austin and Texas A&M University. In fall 2009, 86 percent of students offered admission to the University of Texas at Austin qualified by the top 10 percent rule, a situation that left little room for students to be admitted on the basis of high scores or other talents (such as music or

top 10 percent rule
Texas law gives automatic admission into any Texas public college or university to those graduating in the top 10 percent of their Texas high school class, with limitations for the University of Texas at Austin.

Point/Counterpoint

THE ISSUE To promote diversity in Texas colleges and universities without using race as an admission criterion, the state legislature in 1997 passed a law guaranteeing admission to any public college or university in the state to Texas students who graduate in the top 10 percent of their high school class. The law sought to promote greater geographic, socioeconomic, and racial/ethnic diversity. The law applies to all public colleges and universities in the state, but it has had its greatest effect on the two flagship universities, the University of Texas at Austin and Texas A&M University—prestigious schools with more qualified applicants than they can admit. The rule has increased minority representation at both schools but more so at the University of Texas. In 2009, the legislature capped automatic admission to the University of Texas at Austin at 75 percent through the 2015–2016 academic year.

Arguments For the Top 10 Percent Rule

1. The rule is doing what it was designed to do—increase diversity among highly qualified students.
2. Virtually all top *20* percent students from competitive high schools who choose UT-Austin or Texas A&M gain admission there.
3. The problem is not that Texas has too many students entering schools under automatic admission. Rather, there are too few flagship universities to accommodate the number of qualified students.

Arguments Against the Top 10 Percent Rule

1. The rule unfairly puts students who attend high schools with rigorous standards at a disadvantage. Thus, they are tempted to take lighter loads or attend less demanding high schools.
2. So many students are admitted under this one criterion that the universities have too little discretion, and students with other talents (such as music and the arts) are left out.
3. The rule is creating a brain drain. Many top students are leaving Texas to attend college in other states, where they often remain after graduation.

✔ **10.2 Learning Check**

1. Which two state government entities are most important for public schools?
2. What is the "top 10 percent rule" in Texas higher education?

Answers on p. 402.

leadership). According to the university's president, even football might have had to be abolished. In response, the 2009 legislature modified the rule so that UT-Austin would not have to admit more than 75 percent of its students on the basis of class standing. The class standing that the university chose for admission varied by year: top 8 percent for fall 2011 and 2013, 9 percent for 2012, and 7 percent for 2014 and 2015. The 75 percent cap is in effect only through the 2015 school year, unless it is renewed by the legislature.

Health and Human Services

★ **LO10.3** Describe the health and human services programs in Texas and discuss how efforts to address the needs of its citizens have been approached.

Most people think of Texas as a wealthy state, and indeed there are many wealthy Texans and a substantial middle class. Texas, however, also has long been among the states with the largest proportion of its population in poverty. Texas's 2011–2012 poverty rate was the sixth highest in the nation at 23 percent. From 1980 to 2012, Texas's poverty rate varied from 15 to 23 percent of the population. Poverty is particularly high for children and minorities, as can be seen in detail in Table 10.3. Poverty is defined in terms of family size and income. In 2014, for a family of three, poverty was an annual family income of less than $19,790; for a family of four, it was $23,790.

Even more Texans are low income, meaning they earn an income above the poverty line but insufficient income for many "extras," such as health insurance. (A common measure of low income is an income up to twice the poverty level. In 2010, more than one in five Texans fell into this category—that is, between 101 and 200 percent of the poverty level.)

Access to health care is a national issue that is even more acute in Texas. Although the state's major cities have outstanding medical centers, they are of little use to those who lack the resources to pay for care.[31] For at least the last decade, studies comparing health care in the various states consistently rank Texas near the bottom. For example, from 2007 to 2014, the Commonwealth Fund, a well-respected foundation, did five state-by-state comparisons of various aspects of health system performance. All ranked Texas in the bottom quarter of the states. In 2014, the Lone Star State ranked 44th.[32] A key factor in access to health care is health insurance. Texas has led the nation in the proportion of people without health insurance since at least 1988. About one in four Texans has no health insurance, as compared with one in six in the nation. Texas also leads in the proportion of uninsured children.

The Patient Protection and Affordable Care Act (popularly known as ACA or Obamacare), passed by Congress in 2010, is aimed at improving this situation. Some provisions of the act are widely supported: for example,

Table 10.3 Who's in Poverty in Texas and the United States? (2011–2012)			
	Texas		**U.S.**
	Number (million)	**%**	**%**
Individuals	5.8	23	20
Anglos	1.3	12	13
Hispanics	3.4	33	33
African Americans	0.9	29	35
Children 0–18	2.2	30	27
Age 65 and older	0.4	16	13

Source: Kaiser Family Foundation, "State Health Facts," 2014, http://kff.org/other/state-indicator/poverty-rate-by-raceethnicity/. Based on U.S. Census Bureau, March 2012 and 2013 Current Population Surveys.

CRITICAL THINKING

Why is poverty so substantial and persistent in Texas?

young adults up to age 26 can be on their parents' insurance, preexisting conditions are covered in many cases, and caps on lifetime benefits have been lifted.

The heart of the ACA is an attempt to provide health insurance to almost all Americans: requiring those who can afford it to purchase health insurance and expanding Medicaid to cover those who cannot afford to buy insurance on their own. Both provisions have met with controversy.

For individuals who do not already have a health insurance plan that meets ACA requirements, states can provide insurance "exchanges" or "marketplaces" to assist them. For states such as Texas that opt not to have an exchange, the federal government's exchange provides the assistance. Major technical difficulties in the rollout of the federal exchange provoked a storm of criticism. However, the problems were fixed, and most people met the 2014 enrollment deadline.

The second major effort of the ACA was to expand the coverage of Medicaid, the joint federal-state program to provide medical care to the poor. In June 2012, the U.S. Supreme Court upheld most of the Affordable Care Act in a suit brought by Texas and 25 other states (*National Federation of Independent Business v. Sebelius*, 132 S.Ct. 2566 [2012]). However, very importantly, the court held that the national government could not use the threat to cut existing Medicaid funds to coerce states into expanding Medicaid coverage. This allowed Texas and other states to opt out of the Medicaid expansion. (There is more discussion of Medicaid and the consequences of Texas not expanding its coverage in the Health and Mental Health Services section that follows.)

Since the Great Depression of the 1930s, state and national governments have gradually increased efforts to address the needs of the poor, the elderly, and those who cannot afford adequate medical care. In the 20th century, social welfare became an important part of the federal relationship (see Chapter 2, "Federalism and the Texas Constitution," and Chapter 3, "Local Governments"). Over time, the national government has taken responsibility for relatively popular social welfare programs, such as Social Security, Medicare, and aid to the blind and disabled. The states, on the other hand, have responsibility for less popular welfare programs that have less effective lobbying behind them, such as Medicaid, Supplemental Nutrition Assistance Program (SNAP, formerly food stamps), and Temporary Assistance for Needy Families (TANF). The federal government pays a significant part of the cost of state social welfare programs, but within federal guidelines the states administer them, make eligibility rules, and pay part of the tab.

Health and human services programs are at a disadvantage in Texas for two reasons. First, the state's political culture values individualism and self-reliance; thus, anything suggesting welfare is difficult to fund at more than a minimal level. In addition, the neediest Texans lack the organization and resources to compete with the special interest groups representing the business elite and the middle class. Thus, the Lone Star State provides assistance for millions of needy Texans, but at relatively low benefit levels. And many people are left out.

The Texas Health and Human Services Commission (HHSC) coordinates social service policy. Sweeping changes were launched in 2003 when the 78th Legislature consolidated functions of 12 social service agencies under the **executive commissioner of the Health and Human Services Commission**. This legislation also began a process of privatizing service delivery, creating more administrative barriers to services, and slowing the growth of expenditures.

The executive commissioner of the HHSC is appointed by the governor for a two-year term and confirmed by the Senate. This official controls the agency directly and is not under the direction of a board; instead, executive commissioners tend to respond to the governor. The executive commissioner appoints, with the approval of the governor, commissioners to head the four departments of the HHSC: Department of State Health Services, Department of Aging and Disability Services, Department of Assistive and Rehabilitative Services, and Department of Family and Protective Services. See Figure 10.1 for the commission's organization chart and major tasks of the departments. The HHSC itself handles centralized administrative support services, develops policies, and makes rules for its agencies. In addition, the commission determines eligibility for TANF, SNAP, the Children's Health Insurance Program (CHIP), Medicaid, and long-term care services. For the 2014–2015 biennium, the legislature authorized 58,000 employees for HHSC and its four departments.

The legislature not only consolidated agencies under HHSC in 2003, but it also mandated a major change in the state's approach to social services—**privatization**. The belief is that private contractors can provide public services more cheaply and efficiently than can government. Under the legislative mandate, local social services offices and caseworkers were replaced with call centers operated by private contractors. Applicants for social services were encouraged to use the telephone and Internet to establish eligibility for most social services. A similar but much smaller privatized system had worked reasonably well in 2000. However, this new, larger system performed poorly. After 2003, the number of children covered by insurance dropped sharply, and eligible people faced long waits and lost paperwork. In response to these problems, the offshore private contractor was replaced, many state employees were rehired, and attempts were made to bring children back into the system. Yet in 2010, a federal official complained about Texas's "five-year slide" to last place among the states in the speed and accuracy of handling food stamp applications after privatization. Promised savings and better service have yet to appear.

State officials say the problem is that privatization is still a work in progress and that there is no turning back. Critics argue that profit incentives for contractors and social services for the public are inherently in conflict.[33] Officials have continued to promote privatization, but more gradually, with the result that some Texas social services are a mixture of public and private administration. Private contractors are both for-profit and nonprofit. An example is foster care. With too little money, too few caseworkers, and inadequate accountability, foster care in Texas has performed poorly under both public and privatized management. Child welfare advocates see the current

Executive commissioner of the Health and Human Services Commission
Appointed by the governor with Senate approval, the executive commissioner administers the HHSC, develops policies, makes rules, and appoints (with approval by the governor) commissioners to head the commission's four departments.

Privatization
Transfer of government services or assets to the private sector. Commonly, assets are sold and services contracted out.

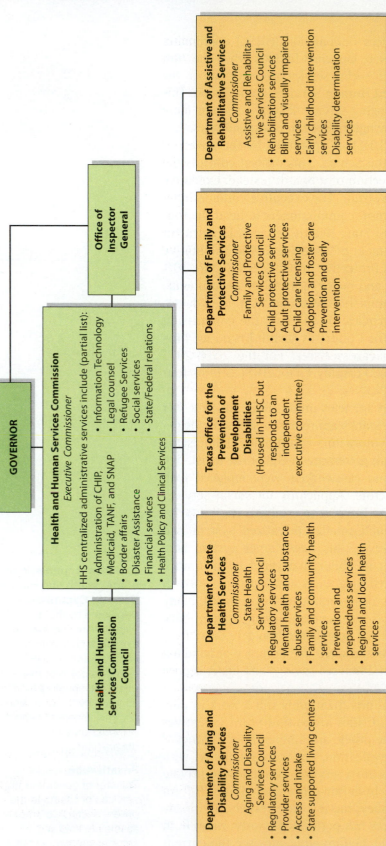

Figure 10.1   The Consolidated Texas Health and Human Services System

Based on Texas Health and Human Services Commission, March 2014, http://www.hhsc.state.tx.us/about_hhsc/index.shtml.

CRITICAL THINKING

Draw on this organization chart and the discussion of the commissioner in the text. What are the strengths and weaknesses of the executive commissioner in shaping Texas health and human services policy?

heavily privatized plan stretching limited resources even thinner and adding a layer of private bureaucracy.[34]

Human Services

The Health and Human Services Commission administers a variety of programs, three of which have long received a great deal of attention and debate: Temporary Assistance for Needy Families, Supplemental Nutritional Assistance Program, and Medicaid. All three are administered by the executive commissioner within federal guidelines and are funded by the federal government and to a lesser extent by the state. In the words of budget analyst Eva DeLuna Castro, eligibility for these and other "public assistance programs in Texas is very restrictive compared to other states, the benefits are lower, and health benefits for poor adults are more limited. As a result, a smaller share of the poor in Texas receives any public assistance."[35] In addition, all three programs suffered financially from the budget cutbacks carried out by the 2011 legislature and only partially recovered in 2013.

The executive commissioner has direct responsibility for the **Temporary Assistance for Needy Families (TANF)** program. In Texas, this program provides limited support for extremely poor families. For a family of three in 2014, the poverty level was $19,790. To receive TANF that year, a family of one parent and two children could earn no more than $2,256 a year (less than 12 percent of the poverty level). The family received $277 a month. Along with other requirements, caretakers must be U.S. citizens or legal residents and agree to work or to enroll in a job training program. According to HHSC, the "most common" TANF caretaker is a woman about 30 years old with one or two children younger than age 11. She is unemployed, has no other income, and receives a TANF grant of $277 or less per month for fewer than 12 months. In addition to the small amount of cash provided by TANF, recipients may receive benefits from other programs, such as SNAP and Medicaid.

A second federal-state program administered by the executive commissioner is the **Supplemental Nutritional Assistance Program (SNAP)**, formerly called food stamps. It makes food available to elderly or disabled people, families, and single adults who qualify because of low income of up to 130 percent of the poverty level. Approximately 80 percent of those who benefit from SNAP receive no TANF support. Benefits vary, depending on income and the number of people in a household. In 2014, for example, a qualified Texas household composed of three people could earn up to $2,686 a month and obtain groceries costing up to $497 each month. To reduce fraud, the program replaced paper stamps used for purchases with a plastic Lone Star Card, which functions like a debit card.[36]

To assist in connecting eligible Texans to service providers, several private groups use social media sites such as Twitter and Facebook, as well as blogs. A Fighting Chance for Texas Families provides information about resources and encourages users to share their stories of what it takes to survive in poverty in Texas.

Temporary Assistance for Needy Families (TANF)
Provides financial assistance to the poor in an attempt to help them move from welfare to the workforce.

Supplemental Nutritional Assistance Program (SNAP)
Joint federal-state program administered by the state to provide food to low-income people.

Health and Mental Health Services

The third major federal-state program administered by the executive commissioner is **Medicaid**. Part of President Lyndon B. Johnson's Great Society initiatives in the 1960s, Medicaid is designed to provide medical care for persons whose income falls below the poverty line. Resources not counted against the poverty level limit are a home, personal possessions, and a low-value motor vehicle. Not to be confused with Medicaid is **Medicare**, another Great Society initiative. A federal program providing medical assistance to qualifying applicants age 65 and older, Medicare is administered by the U.S. Department of Health and Human Services without use of state funds. Because Medicaid is considered welfare and serves the poor, it has much less political clout than Medicare, which serves a more middle-class clientele. Medicaid has much more difficulty gaining funding, and benefits for clients and reimbursements for service providers tend to be lower. Benefits are so low that the majority of Texas doctors now refuse new Medicaid patients, and nursing homes have trouble covering their costs.

Under the 2010 national Affordable Care Act, states were required to expand Medicaid coverage to virtually all nonelderly adults and children earning up to 133 percent of the poverty line. States that did not provide the expanded coverage risked losing their existing federal Medicaid funds. However, the U.S. Supreme Court held that the federal government could not use the threat of withholding the existing funding to coerce expansion of Medicaid for adults. Thus, states have the option of participating in the expansion or keeping their existing adult programs. Coverage of children must be expanded. Editorials in most of Texas's major newspapers supported the expansion; however, in July 2012, Governor Perry informed federal authorities that Texas would not participate in the expansion of Medicaid. As of June 2014, some 26 states were implementing the Medicaid expansion, 19 (including Texas) were not, and 5 were still debating it. For those states participating, the federal government pays the entire cost of expansion for the first three years and at least 90 percent beyond that. Payments for primary care physicians are also raised to Medicare levels.

Without the expansion of Medicaid, Texas remains a national leader in number of uninsured. About 1 million Texans were affected by the decision. Several studies have examined the consequences of the decision and concluded that it will lead to preventable deaths. In Texas, one projection is that 9,000 lives a year could be lost.[37]

The Department of State Health Services (DSHS) performs a wide variety of functions, including public health planning and enforcement of state health laws. As with public assistance, state health policies are closely tied to several federal programs. One example is the Special Supplemental Nutrition Program for Women, Infants, and Children (WIC), a delivery system for healthy foods, nutritional counseling, and health care screening.

In September 2014, Texas's first Ebola case received great publicity and posed a challenge to the DSHS, which educates Texans on infectious diseases. An existing problem in Texas is acquired immunodeficiency syndrome (AIDS) caused by the human immunodeficiency virus (HIV). It is commonly

Medicaid
Funded in large part by federal grants and in part by state appropriations, Medicaid is administered by the state. It provides medical care for persons whose incomes fall below the poverty line.

Medicare
Funded entirely by the federal government and administered by the U.S. Department of Health and Human Services, Medicare provides medical assistance to qualified applicants age 65 and older.

transmitted by sexual contact (both homosexual and heterosexual) and contaminated needles used by drug abusers. AIDS is an international epidemic but more stable in Texas. According to the department's comprehensive 2010 report on AIDS/HIV:

> Since 2004, the number of persons living with HIV (PLWH) in Texas has increased steadily, by about 5 percent each year.... In Texas, the number of new HIV diagnoses and deaths among PLWH has remained largely stable in the past seven years, averaging around 4,180 new diagnoses and 1,470 deaths per year.... The increase ... in PLWH over time reflects continued survival due to better treatment, not an increase in new diagnoses. In an environment of increasing numbers of PLWH, the fact that new diagnoses have remained level speaks to successful prevention and treatment efforts, but more must be done in order to actually reduce the number of new HIV diagnoses.[38]

In 2012, among the 73,000 Texans living with HIV, 78 percent were male, 29 percent Anglo, 38 percent African American, and 29 percent Latino. HIV is the state's seventh leading cause of death among Texans ages 25–44. (For comparison, first is accidents, second is suicide, and sixth is homicide).[39]

A related problem is the continuing increase in the number of cases of sexually transmitted diseases (STDs) other than HIV/AIDS reported in Texas each year. This number reached almost 158,000 in 2012. Persons between 15 and 24 years of age account for the majority of this total. The actual STD numbers are probably higher, because not all STDs must be reported, and many reportable cases are unreported.

The Texas departments of State Health Services and Aging and Disability Services provide public mental health programs for persons unable to afford private therapy for emotional problems. However, Texas's per capita funding for mental health programs has ranked 47th to 50th among the 50 states for years (in fiscal year 2010, $39 per capita, compared to the national average of $121).[40] As a result, the state serves only a fraction of those needing assistance. For example, in Harris County (Houston) in 2013, 8,500 adults received care out of approximately 180,000 who needed care. Thousands are on waiting lists, and an unknown number of the mentally ill are detained in jails and prisons or living on the streets.[41]

Like most states, Texas relies heavily on community outpatient services for mental health treatment, which is the cheaper and medically preferred option for most patients. The number of patients receiving community mental health services has been relatively flat, fluctuating from 62,000 to 68,000 annually during the 2007–2013 period. Approximately 2,400 patients are in state mental health hospitals, and 4,000 are in state-supported living centers. In addition to a long-standing debate about whether these large facilities are appropriate for all patients, reports of abuse in the living centers brought an agreement in 2009 between the U.S. Justice Department and Texas to increase the number of workers and federal inspections. Since then, the number of workers has increased, but the failure to increase wages for direct care workers has contributed to continuing high rates of neglect.

Employment

Texas's state employment services cut across three areas of policy: human services, education, and economic development. The **Texas Workforce Commission (TWC)** receives appropriations from the legislature in the category of business and economic development, which probably works to its advantage because of the legislature's more friendly view of business and development. The agency serves both employers and workers. For employers, TWC offers recruiting, retention, training and retraining, outplacement services, and information on labor law and labor market statistics. For job seekers, TWC offers career development information, job search resources, training programs, and unemployment benefits. As part of this effort, the TWC matches unemployed workers with employers offering jobs. The TWC also collects an employee payroll tax paid by employers, which funds weekly benefit payments to unemployed workers covered by the Texas Unemployment Compensation Act. The amount paid to the unemployed depends on wages earned in an earlier quarter (three months). In 2014, the maximum weekly compensation was $454, and the minimum was $63. In the same year, the average tax rate paid by employers was 1.66 percent of the first $9,000 of each employee's salary. The Great Recession increased unemployment and claims, although Texas unemployment remained below the national average.

The TWC is directed by three salaried commissioners appointed by the governor, with consent of the Senate, for overlapping six-year terms. One member represents employers, one represents labor, and one is intended to represent the general public.

Since 1913, Texas has had a **workers' compensation** program to help workers injured on the job receive medical care and recover some lost wages. The way the system works is that employers purchase insurance from private companies that covers expenses of those injured or sickened at work. By the mid-1980s, the program had become highly controversial, with charges of low benefits for injured workers and high insurance premiums for employers. A two-year lobbying and legislative struggle produced a major modification of the program in 1989. A coalition of employers and insurance companies defeated a coalition of plaintiffs' lawyers and labor unions. The process for injured workers became more administrative and less judicial. Workers were less likely to win and more likely to receive lower benefits. The major source of the problem, Texas's dangerous workplaces, received scant improvement.

The workers' compensation system is governed by the Division of Workers' Compensation (DWC) of the Texas Department of Insurance. It is headed by the Commissioner of Workers' Compensation, who is appointed by the governor for a two-year term. Since creation of the DWC in 2005, lawyers who represent injured workers have complained that the agency is too close to the insurance companies; and the commissioner testified in 2014 that workers are losing an increasing proportion of disputes in the agency's court-like system that resolves disputes. The number of claims by workers and insurance rates charged employers have declined.

Texas Workforce Commission (TWC)
A state agency headed by three salaried commissioners that oversees job training and unemployment compensation programs.

workers' compensation
A system of insurance that pays benefits to workers injured by their work.

Texas is the only state in the union that does not require employers to provide workers' compensation insurance. Failure to provide the insurance puts the employer at risk for expensive court suits, which are generally forbidden by law if the employer provides workers' compensation insurance. About two-thirds of Texas employers provide the insurance.

Economic and Environmental Policies

LO10.4 Compare the roles of government in generating economic development while maintaining a safe and clean environment for the state's residents.

Education, health, and human services receive three-fourths of Texas state government expenditure. Business, economic development, and regulation together account for 14 percent of the budget, but they have a substantial and often direct effect on the lives of Texans. The state tries to generate economic development that, when successful, produces jobs and profits. Regulations affect the prices we pay for electricity and insurance, as well as the quality of the air we breathe. Historically, regulation was supported as a means to protect the individual, the weak, and the general public against the economically powerful and the special interests. In practice, this protection has been difficult to achieve because the benefits of regulation tend to be diffuse and the costs specific. For example, cleaner air benefits a broad range of the public, but few can put a dollar amount on their own benefit. On the other hand, companies that must pay to clean up their air emissions see a specific (and sometimes large) cost. Thus, they may perceive more incentive to spend money to fight regulation than do those who benefit from it. Moreover, businesses are better organized and have more connections to policymakers than does the public. For most of Texas's history, economic and regulatory policies have tilted toward business. The Republican ascendancy in recent years has enhanced this tendency, although consumer, environmental, and labor advocates are increasingly heard.

Economic Regulatory Policy

Have you ever complained about a high telephone bill, a big automobile insurance premium, or the cost of a license to practice a trade or profession for which you have been trained? Welcome to the Lone Star State's regulatory politics. For businesses seeking to boost profits or professional groups trying to strengthen their licensing requirements, obtaining or avoiding changes in regulations can be costly but rewarding. Less organized consumers and workers often believe they are left to pick up the tab for higher bills and fees and, on occasion, inferior service.

Traditionally, government regulation focused on prohibitions or requiring certain procedures to be followed. However, in the last decade, Texas regulators have increasingly sought to use economic competition to bring

10.3 Learning Check

1. Why are health and human services programs at a disadvantage in Texas?
2. Which program is better funded, Medicaid or Medicare?

Answers on p. 402.

down costs to consumers and prevent harmful practices. This policy has produced great controversy. Although Texans tend to believe strongly in the merits of competition in much of the economy, there is not as much agreement that competition works for utilities and in protection of the environment. The reader will see this conflict played out across most of the areas of this section.

Business Regulation The Railroad Commission and the Public Utility Commission are among Texas's most publicized agencies. The former regulates the oil and gas industry, which is experiencing a spectacular resurgence in its influence on the Texas economy, and the latter affects the telephone and electric power bills paid by millions of Texans.

The **Railroad Commission of Texas (RRC)** functions in several capacities, none of which has anything to do with railroads. Established in 1891 to regulate the railroads, it is the oldest regulatory agency in the state. However, in 2005, it lost its last responsibilities for railroads. Today, the commission focuses primarily on the oil and gas industry. It grants permits for drilling oil and gas wells, regulates natural gas rates in rural areas, hears appeals of municipally set gas rates for residential and business customers, tries to prevent waste of petroleum resources, regulates pipeline safety, and oversees the plugging of depleted or abandoned oil and gas wells. The RRC also has jurisdiction over surface coal mining and uranium exploration.

Textbooks often cite the RRC as the classic case of "agency capture," a situation in which the regulated industry exerts excessive influence over the agency intended to regulate it. Despite legislation requiring protection of consumers and the environment, the RRC has long seen its major function as maintaining the profitability of the state's oil and gas industry. The industry's earlier decline and the state's greater economic diversity reduced industry dominance somewhat. However, the resurgence of the industry is enhancing its political power and influence. Some of the consequences of the oil boom are discussed in the reading at the end of this chapter.

Under law, the three commissioners are elected to six-year terms with one commissioner seeking election every two years. However, the RRC is often considered a way station in the career of rising politicians. Only a few stay six years, so many commissioners take office as a result of gubernatorial appointment. A high proportion come to office with much of their career in the oil and gas industry. The commissioners are full-time and earn $137,500 a year.

In 2009–2010, drilling for natural gas in the Barnett Shale put more than 1,000 wells within Fort Worth's city limits, creating a variety of public concerns—environmental pollution, pipeline rights-of-way, drilling near homes, and even earthquakes. The outcry contributed to the defeat of RRC Chair Victor Carrillo in the 2010 Republican primary—an unusual occurrence. (Carrillo complained that his Spanish surname also played a role in his defeat.)

A related controversy facing the RRC is hydraulic fracturing (generally called fracking). This process involves injecting large amounts of water,

Railroad Commission of Texas (RRC)
A popularly elected three-member commission primarily engaged in regulating natural gas and petroleum production.

sand, and chemicals underground at high pressure to break up shale formations, allowing oil or gas to flow up the wellbore. Fracking and horizontal drilling have been key to the rebirth of the oil and gas industry in the state and nation. However, there are major questions about fracking's effect on the environment, including the safety of the underground water supply and the disposal of contaminated water that returns to the surface. The topic is debated in the Point/Counterpoint feature of Chapter 1.

Given the state's growing water shortage, this additional major use for water is causing concern. Another problem arising from the growing exploration and production is the damage to roads in the area of the Eagle Ford Shale (in South Texas). Given the tendency of state agencies to define their role narrowly, neither problem may be readily addressed. Fracking has had at least two major long-term consequences. First, it has extended the use of fossil fuels for decades. Second, the availability of relatively cheap and clean natural gas has reduced the carbon emissions created by much dirtier coal but also made it more difficult for clean, renewable sources of energy such as wind and solar to compete.[42]

Regulation of Public Utilities State regulation of Texas's utility companies did not begin until 1975 with the creation of the **Public Utility Commission of Texas (PUC)**. Its three members are appointed by the governor, with Senate approval, to overlapping six-year terms. They work full-time and earn $150,000 a year.

The PUC's regulatory authority is limited by both national and state policies. Its two major responsibilities are local phone service and electric utilities. It does not regulate long distance calling, wireless, or cable TV (regulated by the Federal Communications Commission [FCC]); natural gas utilities (Railroad Commission); water utilities (Texas Commission on Environmental Quality [TCEQ]); or municipal electric utilities (locally regulated).

Today, PUC operations follow recent trends in regulatory policies nationwide. Traditionally, the rates of utility companies, such as those providing electricity and water, were set or approved by government regulators. (Prices were said to be *regulated*.) Since the early 2000s, Texas regulators have embraced **deregulation**, under which business practices (such as setting rates) formerly strongly influenced by government rules are governed more by market conditions. The belief is that competition will produce fair prices and protect the public interest.

During the past decade, the Texas legislature has caused the PUC to shift from setting rates that telephone and electric power companies may charge to a policy of deregulation. Allowing consumers to choose their telephone service supplier was expected to result in reasonable telephone bills and reliable service from companies that must compete for customers. With the growth of competition from cell phones, this system seems to work.

According to critics, however, deregulation of most Texas electricity suppliers has raised rates in comparison to those of other states—a reversal of two decades of lower-than-average rates under state regulation. In 2013, Texas rates ranked in the middle of the 50 states. Texans in the deregulated

Public Utility Commission of Texas (PUC)
A three-member appointed body with regulatory power over electric and telephone companies.

deregulation
The elimination of government restrictions to allow free market competition to determine or limit the actions of individuals and corporations.

390 Chapter 10 ★ Public Policy and Administration

sector paid more for electricity than Texas consumers served by regulated entities (such as municipal power companies in, for example, Austin and San Antonio).[43] In 2012–2014, the PUC faced major concerns over the reliability of the flow of electricity. To avoid blackouts during periods of high usage, such as the summer air conditioning season, the commission considered raising rates substantially to encourage the construction of additional generating plants.[44] Critics saw this as one more failure of deregulation.

Insurance Regulation The **commissioner of insurance** heads the Texas Department of Insurance (TDI), which regulates to some degree the $50 billion insurance industry in the Lone Star State. The commissioner is appointed by the governor for a two-year term and earns $164,000 a year. The Office of Public Insurance Counsel represents consumers in rate disputes. The TDI deals with the wide range of insurance, including auto, health, home, life, wind, flood, and workers' compensation. It has a role in setting insurance rates, licenses agents and adjustors, and houses the state fire marshal.

At the beginning of 2003, Texans who owned homes and automobiles paid the highest insurance rates in the country. Rates were unregulated and rising rapidly. In response to the public outcry, the 2003 legislature gave the commissioner of insurance authority to regulate all home insurers doing business in Texas. The following year, Texas began a largely deregulated "file and use" system for auto and homeowners insurance. Insurers set their own rates, but the commissioner of insurance is authorized to order reductions and refunds if rates are determined to be excessive. Advocates of this system expected it to produce reasonable rates by promoting competition among insurance companies; however, by 2014, Texas homeowner insurance rates were third highest in the nation, more than $300 above the national average. In the more competitive car insurance industry, during the period 2010 to 2014, Texas fluctuated between the middle of the 50 states in average cost and being significantly higher.[45]

Because of natural disasters such as hurricanes, hail, and mold, insurance rates in Texas tend to be high. But are they higher than necessary, as consumer groups argue? The "loss ratio," which is considered the best measure of insurance company profitability, is what a company pays in benefits as a percentage of the premium money it receives. From 1992 to 2009, the average loss ratio for Texas insurance companies was 68 percent—greater than the 60 percent the industry prefers and lower than consumer advocates desire.[46]

Business Promotion

Some cynical observers contend that the business of Texas government is business. Others argue that boosting business strengthens the economy and creates jobs that benefit the lives of all Texans. Certainly, the state's political culture and the strength of business lobbyists make government highly

commissioner of insurance
Appointed by the governor, the commissioner heads the Texas Department of Insurance, which is responsible for ensuring the industry's financial soundness, protecting policyholders, and overseeing insurance rates.

responsive to business. In 2012, Texas was ranked third among the 50 states in "policy environment" for entrepreneurship, behind South Dakota and Nevada and far ahead of neighboring states.[47] State agencies in at least three policy areas—transportation, tourism, and licensing—are administered in ways that promote and protect economic interests.

Highways The **Texas Department of Transportation (TxDOT)** deals with a wide range of transportation issues. Its major focus is the planning, design, construction, and maintenance of the state's highways and bridges (currently 80,000 miles). However, it is also involved, though to a much lesser degree, with aviation, maritime, rail, public transportation, safety, and toll roads. The agency is headed by a five-member commission appointed by the governor, with Senate concurrence, to six-year overlapping terms. Drawing no state salary, each commissioner must be a "public" member without financial ties to any company contracting with the state for highway-related business. The commission selects an executive director who administers the department and maintains relations with the legislature and other agencies. For the 2014–2015 biennium, TxDOT was authorized 12,000 full-time-equivalent employees and a $22.1 billion budget.

Texans' love affair with their cars and pickups has led to traffic congestion and accidents. In recent years, Texans spent an average of 25 minutes commuting to work (one way), just at the national average. However, this number conceals huge differences—from a few minutes in small towns to much more than the average in densely populated areas and some suburbs. On the other hand, since 2000, the percentage of workers commuting by private vehicle has declined slightly in Texas's major cities.

With an increasing number of cars and trucks on the road, total accidents tend to increase. However, from 1935 to 2012, traffic deaths per 100 million miles driven declined in the nation and Texas (for the state, from 16.6 deaths to 1.43). The reasons for the decline, according to research, are safer roads, vehicles, and behavior by drivers (such as use of seatbelts and designated drivers). In 2012, alcohol was involved in 38 percent of Texas traffic deaths compared to 31 percent for the nation.

TxDOT is widely viewed as one of the most successful state agencies in lobbying the legislature for appropriations. However, it too follows the state pattern of scarce resources for government agencies. Highway mileage and public transportation have not kept up with population growth, and road and bridge maintenance has lagged seriously. Testimony in 2014 by Texas A&M Transportation Institute researchers indicated that Texas would need to spend $4-7.4 billion more each year to maintain 2010 mobility levels.[48]

In the face of strong legislative opposition to new taxes, how should improvements be financed? Texas has made heavy use of bonds but is finding that this avenue is approaching its limits. Texas officials have shown a marked preference for toll roads built and run by private companies. However, there has been strong public opposition to toll roads, particularly to privately run toll roads. In 2007, the legislature passed a loophole-laden bill that has slowed the movement toward private toll roads, though public

Texas Department of Transportation (TxDOT)
Headed by a five-member appointed commission, the department maintains almost 80,000 miles of roads and highways and promotes highway safety.

toll roads continue to expand. For a discussion of infrastructure financing, see Chapter 13, "Finance and Fiscal Policy."

In keeping with state encouragement of private transportation efforts, a developer is planning a high-speed passenger rail for a 90-minute trip between Dallas and Houston. Texas made an unsuccessful push for such a project in the 1990s. If it comes to fruition in 2021 as planned, the bullet train will be the first in the nation.

Compared with highways, public transportation has less public and official support. Only a few Texas cities have light rail (such as Austin's Capital MetroRail) for public transportation. In Texas, 95 percent of public transportation is by bus. Statewide, the proportion of commuters using public transit has increased slightly since 2000, but there has been variation by city (El Paso and Austin up but Dallas and Houston down).

In 2014 Texas had eight large urban transit agencies serving areas with 200,000 or more residents. These agencies provide around 90 percent of Texans' public transit trips. The most common organizational form (7 of 8) is a metropolitan transit authority (MTA), which is a local regional government that can impose taxes and service the central city and the surrounding suburbs. TxDOT has little role in the planning, finance, or operation of MTAs. In 2014, there were also 30 small urban transit agencies and 39 rural transit systems serving smaller communities, as well as more than 135 operators providing transportation services to the elderly and to individuals with disabilities under varying arrangements.[49]

Tourism, Parks, and Recreation Responsibility for preserving Texas's natural habitats and managing public recreational areas lies with the **Texas Parks and Wildlife Department**. The nine members of its governing commission are appointed by the governor with Senate approval. The governor also designates the chair of the commission from among the members. Fees for fishing and hunting licenses and entrance to state parks are set by the commission. Game wardens, under the department, enforce state laws and departmental regulations that apply to hunting, fishing, and boating; the Texas Penal Code; and certain laws affecting clean air and water, hazardous materials, and human health.

Tourism is the third largest industry in the Lone Star State. The state park system attracts 7 to 10 million visitors a year (both Texans and out-of-state tourists) and usually generates over $1 billion a year for the economy. (Wildlife recreation produced over $6 billion for the state in 2011.) With Texas ranked 49th in state money spent on parks in the first years of this century, however, state parks were suffering deterioration in quality and services. Fewer parks and park amenities hurt business and were a loss to middle- and working-class Texans, many of whom depend on public parks for recreation. Since 2007, appropriations for Parks and Wildlife have experienced a roller coaster of ups and downs. In 2007, Parks and Wildlife leaders orchestrated a publicity campaign that convinced the legislature to boost the budget from $439 million to $665 million for the biennium. The 2009 legislature kept the increased level of funding, but the revenue-strapped 2011 legislative session

Texas Parks and Wildlife Department
Texas agency that runs state parks and regulates hunting, fishing, and boating.

cut the budget by $153 million. The 2013 session increased appropriations to just under $600 million. Thus, state parks continue to struggle.

Certification of Trades and Professions Citizens in more than 40 occupations—half of which are health related—are certified (licensed) to practice their profession by state boards. Each licensing board has at least one "public" member (not from the regulated occupation). All members are appointed to six-year terms by the governor with approval of the Senate. In addition to ensuring that practitioners qualify to enter a profession (giving them a license to practice), the boards are responsible for ensuring that licensees continue to meet professional standards. For example, the Texas Board of Nursing (formerly called the Board of Nurse Examiners) licenses nurses to practice. According to investigative reporter Yamil Berard, it "is perhaps the most aggressive healthcare regulator in Texas, taking patient safety to heart."[50] Because of a shortage of legal staff, this board has been criticized for having a backlog of cases. Ironically, it and the Texas Medical Board, which regulates doctors, receive criticism from legislators and medical practitioners for being too tough while simultaneously receiving public criticism for not being tough enough.

Environmental Regulation

Among Texas's many public policy concerns, none draws sharper disagreements than how to maintain a clean and safe environment while advancing business development that will provide jobs and profits. Because of the nature of its industries and the love for driving, Texas has been among the most polluted states for years. Our industries, for example, produce more toxic contaminants (chemical waste) than do those of any other state. This grim reality confronts local, state, and national policymakers, and the decisions of all three affect the quality of air and water.

Since the early 1970s, federal policies have driven state and local environmental efforts, with Texas state and local officials generally trying to resist or slow the impact of federal policies. Mandates come from the national level through the U.S. Environmental Protection Agency (EPA) and congressional directives in the Clean Air and Clean Water Acts. Under the Obama administration, the EPA became more vigorous, and the number of conflicts with Texas officials increased. Responses by Texas officials have included public complaints, legislation introduced by the state's representatives in Congress, requests for waivers, and state-filed lawsuits. Concern about climate change and Texas's substantial greenhouse gas emissions have also increased federal-state conflict.

Texas businesspeople usually support state policies designed to forestall federal regulations. Tracking corporate Texas's every step, however, is a growing army of public "watchdogs" (such as the Sierra Club), who do much to inform the public concerning environmental problems. By about 2012, environmental groups had begun to embrace the former enemy-technology to aid their cause. Cell phone cameras and GPS helped documentation, and social media became major tools for organizing and getting the word out.

Texas Commission on Environmental Quality (TCEQ)

The state agency that coordinates Texas's environmental regulation efforts.

Air and Water The Texas Commission on Environmental Quality (TCEQ), commonly called "T-sec," coordinates the Lone Star State's environmental policies. Three full-time commission members earning $150,000 per year, an executive director earning $145,000 a year, and about 2,700 employees oversee environmental regulation in Texas. The commissioners are named by the governor for six-year staggered terms. The governor designates one of the commissioners as chair, and the commissioners choose the executive director. As with actions of other regulatory bodies, TCEQ's decisions can be appealed to state courts. For the 2014–2015 biennium, the agency received an appropriation of $729 million, which restored little (13 percent) of the major cuts made by the legislature in 2011. This was seen as a problem by environmentalists who thought the agency was underfunded and understaffed before the 2011 cuts.

Like the Railroad Commission, TCEQ has come under so much influence from the businesses it is intended to regulate that it is accused of being another instance of agency capture. For example, there are numerous cases of technical staff and specialists being overruled by the TCEQ's top leadership when the staff recommendation goes against interests with strong connections. This happened with the permitting of a West Texas nuclear waste site. The TCEQ's executive director ordered the license issued against the unanimous recommendation of staff specialists. He soon left the agency and six months later went to work for the operator of the waste site. From 1993 to 2010, "former TCEQ higher-ups—including commissioners, general counsels, and a deputy director ... earned as much as $32 million lobbying for the industries they once policed."[51]

State policymakers must balance federal directives and state law with pressures from businesses and environmentalists, a major challenge. In recent years, TCEQ has pushed the state's metropolitan areas to meet federal air standards, with moderate success. However, Texas missed a 2009 federal deadline, which was then extended to 2012 and missed again. In 2014, the Sierra Club filed a federal suit over the second missed deadline. After changing its approach in 2005, Houston met federal smog standards in 2009 for the first time in 35 years. By 2014, it was meeting standards some days but missing them more often. Air quality in San Antonio has declined since 2008 and by 2014 was threatened with "noncompliance" status. In 2013, the American Lung Association named Houston (7th) and Dallas (8th) among the 10 U.S. cities with dirtiest air. (California had 7 of the 10!)

Cracks in the dry bed of Lake Lavon, northeast of Dallas. Texas's alternating periods of drought and flooding, together with the highly unequal distribution of rainfall from one region to another, make water policy a critical element of the state's development.

AP Images/Matt Slocum

CRITICAL THINKING

We can't control the weather. What can we do to better deal with alternating drought and flooding?

Another recent issue is how to generate more electrical power for Texas's growing population and economy. Many of the recent environmental conflicts between the EPA and Texas have related to the pollution produced by coal-burning plants. Significantly cleaner natural gas is becoming the preferred fuel for generating plants in Texas and elsewhere, and wind and solar power are making small but growing inroads.

Water is another important issue in a state that is largely arid. Texas's growing population, industry, and irrigation-based agriculture face serious water shortages; in addition, drought and flooding are regular problems for many areas. TCEQ, working with local prosecutors, deals with contamination of waterways. Major sources of water pollution include industry (through both air emissions and improper disposal of toxic waste), agriculture (particularly from fertilizer, manure, and pesticide runoff), and poorly treated sewage. The six-member Texas Water Development Board (TWDB) and its staff develop strategies, collect data, and administer grants and loans to support water supply, wastewater treatment, and flood control projects. Three sets of interconnected issues frame the water supply debate:

- Conflicts over who controls the water: Under Texas law, surface water (in lakes and rivers) belongs to the state, but citizens and other entities may be granted rights to it. Water is overappropriated—that is, if every entity actually received the amount it has been allocated by the state, lakes and rivers would be dry. Underground water (called groundwater) has almost no regulation. Under the legal concept known as the rule of capture, landowners own the water below their property. But problems arise when upstream landowners pump so much water that downstream landowners' wells and springs dry up.

- The desire of metropolitan areas and drier Central and Western Texas to build lakes and pipelines to capture and move water from wetter areas, such as East Texas: Many communities want to keep their water. Others object to loss of land to lakes and damage to rivers and wetlands. Closely related are conflicts among the users of water—agriculture, cities, and industry—and with environmentalists over who gets priority over water.

- Maintenance of the quality and quantity of underground water, such as the Ogallala and Edwards aquifers, on which many cities, farms, and rivers depend.

One thing on which most sides of the water disputes agree is that Texas needs an effective water plan. The state has had a series of water plans, but they have had

Flooding in Corpus Christi. While experiencing periodic drought, the Corpus Christi area also suffered 12 "flood events" in the period 2001–2013.

Todd Yates/Black Star/Newscom

CRITICAL THINKING

What factors make it easier or harder to reduce flooding and to deal with its consequences?

little impact. In 2013, the legislature agreed to a two-pronged approach. With the approval of the voters, $2 billion from the state's Rainy Day Fund would be used (1) to encourage conservation and (2) to build new water projects such as reservoirs. Neither side believes that the plan will solve the problem, but some people on both sides are encouraged that some action is being taken. With the continued growth of population and the needs of agriculture and industry, the water fights continue to grow in importance.[52] The issue of water supply is made worse by Texas's periodic droughts, which are often followed by flooding. The 1950–1957 drought cost the state's agriculture $22 billion (in 2011 dollars), and the 2010–2011 drought cost at least $8 billion and saw fires char 4 million acres. Since 1945, the state has experienced six periods of severe drought and two of extreme drought.[53] Water problems are also discussed in Chapter 1, "The Environment of Texas Politics," and financial implications are covered in Chapter 13, "Finance and Fiscal Policy."

Hazardous Waste Hazardous waste is a fact of modern life. From the use of low-level radioactive materials for disease diagnosis in hospitals to industrial production of plastics and chemicals on which we depend, we generate large quantities of dangerous waste. This waste ranges in danger from high-level radioactive material with potential toxicity for thousands of years to nonradioactive hazardous waste. Those who produce hazardous materials want to get rid of waste as cheaply as possible, and they have the money and incentive to succeed in keeping the costs of disposal low. Although environmental groups in Texas have grown in power and political skill, they generally can only delay and modify actions favored by pollution producers. For its part, much of the public simply says "Not in my backyard" (NIMBY).

In the case of low-level radioactive waste, there have been a series of political skirmishes stretching back to the 1970s, a lack of a coordinated plan, and a growing amount of waste. By 2009, a private radioactive waste dumpsite had been built in sparsely populated Andrews County near the border with New Mexico and a permit issued by TCEQ. By 2012, the first loads of waste had arrived. Initially, the waste was to be from Texas and Vermont, based on an interstate compact. However, 29 states depended on the site in 2014, and the number could rise to 38 or more. The substantial campaign contributions and lobbying by the site's developer, Waste Control Specialists, and its owner led to charges of crony capitalism (government officials favoring and subsidizing their friends in the private sector who have helped them). In 2014, the Texas site was the only one in the nation serving the estimated $30 billion a year demand for disposal.[54]

Generated largely by Texas's petrochemical industry, nonradioactive hazardous waste stored in landfills presents another environmental dilemma. Poorly stored materials may leak into the water table or nearby waterways or contaminate the dirt above them. Some housing and commercial land developers covet landfill sites for their building projects because of costs and location. TCEQ has tended to approve less restrictive guidelines for these sites. As the state's population increases in the years ahead, even greater demands will be placed on the quality of its air, water, and land.

✔ **10.4 Learning Check**

1. True or False: Business regulation in Texas tends to be tough on businesses.
2. What are some demands that state environmental policy-makers must balance?

Answers on p. 402.

Selected Reading

Fracking the Eagle Ford Shale—Big Oil and Bad Air on the Texas Prairie

Terrence Henry

In Texas, big oil and the chance to make money have always carried a lot of weight, in both public and private life. With the resurgence of oil production in recent years, oil companies are gaining more power, and public officials are reluctant to take on the "big guys" or to threaten the golden goose that is revitalizing the state's economy. This reading gives a taste of the impact on people of the boom mentality, the reluctance to be regulated, and the tendency of government officials to not want to share information, particularly if it might put them or someone of importance in a bad light.

A new joint investigation out this week on air quality in the Eagle Ford Shale has brought up troubling questions about the effect fracking in South Texas is having on the health of residents. Inside Climate News, the Center for Public Integrity, and the Weather Channel cooperated on the report, which took eight months.

Among the report's findings:

- "Texas' air monitoring system is so flawed that the state knows almost nothing about the extent of the pollution in the Eagle Ford. Only five permanent air monitors are installed in the 20,000-square-mile region, and all are at the fringes of the shale play, far from the heavy drilling areas where emissions are highest."

- "Thousands of oil and gas facilities, including six of the nine production sites near the Buehrings' house [a family with severe respiratory problems discussed in an article accompanying the report], are allowed to self-audit their emissions without reporting them to the state. The Texas Commission on Environmental Quality (TCEQ), which regulates most air emissions, doesn't even know some of these facilities exist. An internal agency document acknowledges that the rule allowing this practice '[c]annot be proven to be protective.'"

- "Companies that break the law are rarely fined. Of the 284 oil and gas industry-related complaints filed with the TCEQ by Eagle Ford residents between Jan. 1, 2010, and Nov. 19, 2013, only two resulted in fines despite 164 documented violations. The largest was just $14,250. (Pending enforcement actions could lead to six more fines)."

The report also notes that the TCEQ's budget has been slashed, reducing their ability to conduct inspections and air monitoring. Simultaneously, there has been a "100 percent statewide increase in unplanned, toxic air releases associated with oil and gas production since 2009." These "are usually caused by human error or faulty equipment," the report notes, and can be fixed.

The oil and gas industry wasted no time in issuing a response dismissing the investigation through the industry-funded Energy In Depth, saying it is "based on phony science and a deliberate misreading of the regulatory regime."

Also of note are the roadblocks the team faced from state regulators and the oil and gas industry itself. While these obstacles are familiar to anyone who's ever reported on the fracking boom in Texas, they raise questions about what the state and industry are trying to hide:

- "The agency responsible for regulating air emissions—the TCEQ—refused to make any of its commissioners, officials or investigators available for interviews. Instead, we had to submit questions via emails that were routed through agency spokespeople. It's unclear if the spokespeople passed our questions along to the agency's experts. We received answers to most of our emails, often in some detail. But some of our questions were ignored or answered with talking points on general topics. The TCEQ employees who dealt with our public records requests were helpful and responsive, however. They discussed the filing process over the phone and answered questions about our requests."

- "When a reporter called TCEQ field inspectors at their homes—a commonly used reporting technique—TCEQ spokeswoman Andrea Morrow left the reporter a message saying, 'Under no circumstances are you to call our people and harass them at home.' Morrow also blocked the reporter from approaching the agency's chairman, Bryan Shaw, at a public meeting in Austin."

- "The agency's public records pricing system was puzzling. We were charged as little as 20 cents for one document but were asked for more than $10,000 to provide a batch of documents that had been given to another news agency years ago. We withdrew our request."

- "The Texas Railroad Commission, which regulates drilling and all other aspects of the industry, made Commissioner David Porter available for a 10-minute phone interview. The Weather Channel later scheduled an on-camera interview with Porter, but when the producers arrived at the appointed time, they were told Porter was sick and would not be available for the next month. Like the TCEQ, the Railroad Commission spokespeople refused to discuss anything on the phone, including even technical questions about the mapping data we purchased from the agency. Nor would they make Porter or other top officials available for final, pre-publication phone interviews."

- "Industry officials in Texas were as reluctant as regulators to meet face-to-face or go on camera. Most insisted that all queries be submitted in writing. No tours of Eagle Ford operations were allowed, despite several requests. No on-the-ground discussions of air pollution were facilitated. Hunt Oil was the exception. When we asked about a problem at one of its processing plants, the company set up a phone interview with an executive who answered our questions."

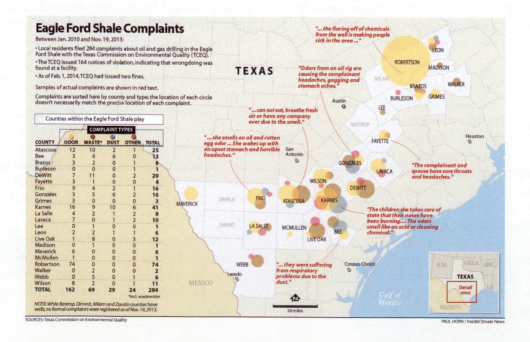

Eagle Ford Shale Complaints

Between Jan. 2010 and Nov. 19, 2013:

- Local residents filed 284 complaints about oil and gas drilling in the Eagle Ford Shale with the Texas Commission on Environmental Quality (TCEQ).
- The TCEQ issued 164 notices of violation, indicating that wrongdoing was found at a facility.
- As of Feb. 1, 2014, TCEQ had issued two fines.

Samples of actual complaints are shown in red text.

Complaints are sorted here by county and type; the location of each circle doesn't necessarily match the precise location of each complaint.

Counties within the Eagle Ford Shale play

COUNTY	ODOR	WASTE*	DUST	OTHER	TOTAL
Atascosa	12	10	2	1	25
Bee	3	4	6	0	13
Brazos	3	2	0	1	6
Burleson	0	0	0	1	1
DeWitt	7	11	0	2	20
Fayette	3	1	0	0	4
Frio	9	4	2	1	16
Gonzales	3	5	6	2	16
Grimes	3	0	0	0	3
Karnes	16	9	10	6	41
La Salle	4	2	1	2	9
Lavaca	7	0	1	2	10
Lee	0	1	0	0	1
Leon	2	2	1	1	6
Live Oak	1	8	0	3	12
Madison	0	1	0	0	1
Maverick	6	0	0	0	6
McMullen	1	0	0	0	1
Robertson	74	0	0	0	74
Walker	0	2	0	0	2
Webb	0	5	0	1	6
Wilson	8	2	0	1	11
TOTAL	162	69	29	24	284

*incl. wastewater

"...the flaring off of chemicals from the well is making people sick in the area..."

"Odors from an oil rig are causing the complainant headaches, gagging and stomach aches."

"...can not eat, breathe fresh air or have any company over due to the smell."

"...she smells an oil and rotten egg odor...She wakes up with an upset stomach and horrible headaches."

"The complainant and spouse have sore throats and headaches."

"The children she takes care of state that their noses have been burning....The odors smell like an acid or cleaning chemical."

"...they were suffering from respiratory problems due to the dust."

TEXAS

NOTE: While Bastrop, Dimmit, Milam and Zavala counties have wells, no formal complaints were registered as of Nov. 19, 2013.

SOURCES: Texas Commission on Environmental Quality

PAUL HORN / InsideClimate News

Selected Reading Learning Check

1. Does the reading indicate that the two major state agencies involved in regulation are more supportive of the needs of industry or of local residents?

2. Texas has a law requiring public access to government records. Do the two agencies appear to be in compliance with the spirit of this law?

Answers on p. 402.

....

Source: Terrence Henry, ''Fracking the Eagle Ford Shale—Big Oil and Bad Air on the Texas Prairie,'' NPR, February 20, 2014, http://stateimpact.npr.org/texas/2014/02/20/watch-fracking-the-eagle-ford-shale-big-oil-and-bad-air-on-the-texas-prairie/. Printed by permission. Terrence Henry reports on energy and the environment for StateImpact, a collaborative project of National Public Radio and member stations to examine the impact of state issues and policies on people's lives.

Conclusion

The state's public policies affect many aspects of Texans' lives. The Texas education system faces challenges created by serving large numbers of disadvantaged students, coupled with a reluctance to devote sufficient state resources to education. The state has a large proportion of poor and working-class citizens in need of help in health and human services; this segment of the population has little political power to effectively satisfy their needs. In the areas of economic development and regulation, public policy has often tended to serve the interests of business over those of consumers.

Chapter Summary

LO 10.1 **Describe the role of bureaucracy in making public policy in Texas**. Public policymaking is a dynamic process in which bureaucracy plays a vital role in shaping the nature of policy. Texas's political culture and political process produce public policies that are responsive to business and government elites but that provide a weaker social safety net than the majority of other states. Most of the state's budget is spent on four areas: education, health and human services, business and economic development, and public safety and corrections. The sunset review process requires periodic review of state agencies by the legislature. Although producing few major changes in state government, it has had positive effects. The state's numerous agencies provide a variety of services to Texans, including public and higher education, social services, and business regulation and promotion. State agencies and their employees (bureaucrats or public administrators) carry out laws passed by the legislature but add their own influence by interpreting and applying the laws to specific situations. The success of agencies in Texas is influenced by the vigor of their leaders, the lack of resources for most agencies, and elite access. State employees are Texas's largest work group. Texas state government has done better than the private sector in providing access to employment for women and African Americans, but access for Latinos has been more mixed.

LO 10.2 **Analyze the major challenges faced by the Texas education system**. Whether in public school districts, institutions of higher education, or the legislature, policymakers face the challenge of achieving educational excellence at a price that Texas taxpayers can afford and that voters will support. Texas schools face the challenge of a changing student body—more ethnically diverse and from less affluent families. Failure to respond to the challenge is likely to damage the state's economy. The State Board of

Education is limited and highly controversial. The greater state role in education is handled by the commissioner of education, who heads the Texas Education Agency. Testing remains a major tool for trying to improve education in the state. It is also a source of great controversy. The Texas Higher Education Coordinating Board coordinates all institutions of higher education; boards of regents govern universities; and local boards make policy for community colleges. Affirmative action and the top 10 percent rule have been major issues in college admissions.

LO 10.3 **Describe the health and human services programs in Texas and discuss how efforts to address the needs of its citizens have been approached.** State responsibility for many public assistance programs and the state's high poverty rate continue to place demands on Texas's social service agencies to assist needy families and those physically or mentally ill, aged, or disabled. Health and human services programs in Texas are politically weak and poorly funded. They are coordinated by the Health and Human Services Commission.

LO 10.4 **Compare the roles of government in generating economic development while maintaining a safe and clean environment for the state's residents.** Privatization of service delivery has a mixed record in Texas, with some major failures. It remains to be seen whether deregulation (the current direction of regulators) will be more effective than regulation in protecting the public interest; meanwhile, Texas consumers demand low-cost utilities, safe and plentiful drinking water, and cleaner air. State regulators tend to be protective of the industries they are charged to regulate. The deterioration of state parks because of funding shortages may cause Texas to lose tourist dollars. Texas has long had major pollution problems and public policies that have done little to improve the environment. Challenges to polluters are increasing, but change is slow. The ownership, protection, use, and availability of water have become major public policy issues.

Key Terms

public policy, p. 358
sunset review process, p. 360
public administration, p. 361
bureaucrats, p. 361
elite access, p. 362
patronage system, p. 364
merit system, p. 364
State Board of Education (SBOE), p. 367

Texas Education Agency (TEA), p. 370
commissioner of education, p. 370
Texas Essential Knowledge and Skills (TEKS), p. 371
State of Texas Assessment of Academic Readiness (STAAR), p. 371

Texas Higher Education Coordinating Board (THECB), p. 374
equal opportunity, p. 376
affirmative action, p. 376
top 10 percent rule, p. 377
Executive commissioner of the Health and Human Services Commission, p. 381

Learning Check Answers

10.1 1. False. Public administrators must make many decisions not clearly specified in the law. Their own views, their bosses' preferences, and their agency culture all make a difference in how they apply laws passed by the legislature.

2. The vigor of agency leaders, resources, and elite access are particularly important in determining how successful agencies are in achieving their policy goals.

10.2 1. The State Board of Education and the Texas Education Agency under the direction of the commissioner of education are the most important state entities for public schools.

2. According to the top 10 percent rule, Texas students graduating in the top 10 percent of their high school class must be admitted to the public college or university of their choice.

10.3 1. Health and human services programs are at a disadvantage in Texas because of the state's political culture and the lack of resources and organization of those needing the services.

2. Medicare is better funded than Medicaid.

10.4 1. False. Regulation of business in Texas tends not to be tough on businesses (consider the Railroad Commission, for example).

2. State environmental policymakers must balance federal directives, business pressures, and demands from environmental groups.

Selected Reading Learning Check

1. Industry. Monitoring is minimal, and punishments for violations are minimal.

2. It is not clear whether the public agencies complied with the letter of the law, but they were hardly in compliance with its spirit. They consistently put roadblocks in the way of reporters gathering information about the agencies' actions and what was happening in the oil patch.

11

The Judicial Branch

SARGENT © 1998 Austin American-Statesman. Reprinted with permission of UNIVERSAL UCLICK. All rights reserved.

CRITICAL THINKING

Does the popular election of judges affect the quality of justice Texans receive?

Learning Objectives

11.1   Identify the sources of Texas law.

11.2   Compare the functions of all participants in the justice system.

11.3   Describe the judicial procedure for the adjudication of civil lawsuits.

11.4   Describe the judicial procedure for the adjudication of criminal cases.

In 2014, only two of nine justices on the Texas Supreme Court, the state's highest appellate court for civil cases, were women. Yet in 1925, Texas became the first state to have an all-female supreme court. Governor Pat Neff appointed the all-female court to hear the appeal of a case involving the Woodmen of the World (W.O.W.), a fraternal organization to which almost all lawyers and judges in the state belonged. Judges must recuse themselves if they have a bias in a case. No male judge could be found who was not also a member of the W.O.W.; therefore, no one was available to render an unbiased judgment. Because women could not belong to the W.O.W., selecting female justices became the only option. Locating three women who met the qualifications to serve on the supreme court was a challenge. Two of Governor Neff's initial appointees failed to qualify, having less than seven years' legal experience (Texas supreme court justices must now have been practicing attorneys or judges for at least 10 years). Finally on January 8, 1925, the elected Chief Justice of the Texas Supreme Court, C. M. Cureton, administered the oath of office in which, among other affirmations, each female justice swore she had never fought a duel. The court then met and granted the writ of error in the case of *Johnson v. Darr* (114 Tex. 516). Their work was completed by May 1925, when they announced their decision in favor of the W.O.W. and delivered their written opinions. Chief Justice Hortense Sparks Ward, the first woman to pass the state bar exam, wrote the majority opinion for the court. Associate Justice Hattie Leah Henenberg, who practiced law in Dallas until 1966, and Associate Justice Ruth Virginia Brazzil, who reportedly opposed women's suffrage and women's rights, wrote concurring opinions. Once the opinions were delivered, Governor Neff dissolved the court.[1]

Not until 1991 was a woman elected to serve on the Texas Supreme Court. Since the election of Justice Rose Spector in that year, five women have won elections to serve on the high court. Among the problems often cited by those who oppose the popular, partisan election of judges and justices is that many qualified candidates do not win because they do not appear judicial to the voters. Women may fall victim to this bias. The opening cartoon to this chapter highlights another complaint—requiring judges to raise campaign donations to win elections calls into question the fairness of a judge's decisions. When commentator Mike Wallace argued that "justice was for sale in Texas" in the 1990s, he reinforced concern about judicial bias. As you learn about Texas's judicial system, consider the role of courts and whether the current method of selecting judges has a negative or positive effect on that role.

State Law in Texas

★ **LO11.1** Identify the sources of Texas law.

Texans have given substantial power to their justice system. The Texas Constitution and state statutes grant government the authority, under appropriate circumstances, to take a person's life, liberty, or property. It is the role of the judicial branch to interpret and apply state constitutional provisions, statutory laws, and agency regulations. Through these interpretations, judges are involved in the policymaking process. Yet judges attract less public attention than state legislative and executive officials, even though their decisions affect Texans every day. It is therefore important that the state's residents understand the purpose and workings of the judicial branch.

With approximately 4,000 justices and judges, and almost that many courts, Texas has one of the largest judicial systems in the country. Including traffic violations handled in lower courts, millions of cases are processed each year. Texas courts deal with cases involving **civil law** (for example, disputes concerning business contracts, divorces and other family issues, and personal injury claims). They also hear cases involving **criminal law** (proceedings against persons charged with committing a **misdemeanor**, such as using false identification to purchase liquor, which is punishable by a fine and jail sentence; or a **felony**, such as armed robbery, which is punishable by a prison sentence and a fine). A court's authority to hear a particular case is its **jurisdiction**.

Sources of Law

Regardless of their jurisdiction, Texas courts interpret and apply state law.[2] These laws include the provisions of the Texas Constitution, statutes enacted by the legislature, regulations adopted by state agencies, and judge-made common law based on custom and tradition dating back to medieval England. A court may apply a constitutional provision, statute, regulation, and common law all in the same case. Procedures for filing a case, conducting a trial, and appealing a judgment depend on whether the case is civil or criminal.

The Texas Constitution and statutes are available at Texas Legislature Online. Thomson Reuters Westlaw publishes the same information in *Vernon's Texas Statutes and Codes Annotated*. Newly enacted laws passed in each legislative session are compiled and made available through the Office of the Secretary of State's website. Agency regulations are codified in the *Texas Administrative Code*.

Code Revision

In 1963, the legislature charged the Texas Legislative Council with the responsibility of reorganizing Texas laws related to specific topics (such as education or taxes) into a systematic and comprehensive arrangement of legal codes. More than 50 years later, the council continues to work on this project. In addition to piecemeal changes resulting from routine legislation, the legislature also sometimes undertakes extensive revision of an entire legal code. In 2003, the 78th Legislature authorized the council to compile all statutes related to local governments into the Special District Local Laws Code, a project that remained ongoing in 2015.

civil law
The body of law concerning noncriminal matters, such as business contracts and personal injury.

criminal law
The body of law concerning felony and misdemeanor offenses by individuals against other persons and property, or in violation of laws or ordinances.

misdemeanor
Classified as A, B, or C, a misdemeanor may be punished by fine and/or jail sentence.

felony
A serious crime punished by fine and prison confinement.

jurisdiction
A court's authority to hear a particular case.

✔ **11.1 Learning Check**

1. True or False: Civil law cases involve misdemeanors and felonies.
2. True or False: Texas state law includes judge-made common law based on custom and tradition.

Answers on p. 434.

Courts, Judges, Lawyers, and Juries

LO11.2 Compare the functions of all participants in the justice system.

Article V of the Texas Constitution, "Judicial Department," vests all state judicial power "in one Supreme Court, in one Court of Criminal Appeals, in Courts of Appeals, in District Courts, in County Courts, in Commissioners Courts [which now have no judicial authority, as discussed in Chapter 3, "Local Governments"], in Courts of Justice of the Peace and in such other courts as may be provided by law." (See the Selected Reading for this chapter.) In exercising its constitutional power to create other courts, the Texas legislature has established municipal courts, county courts-at-law, and **probate** courts (probate matters relate specifically to decedents' estates, primarily establishing the validity of their wills; however, courts with probate jurisdiction also handle guardianship proceedings and mental competency determinations). These courts are referred to as statutory courts.[3] The legislature has also authorized the creation of a number of specialty courts to meet specific needs of particular groups of the state's residents.

Trial and Appellate Courts

Texas's judicial system is complex. (See the structure of the current judicial system presented in Figure 11.1.) The law creating a particular court fixes the court's subject matter jurisdiction (civil, criminal, or both). Further, constitutional provisions or statutes determine whether a court has **original jurisdiction**, authority to try cases being heard for the first time; **appellate jurisdiction**, authority to rule on lower court decisions; or both. A court may have both exclusive and concurrent jurisdiction. A court that has **exclusive jurisdiction** is the only court with the authority to decide a particular type of case. **Concurrent jurisdiction** means that more than one court has authority to try a specific dispute. In that instance, a plaintiff selects the court in which to file the case. Qualifications and compensation for judges vary among the different courts, as shown in Table 11.1. In an effort to bring greater uniformity and efficiency to the Texas court system, the 82nd Legislature, meeting in special session in 2011, passed HB 79, "the most comprehensive court reorganization bill to be adopted in many years."[4]

Local Trial Courts The courts with which Texans are most familiar are **municipal courts** and **justice of the peace** courts. Together, these local trial courts handle, among other types of cases, charges involving Class C misdemeanors (including most traffic violations), which are the least serious category of criminal offenses. Both municipal judges and justices of the peace, like other Texas justices and judges, may perform marriages. They also serve as magistrates of the state. In this latter capacity, these officials issue warrants for the arrest of suspects and conduct hearings to determine whether a person charged with a criminal act will be released on bail or jailed pending further court action.

Sidebar glossary

probate
Proceedings that involve the estates of decedents. Additionally, courts with probate jurisdiction (county courts, county courts-at-law, and probate courts) handle guardianship and mental competency matters.

original jurisdiction
The power of a court to hear a case first.

appellate jurisdiction
The power of a court to review cases after they have been tried elsewhere.

exclusive jurisdiction
The authority of only one court to hear a particular type of case.

concurrent jurisdiction
The authority of more than one court to try a case (for example, a civil dispute involving more than $200 but less than $10,000 may be heard in either a justice of the peace court, a county court (or county-court-at-law), or a district court).

municipal court
City-run court with jurisdiction primarily over Class C misdemeanors committed within a city's boundaries.

justice of the peace
A judge elected from a justice of the peace precinct who handles minor civil and criminal cases.

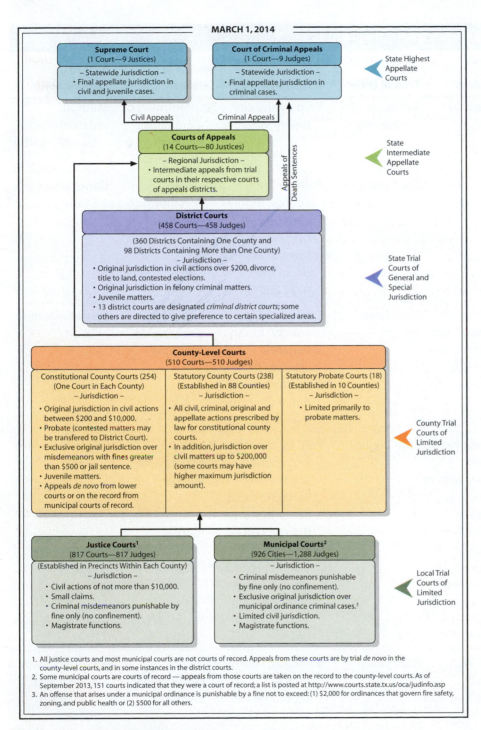

MARCH 1, 2014

Supreme Court (1 Court—9 Justices)
– Statewide Jurisdiction –
• Final appellate jurisdiction in civil and juvenile cases.

Court of Criminal Appeals (1 Court—9 Judges)
– Statewide Jurisdiction –
• Final appellate jurisdiction in criminal cases.

State Highest Appellate Courts

Civil Appeals | Criminal Appeals

Courts of Appeals (14 Courts—80 Justices)
– Regional Jurisdiction –
• Intermediate appeals from trial courts in their respective courts of appeals districts.

State Intermediate Appellate Courts

Appeals of Death Sentences

District Courts (458 Courts—458 Judges)
(360 Districts Containing One County and 98 Districts Containing More than One County)
– Jurisdiction –
• Original jurisdiction in civil actions over $200, divorce, title to land, contested elections.
• Original jurisdiction in felony criminal matters.
• Juvenile matters.
• 13 district courts are designated *criminal district courts*; some others are directed to give preference to certain specialized areas.

State Trial Courts of General and Special Jurisdiction

County-Level Courts (510 Courts—510 Judges)

Constitutional County Courts (254) (One Court in Each County)
– Jurisdiction –
• Original jurisdiction in civil actions between $200 and $10,000.
• Probate (contested matters may be transfered to District Court).
• Exclusive original jurisdiction over misdemeanors with fines greater than $500 or jail sentence.
• Juvenile matters.
• Appeals *de novo* from lower courts or on the record from municipal courts of record.

Statutory County Courts (238) (Established in 88 Counties)
– Jurisdiction –
• All civil, criminal, original and appellate actions prescribed by law for constitutional county courts.
• In addition, jurisdiction over civil matters up to $200,000 (some courts may have higher maximum jurisdiction amount).

Statutory Probate Courts (18) (Established in 10 Counties)
– Jurisdiction –
• Limited primarily to probate matters.

County Trial Courts of Limited Jurisdiction

Justice Courts[1] (817 Courts—817 Judges)
(Established in Precincts Within Each County)
– Jurisdiction –
• Civil actions of not more than $10,000.
• Small claims.
• Criminal misdemeanors punishable by fine only (no confinement).
• Magistrate functions.

Municipal Courts[2] (926 Cities—1,288 Judges)
– Jurisdiction –
• Criminal misdemeanors punishable by fine only (no confinement).
• Exclusive original jurisdiction over municipal ordinance criminal cases.[3]
• Limited civil jurisdiction.
• Magistrate functions.

Local Trial Courts of Limited Jurisdiction

1. All justice courts and most municipal courts are not courts of record. Appeals from these courts are by trial *de novo* in the county-level courts, and in some instances in the district courts.
2. Some municipal courts are courts of record — appeals from those courts are taken on the record to the county-level courts. As of September 2013, 151 courts indicated that they were a court of record; a list is posted at http://www.courts.state.tx.us/oca/judinfo.asp
3. An offense that arises under a municipal ordinance is punishable by a fine not to exceed: (1) $2,000 for ordinances that govern fire safety, zoning, and public health or (2) $500 for all others.

Figure 11.1 Court Structure of Texas

Source: Office of Court Administration, 2014, available at http://www.txcourts.gov/media/654201/Court-Structure-Chart-for-publication9_1_14b.pdf.

CRITICAL THINKING

How could Texas simplify its court system?

Table 11.1	Texas Judges and Justices				
Court	**Judicial Qualifications**	**Term of Office**	**Annual Salary**	**Method of Selection**	**Method of Replacement**
Local Courts Municipal Courts	Varies; set by each city	Varies; set by each city	Paid by the city; highly variable	Appointment or election, as determined by city charter	Method determined by city charter
Justice of the Peace Courts	None	Four years	Paid by the county; highly variable, ranging from a few thousand dollars to $125,000	Partisan precinctwide elections	Commissioners Court
County Courts Constitutional County Courts	Must be "well informed" in Texas law; law degree not required	Four years	Paid by the county; highly variable, ranging from a few thousand dollars to more than $150,000	Partisan countywide elections	Commissioners Court
Statutory County Courts (courts-at-law and probate courts)	Age 25 or older; licensed attorney with at least four to five years' experience, depending on statutory requirements; two years' county residence	Four years	Paid by the state and county; somewhat variable; must be no more than $1,000 less than district judge in same county	Partisan countywide elections	Commissioners Court
State Courts District Courts	Ages 25–74; licensed attorney with at least four years' experience; two years' county residence	Four years	$140,000; county salary supplements; must be $5,000 less than court of appeals justices' salaries	Partisan districtwide elections	Governor, with advice and consent of Senate

Table 11.1	(Continued)				
Court	**Judicial Qualifications**	**Term of Office**	**Annual Salary**	**Method of Selection**	**Method of Replacement**
Courts of Appeals	Ages 35–74; licensed attorney with at least 10 years' experience	Six years	$154,000 (justices); $156,500 (chief justices); county salary supplements; must be $5,000 less than Texas Supreme Court justices' salaries	Partisan districtwide elections	Governor, with advice and consent of Senate
Court of Criminal Appeals	Ages 35–74; licensed attorney with at least 10 years' experience	Six years	$168,000 (judges); $170,500 (presiding judge)	Partisan statewide elections	Governor, with advice and consent of Senate
Supreme Court	Ages 35–74; licensed attorney with at least 10 years' experience	Six years	$168,000 (justices); $170,500 (chief justice)	Partisan statewide elections	Governor, with advice and consent of Senate

Sources: Compiled from Harris County, Texas, Human Resources and Risk Management, "Judicial Salaries," August 13, 2013; Texas Legislature Online, http://www.capitol.state.tx.us.

CRITICAL THINKING

Should all judges and justices be required to have the same qualifications?

More than 900 incorporated cities, towns, and villages in Texas have municipal courts. Although mayors of a general law city have the authority to preside over municipal courts (unless the city council provides for the election or appointment of someone to perform this function), only 2 percent of municipal judges are mayors. Usually, municipal court judges of home rule cities are named by city councils for two-year terms. State law does not require municipal judges to be licensed attorneys unless they preside over a municipal **court of record** (a court with a court reporter or electronic device to record the testimony and proceedings). City councils, however, set professional qualifications, as well as determine the number of judges and set judicial salaries for their municipalities.

Municipal courts have limited civil jurisdiction in cases involving owners of dangerous dogs. These courts have no appellate jurisdiction. Their

court of record
A court that has a court reporter or electronic device to record testimony and proceedings.

original and exclusive criminal jurisdiction extends to all violations of city ordinances, and they have criminal jurisdiction concurrent with justice of the peace courts over Class C misdemeanors committed within city limits. Individuals dissatisfied with the result of a municipal court ruling can appeal the decision to the county court or a county court-at-law.

Approximately 10 percent of municipal courts are courts of record. Appeals from those courts are based on a transcript of trial proceedings. If a court is not a court of record, appeals receive a trial de novo (a completely new trial).

A justice of the peace, often called a JP, is elected by voters residing in a precinct with boundaries created by the county commissioners court. The Texas Constitution mandates the minimum number of precincts per county (one to four) according to population. County commissioners may exceed this minimum by creating up to eight precincts (also based on population) and establish the number of JPs (one or two) per precinct. In recent years, a few commissioners courts have abolished some justice courts to save money for their counties.[5]

The position of JP requires neither previous legal training nor experience. Approximately 10 percent of Texas's JPs (usually in large cities) are lawyers who may engage in private legal practice while serving as a justice of the peace. Within a year after election, a justice of the peace who is not a lawyer must complete an 80-hour course in performing the duties of that office. Thereafter, the JP is supposed to receive 20 hours of instruction annually, 10 hours of which must include topics related to civil trial procedure. Failure to complete annual training violates a JP's duties under the law. The State Commission on Judicial Conduct, a state agency that has the authority to recommend removal, can order justices who do not comply to complete mandatory education.

In urban areas, being a justice of the peace is a full-time job, whereas justices in many rural precincts hear few cases. In addition to presiding over the justice court, a justice of the peace serves as an ex officio notary public (someone who verifies signatures on legal documents). A JP also functions as a coroner, determining cause of death when the county commissioners court has not named a county medical examiner. Justice of the peace courts have both criminal and civil jurisdiction. In all cases, their jurisdiction is original. In criminal matters, these local courts try Class C misdemeanors; however, any conviction may be appealed to the county court or a county court-at-law for a new trial.

Justices of the peace have jurisdiction over four types of civil cases: evictions, debt claims, repair and remedies, and small claims (civil disputes with less than $10,000 in controversy). When justice courts were reorganized in 2013, newspapers described the action as "abolishing small claims courts." Actually, small claims proceedings were merely combined with the other types of cases handled by justice courts. Rules followed in small claims courts were not as formal as in other court proceedings so lay litigants could represent themselves more easily, thus earning these courts the nickname "the people's court." The more relaxed rules were made uniform and extended to most civil cases decided by justice courts. A justice may question witnesses directly to develop the facts in a case and limit the types and amount of potential evidence each party must provide the other prior to trial (a process called discovery). The legislature's goal was to make justice courts more accessible and understandable to the general public.[6] More formal rules still apply to most debt collection cases.

Exclusive civil jurisdiction of JP courts is limited to cases in which the amount in controversy is $200 or less, not including interest. Concurrent civil jurisdiction is shared with county courts (for amounts in controversy in excess of $200) and district courts (for amounts in controversy in excess of $500), so long as the disputed amount does not exceed $10,000. Appeals from JP courts, in which more than $250 is in controversy, are taken to the county level. The justice of the peace court is the court of last resort if the amount in controversy does not exceed $250, thus making their decisions final in these cases.

County Trial Courts Each of Texas's 254 counties has a county court and a county judge, as prescribed by the state constitution. In the more than 80 counties that have one or more county-level courts created by statute, county judges generally do not have a judicial function. Judges of constitutional county courts need not be attorneys. Statutory county court judges must be experienced attorneys. All county-level judges who preside over courts must take Texas Supreme Court–approved courses in court administration, procedure, and evidence, along with judges of county courts-at-law, district courts, and appellate courts.

Most constitutional county courts have original and appellate jurisdiction, as well as probate, civil, and criminal jurisdiction. Original civil jurisdiction is limited to cases involving between $200 and $10,000. Original criminal jurisdiction includes all Class A and Class B misdemeanors.

Appellate criminal jurisdiction extends to cases originating in JP courts and municipal courts. A constitutional county court's appellate jurisdiction is final with regard to criminal cases involving fines of $100 or less. For cases in which greater fines are imposed, the plaintiff may appeal to a court of appeals. Civil cases are heard on appeal from JP courts.

In counties with large populations, the legislature has authorized more than 200 statutory courts (most commonly called county courts-at-law) to relieve constitutional county court judges of some or all courtroom duties. With few exceptions, the criminal jurisdiction of county courts-at-law is limited to misdemeanors. Civil jurisdiction of most county courts-at-law is limited to controversies involving amounts of $200 to $200,000. In 10 urban counties throughout the state, the legislature has created statutory county probate courts to handle guardianship and competency proceedings, as well as the admission of wills to probate.

State Trial Courts Texas's principal trial courts are composed of district-level courts of general and special jurisdiction. Most state trial courts are designated simply as district courts, but a few are called criminal district courts. Each district-level court has jurisdiction over one or more counties. Heavily populated counties may have several district courts with countywide jurisdiction.

Most district court judges are authorized to try both criminal and civil cases, though a statute creating a court may specify that the court give preference to one or the other. All criminal cases are matters of original jurisdiction. Misdemeanor jurisdiction is limited to cases transferred from constitutional county courts, cases specifically authorized by the state legislature, and offenses involving misconduct by government officials while acting in an official capacity. Felony jurisdiction extends to all types of felonies. Appeal after a death penalty sentence is taken directly to the Court of Criminal Appeals. Other criminal convictions are appealed to an intermediate appellate court.

District courts have exclusive original jurisdiction over civil cases involving divorce, land titles, contested elections, contested wills, slander, and defamation of character. They have original civil jurisdiction in controversies involving $200 or more. Thus, concurrent jurisdiction with lower courts begins at this level; above the maximum "dollar amount" jurisdiction of those courts, district courts exercise exclusive civil jurisdiction. Appeals of civil cases go to courts of appeals.

Intermediate Appellate Courts The legislature has divided Texas into 14 state court of appeals districts and has established a court of appeals in every district. Each of these courts has three or more judges or justices (a chief justice and from 2 to 12 justices). Their six-year terms are staggered so that one-third of the members are elected or reelected every two years. This arrangement helps ensure that at any given time—barring death, resignation, or removal from office—each appellate court will have two or more judges

How Do We Compare...in Salaries of Highest Court Justices and Judges?

Annual Salaries of Highest Court Justices and Judges (in dollars as of 2013)

Most Populous U.S. States	Amount*	U.S. States Bordering Texas	Amount*
California	$221,292	Arkansas	$148,108
Florida	$161,200	Louisiana	$150,772
New York	$184,800	New Mexico	$124,928
Texas	**$168,000****	Oklahoma	$137,655

*In most states (including Texas), the chief presiding judge or justice receives a supplement due to the additional workload. In Texas the amount is $2,500.
**Salaries for Texas appellate justices and judges reflect increases effective September 1, 2013.
Source: Judicial Salary Resource Center (July 2013), http://www.ncsc.org.

CRITICAL THINKING

What is fair compensation for a judge or justice?

with experience on that court. Decisions are reached by majority vote of the assigned judges after they examine the written record of the case, review briefs (written arguments) prepared by the parties' attorneys, and hear oral arguments by the attorneys. These courts hear appeals of civil and criminal cases from district courts and county courts (but not appeals involving the death penalty or DNA-forensic testing for individuals sentenced to death).

Final jurisdiction includes cases involving divorce, slander, boundary disputes, and elections held for purposes other than choosing government officials (for example, bond elections). Courts must hear appeals in panels of at least three justices. A decision requires a majority vote of a panel of justices.

Highest Appellate Courts Texas and Oklahoma are the only states in the Union that have **bifurcated** (divided) court systems for dealing with criminal and civil appeals. Texans continue to resist the creation of a unified judicial system, which would have a single appellate court of last resort for both criminal felony cases and complex civil cases.[7] Both of Texas's highest courts have nine justices (Supreme Court) or judges (Court of Criminal Appeals) who serve six-year terms. One-third of the positions on each court are open for election or reelection in each general election. Members of the courts are elected on a statewide basis. The Supreme Court of Texas and the Court of Criminal Appeals are authorized to answer questions about Texas law asked by federal appellate courts (for example, the U.S. Fifth Circuit Court of Appeals or the U.S. Supreme Court).

In Texas, the highest tribunal with criminal jurisdiction is the Court of Criminal Appeals. This court hears criminal appeals exclusively. Most appeals

bifurcated
A divided court system in which different courts handle civil and criminal cases. In Texas, the highest-level appeals courts are bifurcated.

(left) The Texas Supreme Court as constituted in 2014. Chief Justice Nathan Hecht is seated in the center of the first row. (right) The Texas Court of Criminal Appeals as constituted in 2014. Presiding Judge Sharon Keller is seated in the center of the first row.

(left) The Supreme Court of Texas; (right) Texas Court of Criminal Appeals

CRITICAL THINKING

Would Texas benefit from greater racial, ethnic, gender, and political diversity on its highest courts?

come to the court from courts of appeals. Death penalty defendants in capital felonies or DNA forensic testing cases have an automatic right of appeal from the district court to the Court of Criminal Appeals. Of the 229 direct appeals resolved by the court in 2013, only 11 involved death penalty cases. The court affirmed all 11 of these lower court decisions.

Voters elect one member of the Court of Criminal Appeals as presiding judge. Sharon Keller became the first woman to head the Texas Court of Criminal Appeals in 2000. As of 2014, four of the other eight judges were women. Judge Elsa Alcala became the first Latina judge on the court when she was appointed in 2011. She was elected to a full term in 2012. As of 2014, no African Americans were on the Court of Criminal Appeals. All members of the court were originally elected as Republicans, but in December 2013, Justice Lawrence Meyers announced he would seek election to the Texas Supreme Court as a Democrat in the 2014 election.[8] This switch in party affiliation made Judge Meyers the first Democrat to hold statewide office since 1998. Meyers's term on the Texas Court of Criminal Appeals does not expire until January 2017.

Officially titled the Supreme Court of Texas, the state's highest court with civil jurisdiction has nine members: one chief justice and eight justices. No Democrats have served on the Texas Supreme Court since 1998. When Governor Rick Perry appointed Wallace Jefferson to the Texas Supreme Court in 2001, Jefferson became the first African American to serve on the court. His elevation to chief justice in 2004 marked another first for African Americans on the court. In 2015, the court was less diverse than it had been throughout the 21st century. The nine-member court included no African Americans and two women (one Latina and one Anglo). All of the justices were Republican.

This high court is supreme only in cases involving civil law. Because it has severely limited original jurisdiction (for example, cases involving denial of a place on an election ballot), nearly all of the court's docket involves appeals of cases that it determines must be heard. Much of the supreme court's work involves handling petitions for review, which can be requested by a party who argues that a court of appeals made a mistake on a question of law. If as many as four justices favor granting an initial review, the case is scheduled for argument in open court. In 2013, the Texas Supreme Court granted an initial review for approximately 12 percent of the almost 800 petitions that were filed, a 30-year low. Justices do not make public their votes to accept or deny a petition for review.

Other functions of the supreme court include establishing the rules of civil procedure for the state's lower courts and transferring cases for the purpose of equalizing workloads among the courts of appeals. Early in each regular session of the Texas legislature, the chief justice is required by law to deliver to the legislature a State of the Judiciary message, either orally or in written form.

 The Texas Supreme Court has taken a leadership role in the use of technology as a way to make courts with civil jurisdiction more efficient and to make court proceedings more accessible. In 2012, when the supreme court launched its mandatory e-filing program, former Chief Justice Wallace Jefferson declared,

"The era of big paper is over."[9] As of 2016, all documents used in civil cases (except for juvenile cases) must be submitted online through efiletexas.gov. For those interested, podcasts of oral arguments are available for downloading. The court's activities may also be followed through RSS feeds.

Specialty Courts Over the last decade, Texas has followed the national trend of developing **specialty courts** to deal with particular types of problems or specific populations. (See this chapter's Point/Counterpoint feature.) Among the approximate 150 specialized courts are "cluster courts," which are traveling courts that adjudicate only Children's Protective Services cases; drug courts, which focus on treatment options rather than incarceration for substance abusers; and veterans' courts, which deal with offenders who have suffered some type of mental disorder related to their military service experiences.[10]

Specialty courts are created by county commissioner's courts and with regard to drug courts, municipalities, as well. The courts have a dual rationale: efficiency and therapy.[11] Courts with a nontherapeutic purpose, such as Children's Protective Services courts, are intended to increase the court system's efficiency by placing foster children into permanent homes more quickly. Others, such as drug courts, mental health courts, or veterans' courts, are designed with a therapeutic rationale. Their goal is to improve outcomes for participants through individualized treatment plans developed and monitored by attorneys, judges, and treatment personnel. If treatment is successful, the presiding judge can enter an order of nondisclosure for most offenders, thus keeping the public from learning about an offense. Laws passed by the 83rd Legislature in 2013 now provide both legislative and executive supervision of specialty courts.

Alternative Dispute Resolution The state has adopted several methods to encourage litigants to resolve their disputes without going to trial. To reduce workloads, speed the handling of civil disputes, and cut legal costs, each county is authorized to set up a system for **alternative dispute resolution (ADR)**. This procedure allows an impartial third party who has training as a mediator or arbiter to negotiate disputes between and among litigants. ADR is frequently cited as a significant factor in the "vanishing jury trial."[12]

Collaborative divorce is another nonadversarial method for resolving disputes outside the courtroom. If either spouse elects to litigate after the process begins, both attorneys must resign. Under the Texas Family Code, families with children are encouraged to use collaborative procedures. If family violence is involved, however, the abuse victim must expressly request using a collaborative process, and the victim's lawyer must work with the client to devise procedures to limit the possibility of further violence.

Selecting Judges and Justices

Texas, along with Alabama, Louisiana, and West Virginia, chooses all judges (except municipal judges) in partisan elections. Many commentators (including the last three chief justices of the Texas Supreme Court) oppose this practice.

specialty courts
Courts designed to deal with particular types of problems, such as drug-related offenses, or specific populations, such as veterans or foster children.

alternative dispute resolution (ADR)
Use of mediation, conciliation, or arbitration to resolve disputes among individuals without resorting to a regular court trial.

Point/Counterpoint

Though … specialty courts are still experiments that require careful monitoring and improvement, they are a brave attempt to deal with situations in which the traditional justice system is not working well enough.

Patrick J. McClain

Is a System of Specialty Courts for Particular Populations Fair?

THE ISSUE   Approximately 150 specialty courts (or "problem-solving courts") had been established in Texas as of 2014. Specialty courts deal with particular types of problems or populations within a county or city. A rapid increase in the number of these courts requires consideration of their advantages and disadvantages.

Arguments For Specialty Courts

1. Recidivism rates are substantially lower for participants in therapeutic specialty court programs. Studies of specialty drug courts reflect recidivism rates as low as 4 percent for participants compared to 27 percent for nonparticipants.
2. Per capita costs are lower for rehabilitation programs than for incarceration.
3. Life outcomes, as measured by educational outcomes, are more positive for foster children whose cases are handled by specialty courts.
4. Special populations, such as veterans and children, deserve better treatment by the judicial system because of service to country or vulnerability.

Arguments Against Specialty Courts

1. Success rates for specialty court rehabilitation programs are suspect. Program participants must meet special criteria to qualify and only those most likely to succeed are admitted. Further, unlike in the general population, recurring offenses do not necessarily result in immediate incarceration.
2. The programs are costly and unfair. Devoting taxpayer dollars to supporting programs available to only a select few is not fair. Many courts must rely on grants for all or a part of their funding. This model is not fiscally sustainable.
3. The collaborative process required to develop and maintain individualized treatment plans weakens the adversarial process of having strong advocates for accuser and accused.
4. Extensive use of nondisclosure orders conflicts with the public's right to know that someone has committed a crime.

In discussing "the peculiar [American] institution" of electing judges, Harvard Law professor Jed Handelsman Shugerman observed that although a number of foreign countries have adopted the American legal system, few have chosen to follow the practice of popular election of judges.[13] A strong complaint is the appearance that "justice is for sale" in Texas to the highest campaign donor.[14]

Judicial selection methods are far from uniform, with at least 15 different processes in use across the country.[15] Many opponents of the popular election of judges favor some version of the merit selection process initiated by the state of Missouri in 1940. The **Missouri Plan** features a nominating commission that recommends a panel of names to the governor whenever a judicial vacancy is to be filled. The appointee then serves for a year or so before the voters decide, based on his or her judicial performance record, whether to give the new judge a full term or to allow the nominating commission and governor to make another appointment on a similar trial basis.

Others, especially some Texas legislators, favor an **appointment-retention system** for all courts of record. In this system, the governor appoints a judge and voters determine whether to retain the appointee. Reform proposals have consistently failed in the Texas legislature. At the very least, reformers argue, judicial elections should not be partisan. They agree with former Chief Justice Wallace Jefferson who observed, "a justice system built on some notion of Democratic judging or Republican judging is a system that cannot be trusted."[16] The 83rd Legislature approved a task force to study this issue and provide recommendations to the 84th Legislature when it met in 2015.

Disciplining and Removing Judges and Justices

Each year, a few of Texas's judges and justices commit acts that warrant discipline or removal. These judges can be removed by the voters at the next election; by trial by jury; or if they are state court judges, by legislative address or impeachment. The State Commission on Judicial Conduct, however, plays the most important role in disciplining the state's judiciary. This 13-member commission is composed of six judges, each from a different level court; two attorneys; and five private citizens who are neither attorneys nor judges.

The commission has often been criticized for being too lenient in resolving complaints.[17] In 2013, the commission resolved almost 1,100 complaints. Of the 42 cases that were not dismissed, only one judge received a public sanction. Four judges resigned to avoid disciplinary action, including District Judge Elizabeth E. Coker (Polk, San Jacinto, and Trinity Counties). Complainants charged that while presiding over a case, Coker texted instructions from the bench to the district attorney's office on how best to question witnesses appearing in the case. After her resignation, Coker ran unsuccessfully for district attorney.[18] Table 11.2 provides an overview of the number of complaints and disciplinary actions by court type. Parties to a lawsuit—either litigants or criminal defendants—file most complaints.

The commission's jurisdiction extends to judges and justices at all levels of the court system. Both the presiding judge of the Court of Criminal Appeals, Sharon Keller, and the chief justice of the Texas Supreme Court, Nathan Hecht, have been disciplined by the commission. Both disciplinary actions were reversed in appellate proceedings.[19]

In addition to a public reprimand, any judge can receive a private reprimand or be ordered to take additional training. These rulings can be appealed to the chief justice of the Texas Supreme Court, who appoints a Special Court of Review (a three-judge panel of appellate judges) to hear the appeal. The commission has the authority to recommend removal of a judge. Such a recommendation is considered by a seven-member tribunal

Missouri Plan
A judicial selection process in which a commission recommends a panel of names to the governor, who appoints a judge for one year or so before voters determine whether the appointee will be retained for a full term.

appointment-retention system
A merit plan for judicial selection in which the governor makes an appointment to fill a court vacancy for an interim period, after which the judge must win a full term in an uncontested popular election.

Table 11.2	Disposition of Cases by Judge Type, 2013				
Judge Type	Number of Judges	Number of Complaints	Portion of Total Complaints	Number of Disciplinary Actions	Portion of Total Actions
Municipal	1,586	84	7%	10	24%
Justice of the peace	817	193	17%	19	45%
Constitutional county court	254	45	4%	0	0%
Statutory county court	256	120	11%	5	12%
District court	457	547	48%	7	17%
Appellate	98	28	3%	0	0%
Senior or retired	314	61	5%	0	0%
Associate*	142	54	5%	1	2%
Total	3,924	1,132	100%	42	100%

*Full- or part-time judges appointed as masters, magistrates, or referees to assist with specific types of cases.

Source: State Commission on Judicial Conduct, *Fiscal Year 2013 Annual Report*, http://www.scjc.state.tx.us/pdf/rpts/AR-FY13.pdf.

CRITICAL THINKING

Does the Commission on Judicial Conduct appear too lenient in handling complaints against judges?

appointed by the Texas Supreme Court. If the tribunal votes to remove the judge, the decision may be appealed to the Texas Supreme Court.

The State Commission on Judicial Conduct also oversees an employee assistance program called Amicus Curiae. The program locates service providers for judges suffering from substance abuse or mental or emotional disorders. Judges receiving services through Amicus Curiae may do so through a self-referral or be referred by the commission. In all instances, participation is voluntary.

Lawyers

Both the Texas Supreme Court and the State Bar of Texas play roles in regulating the 90,000 practicing attorneys licensed by the State of Texas. Through the Board of Law Examiners, the supreme court supervises the licensing of lawyers. Accreditation of the state's nine law schools is largely a responsibility of the American Bar Association. (The University of North Texas Law School, the state's tenth law school, began the accreditation process in 2014 when it opened for classes.) The State Bar of Texas oversees the state's lawyers.

State Bar of Texas To practice, a licensed attorney must be a member of the State Bar of Texas and pay dues for its support. The state bar is known for both its lobbying activities and its role in enforcing ethical standards for Texas lawyers. As an administrative agency of the state, the organization is authorized to discipline, suspend, and disbar attorneys. The advent of social media has presented special challenges for attorneys. Some have failed to

Students  in Action

> "With help from … the UT Domestic Violence Clinic … I am no longer a victim of domestic violence … I am a SURVIVOR."
>
> *Client comment*

Law school can be more than attending classes and taking exams. The University of Texas School of Law prides itself on offering students "real cases, real experience" through its 17 legal clinics. Many programs are interdisciplinary and involve law students and graduate students from other departments within the university. Students receive course credit while working on cases involving real clients and addressing major legal issues.

The clinics cover a variety of legal topics such as criminal law, children's rights, and international law. Student lawyers, working under the supervision of practicing attorneys and law school professors, prepare documents used in court proceedings. In addition, they write reports on significant issues.

Clients include children, domestic violence victims, undocumented immigrants, criminal defendants, convicted felons, and nonprofit organizations. Students have helped children in cases in which a judge is terminating parental rights for child abuse. They have assisted in obtaining exonerations for wrongfully convicted prisoners and obtaining new trials for those whose constitutional rights were ignored in the original proceeding.

One of the more active clinics is the Human Rights Clinic. In 2014, students published a report on the physical harm caused by extreme heat in Texas prison facilities (see Chapter 12, "The Criminal Justice System"). Student-developed reports on human rights abuses have been presented to the United Nations and the Inter-American Commission on Human Rights. On a more local level, student efforts resulted in the Austin City Council's and the Travis County Commissioners' Court's approving resolutions to place a higher priority on domestic violence issues.

Students describe their work with the clinics as "transformative" and "the academic experience of a lifetime." Clients express deep gratitude for the students' work. Law students' efforts have made a difference in individual clients' lives as well as local, state, national, and international legal systems.

Source: "Clinical Education at UT Law," School of Law, The University of Texas at Austin, http://www.utexas.edu/law/clinics/.

© Andresr/Shutterstock.com

recognize that maintaining a blog touting courtroom accomplishments is advertising. Others have not considered that communicating through a Facebook page with a judge presiding over a lawyer's case is prohibited.[20] Information about an attorney's professional disciplinary record is available from the Find-A-Lawyer link on the state bar's website. In addition, the entity oversees an extensive continuing legal education program.

Legal Services for the Poor Many attorneys and judges agree with former U.S. Supreme Court justice Lewis Powell that "[e]qual justice under law is … one of the ends for which our entire legal system exists.… [I]t is fundamental that justice should be the same, in substance and availability, without regard to economic status."[21] Under the Bill of Rights in the Texas Constitution and the Sixth Amendment to the U.S. Constitution, indigent individuals who are accused of a felony are entitled to representation by an attorney at the state's expense. A person whose claim arises from a physical injury may be able to hire an attorney on a **contingency fee** basis, in which the lawyer is paid from any money recovered in a lawsuit. Representation in legal matters such as divorce, child custody, or contract disputes, however, requires the client to make direct payment to the attorney before or at the time services are performed. When free legal help is provided for civil cases, it is often through an attorney with the Legal Services Corporation, more commonly referred to as Legal Aid. Limited funding in recent years has reduced the assistance available through this program. In 2013, legal aid attorneys in Texas turned away more than half of the eligible clients who sought their help.

The Texas Access to Justice Commission, created by the Texas Supreme Court, works to coordinate and increase delivery of legal services to the state's poor. The 15-member commission includes judges, lawyers, and private citizens. The State Bar of Texas and the Texas Access to Justice Foundation support and collaborate with these efforts. The foundation maintains a website that provides information, forms, and links to low- and no-cost legal services providers.

Attorney volunteers fill some of the representation gap. Special programs, such as Texas Lawyers for Texas Veterans, target particular populations for legal services provided by these private attorneys. State bar officials recommend that lawyers donate 50 hours per year assisting needy clients. In 2013, the state's lawyers provided almost 2.5 million hours of free legal assistance, more than 2 million hours of reduced-fee legal work, and approximately $1 million in donations to the Access to Justice Foundation.[22]

For-profit companies provide options for low-cost legal services through online self-help legal materials. Some of the sites include lawyer referrals in the event purchasers decide they want assistance. Interactive software and legal self-help books allow a person to write a will, obtain a divorce, or create a corporation. Legal documents that would cost hundreds, and sometimes thousands, of dollars if prepared by an attorney can be completed at little or no cost with self-help products.

Juries

A jury system lets citizens participate directly in the administration of justice. Texas has two types of juries: grand juries and trial juries. The state's Bill of Rights guarantees that individuals may be charged with a felony only by grand jury indictment. It also provides that anyone charged with either a

contingency fee
A lawyer's compensation paid from money recovered in a lawsuit.

felony or a misdemeanor has the right to trial by jury. If requested by either party, jury trials are required in civil cases. In recent years, the number of civil jury trials in Texas has steadily declined.

Grand Jury Composed of 12 citizens, a **grand jury** may be either chosen at random or, in a method known as the "key-man system," selected by a judge from a list of 15 to 40 county residents recommended by a judge-appointed grand jury commission. Most states and the federal government only use random selection to choose grand jurors. Members of a Texas grand jury must have the qualifications of trial jurors and not be a complainant in a grand jury proceeding. County commissioners determine the pay for grand jurors. Some counties, like Harris County, offer extra benefits to grand jurors, including opportunities to ride with police officers and tours of the county's morgue. The district judge appoints one juror to serve as presiding juror or foreman of the jury panel. A grand jury's life lasts for a district court's term, which is six months in length, though a district judge may extend a grand jury's term. During this period, grand juries have the authority to inquire into all criminal actions but devote most of their time to felony matters.

Jurors and witnesses are sworn to keep secret all they hear in grand jury sessions, although the subject of a grand jury proceeding is often publicized. Well-known individuals, like Governor Rick Perry, may prefer to avoid the notoriety created by a grand jury investigation. When Perry was investigated for abuse of power for his veto of funding for the state's public integrity unit (see Chapter 9, "The Executive Branch"), his request to allow him to enter the Travis County courthouse through District Attorney Rosemary Lehmberg's office was denied. The accusations against Perry and his subsequent indictment arose from his attempts to force Lehmberg's resignation to avoid the funding veto.[23]

If, after investigation and deliberation (often lasting only a few minutes), at least nine grand jurors decide there is sufficient evidence to warrant a trial, an indictment is prepared with the aid of the prosecuting attorney. The indictment is a written statement accusing some person or persons of a particular crime (for example, burglary of a home). An indictment is referred to as a true bill; failure to indict constitutes a no bill. In a misdemeanor case, a grand jury information (with the same effect as an indictment in a felony case) may be prepared, but is not required, for prosecution.

Petit Jury Although relatively few Texans ever serve on a grand jury, a greater number can expect to be summoned for duty on a trial jury (**petit jury**). Official qualifications for jurors are not high. To ensure that jurors are properly informed concerning their work, the court gives them brief printed instructions (in English and Spanish) that describe their duties and explain basic legal terms and trial procedures. In urban counties, these instructions are often shown as a video in English and other languages common to segments of the county's population, such as Spanish or Vietnamese.

grand jury
Composed of 12 persons with the qualifications of trial jurors, a grand jury serves six months while it determines whether sufficient evidence exists to indict persons accused of committing crimes.

petit jury
A trial jury of 6 or 12 members.

Qualifications, Selection, and Compensation of Jurors A qualified Texas juror must be

- A citizen of the United States and of the State of Texas
- 18 years of age or older
- Of sound mind
- Able to read and write (with no restriction on language), unless literate jurors are unavailable
- Neither convicted of a felony nor under indictment or other legal accusation of theft or any felony

Qualified persons have a legal responsibility to serve when called, unless exempted or excused. Exemptions include

- Being age 70 or older
- Having legal custody of a child or children younger than age 10
- Being enrolled in and attending a university, college, or secondary school
- Being the primary caregiver for an invalid
- Being employed by the legislative branch of state government
- Having served as a petit juror within the preceding two years in counties with populations of at least 200,000 or the preceding three years in counties with populations of more than 250,000
- Being on active military duty outside the county

Judges may excuse others from jury duty in special circumstances. A person who is legally exempt from jury duty may file a signed statement with the court clerk at any time before the scheduled date of appearance. In most counties, prospective jurors complete necessary exemption forms online. Anyone summoned for jury duty can reschedule the reporting date once (at least twice in urban counties), as long as the new date is within six months of the original. Subsequent rescheduling requires an emergency that could not have been previously anticipated, such as illness or a death in the family. Failure to report for jury duty or falsely claiming an exemption is punishable as contempt of court, and a guilty individual can be fined up to $1,000.

A **venire** (panel of prospective jurors) is chosen by random selection from a list provided by either the secretary of state, another governmental agency, or a private contractor selected by the county commissioners court. The list includes the county's registered voters, licensed drivers, and persons with identification cards issued by the Department of Public Safety. A trial jury is composed of 6 or 12 citizens, one of whom serves as foreman or presiding juror: 6 serve in a justice of the peace court, municipal court, or county court, whereas 12 serve in a district court. A jury panel generally includes more than the minimum number of jurors.

Attorneys question jurors through a procedure called **voir dire** (which means "to speak the truth") to identify any potential jurors who cannot be fair and impartial. Prospective jurors can expect to be asked about their social media habits, such as who they follow on Twitter. In some instances,

venire
A panel of prospective jurors drawn by random selection. These prospective jurors are called veniremen.

voir dire
Courtroom procedure in which attorneys question prospective jurors to identify any who cannot be fair and impartial.

attorneys will have reviewed veniremen's Facebook accounts and other social media sites. An attorney may challenge for cause any venire member suspected of bias. If the judge agrees with the attorney, the prospective juror is excused from serving. Some individuals try to avoid jury duty by answering voir dire questions in a way that makes them appear biased.

An attorney challenges prospective jurors either by peremptory challenge (up to 15 per side, depending on the type of case, without having to give a reason for excluding the venire members) or by challenge for cause (an unlimited number). Jurors may not be eliminated on the basis of race or ethnicity. For a district court, a trial jury is made up of the first 12 venire members who are neither excused by the district judge nor challenged peremptorily by a party in the case. For lower courts, the first six venire members accepted form a jury. A judge may direct the selection of alternate jurors to replace any seated juror who can no longer serve. Once impaneled, jurors are sworn in and receive further instructions from the court. They will be instructed to avoid communication with others about the trial during the proceedings. Not only is direct communication disallowed, jurors are also prohibited from sending information about the trial through tweets, Facebook postings, or blogs. Attempts to communicate with parties to the trial such as friending them on social media sites is also prohibited.

Although daily pay for venire members and jurors varies from county to county, minimum pay for juror service is $6 for all or part of the first day of jury duty and $40 for each subsequent day. Under state law, counties fund the first $6 per juror each day, and the state reimburses the counties up to $34 per juror for each subsequent day of service. Employers are not required to pay wages to an employee summoned or selected for jury duty; however, they are prohibited by law from discharging permanent employees for such service.

Judicial Procedures in Civil Cases

LO11.3 Describe the judicial procedure for the adjudication of civil lawsuits.

The term civil law generally refers to matters not covered by criminal law. The following are important subjects of civil law: **torts** (for example, unintended injury to another person in a traffic accident); contracts (for example, agreements to deliver property of a specified quality at a certain price); and domestic relations or family law (such as divorce). Civil law disputes usually involve individuals or corporations in lawsuits that seek money damages or injunctive relief (requiring someone to do or cease doing something). In criminal cases, a person is prosecuted by the state.

The state legislature frequently changes both criminal and civil law. In recent years, the state legislature, through statutes and proposed constitutional amendments, and the people of Texas, by ratification of constitutional amendments, have greatly limited money damage recoveries in tort cases.[24]

✓ 11.2 Learning Check

1. A court must have jurisdiction to hear a case. What does this mean?
2. True or False: It is the responsibility of the grand jury to determine whether a defendant is guilty.

Answers on p. 434.

---

tort
An injury to a person or an individual's property resulting from the wrongful act of another.

In civil cases, plaintiffs may be eligible to recover for three different types of damages:

- Economic damages, which include lost wages and actual expenses (for example, hospital bills)
- Noneconomic damages, which include a loss in quality of life, such as disfigurement, mental anguish, and emotional distress
- Exemplary or punitive damages, which are intended to punish the defendant

Originally juries determined the maximum amount of money judgments. Now, these recovery amounts, especially for noneconomic and exemplary damages, are restricted by law.

A major justification for limiting recoveries in tort cases is that individuals and businesses must pay high liability insurance premiums for protection against the risk of lawsuit judgments. After limitations were placed on recoveries in medical malpractice cases, many insurers reduced their malpractice insurance rates, and the number of physicians relocating to Texas increased. Likewise, between 2003 (the year the law was enacted) and 2011 (the most recent year for which information is available), the number of filed lawsuits dropped by two-thirds and recoveries were cut by about one-fourth.[25] Skeptics note that the cost of health care and health insurance premiums for consumers has continued to rise.[26] Additionally, according to some observers, the most vulnerable patients, those in nursing homes and children, are denied access to the courts because their economic losses are small since they have no lost income, even though their nonecomonic losses, such as pain and suffering, may be immense.

Recoveries for other types of torts, such as those arising from trucking accidents, have not been so restricted. Texas's recent oil and gas boom has led to increased road usage and more injuries and deaths on roadways in the areas of the state with the highest levels of oil and gas activity. In March 2014, a Dimmitt County jury (in Southwest Texas) awarded a decedent's family $281 million for his wrongful death from a trucking company's improper maintenance of one of its vehicles. The truck's driveshaft broke off the engine and flew through the windshield of a nearby pickup. The trucking company appealed and argued that the award was excessive based on current "judicial norms."[27] In August 2014, the parties settled the lawsuit for an undisclosed amount.

Civil Trial Procedure

plaintiff
The injured party who initiates a civil suit or the state in a criminal proceeding.

defendant
The person sued in a civil proceeding or prosecuted in a criminal proceeding.

The Supreme Court of Texas makes rules of civil procedure for all courts with civil jurisdiction. These rules, however, cannot conflict with any general law of the state. Rules of civil procedure are enacted unless they are rejected by the legislature.

Civil cases normally begin when the **plaintiff** (injured party) files a petition, or a document containing the plaintiff's complaints against the **defendant** and the remedy sought—usually money damages. This petition is filed with the clerk of the court (through efiletexas.gov in most counties) in which the lawsuit is contemplated, and the clerk issues a citation. The citation is delivered to the defendant, directing that person to answer the charges. To contest the suit, the defendant must file an answer to the plaintiff's charges. The answer explains why the plaintiff is not entitled to the remedy sought and asks that the plaintiff be required to prove every charge made in the petition.

Some individuals represent themselves pro se (without a lawyer) and file multiple frivolous lawsuits. If a defendant prevails in having the plaintiff declared a vexatious litigant by a court, the person's name is placed on a list maintained online by the Office of Court Administration. Vexatious litigants must either file a bond with the court or, in some instances, obtain prior permission before proceeding with a lawsuit.

Before the judge sets a trial date (which may be many months or even years after the petition is filed), all interested parties should have had an opportunity to file their petitions, answers, or other pleas with the court. These instruments constitute the pleadings in the case and form the basis of the trial. Prior to the trial, the parties also have the opportunity to gather information related to the pending case from each other. This process, known as **discovery**, includes examining documents, obtaining written and oral answers to questions, inspecting property under the control of the other party, and similar activities. Information obtained during discovery may become evidence in the case. Among the items attorneys research are any electronic communications, such as email, a party might have created or received, as well as postings on social media sites. Some unethical practitioners have attempted to friend a party to get into the more private areas of these sites.

Either party has the option to have a jury determine the facts. Over the past 25 years, the number of cases decided by a jury has decreased by more than 60 percent.[28] Less than 0.4 percent of civil lawsuits are tried to a jury. After the jury determines the facts, the judge applies the law to that version of the facts. If no one demands a jury, the trial judge decides all facts and applies the law. Fewer than one-third of all filed lawsuits are tried to the judge in a proceeding known as a bench trial. In recent years, the number of bench trials has also been in rapid decline while the number of cases settled by agreement between the plaintiff and defendant has increased. The remaining cases are dismissed.

Trial and Appeal of a Civil Case

As a trial begins, lawyers for each party make brief opening statements. The plaintiff's case is presented first. The defendant has an opportunity to contest all evidence introduced and may cross-examine the plaintiff's witnesses. After the plaintiff's case has been presented, it is the defendant's turn to offer evidence and the testimony of witnesses. The plaintiff may challenge this evidence and testimony. The judge is the final authority as to what evidence and testimony may be introduced by all parties, though objections to the judge's rulings can be used as grounds for appeal.

In a jury trial, after all parties have concluded, the judge writes a charge to the jury, submits it to the parties for their approval, makes any necessary

discovery
Gathering information from the opposing party and witnesses in a lawsuit, including examination of relevant documents, obtaining written and oral answers to questions, inspecting property under the control of the other party, and similar activities.

changes they suggest, and reads the charge to the jury. In the charge, the judge instructs the jury on the rules governing their deliberations and defines various terms. After the charge is read, attorneys make their closing arguments to the jurors; then the jury retires to elect one of its members to serve as the presiding juror (commonly referred to as foreman) and to deliberate.

The jury will not be asked directly whether the plaintiff or the defendant should win. Instead, the jury must answer a series of questions that will establish the facts of the case. These questions are called **special issues**. Judgment is based on jurors' answers. To decide a case in a district court, at least 10 of the 12 jurors must agree on answers to all of the special issues; in a county court or JP court, five of six must agree. If the required number of jurors cannot reach agreement, the foreman reports a hung jury. If the judge agrees, the jury is discharged. Any party may then request a new trial, which will be scheduled unless the case is dismissed. If the judge disagrees with the foreman's report, jurors continue to deliberate.

A jury's decision is a **verdict**. When there is no jury, the judge arrives at a verdict. In either case, the judge prepares a written decision, or the **judgment** or decree of the court. Any party may then file a motion for a new trial based on the reasons the party believes the trial was unfair. If the judge agrees, a new trial is ordered; if not, the case may be appealed to a higher court. A complete written record of the trial is sent to the appellate court. The usual route of appeals is from a county or district court to a court of appeals and then, in some instances, to the Texas Supreme Court.

> ✔ **11.3 Learning Check**
>
> 1. What are the parties to a civil lawsuit called?
> 2. True or False: In a civil jury trial, jurors will be asked to decide which party should win.
>
> Answers on p. 435.

Judicial Procedures in Criminal Cases

★ LO11.4 Describe the judicial procedure for the adjudication of criminal cases.

Criminal cases occur when someone violates the rules of society by committing an offense for which the government can seek the offender's life, liberty, or property. Because a defendant risks losing his or her natural rights, the rules and procedures in criminal cases include many more checks on the system than in civil cases. From the moment a person is taken into custody until all appeals have been exhausted, the law is designed to assure the highest level of protection for the defendant's rights.

Criminal Justice System

Rules of criminal procedure are made by the legislature. The Texas Code of Criminal Procedure is written to comply with U.S. Supreme Court rulings regarding confessions, arrests, searches, and seizures. Additional rules of procedure have been adopted to promote fairness and efficiency in handling criminal cases.

It is likely that millions of illegal acts (including traffic violations) are committed daily in Texas. After an arrest and before questioning, police

special issues
Questions a judge gives a trial jury to answer to establish facts in a civil case.

verdict
A jury's decision about a court case.

judgment
A judge's written opinion based on a verdict.

must advise suspects of their constitutional rights to remain silent and to have an attorney present (a procedure commonly known as a *Miranda* warning). When a prosecuting attorney files charges, a suspect must appear before a judicial officer (usually a justice of the peace), who names the offense or offenses charged and provides information concerning the suspect's legal rights. A person charged with a noncapital offense may be released on personal recognizance (promising to report for trial at a later date), released on bail by posting personal money or money provided for a charge by a bail bond service, or denied bail and jailed.

People who cannot afford to hire a lawyer must be provided with the services of an attorney in any felony or misdemeanor case in which conviction may result in a prison or jail sentence. The 13-member Texas Indigent Defense Commission, comprised of judges, attorneys, and legislators, oversees the development of statewide policies and procedures for the representation of the poorest defendants. In addition, it monitors county compliance and coordinates state monetary assistance for these programs. County taxpayers, however, bear the major burden of this expense.

Private attorneys, appointed by judges, provide most of the defense for indigent defendants, but an increasing number of counties maintain public defenders' offices to meet some of the representation needs of the poor. A study of the results achieved by the public defenders' office in Harris County found that although per case cost was higher for public defender representation ($946 versus $550), fewer defendants received guilty verdicts. Private criminal defense attorneys often oppose the creation of public defenders' offices; however, the Harris County office represented only 6 percent of indigent criminal defendants.[29] The Texas Fair Defense Act requires counties to devise standards for appointed counsel and establishes minimum attorney qualifications for the appointment of counsel for indigent defendants charged with capital crimes.

Under Texas law, the right to trial by jury is guaranteed in all criminal cases. Except in death penalty cases, defendants may waive jury trial (if the prosecuting attorney agrees), regardless of the plea—guilty, not guilty, or nolo contendere (no contest). To expedite procedures, prosecuting and defense attorneys may engage in plea bargaining, in which the accused pleads guilty in return for a promise that the prosecutor will seek a lighter sentence or will recommend community supervision. Usually, a judge will accept a plea bargain. If the defendant waives a trial by jury and is found guilty by a judge, that judge also determines punishment.

Criminal Trial and Appeal

After the trial jury has been selected, the prosecuting attorney reads an information (misdemeanor) or an indictment (felony) to inform the jury of the basic allegations of the state's case. The defendant then enters a plea.

As plaintiff, the state begins by calling its witnesses and introducing any evidence supporting the information or the indictment. The defense may then challenge evidence and cross-examine witnesses. Next, the defense presents its case, calling witnesses and submitting evidence that, in turn, the prosecution attacks. After all evidence and testimony have been presented, the judge charges the jury by instructing jurors on rules governing their deliberations and explaining the law applicable to the case. Both prosecuting and defense attorneys then address final arguments to the jury before it retires to reach a verdict.

The jury must reach a unanimous decision to return a verdict of guilty or not guilty. If jurors are hopelessly split, the result is a hung jury. In that event, the judge declares a mistrial and discharges the jurors. When requested by the prosecuting attorney, the judge orders a new trial with another jury.

If a jury brings a verdict before a court, the judge may choose to disregard it and order a new trial on the grounds that the jury failed to arrive at a verdict that achieves substantial justice. In a jury trial, the jury may fix the sentence if the convicted person so requests; otherwise, the judge determines the sentence. A separate hearing on the penalty is held, at which time the person's prior criminal or juvenile record, general reputation, and other relevant factors may be introduced, such as facts concerning the convicted person's background and lifestyle as determined by a presentence investigation.

A convicted defendant has the right to appeal on grounds that an error in trial procedure occurred. All appeals (except for death penalty cases) are heard first by the court of appeals in the district in which the trial was held. A few of these appeals are ultimately reviewed by the Texas Court of Criminal Appeals. Death penalty appeals are made directly to the Texas Court of Criminal Appeals.

✓**11.4 Learning Check**

1. True or False: A majority of jurors must return a verdict of guilty or not guilty.
2. A capital felony for which the defendant received the death penalty is appealed to which court?

Answers on p. 435.

A Short History of Texas Courts

Honorable J. D. Langley, Judge, 85th District Court

Just as Texas represents the cultures of the countries that have claimed the area over the past 300 years, so too do its courts. In this brief historical account, District Judge J. D. Langley reviews the influence of the Spanish, Mexican, and U.S. court systems on the state's modern-day court structure.

From the time the first Europeans arrived in the area known as Texas to discover only native tribes and wild animals until its growth to a current population of more than 27 million, judges and courts of many kinds have served the inhabitants. The lure of undiscovered wealth, inexpensive land, good climate, and the possibility of a bright future brought a diverse group of settlers into Texas. With growth came conflicts between people competing to achieve wealth and happiness—conflicts that required resolution by judicial action.

New Spain (1716–1821)

After the expeditions of Pineda, Cabeza de Vaca, Coronado, de Soto, and Moscoso, the vast region that became Texas was the *frontera* or frontier of New Spain. "*Frontera*" in 18th century Spain meant "a fixed border area." To defend its claim to this vast frontier, Spain created *municipios*, or municipalities to provide for both a centralized government and defense against hostile attacks and invasions.

The municipalities were established under the *Recopilación de las leyes de los reinos de las Indias* (*Compilation of the Laws of the Kingdom of the Indies*), a code of Spanish laws. This code specified the duties of officials and procedures for municipalities. It was first issued in 1680, and revised in 1772, 1791, and 1805.

Each municipality was governed by an elected council called an *ayuntamiento* that consisted of citizen members called *regidores* and one or more elected leaders called an *alcalde*. The size of the ayuntamiento depended on a municipality's population. Larger *municipios* had up to two alcaldes and 12 regidores, plus two *escribanos* or clerks. The ayuntamiento could also appoint a *síndico procurado*, similar to today's city or county attorney; an *aguacil* (sheriff or police chief); two *escribanos* (clerks); and a *mayordomo* (supervisor of public land and its use).

The alcalde acted as the local magistrate or judge and presided over the ayuntamiento. Each alcalde had primary jurisdiction in both civil and criminal cases in his municipality. By the time Moses Austin arrived in San Antonio de Bexar in December 1820, there were three municipios established in the province of Tejas: Bexar (established in 1716), Nacogdoches (established in 1716), and Laredo (established in 1787).

Tejas (1821–1836)

The Spanish legal tradition became the basis for Tejano legal thought when the Mexican Federation was established in 1821. Under Mexico's constitution, authority to create municipios was delegated to the State of Coahuila y Tejas. As contractual grants were issued to *empresarios* for the settlement of Tejas by U.S. immigrants, each empresario was given authority by the legislature to establish a judicial system in the area covered by his grant. Stephen F. Austin, the first empresario in Tejas, initially created a justice of the peace for his jurisdiction, but that position was supplanted by the Mexican government's return to the ayuntamiento system with elected alcaldes for each of the municipalities. Any area with at least 40 families could establish a municipio; and when the population reached 200 (later 500), residents could elect their own ayuntamiento. Elected alcaldes had civil and criminal jurisdiction and reported their judgments to the legislative branch. Cases involving members of native tribes and people in religious orders were disposed in the canonical courts of the church. The alcaldes continued to be the primary judiciary for cases arising in Texas until the constitutional convention of the new republic in late 1836.

The Republic (1836–1845)

After Texas achieved its independence from Mexico, the Constitution of 1836 authorized a simple four-tiered court system patterned after those found in the United States, consisting of a Supreme Court, District Courts, County Courts, and Justices of the Peace. A Chief Justice and the District Judges, who served as judges in their judicial districts and as Associate Justices on Texas's Supreme Court, were initially appointed to four-year terms by a majority vote of a joint session of the Republic's Congress. The Supreme Court held annual sessions and had virtually unlimited appellate jurisdiction. The new Congress divided the state into four judicial districts, which grew to seven judicial districts by 1845.

Once selected, a District Judge was required to live in his judicial district and hold court in each county in his district at least twice per year. The District Courts were courts of general jurisdiction, meaning they could hear criminal cases and civil cases where the amount in controversy exceeded $100, unless specific jurisdiction was granted to another court. Jury trials were guaranteed for all civil and criminal cases in District Court. Appeals from District Court decisions were heard by the Supreme Court.

By the end of 1836, the republic had created 23 counties, each of which roughly surrounded the existing municipios. Over the next 30 years, a political struggle ensued for control of county government between the Justices of the Peace and what would later become known as County Commissioners.

The Congress initially created a County Court for each county composed of a Chief Justice, chosen by joint ballot of both houses of Congress, and two Associate Justices, chosen by a majority vote of the Justices of the Peace in the county. The County Court had concurrent jurisdiction with the District Court in civil cases involving more than $100, and appellate jurisdiction over cases decided by the Justices of the Peace in the county.

Two Justices of the Peace were elected by the people in each militia captain's district (later to become precincts). Each Justice of the Peace issued arrest and search warrants, set bail, and tried civil cases involving $100 or less. Additionally, the Chief Justice of the County together with all the Justices of the Peace acted as a county board of commissioners to manage the county's roads, bridges, and ferries, as well as care for the poor.

In 1841, the people of the county gained the power to elect the Chief Justice of the County Court. By 1844, the Congress replaced the original County Court structure with a County Court consisting of a Chief Justice and four County Commissioners, all elected by the county's voters.

The judiciary of the Republic of Texas were not required to be lawyers by profession; however, over its more than 10-year history, the reality became that the justices and judges of the Supreme Court and District Courts were all lawyers. Conversely, less than 10 percent of all people who served as Chief Justices of the County Court were lawyers. This distinction in fact would become a distinction in law.

Statehood (1845–1861)

When Texas was admitted as the 28th state of the United States, the Constitution of 1845 modified the composition of the Supreme Court to consist of a chief justice and two associate justices (who were not also serving as District Court Judges). The manner for selection of the Justices of the Supreme Court and the Judges of the District Courts changed to appointment by the governor with the advice and consent of two-thirds of the Texas Senate.

The County Court received little reference in the 1845 constitution. Its existence, powers, duties, and composition were left entirely to the discretion of the state legislature. The structure became one chief justice and four county commissioners, each from a separate precinct in the county. The Justices of the Peace were mentioned in the constitution, but their powers and duties were mostly left to legislative discretion.

Most civil and criminal trial jurisdiction during this period of Texas history was exercised by the Justices of the Peace and the District Courts. The duties of the County Chief Justice and Board of Commissioners were primarily the management of the county, but it retained some jurisdiction over probate, estates, and guardianships.

The Confederacy (1861–1866)

Upon secession from the Union and admission to the Confederacy, the Constitution of 1861 made few changes to the judicial branch. Judges were required to take an oath that they would "faithfully and impartially discharge and perform all duties" under the Constitution and laws of the Confederate States of America.

Reconstruction (1866–1876)

During Reconstruction the state's Supreme Court continued to consist of three judges who were appointed by the Governor, but both the Supreme Court and District Judges only needed a majority vote in the Texas Senate to be confirmed. In addition to one District Judge in each judicial district, the Constitution of 1866 authorized the legislature to create specialized criminal courts in counties with major cities. This experiment in the creation of statutory courts to address specific needs resurfaced when Texas began to urbanize.

The most significant change following the Civil War was to the county court structure. The Constitution of 1866 required every county to elect five Justices of the Peace who together would act as the County Court and "have such jurisdiction, similar to that heretofore exercised by County Commissioners and Police Courts." Under the Constitution of 1869, all Justices of the Peace were appointed by the Governor. After appointment, one of the Justices of the Peace was required to reside at the county seat. The Justice of the Peace who resided at the county seat acted as the Presiding Judge of the County Court.

Urbanization (1876–Now)

After Reconstruction, the citizens of Texas were eager to recover control over their government. The Constitution of 1876 was a wholesale remodeling to limit the power of the governor and legislative branch and return control to the voters. Since 1876, all judges (except municipal judges) have been elected by the state's voters. All four tiers of the court system, as well as the qualifications, powers, and duties of judges, were detailed in the constitution, limiting the power of the legislature and governor to exert control over the judicial branch.

Appellate Courts

To deal with the rising appellate caseload, criminal appeals were removed from the jurisdiction of the Texas Supreme Court in 1876. While the number of justices remained the same (a Chief Justice and two Associate Justices), the appellate jurisdiction of the Supreme Court was limited to civil cases. The civil appeal caseload continued to increase, and in 1918 the legislature authorized commissioners to assist the court in handling its caseload. The statutory commissioners were converted to Associate Justices by constitutional amendment in 1945 when the number of Associate Justices was set at its current number: eight.

The Constitution of 1876 created one Court of Appeals limited to three judges to hear appeals in all criminal cases and in certain civil appeals from County Courts. By constitutional amendment ratified in 1891, the Texas Court of Criminal Appeals was created as the state's highest criminal appellate court with three judges elected statewide to six-year terms of office.

By 1925, because of an increase in the criminal appellate caseload, the legislature authorized the governor to appoint a two-judge Commission of Appeals to assist the Court of Criminal Appeals. Nine years later, the legislature allowed the Court of Criminal Appeals to appoint the commissioners. The commissioners were converted to judges on the court by constitutional amendment in 1966, thus increasing the number of judges on the court to five. That same amendment allowed the voters, instead of the judges on the court, to choose the

Presiding Judge of the Court of Criminal Appeals. In 1969, a growing caseload again caused the legislature to temporarily bring back the Commission of Appeals for nine years. A constitutional amendment in 1977 increased the size of the Court of Criminal Appeals to its current number: nine judges, including the Presiding Judge.

In addition to creating the Court of Criminal Appeals, the 1891 amendment authorized the legislature to create regional Courts of Civil Appeals with intermediate appellate jurisdiction over civil cases only. Each court required a minimum of three justices—one Chief Justice and at least two Associate Justices. The latest measure to address the caseload of the court occurred by constitutional amendment in 1981 to add intermediate criminal appellate jurisdiction to the Courts of Appeals. There are today 14 Courts of Appeals with 80 justices determining appeals in panels of at least three justices.

Trial Courts

The Constitution of 1876 gave the legislature the authority to create trial courts as necessary. This power extended to three tiers of the court system: District, County, and Justice of the Peace Courts. In 1876, the constitution specified 26 judicial districts. The legislature (through 2014) had created 458 district courts. Additionally, the legislature had created 256 statutory courts (through 2014), including county courts-at-law and probate courts.

There were 220 counties in Texas when the Constitution of 1876 became effective. In 1931, the Texas legislature reestablished Loving County (on the Texas–New Mexico border), thus establishing 254 counties. Although every county is required to have a County Judge, in those counties where a statutory county court exists, the County Judge generally only presides over the Commissioners Court and manages the county's affairs. Under the Constitution of 1876, each county was also required to divide into no fewer than four Justices of the Peace precincts. By a 1983 constitutional amendment, the number of Justice of the Peace precincts was established as one to eight depending on a county's population. Today, voters elect one (or two) Justice(s) of the Peace in each precinct in the state.

Conclusion

Over the last 300 years, the Texas economy has developed from a land speculator base to an agriculture base to an oil base and has now achieved a relatively balanced economy that continues to lure migration over its borders. Throughout that time, the thriving economy brought attendant increases in conflicts between all who were trying to own and use the increasingly scarce resources of Texas. Numerous governments have grappled with creating and developing judicial resources to resolve these disputes. The result frequently leaves those unfamiliar with the history of the Texas judicial system curious about why it is so complex. The answer is simply that the history of the Texas courts is—like Texas itself—a growing, vibrant, and ever-changing enterprise.

✔ **Selected Reading Learning Check**

1. True or False. Since the days of the Republic, Texas has had a four-tiered court system.
2. How did the Constitution of 1876 limit the power of the governor and legislature over the judicial branch?

Answers on p. 435.

....

The Honorable J. D. Langley presides over the 85th District Court in Brazos County and teaches government at Blinn College–Bryan. This article was specially commissioned for *Practicing Texas Politics*.

Conclusion

The Texas legal system is indeed confusing. From sorting out overlapping court jurisdictions to identifying elected judges and justices—the system appears to be shrouded in mystery and anonymity. Often understood only by those who use the system daily—Texas lawyers—decisions of criminal and civil court judges affect every Texan. It is therefore critical that Texans understand this complex system. Technology has affected all aspects of the judicial branch. The ability of computers to process and organize large volumes of data has made the system more efficient. Ease of communication through alternative media has sometimes confused its users, whether judges, lawyers, or jurors. The move into the 21st century has included problems not contemplated by those who designed the judicial branch.

Chapter Summary

LO 11.1 **Identify the sources of Texas law**. The role of courts is to interpret and apply the law. Texas state law includes both civil law and criminal law. The sources of law include the state's constitution, its statutes, regulations, and the common law (judge-made law). In an attempt to organize its laws, the legislature has instructed the Texas Legislative Council to place laws that cover specific topics into codes. This work has been ongoing for more than 50 years.

LO 11.2 **Compare the functions of all participants in the justice system**. Both constitutional and statutory laws have been used to create the state's court system. Courts may have original or appellate jurisdiction, or both. Texas has local, county, trial, and appellate courts. Some trial courts are now specialty courts that provide more direct oversight of particular types of cases or proceedings involving specific populations. The state's emphasis on parties' resolving their disputes outside the courtroom has resulted in fewer trials. Almost all Texas judges are elected through popular, partisan elections, a system followed in only three other states. Once in office, a judge, as well as the lawyers who appear before him or her, are subject to regulation and discipline. There are two types of juries: grand juries (which determine if adequate cause exists to bring a defendant to trial in a criminal case) and petit juries (which determine the facts in criminal and civil cases).

LO 11.3 **Describe the judicial procedure for the adjudication of civil lawsuits**. The civil justice system includes contract cases, tort cases, family law matters, and juvenile justice cases. The Texas legislature has limited the amount of punitive and noneconomic damages in tort cases. In jury trials for civil cases, the jury determines the facts of the case by answering special issues and the judge applies the law. In Texas's bifurcated court system, the highest appellate court for civil cases is the Texas Supreme Court.

LO 11.4 **Describe the judicial procedure for the adjudication of criminal cases**. Criminal law regulates many types of behavior. Protections that are built into the law, for felony cases in particular, include a defendant's being advised of his or her *Miranda* rights, the right to appointed counsel if someone is indigent, the right to a grand jury indictment, and the right to trial by jury. Except in capital murder cases, a defendant can waive the right to a jury trial. Jury verdicts in criminal cases must be unanimous. In Texas's bifurcated court system, the highest appellate court for criminal cases is the Texas Court of Criminal Appeals.

Key Terms

civil law, p. 405
criminal law, p. 405
misdemeanor, p. 405
felony, p. 405
jurisdiction, p. 405
probate, p. 406
original jurisdiction, p. 406
appellate jurisdiction, p. 406
exclusive jurisdiction, p. 406
concurrent jurisdiction, p. 406
municipal court, p. 406

justice of the peace, p. 406
court of record, p. 409
bifurcated, p. 413
specialty courts, p. 415
alternative dispute resolution (ADR), p. 415
Missouri Plan, p. 417
appointment-retention system, p. 417
contingency fee, p. 420
grand jury, p. 421

petit jury, p. 421
venire, p. 422
voir dire, p. 422
tort, p. 423
plaintiff, p. 424
defendant, p. 424
discovery, p. 425
special issues, p. 426
verdict, p. 426
judgment, p. 426

Learning Check Answers

11.1 1. False. Misdemeanors and felonies are considered criminal law cases.
2. True. Texas courts interpret and apply judgemade common law based on custom and tradition dating back to medieval England, in addition to state laws that include the provisions of the Texas Constitution, statutes enacted by the legislature, and regulations adopted by state agencies.

11.2 1. Jurisdiction means that the court has the authority to hear a particular kind of case. Jurisdiction may be granted in the Texas Constitution or in the statute creating a court.
2. False. A grand jury only determines if there is enough evidence to go to trial in a criminal case. A petit jury determines if a defendant is guilty.

11.3 1. The parties to a civil lawsuit are the plaintiff, who is the injured party bringing the lawsuit, and the defendant, who is the person being sued.

2. False. In a civil jury, trial jurors answer special issues, or a series of questions about the facts in the case. The judge then applies the law to the answers to the special issues and renders a judgment establishing who won the case.

11.4 1. False. A jury verdict in a criminal case, whether guilty or not guilty, requires a unanimous decision by the jury.

2. A capital felony for which the defendant received the death penalty is appealed to the Court of Criminal Appeals.

Selected Reading Learning Check

1. True. The Constitution of 1836 established a four-tiered court system including the supreme court, district courts, county courts, and justice of the peace courts.

2. The Constitution of 1876 took appointive power for judges away from the governor and legislature and gave the people the power to elect all judges (except some municipal judges).

The Criminal Justice System

Learning Objectives

12.1 Describe the different classifications of criminal offenses.

12.2 Analyze issues of the death penalty in Texas.

12.3 Explain the role of Texas's jail and prison system in handling corrections and rehabilitations.

12.4 Compare the juvenile justice system to the adult correctional system.

12.5 Evaluate the fairness of Texas's justice system.

Nick Anderson Editorial Cartoon used with the permission of Nick Anderson, the Washington Post Writers Group and the Cartoonist Group. All rights reserved.

CRITICAL THINKING

Take a close look at the cartoon. If people think of Texas as the execution capital, what impact does that perception have on the state?

In the early morning hours of August 18, 1992, four children under the age of eight years old and two adults were brutally murdered in Somerville, a small community northwest of Houston. Two of the children were bludgeoned to death, one child was shot, and all six of the victims were stabbed multiple times. Gasoline was poured over the bodies, along with the house, and then set on fire. At the funeral, Robert Carter, the father of one of the victims, showed up with burns and abrasions. Immediately Carter became a suspect and was brought in for questioning by the Texas Rangers. Carter's story to the authorities was implausible. He consented to a polygraph test and failed. Although polygraph tests are not admissible in courts, they can help direct an investigation.

When investigators confronted Carter about the failed polygraph and his inconsistent story, he implicated his wife and Anthony Graves, his wife's cousin. Carter gave the Rangers a detailed account of how Graves went room to room on a killing spree while he watched. During the interrogation the officers honed in on Graves and issued a warrant for his arrest based on Carter's account of events. Immediately after Carter's confession, he and Graves were arrested.

Although Graves had an alibi and Carter recanted his story before the grand jury and multiple times before his execution in 2000,[1] Graves was convicted, sentenced to death, and incarcerated. Several factors contributed to Graves's conviction and sentence. A report of the case filed by Texas Ranger Ray Coffman omitted any reference to Grave's alibi and those who could support it, including family members and an employee of a Brenham Jack-in-the-Box. (Brenham is approximately 15 miles from the murder scene.) Pressure on the district attorney, Charles Sebesta, to get a conviction and a death penalty sentence was high. After Robert Carter claimed he acted alone and wavered on testifying against Anthony Graves, the prosecutor promised Carter that if he provided testimony against Graves, no questions would be raised about the possible involvement of Carter's wife in the murders. Although Sebesta stated that he advised the defense attorneys about Carter's admission, Graves's attorneys maintained they were never told. Under the U.S. Supreme Court's decision in *Brady v. Maryland*, 373 U.S. 83 (1963), prosecutors must disclose **exculpatory evidence** that could be favorable to an accused.

On November 1, 1994, jurors found Graves guilty of capital murder. During the penalty phase, he was sentenced to death in less than two hours. On May 31, 2000, Carter was executed. In his last words, he claimed Graves's innocence and stated that he acted alone. Sebesta retired in 2000.

On March 3, 2006, the U.S. Court of Appeals, Fifth Circuit set aside Graves's conviction and sentence. Sebesta was faulted for his failure to provide exculpatory evidence to Graves's defense attorneys. After a lengthy reinvestigation of the case, Burleson-Washington County District Attorney Bill Parham dropped all charges against Graves, noting, "This man is not guilty." Special prosecutors determined that Charles Sebesta had misled jurors, fabricated, and concealed evidence of Graves's innocence. Sebesta maintains a website to explain his actions in this case.

exculpatory evidence
Evidence that helps a defendant and may exonerate the defendant in a criminal trial.

On October 27, 2010, Anthony Graves was released after spending 18 years incarcerated for a crime he did not commit. In 2011, he was awarded $1.4 million in restitution for wrongful incarceration. Graves filed a grievance with the State Bar of Texas against Charles Sebesta for the former district attorney's actions in his wrongful prosecution. In July 2014, the State Bar of Texas found there is "just cause" to look into allegations of misconduct by Sebesta.

In his opinion in *Brady v. Maryland*, U.S. Supreme Court Justice William O. Douglas observed, "Society wins not only when the guilty are convicted but when criminal trials are fair; our system of the administration of justice suffers when any accused is treated unfairly." Fairness becomes even more critical in cases that involve the death penalty. Cases such as that of Anthony Graves remind us that, unlike the proviso in the cartoon that opens this chapter, we must continue to ask if anyone convicted of a felony might be innocent. As you learn about Texas's justice system, consider what the state does to make the system fair and what practices might interfere with that goal.

Elements of the Criminal Justice System

LO12.1 Describe the different classifications of criminal offenses.

The Texas **criminal justice system** classifies different types of crimes as either felonies or misdemeanors (discussed in Chapter 11, "The Judicial Branch"). The **Texas Penal Code** is a codified body of laws that covers crime and its punishment. After each legislative session, the State of Texas updates its penal code to include new laws while keeping the core chapters and titles the same. The punishment of crimes in Texas varies from a fine to imprisonment based on the severity and category of a crime. Arguments have been made for continuing to strengthen criminal justice laws and policies while at the same time examining concerns about how Texas carries out justice. Laws may be applied differently based on the resources of local law enforcement and the prevailing attitudes of one's community.

Criminal Justice Law

As of 2014, the State of Texas identified 2,623 crimes as felonies.[2] Less serious offenses are classified as misdemeanors. Features of the Texas Penal Code include **graded penalties** for noncapital offenses and harsher penalties for repeat offenders. First-, second-, and third-degree felonies may involve imprisonment and fines in cases involving the most serious noncapital crimes. Some lesser offenses (especially those involving alcohol and drug abuse) are defined as state-jail felonies (so-called fourth-degree felonies) and are punishable by fines and confinement in jails operated by the state. The three classes of misdemeanors (A, B, and C) may involve county jail sentences and/or fines. (See Table 12.1 for categories of noncapital offenses

criminal justice system
The system involves prosecution, defense, sentencing, and punishment of those suspected or convicted of committing a crime.

Texas Penal Code
The body of Texas law covering crimes, penalties, and correctional measures.

graded penalties
Depending on the nature of the crime, noncapital felonies are graded as first degree, second degree, third degree, and state jail; misdemeanors are graded as A, B, and C.

Table 12.1	Selected Texas Noncapital Offenses, Penalties for First Offenders, and Courts Having Original Jurisdiction		
Selected Offense	**Offense Category**	**Punishment**	**Court**
Murder Theft of property valued at $200,000 or more	First-degree felony	Confinement for 5–99 years or life Maximum fine of $10,000	District court
Theft of property valued at $100,000 or more but less than $200,000 Aggravated assault, including of a spouse	Second-degree felony	Confinement for 2–20 years Maximum fine of $10,000	District court
Theft of property valued at $20,000 or more but less than $100,000 Impersonating someone online	Third-degree felony	Confinement for 2–10 years Maximum fine of $10,000	District court
Theft of property valued at $15,000 or more but less than $20,000 Possession of 4 ounces to 1 pound of marijuana	State-jail felony	Confinement for 180 days to 2 years Maximum fine of $10,000	District court
Theft of property valued at $500 or more but less than $1,500 Resisting arrest	Class A misdemeanor	Confinement for 1 year Maximum fine of $4,000	Constitutional county court and county court-at-law
Theft of property valued at $20 or more but less than $500 Terroristic threat	Class B misdemeanor	Confinement for 180 days Maximum fine of $2,000	Constitutional county court and county court-at-law
Theft of property valued at less than $20 Sexting (sending or possessing sexually explicit images of people 17 or younger by a minor)	Class C misdemeanor	No confinement Maximum fine of $500	Justice of the peace court and municipal court (if offense committed within city limits)

and ranges of penalties.) People who engage in organized criminal activity, repeat offenders, and those who commit hate crimes (crimes motivated by bias against a person's race, ethnicity, religion, age, gender, disability, or sexual preference) are punished as though the offender had committed the next higher degree of felony. This practice is called **enhanced punishment**.

Under the Texas Penal Code, a person commits murder if there is evidence of intent to kill or cause serious bodily harm to the victim. The presence of additional circumstances, such as the victim's age or role as a law enforcement official, makes the crime a **capital felony**, for which the death penalty may be applied.

Criminal Justice Policy

Policymaking in Texas takes into account public opinion, the state's budget, and federal court rulings. The Lone Star State's political culture requires elected officials to be seen as "tough on crime." Lengthy imprisonment is expensive, however; and Texas has one of the highest incarceration rates in the nation. Detention practices that do not result in cruel and unusual punishment (including provision of adequate facilities, health care, and prisoner safety) add to the cost of confinement. Increasing racial and ethnic diversity of Texas also creates tension among all its residents. These factors influence the state's policies with regard to criminal law.

Drug Crimes Since the 1980s, arrests for drug possession have ballooned in Texas. Most arrests are for possession of a controlled substance. Many people who are prosecuted for low-level drug crimes are dealing with a range of other issues, including mental illness, homelessness, and poverty. Prisons and jails are not equipped to treat these problems; untreated inmates are more likely to continue using drugs and commit other crimes when released. Texas relies heavily on incarceration as a primary response to drug offenses.

In the current century, state legislators have searched for less costly and more effective ways to address high incarceration rates for drug offenses. Solutions include easing parole criteria for nonviolent offenders, establishing in-prison treatment options, and creating specialty drug courts (see Chapter 11, "The Judicial Branch"). Since reforming its criminal justice policies, the state has experienced a nearly 20 percent reduction in crime.

All Texas counties with populations over 550,000 must establish drug courts. Research has shown that drug courts provide more extensive supervision than other programs. An example of a successful drug court is in Tarrant County, where SWIFT (Supervision With Intensive enForcemenT) Court was created in 2012. In a program described as "probation on steroids," offenders are closely monitored for strict compliance with probation conditions.

Inefficiencies in the criminal justice system occur even before trial. A yearlong study in Harris County examined more than 6,500 felony and misdemeanor cases. Many defendants spent weeks or months in county jail awaiting punishment for minor offenses, including possession of small

enhanced punishment
Additional penalties or prison time for those who engage in organized crime or hate crimes, and for repeat offenders.

capital felony
A crime punishable by death or life imprisonment without parole.

amounts of drugs.[3] By prosecuting and incarcerating Texans who suffer from addiction, the county and state limit their ability to become healthy, productive members of the community. The cost is much lower for drug treatment programs: under $4,000 per inmate per year, compared to state incarceration at nearly $19,000 per inmate per year.[4]

Hate Crimes Since 1993, Texas law has provided enhanced punishment for criminal acts against another person motivated by bias or prejudice against a group of which the victim was a member, also called hate crimes. Texas's first hate crimes law was vague and likely unconstitutional. In 1998, one of Texas's most horrific hate crimes occurred in Jasper, located in East Texas. James Byrd Jr., an African American man, was chained by his ankles to the back of a pickup truck and dragged for miles to his death by three white men. Authorities believe that he was conscious throughout the incident until his head hit the side of the road and he was decapitated. In response, the legislature passed the James Byrd Jr. Hate Crimes Act in 2001. This law strengthened Texas law by identifying specific targeted groups.

Violent acts that are perpetrated on specific groups of Texans are a threat to all Texans. The Texas Department of Public Safety (DPS) maintains a log of law enforcement agency reports on hate crimes. The record includes information on motivation for the crime, its location, the offender, the victim, and the type of offense committed.

In 2012, DPS classified 169 criminal incidents as hate crimes, an increase of 15 percent from 2011. Race was identified as the primary motivation for hate crimes, followed by hate crimes based on sexual orientation. DPS data indicate that one is more likely to become the victim of a hate crime in Dallas than in Houston or Austin.[5] The information that DPS collects can help policymakers determine if laws and policies are effective.

It is noteworthy that district attorneys determine which cases are prosecuted as hate crimes. Their reluctance to use this law is reflected in the fact that there has been roughly one conviction per year in which the statute has been officially invoked. Often prosecutors have used the law as leverage for a **plea bargain**. In response, civil rights groups have called for a law that would require the Texas attorney general's office to conduct a study analyzing the effectiveness of the Hate Crimes Act.

plea bargain
A deal between the prosecutor and the defendant in a criminal case in which the defendant agrees to plead guilty to a specific charge and in return will get certain concessions from the prosecutor.

12.1 Learning Check

1. What types of crimes may receive "enhanced punishment," and what does that mean?
2. True or False: Most low-level drug offenders have complicating issues such as homelessness and poverty.

Answers on p. 462.

The Death Penalty

★ **LO12.2** Analyze issues of the death penalty in Texas.

The death penalty has taken many forms in Texas. Before 1923, counties carried out executions by hanging. After 1923, the legislature required the state to execute offenders by electrocution. Due to a series of court challenges, no executions occurred in Texas between 1964 and 1982. In 1972, in the case of *Furman v. Georgia*, 408 U.S. 238 (1972), the U.S. Supreme Court ruled that the state's use of the death penalty was unconstitutional because its use was arbitrary and racially biased.

Reinstitution of the Death Penalty

Following the *Furman* decision, Texas rewrote its death penalty laws in 1973 to meet the U.S. Supreme Court's demands for standardization and fairness. The first execution under the new law occurred in 1982, when Texas became the first state in the nation to use a lethal injection. During the past three decades, no state has executed more capital felons than Texas (512 men and six women executed from January 1982 to October 2014).

A capital murderer can receive the death penalty in a variety of circumstances. Murder becomes a capital felony if the victim was younger than 10, or a police officer, firefighter, or prison employee acting in his or her official capacity. In addition, murders become capital felonies when they occur during the commission of another felony. Murder for hire, serial murders (including killing an unborn child), and inmate-on-inmate murder are also capital felonies. Although state law also allows the death penalty for a second conviction for rape of a child under the age of 14, legal commentators argue this law is unconstitutional. The U.S. Supreme Court has ruled that the death penalty can only be imposed for murder.

After a jury has found a defendant guilty of a capital offense, jurors must unanimously determine whether the accused represents a continuing threat to society and whether circumstances in the defendant's life warrant life imprisonment rather than death. The minimum sentence for a capital felony is life imprisonment without parole. If the state seeks the death penalty, all jurors must agree to the sentence. The death certificate of someone who has been executed lists the cause of death as "judicially ordered execution." Capital punishment remains controversial.[6]

The issue of racial bias has never been fully resolved. Courts have allowed testimony that a person's race may make the accused a continuing threat to society. Research suggests that the victim's race and gender (white females) is significant in determining whether the defendant receives the death penalty, regardless of the race of the accused. In addition to questions regarding racial bias and the possible innocence of some of the individuals executed, concerns remain about the method used to execute capital felons. From December 1982 through July 2012, Texas used a three-drug process that first rendered a prisoner unconscious, then induced paralysis, and finally stopped the heart. Currently, Texas prison officials give a lethal injection of pentobarbital, the same drug used to euthanize animals. State officials stockpiled pentobarbital (sold under the trade name Nembutal) when European pharmaceutical manufacturers announced they would no longer produce the drug for use in human executions.[7] When Texas ran out of the drug in September 2013, the state turned to compounding pharmacies for custom-made pentobarbital. Compounding pharmacies are unregulated by the U.S. Food and Drug Administration (FDA). In October 2013, several death row inmates in Texas filed a federal civil complaint against the Texas Department of Criminal Justice (TDCJ). The complaint alleged that TDCJ had falsified a prescription for pentobarbital, purchased from a Houston compounding pharmacy, for an inmate and facility that did not exist. Attorneys for the inmates argued that using untested drugs from unregulated pharmacies is against the Eighth Amendment's ban on "cruel and unusual punishment." TDCJ did not get a prescription for the compounded drugs from a physician, required by state law in most cases, and the pharmacy requested return of the drugs. TDCJ refused to return the pentobarbital. In mid-2014, Attorney General Gregg Abbott refused to release the names of the state's drug suppliers, maintaining that to do so would compromise the physical safety of employees. Further complicating this issue is the lack of uniformity and oversight of death penalty practices.

Reviewing the Death Penalty

Imposition of the death penalty has declined across the United States and in Texas in recent years. Concerns about the possible execution of innocent people have had some effect. (From 1973 through mid-2014, Texas had released 12 wrongfully convicted death row inmates.) In addition, the option of life without parole has provided an alternative punishment for capital felons.

Some states have placed a moratorium on the death penalty.[8] A **moratorium** is a delay or suspension of an activity or law. Although the American Bar Association has encouraged other states with death penalty laws to do the same, Texas legislators have consistently rejected the idea. An interest group that has worked in Texas for a moratorium is the Texas Moratorium Network (TMN). This special interest group argues that if more Texans were educated on the death penalty a moratorium would be possible.

One factor that supports continued use of the death penalty is deterrence. A 2009 study of the relationship between executions in Texas and subsequent homicides suggested that reductions occur in murders for a short time after an execution.[9] These findings have been challenged, however, as not establishing a causal relationship between executions and deterrence.[10] A problem in determining whether the death penalty deters crime is that the time between sentencing and execution is quite lengthy. According to the TDCJ, the average time spent on death row prior to execution is nearly 11 years.[11] Some argue the punishment loses its deterrent effect because people do not see the immediate impact of the death penalty. Former Texas attorney general Jim Mattox interviewed several condemned inmates who were ultimately executed. Based on the inmates' responses, Mattox concluded, "It is my own experience that those executed in Texas were not deterred by the existence of the death penalty. I think in most cases you'll find that the murder was committed under severe drug and alcohol abuse."[12]

Some capital defendants are exempt from the death penalty. As the result of U.S. Supreme Court decisions and state law, for example, the death penalty cannot be used as punishment for anyone who was younger than 18 when committing a capital crime (*Roper v. Simmons*, 543 U.S. 551 [2005]) or anyone who is "mentally retarded" (now classified as intellectually disabled) (*Atkins v. Virginia*, 536 U.S. 304 [2002]). This penalty cannot be imposed if a defendant is found to have been mentally incompetent at the time of committing a capital crime.

moratorium
The delay or suspension of an activity or law. A moratorium may be imposed when something is seen as needing improvement.

Point/Counterpoint

THE ISSUE   The United States is an industrialized democratic nation that uses the death penalty in its criminal justice system. Countries like Iran, China, India, Thailand, and Jordan also employ this sentence. Seventeen U.S. states have barred state-sanctioned executions. Some observers argue that the death penalty is cruel, barbaric, and unfairly applied and should therefore be replaced by life imprisonment without the possibility of parole. This alternative is available under Texas law.

Is Life Imprisonment Without Parole a Better Option Than the Death Penalty?

Arguments For Life Imprisonment Without Parole

1. "The death penalty costs more, delivers less, and puts innocent lives at risk. Life without parole provides swift, severe, and certain punishment. It provides justice to survivors of murder victims and allows more resources to be invested into solving other murders and preventing violence." *American Civil Liberties Union*

2. Life without parole (LWOP) takes away the risk of a wrongful execution and is far less expensive than the trial and appeals processes used in death penalty cases. Some officials estimate that a capital punishment case costs as much as $3 million. By comparison, the cost of both trial and incarceration for a person sentenced to life without parole is approximately $500,000.*

3. LWOP may be a more severe punishment since it is by no means a lenient sentence. Sometimes called "death by incarceration," the prisoner has to live out his or her life behind bars.

Arguments Against Life Imprisonment Without Parole

1. The death penalty has a deterrent effect and prevents future lives from being taken. One study suggests that each execution prevents some 18 murders, on average.

2. Incarceration doesn't prevent a murderer from taking other lives. Inmates can kill other inmates, prison guards, or prison staff.

3. Inmates fight their death penalty convictions, doing anything in order to avoid a death sentence. Experts suggest murderers fear death more than prison and therefore the ultimate punishment should be available for committing the ultimate crime.

* See Peter Kendall, "Judge Favors Sentence Other Than Death," *Cleburne Times-Review*, April 13, 2009.

The death penalty cannot be carried out on a convicted individual who is mentally ill. What constitutes mental illness in Texas requires significant evidence. For example, Andre Thomas, who murdered his estranged wife, his 4-year-old son, and her 13-month-old daughter in Grayson County, claimed that God told him to murder his family. Nearly a week after the multiple homicide, while incarcerated, Thomas removed one of his eyes with his bare hands. A few years later, his mental illness seemed to have worsened when he removed his other eye and ate it.

Thomas's case was appealed to the Texas Court of Criminal Appeals, where Judge Cathy Cochran stated he "is clearly 'crazy,' but he is also 'sane' under Texas law,"[13] and therefore subject to being put to death. Thomas's attorneys appealed the ruling to the U.S. Court of Appeals, Fifth Circuit. Their appeal focused on Thomas's mental illness both at the time of the murder in 2004 and at the time of the appeal. His attorneys argued that Thomas's execution would violate the ban on "cruel and unusual punishment." As of late 2014, no final determination had been reached.

✔ 12.2 Learning Check

1. Which Supreme Court case deemed the death penalty unconstitutional in 1972?
2. According to the Texas Department of Criminal Justice, what is the average time spent on death row before an execution?

Answers on p. 462.

Correction and Rehabilitation

★ **LO12.3** Explain the role of Texas's jail and prison system in handling corrections and rehabilitations.

Confinement in a prison (either a penitentiary or a state jail) or in a county or municipal jail is designed to punish lawbreakers, deter others from committing similar crimes, and isolate offenders from society, thus protecting the lives and property of citizens who might otherwise become victims of criminals.[14] Ideally, while serving a sentence behind bars, a lawbreaker will be rehabilitated and, after release, will obey all laws, find employment, and make positive contributions to society. In practice, approximately 25 percent of convicted adult criminals violate the conditions of their release or commit other crimes after being released, for which they are resentenced to prison. Juvenile justice systems, which actually conduct their proceedings as civil cases and are, therefore, outside the criminal justice system, have a similar design but with a greater emphasis on rehabilitation rather than punishment. Descriptions of the criminal justice system in this section relate to adults; references to the juvenile justice system include individuals between the ages of 10 and 16.

The number of adult Texans either imprisoned or supervised by local and state criminal justice authorities is larger than in any other state. In 2013, approximately 640,000 Texans were incarcerated, on parole, or under community supervision (formerly known as probation). In response to high crime rates at the end of the 20th century, the Texas legislature and the Texas Board of Pardons and Paroles concentrated resources on incarceration and punishment. A few years later, the legislature shifted its emphasis to rehabilitation.

The Texas Department of Criminal Justice

The principal criminal justice agencies of the state are organized within the Texas Department of Criminal Justice (TDCJ). This department has a four-part mission:

- To provide public safety
- To promote positive behavioral changes
- To reintegrate offenders into the general society
- To assist crime victims

The organizational structure of TDCJ includes governance by the nine-member nonsalaried Texas Board of Criminal Justice; a full-time executive director hired by the board; and directors of the department's divisions, who are selected by the executive director. Each division director is responsible for hiring division personnel. Nearly 40,000 Texans worked for TDCJ in 2013. These employees are responsible for a prison population of approximately 150,000 inmates and more than 87,000 parolees. The Community Justice Assistance Division monitors local community supervision programs that oversee an additional 404,000 offenders on probation.

Providing Public Safety For many years, the primary focus of the Texas legislature, and therefore the TDCJ, was on providing public safety. Legislators classified an increasing number of actions as felonies, lengthened sentences for all types of crimes, funded construction of additional prison units, and balanced the state's budget by reducing drug treatment programs and other interventions intended to alter an individual's behavior. Because a large prison population and high recidivism rates proved costly, a bipartisan legislative effort redirected funding efforts to expand treatment and counseling services.

The current focus on rehabilitation and reentry has reduced the escalating imprisonment rates the state experienced in the 20th century. Reversing a decades-long trend, Texas's adult and juvenile prison populations declined in 2010 and 2011. State officials predict that the number of inmates in the state's prisons will increase by approximately 3 percent between 2013 and 2018.[15] In a longer period (2013–2020), the state's population is expected to increase by 5 percent.[16] Since 2011, Texas has closed three state prisons, suggesting that increasing the use of probation and job training is a smart fiscal choice. The state has also utilized programs to help inmates adapt to

How Do We Compare...in Prison Incarceration Rates?

Number of Prisoners per 100,000 State Residents (as of December 2012)

Most Populous U.S. States	Number of Prisoners per 100,000 Residents	U.S. States Bordering Texas	Number of Prisoners per 100,000 Residents
California	480	Arkansas	494
Florida	524	Louisiana	893
New York	298	New Mexico	315
Texas	**601**	Oklahoma	648

Source: E. Ann Carson and Daniela Golinelli, *Bureau of Justice Statistics Bulletin: Prisoners in 2012 Advance Counts* (Washington, DC: U.S. Department of Justice, July 2013), http://www.ojp.usdoj.gov.

life after incarceration. Between 2010 and 2014, lower numbers of prisoners and fewer prison facilities saved taxpayers more than $2 billion.

The sector of TDCJ responsible for ensuring public safety is the Correctional Institutions Division. Staff members in this division supervise the operation and management of state prisons, state jails, and other specialized facilities. Private contractors operate seven prisons, five state jails, and various prerelease, work, substance abuse, and intermediate sanctions facilities. Figure 12.1 shows the location of prison and state jail units in Texas.

Maintaining a trained workforce to provide security has been an ongoing problem for the Correctional Institutions Division. Historically, difficult working conditions and low pay produced annual turnover rates for correctional officers of more than 25 percent. Salary increases, signing bonuses, and a depressed economy temporarily improved staff retention;

Figure 12.1   Facilities of the Texas Department of Criminal Justice, 2013.

Source: Texas Department of Criminal Justice.

CRITICAL THINKING

How does having a state jail or prison facility in or near a community affect the community?

The Darrington Unit Gospel Choir sings at a convocation ceremony.

AP Images/Pat Sullivan

CRITICAL THINKING

Should an inmate receive a reduced sentence for completing a rehabilitation program?

Southwestern Baptist Theological Seminary operates an extension program at the Darrington Unit, a maximum-security prison near Houston. Inmates are able to complete a four-year program for a bachelor of science in biblical studies that prepares them to assist chaplains and help counsel inmates. Although prison officials report a reduction in prison violence since the program began, Baylor University is sponsoring a study to quantify results. Unlike most inmate education programs that are designed to prepare prisoners for parole, Darrington Unit Seminary targets inmates who will likely never be released.

More than one-half of Texas prisoners are enrolled in vocational and academic classes offered through the prison system's Windham School District. In addition, some prisoners take community college and university courses. In 2013, approximately 2,200 prisoners completed workforce training through community colleges. Almost 400 inmates graduated with degrees ranging from associate's to master's. The state pays tuition costs for vocational training, but once released, the former inmate must reimburse the state. Tuition for academic courses must be paid by the prisoner.

Reintegrating Offenders A major goal of treatment and education programs is to equip prisoners with the skills to succeed upon release. The Reentry and Integration Division provides extensive support to released offenders. This division has more than 60 reentry counselors located throughout the state to assist released inmates.

Two agencies are responsible for convicted criminals who serve all or a part of their sentences in the community: the Community Justice Assistance Division and the Parole Division. The Community Justice Assistance Division establishes minimum standards for county programs involving community supervision and community corrections facilities (such as a boot camp or a restitution center). In cases involving adult first-time offenders convicted of misdemeanors and lesser felonies, jail and prison sentences are commonly commuted to community supervision (formally called adult probation). These convicted persons are not confined if they fulfill certain court-imposed conditions. Through specialty courts, judges have also become directly involved in community supervision (see Chapter 11, "The Judicial Branch").

The Parole Division manages Texas's statewide parole and mandatory supervision system for convicted felons. The seven-member Board of Pardons and Paroles recommends acts of clemency (such as pardons) to the governor and grants or revokes paroles. The board's presiding officer employs and supervises 12 commissioners, who assist the board with parole and revocation decisions. A three-member panel, comprised of at least one parole board member along with one or more commissioners, reviews inmate applications and decides whether to grant or deny parole. The board may impose restrictions that it deems necessary to protect the community. If a parolee violates any conditions of release, a board panel determines whether to revoke parole.

Prisoners who have served some portion of their sentences may be eligible for parole. Felons who commit serious, violent crimes, such as rape or murder, must serve 30 to 40 years of "flat time" (without the possibility of having prison time reduced for "good-time" credit for good behavior). Other offenders may apply for parole after serving one-fourth of a sentence or 15 years, whichever is less (minus good-time credit).

Successful reintegration of offenders is complicated by a number of barriers to reentry. Not only do those convicted of felonies lose many civil rights, such as the right to serve on juries and administer estates, they, along with those convicted of misdemeanors, also encounter lifetime impediments to employment. According to the Equal Employment Opportunity Commission (EEOC), the use of blanket exclusions against applicants with arrest or conviction records could violate civil rights laws. The EEOC noted that Texas's sweeping anti-felon policies may be flawed because they fail to distinguish between candidates who are a risk to society versus those who pose little risk. In November 2013, Texas filed a lawsuit against the EEOC to protect state hiring laws and policies. On August 20, 2014, a Federal Judge dismissed the state's case. The judge ruled Texas lacked standing since it was not facing any immediate penalties related to the EEOC's guidance on criminal screening in hiring. Texas has appealed the case to the U.S. Court of Appeals, Fifth Circuit.

Assisting Victims The fourth prong of TDCJ's mission directs attention to crime victims and their close relatives. The Victim Services Division provides information to crime victims about any change in the offender's status within the TDCJ system, as well as notification of pending parole hearings. Upon a finding of guilt, and before sentencing, victims may deliver victim impact statements in open court. They may also complete written statements that remain available to prison and parole officials. When an inmate is executed, up to five family members and close friends of the victim may witness the execution.

The State of Texas maintains a Crime Victims' Compensation Fund that provides up to $50,000 to victims and their families for expenses related to a crime ($125,000 in the event of total disability). Covered costs include medical treatment, counseling, and burial expenses. The program is funded by court costs, fees, and fines collected from convicted offenders and is administered by the Office of the Attorney General.

Local Government Jails

In addition to prisons and state jails operated by the Texas Department of Criminal Justice, counties and cities across the state operate jails. These facilities are financed largely by county and municipal governments, respectively. Like penal institutions of the TDCJ, local government jails are used to control lawbreakers by placing them behind bars.

All but 19 Texas counties maintain a jail. Some counties have contracted with commercial firms to provide "privatized" jails, but most counties maintain public jails operated under the direction of the county sheriff. Originally established to detain persons awaiting trial and to hold individuals serving sentences for misdemeanor offenses, county jail facilities vary in quality and, except in some urban areas, do not offer rehabilitation programs. The Texas Commission on Jail Standards has oversight responsibility for county jails.

Texas also has approximately 350 municipal jails, most of which are not regulated by the state. In large cities, these facilities often house hundreds of inmates who have been arrested for a variety of offenses ranging from Class C misdemeanors to capital murder. Those charged with more serious crimes are usually held temporarily until they can be transferred to a more secure county jail.

Private Prisons

Both state and local governments have contracted with private companies to construct and operate prisons and direct prerelease programs. Texas now has more privately operated facilities than any other state. Approximately 10 percent of Texas's inmates are housed in private prisons. These facilities are under the supervision of the Private Facility Contract Monitoring/ Oversight Division of the TDCJ. The Texas Juvenile Justice Department oversees community-based private contract juvenile facilities. In addition to prisons and jails, private contractors also provide substance abuse treatment programs and halfway houses, where state and county prisoners are incarcerated in privately operated units. The reduced number of prison inmates has also affected privately owned facilities. In 2013, two private prisons were closed in Mineral Wells and downtown Dallas because they were no longer needed.

✔ **12.3 Learning Check**

1. What are the two primary means of combating recidivism?
2. How has the change in the state's prison population affected private prisons?

Answers on p. 462.

Juvenile Justice

★ **LO12.4** Compare the juvenile justice system to the adult correctional system.

Texas's juvenile justice system clearly distinguishes between youthful pranks and violent, predatory behavior. In general, young Texans at least 10 years of age but younger than 17 are treated as "delinquent children" when they commit acts that would be classified as felonies or misdemeanors if committed by adults. Children are designated as "status offenders" if they commit noncriminal acts such as running away from home, failing to attend school, or violating a curfew established by a city or county. From 1957 to 2011, the Texas Youth Commission (TYC) was the agency responsible for the rehabilitation and training of delinquent youth. After several years of scandal highlighting deficiencies in the agency, the 82nd Legislature (2011) abolished the TYC. The Texas Juvenile Probation Commission, the agency that oversaw county juvenile probation departments, was abolished at the same time. As a part of the sunset review process (see Chapter 10, "Public Policy and Administration"), the legislature created the Texas Juvenile Justice Department (TJJD) to assume the responsibilities of the abolished agencies. The 11-member board of TJJD, appointed by the governor with the consent of the Senate, is charged with unifying juvenile justice services from an individual's entry into the system through departure.

State and Local Agencies

Each county has a juvenile probation board that designates one or more juvenile judges, appoints a chief juvenile probation officer, and makes policies carried out by a juvenile probation department. When youth must be incarcerated, the responsibility rests with the TJJD. Here, the goal has shifted from sending juveniles to facilities far from their families to keeping them within their local area. If children must be removed from family settings, the law reflects a preference for group homes over correctional facilities.

In mid-2012, an increase in youth-on-youth and youth-on-staff violence focused attention on security within TJJD facilities. A new program to isolate the most aggressive inmates in a separate facility was announced. Youth advocates claimed this practice represented a return to unsuccessful methods used in the previous decade. Legislators and some juvenile detention officials argued that inadequate security substantially reduced the success of treatment programs. In 2013, a study conducted by the LBJ School of Public Affairs at the University of Texas found that reforms at TJJD facilities had not quelled violent offenses by inmates. The report stated that TJJD officials may have overused isolation methods to manage youth behavior, which could have led to increased misconduct. Juveniles in isolation do not receive access to programs or treatment. The study provided TJJD officials and the Texas legislature with recommendations for further reform.[23]

Procedures

Although juvenile offenders are arrested by the same law enforcement officers who deal with adult criminals, they are detained in separate facilities. Counseling and probation are the most widely used procedures for dealing with juvenile offenders, but residential treatment and commitment to TJJD facilities remain options. An arresting officer has the discretion to release a child or refer the case to a local juvenile probation department. Other referrals come from public school officials, victims, and parents. Approximately 100,000 Texas youths enter the state's juvenile justice system annually.

Trials in juvenile courts are termed **adjudication hearings**. Juvenile courts are civil rather than criminal courts; therefore, any appeal of a court's ruling will be made to a higher court with civil jurisdiction. A few cases are ultimately appealed to the Texas Supreme Court.

A juvenile determinate sentencing law covers more than 20 serious offenses. Under this sentencing provision, juveniles who commit offenses such as capital murder or aggravated sexual assault can be transferred to adult prisons when they reach age 19 and can be held there for as long as 40 years. In addition, approximately 1 percent of juveniles charged with serious crimes stand trial and are punished as adults. Prior to a determination of guilt, these young offenders remain in juvenile facilities "separated by sight and sound" from adult offenders; but once found guilty, convicted youth are transferred to the adult prison system.

An issue Texas legislators are trying to resolve is whether to raise the age of adulthood to 18 for criminal matters. Researchers and lawmakers find that steering 17-year-olds to juvenile courts and lockups instead of adult jails would save money, reduce arrest rates, and help to streamline the process. Texas is one of eight states that automatically direct 17-year-olds into the adult criminal justice system. Many argue that adulthood should start at age 18, which is considered an adult age in 40 states.

adjudication hearing
A trial in a juvenile court.

12.4 Learning Check

1. What agency oversees Texas's juvenile justice system?
2. True or False: Young Texans at least 6 years of age but younger than 19 are treated as "delinquent children" when they commit offenses that would be classified as felonies or misdemeanors if committed by adults.

Answers on p. 462.

Problems and Reforms: Implications for Public Policy

LO12.5 Evaluate the fairness of Texas's justice system.

Legislators must deal with the 21st-century issues of overcrowding and mental illness in prisons, electronic and scientific technology, changing demographics, and misconduct by district attorneys. It is important for our policymakers to respond to issues within the criminal justice system that will assure fairness for all.

Overcrowding and Mental Illness in Prison

Overcrowding and high rates of inmates suffering from mental illness are recurring problems for many prisons and jails. The Harris County jail system is the third largest in the country. Its jail population is frequently at or near capacity, ranging between 8,500 and 9,500 inmates at any point in time. Many of the inmates have complicating conditions such as mental illness.[24]

In Texas, based on the availability of psychiatric facilities, an individual with a serious mental illness is eight times as likely to be incarcerated as to receive treatment.[25] Harris County Judge Ed Emmett estimates that approximately one-third of inmates housed in county facilities are mentally ill. The county spends about $54 million a year to incarcerate those with mental illness. Many offenders have undiagnosed or untreated mental illnesses that may lead them to commit crimes. Although many receive treatment during their incarceration, once they are out of the system they are left with little assistance. In a pilot program approved by the 83rd Legislature in 2013, Harris County and the Texas Department of State Health Services (DSHS) have joined together to provide mental health services to county jail inmates. An evaluation of the program's effect on lowering recidivism rates, repeat arrests, and incarceration of the mentally ill will determine its success. DSHS will provide the evaluation to legislators by December 2016.

Technology

Technology now touches many areas of the criminal justice system. Websites and social media provide different avenues for inmates to communicate with each other and the outside world. Forensic science, and especially DNA testing, has been a resource that aids both defendants and prosecutors.

Since March 1980, Houston's KPFT has aired *The Prison Show* on Friday nights. The show can also be heard live online and downloaded as a podcast. Families and inmates have an opportunity to communicate through the show's format. Friends and family members call in to the show while inmates listen. In fact, Anthony Graves, whose story opened this chapter, has served as a cohost of the program. Sometimes the messages on the show are words of encouragement and support; at other times, callers use the time to update an inmate about family matters such as a child's doctor visit.

Many inmates have a Facebook page, often created by their families or friends. In 2012, prison officials fired a correctional officer for "friending" an inmate on Facebook. TDCJ has a policy of no fraternizing between inmates and correctional staff. The officer appealed the decision because he knew the man in high school and had no idea he was an inmate. Upon review, officials determined the officer had only friended the inmate, and no real relationship existed between the two. On further review, investigators discovered that other correctional officers had also friended the inmate. TDCJ now permits staff and inmates to be "friends" on Facebook. Difficulty in monitoring online sites led to TDCJ's decision.

Gawker.com is an online weblog that started a "Letters from Death Row" series in 2012. One of the site's most popular letters was written by death row inmate Ray Jasper from San Antonio, who was executed in March 2014. Jasper's first letter to the site, written in December 2013, detailed life on death row. His second letter was his last statement before execution. It complains about how prisoners are slaves of the prison system and how his case was race-based. The victim's brother responded to Jasper's letter on Gawker. The brother recounted David Alejandro's death, the trial, and the lack of remorse in Jasper's letter. He refuted Jasper's claim of innocence. The website offers letters from death row inmates throughout the United States.

DNA testing, developed by geneticist Alec Jeffreys, transformed the criminal justice system. Biological evidence is used to identify suspects, as well as to exonerate the innocent. The state maintains a DNA database. Both TDCJ and TJJD collect DNA samples from all inmates convicted of felony-level offenses. Convicted felons who receive community supervision must provide DNA samples, as do juveniles released on probation who have committed the most serious offenses (for example, murder, rape, or aggravated robbery) or who used a weapon to commit their offenses. Crime scene evidence can then be tested against the state's database samples. DNA evidence not only aids in identifying the guilty, it may also establish innocence, which is what occurred in the Michael Morton case. Morton was found guilty of murdering his wife in 1986 and spent 25 years in prison for a crime he did not commit. After Morton's attorneys were able to have a bloody bandana found at the crime scene tested for DNA evidence, the results set him free.[26] Delays that Morton experienced in having evidence submitted for testing are no longer possible due to laws passed by the 82nd Legislature.

Laws, agencies, and commissions have been established by the state to prevent the miscarriage of justice. For example, state law requires all public crime labs to be accredited and DNA evidence to be held for retesting. An 11-member Texas Forensic Science Commission, appointed by the governor, investigates charges of negligence and misconduct.

Exoneration Issues

The Fourteenth Amendment to the U.S. Constitution guarantees that no state can "deprive any person of life, liberty, or property without due process of law." Rules and procedures that must be followed in criminal cases are specifically designed to protect people from losing their lives, liberty, or property as a result of arbitrary acts by the government. According to the Innocence Project at New York's Cardozo Law School, more than 315 inmates across the nation were exonerated between 1989 and mid-2014 after DNA analysis proved their innocence. Forty-eight of those individuals were from Texas.

Although DNA test results have contributed to the release of innocent prisoners, this evidence is not the panacea that will eliminate all wrongful

imprisonment. In fact, 35 individuals who were released from prison between 1992 and 2012 had no DNA evidence to exonerate them. More than 75 percent of exonerees across the nation were victims of mistaken eyewitness identification, a form of evidence jurors consider highly reliable. Research now indicates several flaws in this type of evidence, including overlooking facial features of people of different races, transference to an individual encountered in a different setting, and poor recall due to the stress of being a crime victim or witness.[27] In response to these concerns, the 82nd Legislature revised state law in 2011 to require police departments and other agencies to develop written procedures for conducting photo and live lineups.

Although most people convicted of a crime are guilty, the probability of exoneration is remote, even for the innocent. The political reality is that to obtain a pardon and be fully exonerated requires the agreement of district attorneys, judges, the Board of Pardons and Paroles, and the governor. Posthumous pardons can be granted, should someone be exonerated after his or her death. The State of Texas compensates individuals wrongfully incarcerated. Someone found innocent after being imprisoned is entitled to $80,000 for each year he or she was wrongly incarcerated, $25,000 for each year on parole or required registration on a sex offender registry, tuition for training or college, a lifetime annuity, assistance in accessing social service providers, and health insurance. Since 1992, the state has paid more than $61 million to 89 exonerated individuals. Lump sum payments can be made to the heirs of those exonerated after death. Even though the state funds innocence projects at its public law schools, the legislature has consistently rejected establishing an innocence commission to examine the causes of wrongful conviction.

Racial Bias in the Criminal Justice System

Changes in the state's demography have affected its justice system. The underrepresentation of African Americans and Latinos in elected and appointed leadership positions is matched by their overrepresentation in the criminal justice system.[28] If the race or ethnicity of those enforcing the law is consistently different from those against whom the law is enforced, the system has less credibility and may be viewed as unfair.

Studies in the early part of the past decade provided evidence that more than two-thirds of Texas law enforcement agencies targeted members of historical minority groups for stops and searches. More recent studies reflect a reduction in the disparity between consent searches of minorities and Anglos. Perhaps a contributing factor to this reduction is the requirement that law enforcement agencies provide annual racial profiling reports to their governing bodies and to the Texas Commission on Law Enforcement Standards and Education. These reports make public the number of traffic stops by race, gender, and age, as well as subsequent action, such as searches and arrests, that resulted from the stops. Instances of racial and ethnic bias are the subject of growing concern as Texas has evolved into a

Students in Action

Correctional System Intern, Travis County Jail

Arisbeth Garcia, in her senior year at an Austin high school, wanted to intern for the Travis County jail. This internship was Arisbeth's opportunity to get a closer look at the criminal justice system and help decide her career path. As a correctional system intern, she shadowed a correctional officer. With 40 inmates in a "cube" area, Arisbeth was responsible for helping the officer with roll call, distributing lunches to prisoners, and generally helping monitor inmates.

Arisbeth learned a lot about the criminal justice system during that year as an intern. She noticed that many of the inmates were young. She's hoping to work with people, particularly youth, as a social worker to prevent them from becoming inmates.

Arisbeth's advice to students is to look for an internship in a field you are interested in; it's the best way to figure out what path you may want to pursue. She had a great experience interning with the Travis County jail and would recommend the internship program to any student planning a career in criminal justice. Arisbeth believes it's important to know different aspects of the system, whether one plans on becoming a social worker, correctional officer, or youth services provider. She wasn't sure what she wanted to do until she worked for the Travis County jail.

While she learned a great deal from her internship, it also helped her know that she did not want to work in corrections directly. She believes internships are also good for helping students decide if a field of study is right for them. Students often spend years pursing a degree and later find they do not like the work in their field of study. Arisbeth's internship helped her when it was time to select a major in social work. It further helped her decide to use her education to find what would help youth stay out of prison.

Interview conducted with Arisbeth Garcia on April 25, 2014.

© Andresr/Shutterstock.com

state in which two historical minority groups, African Americans and Latinos, make up the majority population, and the state's Latino population continues movement toward becoming the majority.

Misconduct by District Attorneys

The main responsibility of a district attorney (DA) is to represent the State of Texas in criminal cases. The DA works with law enforcement to put together a criminal case that may be brought before criminal courts. Although most district attorneys are fair and effective, some unfortunately misuse their power. According to the *Texas Tribune*, there were at least 91 criminal cases

Anthony Graves has filed a petition for official misconduct with the State Bar against former district attorney Charles Sebesta. Here Graves is flanked by State Senators Rodney Ellis (D-Houston) and John Whitmire (D-Houston).

AP Images/Houston Chronicle/Marie D. De Jesus

CRITICAL THINKING

What repercussions should district attorneys face for misconduct as described in the Anthony Graves case?

between 2004 and 2012 in which "prosecutors committed misconduct, ranging from hiding evidence to making improper arguments to the jury."[29]

The Code of Criminal Procedure requires that DAs not focus on convictions, but instead see that justice is done. Charles Sebesta, the DA in the Anthony Graves case, has been described as ignoring the primary focus of achieving justice. The U.S. Court of Appeals, Fifth Circuit ruled that he withheld exculpatory evidence and obtained false statements from witnesses in his efforts to send Graves to death row. Another example of injustice by a DA can be observed in the case of Michael Morton. As a result of his failure to disclose exculpatory evidence to both the trial judge and Morton's attorneys, former Williamson County DA Kenneth Anderson was found in contempt of court. Further, the State of Texas brought a civil lawsuit accusing Anderson of official misconduct in the case. In November 2013, Anderson agreed to spend 10 days in jail, serve 500 community service hours, and pay a $500 fine to resolve the contempt case. In addition, his law license was revoked.

The district attorney is a powerful figure in the criminal justice system. He or she has the authority to ask the courts, on behalf of the state, to take someone's life, liberty, or property. Many criminal justice advocates argue there should be strict repercussions for misuse of that power.

✔ 12.5 Learning Check

1. Most individuals who have been exonerated were sent to prison based on what type of evidence?
2. True or False: The Code of Criminal Procedure requires district attorneys to give primary importance to convicting a criminal defendant.

Answers on p. 462.

Report: Texas Leads Nation in 2013 Exonerations

Edgar Walters

Texas has been in the national spotlight for wrongful convictions and executions for years. This article looks at the problems that may cause wrongful convictions and the need for reform.

Texas in 2013 exonerated more people who were wrongfully convicted of crimes than any other state, according to a new report from the National Registry of Exonerations. Thirteen Texans were officially absolved of wrongdoing last year for crimes ranging from murder to drug possession. The state with the second-most exonerations was Illinois, with nine, followed by New York, with eight.

The national registry, a joint project of the University of Michigan Law School and the Center on Wrongful Convictions at the Northwestern University School of Law, was launched in 2012. It tracks every known exoneration in the United States since 1989. Texas has 133 exonerations listed. Only New York, with 152, and California, with 136, have more.

The report found that while the number of exonerations in 2013 was a record high (87 across the country), the percentage based on DNA evidence dropped. Rebecca Bernhardt, policy director for the Texas Defender Service, said the report demonstrates the importance of high-quality defense in all criminal trials. The registry attributes "inadequate legal defense" as a contributing factor to four of the 13 wrongful convictions. "It's not so much about good lawyers versus bad lawyers," Bernhardt said. "Every time the court doesn't give you the resources you need for investigations, you lose the tools necessary to prove that your client either wasn't guilty or deserves mercy."

State Sen. Rodney Ellis, D-Houston, who has authored legislation aimed at preventing wrongful convictions, including last year's Michael Morton Act, called on the state to provide higher quality legal representation to the poor. "Unfortunately, in everyday Texas, quality of justice is too often contingent on your wealth and the attorney you can afford," he said. The registry includes a racial/ethnic breakdown of known wrongful convictions. At 47 percent of exonerees, blacks are overrepresented, while whites and Hispanics make up 40 and 11 percent, respectively.

Others have called for tougher punishments against prosecutors who behave unethically in order to reduce wrongful convictions. They point to cases like that of Kenneth Wayne Boyd Jr., who was convicted in 1999 of a triple murder and sentenced to life in prison. Boyd appealed, and more than a decade later, in 2013, Texas' highest criminal court exonerated him, ruling that his prosecutor had suppressed favorable evidence and knowingly presented false evidence.

The registry lists "official misconduct" as a contributing factor in two of Texas' exonerations last year. Shannon Edmonds, director of governmental relations for the Texas District and County Attorneys Association, said that prosecutorial misconduct accounted for just a "fraction" of wrongful convictions. According to the report, many cases in 2013 relied on faulty forensic evidence, often related to drug testing. "To ensure that the system works as it's intended, both sides have to have good advocates to investigate the cases," Edmonds said. Compared to the roughly 1 million criminal cases processed in Texas each year, Edmonds called the 13 known wrongful convictions a "pretty small number." "And yet, even one is too many," he said. "We strive for perfection."

✔ **Selected Reading Learning Check**

1. Texas had the highest number of exonerations in 2013. Which state was second?
2. Texas Senator Rodney Ellis believes the quality of justice in Texas is based on what?

Answers on p. 462.

....

Source: This article first appeared in the *Texas Tribune* on February 4, 2014, http://www.texastribune.org/2014/02/04/report-texasleads-nation-2013-exonerations/.

Conclusion

The Texas criminal justice system is complex. Issues of fairness and efficiency remain paramount in ensuring that residents accept the legitimacy, or authority, of the criminal justice system. In recent years, the shift in Texas from punishment to rehabilitation appears to have made the state a leader in reducing the number of prisoners and lowering the cost of the criminal justice system. The legal system, however, is not error-free. Issues of concern with criminal justice policies, the death penalty, rehabilitation, and fairness of the process need to be addressed. Only by understanding the system can citizens and lawmakers develop effective solutions.

Chapter Summary

LO 12.1 Describe the different classifications of criminal offenses. Criminal law regulates many types of behavior. Less severe crimes are classified as Class A, B, or C misdemeanors and result in fines or detention in a county jail. More severe crimes include state-jail felonies; first-, second-, and third-degree felonies; and capital felonies. Policies have been adopted to deal with different criminal justice issues such as substance abuse and hate crimes.

LO 12.2 Analyze issues of the death penalty in Texas. Texas is one of 32 states in the United States that use the death penalty. There are problems and concerns with the method and usage of the death penalty. The number of death penalty cases has declined, but concerns remain about whether innocent people could be executed and the proper handling of the mentally ill who are on death row.

LO 12.3 Explain the role of Texas's jail and prison system in handling corrections and rehabilitations. Approximately 640,000 Texans were under the supervision of state and local judicial or correctional officers in 2013. Recent changes in state laws have emphasized the rehabilitative role of incarceration. The Texas Department of Criminal Justice has a four-pronged mission to handle issues of correction and rehabilitation.

LO 12.4 Compare the juvenile justice system to the adult correctional system. The juvenile justice system deals with correction and rehabilitation for juveniles (those between ages 10 and 16) and is administered through the Texas Family Code. Years of scandal at Texas Youth Commission (TYC) facilities resulted in abolition of the TYC and the Texas Juvenile Probation Commission. The Texas Juvenile Justice Department replaced those agencies in 2011.

LO 12.5 Evaluate the fairness of Texas's justice system. A number of issues remain problematic for the Texas justice system. These problems include overcrowding and mental illness in prisons, the effect of technological and scientific advances, the probable innocence of some inmates, possible racial and ethnic bias in the justice system, and misconduct among district attorneys.

Key Terms

exculpatory evidence, p. 437
criminal justice system, p. 438
Texas Penal Code, p. 438
graded penalties, p. 438

enhanced punishment, p. 440
capital felony, p. 440
plea bargain, p. 441
moratorium, p. 443

administrative segregation, p. 448
recidivism, p. 449
adjudication hearing, p. 454

Learning Check Answers

12.1 1. People who engage in organized criminal activity, repeat offenders, and those who commit hate crimes may receive enhanced punishment. This means the offender will be punished as though he or she had committed the next higher degree of felony.
2. True. Most low-level drug offenders are dealing with other issues like homelessness and poverty.

12.2 1. The Supreme Court ruled in *Furman v. Georgia* that the death penalty was unconstitutional because there was racial bias in its application.
2. According to the TDCJ, the average time spent on death row is nearly 11 years.

12.3 1. Discipline and education are the primary means of combating recidivism.
2. Private prisons are closing as the prison population decreases.

12.4 1. The legislature created the Texas Juvenile Justice Department (TJJD) to assume the responsibilities of the abolished Texas Youth Commission (TYC) and the Texas Juvenile Probation Commission.
2. False. In general, young Texans at least 10 years of age but younger than 17 are treated as "delinquent children" when they commit crimes labeled felonies or misdemeanors if committed by adults.

12.5 1. More than 75 percent of convicted felons who have been exonerated in the United States were convicted in part because of mistaken eyewitness identification.
2. False. According to the Code of Criminal Procedure, a district attorney's primary responsibility is to seek justice, not convictions.

Selected Reading Learning Check

1. The state with the second most exonerations in 2013 was Illinois with nine.
2. State Senator Rodney Ellis believes the quality of justice in Texas is often based on one's wealth and the attorney one can afford.

13

Finance and Fiscal Policy

John Branch

Learning Objectives

13.1 Assess the fairness of Texas's budgeting and taxing policies.

13.2 Describe the sources of Texas's state revenue.

13.3 Describe the procedure for developing and approving a state budget.

13.4 Evaluate the effectiveness of the state's financing of public services.

CRITICAL THINKING

Do you believe Texas should spend more or less money building and maintaining roads and bridges?

Bad roads and traffic jams aren't just an inconvenience; they cost money. A 2012 study by the Road Information Program placed that cost at $23.2 billion annually for all Texans. In Houston, wasted time, vehicle wear-and-tear, and extra fuel expenses totaled $1,900 per driver; in Dallas, $1,550; in San Antonio, $1,425; and in Austin, $1,235.[1] Urban Texans spend as much as 37 additional hours in traffic each year because of road congestion. Outdated and unsafe roads and bridges account for 45 percent of the state's transportation infrastructure. The oil and gas boom that has fostered a strong economy in rural areas has also damaged or destroyed roads. The 1,500 new Texans who arrive each week add to traffic congestion. If funding for transportation needs continues at current levels, Texas A&M University's Texas Transportation Institute predicts that within 15 years urban Texans will spend approximately 75 hours per year waiting in traffic jams.[2]

The third special session of the 83rd Legislature asked Texans to address the problem of inadequate funding for road repair and construction in the state. In November 2014, Texas voters amended the state's constitution to allow the diversion of some money intended for the Rainy Day Fund, the state's savings account, to the State Highway Fund. Although an improvement over previous funding levels, as the opening cartoon to this chapter indicates, this solution was only a Band-Aid approach to a much more substantial problem. Texans, who abhor high taxes, also demand good roads.

This chapter examines the balance between costs and services; it provides an overview of the Lone Star State's fiscal policies, budgeting processes, and most costly public policy areas. Taxing, public spending, and governmental policy priorities will continue to have significant impacts on 21st-century Texans.

Fiscal Policies

★ **LO13.1** Assess the fairness of Texas's budgeting and taxing policies.

During the 83rd legislative session in 2013, Texas's traditional low-tax approach to **fiscal policy** (public policy that concerns taxes, government spending, public debt, and management of government money) faced key challenges. Students at all levels of publicly financed education, uninsured Texans, a decaying infrastructure, and water needs competed for state funding. A rapidly improving economy provided more funds to address these needs than had been available to the 82nd Legislature, but the session was not without conflict about the appropriate use of state revenue.

Tax revenue includes state sales taxes, as well as taxes on specific items such as cigarettes, motor vehicles, and gross receipts from businesses. Revenue sources other than taxes include oil and gas royalties, land sales, and federal grants-in-aid. The 82nd Legislature used a number of accounting maneuvers, such as delaying some mandatory payments beyond August 31, 2013 (the end of the biennial budget period), encouraging early payment of taxes to speed up revenue collection, and intentionally underfunding high-cost items such as

fiscal policy
Public policy that concerns taxing, government spending, public debt, and management of government money.

Medicaid, to achieve a balanced budget.[3] Spending was reduced for public education, higher education, health care programs, children's protective services, and all other areas of the budget except natural resources and economic development. Because of an improved economy, the 83rd Legislature was able to reverse many of these accounting devices, or "tricks." Even with an improving economy, state agencies were directed in 2012 to reduce their upcoming budget requests to the 83rd Legislature by 10 percent. The 84th Legislature, meeting in 2015, faced no such limitations.

Texans remain committed to pay-as-you-go spending and low taxes, no matter the strength of the economy. The Lone Star State's fiscal policy has not deviated from its 19th-century origins. Today, the notion of a balanced budget, achieved by low tax rates and low to moderate government spending levels, continues to dominate state fiscal policy. Consequently, state government, its employees, and its taxpayers face the daily challenge of meeting higher demands for services with fewer resources.

The state's elected officials appear to adopt the view expressed by economist and Nobel Prize winner Milton Friedman (1912–2006) that "the preservation of freedom requires limiting narrowly the role of government and placing primary reliance on private property, free markets, and voluntary arrangements."[4] Texas legislators and other state leaders have repeatedly demonstrated a willingness to reduce services, outsource governmental work to decrease the number of employees on the state's payroll, and maintain or lower tax rates as solutions to the state's fiscal problems.

Taxing Policy

Texans have traditionally opposed mandatory assessments for public purposes, or **taxes.** Residents have pressured their state government to maintain low taxes. When additional revenues have been needed, Texans have indicated in poll after poll their preference for **regressive taxes,** which favor the rich and fall most heavily on the poor ("the less you make, the more government takes"). Under such taxes, the burden decreases as personal income increases. Figure 13.1 illustrates the impact of regressive taxes on different levels of income. Under the current tax structure, the poorest 20 percent of Texans pay more than four times as much of their income in taxes as the wealthiest 20 percent.

Texas lawmakers have developed one of the most regressive tax structures in the nation. A general sales tax and selective sales taxes have been especially popular. **Progressive taxes** (taxes in which the impact increases as income rises—"the more you make, the more government takes") have been unpopular. Texas officials and citizens so oppose state income taxes that the state constitution requires a popular referendum before an income tax can be levied. Newspaper columnists often observe that any elected official who proposes a state income tax commits political suicide.

To finance services, Texas government depends heavily on sales taxes, which rank among the highest in the nation. In addition, the Lone Star State has a dizzying array of other taxes. The Texas state comptroller's office

tax
A mandatory assessment exacted by a government for a public purpose.

regressive tax
A tax in which the effective tax rate falls as the tax base (such as individual income or corporate profits) increases.

progressive tax
A tax in which the effective tax rate increases as the tax base (such as individual income or corporate profits) increases.

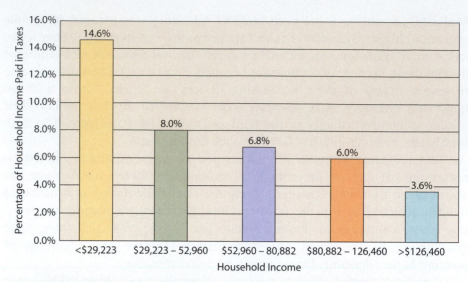

Figure 13.1   Percent of Average Annual Family Income Paid in Local and State Taxes in Texas (FY2011).

Source: Chandra King Villanueva, ''Who Pays Texas Taxes?'' (Austin: Center for Public Policy Priorities, September 25, 2012), http://library.cppp.org/research.php?aid=1060.

CRITICAL THINKING

What are the benefits and problems of a regressive tax system?

collects more than 60 separate taxes, fees, and assessments on behalf of the state and local governments.[5] Yet the sales tax remains the most important source of state revenue.

Many observers have criticized the regressive characteristics of Texas's tax system as being unfair. An additional concern is that the state primarily operates with a 19th-century land- and product-based tax system that is no longer appropriate to the knowledge- and service-based economy of the 21st century. Local governments rely heavily on real estate taxes for their revenue. More than half of the state's general revenue tax collections are sales and use taxes. Until 2006, business activities of **service sector** employers (including those in trade, finance, and the professions) remained tax-free. In that year, however, the state altered the franchise tax law to require most Texas businesses to pay taxes calculated on their profit margins. This extension of the franchise tax subjected many service sector entities to taxation.

Texas is recognized as one of the "top performers" in the nation in the ability of its tax system to respond to shifts in the economy.[6] Even so, a comparison of sales and use tax collections ($50 billion) and franchise tax collections ($9.3 billion) for the 2012–2013 biennium reflects the extent to which the Lone Star State persists in relying on sales tax revenue. Changes in Texas's economy, without corresponding changes in its tax system, are projected to continue to erode the tax base. Under the current structure, the part of the economy generating the greatest amount of revenue frequently pays the least amount in taxes.

service sector
Businesses that provide services, such as finance, health care, food service, data processing, or consulting.

In addition, the state charges special fees and assessments that are not called taxes but that represent money the state's residents pay to government. Texas legislators, reluctant to raise taxes, have often assessed these fees and surcharges. Is a **fee**, defined as a charge "imposed by an agency upon those subject to its regulation,"[7] different from a tax? Some argue that these assessments represent an artful use of words, not a refusal to raise taxes, and that these charges meet the definition of a tax if the proceeds benefit the general public. For example, the state requires attorneys to pay an annual legal services fee to fund legal assistance for the poor. Attorneys who fail to pay this fee lose their right to practice law in the state. No matter the designation, this mandatory fee is money that an attorney must pay to finance government services for the general public.

Budget Policy

Hostility to public debt is demonstrated in constitutional and statutory provisions that are designed to force the state to operate with a pay-as-you-go **balanced budget**. The Texas Constitution prohibits the state from spending more than its anticipated revenue "[e]xcept in the case of emergency and imperative public necessity and with a four-fifths vote of the total membership of each House."[8] In addition, the cost of debt service limits the state's borrowing power. This cost cannot exceed 5 percent of the average balance of general revenue funds for the preceding three years.

To ensure a balanced budget, the comptroller of public accounts must submit to the legislature in advance of each regular session a sworn statement of cash on hand and revenue anticipated for the succeeding two years. Appropriation bills enacted at that particular session, and at any subsequent special session, are limited to not more than the amount certified, unless a four-fifths majority in both houses votes to ignore the comptroller's predictions or the legislature provides new revenue sources.

Texas accounts for the state's revenue and spending in several different budgets. The All Funds Budget includes all sources of revenue and all spending. It is the All Funds Budget that must be balanced each biennium. Additionally, reference is often made to the General Revenue Funds Budget. This budget includes the nondedicated portion of the **General Revenue Fund** (money that can be appropriated for any legal purpose by the legislature) plus some of the funds used to finance public education (Available School Fund, the State Instructional Materials Fund, and the Foundation School Fund). Casual deficits (unplanned shortages) sometimes arise in the General Revenue Fund. Like a thermometer, this fund measures the state's fiscal health. If the fund shows a surplus (as occurred in FY2012–2013), fiscal health is good; if a deficit occurs (as occurred in FY 2010–2011), then fiscal health is poor. Less than one-half of the state's expenditures come from the General Revenue Fund; the remainder comes from other funds that state law designates for use for specific purposes.

The General Revenue–Dedicated Funds Budget includes more than 200 separate funds. Because of restrictions on use, these accounts are defined as **dedicated funds**. In most cases, the funds can only be used for their

fee
A charge imposed by an agency upon those subject to its regulation.

balanced budget
A budget in which total revenues and expenditures are equal, producing no deficit.

General Revenue Fund
An unrestricted state fund that is available for general appropriations.

dedicated fund
A restricted state fund that has been identified to fund a designated purpose. If the fund is consolidated within the general revenue fund, it usually must be spent for its intended purpose. Unappropriated amounts of dedicated funds, even those required to be used for a specific purpose, can be included in the calculations to balance the state budget.

designated purposes, though in some instances money can be diverted to the state's general fund. Even amounts that can only be spent for a designated purpose may be manipulated to satisfy the mandate for a balanced budget. The legislature can incorporate any unspent balances into its budget calculations. In the 82nd legislative session, for example, the legislature refused to appropriate more than $5 billion in General Revenue–Dedicated Funds in order to give the appearance of a balanced budget. State lawmakers justify these actions by noting that the high costs of programs such as Medicaid force them to freeze these balances. State Representative Sylvester Turner has characterized this practice somewhat differently, calling it "dishonest governing,"[9] because it is an accounting trick that makes money appear available on paper that in fact is not available. The 83rd Legislature limited this practice and in 2014, Speaker Joe Straus announced that the 84th legislature would only use the State Highway fund to build and maintain transportation infrastructure.

The Federal Funds Budget includes all funding from the federal government. These amounts must be spent for their designated purposes. Likewise, the Other Funds Budget includes an additional 200-plus dedicated funds, each of which must be spent for its stated purpose, such as the Property Tax Relief Fund that must be used to fund public education.

Spending Policy

Historically, Texans have shown little enthusiasm for state spending. In addition to requiring a balanced budget, the Texas Constitution restricts increases in spending that exceed the rate of growth of the state's economy and limits welfare spending in any fiscal year to no more than 1 percent of total state expenditures. Consequently, public expenditures have remained low relative to those of other state governments. Texas has consistently ranked between 48th and 50th in state spending per capita. Although the state's voters have indicated moderate willingness to spend for highways, roads, and other public improvements, they have demonstrated much less support for welfare programs, recreational facilities, and similar social services.

✔ **13.1 Learning Check**

1. What are three characteristics of Texas's fiscal policy?
2. The state of Texas has one of the highest sales tax rates in the nation. It does not have a state income tax. Is Texas's tax structure an example of a regressive or a progressive tax system?

Answers on p. 502.

Revenue Sources

LO13.2 Describe the sources of Texas's state revenue.

Funding for government services primarily comes from those who pay taxes. In addition, the state derives revenue from fees for licenses, sales of assets, investment income, gambling, borrowing, and federal grants. When revenue to the state declines, elected officials have only two choices: increase taxes or other sources of revenue or decrease services. In times of projected budget shortfalls, as occurred prior to the 2012-2013 biennium, the legislature's first response has been to decrease services. When revenue is plentiful, as was the situation at the end of that biennium, pressure builds to reduce taxes.

Point/Counterpoint

THE ISSUE In December 2013, Comptroller of Public Accounts Susan Combs certified that the 2012–2013 state budget had $2.6 billion in unspent revenue at the end of the budget cycle. Some observers believed this excess represented a surplus that should be returned to the people through reduced sales taxes. Others argued that this amount was not a surplus but the result of the legislature's failing to meet the needs of Texas's population.

How Should the State Use a Budget Surplus?

Arguments For Refunding Tax Collections Above Budgeted Amounts

1. Collecting more money than the state included in its budget is a sign the state is overcollecting taxes.
2. Additional money should not be spent on public education. The state's teacher-student ratio is better than the national average. "Public education needs reform not additional dollars."
3. Additional money should not be spent on welfare. When adjusted for the cost of living, Texas's poverty rate is almost at the national average (16.4 percent vs. 16 percent), and much lower than California's (23.8 percent) with its higher taxes and higher benefits.
4. Temporarily reducing the state's portion of the sales tax from 6.25 percent to 5.75 percent would save the average family $132 per year, providing a tangible reward for the state's frugality.

Source: Chuck DeVore, "Texas Needs to Refund Its Surplus Taxes," *Houston Chronicle,* April 13, 2014.

Arguments Against Refunding Tax Collections Above Budgeted Amounts

1. Texas has no "surplus" because legislators chose not to spend $4 billion in dedicated funds in 2014–2015 in an effort to make the budget appear balanced. That amount should be subtracted from any reported surplus.
2. Because of population growth, on a per capita basis Texas spent less on state services in 2013 than it did in 2011.
3. A reduction in state taxes may result in an increase in local property taxes as local governments try to meet the service needs of their populations.
4. The state has many needs (including education, health care, and transportation) that should be addressed by state government to assure a high-quality future for the Lone Star State's population. Surplus revenue should be spent to meet these needs.

Source: Dick Lavine and Eva Deluna Castro, "State Should Invest More Funding for Future Growth," *Houston Chronicle,* April 13, 2014.

The Politics of Taxation

Taxes are but one source of state revenue. According to generally accepted standards, each tax levied and the total tax structure should be just and equitable. Opinions vary widely about what kinds of taxes and what types of structures meet these standards. Conflicts are most apparent in the struggle to finance the state's public schools as elected officials strive to lower real estate taxes for the state's property owners and replace local funding with additional state-level taxes. Texas has a constitutional mandate to provide "an efficient system of public free schools," and the state's courts have defined adequate funding as a key element of this requirement. Determining who should pay taxes to finance public education is a challenge.

In 2006, despite resistance from several large law firms, the 79th Legislature modified and expanded the business franchise tax. It also imposed an additional $1 tax on cigarettes, increased taxes on other tobacco products (except cigars), and required buyers to pay a tax on used cars at their presumptive value as determined by publications such as *Kelley Blue Book*. Since 2006, legislators have yielded to the demands of small business owners by reducing the number of businesses subject to the franchise tax and lowering the tax rate. Concomitantly, the legislature has increased taxes on tobacco products. These modifications reflect both the political strength of business owners and the ease of raising taxes on items that some people deem morally questionable.

general sales tax
Texas's largest source of tax revenue, applied at the rate of 6.25 percent to the sale price of tangible personal property and "the storage, use, or other consumption of tangible personal property purchased, leased, or rented."

Sales Taxes By far the most important single source of state tax revenue in Texas is sales taxation. (See Figure 13.2 for the sources of state revenue.) Altogether, sales taxes accounted for more than 55 percent of state tax revenue and 26 percent of all revenue in fiscal years 2014–2015. These sales taxes function as a regressive tax, and the burden they impose on individual taxpayers varies with spending patterns and income levels.

For more than 50 years, the state has levied and collected two kinds of sales taxes: a **general sales tax** and several selective sales taxes. First imposed in 1961, the limited sales, excise, and use tax (commonly referred to as the general sales tax) has become the foundation of the Texas tax

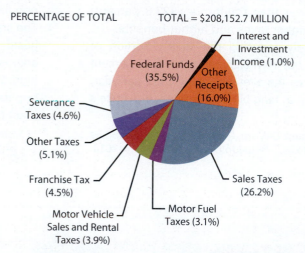

PERCENTAGE OF TOTAL   TOTAL = $208,152.7 MILLION

Interest and Investment Income (1.0%)
Federal Funds (35.5%)
Other Receipts (16.0%)
Severance Taxes (4.6%)
Other Taxes (5.1%)
Franchise Tax (4.5%)
Motor Vehicle Sales and Rental Taxes (3.9%)
Motor Fuel Taxes (3.1%)
Sales Taxes (26.2%)

Figure 13.2   Projected Sources of State Revenue, Fiscal Years 2014–2015.

Note: Amounts are in billions of dollars.

Source: Legislative Budget Board, *Fiscal Size-up, 2014–15 Biennium* (Austin: Legislative Budget Board, February 2014), 29, http://www.lbb.state.tx.us/Documents/Publications/Fiscal_SizeUp/Fiscal_SizeUp.pdf.

CRITICAL THINKING

What other sources of revenue do you believe are available to the State of Texas?

system. The current (2014) statewide rate of 6.25 percent is one of the nation's highest (ranking as the 12th-highest rate among the 45 states that imposed a sales tax as of midyear 2014). Local governments have the option of levying additional sales taxes for a combined total of state and local taxes of 8.25 percent (see Chapter 3, "Local Governments"). The base of the tax is the sale price of "all tangible personal property" and "the storage, use, or other consumption of tangible personal property purchased, leased, or rented." Among exempted tangible property are the following: receipts from water, telephone, and telegraph services; sales of goods otherwise taxed (for example, automobiles and motor fuels); food and food products (but not restaurant meals); medical supplies sold by prescription; nonprescription drugs; animals and supplies used in agricultural production; and sales by university and college clubs and organizations (as long as the group has no more than one fundraising activity per month).

Two other important items exempt from the general sales tax are goods sold via the Internet and most professional and business services. According to U.S. Supreme Court decisions, a state cannot require businesses with no facilities in the state to collect sales taxes on its behalf because the practice interferes with interstate commerce. Therefore, when a student buys a textbook from an online seller with no facilities in the state, no sales tax is collected. The book is, however, subject to a use tax, which requires the purchaser to file a form with the comptroller's office and pay taxes on items purchased out of state for use in Texas. Because the cost of enforcing such a provision on individual consumers is prohibitive, these transactions remain largely untaxed.

Some online merchants, such as kitchen retailer Williams-Sonoma, Inc., voluntarily collect sales taxes for the states. Other sellers argue that multiple rates and definitions of products subject to state sales taxes create a collection nightmare. Through the Streamlined Sales Tax Governing Board, 24 states, not including Texas, have signed Streamlined Sales and Use Tax Agreements that provide a uniform tax system to overcome these arguments. Approximately 2,000 online retailers voluntarily collect taxes for these states. To force all out-of-state retailers to participate, the U.S. Congress would be required to act because of its authority under the Commerce Clause of the U.S. Constitution. To benefit from such a law, Texas would need to sign a Streamlined Sales and Use Tax Agreement. Based on estimated electronic sales in 2012, Texas lost more than $870 million in tax revenue.[10]

One way to tax online retailers is through affiliate-nexus or "Amazon" laws (a reference to the online retailer Amazon). Under these laws, if an online retailer has a facility or employees in a state, the physical presence of the facility or people creates "a nexus" (or connection with the state). If any goods or services subject to sales tax are sold to the residents of that state, the seller must collect the tax and remit it to the state. Failure to do so subjects the seller to tax liability, interest, and penalties. In 2011, the 82nd Legislature clarified that the mere use of a Texas-based web hosting service was not sufficient to create a nexus with the State of Texas.

Having a distribution center in the state creates a nexus with the state, however. In 2012, State Comptroller Susan Combs settled a long-running dispute with Amazon regarding whether having a distribution center in the Dallas area was sufficient to force collection of sales tax on goods purchased by Texas customers. Under terms of the settlement agreement, the state forgave $269 million in unpaid sales taxes, interest, and penalties. In return, as of July 2012, Amazon began collecting sales taxes on customer purchases by Texans. In addition, the retailer agreed to invest more than $200 million in the state and create an additional 2,500 jobs. In 2013, the company completed construction of three new distribution centers in Texas, each at least 1 million square feet in size, and hired 1,000 workers to staff the centers. Although most of the jobs were hourly wage jobs, Amazon noted they paid higher than retail sales jobs and included health insurance.[11] Additional controversy surrounded this settlement when some legal experts argued that the Texas Constitution prohibited the comptroller's forgiving unpaid taxes. Other attorneys and tax specialists countered that the comptroller had great latitude in resolving tax disputes.

Because the general sales tax primarily applies to tangible personal property, many services are untaxed. Sales taxes are charged for dry cleaning, football tickets, and parking; however, accountants, architects, and consultants provide their services tax-free. Because professional service providers and businesses represent some of the most powerful and well-organized interests in the Lone Star State, proposals that would require these groups to collect a sales tax have faced strong resistance. (See Chapter 7, "The Politics of Interest Groups.") Although the comptroller estimates that eliminating sales tax exclusions for professional and other service providers would generate approximately $6.5 billion in additional annual revenue, even in difficult economic times, legislators made no effort to change the law.[12]

Since 1931, when the legislature first imposed a sales tax on cigarettes, many items have been singled out for **selective sales taxes**. These items may be grouped into three categories: highway user taxes, **sin taxes**, and miscellaneous sales taxes. Highway user taxes include taxes on fuels for motor vehicles that use public roads and registration fees for the privilege of operating those vehicles. The principal sin taxes are those on cigarettes and other tobacco products, alcoholic beverages, and mixed drinks. One of the most contested taxes is the $5 fee added to admission fees to so-called gentlemen's clubs. The Texas Supreme Court rejected club owners' arguments that the law interfered with exotic dancers' free speech rights. In 2014, the Third Court of Appeals (Austin) found that the fee was a valid excise tax. The state collected approximately $17 million from this tax source between 2008 (when the law took effect) and 2013.[13] Additional items subject to selective sales taxes include hotel and motel room rentals (also called a "bed tax") and retail sales of boats and boat motors.

Business Taxes As with sales taxes, Texas imposes both general and selective business taxes. A general business tax is assessed against a wide range of business operations. Selective business taxes are those levied on businesses engaged in specific or selected types of commercial activities.

selective sales tax
A tax charged on specific products and services.

sin tax
A selective sales tax on items such as cigarettes, other forms of tobacco, alcoholic beverages, and admission to sex-oriented businesses.

Commercial enterprises operating in Texas have historically paid three general business taxes:

- Sales taxes, because businesses are consumers
- **Franchise taxes**, because many businesses operate in a form that attempts to limit personal liability of owners (that is, corporations, limited liability partnerships, and similar structures)
- Unemployment compensation payroll taxes, because most businesses are also employers

The franchise tax, which has existed for almost 100 years, is imposed on businesses for the privilege of doing business in Texas. As a part of the restructuring of the state's school finance system, the legislature expanded the franchise tax to include all businesses operating in a format that limited the personal liability of owners. Sole proprietorships, general partnerships wholly owned by natural persons, passive investment entities (such as real estate investment trusts or REITs), and businesses that make $1 million or less in annual income or that owe less than $1,000 in franchise taxes are exempt. The tax is levied on a business's taxable margin, which is an amount equal to the least of (1) total revenue minus the cost of goods sold, (2) total revenue minus compensation and benefits paid to employees, (3) 70 percent of total revenue, or (4) total revenue minus $1 million.

Although proponents estimated that this tax would produce about $6 billion in state revenue each fiscal year, actual collections have been far less. In FY2013, franchise tax collections were $4.8 billion. For the two-year period covering the 2014–2015 biennium, the comptroller projected total collections of $9.2 billion (or approximately $4.6 billion per fiscal year). Thus, collections remain below the amounts predicted by the tax's original proponents. Several reasons have been cited for this shortfall, including a weak economy, the increase in the exemption from tax liability to include businesses earning less than $1 million, and a definition of "cost of goods sold" that includes deductions not available under federal law. The tax is highly unpopular among small business owners, who continue to seek its repeal.[14]

All states have unemployment insurance systems supported by **payroll taxes**. Paid by employers, these taxes are levied against a portion of the compensation paid to workers to insure employees against unemployment. Although collected by the state, the proceeds are deposited into the Unemployment Trust Fund in the U.S. Treasury. Benefits are distributed to qualified workers who lose their jobs.

The most significant of the state's selective business taxes are levied on the following:

- Oil and gas production
- Insurance company gross premiums
- Public utilities gross receipts

Selective business taxes accounted for approximately 15 percent of the state's tax revenue in FY2008, when the economy was strong and oil and gas prices and production were high. When the economy floundered and oil

franchise tax
A tax levied on the annual receipts of businesses that are organized to limit the personal liability of owners for the privilege of conducting business in the state.

payroll tax
An employer-paid tax levied against a portion of the wages and salaries of workers to provide funds for payment of unemployment insurance benefits in the event employees lose their jobs.

and gas prices and production declined, these taxes amounted to only 10 percent of tax collections for the 2010–2011 biennium. By 2014–2015, primarily due to the recovery of the oil and gas industry, revenue from these sources rebounded to comprise 14 percent of the state's revenue.

One of the more important selective business taxes is the **severance tax.** Texas has depended on severance taxes, which are levied on a natural resource, such as oil or natural gas, when it is removed from the earth. Texas severance taxes are based on the quantity of minerals produced or on the value of the resource when removed. The Texas crude oil production tax and the gas-gathering tax were designed with two objectives in mind: to raise substantial revenue and to regulate the amount of natural resources mined or otherwise recovered. Each of these taxes is highly volatile, reflecting dramatic increases and decreases as the price and demand for natural resources fluctuate. Current production in Texas relies heavily on hydraulic fracture stimulation (fracking) to recover oil and gas reserves. Controversies about the environmental impact of this recovery method on groundwater and on underground stability and water supply could reduce production and, therefore, decrease revenue to the Lone Star State.[15]

Inheritance Tax Because of changes to federal law, no inheritance or estate tax (frequently called a death tax) is collected on the estates of individuals dying on or after January 1, 2005. Some states have enacted laws imposing a tax on estates. It is unlikely that Texas will do so.

Tax Burden The Tax Foundation places Texas well below the national average for the state tax burden imposed on its residents. In 2011, when state taxes alone were considered, the Lone Star State's tax burden ranked 45th among the 50 states. A candidate's "no new taxes" pledge remains an important consideration for many Texas voters and will likely result in state officials' continuing to choose fewer services over higher taxes to balance the state budget.

Tax Collection As Texas's chief tax collector, the comptroller of public accounts collects more than 90 percent of state taxes, including those on motor fuel sales, oil and gas production, cigarette and tobacco sales, and franchises. Amounts assessed by the comptroller's office can be challenged through an administrative proceeding conducted by that office. Taxpayers dissatisfied with the results of their hearings can appeal the decision to a state district court.

Some taxpayers commit tax fraud by not paying their full tax liability. Electronic sales suppression devices and software, like zappers and phantom-ware, are used to report fewer sales than retailers actually have. These devices allow users to maintain an electronic set of books for tax purposes that erases some credit card and cash transactions from the register's memory. The devices and software are difficult to detect. Their use reduces the payment of any taxes based on a business's receipts, such as sales taxes, mixed drink taxes, and the gross margins or franchise tax. Although through May 2014 Texas

severance tax
An excise tax levied on a natural resource (such as oil or natural gas) when it is severed (removed) from the earth.

had no reported cases of electronic tax fraud, one estimate suggests the state may lose as much as $1.6 billion per year from this type of fraud. More than 10 states have made some form of the use, installation, or sale of zappers and phantomware a crime. Texas is not one of them.[16] Retailers and restaurateurs are not the only sources of tax fraud. Motor fuels are also subject to taxation and therefore tax fraud. An additional consequence of Governor Rick Perry's line-item veto of funding for the state's Public Integrity Unit was the elimination of the motor fuels fraud enforcement division. Enforcement of motor fuels tax fraud is now the responsibility of local district attorneys' offices.[17]

Other agencies also collect taxes on behalf of the state. The Department of Motor Vehicles collects motor vehicle registration and certificate-of-title fees through county tax collectors' offices; the State Board of Insurance collects insurance taxes and fees; and the Department of Public Safety collects driver's license, motor vehicle inspection, and similar fees. The Texas Alcoholic Beverage Commission collects state taxes on beer, wine, and other alcoholic beverages. Although taxes represent the largest source of state revenue, Texas has other funding means.

Revenue from Gambling

The Lone Star State receives revenue from three types of gambling operations (called "gaming" by supporters): horse racing and dog racing, a state-managed lottery, and bingo. Owners of horse racing operations have lobbied politicians for legalization of slot machines at their tracks. In addition, the state's three Native American tribes (the Kickapoo nation near Eagle Pass, the Alabama-Coushatta in East Texas, and the Tigua near El Paso) continue to argue for the right to operate Las Vegas–style casinos. Opposition from both social conservatives and many Democrats remains strong. This opposition is not restricted to casino gambling. In 2013, the Texas House of Representatives voted to abolish the Texas Lottery Commission. When proponents argued the legislature would have to replace $2.2 billion in funding for public schools if the lottery were eliminated, some opponents changed their votes.[18] As a result, the Texas Lottery Commission will continue in existence through 2025, although the same bill created the Legislative Committee to Review the Texas Lottery and Texas Lottery Commission. Among the committee's responsibilities is investigating the viability of phasing out the lottery.

Racing Pari-mutuel wagers on horse races and dog races are taxed. This levy has never brought Texas significant revenue. Proceeds from uncashed mutuel tickets, minus the cost of drug testing the animals at the racing facility, revert to the state. In most years, the Racing Commission collects far less revenue than its operating expenses. Texas has four types of horse racing permits, ranging from Class 1 (with no limit on the number of race days per year) to Class 4 (limited to five race days annually). As of 2014, the Lone Star State had 10 permitted horse racing tracks (four that were active and six that were inactive) and three dog tracks providing live and simulcast racing events on which people could wager legal bets.

Lottery Texas operates one of 43 state-run lotteries as well as the multistate lotteries, Mega Millions and Powerball. Through April 2014, Texans had won more than $43 billion in prizes. Chances of winning the state lottery jackpot, however, are 1 in 26 million. No Texan has won a Mega Millions jackpot, and only one has won a Powerball jackpot since the state began participating in these lotteries in 2003. Chances of winning Mega Millions are 1 in 176 million. Powerball odds are even more daunting: 1 in 195 million.

The Texas Lottery Commission administers the state's lottery. The five-member commission is appointed by the governor for six-year terms. Because the commission also oversees bingo operations, one member must have experience in the bingo industry. Among the commission's functions are determining the amounts of prizes, overseeing the printing of tickets, advertising ticket sales, and awarding prizes. The commission maintains a Twitter account through which the public receives regular updates on winning lottery numbers and upcoming jackpot amounts.

Almost all profits from the lottery are dedicated to public education spending. In 2013, more than $1.1 billion went to the Texas Foundation School Fund. This amount constituted a small portion of the state's budgeted expenditure of more than $26 billion on public education in that same year. Proceeds from a Veteran's Cash scratch-off game benefit the Veterans' Assistance Fund, which received $5.2 million from ticket sales in 2013. Unclaimed prizes from the Texas lottery revert to the state 180 days after a drawing. These funds are transferred to hospitals across the state to provide partial reimbursement for unfunded indigent medical care. Five percent of ticket sale revenue is used to pay commissions to retailers who sell the tickets.

Bingo State law allows bingo operations to benefit charities (for example, churches, veterans' organizations, and service clubs). The 5 percent tax on bingo prizes is divided 50–50 between the state and local governments. State revenue from bingo taxes remains low. Local charities benefit somewhat from the portion of the proceeds that is distributed to them. In 2011, the last year for which information is available, these donations were approximately $29 million. In that same year, the Texas Lottery Commission reported gross receipts from charitable bingo games of $705 million, exceeding all previous years. This increase in gross revenue was not reflected in donations, however. The amount was used to increase winners' prizes. Investigations in the Dallas area identified several bingo operations that paid little, if any, of their proceeds to charitable organizations. One bingo hall collected $1 million in gross receipts from which the charity received $1,600.[19] The Legislative Committee to Review the Texas Lottery and Texas Lottery Commission was required to evaluate the effect of mandatory charitable distributions on charitable bingo.

Other Nontax Revenues

Less than 50 percent of all Texas state revenue comes from taxes and gambling operations; therefore, other nontax revenues are important sources of funds. The largest portion of these revenues comes from federal grants.

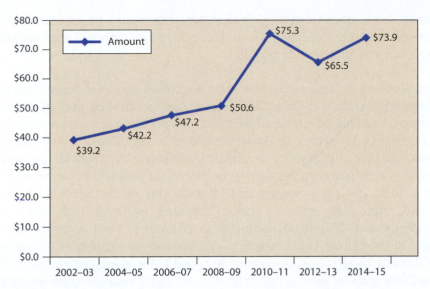

Figure 13.3 Federal Grants to Texas by Biennium (FY2002–2015) (in billions).

Source: Developed from information available from State Comptroller, "Texas Net Revenue by Source, 1973–2010" and "Texas Net Revenue by Source, 2011," and Legislative Budget Board, *Fiscal Size-up: 2014–2015 Biennium.*

CRITICAL THINKING

Is Texas too reliant on federal grants to balance its budget?

Figure 13.3 reflects the growth of this funding source over the last seven biennia. State business operations (such as sales of goods by one government agency to another government agency) and borrowing also are significant sources of revenue. In addition, the state has billions of dollars invested in interest-bearing accounts and securities.

Federal Grants-in-Aid Gifts of money, goods, or services from one government to another are defined as **grants-in-aid**. Federal grants-in-aid contribute more revenue to Texas than any single tax levied by the state. More than 95 percent of federal funds are directed to three programs: health and human services, business and economic development (especially highway construction), and education. For the 2012–2013 biennium, federal funds, including grants, accounted for approximately $74 billion in revenue. In the 2010–2011 biennium, during the Great Recession, the state relied on an additional $12 billion in one-time federal grants to balance the state budget.

State participation in federal grant programs is voluntary. Participating states must (1) contribute a portion of program costs (varying from as little as 10 percent to as much as 90 percent) and (2) meet performance specifications established by federal mandate. Funds are usually allocated to states on the basis of a formula. These formulae usually include (1) lump sums (made up of identical amounts to all states receiving funds) and (2) uniform

grant-in-aid
Money, goods, or services given by one government to another (for example, federal grants-in-aid to states for financing public assistance programs).

sums (based on items that vary from state to state, such as population, area, highway mileage, need and fiscal ability, cost of service, administrative discretion, and special state needs).

Land Revenues Texas state government receives nontax revenue from public land sales, rentals, and royalties. Sales of land, sand, shell, and gravel, combined with rentals on grazing lands and prospecting permits, accounted for approximately 1.1 percent of the state's budget in the 2014–2015 biennium. A substantial portion of revenue from state lands is received from oil and natural gas leases and from royalties derived from mineral production. Volatility of oil and natural gas prices causes wide fluctuations in the amount the state receives from these mineral leases. Projected collections for 2014–2015 represented a $300 million decline from 2012–2013 land revenues. A new source of revenue is lease payments from commercial offshore wind turbines. The General Land Office, the agency responsible for managing the more than 20 million acres of land surface and mineral rights that the state owns, also leases offshore sites for wind power. As of 2013, the state had 52,000 acres in Texas's tidelands under lease for wind energy production. Like most other lease payments and royalties derived from the state's public lands, rental amounts are deposited in the Permanent School Fund for the benefit of public schools.[20]

The Tobacco Suit Windfall Early in 1998, the American tobacco industry settled a lawsuit filed by the State of Texas. During a period of 25 years, cigarette makers will pay the Lone Star State $18 billion in damages for public health costs incurred by the state as a result of residents' tobacco-related illnesses. These funds support a variety of health care programs, including the Children's Health Insurance Program (CHIP), Medicaid, tobacco education projects, and endowments for health-related institutions of higher education. Payments averaged approximately $500 million per year through 2011. Because of increases in taxes that have reduced consumption in Texas and other states, revenue from the sale of tobacco products has declined in recent years. As a result, the comptroller predicted that settlement payments from the tobacco lawsuit would decline by $45 million in the 2014–2015 biennium. An additional $2.3 billion is administered as a trust by the state comptroller to reimburse local governments (cities, counties, and hospital districts) for unreimbursed health care costs.

Miscellaneous Sources Fees, permits, and income from investments are major miscellaneous nontax sources of revenue. Fee sources include those for motor vehicle inspections, college tuition, student services, state hospital care, and certificates of title for motor vehicles. The most significant sources of revenue from permits are those for trucks and automobiles; the sale of liquor, wine, and beer; and cigarette tax stamps. During the 2014–2015 biennium, income from these sources increased over the previous biennium, providing further evidence of Texas's return to economic health.

At any given moment, Texas has billions of dollars on hand, invested in securities or on deposit in interest-bearing accounts. Trust funds constitute the bulk of the money invested by the state (for example, the Texas Teacher Retirement Fund, the State Employee Retirement Fund, the Permanent School Fund, and the Permanent University Fund). Investment returns closely track fluctuations in the stock market. Chaos in the financial markets that began in September 2008 had a direct effect on this revenue source. Interest and investment income for the 2014–2015 biennium was less than half of amounts collected during fiscal years 2008 and 2009.

The Texas state comptroller is responsible for overseeing the investment of most of the state's surplus funds. Restrictive money management laws limit investments to interest-bearing negotiable order withdrawal (NOW) accounts, U.S. Treasury bills (promissory notes in denominations of $1,000 to $1 million), and repurchase agreements (arrangements that allow the state to buy back assets such as state bonds) from banks. Interest and investment income was expected to provide 1 percent of state revenue in 2014–2015.

The University of Texas Investment Management Company (UTIMCO) invests the Permanent University Fund and other endowments for the University of Texas and Texas A&M University systems. Its investment authority extends to participating in venture capital partnerships that fund new businesses. Board members for UTIMCO include the chancellor and three regents from the University of Texas System, two individuals selected by the Board of Regents of the Texas A&M University System, and three outside investment professionals. This nonprofit corporation was the first such investment company in the nation affiliated with a public university.

The Public Debt

When expenditures exceed income, governments finance shortfalls through public borrowing. Such deficit financing is essential to meet short- and long-term crises and to pay for major projects involving large amounts of money. Most state constitutions, including the Texas Constitution, severely limit the authority of state governments to incur indebtedness.

Bonded Indebtedness For more than 70 years, Texans have sought, through constitutional provisions and public pressure, to force the state to operate on a pay-as-you-go basis. Despite those efforts, the state is allowed to borrow money by issuing **general obligation bonds** (borrowed amounts repaid from the General Revenue Fund) and **revenue bonds** (borrowed amounts repaid from a specific revenue source, such as college student loan bonds repaid by students who received the funds). Commercial paper (unsecured short-term business loans) and promissory notes also cover the state's cash flow shortages. Whereas general obligation bonds and commercial paper borrowings require voter approval, other forms of borrowing do not. Outstanding bonded debt must be repaid from the General Revenue Fund. This debt, including bonds issued by the state's universities, was approximately $37.9 billion as of FY2013, of which $22.5 billion was issued as revenue bonds and the remainder as general obligation bonds.[21]

general obligation bond
Amount borrowed by the state that is repaid from the General Revenue Fund.

revenue bond
Amount borrowed by the state that is repaid from a specific revenue source.

Bond Review Specific projects to be financed with bond money require legislative approval. Bond issues also must be approved by the Texas Bond Review Board. The four members of this board are the governor, lieutenant governor, Speaker of the House, and comptroller of public accounts. The board approves all borrowings by the state or its public universities with a term in excess of five years or an amount in excess of $250,000.[22]

Economic Stabilization Fund The state's Economic Stabilization Fund (popularly called the **Rainy Day Fund**) operates like a savings account. It is intended for use when the state faces an economic crisis and is used primarily to prevent or eliminate temporary cash deficiencies in the General Revenue Fund. The Rainy Day Fund is financed with one-half of any excess money remaining in the General Revenue Fund at the end of a biennium and with oil and natural gas taxes that exceed 1987 collections (approximately $1.3 billion in that year). This fund has provided temporary support for public education, Medicaid, and the criminal justice system, as well as financing for the Texas Enterprise Fund (TEF), which is designed to attract new businesses to the state, and the Emerging Technology Fund, intended for use by companies engaged in work with medical or scientific technologies. A 2014 audit of TEF disclosed a number of improprieties including noncompetitive funding of grants and unpunished defaults in companies' obligations to create new jobs.

The weakness or strength of the economy is revealed in collections by the Rainy Day Fund. During the two biennia in 2008–2011, the state experienced the effects of the Great Recession and had no budget surpluses to transfer into the fund. By 2013, all sectors of Texas's economy were doing well, especially oil and gas. As a result, Texas had a $2.6 billion budget surplus for the 2013–2014 biennium, one-half of which ($1.3 billion) was deposited in the Rainy Day Fund. The state collected an additional $2.76 billion in excess oil and gas taxes. Because of the constitutional amendment approved in November 2014 that required the use of one-half of this amount for transportation infrastructure needs, the Rainy Day Fund received $1.38 billion. When the 84th Legislature convened in January 2015, the economic stabilization fund totaled $8.1 billion, well below the maximum amount of $14.5 billion that could be held in the fund. Deposits to the Rainy Day Fund are limited to an amount equal to 10 percent of revenue collections from the previous biennium. Should the maximum be reached, the state suspends transfers and deposits earned interest in the General Revenue Fund. The 2014 drop in oil prices made this option unlikely.

Rainy Day Fund
A fund used like a savings account for stabilizing state finance and helping the state meet economic emergencies when revenue is insufficient to cover state-supported programs.

13.2 Learning Check

1. What is the largest source of tax revenue for the state of Texas?
2. What is the stated purpose of the Rainy Day Fund?

Answers on p. 502.

Budgeting and Fiscal Management

LO13.3 Describe the procedure for developing and approving a state budget.

The state's fiscal management process begins with a statewide vision for Texas government and ends with an audit.[23] Other phases of this four-year process include development of agency strategic plans, legislative approval of an appropriations bill, and implementation of the budget. Each activity is important if the state is to derive maximum benefit from the billions of dollars it handles each year.

Budgeting Procedure

A plan of financial operation is usually referred to as a **budget**. In modern state government, budgets serve a variety of functions, each important in its own right. A budget outlines a plan for spending that shows a government's financial condition at the close of one budget period and the anticipated condition at the end of the next budget cycle. Based on estimated revenue, the budget also makes spending recommendations for the coming budget period. In Texas, the budget period covers two fiscal years. Each fiscal year begins on September 1 and ends on August 31 of the following year. The fiscal year is identified by the initials FY (for "fiscal year") preceding the number for the ending year. For example, FY2015 began on September 1, 2014, and ended on August 31, 2015.

Texas is one of only four states that have biennial (every two years) legislative sessions and budget periods. Many political observers argue that today's economy fluctuates too rapidly for this system to be efficient. Voters, however, have consistently rejected proposed constitutional amendments requiring annual state appropriations.

Legislative Budget Board By statute, the **Legislative Budget Board (LBB)** is a 10-member joint body of the Texas House of Representatives and the Texas Senate. Its membership includes as joint chairs the lieutenant governor and the Speaker of the House of Representatives. Assisted by its director and staff, the LBB prepares a biennial (two fiscal years) current services–based budget. This type of budget projects the cost of meeting anticipated service needs of Texans over the next biennium. The comptroller of public accounts furnishes the board with an estimate of the growth of the Texas economy covering the period from the current biennium to the next biennium. Legislative appropriations from tax revenue not dedicated by the Texas Constitution cannot exceed that rate of growth. Based on the comptroller's projections, the LBB capped the growth of appropriations from undedicated revenue at slightly less than 11 percent for the 2014–2015 biennium.

The board's staff also helps draft the general appropriation bill for introduction at each regular session of the legislature. If requested by a legislative committee chair, staff personnel prepare fiscal notes that estimate the potential economic impact of a bill or resolution. Employees of the LBB also assist agencies in developing performance evaluation measures and audits, and they conduct performance reviews to determine how effectively and efficiently agencies are functioning.

Governor's Office of Budget, Planning and Policy Headed by an executive budget officer who works under the supervision of the governor, the Governor's Office of Budget, Planning and Policy (GOBPP) is required by

budget
A plan of financial operation indicating how much revenue a government expects to collect during a period (usually one or two fiscal years) and how much spending is authorized for agencies and programs.

Legislative Budget Board (LBB)
A 10-member body cochaired by the lieutenant governor and the Speaker of the House. This board and its staff prepare a biennial current services budget. In addition, they assist with the preparation of a general appropriation bill at the beginning of a regular legislative session. If requested, staff members prepare fiscal notes that assess the economic impact of a proposed bill or resolution.

statute to prepare and present a biennial budget to the legislature. Traditionally, the governor's plan is policy based. It presents objectives to be attained and a plan for achieving them. As a result of this dual arrangement, two budgets, one legislative in origin and the other executive, should be prepared every two years. Governor Perry submitted separate budgets for each of the first four biennia of his administration (2001–2007). For the last three biennia (2009–2015) of his governorship, however, Perry proposed budgets that were the same or varied only minimally from those prepared by the LBB.[24]

Budget Preparation Compilation of each budget begins with development of a mission statement for Texas by the governor in cooperation with the LBB. That vision for the 2016–2017 biennium, as for the preceding biennium, urged agency personnel to "continue to critically examine the role of state government by identifying core programs and activities necessary for the long-term economic health of our state."[25] Every even-numbered year, each operating agency requesting appropriated funds must submit a five-year strategic operating plan to the GOBPP and to the LBB. These plans must incorporate the state's mission and philosophy of government, along with quantifiable and measurable performance goals. Texas uses performance-based budgeting; thus, strategic plans provide a way for legislators to determine how well an agency is meeting its objectives. For example, in 2012, the Office of the Comptroller submitted a strategic plan in which the agency set a goal of improving taxpayers' voluntary compliance with the Tax Code. One performance measure was to assure that each tax collector had an average of 269 delinquent account closures annually (presumably, if taxpayers believe a high likelihood exists of their being caught for noncompliance, they are more likely to comply with tax laws).

Legislative Appropriation Request forms and instructions are prepared by the LBB. (See Figure 13.4 for a diagram of the budgeting process.) These materials are sent to each spending agency in late spring in every even-numbered year. For several months thereafter, representatives of the budgeting agencies work to complete their proposed departmental requests. An agency's appropriations request must be organized according to strategies that the agency intends to use in implementing its strategic plan over the next two years. Each strategy, in turn, must be listed in order of priority and tied to a single statewide functional goal.

By early fall in even-numbered years, state agencies submit their departmental estimates to the LBB and GOBPP. These budgeting agencies then carefully analyze all requests and hold hearings with representatives of spending departments to clarify details and glean any additional information needed. At the close of the hearings, budget agencies traditionally compile their estimates of expenditures into two separately proposed budgets, which are then delivered to the legislature.

Thus, during each regular session, legislators normally face two sets of recommendations for all state expenditures for the succeeding biennium. Since the inception of the **dual budgeting system**, the legislature has shown a marked preference for the recommendations of its own budget-making agency,

dual budgeting system
The compilation of separate budgets by the legislative branch and the executive branch.

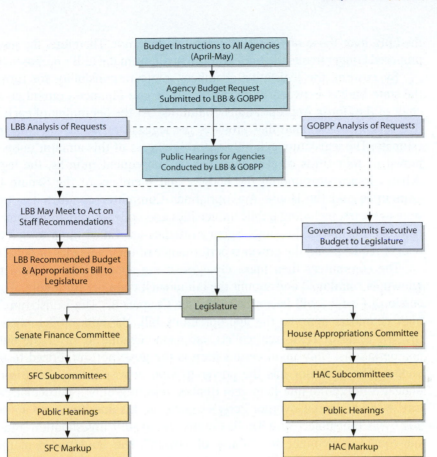

Figure 13.4 Texas Biennial Budget Cycle.

Source: Senate Research Center, *Budget 101: A Guide to the Budget Process in Texas* (Austin: Senate Research Center, January 2013), p. 5, http://www.senate.state.tx.us/SRC/pdf/Budget101WebsiteSecured_2013.pdf.

CRITICAL THINKING

Is Texas's budgeting process efficient?

the LBB, over those of the GOBPP and the governor. Therefore, the governor's proposed budget frequently varies little, if at all, from the LBB's proposed budget.

By custom, the legislative chambers rotate responsibility for introducing the state budget between the chair of the Senate Finance Committee and the chair of the House Appropriations Committee. At the beginning of each legislative session, the comptroller provides the legislature with a biennial revenue estimate. The legislature can only spend in excess of this amount upon the approval of four-fifths of each chamber. In subsequent months, the legislature debates issues surrounding the budget, and members of the Senate Finance Committee and the House Appropriations Committee conduct hearings with state agencies, including public universities and colleges, regarding their budget requests. During the hearings, agency officials are called upon to defend their budget requests and the previous performance of their agencies or departments.

The committees then make changes to the appropriations bill (a practice known as "markup") and submit the bill to each chamber for a vote. (For a discussion of how a bill becomes a law, see Chapter 8, "The Legislature.") After both chambers approve the appropriations bill, the comptroller must certify that the State of Texas will collect sufficient revenue to cover the budgetary appropriations. Only upon certification is the governor authorized to sign the budget. The governor has the power to veto any spending provision in the budget through the line-item veto (that is, rejecting only a particular expenditure in the budget). Governor Perry's exercise of his line-item veto authority in 2013 was the subject of a Travis County grand jury investigation and Perry's subsequent indictment for "abuse of power." The governor demanded the resignation of Travis County District Attorney Rosemary Lembaugh in exchange for an appropriation to the Public Integrity Unit directed by the District Attorney's office. (See Chapter 9, "The Executive Branch.") When she did not comply, he vetoed funding.

Budget approval does not guarantee that funds will remain available to an agency, including public colleges and universities. For example, in January 2010, Governor Perry, Lieutenant Governor David Dewhurst, and House Speaker Joe Straus directed all state-funded entities to identify ways to reduce by 5 percent the portion of their FY2010 and FY2011 budgets funded by the state. Approximately $1.2 billion in reductions were required (cuts amounting to 1.4 percent of state funding).

Budget Expenditures

Analysts of a government's fiscal policy classify expenditures in two ways: functional and objective. The services being purchased by government represent the state's functional budget. An objective analysis is used to report how money was spent for items such as employees' salaries. Figure 13.5 illustrates Texas's proposed functional expenditures for fiscal years 2014 and 2015. For more than five decades, functional expenditures have centered on three principal functions: public education, human services, and highway construction and maintenance (included under business and economic development). The 2014–2015 biennial budget reflected the same priorities.

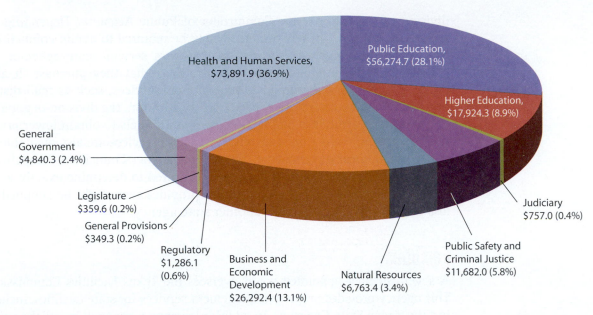

Figure 13.5 All Texas State Funds Appropriations by Function for Fiscal Years 2014–2015 (in millions).

Source: House Research Organization, *Texas Budget Highlights: Fiscal 2014–15,* State Finance Report No. 83-4 (Austin: House Research Organization, May 2, 2014), 3, http://www.hro.house.state.tx.us/pdf/focus/highlights83.pdf.

CRITICAL THINKING

On what services do you believe the state should spend more or less money?

Budget Execution

In most state governments, the governor's office or an executive agency responsible to the governor supervises **budget execution** (the process by which a central authority in government oversees implementation of a spending plan approved by the legislative body). The governor of Texas and the Legislative Budget Board have limited power to prevent an agency from spending part of its appropriations, to transfer money from one agency to another, or to change the purpose for which an appropriation was made. Any modification the governor proposes must be made public, after which the LBB may ratify it, reject it, or recommend changes. If the board recommends changes in the governor's proposals, the chief executive may accept or reject the board's suggestions.

The proper functioning of Texas's budget execution system requires a coordinated effort among the state's political leadership. The board met twice in 2012, in August and November, to receive updates on the state's economic condition. The board met in August 2014 for a similar update through FY2014.

Purchasing

Agencies of state government must make purchases through or under the supervision of the Texas Procurement and Support Services (TPASS), a

budget execution
The process whereby the governor and the Legislative Budget Board oversee (and, in some instances, modify) implementation of the spending plan authorized by the Texas legislature.

division of the Office of the Comptroller of Public Accounts. Depending on the cost of an item, agency personnel may be required to obtain competitive bids. This division places greater emphasis on serving state agencies for which it purchases goods than on controlling what they purchase. It also provides agencies with administrative support services, such as mail distribution and management of vehicle fleets. In addition, the division negotiates contracts with airlines, rental car agencies, and hotels to obtain lower prices for personnel traveling on state business. These services are also available to participating local governments. The seven-member Council on Competitive Government, chaired by the governor, is required to determine exactly what kinds of services each agency currently provides that might be supplied at less cost by private industry or another state agency.

Facilities

A seven-member appointed board oversees the Texas Facilities Commission. This agency provides property management services for state facilities, including the Texas State Cemetery. In addition, agency personnel, in collaboration with the Longhorn Foundation, manage football tailgating on state property in Austin. The agency begins taking online reservations in June of each year.

Accounting

The comptroller of public accounts oversees the management of the state's money. Texas law holds this elected official responsible for maintaining a double-entry system, in which a debit account and a credit account are maintained for each transaction. Other statutes narrow the comptroller's discretion by creating numerous dedicated funds or accounts that essentially designate revenues to be used for financing identified activities. Because this money is usually earmarked for special purposes, it is not subject to appropriation for any other use by the legislature.

Major accounting tasks of the comptroller's office include preparing warrants (checks) used to pay state obligations, acknowledging receipts from various state revenue sources, and recording information concerning receipts and expenditures in ledgers and other account books. Contrary to usual business practice, state accounts are set up on a cash basis rather than an accrual basis. In cash accounting, expenditures are entered when the money is actually paid rather than when the obligation is incurred. In times of fiscal crisis, the practice of creating obligations in one fiscal year and paying them in the next allows a budget to appear balanced. Unfortunately, it complicates the task of fiscal planning by failing to reflect an accurate picture of current finances at any given moment. The comptroller issues monthly and annual reports that include general statements of revenues and expenditures. These reports allocate spending based on the object of expenditures that are the goods, supplies, and services used to provide government programs. Salaries, wages, and employment benefits for state employees consistently lead all objective expenditures.

Auditing

State accounts are audited (examined) under direct supervision of the state auditor. This official is appointed by and serves at the will of the Legislative Audit Committee, a six-member committee comprised of the lieutenant governor; the Speaker of the House of Representatives; one appointed member from the Senate; and the chairs of the Senate Finance Committee, the House Appropriations Committee, and the House Ways and Means Committee. The auditor may be removed by the committee at any time without the privilege of a hearing.

With the assistance of approximately 200 staff members, the auditor provides random checks of financial records and transactions after expenditures. Auditing involves reviewing the records and accounts of disbursing officers and custodians of all state funds to assure compliance with the law. Another important duty of the auditor is to examine the activities of each state agency to evaluate the quality of its services, determine whether duplication of effort exists, and recommend changes. The State Auditor's Office is also responsible for reviewing performance measures that agencies include in their strategic plans to ensure that accurate reporting procedures are in place. The agency conducts audits in order of priority by reviewing activities most subject to potential or perceived abuse first. Its stated mission is to provide elected officials with information to improve accountability in state government.

13.3 Learning Check

1. What is a fiscal year?
2. Texas has a dual budgeting system. What does this mean?

Answers on p. 502.

Future Demands

LO13.4 Evaluate the effectiveness of the state's financing of public services.

Elected officials have worked to keep taxing levels low. As a result, Texas has also kept its per capita spending levels among the lowest in the nation. Some observers believe that this limited funding is merely deferring problems in the areas of education, social services, and the state's infrastructure for years to come. Problems that continue to compete for public money include increasing enrollment in our public schools, colleges, and universities; additional social service needs; and an outdated infrastructure.

Public Education

The state, together with local school districts, is responsible for providing a basic education for all Texas school-age children. State and local spending on public education remains below the national average ($8,275 per student in Texas versus $10,938 nationally for 2012–2013). Public education accounted for 28 percent of the state's projected expenditures (approximately $28 billion per year) for the 2014–2015 biennium. That amount of state funding reportedly accounted for less than 50 percent of the actual cost of public education. Legislators had, however, restored some of the 82nd Legislature's historic $5.4 billion funding reduction from 2011. The cuts had been required to balance the state's budget for the 2012–2013 biennium. All remaining costs for public education must be covered with local taxes and federal grants.

This hybrid arrangement may explain some of the difficulties in operating and financing Texas's schools. Is public education a national issue deserving of federal funding, attention, and standards, similar to the interstate highway system, in which the federal government pays for roads that connect all parts of the nation? Or should education be a state function, similar to the state's role in building and maintaining state highways so that all Texans are entitled to drive on the same quality of paved roads? Or is public education a local responsibility, more akin to city streets so that towns with more money have better-quality streets than their poorer neighbors? Although education appears to integrate all three levels of government—national, state, and local—into one system, confusion and conflict surround the fiscal responsibility and role of each in the state's educational system. When the Texas legislature created the Property Tax Relief Fund in 2006, state leaders predicted that by 2008 state funding would provide at least 50 percent of public school funding. Through 2015, however, the state's share of funding for public schools remained at less than 50 percent.

Sources of Public School Funding Texas state government has struggled with financing public education for more than 40 years.[26] Table 13.1 provides a history of relevant court decisions, state constitutional provisions, and legislative responses that have established funding sources and

Table 13.1   History of Texas Public School Finance in the Courts

Case	Year	Question	Decision	Legislative Response
Rodriguez v. San Antonio (U.S. Supreme Court)	1971	Does Texas's school funding system violate the Equal Protection Clause?	No, because education is not a federally protected right.	None
Edgewood v. Kirby (Texas Supreme Court)	1989	Is Texas's school funding system "efficient" as required by the Texas Constitution?	No, a 9-to-1 difference in per-student funding is inefficient. An efficient system must produce "similar revenue for similar effort."	Decided to study the issue.
Edgewood v. Kirby (Texas Supreme Court)	1991	Is Texas's school funding system "efficient"?	No	Authorized county education districts.

Table 13.1   (Continued)

Carrollton-Farmers Branch v. Edgewood (Texas Supreme Court)	1992	Do countywide education districts create a statewide property tax, a practice prohibited by the Texas Constitution?	Yes	Established a program to recapture wealth from property-rich districts to redistribute to property-poor districts (also known as the "Robin Hood" plan).
Edgewood v. Meno (Texas Supreme Court)	1995	Is a recapture program constitutional?	Yes, because it provides funding for a "general diffusion of knowledge."	None
West Orange-Cove v. Neeley (Texas Supreme Court)	2005	Does the need for most districts to tax at the maximum allowable tax rate create a statewide property tax?	Yes	Lowered the property tax by establishing the Property Tax Relief Fund at the state level.
Texas Taxpayer and Student Fairness Coalition, et al. v. Williams Multiple cases involving more than 600 school districts, parents, the Texas Association of Business, and the Texas Charter School Association (District Court, decision under review by Texas Supreme Court)	2014	Is Texas's school funding system "efficient"? Does the need for most districts to tax at the maximum allowable tax rate create a statewide property tax?	No, because it does not provide for a "general diffusion of knowledge." Yes	Joint interim committee appointed to study school finance in 2012; legislature increased funding by $3.4 billion in 2013.

Sources: Compiled from Albert H. Kauffman, "The Texas School Finance Litigation Saga: Great Progress, Then Near Death by a Thousand Cuts," *St. Mary's Law Journal* 40, no. 2 (2008): 511–579; Morgan Smith, "A Guide to the Texas School Finance Lawsuits," *Texas Tribune*, February 29, 2012, http://www.texastribune.org/texas-education/public-education/how-navigate-texas-school-finance-lawsuits/; Morgan Smith, "Texas School Finance Trial Enters Phase Two," *Texas Tribune*, January 21, 2014, http://www.texastribune.org/tribpedia/school-finance/.

CRITICAL THINKING

What amount of financial support should the state provide for funding public schools?

shaped the ways in which those sources are administered. In promoting public education, Texas state government has usually confined its activity to establishing minimum standards and providing basic levels of financial support. School districts and state government share the cost of three elements—salaries, transportation, and operating expenses. Local funding of school systems relies primarily on the market value of taxable real estate within each school district, because local schools raise their share primarily through property taxes. Average daily attendance of pupils in the district, types of students (for example, elementary, secondary, or disabled), and local economic conditions determine the state's share.

In 1949, the Texas legislature passed the Gilmer-Aiken Law, intended to provide a minimum level of state support for every public school student in Texas. This law established the Minimum Foundation Program (now called the Foundation School Program). Local property taxes fund programs beyond the minimum level of services financed by the Foundation School Program. (For a discussion of school district taxing procedures, see Chapter 3, "Local Government.")

Money to finance the Foundation School Program is allocated to each school system from the Foundation School Fund. This fund accounts for more than 70 percent of state funding for public schools. Other sources of state revenue used to support public schools include:

- The Available School Fund (revenue received from a variety of state taxes and income from the Permanent School Fund, primarily funded by public land proceeds)
- The School Taxing Ability Protection Fund (money appropriated by the legislature to offset revenue reduction incurred by rural school districts)
- The Texas Lottery
- The Property Tax Relief Fund (money appropriated to offset loss of revenue from local property taxes)
- The General Revenue Fund

Funding Equalization As Table 13.1 indicates, a continuing controversy surrounding public school finance in Texas has been court-mandated funding equalization. The legislatively enacted wealth equalization plan, labeled the **"Robin Hood" plan** by its critics, requires wealthier districts (those with a tax base equal to $319,500 or more per student) to choose among a series of options to reduce its wealth per student in a process called recapture. These funds are transferred to the state to redistribute to property-poor school districts. Despite court challenges, the "Robin Hood" plan has been found to be constitutional. One-third of the state-administered Property Tax Relief Fund may be used to equalize funding among districts. Nevertheless, according to evidence presented in *Texas Taxpayer and Student Fairness Coalition, et al. v. Williams* (2014), a $2,124 per student funding gap still exists between the wealthiest and poorest 15 percent of school districts.

At the heart of the dispute regarding how to achieve equalized funding is whether all students in the state are entitled to receive the same quality of education. Although court decisions have granted Texas students the right to equal educational opportunities, these determinations do not address

"Robin Hood" plan
A plan for equalizing financial support for school districts by transferring tax money from rich districts to poor districts.

the reality that not all students enter school equally prepared to succeed. Frequently, parents of economically disadvantaged students are unable to offer their children the same learning opportunities as those provided by more affluent parents. To make up for this difference in preparation, both the state and federal governments provide additional funding to help school districts equalize learning outcomes for low-income students. The number of economically disadvantaged students enrolled in Texas's public schools, however, continues to increase.

Many public officials and education experts have expressed concern that educating an increasing number of students, especially those who are economically disadvantaged, requires increases in the funding of public education. Yet state funding in terms of actual dollars appropriated was lower in 2015 than in 2011, even though school enrollments had increased by 320,000 students. Unless funding levels increase, school districts will continue to struggle in their attempts to provide students with an adequate education to compete in the 21st-century workplace.

Public Higher Education

Like public schools, the public higher education system endures the dual pressures of increasing enrollment and declining state support. The Texas Higher Education Coordinating Board's Closing the Gaps initiative required all public institutions to participate actively in increasing college enrollment levels by an additional 630,000 students over year 2000 enrollment levels by the year 2015. At a time when Texas legislators, like other state legislators across the nation, worked to balance state budgets by reducing funding to higher education, the Closing the Gaps initiative placed additional demands on colleges and universities for faculty, staff, and facilities. Furthermore, the success of this effort depended on more low-income students enrolling in institutions of higher education.

State financial aid for college and university students remains insufficient to meet demand. The 82nd Legislature reduced funding for higher education by more than 9 percent from 2010–2011 funding levels. The 83rd Legislature restored most funding for college operations and financial aid benefits to 2010–2011 levels. Still, the number of eligible students who receive assistance is far lower than the number who are eligible. In an effort to serve more students, higher education institutions have reduced the amount of some awards.[27] At the same time, colleges and universities are increasing tuition to cover their operating costs. Low levels of state funding have forced students to bear more of the costs of their education by paying higher tuition and taking out more and larger loans.

Colleges and universities receive most of their income from the state through formula funding, a method that uses specific factors to calculate how much money each institution receives. In recent years, the governor, the legislature, and the Texas Higher Education Coordinating Board have argued for a change in the factors used to determine the state's portion of funding. Each favors an outcomes-based funding formula that links the amount of state funding for a college or university to the number of students who successfully complete courses and the number of students who graduate (and, if a community college, transfer to a university). Governor Perry addressed the issue in his State of the State speech to the 82nd Legislature. He called on legislators to shift most funding to outcomes-based budgeting because "Texans deserve college graduation for their hard-earned tax dollars, not just college enrollment."[28] The 82nd Legislature complied by passing HB 9, requiring the Texas Higher Education Coordinating Board to develop an outcomes-based formula for funding the state's public universities and colleges. The 83rd Legislature implemented outcomes-based funding for a portion of state money appropriated to community colleges. Proponents maintain that the emphasis on successful outcomes will improve higher education. Opponents argue that such a funding structure will reduce the amount of financial support institutions receive and will have a negative effect on students who need the most assistance.[29]

Community College Funding State financing of public community or junior colleges was restructured by the 83rd Legislature. Each community college district in the state received a minimum of $500,000 in funding. The legislature appropriated an additional amount that is distributed to colleges based on a "contact hour of instruction" rate for vocational-technical and academic courses. This rate is determined by calculating the hours of contact between an instructor and students and represents 90 percent of state funding. The remaining 10 percent is based on student performance, including successful completion of courses, graduation, and transfer to a university. In addition, these two-year institutions use local property tax revenues, tuition, fees, gifts, and state and federal grants to finance their operations. Funding for community colleges remains significantly below 1998 formula funding levels. Since that year, however, costs have increased. This gap in funding has been financed by students and local taxpayers. Having responsibility for managing local tax dollars causes community college boards of regents to be cautious in spending money on campus resources. For a discussion of how one group of students brought attention to these issues, see this chapter's Students in Action feature.

Over the years, the legislature has reduced funding to community colleges by a greater percentage than university funding. One report by the *Texas Public Higher Education Almanac* suggests that 56 percent of undergraduates attend community colleges. The majority of these students are African American and Latino. For some observers, this reduction in funding constitutes inequality between universities and community colleges,[30] and arguably because of student population demographics, unequal treatment based on race.

University Funding Texas's state universities and the Texas State Technical College System obtain basic financing through legislated biennial appropriations from the General Revenue Fund. They also obtain money from fees other than tuition, such as student service and computer use fees (which are deposited in the General Revenue Fund), auxiliary services income (for example, rent for campus housing and food service fees), grants, gifts, and special

 **Students in Action**

"Try. Even though you think you can't, try."

Kelsey Lea

When Professor Gilbert Schorlemmer announced the special interest portfolio group project to his Texas government class at Blinn College-Bryan, Connor Shields was not surprised. In fact, that's why he'd selected Professor Schorlemmer's class. The other members of his team (Kelsey Lea, Samantha Davis, and William Niven) were not so certain. The work sounded overwhelming.

"Government happens outside the classroom," the professor said, "so pick an issue, gather data, and see what you can do to solve it." The group decided to stay local and focus on the problems they encountered every day right on the Blinn campus. They divided the work into academic and nonacademic issues.

Connor, a landscape major, believed much could be done to improve the outward appearance of the college so the campus would look inviting. William noticed a lack of outdoor amenities: "Four outdoor grated tables for a campus of 13,000 students." Kelsey and Samantha were concerned about the limited availability of tutoring and the library's closing just as evening classes ended.

The team went to work gathering data. They conducted a survey of their fellow students. Team members visited Blinn's Brenham campus to compare landscaping, the library, and social areas with their home campus. They interviewed the Student Government Association's president and sponsor, faculty members, and the campus president.

When talking with others about campus issues, they often discovered an ally. The Student Government Association passed six resolutions recommending the requested changes: increased tutoring services, longer library hours, more

computers, improved landscaping, additional outdoor lounge areas, and covered walkways.

In April 2014, the four team members presented their findings to Blinn's Board of Regents. The students received a standing ovation. A faculty member volunteered to sponsor them. The Vice President of Student Services contacted them, asking to set up a meeting. Board members responded that they knew there were problems, but had not realized the magnitude of those issues until the student report.

During the summer of 2014, Blinn installed more tables on the campus and began addressing landscape issues. A new student organization, the Blinn-Bryan Improvement Group, was established as a place for students to identify and work to resolve campus issues. And what's the group's advice to other students? "If you have an issue, talk to people. It doesn't take a lot to get things changed."

Source: Interview with Kelsey Lea, Samantha Davis, William Niven, Connor Shields, and Gilbert Schorlemmer, May 7, 2014.

© Andresr/Shutterstock.com

building funds. The University of Texas and the Texas A&M University systems share revenue from the Permanent University Fund (PUF) investments (approximately $671 million in 2013), with the University of Texas System receiving two-thirds of the money and the Texas A&M University System receiving one-third.

Controversy has surrounded the limited state funding for universities in South Texas and border regions, most especially in the Rio Grande Valley. In 1987, the unequal allocation of state funding for universities was challenged in the case of *Richards v. LULAC*, 868 SW2d 306 (1993). Although the plaintiffs failed to establish racial bias in the funding of higher education to the satisfaction of the Texas Supreme Court, in 1989 the legislature established the South Texas/Border Initiative with a focus on funding parity for higher education in these areas of the state.[31] The 83rd Legislature authorized the creation of a regional comprehensive university in the Rio Grande Valley that includes a new medical school. Combining the campuses of UT-Pan American, UT-Brownsville, and the Regional Academic Health Center, the University of Texas Rio Grande Valley has direct access to PUF money. The university was scheduled to enroll its first class in September 2015.

Tuition Deregulation   In late 2002, the University of Texas System led an effort to eliminate legislative caps on tuition and fees. According to university officials, funding limitations threatened the University of Texas at Austin's ability to remain a premier research institution. Despite fears that escalating tuition and fees would limit access to higher education for Texas's lower-income students, the proposal became law in 2003.

Public universities, as well as public community colleges, quickly moved to raise tuition. Both the dollar increase in tuition and the rate of increase have been dramatic. Since 2003, universities have raised tuition rates and fees approximately 90 percent above their 2003 levels. At the same time, state support of universities and community colleges has declined. Elected officials expressed concern about the dramatic increase in tuition and fees. The 83rd Legislature responded by approving legislation that required public universities to establish programs that locked in tuition rates for four years for entering freshmen who chose to participate. For more on this program, see the Selected Reading for this chapter.

Texas Tomorrow Funds   The Texas Guaranteed Tuition Plan and Tomorrow's College Investment Plan comprise the Texas Tomorrow Funds. The Tuition Plan provides a way for parents to save for their children's education and to lock in the cost of tuition and fees at the state's public colleges and universities. Tuition increases have also affected these programs. The Texas Tomorrow Fund is backed by the full faith and credit of the State of Texas. According to the fund's provisions, approximately 85,000 students must be educated at an anticipated expense to the state of $2 billion. As of 2012 (the last year for which public information is available), the fund had an unfunded liability of $641 million, an amount the state would be required to finance from general revenue. Actuarial projections, an analysis that estimates annual revenue versus cost, indicate the state will be forced to supplement the fund as early as 2020. Because of rapid tuition increases, the state closed the fund to new participants in 2003. The fund reopened as the Texas Tuition Promise Fund in 2008, though at much higher rates. Most important, the Texas Tuition Promise Fund is not guaranteed by the full faith and credit of the State of Texas. College living costs can still be covered by investment in Tomorrow's College Investment Plan.

How Do We Compare...in Tuition and Fees?

Average Tuition and Fees for Academic Year 2013–2014

Most Populous U.S. States	Private University	Public University	Public Community College	U.S. States Bordering Texas	Private University	Public University	Public Community College
California	$36,914	$9,037	$1,424	Arkansas	$19,727	$7,238	$2,960
Florida	$28,087	$6,336	$3,140	Louisiana	$32,649	$6,546	$3,307
New York	$35,484	$6,919	$4,655	New Mexico	$32,948	$5,987	$1,696
Texas	**$29,750**	**$8,522**	**$2,222**	Oklahoma	$23,562	$6,583	$3,290

Note: Tuition rates are for in-state students at public universities and community colleges.
Source: The College Board, "Tuition and Fees by Sector and State over Time," *Trends in College Pricing* (2014), http://trends.collegeboard.org/college-pricing/figures-tables/tuition-and-fees-sector-and-state-over-time.

CRITICAL THINKING

Who should pay the costs of a college education: students or taxpayers?

State Grant and Loan Programs Rather than give money directly to colleges and universities, legislators across the country have preferred to give students the funding and allow them to select the institution at which the funds will be spent. The Texas Tuition Equalization Grants program, created in 1971, subsidizes tuition expenses for eligible students who demonstrate financial need and attend private, nonprofit colleges and universities in Texas. The student must maintain a 2.5 GPA to continue receiving aid. A second type of grant is the **TEXAS Grants Program** (Toward Excellence, Access, and Success), which is the state's largest financial aid program. Qualified students receive grant funding to pay all tuition and fees at any public college or university in the state. Students must be Texas residents, enroll in college within 16 months of high school graduation, show financial need, and have no convictions for a crime involving a controlled substance. Participating students must maintain a 2.5 GPA. The Texas Educational Opportunity Grant Program (TEOG) provides financial aid to financially needy students enrolled in a Texas public two-year college who maintain a 2.5 cumulative GPA and complete 75 percent of attempted hours.

The B-on-Time program provides no-interest loans to eligible students. The loans are forgiven if the student graduates within four years with a 3.0 GPA. The Teach for Texas program provides loan repayment assistance for eligible teachers. Because Texas default rates on student loans exceed the national rate (16.1 percent versus 13.4 percent), the 83rd Legislature directed the Texas Higher Education Coordinating Board (THECB) to develop programs to improve students' financial literacy and understanding of the

TEXAS Grants Program
"Toward Excellence, Access, and Success" is a college financial assistance program that provides funding for qualifying students.

consequences of borrowing to finance college expenses and failing to repay borrowed amounts.

The 2013 Texas legislature adopted changes to the major state financial aid programs to increase flexibility and serve more students, including limiting TEXAS Grants and the B-on-Time Loan Program to university-only programs beginning in FY2015. Previous funding amounts for the TEXAS grants program were transferred to the TEOG program for qualified community college students. Current information about all of these programs is available on the THECB's website. Utilizing social media, the THECB maintains a Twitter account and an interactive web tool, entitled Compare College TX, to help users learn about various aspects of Texas public universities and colleges, including costs.

Public Assistance

Enrolling more students in high-quality public schools and institutions of higher education are ways in which Texas's political leaders hope to combat poverty. Income disparity between the wealthiest 20 percent of Texans and the poorest 20 percent widened throughout the first decade of the 21st century. Even with implementation of the federal Patient Protection and Affordable Care Act in 2014, a higher percentage of Texans lacked health insurance than residents of any other state. The number of children without coverage also ranked the highest in the nation, in both percentage and sheer numbers. Poverty levels remain above the national average. Notable differences in levels of poverty also exist among racial and ethnic groups: African Americans (24.8 percent), Latinos (26.8 percent), and Asians (12.6 percent), compared to Anglos (9.1 percent).

Increasing health care costs for the poor present significant challenges to state government. The percentage of the total state budget dedicated to health and human services is second only to spending on all levels of education ($74.2 billion for education versus $73.9 billion for health and human services in the 2014–2015 biennium). The cost of Medicaid and the **Children's Health Insurance Program (CHIP)** (an insurance program with minimal premiums for children from low-income families) frequently exceeds budget allocations, even though many eligible individuals are not included.

Coverage for children remains a concern for lawmakers. In 2012, the state had the largest number of uninsured children in the nation: 1.1 million.[32] Some observers suggest that up to one-half of uninsured children qualify for Medicaid or CHIP. A third program, created in 2009 and administered by the attorney general's Child Support Division, targets uninsured young Texans. **ChildLINK** purchases insurance coverage with money paid by noncustodial parents who have been ordered to pay medical support for their children. Proponents argued that this program would provide insurance for an additional 200,000 children. Opponents maintained that the coverage had fewer benefits than Medicaid or CHIP.

Limiting access to Medicaid lowers the state's obligation to pay for benefits, but at what cost? The federal government funds almost 60 cents of

Children's Health Insurance Program (CHIP)
A program that provides medical insurance for minimal premiums to children from low-income families.

ChildLINK
A program administered by the Texas Attorney General's Child Support Division in which medical support payments from noncustodial parents are used to provide insurance for their children.

every dollar paid for Medicaid services. In addition, the federal portion of CHIP expenditures is approximately 72 cents of every dollar paid for medical services. The 83rd Legislature increased state funding for Medicaid to accommodate an additional 450,000 recipients by FY2015, because many children previously on CHIP are now eligible for Medicaid under the Affordable Care Act. Although the state refused to extend Medicaid benefits to adults who were not primary caregivers for a minor, it was not allowed to limit extending coverage to more children. According to some observers, state officials' refusal to expand Medicaid coverage to adults likely cost the state $100 billion in federal funding over the 10-year period from 2014 to 2024. Under the expanded program, the federal government was responsible for 100 percent of costs for the first three years of coverage and 90 percent thereafter.

Much of the cost and care burden for uninsured residents, both children and adults, has shifted to local governments, hospitals, and the insured. Counties and hospitals must subsidize unreimbursed costs for treating the uninsured by charging higher rates to the insured, which translates into higher insurance premiums, as well as higher county property taxes. Analysts project a continuing increase in indigent health care costs in the years to come. The ability of local entities to meet the social service needs of the state's low-income residents is one of the key challenges of the 21st century.

Infrastructure Needs

In addition to demands for education, health, and human services, Texans look to state government to meet other needs. The state of Texas has a responsibility to provide an infrastructure for its residents, including both highway and water systems. Limited resources and growing demands are evident in the provision of these services as well.

Transportation Consistent with Texas's pay-as-you-go budget system is its pay-as-you-ride system of financing construction and maintenance of roads and highways. Historically, Texas roads have been financed through a combination of motor fuel taxes, motor vehicle registration fees, and the Federal Highway Trust Fund, to which certain federal highway user taxes are allocated. A 2011 study by the Center for Transportation Research reported that the state would require more than $315 billion to meet its roadway needs through 2031. Authors of the same study noted that only $160 billion was available under current funding strategies.[33] Trucks and heavy equipment used in Texas's burgeoning oil and gas industry have damaged roads and other transportation infrastructure. Legislation passed by the 83rd Legislature allows counties with significant oil and gas production to create County Energy Tax Reinvestment Zones (CETRZ). The CETRZ can then apply for grants from the Transportation Infrastructure Fund, which is administered by the Texas Department of Transportation. To obtain a grant, counties must provide 10 percent of funding (if the county is designated as economically disadvantaged) or 20 percent (if the county is not so designated).

As increases in roadway construction costs have exceeded funding, much of this expense has been transferred to users in the form of tolls. The reality of financing new highway construction with tolls was perhaps best expressed by former Texas Transportation Commission chair Ric Williamson, who described the policy as, "It's the no road, the toll road, or the slow road."[34] Increasing costs have required borrowing concessions, as authorized by Texas voters through constitutional amendment. The Texas Mobility Fund allows the state to issue bonds and use the proceeds for road construction. In 2014, Texas voters amended the Texas Constitution to allow one-half of the amount of oil and gas taxes intended for the Rainy Day Fund to be diverted to the State Highway Fund (also identified as Fund 6). Proponents suggested this approval would provide an additional $1.5 billion annually for highway construction and maintenance, still well below the $4 billion needed for a sufficient and safe infrastructure.[35]

Water The ongoing Texas drought that began in 2007 has highlighted the state's water needs. In 2012, the Texas Water Development Board issued its state water plan. Six years in development, the plan had dire predictions for Texans if efforts were not made to increase the state's water supply in the coming years. The projected cost to provide adequate water supplies for anticipated population growth was $53 billion. If the state took no action, in the event of a significant drought, the report estimated annual losses of $12 billion in income and 115,000 jobs.[36] A constitutional amendment, ratified by voters in 2013, led to the creation of two special funds to finance, through low-interest loans, certain water projects under the State Water Plan to ensure the availability of adequate water resources in the future. In 2014, the comptroller of public accounts focused attention on the continuing need for additional state funding and more reliance on technology, noting that "conservation's not enough."[37] While water supplies dwindled, demand surged. In May 2014, the U.S. Census Bureau reported that 7 of the 15 fastest growing U.S. cities were in Texas.[38] In that same month, *Texas Monthly* reported that because of its severe water shortage, Wichita Falls was constructing the first wastewater treatment plant in the nation to treat toilet water for reuse as drinking water (a method called toilet-to-tap).[39] In July 2014, the system became operational.

13.4 Learning Check

1. True or False: Tuition deregulation resulted in lower tuition at the state's public colleges and universities.
2. What three programs provide health insurance for Texas children?

Answers on p. 503.

Universities to Offer Four-Year Fixed-Tuition Rates

Renée C. Lee

Since the legislature authorized state institutions of higher education to set their own tuition rates in 2003, tuition has increased by more than 90 percent. In 2013, the legislature required universities to provide fixed tuition and rebates for students who graduate within four years. The following article describes how some schools have responded to this challenge.

Incoming freshmen at Texas public universities … have an option to lock in their first-year tuition rate for four years, giving them a bit more control over rising college costs. But there's a small catch: Students must graduate in four years to realize the savings of a fixed-rate tuition plan. Tuition goes up after four years to the current rate.

A new state law, recently signed by Gov. Rick Perry, requires public universities to offer fixed-rate tuition plans to freshmen. It's a concept that's been heavily touted by Perry since last fall [2012] as a way to keep college accessible and affordable. Lawmakers, who passed the legislation during the regular session, say it also will give students and parents some predictability in planning college costs. Texas and Illinois are the only states that mandate fixed-rate tuition at public universities.

Universities are preparing to offer guaranteed tuition in fall 2014. Regents of several university systems have authorized staff to develop plans. "The University of Houston believes that a four-year fixed tuition option sends a strong signal to students that we expect them to graduate in four years and gives them a powerful incentive to do so," said Paula Short, UH senior vice president for academic affairs and provost. "Incoming freshmen who select the fixed-rate option, complete 30 hours per year, and graduate in four years will be rewarded with a lower price for their college degree."

Mixed Results, So Far

Colleges and universities have been under pressure from the Obama administration to improve graduation rates and to lower costs. In Texas, the six-year graduation rate is 49 percent and tuition has increased 90 percent since the state deregulated it in 2003.

The University of Texas at El Paso and UT-Dallas were the first institutions in the state to implement fixed-rate tuition in 2006 and 2007. Results have been mixed. Only 120 students are participating in the UTEP program. Most of the university's students are low income and receive enough financial aid to pay as they go, said Gary Edens, vice president of student affairs. "We have not seen it be overly popular," Edens said. "What we found is that our student population can't commit the time and energy. They have families and jobs. To lock in a structured program is not convenient for them. They would rather work their way through school because they don't want to take on debt."

Students who choose the option have some assurance that their tuition won't go up, he said. But students pay a premium for that assurance. Their tuition at the outset is about 10 percent higher than general tuition. In 2012–13, the fixed-rate tuition at UTEP for incoming freshman was $7,724 per year. General tuition was $7,016. Fixed-rate tuition is generally higher to account for inflation.

Graduation Rate Rises

At UT-Dallas, fixed-rate tuition is mandatory for all students. Each incoming freshman class is locked into a rate based on their first year tuition. Tuition at the university is about 2 percent higher than tuition at other state universities, said Matt Sanchez, director of enrollment services. The university has seen its graduation rate increase by 5 percent since 2008, Sanchez said.

Daniel Hurley with the American Association of State Colleges and Universities said guaranteed tuition isn't necessarily the best tool to keep tuition costs in check. Institutions in Georgia and Michigan have abandoned fixed-rate tuition. Declining state support made it too costly for the colleges and universities to continue offering the option. "I'm not a big fan of it," said Hurley, director of state relations and policy analysis at the association. "It's more popular than it is efficient or productive in the long run," he said. "I think while the conventional wisdom behind them make sense, they probably add greater inefficiency."

It's difficult for institutions to make financial predictions over four years, because a significant change in state funding and enrollment can disrupt the system. And without sufficient state support, annual tuition increases could be larger as a financial precaution, Hurley said.

✔ Selected Reading Learning Check

1. True or False: If a student entering a university chooses a fixed-rate tuition plan, the student's tuition will never increase.
2. Why did universities in Georgia and Michigan stop offering fixed-rate tuition plans?

Answers on p. 503.

....

Source: This article appeared in the *Houston Chronicle* on July 5, 2013.

Conclusion

Economists suggest that a full recovery from the global economic crisis that erupted in 2008 may take as long as 20 years. Yet by 2013, Texas had experienced a remarkable turnaround in its economy. Legislators moved from arguing about how to deal with budget shortfalls to what to do with a budget surplus. Former Governor Rick Perry captured the view of many Texans when he observed, "[W]hether tax receipts are coming in higher than expected or lower than expected, we must always look to cut expenses first." He concluded, "I believe we can continue to be a beacon to those seeking the freedom and liberty to follow their dreams and find success." A far different future was envisioned by Dick Lavine and Eva DeLuna Castro of the Center for Public Policy Priorities when they warned of the pending "consequences of not adequately investing in our schools, health care services, and roads." Which vision prevails in the years ahead remains to be seen.

Chapter Summary

LO 13.1 Assess the fairness of Texas's budgeting and taxing policies. Texas remains a low-cost, low-services state despite an improving economy. The Lone Star State has one of the most regressive tax systems in the United States because of its heavy reliance on the sales tax and its having no state income tax. Texans require that the state operate with a balanced budget, limit borrowing, and limit spending on social services.

LO 13.2 Describe the sources of Texas's state revenue. The state relies on taxes, fees, gambling revenue, sale of assets, oil and gas royalties, investments, and the federal government to fund state services. Rather than raise taxes, Texas's elected officials often increase fees, fines, and other assessments. Voters have restricted the amount of money the state can borrow. Additionally, the state has a Rainy Day Fund that operates like a savings account to provide one-time funding for emergencies.

LO 13.3 Describe the procedure for developing and approving a state budget. Each biennium, the Legislative Budget Board and the Governor's Office of Budget, Planning and Policy are required to prepare proposed budgets. Before a budget can be approved, the comptroller of public accounts must provide an estimate of available revenue for the upcoming biennium and certify that spending will not exceed revenue in the upcoming biennium. Tax collection, investment of the state's surplus funds, and overseeing management of the state's money are responsibilities of the comptroller of public accounts. The state auditor is responsible for examining all state accounts to ensure honesty and efficiency in agency spending of state funds.

LO 13.4 **Evaluate the effectiveness of the state's financing of public services**. State revenue pays for services to Texas's residents. Most state money pays for public education (including higher education) and public assistance, especially Medicaid. Higher numbers of low-income students enrolled in the state's public schools will likely increase the cost of public education. The burden for the cost of higher education and roads is shifting to those who use these services. To repair the state's decaying infrastructure, construct adequate roadways to meet the needs of a growing population, and overcome severe water shortages will be costly to the state's taxpayers in the years ahead.

Key Terms

fiscal policy, p. 464

tax, p. 465

regressive tax, p. 465

progressive tax, p. 465

service sector, p. 466

fee, p. 467

balanced budget, p. 467

General Revenue Fund, p. 467

dedicated fund, p. 467

general sales tax, p. 470

selective sales tax, p. 472

sin tax, p. 472

franchise tax, p. 473

payroll tax, p. 473

severance tax, p. 474

grant-in-aid, p. 477

general obligation bond, p. 479

revenue bond, p. 479

Rainy Day Fund, p. 480

budget, p. 481

Legislative Budget Board (LBB), p. 481

dual budgeting system, p. 482

budget execution, p. 485

''Robin Hood'' plan, p. 490

TEXAS Grants Program, p. 495

Children's Health Insurance Program (CHIP), p. 496

ChildLINK, p. 496

Learning Check Answers

13.1 1. Texas requires a balanced budget, favors low taxes, and spends at low to moderate levels.

2. Texas has a regressive tax system, which means that poor people pay a higher percentage of their incomes in taxes than do wealthier residents.

13.2 1. The general sales tax is the state's largest source of tax revenue.

2. The Rainy Day Fund is to be used when the state faces an economic crisis.

13.3 1. A fiscal year is a budget year. In Texas, it begins on September 1 and ends on August 31 of the following calendar year.

2. A state with a dual budgeting system requires both the executive branch and the legislative branch to prepare and submit proposed budgets to the legislature. In Texas, both the governor and the Legislative Budget Board submit proposed budgets.

13.4 1. False. Since tuition deregulation, student tuition has risen an average of 90 percent over 2003 levels at public colleges and universities.
2. Health insurance is provided to Texas children through Medicaid, CHIP, and ChildLINK.

Selected Reading Learning Check

1. False. Fixed-rate tuition is only in effect for four years. If a student has not graduated within that time, tuition increases to the current rate.
2. Georgia and Michigan abandoned fixed-rate tuition plans because the respective state government's support for higher education decreased and the cost of continuing the programs was too expensive for universities.

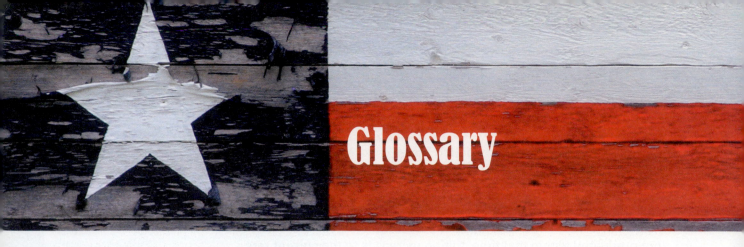

Glossary

Numbers in parentheses indicate the chapter in which the term is found.

adjudication hearing A trial in a juvenile court. (12)

administrative segregation Commonly referred to as solitary confinement, this practice isolates an inmate in a separate cell as punishment, typically for violent or disruptive behavior. (12)

adversarial Reporting featuring opposition and a combative style. Also called *attack journalism*. (6)

affirmative action Takes positive steps to attract women and members of racial and ethnic minority groups; may include using race in admission or hiring decisions. (10)

affirmative racial gerrymandering Drawing the boundaries of a district designed to affect representation of a racial group (e.g., African Americans) in a legislative chamber, city council, commissioners court, or other representative body. (5)

African American A racial classification applied to Americans of African ancestry. The term is commonly applied on the basis of skin color, omitting white Americans whose ancestors immigrated from Africa and including black Americans whose ancestors immigrated from the Caribbean, Latin America, and Europe. (1)

agenda setting Affecting the importance given issues by government and public leaders. (6)

alternative dispute resolution (ADR) Use of mediation, conciliation, or arbitration to resolve disputes among individuals without resorting to a regular court trial. (11)

Anglo As commonly used in Texas, the term is not restricted to persons of Anglo-Saxon lineage but includes those of European ancestry more generally. Traditionally, the term applies to all whites except Latinos. (1)

annex To make an outlying area part of a city. Within a home-rule city's extraterritorial jurisdiction, the city can annex unincorporated areas without a vote by those who live there. (3)

appellate jurisdiction The power of a court to review cases after they have been tried elsewhere. (11)

appointive power The authority to name a person to a government office. Most gubernatorial appointments require Senate approval by two-thirds of the members present. (9)

appointment-retention system A merit plan for judicial selection in which the governor makes an appointment to fill a court vacancy for an interim period, after which the judge must win a full term in an uncontested popular election. (11)

Asian American An ethnic classification for persons whose ancestry originates in the Far East, Southeast Asia, or the Indian subcontinent. (1)

at-large election Members of a policymaking body, such as some city councils, are elected on a citywide basis rather than from single-member districts. (3)

at-large majority district A district that elects two or more representatives. (5)

attack ad An advertisement meant as a personal attack on an opposing candidate or organization. (6)

attorney general The constitutional official elected to head the Office of the Attorney General, which represents the state government in lawsuits and provides legal advice to state and local officials. (9)

balanced budget A budget in which total revenues and expenditures are equal, producing no deficit. (13)

bicameral A legislature with two houses or chambers, such as Texas's House of Representatives and Senate. (8)

bifurcated A divided court system in which different courts handle civil and criminal cases. In Texas, the highest-level appeals courts are bifurcated. (11)

bill A proposed law or statute. (8)

biotechnology Also known as "biotech," this is the use and/or manipulation of biological processes and microorganisms to perform industrial or manufacturing processes or create consumer goods. (1)

block grant Congressional grant of money that allows the state considerable flexibility in spending for a program, such as providing welfare services. (2)

blog A website or Web page on which a writer or group of writers record opinions, information, and links to other sites on a regular basis. (6)

bond A mechanism by which governments borrow money. General obligation bonds (redeemed from general revenue) and revenue bonds (redeemed from revenue obtained from the property or activity financed by the sale of the bonds) are authorized under Texas law. (3)

budget A plan of financial operation indicating how much revenue a government expects to collect during a period (usually one or two fiscal years) and how much spending is authorized for agencies and programs. (13)

budget execution The process whereby the governor and the Legislative Budget Board oversee (and, in some instances, modify) implementation of the spending plan authorized by the Texas legislature. (13)

budgetary power The governor is supposed to submit a state budget to the legislature at the beginning of each regular session. When an appropriation bill is enacted by the legislature and certified by the comptroller of public accounts, the governor may veto the whole document or individual items. (9)

bureaucrats Public employees. (10)

business organization An economic interest group, such as a trade association (e.g., Texas Gaming Association), that lobbies for policies favoring business. (7)

Campaign Reform Act Enacted by the U.S. Congress and signed by President George W. Bush in 2002, this law restricts donations of "soft money" and "hard money" for election campaigns, but its effect has been limited by federal court decisions. (5)

canvass To scrutinize the results of an election and then confirm and certify the vote tally for each candidate. (5)

capital felony A crime punishable by death or life imprisonment. (12)

Capitol press corps Reporters assigned to cover state-level news, commonly working in the state capital. (6)

caucus A meeting at which members of a political party assemble to select delegates and make other policy recommendations at the precinct, county, or state senatorial district and state levels. (4)

ChildLINK A program administered by the Texas Attorney General's Child Support Division in which medical support payments from noncustodial parents are used to provide insurance for their children. (13)

Children's Health Insurance Program (CHIP) A program that provides medical insurance for minimal premiums to children from low-income families. (13)

chubbing A practice whereby representatives engage in lengthy debate for the purpose of using time and thus preventing floor action on a bill that they oppose. (8)

civic engagement Actions by citizens to address issues of public concern. (6)

civil law The body of law concerning noncriminal matters, such as business contracts and personal injury. (11)

closed primary A primary in which voters must declare their support for a party before they are permitted to participate in the selection of its candidates. (5)

colonia A low-income community, typically located in South Texas and especially in counties bordering Mexico, that lacks running water, sewer lines, and other essentials. (3)

commission form A type of municipal government in which each elected commissioner is a member of the city's policymaking body, but also heads an administrative department (e.g., public safety with police and fire divisions). (3)

commissioner of agriculture The elected official, whose position is created by statute, who heads Texas's Department of Agriculture, which promotes the sale of agricultural commodities and regulates pesticides, aquaculture, egg quality, weights and measures, and grain warehouses. (9)

commissioner of education The official who heads the TEA. (10)

commissioner of insurance Appointed by the governor, the commissioner heads the Texas Department of Insurance, which is responsible for ensuring the industry's financial soundness, protecting policyholders, and overseeing insurance rates. (10)

commissioner of the General Land Office As head of Texas's General Land Office, this elected constitutional officer oversees the state's extensive landholdings and related mineral interests, especially oil and gas leasing, for the benefit of the Permanent School Fund. (9)

commissioners court A Texas county's policymaking body, with five members: the county judge, who presides, and four commissioners representing single-member precincts. (3)

commutation of sentence On the recommendation of the Board of Pardons and Paroles, the reduction of a sentence by the governor. (9)

companion bill Filed in one house but identical or similar to a bill filed in the other chamber; speeds passage of a bill because committee consideration may take place simultaneously in both houses. (8)

comptroller of public accounts An elected constitutional officer responsible for collecting taxes, keeping accounts, estimating revenue, and serving as treasurer for the state. (9)

concurrent jurisdiction The authority of more than one court to try a case (for example, a civil dispute involving more than $500 but less than $10,000 may be heard in either a justice of the peace court, a county court (or county-court-at-law), or a district court). (11)

concurrent resolution A resolution adopted by House and Senate majorities and then approved by the governor (for example, a request for action by Congress or authorization for someone to sue the state). (8)

conditional pardon An act of executive clemency, on recommendation of the Board of Pardons and Paroles, that releases a convicted person from the consequences of his or her crime but does not restore all rights, as in the case of a full pardon. (9)

conference committee A committee composed of representatives and senators appointed to reach agreement on a disputed bill and recommend changes acceptable to both chambers. (8)

conservative A person who advocates minimal intervention by government in social and economic matters and who gives a high priority to reducing taxes and curbing public spending. (4)

constable A citizen elected to assist the justice of the peace by serving papers and in some cases carrying out security and investigative responsibilities. (3)

constitutional amendment election Election, typically in November of an odd-numbered year, in which voters are asked to approve one or more proposed constitutional amendments. An amendment must receive a majority of the popular vote to be approved. (2)

constitutional amendment process Process for changing the Texas Constitution in which an amendment is proposed by a two-thirds vote of each chamber of the legislature and approved by a simple majority of voters in a general or special election. (2)

constitutional guarantees Rights and protections assured under the U.S. Constitution. For example, among the guarantees to members of the Union include protection against invasion and domestic uprisings, territorial integrity, a republican form of government, and representation by two senators and at least one representative for each state. (2)

constitutional revision Extensive or complete rewriting of a constitution. (2)

constitutional revision convention A body of delegates who meet to make extensive changes in a constitution or to draft a new constitution. (2)

contingency fee A lawyer's compensation paid from money recovered in a lawsuit. (11)

contingency rider Authorization for spending state money to finance provisions of a bill if it passes. (9)

council of governments (COG) A regional planning body composed of governmental units (e.g., cities, counties, special districts); functions include review and comment on proposals by local governments for obtaining state and federal grants. (3)

council-manager form A system of municipal government in which an elected city council hires a manager to coordinate budgetary matters and supervise administrative departments. (3)

county Texas is divided into 254 counties that serve as an administrative arm of the state and that provide important services at the local level, especially in rural areas. (3)

county attorney A citizen elected to represent the county in civil and criminal cases, unless a resident district attorney performs some of these functions. (3)

county auditor A person appointed by the district judge or judges to check the financial books and records of other officials who handle county money. (3)

county chair Elected by county party members in the primaries, this key party official heads the county executive committee. (4)

county clerk A citizen elected to perform clerical chores for the county courts and commissioners court, keep public records, maintain vital statistics, and administer public elections, if the county does not have an administrator of elections. (3)

county convention A party meeting of delegates held in even-numbered years on a date and at a time and place prescribed by the party's state executive committee to adopt resolutions and to select delegates and alternates to the party's state convention. (4)

county executive committee Composed of a party's precinct chairs and the elected county chair, the county executive committee conducts primaries and makes arrangements for holding county conventions. (4)

county judge A citizen popularly elected to preside over the county commissioners court and, in smaller counties, to hear civil and criminal cases. (3)

county sheriff A citizen popularly elected as the county's chief law enforcement officer; the sheriff is also responsible for maintaining the county jail. (3)

county tax assessor-collector This elected official no longer assesses property for taxation but does collect taxes and fees and commonly handles voter registration. (3)

county treasurer An elected official who receives and pays out county money as directed by the commissioners court. (3)

countywide tax appraisal district The district appraises all real estate and commercial property for taxation by units of local government within a county. (3)

court of record A court that has a court reporter or electronic device to record testimony and proceedings. (11)

criminal justice system The system involves prosecution, defense, sentencing, and punishment of those suspected or convicted of committing a crime. (12)

criminal law The body of law concerning felony and misdemeanor offenses by individuals against other persons and property, or in violation of laws or ordinances. (11)

crossover voting A practice whereby a person participates in the primary of one party, then votes for one or more candidates of another party in the general election. (5)

cumulative voting When multiple seats are contested in an at-large election, voters cast one or more of the specified number of votes for one or more candidates in any combination. It is designed to increase representation of historically underrepresented ethnic minority groups. (3)

dealignment Occurs when citizens have no allegiance to a political party and become independent voters. (4)

decentralized government Decentralization is achieved by dividing power between national and state governments and separating legislative, executive, and judicial branches at both levels. (7)

dedicated fund A restricted state fund that has been identified to fund a designated purpose. If the fund is consolidated within the general revenue fund, it usually must be spent for its intended purpose. Unappropriated amounts of dedicated funds, even those required to be used for a specific purpose, can be included in the calculations to balance the state budget. (13)

defendant The person sued in a civil proceeding or prosecuted in a criminal proceeding. (11)

delegated powers Specific powers entrusted to the national government by Article I, Section 8, of the U.S. Constitution (e.g., regulate interstate commerce, borrow money, and declare war). (2)

deregulation The elimination of government restrictions to allow free market competition to determine or limit the actions of individuals and corporations. (10)

Dillon's Rule A legal principle, still followed in the majority of states including Texas, that local governments have only those powers granted by their state government. (3)

direct primary A nominating system that allows voters to participate directly in the selection of candidates to public office. (5)

discovery Gathering information from the opposing party and witnesses in a lawsuit, including examination of relevant documents, obtaining written and oral answers to questions, inspecting property under the control of the other party, and similar activities. (11)

district attorney A citizen elected to serve one or more counties who prosecutes criminal cases, gives advisory opinions, and represents the county in civil cases. (3)

district clerk A citizen elected to maintain records for the district courts. (3)

district convention Held in even-numbered years on a date and at a time and place prescribed by the party's state executive committee in counties that have more than one state senatorial district. Participants select delegates and alternates to the party's state convention. (4)

district executive committee Composed of county chairs within a district that elects a state senator, U.S. or state representative, or district judge, this body fills a vacancy created by the death, resignation, or disqualification of a nominated candidate. (4)

dual budgeting system The compilation of separate budgets by the legislative branch and the executive branch. (13)

early voting Conducted at the county courthouse and selected polling places before the designated primary, special, or general election day. (5)

economic interest group Interest groups that exist primarily to promote their members' economic self-interest. Trade associations and labor unions are classified as economic interest groups because they are organized to promote policies that will maximize profits and wages. (7)

election judge Official appointed by the county commissioners court to administer an election in a voting precinct. (5)

electioneering Active campaigning by an interest group in support of, or in opposition to, a candidate; actions urging the public to act on an issue. (7)

elections administrator Person appointed to supervise voter registration and voting. (5)

elite access The ability of the business elite to deal directly with high-ranking government administrators to avoid full compliance with regulations. (10)

eminent domain The power of the government to take private property for public uses, so long as just compensation is paid. (1)

enhanced punishment Additional penalties or prison time for those who engage in organized crime or hate crimes, and for repeat offenders. (12)

equal opportunity Ensures that policies and actions do not discriminate on factors such as race, gender, ethnicity, religion, or national origin. (10)

exclusionary zoning The use of local government zoning ordinances to exclude certain groups of people from a given community. (1)

exclusive jurisdiction The authority of only one court to hear a particular type of case. (11)

exculpatory evidence Evidence that helps a defendant and may exonerate the defendant in a criminal trial. (12)

executive commissioner of the Health and Human Services Commission Appointed by the governor with Senate approval, the executive commissioner administers the HHSC, develops policies, makes rules, and appoints (with approval by the governor) commissioners to head the commission's four departments. (10)

executive order The governor issues executive orders to set policy within the executive branch and to create task forces, councils, and other bodies. (9)

extraterritorial jurisdiction (ETJ) The limited authority a city has outside its boundaries. The larger the city's population size, the larger the reach of its ETJ. (3)

federal grants-in-aid Money appropriated by the U.S. Congress to help states and local governments provide needed facilities and services. (2)

fee A charge imposed by an agency upon those subject to its regulation. (13)

felony A serious crime punished by fine and prison confinement. (11)

filibustering A delaying tactic whereby a senator may speak, and thus hold the Senate floor, for as long as physical endurance permits, unless action is taken to end the filibuster. (8)

fiscal policy Public policy that concerns taxing, government spending, public debt, and management of government money. (13)

framing The news media providing meaning or defining the central theme of an issue. (6)

franchise tax A tax levied on the annual receipts of businesses that are organized to limit the personal liability of owners for the privilege of conducting business in the state. (13)

full faith and credit clause Most government actions of another state must be officially recognized by public officials in Texas. (2)

full pardon An act of executive clemency, on recommendation of the Board of Pardons and Paroles, that releases a convicted person from all consequences of a criminal act and restores the same rights enjoyed by others who have not been convicted of a crime. (9)

general election Held in November of even-numbered years to elect county and state officials from among candidates nominated in primaries or (for small parties) in nominating conventions. (5)

general obligation bond Amount borrowed by the state that is repaid from the General Revenue Fund. (13)

General Revenue Fund An unrestricted state fund that is available for general appropriations. (13)

general sales tax Texas's largest source of tax revenue, applied at the rate of 6.25 percent to the sale price of tangible personal property and "the storage, use, or other consumption of tangible personal property purchased, leased, or rented." (13)

general-law city A municipality with a charter prescribed by the legislature. (3)

gerrymandering Drawing the boundaries of a district designed to affect representation of a political party or group in a legislative chamber, city council, commissioners court, or other representative body. (5)

gerrymandering Drawing the boundaries of a district, such as a state senatorial or representative district, to include or exclude certain groups of voters and thus affect election outcomes. (8)

ghost voting A prohibited practice whereby one representative presses the voting button of another House member who is absent. (8)

government A public institution with authority to formulate, adopt, implement, and enforce public policies for a society. (1)

governor's office The administrative organization through which the governor of Texas makes appointments, prepares a biennial budget recommendation, administers federal and state grants for crime prevention and law enforcement, and confers full and conditional pardons on recommendation of the Board of Pardons and Paroles. (9)

graded penalties Depending on the nature of the crime, noncapital felonies are graded as first degree, second degree, third degree, and state jail; misdemeanors are graded as A, B, and C. (12)

grand jury Composed of 12 persons with the qualifications of trial jurors, a grand jury serves six months while it determines whether sufficient evidence exists to indict persons accused of committing crimes. (11)

grandfather clause Although not used in Texas, exempted people from educational, property, or tax requirements for voting if they were qualified to vote before 1867 or were descendents of such persons. (5)

grant-in-aid Money, goods, or services given by one government to another (e.g., federal grants-in-aid to states for financing public assistance programs). (13)

grassroots Local (as in grassroots government or grassroots politics). (3)

group leadership Individuals who guide the decisions of interest groups. Leaders of groups tend to have financial resources that permit them to contribute money and devote time to group affairs. (7)

hard money Campaign money donated directly to candidates or political parties and restricted in amount by federal law. (5)

hard news News that focuses on the facts, provides more depth, and commonly has implications for public policy. (6)

home-rule city A municipality with a locally drafted charter. (3)

homogenization of news Making news uniform regardless of differing locations and cultures. (6)

horserace journalism News that focuses on who is ahead in the race (poll results and public perceptions) rather than policy differences. (6)

impeachment Process in which the Texas House of Representatives, by a simple majority vote, initiates action (brings charges) leading to possible removal of certain judicial and executive officials (e.g., the governor) by the Senate. (8)

implied powers Powers inferred by the constitutional authority of the U.S. Congress "to make all laws which shall be necessary and proper for carrying into execution the foregoing [delegated] powers, and all other powers vested by this Constitution in the government of the United States, or in any department or officer thereof." (2)

independent candidate A candidate who runs in a general election without party endorsement or selection. (4, 5)

independent expenditures Expenditures that pay for political campaign communications that expressly advocate the nomination, election, or defeat of a clearly identified candidate but are not given to, or made at the request of, the candidate's campaign. (5)

independent school district (ISD) Created by the legislature, an independent school district raises tax revenue to support its public schools. Voters within the district elect a board that hires a superintendent, determines salary schedules, selects textbooks, and sets the district's property tax rate. (3)

individualistic culture This culture looks to government to maintain a stable society but with minimum intervention in the lives of the people. (1)

initiative A citizen-drafted measure proposed by a specific number or percentage of qualified voters that becomes law if approved by popular vote. In Texas, this process occurs only at the local level, not at the state level. (2)

initiative A citizen-drafted measure proposed by a specific number or percentage of qualified voters, which becomes law if approved by popular vote. In Texas, this process occurs only in home-rule cities. (3)

interest group An organization that seeks to influence government officials and their policies on behalf of members sharing common views and objectives (e.g., labor union or trade association). (7)

interest group technique An action such as lobbying, personal communication, giving favors and gifts, grassroots activities, electioneering, campaign financing by political action committees, and, in extreme instances, bribery and other unethical practices intended to influence government decisions. (7)

intergovernmental relations Relationships between and among different governments that are on the same or different levels. (3)

interim committee A House or Senate committee appointed by the Speaker or lieutenant governor to study an important policy issue between regular sessions.

Jim Crow laws Ethnically discriminatory laws that segregated African Americans and denied them access to public services for many decades after the Civil War. (1)

joint resolution A resolution that must pass by a majority vote in each house when used to ratify an amendment to the U.S. Constitution. As a proposal for an amendment to the Texas Constitution, a joint resolution requires a two-thirds majority vote in each house. (8)

judgment A judge's written opinion based on a verdict. (11)

jungle primary A nominating process in which voters indicate their preferences by using a single ballot on which are printed the names and respective party labels of all persons seeking nomination. A candidate who receives more than 50 percent of the vote is elected; otherwise, a runoff between the top two candidates must be held. (5)

junior college or community college district Establishes one or more two-year colleges that offer both academic and vocational programs. (3)

jurisdiction A court's authority to hear a particular case. (11)

justice of the peace A judge elected from a justice of the peace precinct who handles minor civil and criminal cases. (3, 11)

labor organization A union that supports public policies designed to increase wages, obtain adequate health insurance coverage, provide unemployment insurance, promote safe working conditions, and otherwise protect the interests of workers. (7)

Latino An ethnic classification of Mexican Americans and others of Latin American origin. When applied to females, the term is Latina. We will use this term throughout the book in addition to the term "Hispanic," which refers to people who trace their ancestry to Spanish-speaking countries. (1)

Legislative Budget Board (LBB) A 10-member body cochaired by the lieutenant governor and the Speaker of the House. This board and its staff prepare a biennial current services budget. In addition, they assist with the preparation of a general appropriation bill at the beginning of a regular legislative session. If requested, staff members prepare fiscal notes that assess the economic impact of a proposed bill or resolution. (13)

legislative caucus An organization of legislators who seek to maximize their influence over issues in which they have a special interest. (8)

legislative power A power of the governor exercised through messages delivered to the Texas legislature, vetoes of bills and concurrent resolutions, and calls for special sessions of the legislature. (9)

liberal A person who advocates government support in social and economic matters and who favors political reforms that extend democracy, achieve a more equitable distribution of wealth, and protect individual freedoms and rights. (4)

lieutenant governor Popularly elected constitutional official who serves as president of the Senate and is first in the line of succession if the office of governor becomes vacant before the end of a term. (9)

line-item veto Action by the governor to eliminate an individual budget item while permitting enactment of other parts of an appropriation bill. (9)

literacy tests Although not used in Texas as a prerequisite for voter registration, the test was designed and administered in ways intended to prevent African Americans and Latinos from voting. (5)

lobbying Communicating with legislators or other government officials on behalf of an interest group for the purpose of influencing decision makers. (7)

local government Counties, municipalities, school districts, and other special districts that provide a range of services, including rural roads, city streets, public education, and protection of persons and property. (2)

maquiladora "Partner plant" on the Mexican side of the border that uses cheap labor to assemble goods and then exports these goods back to the United States. (1)

martial law Temporary rule by military authorities when civil authorities are unable to handle a riot or other civil disorder. (9)

Medicaid Funded in large part by federal grants and in part by state appropriations, Medicaid is administered by the state. It provides medical care for persons whose incomes fall below the poverty line. (10)

Medicare Funded entirely by the federal government and administered by the U.S. Department of Health and Human Services, Medicare provides medical assistance to qualified applicants age 65 and older. (10)

merit system Hiring, promoting, and firing on the basis of objective criteria such as tests, degrees, experience, and performance. (10)

message power The governor's effectiveness in communicating with legislators via the State of the State address at the "commencement" of a legislative session and other messages delivered in person or in writing. (9)

metro government Consolidation of units of local government within an urban area under a single authority. (3)

metropolitanization The development of a residential pattern centered in a core area containing a large population nucleus together with adjacent communities economically and socially integrated with that core. (1)

middle class Social scientists identify the middle class as those people with white-collar occupations (such as professionals and small business workers). (3)

misdemeanor Classified as A, B, or C, a misdemeanor may be punished by fine and/or jail sentence. (11)

Missouri Plan A judicial selection process in which a commission recommends a panel of names to the governor, who appoints a judge for one year or so before voters determine whether the appointee will be retained for a full term. (11)

moralistic culture This culture influences people to view political participation as their duty and to expect that government will be used to advance the public good. (1)

moratorium The delay or suspension of an activity or law. A moratorium may be imposed when something is seen as needing improvement. (12)

motor-voter law Legislation requiring certain government offices (e.g., motor vehicle licensing agencies) to offer voter registration applications to clients. (5)

multimember district A district in which all voters participate in the election of two or more representatives to a policymaking body, such as a state House or state Senate. (8)

municipal (city) government A local government for an incorporated community established by law as a city. (3)

municipal court City-run court with jurisdiction primarily over Class C misdemeanors committed within a city's boundaries. (11)

national supremacy clause Article VI of the U.S. Constitution states, "This Constitution, and the laws of the United States which shall be made in pursuance thereof; and all treaties made, or which shall be made, under the authority of the United States, shall be the supreme law of the land." (2)

Native American A term commonly used for those whose ancestors were living in the Americas before the arrival of Europeans and Africans. Another commonly used term in the United States is "American Indian" or in Canada "First Nations." (1)

neoconservatism A political ideology that reflects fiscal conservatism but accepts a limited governmental role in solving social problems. (4)

neoliberal A political ideology that advocates less government regulation of business but supports more governmental involvement in social matters. (4)

net neutrality A legal principle that Internet service providers and governments should treat all data on the Internet equally, not discriminating or charging differentially and not blocking content they do not like. (6)

news website An Internet site that provides news. These sites are often affiliated with a newspaper or television station, but many are independent. (6)

niche journalism (narrowcasting) A news medium focusing on a narrow audience defined by concern about a particular topic or area. (6)

noneducation special districts Special districts, other than school districts or community college districts, such as fire prevention or municipal utility districts, that are units of local government and may cover part of a county, a whole county, or areas in two or more counties. (3)

nonpartisan election An election in which candidates are not identified on the ballot by party label. (3)

North American Free Trade Agreement (NAFTA) An agreement among Mexico, the United States, and Canada designed to expand trade by eliminating tariffs among the three nations. (1)

off-year or midterm election A general election held in the even-numbered year following a presidential election. (5)

open meetings Meetings of public entities that are required by law to be open to the public. (6)

open primary A primary in which voters are not required to declare party identification. (5)

open records Government documents and records that are required by law to be available to the public. (6)

ordinance A local law enacted by a city council or approved by popular vote in a referendum or initiative election. (3)

organizational pattern The structure of a special interest group. Some interest groups have a decentralized pattern of organization (e.g., the AFL-CIO, with many local unions). Others are centralized (e.g., the National Rifle Association, which is a national body with a group operating in Texas). (7)

original jurisdiction The power of a court to hear a case first. (11)

oversight A legislative function that requires reports from state agencies concerning their operations; the state auditor provides information on agencies' use of state funds. (8)

parliamentarian An expert on rules of order who sits at the left of the presiding officer in the House or Senate and provides advice on procedural questions. (8)

parole Supervised release from prison before completion of a sentence, on condition of good behavior. (9)

patrón system A type of boss rule that has dominated areas of South Texas and Mexico. (1)

patronage system Hiring friends and supporters of elected officials as government employees without regard to their abilities. (10)

payroll tax An employer-paid tax levied against a portion of the wages and salaries of workers to provide funds for payment of unemployment insurance benefits in the event employees lose their jobs. (13)

permanent party organization In Texas, the precinct chairs, county and district executive committees, and the state executive committee form the permanent organization of a political party. (4)

petit jury A trial jury of 6 or 12 members. (11)

plaintiff The injured party who initiates a civil suit or the state in a criminal proceeding. (11)

platform A document that sets forth a political party's position on issues such as income tax, school vouchers, or public utility regulation. (4)

plea bargain A deal between the prosecutor and the defendant in a criminal case in which the defendant agrees to plead guilty to a specific charge and in return will get certain concessions from the prosecutor. (12)

plural executive The governor, elected department heads, and the secretary of state, as provided by the Texas Constitution and statutes. (9)

political action committee (PAC) An organizational device used by corporations, labor unions, and other organizations to raise money for campaign contributions. (5)

political culture Attitudes, habits, and general behavior patterns that develop over time and affect the political life of a state or region. (1)

political party An organization influenced by political ideology whose primary interest is to gain control of government by winning elections. (4)

politics The process of policymaking that involves conflict and cooperation between political parties and other groups that seek to elect government officials or to influence those officials when they make public policy, such as enacting and interpreting laws. (1)

poll tax A tax levied in Texas from 1902 until a similar Virginia tax was declared unconstitutional in 1962; failure to pay the annual tax (usually $1.75) made a citizen ineligible to vote in party primaries or in special and general elections. (5)

pork-barrel politics A legislator's tactic to obtain funding for a pet project, usually designed to be of special benefit for the legislator's district. (9)

postadjournment veto Rejection by the governor of a pending bill or concurrent resolution during the 20 days after a legislative session ends. (9)

power group An effective interest group strongly linked with legislators and bureaucrats for the purpose of influencing decision making and having a continuing presence in Austin as a "repeat player" from session to session. (7)

precinct chair The party official responsible for the interests and activities of a political party in a voting district; typical duties include encouraging voter registration, distributing campaign literature, operating phone banks, and getting out the vote on Election Day. (4)

precinct convention If a political party decides to conduct a precinct convention, this serves as the lowest level of temporary political party organization. Delegates convene in even-numbered years on a date and at a time and place prescribed by the party's state executive committee to adopt resolutions and to select delegates to a county (or district) convention. (4)

president of the Senate Title of the lieutenant governor in his or her role as presiding officer for the Texas Senate. (8)

presidential preference primary A primary in which the voters indicate their preference for a person seeking nomination as the party's presidential candidate. (4)

primary A preliminary election conducted within the party to select candidates who will run for public office in a subsequent general election. (5)

priming The news media indicating how important an issue is or which part of a situation is most important. (6)

prior restraint Suppression of material before it is published, commonly called censorship. (6)

Privatization Transfer of government services or assets to the private sector. Commonly, assets are sold and services contracted out. (10)

privileges and immunities Article IV of the U.S. Constitution guarantees that "citizens of each state shall be entitled to the privileges and immunities of citizens of the several states." According to the U.S. Supreme Court, this provision means that citizens are guaranteed protection by government, enjoyment of life and liberty, the right to acquire and possess property, the right to leave and enter any state, and the right to use state courts. (2)

probate Proceedings that involve the estates of decedents. Additionally, courts with probate jurisdiction (county courts, county courts-at-law, and probate courts) handle guardianship and mental competency matters. (11)

procedural committee These House committees (such as the Calendars Committee and House Administration Committee) consider bills and resolutions relating primarily to procedural legislative matters. (8)

proclamation A governor's official public announcement (such as calling a special election or declaring a disaster area). (9)

professional group An organization of physicians, lawyers, accountants, or other professional people that lobbies for policies beneficial to members. (7)

professionalism Reporting that is objective, neutral, and accurate. (6)

progressive Favoring and working for progress in conditions facing the majority of society or in government. (1)

progressive tax A tax in which the effective tax rate increases as the tax base (such as individual income or corporate profits) increases. (13)

property tax A tax that property owners pay according to the value of real estate and other tangible property. At the local level, property owners pay this tax to the city, the county, the school district, and often other special districts. (3)

Protestant fundamentalism A socially and politically conservative form of Protestant Christianity that arose in the late 1800s as a reaction against modernism. Protestant fundamentalists insist that the Christian Bible is literally true in both religious and historical terms. (1)

public administration The implementation of public policy by government employees. (10)

public interest group An organization claiming to represent a broad public interest (environmental, consumer, political participation, and public morality) rather than a narrow private interest. (7)

public officer and employee group An organization of city managers, county judges, or other public employees or officials that lobbies for public policies that protect group interests. (7)

public policy Government action designed to meet a public need or goal as determined by a legislative body or other authorized officials. More broadly, what government does or does not do to or for its citizens. (1, 10)

Public Utility Commission of Texas (PUC) A three-member appointed body with regulatory power over electric and telephone companies. (10)

racial and ethnic groups Organizations that seek to influence government decisions that affect a particular racial or ethnic group, such as the National Association for the Advancement of Colored People (NAACP) and the League of United Latin American Citizens (LULAC), which seek to influence government decisions affecting African Americans and Latinos, respectively. (7)

racial covenants Agreements by a group of property owners, subdivision developers, or real estate operators in a given neighborhood, binding them not to sell, lease, or rent property to specified groups because of race, creed, or color for a definite period unless all agree to the transaction. (1)

Railroad Commission of Texas (RRC) A popularly elected three-member commission primarily engaged in regulating natural gas and petroleum production. (10)

Rainy Day Fund A fund used like a savings account for stabilizing state finance and helping the state meet economic emergencies when revenue is insufficient to cover state-supported programs. (13)

realignment Occurs when members of one party shift their affiliation to another party. (4)

recall A process for removing elected officials through a popular vote. In Texas, this power is available only for home-rule cities. (3)

recess appointment An appointment made by the governor when the Texas legislature is not in session. (9)

recidivism Criminal behavior that results in reincarceration after a person has been released from confinement for a prior offense. (12)

redistricting Redrawing of boundaries after the federal decennial census to create districts with approximately equal population (e.g., legislative, congressional, and State Board of Education districts in Texas). Local governments must also redistrict for some positions. (3, 8)

redlining A discriminatory rating system used by federal agencies to evaluate the risks associated with loans made to borrowers in specific urban neighborhoods. (1)

referendum A process by which issues are referred to the voters to accept or reject. Voters may also petition for a vote to repeal an existing ordinance. In Texas, this process occurs at the local level in home-rule cities. At the state level, bonds secured by taxes and state constitutional amendments must be approved by the voters. (3)

regressive tax A tax in which the effective tax rate falls as the tax base (such as individual income or corporate profits) increases. (13)

regular session A session of the Texas legislature that is constitutionally mandated and begins on the second Tuesday in January of odd-numbered years and lasts for a maximum of 140 days. (8)

religion-based group An interest group, such as the Texas Freedom Network, that lobbies for policies to promote its religious interests. (7)

removal power Authority to remove an official from office. In Texas, the governor's removal power is limited to staff members, some agency heads, and his or her appointees with the consent of the Senate. (9)

reprieve An act of executive clemency that temporarily suspends execution of a sentence. (9)

reserved powers Reserved powers are derived from the Tenth Amendment of the U.S. Constitution. Although not spelled out in the U.S. Constitution, these reserved powers to the states include police power, taxing power, proprietary power, and power of eminent domain. (2)

revenue bond Amount borrowed by the state that is repaid from a specific revenue source. (13)

right of association The U.S. Supreme Court has ruled that this right is part of the right of assembly guaranteed by the First Amendment to the U.S. Constitution and that it protects the right of people to organize into groups for political purposes. (7)

right to work laws Laws that limit the power of workers to bargain collectively and form and operate labor unions, increasing the power of employers relative to their employees. (1)

"Robin Hood" plan A plan for equalizing financial support for school districts by transferring tax money from rich districts to poor districts. (13)

runoff primary Held after the first primary to allow party members to choose a candidate from the first primary's top two vote-getters. (5)

secretary of state The state's chief elections officer, with other administrative duties, who is appointed by the governor for a term concurrent with that of the governor. (9)

select committee This committee, created independently by the House Speaker or lieutenant governor, may consider legislation that crosses committee jurisdictional lines or may conduct special studies. (8)

selective sales tax A tax charged on specific products and services. (13)

senatorial courtesy Before making an appointment, the governor is expected to obtain approval from the state senator in whose district the prospective appointee resides; failure to obtain such approval will probably cause the Senate to "bust" the appointee. (8)

separation of powers The assignment of lawmaking, law-enforcing, and law-interpreting functions to separate branches of government. (2)

service sector Businesses that provide services, such as finance, health care, food service, data processing, or consulting. (13)

severance tax An excise tax levied on a natural resource (such as oil or natural gas) when it is severed (removed) from the earth. (13)

shield law A law protecting journalists from having to reveal confidential sources to police or in court. (6)

simple resolution A resolution that requires action by one legislative chamber only and is not acted on by the governor. (8)

sin tax A selective sales tax on items such as cigarettes, other forms of tobacco, alcoholic beverages, and admission to sex-oriented businesses. (13)

single-member district An area that elects only one representative to a policymaking body, such as a state House, state Senate, or U.S. Congress. (8)

single-member district election Voters in an area (commonly called a district, ward, or precinct) elect one representative to serve on a policymaking body (e.g., city council, county commissioners court, state House and Senate). (3)

social interest group Groups concerned primarily with social issues, including organizations devoted to civil rights, racial and ethnic matters, religion, and public interest protection. (7)

social media Websites and computer applications that allow users to engage in social networking and create online communities. Social media provide platforms for sharing information and ideas through discussion forums, videos, photos, documents, audio clips, and the like. (1, 6)

soft money Unregulated political donations made to national political parties or independent expenditures on behalf of a candidate. (5)

soft news News that is more entertaining, sensationalized, covers only the surface, and has little connection to public policy. (6)

sound bite A brief statement of a candidate's theme communicated by radio or television in a few seconds. (5)

Speaker of the House The state representative elected by House members to serve as the presiding officer for that chamber. (8)

special district A unit of local government that performs a particular service, such as providing schools, hospitals, or housing, for a particular geographic area. (3)

special election An election called by the governor to fill a vacancy (e.g., U.S. congressional or state legislative office) or to vote on a proposed state constitutional amendment or local bond issue. (5)

special issues Questions a judge gives a trial jury to answer to establish facts in a civil case. (11)

special session A legislative session called by the governor and limited to no more than 30 days. (8)

specialty courts Courts designed to deal with particular types of problems, such as drug-related offenses, or specific populations, such as veterans or foster children. (11)

standing committee A Senate committee appointed by the lieutenant governor for the purpose of considering proposed bills and resolutions before possible floor debate and voting by senators. (8)

State Board of Education (SBOE) A popularly elected 15-member body with limited authority over Texas's K–12 education system. (10)

state convention Convenes every even-numbered year to make rules for a political party, adopt a party platform and resolutions, and select members of the state executive committee; in a presidential election year, it elects delegates to the national convention, names members to serve on the national committee, and elects potential electors to vote if the party's presidential candidate receives a plurality of the popular vote in the general election. (4)

state executive committee Composed of a chair, vice chair, and two members from each senatorial district, this body is part of a party's permanent organization. (4)

State of Texas Assessment of Academic Readiness (STAAR) A state program of end-of-course and other examinations begun in 2012. (10)

statutory county court Court created by the legislature at the request of a county; may have civil or criminal jurisdiction or both, depending on the legislation creating it. (3)

straight-ticket voting Voting for all the candidates of one party. (4)

stratarchy A political system in which power is diffused among and within levels of party organization. (4)

strong mayor-council form A type of municipal government with a separately elected legislative body (council) and an executive head (mayor) elected in a citywide election with veto, appointment, and removal powers. (3)

substantive committee Appointed by the House Speaker, this committee considers bills and resolutions related to the subject identified by its name (such as the House Agriculture Committee) and may recommend passage of proposed legislation to the appropriate calendars committee. (8)

suffrage The right to vote. (2)

sunset review process During a cycle of 12 years, each state agency is studied at least once to see if it is needed and efficient, and then the legislature decides whether to abolish, merge, reorganize, or retain that agency. (10)

super PAC Independent expenditure–only committees that may raise unlimited sums of money from corporations, unions, nonprofit organizations, and individuals. (5)

superdelegate An unpledged party official or elected official who serves as a delegate to a party's national convention. (4)

Supplemental Nutritional Assistance Program (SNAP) Joint federal-state program administered by the state to provide food to low-income people. (10)

tax A mandatory assessment exacted by a government for a public purpose. (13)

tax reinvestment zone (TRZ) An area in which municipal tax incentives are offered to encourage businesses to locate in and contribute to the development of a blighted urban area. Commercial and residential property taxes may be frozen. (3)

Temporary Assistance for Needy Families (TANF) Provides financial assistance to the poor in an attempt to help them move from welfare to the workforce. (10)

temporary party organization Primaries and conventions that function briefly to nominate candidates, pass resolutions, adopt a party platform, and select delegates to party conventions at higher levels. (4)

Tenth Amendment The Tenth Amendment to the U.S. Constitution declares that "the powers not delegated by the Constitution, nor prohibited by it to the States, are reserved to the States, respectively, or to the people." (2)

term limit A restriction on the number of terms officials can serve in a public office. (3)

Texas Bill of Rights Article I of the Texas Constitution, which guarantees protections for people and their property against arbitrary actions by state and local governments. Protected rights include freedom of speech, press, religion, assembly, and petition. (2)

Texas Commission on Environmental Quality (TCEQ) The state agency that coordinates Texas's environmental protection efforts. (10)

Texas Constitution of 1876 The lengthy, much-amended state constitution, a product of the post-Reconstruction era that remains in effect today. (2)

Texas Department of Transportation (TxDOT) Headed by a five-member appointed commission, the department maintains almost 80,000 miles of roads and highways and promotes highway safety. (10)

Texas Education Agency (TEA) Administers the state's public school system of more than 1,200 school districts and charter schools. (10)

Texas Election Code The body of state law concerning parties, primaries, and elections. (5)

Texas Equal Legal Rights Amendment (ELRA) Added to Article I, Section 3, of the Texas Constitution, it guarantees that "equality under the law shall not be denied or abridged because of sex, race, color, creed, or national origin." (2)

Texas Essential Knowledge and Skills (TEKS) A core curriculum (a set of courses and knowledge) setting out what students should learn. (10)

Texas Ethics Commission A state agency that enforces state standards for lobbyists and public officials, including registration of lobbyists and reporting of political campaign contributions. (5, 7)

Texas Grange A farmers' organization, also known as the Patrons of Husbandry, committed to low levels of government spending and limited governmental powers; a major influence on the Constitution of 1876. (2)

TEXAS Grants Program "Toward Excellence, Access, and Success" is a college financial assistance program that provides funding for qualifying students. (13)

Texas Higher Education Coordinating Board (THECB) An agency that provides some coordination for the state's public community colleges and universities. (10)

Texas Parks and Wildlife Department Texas agency that runs state parks and regulates hunting, fishing, and boating. (10)

Texas Penal Code The body of Texas law covering crimes, penalties, and correctional measures for crime in Texas. (12)

Texas Workforce Commission (TWC) A state agency headed by three salaried commissioners who oversee job training and unemployment compensation programs. (10)

third party A party other than the Democratic Party or the Republican Party. Sometimes called a "minor party" because of limited membership and voter support. (4)

top 10 percent rule Texas law gives automatic admission into any Texas public college or university to those graduating in the top 10 percent of their Texas high school class, with limitations for the University of Texas at Austin. (10)

tort An injury to a person or an individual's property resulting from the wrongful act of another. (11)

traditionalistic culture A product of the Old South, this culture uses government as a means of preserving the status quo and its leadership. (1)

two-thirds rule A procedural device to control bringing bills to the Senate floor for debate. (8)

undocumented immigrant A person who enters the United States in violation of federal immigration law and thus lacks proper documentation and identification. (1)

unicameral A one-house legislature, such as the Nebraska legislature. (8)

universal suffrage Voting is open for virtually all persons 18 years of age or older. (5)

urban renewal The relocation of businesses and people, the demolition of structures, and the use of eminent domain to take private property for government development projects. (1)

venire A panel of prospective jurors drawn by random selection. These prospective jurors are called veniremen. (11)

verdict A jury's decision about a court case. (11)

veto power Authority of the governor to reject a bill or concurrent resolution passed by the legislature. (9)

voir dire Courtroom procedure in which attorneys question prospective jurors to identify any who cannot be fair and impartial. (11)

voter registration A qualified voter must register with the county voting registrar, who compiles lists of qualified voters residing in each voting precinct. (5)

voter turnout The percentage of the voting-age population casting ballots in an election. (5)

voting precinct The basic geographic area for conducting primaries and elections; Texas is divided into more than 8,500 voting precincts. (5)

weak mayor-council form A type of municipal government with a separately elected mayor and council, but the mayor shares appointive and removal powers with the council, which can override the mayor's veto. (3)

white primary A nominating system designed to prevent African Americans and some Latinos from participating in Democratic primaries from 1923 to 1944. (5)

women's organization A women's group, such as the League of Women Voters, that engages in lobbying and educational activities to promote greater political participation by women and others. (7)

Workers' Compensation A system of insurance to compensate workers injured by their work. (10)

working class Social scientists identify the working class as those people with blue-collar (manual) occupations. (3)

yellow journalism Journalism that is based on sensationalism and exaggeration. (6)

Endnotes

Chapter 1

1. For a critical view of Texas's influence nationwide, see Gail Collins, *As Texas Goes . . . How the Lone Star State Hijacked the American Agenda* (New York: Liveright, 2012).

2. Daniel Elazar, *American Federalism: A View from the States*, 3d ed. (New York: Harper & Row, 1984), 84–126, 134. For a different view of political culture, see Dante Chinni and James Gimpel, *Our Patchwork Nation: The Surprising Truth about the "Real" America* (New York: Penguin Group, 2010) and its website at http://www.patchworknation.org/. This view identifies 12 political cultures nationally, of which 9 are present in Texas.

3. David Cullen and Kyle G. Wilkison, *The Texas Left: The Radical Roots of Lone Star Liberalism* (College Station: Texas A&M University Press, 2010).

4. See Mike Kingston, "A Brief Sketch of Texas History," edited and expanded by Robert Plocheck, *Texas Almanac 2014–2015* (Denton, TX: Texas State Historical Association, 2014), 52–59. For a description of events that led up to Texas's war for independence from Mexico, see James Donovan, *The Blood of Heroes: The 13-day Struggle for the Alamo—and the Sacrifice That Forged a Nation* (New York: Little Brown, 2012).

5. Kingston, "A Brief Sketch of Texas History," 61; and Rupert N. Richardson, Adrian Anderson, Cary D. Wintz, and Ernest Wallace, *Texas: The Lone Star State*, 10th ed. (Upper Saddle River, NJ: Prentice Hall, 2010), 151–154.

6. For a case study of the patrón system, see J. Gilberto Quezada, *Border Boss: Manuel B. Bravo and Zapata County* (College Station: Texas A&M University Press, 1999).

7. Richard Sandomir, "A Texas-Size Stadium." *New York Times*, July 16, 2009, http://www.nytimes.com/2009/07/17/sports/football/17cowboys.html?_r=0.

8. Katherine Peralta, "Everything's Bigger, and Still Getting Bigger, in Texas," *U.S. News & World Report*, May 22, 2014, http://www.usnews.com/news/articles/2014/05/22/texas-cities-among-nations-fastest-growing-us-census-bureau-says.

9. Mitchell Schnurman, "Oil Boom 2.0 Pumps Up West Texas Economy," *Fort Worth Star Telegram*, May 23, 2012.

10. Marc Seitles, "The Perpetuation of Residential Racial Segregation in America: Historical Discrimination, Modern Forms of Exclusion, and Inclusionary Remedies," *Journal of Land Use & Environmental Law* 14 (Fall 1998), http://www.law.fsu.edu/journals/landuse/Vol141/seit.htm.

11. U.S. Department of Commerce, Census Bureau, "American FactFinder: Results," February 10, 2014, http://factfinder2.census.gov/faces/tableservices/jsf/pages/productview.xhtml?pid=ACS_12_1YR_DP02&prodType=table.

12. Michael O. Emerson, Jenifer Bratter, Junia Howell, P. Wilner Jeanty, and Mike Cline, *Houston Region Grows More Racially/Ethnically Diverse, With Small Declines in Segregation: A Joint Report Analyzing Census Data from 1990,*

2000, and 2010 (March 2012), http://kinder.rice.edu/uploadedFiles/Urban_Research_Center/Media/Houston%20Region%20Grows%20More%20Ethnically%20Diverse%202-13.pdf.

13. Cal Jillson, *Lone Star Tarnished: A Critical Look at Texas Politics and Public Policy* (New York: Routledge, 2012), 154.

14. Frederick Law Olmsted, *A Journey through Texas* (New York: Dix, Edwards, 1857; reprint, Burt Franklin, 1969), 296. For more information on Texas Indian tribes, see Richard L. Schott, "Contemporary Indian Reservations in Texas: Tribal Paths to the Present," *Public Affairs Comment* (Austin: Lyndon B. Johnson School of Public Affairs, University of Texas at Austin) 39 (1993): 1–9; and David LaVere, *The Texas Indians* (College Station: Texas A&M University Press, 2004).

15. Jillson, *Lone Star Tarnished*, 60.

16. Terry G. Jordan, "The Imprint of Upper and Lower South on Mid-Nineteenth Century Texas," *Annals of the American Association of Geographers* 57 (December 1967): 667–690.

17. For links to important documents from Texas history, including the Ordinances of Secession, see http://www.lsjunction.com/docs/secesson.htm.

18. Kent Biffle, "If at First You Don't Secede," *Dallas Morning News*, November 3, 2002.

19. John R. Ross, "Lynching," in The *Handbook of Texas Onlline* http://www.tshaonline.org/handbook/online/articles/jgl01.

20. Jillson, *Lone Star Tarnished*, 61.

21. Arnoldo De León, "Mexican Americans," in *The Handbook of Texas Online*, https://www.tshaonline.org/handbook/online/articles/pqmue.

22. "10 Years Later, Dragging Death Changes Town," *NBC News Online*, June 6, 2008, http://www.nbcnews.com/id/25008925/ns/us_news-life/.

23. Keith Hampton, Lauren Sessions Goulet, Lee Rainie, and Kristen Purcell, "Social Networking Sites and Our Lives," Pew Research Centers Internet American Life Project, June 16, 2011, http://www.pewinternet.org/2011/06/16/social-networking-sites-and-our-lives/.

24. *Racial Attitudes of Young Americans—Hamilton College*, Hamilton College, August 1999, http://www.hamilton.edu/news/polls/racial-attitudes-of-young-americans.

25. Texas Department of State Health Services, "Texas Population, 2013," *Population Data (Projections) for Texas Counties, 2013*, http://www.dshs.state.tx.us/chs/popdat/ST2013.shtm.

26. Ibid.

27. Paul Burka, "The Party Never Ends," *Texas Monthly*, June 2012, 16, 18, 20.

28. Texas Department of State Health Services, "Texas Population, 2013," https://www.dshs.state.tx.us/Layouts/ContentPage.aspx?PageID=35615&id=8589943721&terms=texas+population+2013.

29. The Henry J. Kaiser Family Foundation, "Poverty Rate by Race/Ethnicity," http://kff.org/other/state-indicator/poverty-rate-by-raceethnicity.

30. Texas Legislative Study Group, *Texas on the Brink: A Report from the Texas Legislative Study Group on the State of Our State* (March 2013), http://texaslsg.org/texasonthebrink.

31. To see more about the Democrats' efforts to turn Texas Blue, see http://battlegroundtexas.com/content/home.

32. Richard Dunham, "Exclusive analysis: If trends hold, Texas will be a toss-up state by 2024," *Houston Chronicle*, November 12, 2012, http://blog.chron.com/txpotomac/2012/11/exclusive-analysis-if-trends-hold-texas-will-be-a-toss-up-state-by-2024/#4619101=0.

33. For full discussions of these changes and their implications, see Steve H. Murdock, *Changing Texas: Implications of Addressing or Ignoring the Texas*

Challenge (College Station: Texas A&M University Press, 2014); and Jillson, *Lone Star Tarnished.*

34. See Don Graham, *Kings of Texas: The 150-Year Saga of an American Empire* (Hoboken, NJ: John Wiley & Sons, 2003); Jane Clements Monday and Betty Bailey Colley, *Voices from the Wild Horse Desert: The Vaquero Families of the King and Kenedy Ranches* (Austin: University of Texas Press, 1997); Armando C. Alonzo, *Tejano Legacy: Rancheros and Settlers in South Texas, 1734–1900* (Albuquerque: University of New Mexico Press, 1998); Andrés Tijerina, *Tejano Empire: Life on the South Texas Ranchos* (College Station: Texas A&M University Press, 1998); and Daniel D. Arreola, *Tejano South Texas: A Mexican American Cultural Province* (Austin: University of Texas Press, 2002).

35. Blair Fannin, "U.S. Cowherd Continued to Shrink in 2012," *Texas AgriLife Today,* February 1, 2013, http://today.agrilife.org/2013/02/01/u-s-cowherd-continued-to-shrink-in-2012/.

36. See Kate Galbraith, "Catastrophic Drought in Texas Causes Global Economic Ripples," *New York Times,* October 30, 2011; and Elizabeth Campbell, "'White Gold' Withers in Texas Cotton Fields," *Bloomberg Business Week,* September 15, 2011; Mindy Riffle, "Cotton Crop: Future of Cotton Is Questionable," *Country World* Online Edition, May 29, 2012; and Blair Fannin, "Updated 2011 Texas Agricultural Drought Losses Total $7.62 Billion," *TexasAgriLife Today,* March 21, 2012, http://today.agrilife.org/2012/03/21/updated-2011-texas-agricultural-drought-losses-total-7-62-billion/.

37. Volleen Scherer, "Texas Cotton Crop Suffers Huge Losses," *AG Professional,* August 19, 2013, http://www.agprofessional.com/news/Texas-cotton-crop-suffers-huge-losses-220254351.html.

38. James Cozine, *Saving the Big Thicket: From Exploration to Preservation, 1685–2003* (Denton: University of North Texas Press, 2004).

39. Robert S. Maxwell, "Lumber Industry," *Handbook of Texas Online,* https://www.tshaonline.org/handbook/online/articles/drl02.

40. Ronald H. Hufford, "Tree Farming," *Handbook of Texas Online,* http://www.tshaonline.org/handbook/online/articles/drt04.

41. Texas Comptroller of Public Accounts, "Texas Timber Grows Up," *Fiscal Notes,* October 1999, http://www.window.state.tx.us/comptrol/fnotes/fn9910/fn.html.

42. Nathan Koppel and Daniel Gilbert, "Even after Rain, Texas Drought Persists," *Wall Street Journal,* February 6, 2012.

43. Ricardo Gandera, "Bastrop Park Won't Be Back to Full Glory for Decades, Official Says," *Austin American-Statesman,* October 13, 2011.

44. For an account of the history of the early years of the oil industry in Texas, see Roger M. Olien and Diana Davids Olien, *Oil in Texas: The Gusher Age, 1895–1945* (Austin: University of Texas Press, 2002).

45. "The Exponential Rise in 'Saudi Texas's' Oil Output Continues—Production Has Doubled in Only 27 Months!" *AEIdeas,* American Enterprise Institute, July 31, 2013, http://www.aei-ideas.org/2013/07/the-exponential-rise-in-saudi-texas-oil-output-continues-the-states-oil-production-has-doubled-in-only-27-months/.

46. David Blackmon, "Texas Oil and Gas Numbers Fly Off the Charts," *Forbes,* August 7, 2013, http://www.forbes.com/sites/davidblackmon/2013/08/07/texas-oil-and-gas-numbers-fly-off-the-charts/. See also James Osborne, "Oil Boom Sends Gusher of Cash to Texas Universities," *Dallas Morning News,* May 31, 2014

47. For a broad review of the many studies linking air pollution from the burning of fossil fuels to respiratory and cardiovascular disease, premature birth, infant and adult mortality and more, see Bert Brunekreef and Stephen Holgate, "Air Pollution and Health," *The Lancet* 360 (2002): 1233–1242. For the American Academy of Pediatrics official statement about the impact on

79. Kate Galbraith, "Texas Study Finds Increase in Water Used for Fracking," *Texas Tribune*, January 15, 2013, http://www.texastribune.org/2013/01/15/texas-study-traces-fracking-and-water-use/.

80. Ramit Plushnick-Masti, "It Could Take Years for State's Aquifers to Fill," *San Antonio Express-News*, December 1, 2011.

81. Texas Water Development Board, *Water for Texas: 2012 State Water Plan.*

82. For more information about the effect of this amendment, see Texas Water Resources Institute, "Propositions Up for Vote in November Could Affect Texas' Water Future," http://twri.tamu.edu/publications/new-waves/2011/october/propositions-up-for-vote-in-november.

83. Saskia De Melker, "Two Texas Towns Run Out of Water," PBS, March 20, 2012, http://www.pbs.org/newshour/updates/science-jan-june12-texaswater_03-20/.

84. Texas Comptroller of Public Accounts, "Public Water Supply Conditions," *The Texas Economy: Natural Resources*, October 30, 2013, http://www.thetexaseconomy.org/natural-resources/articles/article.php?name=mapWaterSupply.

85. *Texas on the Brink*, http://texaslsg.org/texasonthebrink.

86. Neena Satija, "High Court to Hear Texas' Challenge to Climate Change Rules," *Texas Tribune*, October 15, 2013, http://www.texastribune.org/2013/10/15/high-court-hear-texas-challenge-climate-change-reg/; and Coral Davenport, "Justices Back Rule Limiting Coal Pollution," *New York Times*, April 29, 2014.

87. For information on all aspects of Texas's environmental problems, see Mary Sanger and Cyrus Reed, comps., *Texas Environmental Almanac*, 2d ed. (Austin: University of Texas Press, 2000); and Texas Center for Policy Studies, http://www.texascenter.org/.

88. Texas Legislative Council, *Texas on the Brink.*

89. Kate Alexander, "Texas Will Not Compete for Federal Education Grant," *Austin American-Statesman*, January 13, 2010.

90. Morgan Smith, "Report Examines How Budget Cuts Affected Texas Schools," *Texas Tribune*, September 27, 2012, http://www.texastribune.org/2012/09/27/report-examine-budget-cuts-affected-texas-schools/. See also Bureau of Labor Statistics website for employment impact.

91. Morgan Smith, "School Finance Trial Reopens, With a Political Backdrop," *Texas Tribune*, January 21, 2014, http://www.texastribune.org/2014/01/21/school-finance-trial-reopens-political-backdrop/.

92. Corrie MacLaggan, "Report: Child Poverty Increases in Texas," *Texas Tribune*, December 3, 2013. For a breakdown of child poverty in Texas, see http://datacenter.kidscount.org/data#TX/2/0.

93. Alemayeshu Bishaw, "Poverty: 2010 and 2011," *American Community Survey Briefs*, U.S. Census Bureau, http://www.census.gov/prod/2012pubs/acsbr11-01.pdf.

94. Corrie MacLaggan, "Texas Rejects Key Provisions of Obama's Health Law," Reuters, Issues & Controversies, Facts On File News Services, July 9, 2012.

95. Vivian Ho and Elena Marks, "Early Effects of the Affordable Care Act on Health Insurance Coverage in Texas for 2014," Rice University's Baker Institute for Public Policy, April 16, 2014, http://bakerinstitute.org/research/early-effects-affordable-care-act-health-insurance-coverage-texas-2014/.

Chapter 2

1. David B. Walker, *The Rebirth of Federalism: Slouching Toward Washington*, 2d ed. (New York: Chatham House, 2000), 260.

2. For a discussion of the history and meaning of this clause, see Gary Lawson, Geoffrey P. Miller, Robert G. Natelson, and Guy I. Seidman, *The Origins of the Necessary and Proper Clause* (New York: Cambridge University Press, 2013).

3. *Garcia v. San Antonio Metropolitan Transit Authority*, 469 U.S. 528 (1985).
4. *U.S. Term Limits v. Thornton*, 514 U.S. 115 (1995).
5. Paul Burka, "The M Word," *Texas Monthly*, January 2006, 14–16.
6. *U.S. v. Windsor*, 570 U.S. 12 (2013).
7. *Kimel v. Florida Board of Regents*, 528 U.S. 62 (2000); *Alden v. Maine*, 527 U.S. 706 (1999); and *Seminole Tribe v. Florida*, 517 U.S. 44 (1996).
8. *Frew v. Hawkins*, 540 U.S. 431 (2004). See also Carlos Guerra, "High Court Orders Texas to Honor Its Word and Pay Up," *San Antonio Express-News*, January 15, 2004.
9. *Kelo v. New London*, 545 U.S. 469 (2005).
10. *United States v. Lopez*, 514 U.S. 549 (1995).
11. *Gonzales v. Raich*, 545 U.S. 1 (2005).
12. Becca Aaronson, Chris Chang, Ben Hasson, and Todd Wiseman, "Interactive: Texas vs. the Federal Government," *Texas Tribune*, July 17, 2013, at http://www.texastribune.org/library/about/texas-versus-federal-government-law-suits-interactive/#dodd_frank-multi_state-challenge.
13. *National Federation of Independent Business v. Sebelius*, 567 U.S.___ (2012).
14. Sanford F. Schram, "Welfare Reform: A Race to the Bottom?" *Publish: The Journal of Federalism* 28 (Summer 1998): 1–8. (Special issue: "Welfare Reform in the United States: A Race to the Bottom?" edited by Sanford F. Schram and Samuel H. Beer.)
15. For a concise study examining the influence of this important law, see Frederick M. Hess and Michael J. Petrilli, *No Child Left Behind* (New York: Peter Lang, 2007). For more information regarding the law, see the National Education Association at http://www.nea.org/esea/more.html. See also Toni Locy, "Judge Dismisses Suit Against No Child Left Behind Law," *Houston Chronicle*, November 24, 2005.
16. Manny Fernandez and Emily Ramshaw, "As States-Rights Stalwart, Perry Draws Doubts," *San Antonio Express-News*, August 29, 2011. See also, Rick Perry, *Fed Up! Our Fight to Save America from Washington* (New York: Little, Brown & Company, 2010), 187–188.
17. For a more detailed account of early Texas constitutions, see John Cornyn, "The Roots of the Texas Constitution: Settlement to Statehood," *Texas Tech Law Review* 26, 4 (1995): 1089–1218. The author served as a member of the Texas Supreme Court and as the state's attorney general before being elected to the U.S. Senate in 2002.
18. Leobardo F. Estrada, F. Chris Garcia, Reynaldo Flores Macias, and Lionel Maldonado, "Chicanos in the United States: A History of Exploitation and Resistance," in *Latinos and the Political System*, ed. F. Chris Garcia (Notre Dame, IN: University of Notre Dame Press, 1988), 28–64. See also, Roberto Juarez, "The American Tradition of Language Rights: The Forgotten Right to Government in a 'Known Tongue'," *Law & Inequality: A Journal of Theory and Practice* 13, 2 (1995): 495–518.
19. Charles William Ramsdell, *Reconstruction in Texas* (New York: Columbia University Press, 1910); and T. R. Fehrenbach, *Lone Star: A History of Texas and the Texans* (New York: Macmillan, 1968), especially chapter 22, "The Carpetbaggers."
20. Patrick G. Williams, *Beyond Redemption: Texas Democrats After Reconstruction* (Austin: University of Texas Press, 2007); Carl H. Moneyhon, *Edmund J. Davis of Texas: Civil War General, Republican Leader, Reconstruction Governor* (Fort Worth: TCU Press, 2010); and Barry A. Crouch, *The Dance of Freedom: Texas African Americans During Reconstruction*, ed. Larry Madaras (Austin: University of Texas Press, 2007).

21. An alternative view on writing Texas's seventh constitution is presented in Patrick G. Williams, "Of Rutabagas and Redeemers: Rethinking the Texas Constitution of 1876," *Southwestern Historical Quarterly* 106, 2 (2002): 230–253.

22. Roy Walthall, "Celebrate Texas's Anniversary with a Reorganized Constitution," *Waco Tribune-Herald*, March 5, 2011.

23. Jane Elliott, "Gay Marriage Ban Put in Texas Constitution," *Houston Chronicle*, November 9, 2005. See also Summary Report of the 2005 Constitutional Election Results at http://www.sos.texas.gov/elections/forms/enrrpts/2005con.pdf.

24. Ralph Haurwitz, "From College to Beach, All Amendments Pass," *Austin American-Statesman*, November 4, 2009; Holly Hacker, "Prop. 4 Would Let Colleges Tap Fund," *Dallas Morning News*, October 4, 2009; and "Constitutional Amendments Proposed for November 2009 Ballot," Focus Report No. 81-8 (Austin: House Research Organization, Texas House of Representatives, August 20, 2009) at http://www.hro.house.state.tx.us/pdf/focus/amend81.pdf.

25. See "Constitutional Amendments Proposed for November 2011 Ballot," Focus Report No. 82-6 (Austin: House Research Organization, Texas House of Representatives, July 20, 2011). See also, Ralph Haurwitz, "Voters to Consider Boosting College Loan Program," *Austin American-Statesman*, October 17, 2011.

26. See "Analyses of Proposed Constitutional Amendments for November 5, 2013 Election" (Austin: Texas Legislative Council, August 2013) at www.tlc.state.tx.us/const_amends.htm.

27. See H2o4Texas.org at www.h2o4texas.org/library/documents-library/ and search for Prop6.

28. *Book of the States, 2013*, at http://knowledgecenter.csg.org/kc/content/book-states-2013-chapter-1-state-constitutions; and the Institute of Initiatives and Referendums at http://www.iandrinstitute.org/.

29. Texas's right-to-work law was enacted in 1947 by the 50th Legislature. The law bans the union shop arrangement whereby newly hired workers must join a union after employment.

30. Jim Lewis, "Getting Around to a New Constitution," *County* (January/February 1999): 11–13. For a profile of Representative Rob Junell and his collaboration with Senator Bill Ratliff, see Janet Elliott, "Maverick in the Middle," *Texas Lawyer* (January 1999): 19–20.

31. For the text of the Ratliff-Junell draft constitution, refer to Texas Legislature Online at http://www.capitol.state.tx.us and search by bill number for the 76th Regular Session, HJR1 or SJR1.

32. See Roy Walthall, "Waco Group Reorganizes Texas Constitution," *Waco Tribune-Herald*, November 15, 2010; Roy Walthall, "Texas Constitution Needs Makeover," *Amarillo Globe-News*, October 23, 2011; and "Waco Group Hoping to Reorganize Texas Constitution," at www.WacoTrib.com, October 31, 2013.

33. For an analysis of amendments proposed between 1976 and 1989, see James G. Dickson, "Erratic Continuity: Some Patterns of Constitutional Change in Texas Since 1975," *Texas Journal of Political Studies* 14 (Fall–Winter 1991–1992): 41–56.

34. For the text of Junell's constitutional proposal, refer to Texas Legislature Online at http://www.capitol.state.tx.us and search by bill for the 77th Legislature, HJR 69.

35. For detailed analyses of the contents of the Texas Constitution, see Janice C. May, *The Texas State Constitution: A Reference Guide* (Westport, CT: Greenwood Press, 1996); and George D. Braden, *Citizen's Guide to the Texas Constitution* (Austin: Texas Advisory Commission on Intergovernmental Relations, 1972).

36. *Santa Fe v. Doe*, 530 U.S. 290 (2000).

37. *Van Orden v. Perry*, 545 U.S. 677 (2005).

38. For details concerning the struggle for equal legal rights, see Rob Fink, "Hermine Tobolowsky, the Texas ELRA, and the Political Struggle for Women's Equal Rights," *Journal of the West* 42 (Summer 2003): 52–57; and Tai Kreidler, "Hermine Tobolowsky: Mother of Texas Equal Rights Amendment," in *The Human Tradition in Texas*, ed. Ty Cashion and Jesus de la Teja (Wilmington, DE: SR Books, 2001), 209–220.

39. Jason Embry, "School Tax System Unconstitutional: State Supreme Court Wants a Fix by June 1," *Austin American-Statesman*, November 23, 2005. See also Gary Scharrer, "Justices Warn That Changes Will Have to Be Significant," *San Antonio Express-News*, November 23, 2005.

Chapter 3

1. *Clinton v. Cedar Rapids and the Missouri River Railroad*, 24 Iowa 455 (1868).

2. *People v. Hurlbut*, 24 Mich. 44, 95 (1871).

3. Jesse J. Richardson Jr., Meghan Zimmerman Gough, and Robert Puentes, "Is Home Rule the Answer? Clarifying the Influence of Dillon's Rule on Growth Management," Brookings Institution, http://www.brookings.edu/research/reports/2003/01/01metropolitanpolicy-richardson.

4. Neena Satija, "Border Towns Struggle to Protect Water Infrastructure," *Texas Tribune*, January 10, 2014, http://www.texastribune.org/search/?q=border+towns+struggle+to+protect+water+infrastructure.

5. See "Local Government Code," http://www.statutes.legis.state.tx.us. A good description of local governments is "Local Government in Texas" by the Texas Municipal League, https://www.tml.org/Handbook-M&C/Chapter1.pdf. The less common but real issue of ending a city government is discussed in Michelle Wilde Anderson, "Dissolving Cities," *Yale Law Journal*, 121 (April 2012): 1346–1447.

6. Enrique Rangel, "Voters in Many Texas Towns Consider Recalls of Elected Officials," *Amarillo Globe-News*, November 30, 2013.

7. "Editorial: Gonzalez's $400,000 Pay Sends Wrong Message at Dallas City Hall." *Dallas Morning News*, February 11, 2014, http://www.dallasnews.com/opinion/editorials/20140210-editorial-gonzalezs-pay-sends-the-wrong-message-at-dallas-city-hall.ece.

8. Alan I. Abramowitz, "Why Section 5 Is Still Needed: Racial Polarization and the Voting Rights Act in the 21st Century," *Sabato's Crystal Ball* (Charlottesville, VA: University of Virginia Center for Politics), March 7, 2013, http://www.centerforpolitics.org/crystalball/articles/why-section-5-is-still-needed-racial-polarization-and-the-voting-rights-act-in-the-21st-century/.

9. The definition of a minority opportunity district varies by source and situation. It is particularly affected by the degree of ethnic polarization in voting. Commonly, it would require that a group be 50 percent of the citizens of voting age, but for Latinos, the percentage may be as high as 65 percent. Rudolph Bush, "Justice Department Approves Dallas Redistricting Plan," *Dallas Morning News*, December 21, 2011, and City of Houston, "Approved City Council Redistricting Plan and Documents," http://www.houstontx.gov/planning/2011/index.html.

10. See Robert Bezdek, David Billeaux, and Juan Carlos Huerta, "Latinos, At-Large Elections, and Political Change: Evidence from the Transition Zone," *Social Science Quarterly* 81 (March 2000): 207–225. Data collected from city websites by author, March 2012.

11. *Directory of Latino Elected Officials* (Los Angeles: NALEO Educational Fund, 2011). Sonia R. García, Valerie Martinez-Ebers, Irasema Coronado, Sharon Navarro, and Patricia Jaramillo, *Politicas: Latina Trailblazers in the Texas Political Arena* (Austin: University of Texas Press, 2008) provides biographical essays on the first Latina elected public officials in Texas; and The Houston Area Survey, http://has.rice.edu, details changes in the attitudes of Houstonians each year from 1982 to 2014 and beyond.

12. Steven Malanga, "Deep in the Debt of Texas," *City Journal*, Spring 2013, http://www.city-journal.org/2013/23_2_snd-texas-debt.html.

13. Daniel Raimi and Richard G. Newell, "Shale Public Finance: Local government revenues and costs associated with oil and gas development," *Duke University Energy Initiative*, May 2014, http://energy.duke.edu/sites/energy.duke.edu/files/files/Shale%20Public%20Finance%20Local%20Revenues%20and%20Costs%20Report%20Final.pdf.

14. Texas Comptroller, *Tax Rates and Levies by County*, http://www.window.state.tx.us/taxinfo/proptax/taxrates/.

15. An interesting account of the problems facing a rural county undergoing population change is Dave Mann, "The Battle for San Jacinto," *Texas Observer*, February 10, 2006, 12–13 and 18–19.

16. Tony Plohetski, "Grand Jury Investigating Gov. Rick Perry Convenes," *Austin American Statesman*, May 16, 2014.

17. Jim Webre, "Treasurer Will Stay until Successor Appointed," *The Sealy News*, December 17, 2004.

18. Tom Bower, "Toyota Incentives Gets County's OK," *San Antonio Express-News*, May 21, 2003; Jack Dennis, "San Antonio Toyota Plant Ceasing Production of Tundras," *San Antonio Headlines Examiner*, January 26, 2010; and Vicki Vaughan, "Toyota Factories Back in High Gear," MySanAntonio.Com, September 14, 2011, http://www.mysanantonio.com/business/article/Toyotafactoriesback-in-high-gear-2170706.php.

19. Gyusuck Geon and Geoffrey K. Turnbull, "The Effect of Home Rule on Local Government Behavior: Is There No Rule Like Home Rule?" Georgia State University, September 2004, http://ayspsprodweb.gsu.edu/drupal/sites/default/files/documents/urag_0405.pdf.

20. Estimates of the number of colonias and of their residents vary. However, as of 2014, the Texas attorney general's website had an interactive list with maps (https://maps.oag.state.tx.us/colgeog/colgeog_online.html#). Likewise, other state agencies keep updated websites (http://www.sos.state.tx.us/border/colonias/index.shtml; and http://www.hhsc.state.tx.us/hhsc_projects/oba/index.shtml).

21. Matthew Waller, "Data Shows Safe Border Regions Before National Guard Deployment", *Corpus Christi Caller-Times*, July 29, 2014, http://www.caller.com/columnists/matthew-waller/data-shows-safe-border-regions-before-natl-guard-deployment_99075946.

22. Texas Education Agency, *Snapshot 2013* (Austin: Texas Education Agency, April 2014), http://ritter.tea.state.tx.us/perfreport/snapshot/2013/state.html

23. "Texas Taxes," Window on State Government, http://www.window.state.tx.us/taxinfo/proptax/.

24. Reeve Hamilton, "Study: Texas Economy Benefits from Community Colleges," *Texas Tribune*, November 26, 2010, https://www.texastribune.org/2010/11/12/study-tx-economy-benefits-from-community-colleges/; and "The Economic Impact of Community Colleges," Window on State Government, http://www.window.state.tx.us/specialrpt/workforce/2008/colleges.php.

25. Enrique Rangel, "Lawmakers, Landowners Keep Eye on Water Rights," *Amarillo Globe-News*, May 31, 2014.